COLLIN COUNTY COMMUNITY COLLEGE

3 1702 00194 5835

84066

10649726

Learning Resources Center
Collin County Community College District
SPRING CREEK CAMPUS
Plano, Texas 75074

DD   Holland, Jack,
859   1959-
H64
1998   Berlin.

$16.95

BAKER & TAYLOR

Berlin

THE ROUGH GUIDE

There are more than one hundred and fifty Rough Guide titles
covering destinations from Amsterdam to Zimbabwe

Forthcoming titles include
Cuba • Ecuador • Las Vegas • Switzerland

Rough Guide Reference Series
Classical Music • Drum 'n' Bass • English Football • European Football
House • The Internet • Jazz • Music USA • Opera
Reggae • Rock Music • World Music

Rough Guide Phrasebooks
Czech • Dutch • Egyptian Arabic • European • French • German • Greek
Hindi & Urdu • Hungarian • Indonesian • Italian • Japanese
Mandarin Chinese • Mexican Spanish • Polish • Portuguese • Russian
Spanish • Swahili • Thai • Turkish • Vietnamese

Rough Guides on the Internet
www.roughguides.com

Rough Guide Credits

Text Editor:	Ann-Marie Shaw
Series Editor:	Mark Ellingham
Editorial:	Martin Dunford, Jonathan Buckley, Samantha Cook, Jo Mead, Kate Berens, Amanda Tomlin, Paul Gray, Chris Schüler, Helena Smith, Kieran Falconer, Judith Bamber, Olivia Eccleshall, Orla Duane, Ruth Blackmore, Sophie Martin (UK); Andrew Rosenberg, Andrew Taber (US)
Online Editors:	Alan Spicer, Kate Hands (UK); Geronimo Madrid (US)
Production:	Susanne Hillen, Andy Hilliard, Judy Pang, Link Hall, Nicola Williamson, Helen Ostick, James Morris
Picture Research:	Eleanor Hill
Cartography:	Maxine Burke, Melissa Flack, Nichola Goodliffe
Finance:	John Fisher, Celia Crowley, Neeta Mistry
Marketing & Publicity:	Richard Trillo, Simon Carloss, Niki Smith (UK); Jean-Marie Kelly, SoRelle Braun (US)
Administration:	Tania Hummel, Alexander Mark Rogers

Acknowledgements

Our thanks for a fine updating job on this edition go to **Andrew Roth**, who in turn would like to express his gratitude to Anni Kloss, Stefan Liebig, Dorothee Kocevar and Elizabeth Koetter. Special thanks again to: Claire Sharp, for vast amounts of help, advice and online access to her endless knowledge of the city; Victor Schröder and Ina Schröder who, despite difficult times, helped so much with the early editions of this book; Ulf Schiefer, for hundreds of corrections to our German spelling; to Michael Jack of the British Bookshop for literary leads, valuable suggestions and entertaining meals in Frankfurt; to Anne McElvoy and Bernd Wöhrle for past hospitality; Katia Pötelt for promoting Anglo-German friendship; Tom Gebhard for bar-crawling assistance and high-rise hospitality; Peter Bork; to Thomas von Arxt and Kerstin Wahala for an arts overview; Wiebke for theatre info. Thanks also, in no particular order, to Beata Gawthrop, Michael Prellberg, Klaus Schindler and Stefan Loose, Wolfgang Zeissner, Peter Rieth, Gordon McLachlan, Marlon Bork, Günther Bork, Petra Stüben, Sean Longden, Martine Klett, David Davies, and Sandy Moritz. Finally, thanks to Margo Daly, Narrell Leffman and Nick Thomson for help with Basics; Rob Humphreys for a comprehensive index; Nichola Goodliffe for careful, patient cartography; Judy Pang for meticulous typesetting and Elaine Pollard for sharp-eyed proofreading.

The publishers and authors have done their best to ensure the accuracy and currency of all information in The Rough Guide to Berlin; however, they can accept no responsibility for any loss, injury, or inconvenience sustained by any traveller as a result of information or advice contained in the guide.

This edition published August 1998 by Rough Guides Ltd, 62–70 Shorts Gardens, London WC2H 9AB.
Reprinted in November 1999. Previous editions published 1990, 1991, 1993 and 1995.
Distributed by the Penguin Group:
Penguin Books Ltd, 27 Wrights Lane, London W8 5TZ.
Penguin Books USA Inc, 375 Hudson Street, New York 10014, USA.
Penguin Books Australia Ltd, 487 Maroondah Highway, PO Box 257, Ringwood, Victoria 3134, Australia.
Penguin Books Canada Ltd, 10 Alcorn Avenue, Toronto, Ontario, Canada M4V 1E4.
Penguin Books (NZ) Ltd, 182–190 Wairau Road, Auckland 10, New Zealand.

Printed in England by Clays Ltd, St Ives PLC
Typography and **original design** by Jonathan Dear and The Crowd Roars.
Illustrations throughout by Edward Briant.

© Jack Holland and John Gawthrop 1998.
368pp. Includes index.

No part of this book may be reproduced in any form without permission from the publisher except for the quotation of brief passages in reviews.

A catalogue record for this book is available from the British Library.

ISBN 1-85828-327-2

Berlin

THE ROUGH GUIDE

Written and researched by
Jack Holland and John Gawthrop

With additional contributions by
Andrew Roth, Claire Sharp and Victor Schröder

THE ROUGH GUIDES

Help us update

We've gone to a lot of trouble to ensure that this new edition of the *Rough Guide to Berlin* is up-to-date and accurate. However, things are still changing at an extraordinary speed in Berlin and if you find we've missed something good or covered something which has now gone, then please write; suggestions, comments or corrections are much appreciated. We'll credit all contributions, and send a copy of the next edition (or any other *Rough Guide* if you prefer) for the best letters.

Please mark all letters "Rough Guide to Berlin update" and send to:
Rough Guides, 62–70 Shorts Gardens, London WC2H 9AB or
Rough Guides, 375 Hudson St, 9th floor, New York, NY 10014.

Email should be sent to:
mail@roughguides.co.uk

Online updates about Rough Guide titles can be found on our Web site at www.roughguides.com

The authors

Following jobs as diverse as insurance collection, beer-barrel rolling and EFL teaching in Greece, **Jack Holland** co-founded the Rough Guides in the mid-1980s. He is co-author of the Rough Guides to New York City and Holland, and lived in Berlin for four years. He can now be found in the Cotswolds, tearing through the countryside in a high-powered sports car. **John Gawthrop** has been a regular visitor to Berlin since 1985, spending much time on the eastern side of the former Wall. He is co-author of the Rough Guide to Turkey, and has written on Estonia, Latvia and Lithuania for the Europe book. He also edits a newsletter on oil in the former Soviet Union.

Thanks

Thanks to those who **wrote letters**: Kevin Armstrong, Sander Berg, Lorna Linnane Boyd and Stephen Boyd, Tim Brown, Jordi Carrasco-Munoz Prats, Anthony German, Peter Haigh and Frédérique Bernard, Amy L. Hess, Mary L. Hind, J. Holland, Nick Kay, Nicole Karsch-Meiborn, Pamela Krämer-North, Charles Lees, Helen Little, Mark Peacock, Luigi Petrucci, Roy Plant, Francesca Rabaiotti, Fran Rout, Tim Ryder, David Satter, Su-Lyn Seah, F. Sellors, Cathy Stedman and Bob Weinreich.

Rough Guides

Travel Guides • Phrasebooks • Music and Reference Guides

We set out to do something different when the first Rough Guide was published in 1982. Mark Ellingham, just out of University, was travelling in Greece. He brought along the popular guides of the day, but found they were all lacking in some way. They were either strong on ruins and museums but went on for pages without mentioning a beach or taverna. Or they were so conscious of the need to save money that they lost sight of Greece's cultural and historical significance. Also, none of the books told him anything about Greece's contemporary life – its politics, its culture, its people, and how they lived.

So with no job in prospect, Mark decided to write his own guidebook, one which aimed to provide practical information that was second to none, detailing the best beaches and the hottest clubs and restaurants, while also giving hard-hitting accounts of every sight, both famous and obscure, and providing up-to-the-minute information on contemporary culture. It was a guide that encouraged independent travellers to find the best of Greece, and was a great success, getting shortlisted for the Thomas Cook travel guide award, and encouraging Mark, along with three friends, to expand the series.

The Rough Guide list grew rapidly and the letters flooded in, indicating a much broader readership than had been anticipated, but one which uniformly appreciated the Rough Guides' mix of practical detail and humour, irreverence and enthusiasm. Things haven't changed. The same four friends who began the series are still the caretakers of the Rough Guide mission today: to provide the most reliable, up-to-date and entertaining information to independent-minded travellers of all ages, on all budgets.

We now publish more than 100 titles and have offices in London and New York. The travel guides are written and researched by a dedicated team of more than 100 authors, based in Britain, Europe, the USA and Australia. We have also created a unique series of phrasebooks to accompany the travel series, along with the acclaimed series of music guides, and a best-selling pocket guide to the Internet and World Wide Web. We also publish comprehensive travel information on our Web site: www.roughguides.com

Contents

List of Maps

MAP SYMBOLS

═══	Major road	ⓘ	Information centre
───	Minor road	⊠	Post office
▬▬	Railway	▓	Built-up area
─ ─ ─	Chapter division boundary	▓	Building
▬ ··	Provincial boundary	⊞	Church
───	River	░	Park
✕	Airport	░	Forest
Ⓤ	U-Bahn	+⁺+	Christian cemetery
Ⓢ	S-Bahn	✿✿	Jewish cemetery
✡	Synagogue		

Introduction

Das gibts nur einmal
Das kehrt nicht wieder
Das ist zu schön, um wahr zu sein!

It happens only once
It will not come again
It is too beautiful to be true!

Berlin is like no other city in Germany, or, indeed, the world. For over a century, its political climate has either mirrored or determined what has happened in the rest of Europe: heart of the Prussian kingdom, economic and cultural centre of the Weimar Republic, and, in the final days of Nazi Germany, the headquarters of Hitler's Third Reich, it is a weather vane of European history. After the war, the world's two most powerful military systems stood face to face here, sharing the spoils of a city later to be split by that most tangible object of the East–West divide, the Berlin Wall. As the Wall fell in November 1989, Berlin was once again pushed to the forefront of world events, ushering in a period of change as frantic, confusing and significant as any the city had yet experienced. It's this weight of history, the sense of living in a hothouse where all the dilemmas of contemporary Europe are nurtured, that gives Berlin its excitement and troubling fascination.

It was, of course, **World War II** that defined the shape of today's city. A seventh of all the buildings destroyed in Germany were in Berlin, Allied and Soviet bombing razing 92 percent of all the shops, houses and industry here. At the end of the war, the city was split into French, American, British and Soviet sectors, according to the agreement made at the Yalta Conference: the Allies took the western part of the city, traditionally an area of bars, hotels and shops fanning out from the Kurfürstendamm and the Tiergarten park. The Soviet zone contained what remained of the pompous civic build-

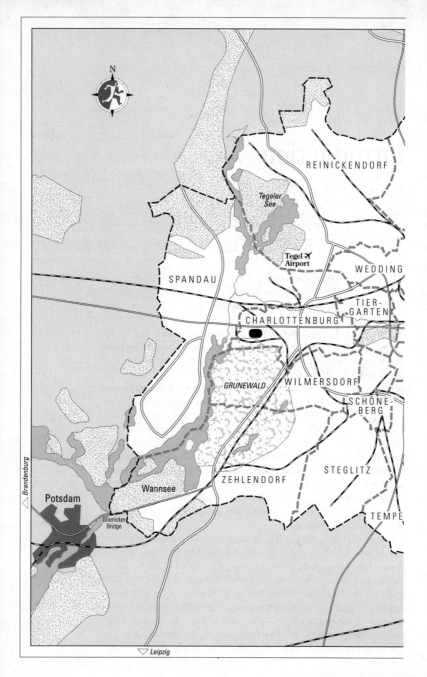

N

Brandenburg

Leipzig

REINICKENDORF

Tegeler
See

Tegel ✈
Airport

SPANDAU

WEDDING

TIER-
GARTEN

CHARLOTTENBURG

GRUNEWALD

WILMERSDORF

SCHÖNE-
BERG

Potsdam

Wannsee

ZEHLENDORF

STEGLITZ

TEMPE

Glienicker
Bridge

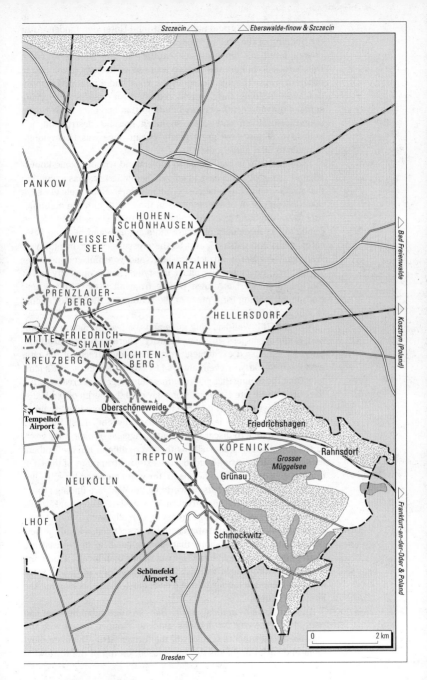

PANKOW

HOHEN-
SCHÖNHAUSEN

WEISSEN-
SEE

MARZAHN

PRENZLAUER-
BERG

HELLERSDORF

MITTE

FRIEDRICH-
SHAIN

KREUZBERG

LICHTEN-
BERG

Oberschöneweide

Friedrichshagen

Tempelhof
Airport

KÖPENICK

Rahnsdorf

TREPTOW

Grosser
Müggelsee

Grünau

NEUKÖLLN

LHOF

Schmockwitz

Schönefeld
Airport

△ Bad Freienwalde

△ Kostryn (Poland)

△ Frankfurt-an-der-Oder & Poland

0   2 km

ings, churches and grand museums around Unter den Linden. After the building of the Wall in 1961, which sealed the Soviet sector and consolidated its position as capital of the young German Democratic Republic, the divided sections of the city developed in different ways. The authorities in the West had a policy of demolition and rebuilding; the East restored wherever possible, preserving some of the nineteenth-century buildings that had once made Berlin magnificent. Even now, after so much massive destruction, it's indicative of just how great a city Berlin once was that enough remains to fill a guidebook.

Though Berlin is impossible to understand without some knowledge of its history, it is easy to enjoy. The unified city has a nightlife that ranks among the most energetic in Europe. Entrepreneurs have taken advantage of planning chaos in the east to move in on empty premises – anything from old fruit and vegetable shops to abandoned public toilets in defunct underground stations – and open up bars, cafés, clubs and galleries. Just as the pressure-cooker mentality of Wall-era West Berlin attracted a large and youthful contingent of would-be dropouts and alternative lifestylers, so the open city feel of the united Berlin has drawn people from all over Germany and Europe, all looking for a piece of the action – or the chance simply to join in the fun.

Now that the Wall has long gone and the two Germanys are unified, Berlin seems less sure of its **identity**. There's a perpetual atmosphere of exhausted excitement in the bars and streets of the city, with the next party or event always just around the corner. It's hard to escape the feeling that you're witnessing a legend in creation, that the Berlin of the late 1990s may one day rival the Berlin of the 1920s in popular mythology. But Berlin is a city with severe identity problems, an inescapable legacy of the past division. East Berliners haven't been able to discard the mental baggage of their forty years in the socialist camp as easily as they were able to bin the Trabant cars and tawdry consumer goods, the external trappings of the GDR era. Westerners, on the other hand, for years cosseted by subsidies and insulated from the outside world by the Wall, are finding it hard to come to terms with the gritty turmoil of post-1989 central Europe.

As a result, east and west Berliners don't really seem to mix. A kind of semi-voluntary **cultural apartheid** has descended: a lot of the new cafés, restaurants and shops that have opened up in the east are geared for west Berliners and tourists rather than locals, with many easterners more concerned with the daily problems of finding work or making enough money to make ends meet, than checking out the latest hip haunts.

Another result of unification was that the **huge subsidies** that had poured into the city for decades suddenly stopped, along with the massive social support schemes of the former GDR. The unemployment and social problems this has caused, on top of the worldwide slump, has had ugly results, as Germans – particularly eastern Germans, already relegated to the status of second-class citizens – find scapegoats in the foreign communites. The attacks on Turks and Jews, which have resulted in several deaths, are too reminiscent of Nazism for comfort, and the **rise of neo-Nazi groups** is a frightening spectacle that many believe the government has done little to stop. Berlin has seen its crime levels rise dramatically, and has had a considerable increase in racially motivated violence.

Still, Berlin exhibits the expectant air of a boom town. Construction projects are a ubiquitous sight as the city expands to make room for the government – relocating here from Bonn – and prepares for a new role as central Europe's economic powerhouse. Museums and art collections are being shifted and reorganized in order to integrate east and west facilities. The long-placid streets of east Berlin are being gussied up to appeal to the tourist trade. Everywhere there is great energy and movement.

What Berlin will be like when the dust settles is anyone's guess. The arrival of the government is sure to make the city more important, but also perhaps a bit straight-laced. The promised economic activity is sure to make at least some residents richer, but will it really benefit the majority? The transformation of the city into a vigorous cultural centre is encouraging, but will it stick? Anxiety and optimism can be found here in equal measure.

Inevitably, the **pace of change** in Berlin, particularly in the eastern part of the city, means that certain sections of this book are going to be out of date even as you read them. New cafés and restaurants open (and close) daily, traffic is rerouted around building sites, and there is much construction on the public transport system.

One great advantage of unification is that, for the first time since the 1930s, the area around Berlin can easily be visited. Potsdam and the magnificent palace of Sansoucci is the obvious day-trip, and it's easy to get into countryside dotted with small towns and villages that preserve a "lost in time" feel.

When to go

Lying in the heart of Europe, Berlin's climate is continental: winters are bitingly cold, summers hot. If you're hanging on for decent weather, April is the soonest you should go: any earlier and you'll

Average temperatures (°F) and rainfall											
	Jan	Feb	Mar	April	May	June	July	Aug	Sept	Oct	Nov	Dec
Min °C	-12	-12	-7	-2	2	6	9	8	4	-1	-4	-9
Min °F	10	10	19	28	36	43	48	46	39	30	25	16
Max °C	9	11	17	22	28	30	32	31	28	21	13	10
Max °F	48	52	63	72	82	86	90	88	82	70	55	50

need to don winter clothing, earmuffs and a decent pair of water-proof shoes; this said, the city (especially the eastern part) does have a particular poignancy when it snows. Ideally, the best time to arrive is in May; June and July can be wearingly hot, though the famed Berlin air (Berliner Luft – there's a song about it) keeps things bracing. The weather stays good (if unpredictable) right up until October.

Part 1

Basics

Getting there from Britain and Ireland

The most convenient and usually best value way to get to Berlin from the UK is to fly – a journey of around ninety minutes. However, taking the train is easier and quicker now that the Channel Tunnel is open: the journey time from London to Berlin via Brussels is around twelve hours. Similarly, if travelling by car you can use the Channel's Le Shuttle services.

There are also ferries to the Hook of Holland and two direct services to Hamburg, from Harwich and Newcastle, which cost significantly less but are often uncomfortable and tiring.

By plane

Direct **scheduled flights** to Berlin are available from British Airways and the new AB Airlines. There are five daily BA flights from London Heathrow to Berlin Tegel, while AB Airlines flies twice daily from London Gatwick to Berlin Schönefeld (for more on both airports, see "Points of arrival", p.15). From regional UK airports, direct flights are limited to British Airways flights from Birmingham (1 daily) and Manchester (Mon–Fri 2 daily, Sun 1 daily). Indirectly, BA flies twice daily via Heathrow from Newcastle, twice daily from Edinburgh with one flight via Birmingham and the other via Heathrow, and twice daily from Glasgow, once via Birmingham and once via Manchester. KLM recently bought Air UK, and the new KLM UK flies to Berlin Tegel via Amsterdam

---

Airlines

AB Airlines ☎ 0345/464748

British Airways ☎ 0345/222111

KLM UK ☎ 0990/074074

Lufthansa ☎ 0345/737747

Discount agents

Campus Travel, 52 Grosvenor Gardens, London SW1W 0AG ☎ 0171/730 3402; branches nationwide and also at YHA shops and on university campuses. *Student/youth travel specialist.*

Council Travel, 28a Poland St, London W1V 3BD ☎ 0171/437 7767. *Flights and student discounts.*

German Travel Centre, 403–409 Rayners Lane, Pinner, Middlesex HA5 5ER ☎ 0181/429 2900. *Discount flight specialist.*

STA Travel, 86 Old Brompton Rd, London SW7 3LH ☎ 0171/937 9962; branches nationwide and on university campuses. *Student/youth travel specialist.*

Trailfinders, 42–50 Earls Court Rd, London W8 6FT ☎ 0171/938 3366; other branches nationwide. *One of the best-informed and most efficient agents for independent travellers.*

Travel Bug, 125a Gloucester Rd London SW7 4SF ☎ 0171/835 2000; 597 Cheetham Hill Rd, Manchester M8 ☎ 0161/721 4000. *Large range of discounted tickets.*

---

from almost every British airport (except Gatwick and Luton) five times daily, and eight times daily from Heathrow. The German airline Lufthansa unfortunately now only flies via Düsseldorf or Frankfurt from Heathrow, Birmingham and Manchester.

Also available, should you want to divide your time between Berlin and other parts of Germany, are the more expensive **open-jaw flights** (fly in to one airport and back from another) and **fly-drive deals**.

The airlines' published **fare** can cost as much as £236. Special offers apart, the least costly way to fly is normally on a **consolidated special fare** which airlines agree with travel agents; restrictions are that you have to stay a Saturday night, can only stay for a maximum of three months, and risk being penalized if you change your schedule. AB Airlines' consolidated direct fare is usually around £129, dropping as low as £99 in January and February. BA can usually offer a special consolidated fare of £150, occasionally bottoming out at £119. Indirect flights on KLM via Amsterdam start at £125, while Lufthansa via Düsseldorf or Frankfurt costs from £141. There are no **seasonal variations** in price. Remember you may have to add £16–20 **airport tax** to any advertised or quoted fares.

You may find a **cheaper flight** by scanning the travel pages of the Sunday or local evening papers, regional listings magazines, and, in London, *Time Out*. There are numerous **discount flight agents and operators** (listed on p.3) offering budget flights – particularly useful to those **under 26** – and specialists like the **German Travel Centre** in London, which consistently has the most attractive prices.

By train

Unless you qualify for one of the discounts listed below, there are no savings to be made travelling to Berlin **by train**: in fact, you'll usually pay more than you would going by plane or bus. Students and those under 26 are best served, with rail discounts offered by specialists like Wasteels and Eurotrain.

By far the **fastest** and most popular train route to Berlin begins with **Eurostar** from London Waterloo to Brussels (2hr 40min), and then onto another train direct to Berlin or via Cologne, a total journey of around twelve hours. Standard return tickets for the complete journey are £169

(with the London–Brussels leg priced at £79, barring special offers, with £69 fares for those under 26); these must be booked three days in advance, require you to spend Saturday night or three nights away, are non-changeable and allow only a 24-hour stopover in Brussels. You can get through ticketing – including the tube journey to Waterloo – from mainline stations in Britain; typical add-on prices are £30 from Edinburgh or Glasgow, £20 from Manchester and £13.50 from Birmingham.

If you are intending to tour en route, **regular return tickets** incorporating a ferry crossing are available from selected mainline train stations and travel agents. These are valid for two months and permit unlimited stopovers along the pre-specified route to Berlin and back. The route from **London via Dover and Ostend** costs £187 (£148 if you're under 26) and takes a minimum of eighteen hours. **London via the Hook of Holland** (changing trains at either Amsterdam or Rotterdam and Amersfoort) costs £194 (under 26, £160) and takes at least 21 hours. Cheapest of all, **London via Harwich to Hamburg** costs £141 (under 26, £88); however, the journey takes a minimum of 26 hours, with twenty hours spent on the ferry.

InterRail, German passes and other offers

If you plan to travel extensively in Europe by train there are better-value options than simply buying a return ticket. Under 26s can invest in an **InterRail** pass, available from any major UK train station or youth/student travel office; the only restriction is that you must have been resident in a European country for at least six months. Since Germany has an extensive train network, InterRail passes are a bargain, even taking into account the extra supplements you may have to pay, especially on intercity services. However, there are some private lines, including eastern Germany's narrow-gauge steam train lines, on which passes are not valid. Passes come in two main forms: the **"All-Zone" pass** (£279), valid for one month on all European railways, and the **"Zonal" pass**, whereby the 26 countries are split into seven zones and you choose the countries you want the pass to be valid for (the UK to Berlin would necessitate a £224 two-zone pass, valid for a month). In addition, all InterRail passes offer discounts on rail travel in the UK and on cross-Channel ferries.

Train information

British Rail International

No longer offers a telephone enquiry/booking service; in London there are British Rail International ticket offices at Kings Cross, Euston, Paddington and Victoria stations.

Eurostar ☎ 01233/617575

Rail Europe ☎ 0990/848848

Eurotrain ☎ 0171/730 3402

German Rail (DB) ☎ 0181/390 8833

Wasteels, Victoria Station London SW1
☎ 0171/834 7066

Bus information

Eurolines, 52 Grosvenor Gardens
(opposite Victoria Train Station), London SW1
☎ 0990/143219

If you are over 26 you can buy an **InterRail "26 Plus" pass** – £275 for a month or £215 for 15 days. This covers only 19 countries in Europe: major exclusions are France, Belgium, Switzerland, Spain, Italy and Portugal.

If you're sixty or over and have a British Rail Senior Card (£18 from any train station), you can get a **Rail Europe Senior Card** for £5, which gives discounts of approximately thirty percent on cross-border train and sea travel in Germany and most of western Europe; both are valid for one year.

Specific **passes for travel in Germany only** must be bought before you go from the DER Travel Service (see box on p.6) and other agents – for a full list contact **German Rail** (see box above), The broadest-ranging is the **EuroDomino**, which offers unlimited travel on the whole train network. Passes are valid for travel for three, five or ten days within any 21-day period (they do not have to be used on consecutive days). Both adult (second-class tickets cost £139 for 3 days, £159 for 5 and £209 for 10) and youth (12–25 years; £109, £119, £159) passes are available.

By bus

Travelling to Berlin by **bus** won't bring any major savings over the cheapest air fares, and the journey will be long and uncomfortable, interrupted every three to four hours by stops at motorway service stations. The one advantage is that you can buy an **open return** at no extra cost.

Services are run by **Eurolines** (see box opposite) from Victoria Coach Station in London, and are bookable through most travel agents and through any National Express agent. At least two buses a week run to Berlin, with daily services in high summer; the journey takes 26 hours and costs £94 return (£85 for students and under-25s), being only slightly cheaper in winter. If you're outside London, Eurolines will book you a National Express coach to London, but with no reductions available on the usual domestic fare. A pass for Europe-wide travel is available for either thirty days (£199/159 under 26) or sixty days (£249/199 under 26) between London and fifteen other European cities including Berlin, Hamburg and Frankfurt.

By car: ferries and Eurotunnel

To take your **car** to Berlin you'll need a vehicle registration document and proof of vehicle insurance.

The cheapest and most frequent (twice daily, daytime only) **Channel crossing** for Berlin is the Stena Line ferry from **Harwich to the Hook of Holland** (3hr 40min). Standard high-season fares (mid-June to mid-Sept) for a medium-sized car and up to five people are £196 one way, £352 return, and in low season £148 one way, £224 return. Five-day returns are substantially cheaper at around £224 in high season and £207 in low, though frequent special offers can bring prices down to £165 in the high season, £99 in the low.

From the Hook, the **best route** is Utrecht–Amersfoort–Hengelo–Osnabrück–Hanover–Helmstedt–Marienborn–Berlin: allow about twelve hours to reach Berlin. Both the AA and RAC publish route maps of the areas you'll be passing through, which are free to members.

Cross-Channel information

Scandinavian Seaways ☎ 01255/241234
(nationwide) or 0191/296 0101

Eurotunnel ☎ 0990/353535

Stena Line ☎ 0990/707070 (nationwide) or
01233/647047

Ferries to Hamburg

Two routes, run by Scandinavian Seaways, ply **directly** from the UK to Germany. Once there, it's a 285km drive to Berlin, making this the best (though most expensive) route if you want to minimize time actually spent driving.

There are services from **Harwich to Hamburg** all year round – three times a week from October to mid-April (low season), and every other day from mid-April to October (high); the crossing takes nineteen hours. At least a couchette berth must be taken, with the cheapest fares booked 21 days in advance avoiding Friday and Saturday; with these fares, each passenger pays £94 per person, rising to £124 in the summer, and car drivers must add on an extra £69, rising to £94 in the high season. Students qualify for a 25 percent reduction on passenger fares.

The second ferry runs from **North Shields**, near Newcastle, taking 23 hours twice a week between May and mid-October only; fares are the same as from Harwich.

Eurotunnel

Probably the most convenient way of getting across the Channel is to take the Channel Tunnel train shuttle – **Eurotunnel** (journey time 35–45min). The tunnel entrance is off the M20 at Junction 11A, just outside Folkestone (emerging outside Calais). Services operate around the clock, 365 days a year, with four services per hour at peak periods: because of the frequency of the service, you don't have to buy a ticket in advance; just arrive and wait to board one of the trains – promised loading time is ten minutes.

Tickets are available through Eurotunnel (see box on previous page) or any travel agent. **Fares** vary with the season, time of day and length of stay: it's cheaper to travel between 10am and 6pm, while the highest fares are reserved for weekend departures and July and August. Apart from special offers, tickets are fully flexible and refundable and are priced per carload: standard returns are £130 (Sept–Easter), £190 (April–June) and £220 (July–Aug). Five-day returns, also fully flexible, offer better value at around £120–135. Look out for special offers when prices can go as low as £55.

Hitching

Most **hitchhikers** who start thumbing in the UK will be expected to pay for their ferry passage, and should aim for the Hook of Holland. For all but the absolutely penniless, it's a smarter idea to buy a bus or boat ticket to the port and start hitching from there, following the route outlined above.

If hitching back from or out of Germany, it's worth contacting one of the many Berlin **Mitfahrzentralen** organizations, whose bureaux put drivers and hikers in touch for a small fee and a contribution towards petrol. There's a valuable safety factor in this system, since all drivers have to notify the agencies of their addresses and car registration. The usual cost of getting from Berlin to London, for example, is about DM60. Mitfahrzentralen can be found at Joachimstaler Str. 17 (☎8 82 76 04; daily 9am–8pm); in Zoo Station U-Bahn station, on the platform for line #2, direction Schlesisches Tor (☎1 94 40; daily 8am–9pm); and in Alexanderplatz U-Bahn station at the crossing from line #8 to line #2 (☎2 41 58 20/1; Mon–Fri 8am–8pm, Sat 8am–6pm, Sun 10am–6pm). More listings for Mitfahrzentralen can be found in *Tip* and *Zitty* magazines (see p.22).

Packages

Since the fall of the Wall, Berlin has featured as a destination for the major **package operators**, and an all-inclusive holiday can prove convenient, if a little pricey, especially for a short break. Prices start from around £250 for a two-night

---

Specialist and package operators

British Airways Holidays, Astral Towers, Betts Way, London Road, Crawley RH10 2XA ☎01293/723100. *City breaks starting at £247 (Jan–March) for two nights in a three-star hotel rising to £257 at various peak times.*

Thomas Cook Holidays ☎01733/418200. *Nationwide holiday company offering competitive packages and flights.*

DER Travel Service, 18 Conduit St, London W1R 9TD ☎0171/290 1111. *The national German travel agency, offering a full range of tours, including city breaks in Berlin for £199.*

Time Off, 2a Chester Close, Chester St, London SW1 7BQ ☎0171/235 8070. *City breaks.*

stay, including flights and accommodation in a centrally located hotel. Any high street travel agent will have details of packages; those offered by the DER Travel Service (see box opposite) are usually reasonable value.

Getting there from Ireland

Flights on Aer Lingus **from Dublin** to Berlin (via Amsterdam) are IR£474: no advance booking is required but you must stay at least one Saturday night. Frequent promotional deals, such as Supersavers (which must be booked 7 days in advance and include a Saturday night), can bring the price down to IR£256. You can also book a flight with Aer Lingus to London (12 flights a day, usually around IR£79) to connect up with one of the British Airways Berlin-bound flights (see p.3). Another money-saving option is to fly to London but book your second flight with one of the London-based **discount travel agents** (see p.3) before you go. However, to do this you'll need to send proof if you are a student or under 26, and if you live in the Republic you'll need a contact in London to collect the tickets and send them to you.

From Belfast most flights are with British Airways via London. Consolidated fares range from £229–253.

Students and anyone under 26 should contact **USIT**, which generally has the best discount deals on flights and train tickets. **Package holidays** and city breaks are mostly routed via

London with an add-on fare for the connection from Ireland.

By car and ferry

Irish Ferries runs services from Rosslare to Roscoff (16hr) and Cherbourg (18hr) on alternate days from April through December. Prices vary according to season and size of car, with prices for a small car and two adults ranging from IR£99–225 one way (return prices are substantially cheaper but generally need to be booked in advance). Brittany Ferries also operates an April to October crossing from Cork to Roscoff (14hr) once or twice a week, from IR£95 one way, IR£155 Saver Return (up to 7 days) to IR£220/355 in August.

Foot passenger prices vary greatly according to season, with one-way fares from IR£35–60 with Irish Ferries, and IR£30–50 with Brittany Ferries; returns on both are roughly double the price.

Insurance

British and other EU nationals are entitled to **free medical treatment** in Germany on production of form E111, available from main post offices, or, in the UK, from the DSS Leaflets Unit, PO Box 21, Stanmore, Middlesex HA7 1AY. Officially, you need to get your E111 at least two weeks before you leave and get it stamped in the post office. Without this form you'll have to pay in full for all medical treatment.

Airlines in Ireland

Aer Lingus

Dublin	☎ 01/705 3333
Belfast	☎ 0645/737747

British Airways

Belfast	☎ 0345/222111
Dublin	☎ 1800/626747

Ferry companies

Brittany Ferries

Cork	☎ 021/277801

Irish Ferries

Dublin	☎ 01/661 0511
Cork	☎ 021/551995
Rosslare	☎ 053/33158
Belfast	☎ 0345/171717

Discount agents and tour operators

Joe Walsh Tours, 8–11 Baggot St, Dublin ☎ 01/678 9555 *General budget fares agent.*

Thomas Cook, 118 Grafton St, Dublin ☎ 01/677 1721; 11 Donegall Place, Belfast ☎ 01232/240833. *Package holiday and flight agent, with occasional discount offers.*

USIT, O'Connell Bridge, 19–21 Aston Quay, Dublin 2 ☎ 01/778 1177; 10–11 Market Parade, Cork ☎ 021/270900; 31a Queen St, Belfast ☎ 01232/242562. *Student and youth specialist for flights and trains.*

Nonetheless, **travel insurance**, covering loss and theft of money or possessions, is a good idea, and policies are sold by almost every travel agent and by specialist insurance companies. STA, USIT and Campus Travel (see p.3 and p.7), and low-cost insurers like Endsleigh and Columbus are usually good value. Policies start around £26.50 a month (including medical cover).

However, before you shell out, check that you're not already covered. Banks and credit cards (particularly Visa and American Express)

Travel insurance suppliers

Columbus, 17 Devonshire Square, London EC2M 4SQ ☎ 0171/375 0011

Endsleigh, 97–107 Southampton Row, London WC1B 4AG ☎ 0171/436 4451

---

often have certain levels of medical or other insurance included. It's also worth knowing that your domestic home insurance policy can sometimes cover your possessions while abroad.

Getting there from North America

Partly as a result of the presence of US military forces, most German cities are well served by US airlines. There are numerous flights to Berlin from nearly all major North American cities, and fares are among the most inexpensive for transatlantic crossings. The majority of flights land at Tegel airport to the west of the city, with some landing at Schönefeld to the east: for details on how to get to the city centre from either airport, see pp.15–16.

The cheapest and most convenient way to fly from the US or Canada to Berlin is to book a **direct flight** (this means booking a ticket for the entire journey with one airline, it doesn't necessarily mean you will be on a nonstop flight). Searching for special deals to another European city first and then booking a second flight with another airline for the final leg to Berlin will usually take longer and rarely result in significant savings. For Canadians there are no major savings to be made by flying to the US first.

If you're visiting Berlin as part of a wider German or European tour, and flying into one of the other mainland European gateway airports, **trains** are the most economical way to get to Berlin. A *Eurail* pass is particularly useful, as it can get you from any part of Europe to Berlin. From England, flying is often just as inexpensive, if not more so, as ground travel.

Shopping for tickets

Barring special offers, the cheapest fare is usually an **Apex** ticket, although this will carry certain restrictions: you will, most likely, have to book – and pay – at least 21 days before departure, spend at least seven days abroad (maximum stay 3 months), and you tend to get penalized if you change your schedule. There are also winter **Super**

Apex tickets, sometimes known as "Eurosavers" – slightly cheaper than an ordinary Apex, but limiting your stay to between 7 and 21 days. Some airlines also issue **Special Apex** tickets to people younger than 24. These will probably cost the same as the lowest Apex fare, but may have an advance purchase requirement of only three days, an "open" return and a maximum stay of a year.

You can normally cut costs further by going through a **discount agent** or **consolidator**, who buys up blocks of tickets from airlines and sells them at a discount. Some agents specialize in **charter flights**, which may be cheaper than any available scheduled flight, but again departure dates are fixed. With all reduced-rate operations, withdrawal penalties are high (check the refund policy).

Especially if you're a **student** or **under 26**, you should contact any of the specialist operators listed below, such as Council Travel, STA, or Travel Cuts in Canada, who may be able to offer substantial discounts on scheduled fares – at the time of writing, low season fares were available for as little as $298 (from New York), $388 (from Chicago) or $458 (from LA).

Airlines

Air Canada	☎ 1-800/776-3000	
Air France	US: ☎ 1-800/237-2747	
	Canada: ☎ 1-800/667-2747	
American Airlines	☎ 1-800/433-7300	
British Airways	US: ☎ 1-800/247-9297	
	Canada: ☎ 1-800/668-1059	
Continental Airlines	☎ 1-800/231-0856	
Delta Airlines	☎ 1-800/241-4141	

Lufthansa	US: ☎ 1-800/645-3880	
	Canada: ☎ 1-800/563-5954	
Northwest/KLM	US: ☎ 1-800/374-7747	
	Canada: ☎ 1-800/361-5073	
Sabena	☎ 1-800/955-2000	
Swissair	US: ☎ 1-800/221-4750	
	Canada: ☎ 1-800/267-9477	
United Airlines	☎ 1-800/538-2929	
US Air	☎ 1-800/622-1015	

Discount travel companies

Council Travel, 205 E 42nd St, New York, NY 10017 ☎ 212/822-2700 or 1-800/226-8624; branches in many other US cities. *Nationwide US organization. Mostly, but not exclusively, specializes in student travel.*

Encore Travel Club, 4501 Forbes Blvd, Lanham, MD 20706 ☎ 1-800/444-9800. *East Coast travel club.*

Interworld, 800 Douglass Rd, Miami, FL 33134 ☎ 305/443-4929 or 1-800/468-3796. *Southeastern US consolidator.*

Moment's Notice, 7301 New Utrecht Ave, Brooklyn, NY 11204 ☎ 718/234-6295 or 212/486-0500. *Discount travel club.*

New Frontiers/Nouvelles Frontières, 12 E 33rd St, New York, NY 10016 ☎ 212/779-0600 or 1-800/366-6387; 1001 Sherbrook East, Suite 720, Montréal, PQ H2L 1L3 ☎ 514/526-8444; branches in LA, San Francisco and Québec City. *French discount travel firm.*

STA Travel, 10 Downing St, New York, NY 10014 ☎ 212/627-3111 or 1-800/777-0112;

branches in several other US cities. *Worldwide specialists in independent travel.*

Travac, 989 Sixth Ave, New York NY 10018 ☎ 1-800/872-8800. *Consolidator and charter broker; has another office in Orlando.*

Travel Avenue, 10 S Riverside, Suite 1404, Chicago, IL 60606 ☎ 1-800/333-3335. *Discount travel agent.*

Travel Cuts, 187 College St, Toronto, ON M5T 1P7 ☎ 416/979-2406 or 1-800/667-2887, or 1-888/238-2887 from US; branches all over Canada. *Canadian student travel organization.*

Travelers Advantage, 3033 S Parker Rd, Suite 900, Aurora, CO 80014 ☎ 1-800/548-1116. *Discount travel club.*

Unitravel, 1177 N Warson Rd, St Louis, MO 63132 ☎ 1-800/325-2222. *Consolidator.*

Worldwide Discount Travel Club, 1674 Meridian Ave, Miami Beach, FL 33139 ☎ 305/534-2082. *Discount travel club.*

Regardless of where you buy your ticket, the fare will depend on the **season**. Fares to Berlin are highest from the beginning of June to the end of September; they drop during the "shoulder" seasons (all of October, mid-March to the end of May and December 1–24), and fall to their lowest level for November and from December 25 to Mid March. But don't be surprised to find further variations; Lufthansa, for instance, divides its "high" season into three further "sub-seasons". In addition, the major carriers periodically offer special limited promotional fares – and it is these which generally offer the best value.

Ticket prices quoted below are for midweek travel. Weekend flights cost around $60 extra. All prices are round-trip, exclusive of taxes and subject to availability and change.

Flights from the US

Although there are direct **nonstop** scheduled flights to Berlin from all the major gateway cities (New York, Atlanta, Boston, Washington DC, Miami, Chicago and LA), you'll usually have to stop over in another European city. At the time of writing, Lufthansa has the most competetive fares and the most non-stop flights.

From the **East Coast**, expect a flying time of approximately 10 hours. From New York a regular APEX fare will cost as little as $410 in low season and up to $1000 in high season; from Atlanta $480 (low) or $1100 (high); from Miami $510 (low) or $1115 (high).

From the **Midwest** flight times are roughly eleven and a half hours. From Chicago fares are around $510 (low) or $1200 (high).

From the **West Coast** the flying time is approximately 14 hours. Flying from Los Angeles, the average fares to Berlin are around $605 in low season and $1320 in high season. From San Francisco $635 (low) or $1320 (high). From Seattle $635 (low) or $1320 (high).

Flights from Canada

Canadians have fewer direct flight options than Americans. The widest selections are out of **Toronto** and **Montréal** (10hr), with fares to Berlin from around CDN$1000 (low season) to CDN$1270 (high season) on the major carriers, although a **discount travel agent**, such as Travel Cuts, may be able to find you a low season fare from the East Coast for as little as CDN$659. From **Vancouver** (12 hours) expect to pay from CDN$1300 (low) to CDN$1530 (high).

Train passes

If you're planning to do much **train travel** across Europe, a **Eurail** pass – which allows unlimited free train travel in seventeen European countries, and must be bought before you leave home – might come in useful. The **Eurail Youthpass** (for under-26s) costs US$376 for fifteen consecutive days, $605 for one month or $857 for two months; if you're 26 or over you'll have to buy a **first-class pass**, available in fifteen-day ($538), 21-day ($698), one-month ($864), two-month ($1224) and three-month ($1512) increments.

You stand a better chance of getting your money's worth out of a **Eurail Flexipass**, good for a certain number of travel days in a two-month period. This, too, comes in under-26/first-class versions, covering ten days, ($444/$634) and fifteen days ($585/$836).

North Americans are also eligible to purchase more specific passes valid for travel in Germany only, such as the **EuroDomino** pass (see "Getting There from Britain"). These and the wider European passes can be purchased through most travel agents, or try the agents listed in the box below.

Rail contacts

CIT Tours, 9501 W Devon Ave, Suite 502, Rosemont, IL 60018 ☎ 1-800/223-7987.

DER Tours/German Rail, 9501 W Devon Ave, Suite 400, Rosemont, IL 60018 ☎ 1-800/421-2929.

Rail Europe, 226 Westchester Ave, White Plains, NY 10604 ☎ 1-800/438-7245.

ScanTours, 1535 Sixth St, Suite 205, Santa Monica, CA 90401 ☎ 1-800/223-7226.

Packages and organized tours

Most **package holidays** combine Berlin with other German and European cities, and if you want something based in Berlin alone, you need to choose carefully. A good starting point for further information on packages is the **German National Tourist Office** (see p.22), and of course, your local travel agent.

Insurance

Before buying an **insurance policy**, check that you're not already covered. Some homeowners' or renters' policies are valid on vacation, and

Tour operators in North America

Unless stated otherwise, all prices quoted below exclude taxes and are subject to change. Where applicable, round-trip flights are from New York and accommodation is priced per person sharing a double room.

American Express Vacations PO Box 1525, Fort Lauderdale, FL 33302 ☎1-800/241-1700. *City breaks from $1120 (7 nights, land/air all taxes included).*

Brendan Tours 15137 Califa St, Van Nuys, CA 91411 ☎818/786-9696 or 1-800/421-8446. *15-day German tour spends two days in Berlin along with Frankfurt, Munich, Dresden etc. (from $1936 land/air).*

Caravan Tours 401 N Michigan Ave, Chicago, IL 60611 ☎312/321 9800 or 1-800/227-2826. *Motorcoach tours. "Berlin to Budapest" spends 2 days in Berlin with stops in Dresden and Prague (11 days from $2995, land only).*

DER Travel Services 9501 West Devon Ave, Rosemont, IL 60018 ☎1-800/782-2424. *Customized tours and packages.*

Euro Lloyd Tours 1640 Hempstead Turnpike, East Meadow, NY 11554 ☎516/794-1253 or 1-800/334-2724. *Customized tours and city packages from $683 (3 nights land/air).*

International Gay Travel Association 4331 N Federal Hwy, Suite 304, Ft Lauderdale, FL 33308 ☎1-800/448-8550. *Trade group with lists of gay-owned or gay-friendly travel agents, accommodations and other travel businesses.*

Maupintour 1515 St. Andrews Drive, Lawrence KS 66047 ☎1-800/255-6162. *"Berlin to Budapest by Train" –14 days from $4680 (land/air).*

Olson-Travelworld 1145 Clark St, Stevens Point, WI ☎715/345-0505 or 1-800/826-4026. *16- day luxury tour of Eastern Europe includes three days in Berlin (from $5375 land only).*

Trafalgar Tours 11 E 26th St, New York, NY 10010 ☎1-800/854-0103. *Berlin included in tours of Germany and Austria.*

Travel Bound 599 Broadway, New York, NY 10012 ☎212/334-1350 or 1-800/456-8656. *Fully inclusive tour package bookable only through a travel agent.*

Vantage Travel 111 Cypress St, Brookline, MA 02146 ☎1-800/322-6677. *Group travel for seniors. River cruises and packages that include Berlin as part of a multi-city itinerary.*

credit cards such as American Express often include some medical insurance, while most Canadians' provincial health plans typically provide limited overseas medical coverage. If you're not covered – or for additional precautions – you might want to contact a specialist travel insurance company; see the box or ask your travel agent for a recommendation.

The best premiums are usually to be had through **student/youth travel agencies** – STA policies, for example, including medical coverage, start at $45 for seven days; $110 for a month.

Note that most North American travel policies apply only to items lost, stolen or damaged while in the custody of an identifiable, responsible third party – hotel porter, airline, luggage consignment, etc. Even in these cases, you will have to contact the local police within 24 hours of the incident to have a complete report made out so that your insurer can process the claim.

Travel insurance companies

Access America, PO Box 90310, Richmond, VA 23230 ☎1-800/284-8300.

Carefree Travel Insurance, PO Box 310, 120 Mineola Blvd, Mineola, NY 11501 ☎1-800/323-3149.

STA Travel, 10 Downing St, New York, NY 10014 ☎212/627-3111 or 1-800/777-0112.

Travel Assistance International, 1133 15th St NW, Suite 400, Washington DC 20005 ☎1-800/821- 2828.

Travel Guard, 1145 Clark St, Stevens Point, WI 54481 ☎1-800/826-1300.

Travel Insurance Services, 2930 Camino Diablo, Suite 300, Walnut Creek, CA 94596 ☎1-800/937-1387.

Getting there from Australia and New Zealand

Few airlines fly direct to Berlin from Australasia; most use Frankfurt as their European gateway. All involve either a transfer or overnight stopover en route in either LA or their Southeast Asian hub city; the chance to rest up should be taken, as flying time is between twenty and thirty hours.

Most airfares to Europe are common rated; you pay the same irrespective of destination, so the carriers below can take you elsewhere in Europe (assuming they fly there of course) for the same price – some airlines offering free flight coupons, car rental or accommodation

---

Airlines

Aeroflot Australia: ☎02/9262 2233; no NZ office

Air France Australia: ☎02/9321 1000; NZ: ☎09/303 3521

Air New Zealand Australia: ☎13 2476; NZ ☎09/357 3000

Alitalia Australia: ☎02/9247 1308; NZ ☎09/379 4457

British Airways Australia: ☎02/9258 3300; NZ: ☎09/356 8690

Garuda Australia: ☎02/9334 9944 or 1-800/800 873; NZ ☎09/366 1855

Japan Air Lines Australia: ☎02/9272 1111; NZ ☎09/379 9906

KLM Australia: ☎02/9231 6333 or 1-800/505 747; no NZ office

Lauda Air Australia: ☎02/9251 6155; no NZ office

Lufthansa Australia: ☎02/9367 3888; NZ ☎09/303 1529

Philippine Airlines Australia: ☎02/9262 3333; no NZ office

Qantas Australia: ☎13 1211; NZ ☎09/357 8900 or 800/808 767

Singapore Airlines Australia: ☎13 1011; NZ ☎9/379 3209

United Australia: ☎13 1777; NZ ☎09/379 3800

Discount travel agents

Anywhere Travel, 345 Anzac Parade, Kingsford, Sydney ☎02/9663 0411.

Brisbane Discount Travel, 260 Queen St, Brisbane ☎07/3229 9211.

Budget Travel, 6 Fort St, Auckland ☎09/366 0061, plus branches around the city (☎0800/808 040).

Destinations Unlimited, 3 Milford Rd, Auckland ☎09/373 4033.

Flight Centres, Australia: 82 Elizabeth St, Sydney, plus branches nationwide ☎13 1600; NZ: 205 Queen St, Auckland (☎09/309 6171), plus branches nationwide.

Northern Gateway, 22 Cavenagh St, Darwin ☎08/8941 1394.

STA Travel, Australia: 702 Harris St, Ultimo, Sydney, and throughout the country (nearest branch ☎13 1776, fastfare telesales ☎1300/360 960); NZ: 10 High St, Auckland ☎09/309 0458 (fastfare telesales ☎09/366 6673), and throughout the country.

Thomas Cook, Australia: 175 Pitt St, Sydney, and throughout the country (local branch ☎13 1771 or telesales ☎1-800/063 913); NZ: 96 Anzac Ave, Auckland ☎09/379 3920.

Tymtro Travel, Level 8, 130 Pitt St, Sydney ☎02/9223 2211 or 1300 652 969.

---

with your ticket. Choose carefully, though, as these perks are often impossible to alter later. Alternatively, you could buy the cheapest possible flight to anywhere in Europe and make your way to Germany by stand-by flight, train or bus, although this rarely works out as cheaply as buying a discounted air fare all the way.

Given the high cost of flights from Australasia a **"round the world"** (RTW) fare is worth considering, if you have plenty of time. Of the airline combinations available, the cheapest is with Qantas–Air France, allowing three stops in each direction (including Africa) for around A$1699/NZ$2099; for greater flexibility Cathay Pacific–United's "Globetrotter'", Air New Zealand–KLM–Northwest's "World Navigator" and Qantas–BA's "Global Explorer" all offer six stopovers worldwide, limited backtracking and additional stopovers (around A$100/NZ$120 each), from A$2699/ NZ$3189 to A$3299/NZ$3799.

Fares

Fares are structured according to **season**, with low season generally defined as mid-January through February and October through November and high season as mid-May through August and December to mid-January; shoulder seasons cover the rest of the year. Flying time is long – between 20 and 30 hours – and can be physically and mentally taxing so consider a stopover.

Flights to Europe are generally cheaper via Asia than the US with fares from major eastern Australian cities usually common rated (flights from Perth via Asia and Africa between $200-400 less and via the Americas about $400 more). Tickets purchased direct from the airlines are usually at published rates – more expensive than some RTW fares. Travel agents offer the best deals on fares and have the latest information on limited special offers. Flight Centres and STA (see box opposite) generally offer the lowest fares, especially for students and those under 26.

From Australia

The most competitive rates for flights via Asia are currently offered by Garuda, starting at A$1600, and Aeroflot, at A$1850. Lufthansa, in conjunction with several other airlines, has the most direct service to Berlin via Bangkok, while KLM, Lauda Air, Swissair, Alitalia and Singapore Airlines – via their home cities – all start around A$1999.

Via North America, United Airlines offers the cheapest deal via LA and either New York, Washington or Chicago from A$2299, while Canadian Airlines–Qantas can take you there via Toronto or Vancouver from around A$2499.

From New Zealand

From Auckland, the choice of airlines flying to Berlin is quite limited, and as with Australia all

---

Specialist agents

There is very little in the way of organized tours to Germany from Australia or New Zealand, and you're better off making arrangements once you're in Europe. However, the agents listed below can help you plan your trip.

Adventure World, 73 Walker St, Sydney ☎ 02/956 7766; 8 Victoria Ave, Perth ☎ 09/9221 2300; 101 Great South Rd, Auckland ☎ 09/524 5118. *Short city-stays and sightseeing tours.*

Creative Tours, bookings through travel agents only. *Escorted bus tours and accommodation.*

European Travel Office, 133 Castlereagh St, Sydney ☎ 02/9267 7727; 122 Rosslyn St, West Melbourne ☎ 03/9329 8844; 407 Great South Rd, Auckland ☎ 09/525 3074. *Five-star accommodation, city stays and cultural tours throughout Germany.*

Insight, bookings through travel agents only. *First-class city accommodation and bus tours.*

Pride Travel, 254 Bay St, Brighton, Melbourne ☎ 03/9596 3566 or 1-800/061 427. *Lesbian and gay tours.*

Silk's Travel, 263 Oxford St, Darlinghurst, Sydney ☎ 02/9380 5835. *Lesbian and gay tours*

Youth Hostel Association, 422 Kent St, Sydney ☎ 02/9261 1111 and branches nationwide; NZ: 36 Customs House, Auckland ☎ 09/379 4224. *Organizes budget accommodation and travel throughout Germany for YHA members.*

make either a transfer or overnight stop in their Asian or US hub city. The best deals are with Garuda, via either Jakarta or Denpasar, from NZ$1899, while the most direct flights are on Lufthansa – which teams up with other carriers to provide a through flight via Bangkok – and Singapore Airlines, via a transfer in Singapore; both for around NZ$2199–2999. Via LA, the best deals are on United Airlines, from NZ$2599.

Trains

If you intend to explore Germany or extend your trip into Europe, it might be worth buying a **rail pass** before you leave home. The **Europass** allows travel in France, Germany, Italy, Spain and Switzerland for A$295/NZ$350 (under 26) or A$440/NZ$525 (over 26) for five days over two months, up to A$700/NZ$830 or A$1030/NZ$1220 for 15 days in 2 months; there's also the option of adding on adjacent countries (Austria, Hungary, Benelux, Portugal and Greece). Passes are available through CIT, 123 Clarence St, Sydney (☎02/9299 4754) or Thomas Cook Rail

Direct (Australia: ☎1300/361 941; New Zealand: ☎09/263 7260).

Insurance

Travel insurance is available from most travel agents, some banks or direct from insurance companies, for periods ranging from a few days to a year or even longer. All are fairly similar in premium and coverage which includes medical expenses, loss of personal property and travellers' cheques, cancellations and delays, as well as most adventure sports. Ready Plan and Cover More usually give the best value coverage. A normal policy for Germany costs around A$100/NZ$110 for two weeks, A$170/NZ$190 for a month.

Travel insurance companies

Cover More, 9/32 Walker St, North Sydney ☎02/9202 8000 or 1-800/251 881.

Ready Plan, 141 Walker St, Dandenong, Melbourne ☎03/9791 5077 or 1-800/337 462; 10/63 Albert St, Auckland ☎09/379 3208.

Red tape and visas

British and other EU nationals can enter Germany on a valid passport or national identity card. The official time limit for stays in Germany is ninety days, but enforcement

of this is fairly lax: it's unlikely, for example, that your passport will be date-stamped on arrival.

US, Canadian, Australian and New Zealand passport holders do not need a visa to enter Germany, and are allowed a stay of ninety days (within any one year). However, you're strongly advised, if you know your stay will be longer than this, to apply for an extension visa from your local German embassy before you go.

Visa requirements vary for nationals of any other country; contact your local German embassy or consulate for information. For details of where to find your own embassy or

---

If you are intending to stay on in Berlin and/or find a job, regulations are complex: see "Staying On", p.35.

consulate when in Berlin, see "Directory" on p.38.

If you want to extend your stay beyond three months, EU, North American and Australasian visitors are expected to **register with the local police** (as is everyone else after their visa has expired). First you'll need a *Polizeianmeldungsformular* ("registration form"), available from newsagents for DM2. Get a friend, who has already registered and understands the complex German on the form, to help; inaccuracies will cause complications when you go to the police station.

Customs

Customs and duty-free restrictions vary throughout Europe, with subtle variations even within the European Community.

Since the inauguration of the EU Single Market, travellers entering Britain from another EU country do not have to make a declaration to Customs at their place of entry. You can effectively bring back as much **duty-paid** wine or beer as you can carry (the legal limits being 90 litres of wine or 110 of beer), though there are still restrictions on the volume of **tax- or duty-free goods** you can bring into the country. The current duty-free allowance for EU citizens is 200 cigarettes, one litre of spirits and five litres of wine; for non-EU residents the

German embassies

Australia 119 Empire Circuit, Yarralumla, Canberra 2600 ☎ 02/6270 1911

Britain 23 Belgrave Square, London SW1X 8PZ ☎ 0171/235 5033

Canada 1 Waverley St, Ottawa, Ontario K2P 0T8 ☎ 613/232-1101
Consulates in Montréal, Toronto and Vancouver.

Ireland 31 Trimelston Ave, Booterstown, Blackrock, Co Dublin ☎ 01/693011

New Zealand 90–92 Hobson St Wellington ☎ 04/736 063

US 4645 Reservoir Rd NW, Washington, DC 20007-1998 ☎ 202/298-4000 or 298-4355
Consulates in New York, Atlanta, Boston, Detroit, Houston, Miami, San Francisco, Seattle, Los Angeles and Chicago.

allowances are usually 200 cigarettes, one litre of spirits and two litres of wine.

Residents of the USA and Canada can take up to 200 cigarettes and one litre of alcohol home, as can **Australian** citizens, while **New Zealanders** must confine themselves to 200 cigarettes, 4.5 litres of beer or wine, and just over one litre of spirits.

Points of arrival

The major points of arrival in Berlin all lie within easy reach of the city centre by public transport. The most distant of the city's three airports is only about 35 minutes away by

S-Bahn, and the main station for those arriving by train – Bahnhof Zoologischer Garten, or Zoo Station – lies at the heart of Berlin's West End and at the western hub of the city's U- and S-Bahn network. Using this, you can reach just about anywhere in the city.

Airports

Chances are you'll arrive at **Tegel airport**, the city's largest: **Schönefeld airport**, on the eastern side of the city, is mainly used by flights from eastern Europe and the Middle and Far East, while **Tempelhof airport** is largely for domestic flights.

Airline offices in Berlin

Aeroflot
Unter den Linden 51
Mitte ☎ 2 26 98 10

Air Canada
Kurfürstendamm 207
Charlottenburg ☎ 8 82 58 79

Air France
Tegel Airport ☎ 0180/5 36 03 70

British Airways
Europa Center
Charlottenburg ☎ 69 10 21

Deutsche BA
Europa Center
Charlottenburg ☎ 2 54 00 00

KLM
Tegel Airport ☎ 0180/5 21 42 01

LTU
Schönefeld Airport ☎ 63 30 62 03

Lufthansa
Kurfürstendamm 220
Charlottenburg ☎ 88 75 88

Sabena
Tempelhof Airport
Tempelhof ☎ 69 51 38 50

Swissair
Kurfürstendamm 206
Charlottenburg ☎ 8 83 90 01

Tegel

Nearly all scheduled and charter flights arrive at the refreshingly small and manageable **Tegel Airport** (☎4 10 11). Here you'll find a small branch of the tourist office, with accommodation booking facilities (see p.211), currency exchange facilities open till 10pm daily (at Berliner Bank, by Gate 1), left luggage (DM10 per item), the usual car rental companies (except Eurorent) and, when you're leaving, scant duty-free shopping.

From Tegel, express #**X9** or regular #**109 buses** run every five to ten minutes directly to **Zoo Station** (see below) at the centre of the West End of the city (journey time 35min; DM3.60). Alternatively, take the #109 bus to Jakob-Kaiser-Platz U-Bahn and transfer to the U-Bahn system (the bus ticket is valid for the U-Bahn journey: see pp.17–18). **Taxis** cover the distance in half the time (depending on the traffic) and cost DM25–35.

Schönefeld

Berlin's second airport, **Schönefeld** (☎6 09 10), lies just beyond the southeastern edge of the city. It mainly serves eastern Europe, Turkey, and the Middle and Far East. Take **bus #171** (DM3.60, ticket also valid on S- and U-Bahn, see pp.17–18) from the terminal building to S-Bahnhof Flughafen Schönefeld, from where S-Bahn line #9 provides a direct link to the city centre, running to Charlottenburg via the Hauptbahnhof, Alexanderplatz, Friedrichstrasse and Zoo Station (journey time to Alexanderplatz approximately 35min).

Alternatively, bus #171 continues to Rudow U-Bahn station (one bus stop further) for transfer to U-Bahn line #7 (change at Hermannplatz for trains to Alexanderplatz, or Berliner Strasse for trains to Zoo Station). A **taxi** into town (for example to Bahnhof Friedrichstrasse) from Schönefeld is prohibitively expensive, costing around DM60.

Tempelhof

Tempelhof (☎6 95 10), the closest airport to the city centre, is currently used mainly by German domestic carriers, some European airlines and scheduled flights by very small operators. However, it's due to close sometime in the next few years and is gradually shutting down; flights are all being switched to Tegel. From the fore-court, **bus #119** links the airport with the Europa Center. A few minutes' walk west is Platz der Luftbrücke U-Bahn station, from where trains on line #6 take under ten minutes to reach Bahnhof Friedrichstrasse in the city centre (or change at Stadtmitte for Zoo Station). A taxi to Friedrichstrasse or Zoo Station would cost about DM20, and probably take longer.

Train stations

Trains from western European destinations go to **Zoo Station** (some trains from the west also stop at Wannsee and Spandau stations). Where you alight depends on where you're staying – if your accommodation is pre-booked, check before arrival. If you have not yet arranged anything, it's probably best to get off at Zoo Station, which, though unpleasantly seedy, is handily located for the city's main tourist office, and has excellent **U- and S-Bahn links** to all parts of the city. At Zoo Station you'll also find exchange and cashpoint facilities (p.25), lockers and left luggage (p.39), a late-opening post office (p.26) and an information kiosk for the city's transport network (p.18).

Bus terminals

International **buses** and those from other German cities mostly stop at the **Zentraler Omnibus Bahnhof** or **ZOB** (central bus station), Masurenallee, Charlottenburg, west of the centre, near the Funkturm; regular #149 buses or U-Bahn line #2 from Kaiserdamm station link it to the city centre, a journey of about 15 minutes.

Getting around

gaps in the U-Bahn system, with buses converging on Zoo Station and Alexanderplatz. Bus #100, which runs between the two, is good for sightseeing purposes. **Night buses** run every twenty minutes or so, although the routes sometimes differ from daytime ones; the **VBB** (Verkehrsgemeinschaft Berlin Brandenburg) supplies a map.

Eastern Berlin's **tram network** survives from prewar days, though thankfully the rolling stock is a little more modern. The main tram **terminus** in the centre of town is at **Hackescher Markt** near Schlossplatz. Tickets are available from machines at the termini or from U-Bahn stations. There's talk, too, of reintroducing trams to western Berlin, such are their environmental advantages.

Public transport

Berlin is a large city, and sooner or later you'll need to use its efficient, if expensive, transport system. The U-Bahn, running both under and over ground, covers much of the centre and stretches into the suburbs: trains run from 4am to between midnight and approximately 12.30am, an hour later on Friday and Saturday. U-Bahn lines #2 and #9 run throughout the night on Friday and Saturday.

The **S-Bahn** system has been extended since unification and these days, though the service is still far less frequent than the U-Bahn, it's better for covering long distances fast – say for heading out to the Wannsee lakes or Potsdam.

You never seem to have to wait long for a **bus** in the city: timetables at the stops are uncannily accurate, and the city network covers most of the

Tickets

Tickets for the U- and S-Bahn system and the bus network can be bought from the orange-coloured machines at the entrances to U-Bahn stations. These take all but the smallest coins, give change and have a basic explanation of the ticketing system in English. Though it's tempting to ride without a ticket, be warned that plain-clothes inspectors frequently cruise the lines (particularly, for some reason, at the beginning of the month), meting out on-the-spot **fines of DM60** for those without a valid ticket or pass. If you're taking a bus after 8pm, you must board by the front door by the driver and purchase or show a ticket.

Single tickets (*Normaltarif*) common to the whole VBB system cost DM3.90, and allow you to travel in any two of the three tariff zones. If you're heading for the outskirts of town or Potsdam, it'll cost DM4.20 to travel through all three tariff zones. Tickets are valid for two hours, enabling you to transfer across the three networks to continue your journey, and to return within that time by a different route. A *Kurzstrecke*, or short-trip ticket, costs DM2.50 and allows you to travel up to three train or six bus stops (no return journeys). On the U- and S-Bahn, tickets other than the passes mentioned below are supposed to be punched before travelling; on the bus the driver may **check** your ticket.

It's possible to save a little money by buying a **day ticket** (*Tageskarte*) for DM7.80 (2 zones) or DM8.50 (3 zones) from any U-Bahn station or the transit authority office on Grunewaldestrasse, Schöneberg, next to Kleistpark U-Bahn station (Mon–Fri 8am–6pm, Sat 7am–2pm). These are valid until 3am of the day following your purchase.

You can also buy a **seven-day ticket** (*Sieben-Tage-Karte*) for DM40–48, depending on the zones through which you travel, or a **monthly ticket** (*Monatskarte*, also known as an *Umweltkarte*) for DM99–120, from any kiosk. A **premium monthly ticket** (*Umweltkarte Premium*), costing DM114–138, allows unlimited travel through all three tariff zones and for one adult and up to three children to travel with you free after 8pm, all day Saturday and Sunday and on public holidays. The monthly cards obviously represent a considerable saving; although tickets begin on the first of each month, not on the date of purchase (however, they are transferable, so you could buy the ticket with someone else or sell it to a friend before leaving). There's also the **Welcome Card** (DM29), which gives unlimited travel across the system for an adult and up to three children for three days. Aimed specifically at visitors to the city, it also gives half-price entry to most of the city's municipally held museums and attractions and is available from around two hundred hotels, ninety VBB stands and city tourist offices.

For **more information** about Berlin's public transport system, and a larger scale U- and S-Bahn map than the one in this guide, it's worth getting hold of the excellent *VBB Atlas* (DM7) either from the cubicle outside Zoo Station or from one of the larger U-Bahn stations. Most U-Bahn stations also provide simple free maps; ask at the kiosk on the platform.

By boat

More an option for messing about on Berlin's numerous canals than a practical mode of trans-port, **boats** run regularly throughout the summer. From the centre of town, Reederei Heinz Riedel, Planufer 78, Kreuzberg (☎6 93 46 46) runs daily trips on the **River Spree**, taking in the Reichstag and the Landwehrkanal. Starting points are the Hansabrücke on the Spree in Moabit and Kottbusser Brücke on the Landwehrkanal in Kreuzberg. Trips cost DM19 and last around three hours. The same company also runs trips out to the **Pfaueninsel** and the **Wannsee** in the west of the city, to the **Müggelsee** in the east, and on the **lakes** surrounding Berlin.

The Stern und Kreis Schiffahrt, Puschkinallee 16–17, Treptow (☎5 36 36 00), offers a variety of city-centre trips with departures from Jannowitzbrücke, Treptower Hafen, the Berliner Dom and the Palastufer (tickets from DM13.50). A number of smaller companies also run cruises along the waterways in and around Berlin, ranging as far afield as **Spandau**, **Potsdam** and **Werder** – details available from the Reederverband der Berliner Personenschiffahrt, Gierezeile 26, Charlottenburg (☎3 42 24 31). Full details and timetables for all Berlin cruise companies are available from city tourist offices.

Taxis

Taxis are plentiful, and though pricey (DM4 plus DM2.20 per kilometre (for the first 6km), rising to DM2.40 from 11pm to 6am and all day Sunday), can work out to be not much more expensive than public transport if you're travelling in small groups. They cruise the city day and night and congregate at useful locations, such as outside the KaDeWe store, on Savignyplatz and by Zoo Station in the West End; and in the city centre at the northern entrance to Friedrichstrasse station and the entrances to Alexanderplatz S-Bahn station. Don't expect the driver necessarily to have an infallible knowledge of the city, as many Berlin taxi drivers are student part-timers or moonlighting second-jobbers.

Taxi phone numbers

☎21 01 01 (24hr service), ☎6 90 22, ☎26 10 26, ☎44 33 22, ☎2 61 70 80 or ☎6 04 83 43.

Driving

Though there's practically no need for a car within the city, you may want to tour around outside Berlin and one way of doing so is by

CAR RENTAL AGENCIES

AUSTRALIA		NEW ZEALAND	
Avis	☎ 1-800/225 533	Avis	☎ 09/526 2847
Budget	☎ 13 2727	Budget	☎ 09/375 2222
Hertz	☎ 13 3039	Hertz	☎ 09/309 0989
BRITAIN		NORTH AMERICA	
Avis	☎ 0990/900500	Alamo	☎ 1-800/522-9696
Budget	☎ 0800/181181	Auto Europe	☎ 1-800/223-5555
Europcar/InterRent	☎ 0345/222525	Avis	☎ 1-800/331-1084
Hertz	☎ 0990/996699	Budget	☎ 1-800/527-0700
Holiday Autos	☎ 0990/300400	Dollar/Europe Car	☎ 1-800/800-6000
Thrifty	☎ 0990/168238	Europe by Car	☎ 1-800/223-1516
		Hertz	☎ 1-800/654-3001
			Canada ☎ 1-800/263-0600
		Holiday Autos	☎ 1-800/422-7737

car. The cheapest way to organize **car rental** is to book before you leave: Holiday Autos (see box above), which acts as an agent for German company Eurorent, guarantees the lowest rates – currently around £87 for a three-day minimum period. Rental rates tend to be higher than in the UK and markedly higher than in the US.

In Berlin itself, the best way to find a good deal is to get the Yellow Pages and look under *Autovermietung* (*PKW an Selbstfahrer*). Phoning around should trawl in something for under DM60 a day, though watch out for hidden extras such as limited mileage. Most rental places do good-value Friday afternoon–Monday morning deals, and most expect to see a credit card and passport. Some inexpensive firms, each charging around DM60 a day, are: ACS Rent a Car, Albrechtstr. 117, Schöneberg (☎7 92 00 15); City Trans, Wönnichstr, 100, Lichtenberg

(☎5 12 71 14); C. Nagel, Bundesallee 176, Wilmersdorg (☎8 54 30 00). International firms have offices at Tegel airport and are listed in the phone book under *Autovermietungen*. Four-star unleaded fuel currently costs around DM1.60 per litre.

Driving rules and traffic problems

The most important rules to bear in mind when driving in Berlin are simple. You drive on the right; main roads have a yellow diamond indicating who has priority; but if you are driving in built-up areas, traffic coming from the right normally has right of way. This is particularly important to remember in the former East Berlin, where **trams** always have the right of way. Unfamiliarity with the traffic system means that unwary visiting drivers are prone to cutting in front of turning trams at junctions – a frightening and potentially lethal error. Also, when trams halt at their designated stops, it's forbidden to overtake until the tram starts moving, to allow passengers time to cross the road and board.

Seatbelts are compulsory in front and rear seats; and children under 12 years must sit in the back. A surviving GDR traffic regulation is the "*Grüner Pfeil*", or green arrow attached to traffic lights at the right-hand turning lane at junctions: it means if the light is red, but no traffic is approaching from the left, you may proceed. The **speed limits** are 50km/h in urban areas, 100km/h out of built-up areas and 130km/h on

---

Some 24-hour filling stations

Aral, Potsdamer Chaussee 6, Zehlendorf

BP, Kurfürstendamm 128, Charlottenburg

Esso, Leibnizstr. corner Mommsenstr., Charlottenburg; Tempelhofer Damm 20, Tempelhof

Minol, Prenzlauer Allee 1–4, Prenzlauer Berg

Minol, Holzmarktstr. 36–42, Friedrichshain

Shell, Uhlandstr. 187, Charlottenburg; Hohenzollerndamm 41, Wilmersdorf

---

the motorways (except where different limits are specified). There are **on-the-spot-fines** for speeding and other offences; for speeding these are calculated on a sliding scale up to about DM75 – after a cutoff point of roughly 25km over the limit, you're charged and taken to court. For failing to wear seatbelts, the immediate fine is DM75. The maximum permitted **blood alcohol level** is 80mg per 100ml.

Thanks to a post-unification boom in car-ownership and extensive road construction projects, Berlin suffers **traffic snarl-ups** that can compete with the worst any other European city has to offer. The authorities seemingly have little clue as to how to control the rush-hour jams that start at around 5pm and are particularly bad on Friday afternoons: don't be surprised if a journey you'd allowed twenty minutes for takes three or four times as long during these periods.

The recent installation of **parking meters** seems to have aided your chances of finding a place to park. The meters, identifiable by their tall grey rectangular solar power umbrellas, cost DM1 per 30min, DM4 in places like Alexanderplatz. You're supposed to move after the hour, and stiff fines are handed out to those without tickets; drivers of cars with foreign plates can expect to be towed away.

Cycling

Cycling is a quick and convenient way of getting around the city, and – if you take your bike on the U- or S-Bahn – exploring the countryside and lakes of the Grunewald and Wannsee areas. To take your bike on a train you'll need an extra ticket costing DM2.50.

Bike rental is available from several shops, though (unlike in cities in the former West Germany) not from the train stations. Try Fahrradstation, with branches at Möckernstr. 92 (☎2 16 91 77), Kreuzberg, and Gipsstr. 7, Mitte (☎2 80 86 20). Prices start at DM18 for an ordinary bike for a day, DM45 for a weekend and DM70 for a week; for a mountain bike it's DM23, DM55 and DM95; and for a tandem, DM40, DM65 and DM175. Their office hours are Mon–Fri 10am–6pm, Sat 10am–2pm, but it's best to phone a reservation through first; they also run bike tours around the city, to Potsdam and the eastern lakes. If you're planning to stay for any length of time, it works out cheaper to **buy** a secondhand machine and sell it when you leave. Try any of the bike shops, or look under *Fahrräder* in the classified ads section of *Zweite Hand* (published Tues, Thurs & Sat), *Die Berliner Morgenpost* (Sun) or *Der Tagesspiegel* (Sun).

Travellers with disabilities

You'll find that access and facilities are good in Berlin, although the western part of the city is currently better equipped than the east, where things are slowly being improved. Most of the major western museums have wheelchair access, as do many other public buildings. The offical U- and S-Bahn map also indicates which stations are accessible by wheelchair.

The **Touristik Union International** has a centralized information bank on many German and Berlin hotels and pensions that cater to the needs of disabled travellers or those with specific dietary requirements. It can also book you onto package tours, provide suitable wheelchairs for train travel, arrange transportation of travellers'

own wheelchairs, and provide transport at airports and stations.

Berlin Tourismus Marketing (tourist information office) also has details on suitable accommodation, and the city boasts one specially adapted **hostel**, *Freizeit- und Bildungsstätte für Körperbehinderte der Fürst-Donnersmarck-Stiftung,* Schäderstr. 9–13, Zehlendorf (☎8 15 60 82). Located in the relatively rural suburb of Zehlendorf, it's convenient to public transport and offers facilities for groups and single guests.

If you are registered disabled then you're allowed to use Berlin's excellent free **Telebus** service, Esplanade 17, Pankow (Mon–Fri 9am–3pm; ☎47 88 20). After being issued with

Contacts for travellers with disabilities

GERMANY

Touristik Union International (TUI), Postfach 610280, 3000 Hannover 61 ☎ 0511/56 70

Deutscher Paritätischer Wohlfahrtsverband, Brandenburgische Str. 80, Wilmersdorf, Berlin ☎ 86 00 10. *Advice on choosing hotels and renting wheelchairs.*

Landesbeauftragter für Behinderte, Sächsische Str. 30, Wilmersdorf, Berlin ☎ 8 67 64 45. *Umbrella group of disabled and self-help organizations, useful for finding addresses of more specific groups.*

AUSTRALIA

ACROD (Australian Council for Rehabilitation of the Disabled), PO Box 60, Curtin, ACT 2605 ☎ 02/62 82 4333. *Regional offices provide lists of travel agencies and tour operators for people with disabilities.*

BRITAIN

Holiday Care Service, 2nd Floor, Imperial Building, Victoria Road, Horley, Surrey RH6 7PZ ☎ 01293/774535, fax 784647, Minicom ☎ 01293/776943. *Free lists of accessible accommodation and information on financial help for holidays.*

Mobility International, 228 Borough High St, London SE1 1JX ☎ 0171/403 5688. *Information, access guides, tours and exchange programmes.*

RADAR (Royal Association for Disability and Rehabilitation), 12 City Forum, 250 City Rd, London EC1V 8AF ☎ 0171/250 3222, Minicom ☎ 0171/250 4119. *Advice on holidays and travel abroad; a guide on European holidays (£5 inc. p&p) is available*

Tripscope, The Courtyard, Evelyn Rd, London W4 5JL ☎ 0181/994 9294, fax 994 3618. *National telephone information service offering free advice on UK and international transport and travel for those with a mobility problem.*

NEW ZEALAND

Disabled Persons Assembly 173–175 Victoria St, Wellington ☎ 04/811 9100

NORTH AMERICA

Directions Unlimited, 720 N Bedford Rd, Bedford Hills, NY 10507 ☎ 1-800/533-5343. *Tour operator specializing in custom tours for people with disabilities.*

Jewish Rehabilitation Hospital, 3205 Place Alton Goldbloom, Chomedy Laval, PQ H7V 1R2 ☎ 514/688-9550, ext 226. *Guidebooks and travel information.*

Mobility International USA, PO Box 10767, Eugene, OR 97440 ☎ 503/343-1284 (voice & TDD). *Information and referral services, access guides, tours and exchange programmes. Annual membership $25 (includes quarterly newsletter).*

Society for the Advancement of Travel for the Handicapped (SATH), 347 Fifth Ave, New York, NY 10016 ☎ 212/447-7284. *Non-profit-making travel industry referral service that passes queries on to its members as appropriate.*

Travel Information Service ☎ 215/456-9600. *Telephone only information and referral service for disabled travellers.*

Twin Peaks Press Box 129, Vancouver, WA 98666 ☎ 206/694-2462 or 1-800/637-2256. *Publisher of the* Directory of Travel Agencies for the Disabled *($19.95), listing more than 370 agencies worldwide;* Travel for the Disabled *($19.95); the* Directory of Accessible Van Rentals *($9.95) and* Wheelchair Vagabond *($14..95), loaded with personal tips.*

---

a pass and number, you call the service and one of their fifty taxis or seventy buses will pick you up and take you to your destination. For people in wheelchairs, the buses need to be booked at least a day in advance, the taxis a few hours.

A café-bar designed especially, but not exclusively, for disabled people, **Blisse 14** (Blissestr. 14, Wilmersdorf; ☎ 8 21 20 79) is a good meeting place with lots of useful information and a wide range of food and non-alcoholic drinks.

Information and maps

Tourist offices in Berlin

Main office: Europa Center (entrance on Budapester Str.), Tiergarten ☎25 00 25. Mon–Sat 8am–10pm, Sun 9am–9pm.

Tegel airport (main hall, left luggage office) ☎41 01 34 26. Daily 5am–10.30pm.

Brandenburg Gate Daily 9.30am–6pm.

Info-Point Dresdener Bank, Unter den Linden 17, Mitte. Mon, Wed & Fri 8.30am–2pm, Tues & Thurs also open 3.30–6pm.

Info-Point KaDeWe, Wittenbergplatz, Charlottenburg. Mon–Fri 9.30am–8pm, Sat 9am–4pm.

Before you set off for Berlin, it's worth contacting the German National Tourist Office, which has a lot of useful information on accommodation, what's on in town and the odd glossy brochure.

Once in the city, the **tourist office**, Berlin Tourismus Marketing, can supply a wider selection of bumph than the national offices, including comprehensive listings of the higher-brow cultural events, and help with accommodation (see "Accommodation" p.211). There are several offices (see below), but the best, in terms of information and service, is the one in the Europa Center.

Additionally, Berlin has a couple of **cultural centres**. The Amerika Haus, Hardenbergstr. 22–24, Charlottenburg (Wed–Fri 1–5pm; ☎31 10 73), has US newspapers, magazines, videos and a well-stocked library, along with regular movies and cultural events. The British Council, Hardenbergstr. 20, Charlottenburg, First Floor (Mon, Wed & Fri 2–6pm, Tues 2–7pm; ☎31 10 99 10), has a small but decent library, and is the best source for British newspapers.

German National Tourist Offices

Australia Level 2, St Andrews House, Sydney Square, Sydney 2000 ☎ 02/9267 8148

Britain 65 Curzon St, London, W1Y 8NE ☎0171/493 0050 (person to person 10am–noon & 2–4pm) or ☎0891/600 1000 (recorded information, 50p per minute)

Canada 175 Bloor St E, Suite 604, North Tower, Toronto, Ontario M4W3R8 ☎416/968 1570

New Zealand PO BOX 80079 Green Bay, Auckland 1 ☎09/620 0601

US 122 E 42nd St, New York, NY 10168 New York, NY 10017 ☎212/308 3300

Listings magazines

Berlin has two essential **listings magazines** – *Tip* (DM4.50) and *Zitty* (DM4) – which come out on alternate weeks. *Zitty* is marginally the better of the two, with day-by-day details of gigs, concerts, events, TV and radio, theatre and film, alongside intelligent articles on politics, style and the Berlin in-crowd, and useful classified ads. The monthly *Prinz* (DM4.50) is unable to compete with the big two (its headquarters are in Munich, and it shows), and relies on titillating covers to entice readers; it's worth picking up only for its eating section. Berlin's diverse arts scene is covered by *Artery Berlin* (DM3.50), a monthly English/German publication with full listings of what's happening

Map and travel book suppliers

AUSTRALIA

Bowyangs, 372 Little Bourke St, Melbourne
☎ 03/9670 4383

The Map Shop, 16a Peel St, Adelaide
☎ 08/8231 2033

Perth Map Centre, 891 Hay St, Perth
☎ 08/9322 5733

Travel Bookshop, Shop 3, 175 Liverpool St,
Sydney ☎ 02/9261 8200

Worldwide Maps and Guides, 187 George St,
Brisbane ☎ 07/3221 4330

BRITAIN

Aberdeen Map Shop, 74 Skene St, Aberdeen,
AB10 1QE ☎ 01224/637999

Blackwell's Map and Travel Shop, 53 Broad
St, Oxford OX1 3BQ ☎ 01865/792792

Heffers Map Shop, 3rd Floor, Heffers
Stationery Department, 19 Sidney St,
Cambridge, CB2 3HL ☎ 01223/568467

James Thin Melven's Bookshop,
29 Union St, Inverness, IV1 1QA
☎ 01463/233500

John Smith and Sons, 57–61 St Vincent St,
Glasgow, G2 5TB ☎ 0141/221 7472

National Map Centre, 22–24 Caxton St,
London SW1H 0QU ☎ 0171/222 2466

Stanfords, 12–14 Long Acre, London WC2E
9LP ☎ 0171/836 1321; Campus Travel, 52
Grosvenor Gardens, SW1W 0AG ☎ 0171/730
1314; British Airways, 156 Regent St, W1R 5TA
☎ 0171/434 4744; 29 Corn St, Bristol BS1 1HT
☎ 0117/929 9966

The Travel Bookshop, 13–15 Blenheim
Crescent, London W11 2EE ☎ 0171/229 5260

*Maps by **mail or phone order** are
available from Stanfords' Long Acre branch,
Heffers and the three Scottish map outlets
listed.*

CANADA

Open Air Books and Maps, 25 Toronto St,
M5R 2C1 ☎ 416/363-0719

Ulysses Travel Bookshop, 4176 St-Denis,
Montréal H2W 2M5 ☎ 514/843 9447

World Wide Books and Maps, 1247 Granville
St, Vancouver V6Z 1G3 ☎ 604/687-3320

NEW ZEALAND

Specialty Maps, 58 Albert St, Auckland
☎ 09/307 2217.

US

Book Passage, 51 Tamal Vista Blvd, Corte
Madera, CA 94925 ☎ 415/927-0960

The Complete Traveller Bookstore, 199
Madison Ave, New York, NY 10016 ☎ 212/685-
9007; 3207 Fillmore St, San Francisco, CA
92123 ☎ 415/923-1511

Elliot Bay Book Company, 101 S Main St,
Seattle, WA 98104 ☎ 206/624-6600

Forsyth Travel Library, 226 Westchester
Ave, White Plains, NY 10604 ☎ 1-800/367-
7984

Map Link Inc., 30 S La Patera Lane, Unit 5,
Santa Barbara, CA 93117 ☎ 805/692-6777

The Map Store Inc., 1636 ISt NW, Washington
DC 20006 ☎ 202/628-2608

Phileas Fogg's Books & Maps, #87 Stanford
Shopping Center, Palo Alto, CA 94304 ☎ 1-
800/533-FOGG

Rand McNally, 444 N Michigan Ave, Chicago,
IL 60611 ☎ 312/321-1751; 150 E 52nd St,
New York, NY 10022 ☎ 212/758-7488; 595
Market St, San Francisco, CA 94105
☎ 415/777-3131 etc

Travel Books & Language Center, 4437
Wisconsin Ave, Washington, DC 20016 ☎ 1-
800/220-2665

Traveler's Bookstore, 22 W 52nd St, New
York, NY 10019 ☎ 212/664-0995

*Note: Rand McNally now has more than 20
stores across the US; call ☎ 1-800/333-0136
ext 2111) for the address of your nearest
store, or for direct mail maps.*

in the city's many galleries. The monthly *Berlin Programm* (DM2.80) has more condensed listings, alongside information on opening times, and national and international train, bus and plane timetables.

Maps

By far the best large-scale **map** of the city is the *VBB Atlas* (DM7), which also has complete listings and timetables for the U- & S-Bahn system, the bus, tram and ferry routes, and postcodes for every street in Berlin and Potsdam. It's available at the larger U-Bahn and S-Bahn stations. If you want to buy a map before you leave home, the ingeniously folded *Falk Plan* (DM9.80, DM11.80 for the better, enlarged version) contains an excellent gazetteer and enlarged plans of the city centre.

Berlin on the Net

Berlin Online
www.BerlinOnline.de
An excellent, all-purpose source for news, business, politics, entertainment, restaurants, listings and the like. All in German, alas.

Zitty Online
www.zitty.de
Web site for one of the city's biweekly listings magazines, this one includes an English-language section of restaurant and club listings.

Spiegel Online
www.speigel.de
The Web site of Germany's leading news magazine includes an English-language summary of articles.

Bundestag
www.bundestag.de
Everything you wanted to know about the country's parliament. German only.

Costs, money and banks

For years massively subsidized by West Germany, the opulent shops and slick restaurants of the former West Berlin mark a sharp contrast to the relative lack of development in the former Eastern sectors of the city. The differences are gradually lessening, but Berlin is still expensive compared to other German cities. Here, as in the rest of the country, people still carry money with them rather than relying on credit cards.

Assuming you intend to eat and drink in moderately priced places, utilize the public transport system sparingly and not stay in the *Hilton*, the **minimum** you could get by on after you've paid for your room is £20/$33 (or around DM45) a day. For this you would get a sandwich (DM3), an evening meal (DM20), three beers (DM10) and one underground ticket (DM3.60), with just over DM9 left for museums, entertainments, etc. A more realistic figure, if you want to see as much of the city as possible (and party at night), would be at least twice that amount.

Accommodation, **transport** and **nightlife** are the most likely to run your budget up. The cheapest hostel dormitory or basic room is around £11/$18 a night; the flat fares of around £1.50/$2.50 on the bus and U- and S-Bahn network quickly mount up. **Drink** is a little more expensive than most are used to, particularly in the city's more enjoyable nightspots; but the quality – especially of the beer – is significantly higher.

Eating is comparatively cheap, cheerful and varied (food is good value in the shops and in restaurants) for British visitors. North Americans will, however, find prices marginally higher than they are used to. However, many **museums** are free, with others softening their entrance fees for students with ID.

Money

The currency of Germany is the **Deutschmark**, which comes in **notes** of DM5 (rarely encountered these days), DM10, DM20, DM50, DM100, DM200, DM500 and DM1000; and **coins** of DM0.01 (one *Pfennig*), DM0.02, DM0.05, DM0.10, DM0.50, DM1, DM2 and DM5.

The current **exchange rate** is around DM2.95 to the pound sterling, DM1.75 to the US dollar. You can bring as much currency as you want into Berlin.

Travellers' cheques and credit cards

Travellers' cheques are the safest way of carrying your money. They can be cashed in any bank or exchange office and used in the flashier shops. For British travellers, **Eurocheques** (issued by most British banks with a Eurocheque card) can be used in banks and shops or restaurants. If you use them to get cash you pay a 1.6 percent fee to the bank, plus a small handling fee chargeable to your bank account.

Surprisingly, **credit and charge cards** are little used in Berlin: only the major cards will be accepted, and then only in large department stores and mid- to upmarket restaurants (though almost all petrol stations take cards). Should you want to get **cash** on your plastic, various banks will give an advance against Visa and Mastercard (Access) cards, subject to a minimum of the equivalent of £60/$100 – stickers in the bank windows indicate which credit cards they're associated with. You can also use the various **ATMs** (cashpoints) without fear of your card being gobbled up – provided you know

Emergency numbers for lost credit cards	
Access/Mastercard/Eurocard	☎069/7 93 30
American Express	☎069/72 00 16
Diner's Club	☎069/2 60 30
Visa	☎069/79 20 13 33

your PIN number and match your card with the correct machine. American Express card holders can use that company's facilities at Friedrichstr. 172, Mitte (Mon–Fri 9am–6pm, Sat 10am–1pm; ☎2 01 74 00).

Banks and exchange

Banking hours are usually Monday to Friday from 9am to noon and two afternoons a week from 2 to 6pm; though this varies from bank to bank. Branches of the Berliner Bank have the longest hours: the airport branch at Tegel is open daily from 8am to 10pm, and the branch at Kurfürstendamm 24, Charlottenburg, is open Monday to Friday from 9.30am to 6.30pm, and on Saturday from 9.30am to 1.30pm. Deutsche Bank's late opening days are Tuesday and Thursday. It may be worth shopping around several banks (including the savings banks or Sparkasse), as the rates of exchange offered can vary, as can the amount of commission deducted. The latter tends to be a flat rate, meaning that small-scale transactions should be avoided whenever possible. In any case, the **Wechselstuben** (bureaux de change) around Zoo Station offer better rates, as well as being open outside normal banking hours.

Perhaps the most useful and central place for **currency exchange** is the Reisebank at the main entrance to the **Zoo Station** (Mon–Sat 7.30am–10pm, Sun 8am–10pm; ☎8 81 71 17). This will cash travellers' cheques and give cash advances on major credit cards, though subject to a minimum of DM200. There's a 24-hour ATM that will give cash advances on Visa and American Express cards; and it's also possible to transfer cash to or from any Western Union office here; for more information, call the main office (☎069/2 64 82 01). Similiar services are available at the Hauptbahnhof station (Mon–Fri 7am–10pm, Sat 7am–6pm, Sun 8am–4pm; ☎2 96 43 93).

Post, phones and the media

Post

Central Berlin's most conveniently situated central post offices (Postämter) are inside Zoo Station (Mon–Sat 6am–midnight, Sun 8am–midnight), and at Rathausstr. 5, Mitte (Mon–Fri 7am–6pm, Sat 8am–1pm), in the complex of shops just to the southeast of the TV Tower. These are the easiest (and quickest) places to send letters home: mail to the UK usually takes 3–4 days; to North America one to two weeks; and to Australasia over two weeks. There are also separate parcel offices (marked Pakete), usually a block or so away.

There's a late-opening post office at Tegel airport (Mon–Fri 7am–7pm, Sat & Sun 8am–8pm),

and another office at Strasse der Pariser Commune 8–10, Friedrichshain, which is open daily until 9pm. Other offices (Mon–Fri 8am–6pm, Sat 8am–1pm) are dotted around town; you can also buy stamps from the small yellow machines next to some postboxes. **Postboxes** themselves are everywhere and unmissable, painted bright yellow. When posting a letter, make sure you distinguish between the slots marked for various postal codes. Boxes marked with a red circle indicate collections late in the day and on Sunday.

The two main post offices are also the places to send and collect letters **poste restante**: letters should be sent to: (Recipient's Name), Postamt 120, Postlagernd, Berlin 10612, or Postlagernde Sendungen, Postamt Rathausstrasse, 10178, and collected from the counter marked "Postlagernde Sendungen" (take your passport). **Telegrams** can be sent either by ringing ☎0 11 31, or from any post office. The major post offices also offer **fax services**, and at a cheaper rate than in copy shops and the like.

Telephones

Believe it or not, there are more **telephones** in Berlin than there are people. You can make **international calls** from most phone boxes in the city, which are usually equipped with basic instructions in English. Virtually every pay phone you'll find takes **cards**. These cost DM12 or DM50 and are available from all post offices and some shops. Very few of the old coin-operated telephones remain; those that do usually take DM0.50, DM1 and DM5 coins. If you don't have a card and need to make a phone call, most cafés have a coin-operated phone. Another option is to use the **direct phone service** facility

---

Berlin postcodes

Each Berlin address has a five-digit post code, which doesn't really give much idea of the location of that address. In our Listings chapters we've given the district name for each address: this is important since certain street names recur across the city. To find out where each district lies, see our map on pp.x–xi.

However, where you may need to write to a given address, we have included the post code. A complete list of city post codes may be found in the inexpensive *VIBB Atlas*, see "Information and Maps".

To call Berlin **from the UK** dial ☎00 49 30 followed by the number; **from the US** dial ☎011 49 30 followed by the number; **from Australia** dial ☎0011 49 30 followed by the number; **from New Zealand** dial ☎00 49 30 followed by the number; **from elsewhere in Germany** dial ☎030 followed by the number.

Phoning abroad from Berlin

Dial ☎ 00 + IDD country code + area code minus first 0 + subscriber number

IDD codes

Britain ☎ 44	USA ☎ 1	New Zealand ☎ 64
Ireland ☎ 353	Canada ☎ 1	Australia ☎ 61

Time

Germany is one hour ahead of GMT, 9 hours ahead of US Pacific Standard Time and 6 hours ahead of Eastern Standard Time. Clocks are turned an hour forward at the end of March and an hour back at the end of September.

Useful numbers within Berlin

Directory enquiries ☎ 1 18 33	Police ☎ 1 10
International directory enquiries ☎ 1 18 34	Ambulance ☎ 1 12
Operator wake-up call ☎ 0 11 41	Fire ☎ 1 12

of the main post offices: a phone booth will be allocated to you from the counter marked *Fremdgespräche*, which is also where you pay once you've finished.

Some of the public boxes are marked *International*, with a ringing bell symbol to indicate that you can be called back on that phone. There are international and local phones next to the post office in Zoo Station. The cheapest time to call abroad is between 9pm and 8am.

The media

English being the prevalent second language in Berlin, you'll find a good range of newspapers and magazines and – if you're prepared to search – some English-language programmes on the TV and radio.

Newspapers

It's relatively easy to find **British and US newspapers** in Berlin: most of the London-printed editions can be found at lunchtime on the same day and the *International Herald Tribune* is also readily available. *Internationale Presse* (inside Zoo Station; daily 9am–midnight) has a good selection of international newspapers and magazines, as does the British Council on Hardenbergstrasse (see p.22).

Berlin has three **local newspapers**. Two of these are from the presses of the right-wing Springer Verlag: the *Berliner Morgenpost* is a staid, conservative publication and *BZ* is a trashy tabloid. The other main local paper is the newsy

Berliner Zeitung, originally an East Berlin publication, which covers national and international news as well as local stories.

Of the **national** dailies, the two best-sellers are also from the Springer presses: *Die Welt* is a right-wing heavyweight, while the tabloid *Bild* is a reactionary, sleazy and sensationalist rag. Recommendable are the Berlin-based *Tagesspiegel*, a good Liberal read, and the left-centre *Tageszeitung*, known as *taz* – not so hot on solid news, but with good in-depth articles on politics and ecology, and an extensive Berlin listings section on Friday. It has the added advantage of being a relatively easy read for non-native German speakers. The *Frankfurter Allgemeine*, widely available in the city, is again conservative, appealing to the business community in particular. Hamburg-based *Die Zeit* appears every Thursday and, while left-wing in stance, includes a number of independently written reports on a variety of subjects. A few other papers from the old GDR hang on, like *Junge Welt*, the former paper of the Freie Deutsche Jugend (the official GDR youth organization), one of the first to openly criticize the old order in the autumn of 1989. A recent staff row produced a breakaway publication called *Jungle World*; the future of both is uncertain.

If you're in Berlin for the club scene, you might want to check out *Frontpage*, a monthly

For details of Berlin's **listings magazines**, see p.22.

guide to all things techno, though the stream-of-consciousness editorial style and "rave as a force for world change" philosophy of the magazine make it all a bit impenetrable, even for German speakers.

TV channels

Berlin has **five main TV channels**: ARD and ZDF somewhat approximate British channels or a downmarket PBS; VOX and B1 are primarily entertainment channels; ORB is basically a local channel for Berlin and Brandenburg, risen from the ashes of the ex-GDR's two TV stations. All channels seem to exist on a forced diet of US reruns clumsily dubbed into German. With cable TV, available in larger hotels, you'll be able to pick up the locally available **cable channels** (over 20 to choose from, including MTV and CNN), which serve the US, British and French armed forces. Of the cable channels, FAB (*Fernsehen aus Berlin* – "TV from Berlin") is a local channel with news footage, celebrity interviews and the infamous "Partnerwahl" dating service.

There's a good chance of catching a **foreign film** on any of the above-mentioned channels. If it's listed in the newspaper as *OF* it will be in the original language (usually English, American or French); *OmU* means that it has German subtitles.

Radio stations

The only English-speaking **radio** stations are the BBC World Service (90.2FM), and Star Radio (87.9FM), which daily combines American rock and country music with the *Voice of America* radio programme, and has to be heard to be believed. Berlin's radio output is fairly dreadful, with a multitude of stations churning out light music and soft rock, and little else. The best (and that's not saying much) local music station is Fritz Radio (102.6FM), with some decent dance music and rap shows (mainly late at night). For the latest bland pop, try R. S. 2 (94.3FM), and for hits from the last couple of decades try RTL (104.6FM). Also listenable is SFB4 MultiKulti (106.8FM), which has popular music from around Europe and occasionally elsewhere. Best of the classical music stations is Klassik Radio (101.3FM). Jazz Radio Berlin (101.9FM) a newcomer, offers jazz and blues and even a couple of English-speaking DJs.

Opening hours, public holidays and festivals

Shops in central Berlin are open Monday to Friday from 9 or 10am to 8pm, on Saturday from 9 or 10am to 4pm, while those outside the centre usually close a little earlier.

British and American visitors will be surprised by the rigidity of Berlin's closing rules: you won't find late-night corner shops or Sunday morning newsagent-grocers here. A few supermarkets, located in U-Bahn stations (and in Zoo Station), **open late** and on Sunday (see "Shopping" in Listings) though you pay for the privilege of after-hours shopping; alternatively, you can stock up on basics in any of the Turkish shops of Kreuzberg on Saturday or Sunday afternoons. Additionally, lots of bakers open on Sunday from 2 to 4pm.

Public holidays

New Year's Day (Jan 1); Good Friday (changes annually); Easter Monday (changes annually); May Day (May 1); Ascension Day (changes annually); Whitsun (changes annually); Reunification Day (Oct 3); Day of Prayer and National Repentance (3rd Wed in Nov); Christmas Eve (Dec 24); Christmas Day (Dec 25); Boxing Day (Dec 26).

Many **museums** follow a general pattern of opening 9am–5pm daily except Monday. This, however, cannot be taken as a rule, and to avoid disappointment it's a good idea to double check opening times before setting off to visit a particular museum. They're open on all the public holidays listed above (even Christmas), but usually close the following day.

Remember that almost nothing else opens on public holidays other than cafés, bars and restaurants, so stock up on groceries the day before.

Festivals and events

Berlin's **festivals** are, in the main, cultural affairs, with music, art and the theatre particularly well catered for. Best place to find out what's on and where (and, occasionally, to book tickets) is the **tourist office** in the Europa Center (see p.22): all mainstream events are well publicized in its leaflets and in brochures like Berlin Programm.

Other events, apart from the giant techno street party that is the **Love Parade** (usually some time in July), tend to be rather staid: one thing to look out for is the Volksfeste, small, local street festivals you often come across by chance from July to September. Most city districts, in the east especially, have their own Volksfeste, which are usually an excuse for open-air music, beer-swilling and Wurst-guzzling. The Feste an der Panke in **Pankow** in September can be fun; the Köpenicker Sommer, held in **Köpenick** in the second half of June, features a re-enactment of the robbery of the Rathaus safe in 1906 by Friedrich Wilhelm Voigt, a cobbler and ex-convict who, disguised as an army officer, conned a detachment of soldiers into accompanying him.

Calendar of events

JANUARY
Grüne Woche Berlin's annual agricultural show, held in the Messegelände, with food goodies to sample from all over the world.

FEBRUARY
Berlin International Film Festival Various cinemas around town; check Tip and Zitty for listings. After Cannes and Venice, the largest film festival in the world, with around 12 days of old and new movies, art house cinema and more mainstream entertainment. Films are usually shown in the original versions with German subtitles. Book tickets in advance from Internationale Filmfestspiele Berlin, Budapesterstr. 50, Tiergarten (☎ 25 48 90); remaining tickets are sometimes available from the festival office or participating theatres.

MARCH
Internationale Tourismus Börse (ITB) Funkturm Exhibition Halls. Information and goodies from over 100 countries.

APRIL
Free Berlin Art Exhibition Early April to early May in the Funkturm Exhibition Halls. Berlin artists show their most recent work. Painting areas for children, too.

MAY
Berlin Drama Festival Various theatres. Large, mainly German-speaking theatre event that has tended towards the experimental in recent years.

German Open Tennis Championship See "Sport" in Listings.

Deutsche Pokalendspiel (German Football Cup Final) From May to June. See "Sport" in Listings.

JUNE
Christopher Street Day Held on June 26, the parade at the centre of Gay Action Week.

Jazz in the Garden Four weeks of the best international jazz artists in the gardens of the Neue Nationalgalerie.

continued overleaf

Calendar of events (continued)

Festival of World Cultures Every fourth year, next in 2000. Massive programme of events, exhibitions, concerts and the like centred around one great culture or civilization.

Youth Drama Festival Late May to early June. Various venues. Experimentalism rather than professionalism is the name of the game here.

JULY

Love Parade Dates variable. Huge techno event that takes over much of the city centre and draws determined party people from all over Germany and the rest of Europe.

Berlin Barrel Organ Festival In the city centre for one weekend; check with tourist office for exact date and location. A gathering of the devices that people either love or hate.

The Bach Days Second week of July. Celebration of the great Baroque composer and musician in concerts throughout the city.

A Midsummer Night's Dream From July to August. A medley of classical music, contemporary art displays, street entertainment and rock concerts, with no real theme or purpose other than to add spice to summer evenings.

German-American Festival Truman Plaza (behind Oskar-Helene-Heim U-Bahn). One of the most popular events of the year. Eat junk food and gamble away your marks.

German-French Festival Late July to mid-August. Kurt-Schumacher-Damm (near Tegel Airport). Mini-fair with food and music and a reconstruction of a different French town each year.

SEPTEMBER

Berlin Festival Weeks Various venues. A wide variety of events and international performers celebrate a different highlight from the history of the arts each year.

ADAC Rennen A chance for motor-racing enthusiasts to hurtle down the Avus, an arrow-straight stretch of autobahn, in their Porsches. Call ☎ 8 68 62 84 for details.

OCTOBER

Berlin Marathon First Sunday of the month. The race begins on Strasse des 17 Juni and ends nearly 50km later, after passing through Dahlem

and along the Ku'damm, back at the Kaiser-Wilhelm Memorial Church. To enter, write to SCC Berlin, Berlin Marathon, Waldschuleallee 34, 14055 Berlin (☎ 3 02 53 70): closing date for entries is one month before the marathon.

AAA Exhibition Early October for nine days; Funkturm Exhibition Halls. Motor show organized by the German equivalent of the Automobile Association.

Lesbian Weeks Mehringhof, Gneisenaustr. 2, Kreuzberg. International forum for discussion, dance, music and celebration of lesbian culture.

Jazz Festival Late October to early November. Jazz of every form and style. Different venues each year; check programme available from the tourist office.

Six-day Non-stop Cycle Race In the Deutschlandhalle. A Berlin tradition that's been going since the 1920s.

NOVEMBER

Festival of Young Songwriters Five days in early November; ask at tourist office for venue. Forum for young songwriters to discuss and perform their work. Strongly international (and political) in tone.

International Indoor Show-Jumping An annual event that attracts big names from the show-jumping world to the Deutschlandhalle.

DECEMBER

Christmas Street Market Twee Christmas market from the first Sunday in December to December 24 in Breitscheidplatz, between the Europa Center and the Memorial Church.

Rixdorfer Christmas Market Richardplatz, Karl-Marx-Strasse U-Bahn. Pretty Christmas market on one of the oldest surviving squares in Berlin.

Spandau Christmas Market In Spandau's old centre from the end of November and on weekends in the run-up to Christmas.

People, Animals, Sensations. Circus in the Deutchslandhalle, near the Funkturm.

New Year's Eve Run December 31. Annual run organized by the Berlin Marathon authorities. Contact SCC Berlin, Waldschuleallee 34, 14055 Berlin (☎ 3 02 53 70).

Police and trouble

Central Berlin police stations

Headquarters:

Platz der Luftbrücke 6, Tempelhof ☎ 69 95

Jägerstr. 48, Mitte ☎ 39 71

Bismarckstr. 111, Charlottenburg ☎ 30 71

Friesenstr. 16, Kreuzberg ☎ 69 95

Hauptstr. 44, Schöneberg ☎ 77 71

Kurfürstendamm 142, Charlottenburg ☎ 30 71

The Berlin police (*Polizei*) maintain a low profile; they're not renowned for their friendliness, but they usually treat foreigners with courtesy. They're unlikely to make their presence much felt unless ordered to from on high (which usually happens during demonstrations), in which case the Prussian military mentality goes into automatic pilot, resulting in robotic-type gratuitous violence.

Generally though, the police are very correct, and shouldn't subject you to any unnecessary chicanery – in this country of rule and order it's more likely to be the ordinary citizen who'll spot you jaywalking and tick you off before the police even have a chance to get there.

Although crime in the city has risen rapidly since the fall of the Wall, probably the worst thing you'll encounter is **bag snatching** in one of the main shopping precincts. Keep a tight grip on your belongings, however, and you should be OK. If you do have something **stolen** (or simply lost), you'll need to register the details at the local police station: this is usually straightforward, but inevitably there'll be a great deal of bureaucratic bumph to wade through.

Racial attacks

Since unification, **racial attacks** on guest workers (anyone who comes into Germany to do menial work), eastern Europeans, naturalized Germans from other countries, and anyone non-White have become an ugly fact of life in Germany. Attacks have been most prevalent in the east, where unemployment and dissatisfaction with the failure of unification to deliver the promised good life have prompted so-called neo-Nazis and skinheads, and a fair number of "normal people", to take out their frustrations on the usual scapegoats. In September 1991, asylum seekers in the town of Hoyerswerda had to be removed en masse following repeated racist attacks on their temporary living quarters; and in Rostock in August 1992 a skinhead mob attacked a hostel full of eastern European asylum seekers, to the open applause of the locals – and with little opposition from the police. The media, too, play their part. Officially, TV channels and newspapers play down racial attacks or fail to mention them entirely, since this would "incite racial hatred". Critics say that this is officialdom's way of turning a blind eye to the problem – and thereby tacitly condoning it.

In Berlin, racial violence, though fairly rare in central parts of the east, is definitely a risk in outlying areas like **Lichtenberg** or **Marzahn**, which are perceived as neo-Nazi/skinhead strongholds. Such thugs are likely to pick on anyone who stands out – and not only because of their skin colour. Simply being "foreign" or looking unusual is reason enough to be at the rough end of their attentions.

The **emergency phone number** for the police is ☎1 10. Occasionally you'll see **emergency posts**; these are about head-high with a button that you press to alert the nearest police station. For an **ambulance** or the **fire brigade**, call ☎1 12.

Personal safety

As far as **personal safety** is concerned, most parts of the city are safe enough, though it's wise to be wary away from the centre, as muggings and casual violence are becoming depressingly frequent. On the whole though, providing you use common sense, you'll be safe walking virtually anywhere alone by day in the city centre. In the suburbs by night, particularly those in the **eastern part of the city**, and on the more far-flung stretches of the public transport system (especially if you're female and/or alone), it's wise to exercise the same caution as you would at home: work out beforehand exactly where you're going so that you don't look lost and vulnerable, don't walk anywhere unlit, always travel with a friend if possible and don't wear or carry anything obviously valuable.

Drugs

Most dealing of hard and soft **drugs** goes on around the back of the Gedächtniskirche and at the junction of Kurfürstenstrasse and Potsdamer Strasse. Possession of any of the usual substances is illegal, and anyone caught with them will face either prison or deportation: consulates will not be sympathetic towards those on drug charges. There's an emergency service for addicts and the "drug endangered" at Ansbacher Str. 11, Schöneberg (☎2 18 31 70; 24hr emergency number ☎1 92 37).

Women's Berlin

There are around 100 women's organizations and permanent venues in Berlin, offering information and advice, courses, performances and partying. They're testimony to a struggle for equal rights which began before the revolution of 1848 and sidestepped a complete ban from 1850 to 1908 on women's right to political assembly.

Not that women can yet afford to rest on their laurels. The election of a Red-Green senate a few years ago briefly opened the public purse to hitherto voluntary-funded women's organizations but proved, perhaps inevitably, to contain more promises than pfennigs. Similarly, recent improvements in maternity provision – while long overdue and very welcome – were fuelled primarily by a concern for the falling birthrate. They also help underpin a "return to family values" which, given the present unforeseen strain on resources and employment, along with the increased electoral support for right-wing parties, could mean that further improvements to the welfare provision for women are unlikely.

Harassment

Compared to many other European cities, Berlin is generally safe for women to visit. **Sexual harassment** is rare, and, with caution, it's safe to use the U- and S-Bahn and walk around at night: streets are well lit, and dawdling for hours in late-night cafés is standard practice. Obviously you should use common sense, but even the rougher neighbourhoods (say East Kreuzberg or Prenzlauer Berg) feel more dangerous than they actually are: the run-down U-Bahn stations at Kottbusser Tor and Görlitzer Bahnhof (both in largely immigrant districts) look alarming when compared to the rest of the system, but wouldn't stand out in most other European cities. Kurfürstenstrasse U-Bahn is in a small (but rapidly growing) red-light district, and worth avoiding if you're on your own at night. See also "Racial Attacks", p.31.

The listings below cover a cross-section of women's groups: don't worry if your German is nonexistent – there's always someone who speaks English. The majority of the following listings are in western Berlin. For **women-only bars and cafés**, see "Cafés and Bars" in Listings.

Health and crisis centres

Feministisches Frauengesundheitszentrum, Bamberger Str. 51, Schöneberg ☎2 13 95 97 (Tues 10am–1pm, Thurs 10am–1pm & 5–7pm). Well-organized feminist health centre for advice, therapy and seminars.

Frauenkrisentelefon, ☎6 15 42 43 (Mon & Thurs 10am–noon, Tues, Wed & Fri 10am–noon & 7–9pm Sat & Sun 5–7pm). Phone-in service offering sympathy and practical advice in a crisis.

Pro Familia, Ansbacherstr. 11, Schöneberg ☎2 13 90 13 (Mon–Thurs 6–9pm, Sun noon–2pm). Impartial abortion referral clinic, advice on pregnancy and the morning-after pill.

Rape Crisis Line ☎2 51 28 28 (Tues & Thurs 6–9pm, Sun noon–2pm).

Selbstverteidigung für Frauen, Hauptstr. 9, 3rd Gartenhaus, 5th floor, Schöneberg ☎7 81 94 32 (Mon 4–6pm, Thurs 5.30–7pm also first Wed in month until 7.30pm). Fairly strenuous courses in self-defence.

Women's centres

Frauenzentrum Berlin, Stresemannstr. 40, Kreuzberg ☎2 51 09 12. Friendly and well-organized help and information centre.

Schokofabrik, Naunynstr. 72, Kreuzberg ☎6 15 29 99 (Mon–Fri & Sun 11am–10pm). One of Europe's largest women's centres, with a café/gallery, sports facilities (including a

women-only Turkish bath, see p.259) and diverse events.

Wildwasser e.V. Beratungsstelle, Mehringdamm 50, Kreuzberg ☎7 86 50 17. Advice centre.

Archives

FFBIZ (Archive of the Women's Research, Education and Information Centre), Danckelmannstr. 15 & 47, Charlottenburg ☎3 22 10 35 (Tues 2–6pm, Fri 3–10pm). The place to make contact with the Berlin Historians' Network, and for guided tours of Women's Berlin. On Tuesday between 10am and 1pm there's a breakfast served for women only.

See also Spinnboden archive in "Gay and lesbian Berlin", p.35.

Galleries, bookshops and cultural centres

Begine, Potsdamer Str. 139, Schöneberg ☎2 15 43 25. Earnest lectures and films (Sept–May), and excellent performances by women musicians and dancers. Also runs a women's travel service, *Frauen Unterwegs Reisen* (☎2 15 10 22).

Cinema Walter-Screiber Platz, Bundesallee 111, Schöneberg ☎8 52 30 04. Cinema screening work by and for women.

Ladengalerie, Kurfürstendamm 64, Charlottenburg ☎8 82 42 14. Exhibitions with an emphasis on work by women artists.

Lärm und Lust, Schwedenstr. 14, Wedding ☎4 91 53 04. A venue for women musicians and bands.

Lilith, Knesebeckstr. 86–87, Charlottenburg ☎3 12 31 02. Feminist books and records, international newspapers and a good selection of fiction written by women. Also stocks a range of English-language books.

Das Verborgene Museum, Schlüterstr. 70, Charlottenburg ☎3 13 36 56 (Wed & Fri 3–7pm, Sat & Sun noon–4pm). A gallery founded by women artists for research, documentation and exhibition of women's art.

Accommodation

Hotel Artemisia, Brandenburgische Str. 18, Wilmersdorf ☎8 73 89 05. The first women-only hotel in the city, with a roof garden and exhibitions. DM100 per person (includes breakfast); it's advisable to book in advance.

Gay and lesbian Berlin

Despite the horrors of the past, Berlin has a good record for tolerating an open and energetic gay and lesbian scene. As far back as the 1920s, Christopher Isherwood and W.H. Auden both came here, drawn to a city where, in sharp contrast to the oppressiveness of London, there was a gay community who did not live in fear of harassment and legal persecution. And if Berlin's gay and lesbian communities are not as immediately noticeable as those of Amsterdam or Paris, it's still a city where there's plenty going on.

The easy-going, easy-living attitude stretches into the straight community, too, and it's not uncommon to see transvestites at their glitziest dancing atop tables at even the most conservative of bashes. The best time to arrive and plunge yourself into the hurly-burly is during **Gay Action Week**, centred around the gay pride **Christopher Street Day** parade on June 26 every year. The Love Parade held annually in July (see "Festivals and Events") also has a strong gay presence. For detailed **information** on the gay scene in Berlin, contact **Aha**, Mehringdamm 61, Kreuzberg (meetings on Wed & Fri at 8pm, Sun at 3pm; ☎6 92 36 00), or pick up a copy of the German/English *Berlin von Hinten* (DM22.80), the city's most useful gay guide. *Siegessäule*, a monthly gay magazine, has listings of events and an encyclopedic directory of gay contacts and groups on its back cover. It's available free from all of the groups below and most gay bars (see "Cafés and Bars" in Listings), as well as at the *Prinz Eisenherz* bookshop. You'll also find *Die Andere Welt*, another free lesbian and gay magazine with a variety of articles, news and letters.

For **hotels** friendly to gays, plus details of the accommodation services, see "Accommodation" in Listings.

Lesbian Berlin

As in many other large cities, **lesbians** in Berlin have a much lower profile than gay men. Perhaps because of this, there's no real distinction between bars and cafés for lesbians and straight women – see "Cafés and Bars" in Listings. *Blattgold* (DM8), a monthly publication

listing all lesbian groups and events, together with *UKZ* (*Unsere Kleine Zeitung*; DM6), are the main newspapers, available from feminist meeting places and bookshops (see p.33).

The most important event of the year is the annual **Lesbian Weeks** at the Mehringhof, Gneisenaustr. 2, Kreuzberg, a one-week international festival of music, dance and political discussion held in October. For more information, call ☎6 91 29 71.

Contacts and information

Lesben Beratung Kommunikations und Beratungs-zentrum, Kulmer Str. 20a, 2nd Gartenhaus, 4th floor, Schöneberg (Mon–Thurs 5–8pm; ☎2 15 20 00). Lesbian advisory service for those coming out.

Lied-Strich Schwules Kulturbüro e.V., Kulmer Str. 30, Schöneberg ☎2 16 28 78. An organization that promotes gay art in the city, and arranges exhibitions specifically for gays and lesbians.

Man-O-Meter Information und Treffpunkt für Schwule, Motzstr. 5, Schöneberg ☎2 16 80 08 (Mon–Sat 5–10pm, Sun 5–9pm). An information centre, meeting point and very successful gay accommodation service.

SchwuZ, Mehringdamm 61, Kreuzberg ☎6 93 70 25. Evening meeting point that can get pretty wild, especially at weekends. During the week a venue for workshops and theatre groups. Highly recommended.

Vorspiel Schwuler Sportverein (SSV) ☎3 32 17 77. Berlin's gay sports club, offering a variety of activities. Call for current details, since the address is not publicized.

Health and advice centres

Deutsche AIDS-Hilfe e.V., Dieffenbachstr. 33, Kreuzberg ☎6 90 08 70 (Mon–Fri 10am–1pm). Constructive help & information on AIDS.

Kommunikations-und-Beratungszentrum homosexueller Frauen und Männer e.V., Kulmer Str. 20a, Schöneberg ☎2 15 37 42 (Mon, Wed & Thurs 5–8pm, Tues & Fri 3–6pm). Comprehensive advice and information centre, offering single and group consultations, a small café, a telephone advisory service and lists of gay bars, activities, doctors and therapists.

Bookshops and galleries

Galerie Janssen, Pariser Str. 45, Wilmersdorf (on Ludwigkirch Platz; Mon–Fri 11am–6.30pm, Sat 11am–2pm). Men's art gallery, also selling posters, postcards and some art books. The building next door contains Janssen's photographic gallery, devoted to exhibiting "classical and contemporary" gay photography.

Prinz Eisenherz Buchladen GmbH, Bleibtreustr. 52, Charlottenburg ☎3 13 99 36. Friendly and informative gay bookstore with helpful assistants. Excellent for relaxed browsing and for free magazines, what's-on posters and leaflets about the current gay scene in the city.

Archives

Lila Archiv e.V., c/o Ursula Sillge, Chorinerstr. 9, Prenzlauer Berg ☎4 48 57 13. Information on the women's movement and gay and lesbian lifestyles, particularly within the former GDR and eastern Europe as a whole.

Schwules Museum, Mehringdamm 61, Kreuzberg, 2nd Hinterhof ☎6 93 11 72 (Wed–Sun 2–6pm). An interesting and relatively unknown museum with changing exhibitions on local and international gay history. Library and archive material is also available to browse through.

Schwules Pressearchiv im ASTA/FU, c/o SchwulZ, Mehrindgamm 61 ☎69 40 17 23. Newspaper cuttings reflecting the German-language media's attitude to homosexuality. Monthly samples of the latest snippets are available from the *Prinz Eisenherz* bookshop and some gay bars.

Spinnboden ("Archive and Treasury for Womanlove"), Anklamer Str. 38, Mitte (Mon & Fri 2–9pm ☎4 48 58 48 (U-Bahn Bernauer Str.; donation expected for each visit). A comprehensive archive of every aspect of lesbian experience, with a beautifully housed collection of 5000 books, videos, posters and magazines. Foreign visitors are welcome.

Staying on

Berlin acts as a magnet for young people from Germany and all over Europe. Its reputation as a politicized, happening city, with a high profile in the arts and a more relaxed and tolerant attitude than its parent state, means that many people come here to live and work. That the English-speaking community – Americans, Brits and Irish – is a large one will work to your advantage when it comes to finding out the latest situation for jobs and housing; and to your disadvantage in terms of competition.

An important **caveat** to the notes below is that things change quickly in this city, and with massive unemployment among former GDR citizens since unification, it seems likely that rules, regulations and openings will have changed at least subtly by the time you read this.

Work

If you don't mind what you do (or what hours you do it), and are prepared to work "black" (without a contract, taxes or insurance), finding **work** in Berlin shouldn't pose too much of a problem. **Work permits** aren't required by EU nationals, though everyone else will need one – and, theoretically, should not even look for a job without one.

However, the paperwork and bureaucracy are complicated and tedious. The following notes cover only the initial stages of the process you'll need to follow: it's essential to seek advice from an experienced friend, especially when completing official forms – writing the wrong thing could land you in a lot of unnecessary trouble. The best official place for advice is the **Ausländer Beauftragte des Senats** at Potsdamer Str. 65, Tiergarten (☎ 26 54 23 51).

If you're an **EU national** and want to stay in Berlin for longer than three months, you only need to prove that you have a roof over your head to satisfy the authorities. Do this by completing a *Polizeianmeldungsformular* ("registration document"), available from any newsagent for DM2. Then fill in the address details and get it signed by your landlord or equivalent – this is the tricky bit since not all lets are legal, especially if you find yourself subletting. You then go to your local police station and get the thing stamped. Providing they have a *Polizeianmeldungsformular*, EU nationals don't need a work permit either to look for or take up a job. The next stage is to get an **Aufenthaltserlaubnis** ("permission to stay") from the Landeseinwohneramt, Friedrich-Krause-Ufer 24, Tiergarten (Mon, Tues & Thurs 7.30am–1pm, Fri 7.30am–noon). Officially you can't get one until you have a job – but you can't get a job without one. The loophole to this catch-22 situation is that most employers aren't too concerned about the *Aufenthaltserlaubnis* if you're an EU citizen – plus the fact that you can only get one six months after you've registered with the police.

For **non-EU nationals** – North Americans, Australasians and everybody else – finding legal work is much more difficult, unless you've secured the job legally before arriving in Germany. The best advice is to approach the German embassy or consulate in your own country.

Finding a job

Since long-term accommodation can work out quite cheap in Berlin, it's possible to live reasonably well on comparatively little here. Indeed, it's possible to get by on a take-home pay of DM1500–2000 a month.

Numerous **Arbeitsbüro** (job agencies) offer both temporary and permanent work – usually secretarial – but you'll obviously be expected to have a good command of German and fast typing speeds. Other than that, there are also several cleaning agencies (look in the Yellow Pages under *Reinigungsfirmen*) where only a minimal knowledge of the language is needed.

However, the best sources of both temporary and permanent work are certain **newspapers and magazines**: *Zweite Hand* (published on Tues, Thurs & Sat), *Tip* or *Zitty* (bimonthly on alternate weeks, first copies on sale Wed). Other than personal contacts, these are also the best places to find English-language **teaching work** – either privately or in a school. For private work, the normal rate is DM25–30 per hour – don't be beaten down to anything less than that. Previous experience is not always necessary (particularly for private lessons). You can place an advert for your services free in *Zweite Hand* or for a small fee in *Tip*, *Zitty* or *Prinz*, and both the British Council and Amerika Haus (p.22) have noticeboards where an ad can be pinned for a small fee. Or you can approach the city's many language schools directly; look in the above-mentioned magazines for names and addresses.

Otherwise, Berlin's innumerable **cafés and restaurants** often look for workers. You'll need to tramp around town a bit first, and they'll expect a decent working knowledge of German, but you can often work black. If you do sign a contract with them, it's likely that you'll need a *Gesundheitspass* (health certificate), information about which can be found at any local **Bezirksamt**. These local official information offices (they're listed under *Senat* in the phone book, and are usually located in the local town hall) can also advise on claiming social security and unemployment benefit.

One last tip: pick up the Sunday *Berliner Morgenpost* late on Saturday evening around Zoo Station and scan the job (*Stelle*) section – some jobs are advertised in English, and the best ones always go quickly.

Accommodation

As Berlin gears up to become *de facto* capital of Germany and accommodation is needed for bureaucrats formerly housed in Bonn, **apartments** in Berlin are becoming increasingly expensive to rent and difficult to find. You'll need to search hard to find a decent affordable place, and get used to the frequent moves necessitated by the preponderance of short-term lets. **Permanent accommodation** is even harder to come by, normally requiring an illegal takeover fee known as an *Abstand*. This can range from DM4000 to DM30,000 or even more, depending on the fittings and the amount of decorating that has been carried out. (It can in turn, and again illegally, normally be extracted from the person who moves in when you leave.) A *Kaution* (deposit), usually in the form of three months' refundable rent, is also required.

Apartment-hunting

Although *Tip*, *Zitty*, *Zweite Hand* and the Sunday *Berliner Morgenpost* advertise apartments and rooms, it's much quicker and less traumatic to sign on at one of the several **Mitwohnzentralen**, accommodation agencies that specialize in long-term sublets in apartments throughout the city. (For full details, see "Accommodation" in Listings.) Wherever you look, expect to pay between DM750 and DM1100 for a self-contained one- or two-roomed apartment, or between DM300 and DM600 for a room in a shared apartment. In listings or adverts, the word *Warm* means that the rent is inclusive of heating and other charges; *Kalt*, non-inclusive. Incidentally, Berlin is the only city in Germany with a large number of apartments that have coal-fuelled burners for heating (*Ofenheizung* in German). These are messy and inconvenient as they require constant stoking up – if you're out of the house for more than a few hours, be prepared to come back to Arctic temperatures during the bitterly cold Berlin winter.

Once you've been here a few months and made contact with people, **word of mouth** also works well if you're searching for somewhere better (or cheaper) to stay: tell everyone you meet you're on the lookout and something will usually become available surprisingly quickly – there's a high turnover in apartments here.

When you finally find a place to live, you need to buy an *Anmeldungsformular* (registration form; see opposite). Ask your landlord or landlady to complete this (if you don't have an apartment or room, friends will usually sign – illegally – that you're living at their home), take it to the local police station to be stamped, and you'll be able to apply to the Foreign Police for your resident's permit.

Squatting and communal living

The tolerant attitude of the 1980s is very much a thing of the past, and although a few **radical squats** still exist, the hassle you're likely to get from the authorities isn't really worth it for the money saved. Squatting is more of a **political gesture** than a practical alternative, and the organized groups here will want to see real evidence of commitment to their ideals before, as a foreigner, you'll be allowed to join. Best chances of finding somewhere are in Kreuzberg (see p.127), or, in the east, Prenzlauer Berg or Friedrichshain – but you'll need luck and contacts.

Originating in the events of 1968, the **Wohngemeinschaften** (literally "communities") are now a firmly established part of the "alternative" scene in what used to be West Berlin. Nothing like the hippy communes of yore, they consist of four to eight people (often with a few children thrown in), who share rent, food and, supposedly, a few ideals. In the independently minded 1990s, however, the stringent requirements of being home every evening at a certain time to eat with "the family", cooking and cleaning to a strict weekly rota, the lack of privacy and heavy "talks" if you don't fulfil community expectations can be too much for some. Having said this, the **Wohngemeinschaften** often advertise rooms to rent and, once you're in, these can be as permanent as you like.

Finally, **council apartments** (*Sozialwohnungen*) are few and far between, have long waiting lists and, with the influx of GDR citizens that began in 1989, are now almost beyond hope. It's worth enquiring at your local *Bezirksamt* on arrival, though, particularly if you have a "social problem" (eg pregnancy), as they're then required to find something as soon as possible.

Directory

ADDRESSES The street name is always written before the number and all Berlin addresses are suffixed by a five-figure post code. *Strasse* (street) is commonly abbreviated to *Str.*, and often joined on to the end of the previous word. Other terms include *Weg* (path), *Ufer* (river bank), *Platz* (square) and *Allee* (avenue). Berlin apartment blocks are often built around courtyards with several entrances and staircases: the *Vorderhaus*, abbreviated as *VH* in addresses, is as the name suggests, the front building; the *Gartenhaus* (garden house) and the *Hinterhof* (*HH*; back house) are at the rear of the building. *EG* means the ground floor, *1 OG* means the first floor, etc. *Dachwohnung* means the "flat under the roof" – ie the top floor.

AIRPORT TAX Tax varies from DM10 to DM120 depending upon destination and time of travel.

BEACHES Berlin has one of the largest inland beaches in Europe, on the Havel River at Wannsee to the west of the city centre (see p.153). To the east, the best beaches are on the northern shore of the Müggelsee near the small town of Rahnsdorf (see p.183). Both these beaches include an *FKK* (nudist) stretch. There are also possibilities in Grünau and, just outside Berlin, on the lakes south of Potsdam.

CONDUCTED TOURS A cop-out really, since there's little you can't see more fully, and more

enjoyably, under your own steam. By far the best company is Berlin Walks, Harbig Str. 26, Charlottenburg (☎3 01 91 94), which runs themed walks in English on the Third Reich, Jewish life and the Wall. Yellow Walking Tour Company, Boppstr. 3, Kreuzberg offers regular English-language tours that include discounts to some restaurants and museums.

CONTRACEPTION A glowing spectrum of condoms is available from supermarkets, anywhere selling toiletries, and vending machines in bar toilets (though best from the *Condomi* at Kantstr. 38, Charlottenburg – see "Shopping" in Listings). To get a prescription for the pill you'll need to see a doctor, so again it's worth stocking up before leaving.

DOCTORS AND PHARMACIES Doctors are likely to be able to speak English, but if you want to be certain, your embassy (see below) will provide a list of English-speaking doctors. For an emergency doctor, call ☎31 00 31; for an emergency dentist, ☎89 00 43 33. In the event of a general emergency, phone ☎1 10 for the police, who will call an ambulance. To get a prescription filled, go to an *Apotheke*: pharmacists are well trained and often speak English. Outside normal hours a notice on the door of any *Apotheke* indicates the nearest one open, meaning there's a round-the-clock service. These chemists aren't open for browsing; you'll be served through a small hatch in the door, so don't be put off by the shops' closed appearance.

ELECTRICITY The supply is 220 volts, though anything requiring 240 volts (all UK appliances) will work. American visitors, however, will need a voltage converter to run appliances. Sockets are of the two-pin variety, so a travel plug is useful.

EMBASSIES AND CONSULATES Australia, Uhlandstr. 181–183, Charlottenburg, (☎8 80 08 80); Britain, Unter den Linden 32–34, Mitte (☎20 18 40); Ireland, Ernst-Reuter-Platz 10, Charlottenburg (☎34 80 08 22); Canada, Internationales Handelszentrum, Friedrichstr. 95, Mitte (☎2 61 11 61); New Zealand, offices in Bonn: Bundeskanzlorplatz 2–10, 53113 (☎02 28 22 80 70); USA, Neustädtische Kirchstr. 4–5,

Mitte (☎2 38 51 74), visa section Clayallee 170, Zehlendorf (☎8 19 74 54).

HOSPITALS If you're in need of immediate medical attention, head for one of the major hospitals: Charité, Schumann Str. 20–21, Mitte (☎2 80 20); Krankenhaus Am Urban, Dieffenbachstr. 1, Kreuzberg (☎69 71); *Krankenhaus Moabit*, Turmstr. 21, Tiergarten (☎3 97 60); Krankenhaus Neukölln, Rudower Str. 48, Neukölln (☎6 00 41); *St* Joseph Krankenhaus, Bäumerplan 24, Tempelhof (☎7 88 20).

ID Bits of official-looking paper go down well in Berlin. It's a legal requirement that you carry your passport with you and essential that you carry all your documentation when driving – failure to do so may result in an on-the-spot fine.

JAYWALKING This is illegal and you can be fined if caught. Even in the irreverent atmosphere of Berlin, locals stand rigidly to attention until the green signal comes on – even when there isn't a vehicle in sight. Cars are not required to stop at crossings; although walking on one should give you right of way, use your judgement and be careful.

LAUNDRIES Dahlmannstr. 17, Charlottenburg (Mon–Fri 9am–1pm & 3–6pm); Uhlandstr. 53, Charlottenburg (6.30am–10.30pm); Hauptstr. 151, Schöneberg (7.30am–10.30pm). Other addresses are listed under *Wäschereien* in the Yellow Pages.

LEFT LUGGAGE Lockers at Zoo Station (DM2 or DM4 for the extra large size; Mon–Fri 6am to midnight, Sat & Sun 6am–5.40pm & 6pm to midnight); do not accept rucksacks. The lockers, on the ground and first floor, are often full, so you may need to use the left luggage office (DM4 per item per day). There are also 24hr luggage lockers at Friedrichstrasse and Alexanderplatz stations (DM4).

LOST PROPERTY Police lost and found, Platz der Luftbrücke 6, Tempelhof (☎69 95). For items lost on public transport, contact the BVG Fundbüro, Fraunhoferstr. 33-36, Charlottenburg (☎25 62 30 40), and for items lost on the S-Bahn system try the Fundbüro at S-Bahn station Schönefeld (☎29 72 96 12).

TIPPING In smarter restaurants, or places where the service has been particularly good, 5–10 per-cent of the bill is the going rate; if there's a figure against the word *Bedienung* on the bill, or if it says *Service inclusiv*, it means that service is included. If the service was appalling, however, there's absolutely no need to tip. In taxis, add a mark or two to the total.

TRAVEL AGENTS Autopia Reiseladen, Kurfürstenstr. 153, Schöneberg (☎2 61 18 21) offers lots of cheap flights at youth fares.. Express Travel, Giesebrechtstr. 18, Charlottenburg (☎3 24 94 20), is a British travel agent. Titanic Reisen, Zossener Str. 20, Kreuzberg (☎69 04 05 22), offers good deals worldwide. Flugbörse, Nollendorfstr. 28, Schöneberg (☎2 16 30 61) is a chain with over half a dozen shops in the city offering last-minute tickets. Team Reisen, Potsdamer Str. 109, Tiergarten (☎2 61 12 71), offers the benefit of instant ticketing for most flights (apart from same-day departures).

VACCINATIONS None needed for Berlin or Germany.

Berlin: The Guide

Chapter 1

Introducing the city

No one in their right mind should come to Berlin for light-hearted sightseeing: in its western reaches especially, this is a profoundly scarred city. Even in the flashiest sections of the West End, around the Memorial Church, it still seems half-built, the modern buildings somehow making it look less finished and more ugly. Unlike Paris, Amsterdam, or Munich, Berlin isn't a city where you can simply stroll and absorb the atmosphere. You need to plan your trips and target your points of interest, using the city's transport system (described in detail on p.17) to cover what can be longish distances. Those points of interest are, almost without exception, sombre: the Reichstag, looming symbol of the war years; the remains of the Wall, facet of its aftermath; and several museums which openly and intelligently try to make sense of twentieth-century German history. The eastern part of the city is, in fact, the real Berlin, cut off by the Wall for thirty years. The area east of the Brandenburg Gate, along Unter den Linden, is only now beginning to regain its original place as centre of the city. This neighbourhood, and the eastern districts of Mitte and Prenzlauer Berg, have emerged as dynamic magnets for shopping and entertainment. Here especially, the rapid transformation of Berlin into capital city and, the city fathers hope, economic and cultural powerhouse, is evident. Many Berliners remain apprehensive. Exactly how the extreme pressures of a weakening economy along with the ominous rise of xenophobic nationalism will alter the development of the new reunited Berlin remains to be seen: for the moment at least, they once again give the city its sense of vital excitement.

Some orientation

Wartime damage has left the **West End** of Berlin (Chapter 2) with the appearance of a badly patched-up skeleton: beneath the surface the former street plan survives, but in a haphazard fashion and fractured by the erstwhile course of the Wall. The heart of the area is the

Zoologischer Garten, or more properly the adjacent combined U-Bahn, S-Bahn and train **Zoo Station**. A stone's throw from here is the centre's single notable landmark, the rotting tusk of the **Kaiser-Wilhelm-Gedächtniskirche** (Kaiser Wilhelm Memorial Church); the **Kurfürstendamm**, an upmarket shopping boulevard, targets in on the church from the west. To the north and east of the Zoo is the **Tiergarten park**, ending in the east with the old **Reichstag** building and the **Brandenburg Gate**. Just south is one of Berlin's three important cultural collections, the **Tiergarten museum district**.

Unter den Linden (Chapter 3) runs east of the Brandenburg Gate, a great strip of stately Neoclassical buildings that lies at the new centre of Berlin. A few hundred metres beyond the Brandenburg Gate, Unter den Linden intersects with **Friedrichstrasse**, which cuts north–south across this part of the city. A left turn from here leads north to **Bahnhof Friedrichstrasse**, while heading south takes you down through magnificently restored architecture to what used to be Checkpoint Charlie.

Continuing along Unter den Linden from the Friedrichstrasse intersection leads, by way of some of Berlin's finest eighteenth- and nineteenth-century architecture, to **Schlossplatz and the Museum Island** (Chapter 4), home to eastern Berlin's leading museums. At the Museum Island, Unter den Linden becomes **Karl-Liebknecht-Strasse**, which leads to **Alexanderplatz** (Chapter 5), the eastern commercial and transport hub, from where rail and bus links run out to the suburbs. North from here, the swathe of land of the **Scheunenviertel** (Chapter 6) contains what was once the heart of the city's Jewish community, and has some fascinating remainders from those days along Grosse Hamburger Strasse and Oranienburger Strasse.

Two districts make up the area described as **South of the centre** (Chapter 7): **Kreuzberg** is an enclave of immigrant workers, "alternative" living, and one of the most vibrant areas at night; **Schöneberg**, while being a mainly residential area, competes with Kreuzberg for nightlife – though the discos, bars and restaurants here are that little bit smarter. By day there's plenty to see, much of it, like the **Resistance to National Socialism** exhibition, of historic interest.

The area **West of the centre** (Chapter 8) is one of Berlin's most attractive – and most overlooked by visitors. A huge region stretching from the museums and gardens around **Schloss Charlottenburg** at the city's edge to the medieval town of **Spandau** 10km away, much of it comprises woodland (the Grunewald) and lakes (the Havel and Wannsee), a reminder that about a third of the western part of Berlin is either forest or park. It's also where, to the southwest, you'll find the superlative **Dahlem museum complex** (displaying everything from German folk art to Polynesian huts); to the northwest is the **Olympic Stadium** and another grim reminder of the war years, **Plötzensee prison**.

The land to the **East of the centre** (Chapter 9) is quite different. The suburbs look like an endless sprawl of prewar tenements punctuated by high-rise developments and heavy industry. However, much of the atmosphere of prewar Berlin has been preserved to the immediate northeast of the centre in the cobbled streets of **Prenzlauer Berg**, while **Friedrichshain** to the east offers some unusual architectural leftovers from the 1950s, and one of eastern Berlin's larger parks. Moving out to the northern edge of the city, the airy suburbs of **Pankow** and **Weissensee** contrast sharply with the inner-city tenement districts. Industrial grime and high-density living reassert themselves in **Lichtenberg**, east of Friedrichshain, but compensation is offered by riverside parkland and open spaces in **Treptow** to the south. **Köpenick**, at the city's southeastern edge, with its lakes and woodland, dotted with small suburban towns and villages, offers the truest break from the city, to the extent that it's easy to forget that this area still belongs to Greater Berlin. For further ventures out of the city **Potsdam** (Chapter 10) is the best target, where Frederick the Great's palace and gardens of **Sanssouci** have long been a major – and deserved – tourist draw.

Nowhere in the city is more than a stone's throw from a bar, be it a corner *Kneipe* or a slick upscale café – indeed, the variety of bars and restaurants is one of the city's great strengths. The **listings** of our favourite places to stay, eat, drink and shop follows the guide, along with chapters on nightlife and information on children's activities and sport.

Chapter 2

The West End

L atterly regarded as the centre of Western Berlin, the area around Zoo Station is gradually reverting to its prewar role. In Wilhelmine and Weimar Berlin, this was the city's **WEST END**. Far from the municipal grandeur of the poorer working-class residential neighbourhoods to the south and east, the West End was based, then as now, on the slick shops of the **Kurfürstendamm**. It was a centre for cinemas, cabaret and clubs by night, cafés and shops by day: even in the grim first few years after the war, a few shops managed to struggle on here. With the coming of the Berlin Wall, the West End had a new role forced upon it, one it played poorly. West Berlin was a city without a true centre, and no amount of showcase building could transform the area into the heart of a great late twentieth-century metropolis. Now, with the balance of the city restored, the West End should regain its proper role as complement to the new centre further to the east.

Roughly speaking, the West End stretches from the landmark of the **Reichstag** in the north to the Landwehrkanal in the south. Zoo Station lies at its western edge, and the excellent group of museums known as the **Tiergarten Complex** marks its easternmost point. While no one could call the area immediately around Zoo Station attractive, the Tiergarten is one of the prettier spots in the city, especially in spring and summer; and though first impressions suggest little more than a glorified (though scruffy) shopping precinct run up against third-rate modern architecture, there's plenty to explore – once you've scratched below the surface.

Around Zoo Station: the Kurfürstendamm and Tiergarten

Whether you come by train or coach, or on the bus from Tegel airport, chances are you'll arrive at Bahnhof Zoologischer Garten – **Zoo Station**. Perched high above the street, and with views across to the zoo itself, the train station is an exciting place to end a journey, conjuring memories of prewar steam trains under its glassy roof. At

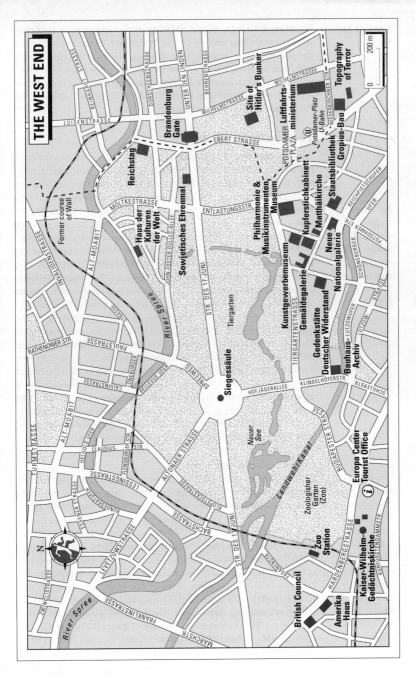

THE WEST END

street level, though, it's an unkempt and conspicuously lavatorial-smelling place that used to be run by the East Berlin authorities. By day, but chiefly by night, it's the meeting place for the city's drunks and dope pushers, but has been cleaned up since a few years back when it was a marketplace for heroin dealing and child prostitution. A few glossy, late-opening stores like Body Shop and Internationale Presse go some of the way to improve things.

The Kurfürstendamm

*For more on
shopping
around Zoo
Station and
along the
Ku'damm, see
"Shopping" in
Listings.*

Step out east from Zoo Station and you're in the centre of the city's maelstrom of bright lights, traffic and high-rise buildings. A short walk south and you're at the eastern end of the **Kurfürstendamm** (universally known as the **Ku'damm**), a 3.5-kilometre strip of ritzy shops, cinemas, bars and cafés that homes in on the centre like the spoke of a broken wheel. The great landmark here, the one that's on all the postcards, is the **Kaiser-Wilhelm-Gedächtniskirche** (Kaiser Wilhelm Memorial Church), built at the end of the nineteenth century and destroyed by British bombing in November 1943. Left as a reminder, it's a strangely effective memorial, the crumbling tower providing a hint of the old city. It's possible to go inside what remains of the nave (Mon–Sat 10am–4.30pm): there's a small exhibit showing wartime destruction and a "before and after" model of the city centre. Adjacent, a modern **chapel** contains the tender, sad *Stalingrad Madonna*, while at the back the blue glass campanile of the chapel has gained the nickname of the "Lipstick" or the "Soul-Silo": its base contains a shop selling Third World gifts. The area around the church acts as a focal point for western Berlin's punks and down-and-outs, who threaten the well-heeled Ku'damm shoppers with demands for cash. It's a menacing, unfriendly spot and **Breitscheidplatz**, the square behind, isn't much better, a dingy concrete slab usually filled with skateboarders, drug dealers and street musicians.

Around the Europa Center

*Berlin
Tourismus
Marketing
supplies free
information
on what's on
in the city,
and can help
find accommo-
dation. See
p.211 for
details.*

Breitscheidplatz marks the beginning of Tauentzienstrasse, with the **Europa Center**, a huge shopping centre that contains the Berlin Tourismus Marketing (tourist office; Mon–Sat 8am–8pm) on its northern side. There's nothing much of interest in this rather generic mall, which was built in the 1960s as a capitalist showcase for West Berlin, topped by a huge, rotating Mercedes-Benz symbol. Further down Tauentzienstrasse, and claiming to be the largest store on the continent, is the *KaDeWe*, an abbreviation of *Kaufhaus Des Westens* – "the Department Store of the West". It's an impressive statement of the city's standard of living, and the sixth-floor food hall is a mouthwatering inducement to sample the many exotic snacks sold there. A little further down, **Wittenbergplatz U-Bahn station** has been likeably restored to its prewar condition both inside (1920s kitsch) and out (Neoclassical pavilion). Near the entrance, a tall sign

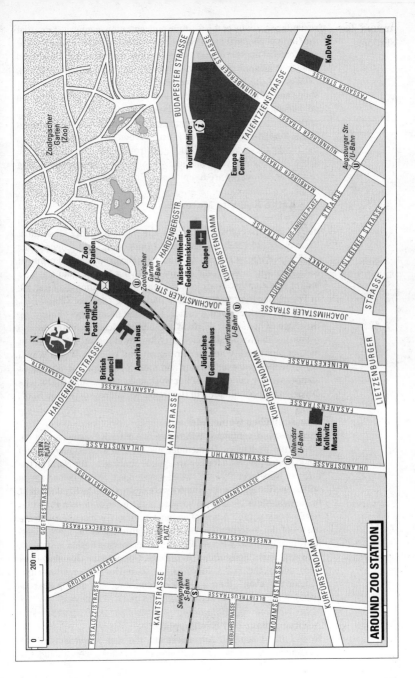

reminds passers-by of the wartime concentration camps: it states that the German people must never be allowed to forget the atrocities that were carried out there, and lists the names of the camps. It's an odd memorial, and one that goes largely unnoticed by Ku'damm shoppers.

West of the Europa Center, the Ku'damm begins its stretch of shops and cafés, which tend to be less expensive the further west you go, blazing a trail at night in a dazzle of neon. The Ku'damm was built under Bismarck in the nineteenth century, and Thomas Wolfe called it "the largest coffee-house in Europe" when spending time here in the 1920s; these days there's little left from either man's time. If the shops are beyond your budget, some of the street stalls selling clothes and jewellery are fun places to find trinkets.

The Käthe Kollwitz Museum

There's little to do on the Ku'damm other than spend money, and there's only one cultural attraction, the **Käthe Kollwitz Museum** at Fasanenstr. 24 (daily except Tues 11am–6pm; DM6, concessions DM3; bus #109, #119, #129 & #219). The drawings and prints of Käthe Kollwitz are among the most moving works from the first half of this century. Born in 1867, she lived for almost all her life in Prenzlauer Berg in the eastern part of the city (see Chapter 9), where her work evolved a radical left-wing perspective. Following the death of her son in World War I, her woodcuts, lithographs and prints became explicitly pacifist, often dwelling on the theme of mother and child. When her grandson was killed in World War II her work became even sadder and more poignant. The museum's comprehensive collection of her work makes it possible to trace its development, culminating in the tragic sculptures on the top floor.

The Jüdisches Gemeindehaus

Fasanenstrasse continues on the other side of the Ku'damm, and at no. 79–80 the **Jüdisches Gemeindehaus** (Jewish Community House) incorporates parts of a former synagogue attacked by the Nazis on the night of November 9, 1938, when synagogues, Jewish-owned shops and homes throughout the country were destroyed – the *Kristallnacht* or "Crystal Night", so-named because of the mass of broken glass that resulted (see p.114). A wall of an inner courtyard is inscribed with the names of the concentration camps and wartime ghettos; more cheerfully, the Community House also has an interesting kosher restaurant – for which see "Restaurants" in Listings. Opposite the Gemeindehaus (just under the rail bridge) is the **Zille-Hof** flea market-cum-junk/antique shop – there's plenty of interesting stuff among the rubbish, but the pleasure is in rummaging as much as in buying.

Adenauerplatz and Savignyplatz

By the time you reach **Adenauerplatz**, the slick showrooms of the Ku'damm have died out and the bars become affordable: although the clientele tends to consist of loud and brash teenagers, it's not a bad starting point for an evening's boozing. Best of all for eating, drinking and nightlife, though, is the squashed rectangle of streets south and west of Zoo Station, roughly bordered by Kantstrasse, Hardenbergstrasse and Leibnizstrasse, and focusing on **Savignyplatz** (see "Cafés and bars", "Restaurants" and "Clubs and live venues" in Listings).

Hardenbergstrasse itself runs from Zoo Station, past the conveniently grouped **British Council** and **Amerika Haus** (see "Information and maps" in Basics), to Ernst-Reuter-Platz, a blandly modern oval named after the city's first postwar governing mayor. To the east, the **Technische Universität** (most striking of whose buildings is the huge, brilliantly painted **Umlauftank**, a hydraulics research centre at the edge of the Tiergarten) marks an uncompromisingly modern start to Strasse des 17 Juni; a collection of old clothes and new crafts makes the weekend **flea market** on the north side of the street a good place to browse.

The Tiergarten

Back in the centre, the **Zoologischer Garten** (daily 9am–6.30pm; DM11, children DM5.50, Aquarium DM11/5.50, combined ticket DM18/9) forms the beginning of the **Tiergarten**, a restful expanse of woodland and lakes. Designed by Peter Lenné, the park was laid out under Elector Friedrich III as a hunting ground and destroyed during the Battle of Berlin in 1945 – though so successful has its replanting been that these days it's hard to tell it's not original. The zoo and its aquarium are like any the world over, and expensive to boot (see "Children's Berlin" in Listings): better to wander through the Tiergarten, tracing the course of the **Landwehrkanal**, an inland waterway off the River Spree.

Near the Corneliusbrücke, a small, odd sculpture commemorates the radical leader **Rosa Luxemburg**. In 1918, along with fellow revolutionary Karl Liebknecht (see p.86), she reacted against the newly formed Weimar Republic and especially the terms of the Treaty of Versailles, declaring a new Socialist Republic in Berlin along the lines of Soviet Russia (she had played an important part in the abortive 1905 revolution). The pair were kidnapped by members of the elite First Cavalry Guards: Liebknecht was gunned down while "attempting to escape", Luxemburg was knocked unconscious and shot, her body dumped in the Landwehrkanal at this point.

Just to the north, a pretty little group of ponds makes up the grand-sounding **Neuer See**; in summer there's a popular beer garden here, and it's possible to rent **boats** by the hour.

The broad avenue that cuts through the Tiergarten to form the continuation of Unter den Linden's triumphal way was originally named Charlottenburger Chaussee. Once known as the **East–West Axis**, it was a favourite strip for Nazi processions: indeed Hitler had the stretch from the Brandenburg Gate to Theodor-Heuss-Platz (formerly Adolf-Hitler-Platz) widened in order to accommodate these mass displays of military might and Nazi power; on his birthday in 1938, 40,000 men and 600 tanks took four hours to parade past the Führer. Later, in the final days of the war, Charlottenburger Chaussee became a makeshift runway for aeroplanes ferrying Nazi notables to and from the besieged capital. Now called Strasse des 17 Juni, its name commemorates the day in 1953 when workers in the East rose in revolt against the occupying Soviet powers, demanding free elections, the removal of all borders separating the two Germanys, and freedom for political prisoners. Soviet forces were quickly mobilized, and between two and four hundred people died; the authorities also ordered the execution of twenty-one East Berliners and eighteen Soviet soldiers – for "moral capitulation to the demonstrators".

The Siegessäule

By night, the area around the Siegessäule is one of the city's principal cruising points for gay men. See "Gay and lesbian Berlin" in Basics.

At the centre of Strasse des 17 Juni is the **Siegessäule** (Mon 1–6pm, Tues–Sun 9am–6pm, last admittance 5.45pm; DM2, concessions DM1; bus #100, #187 & #341), the victory column celebrating Prussia's military victories (chiefly that over France in 1871). It was shifted to this spot on Hitler's orders in 1938 from what is today known as Platz der Republik. Though the boulevard approaches exaggerate its size, it's still an eye-catching city monument: 67m high and topped with a gilded winged victory that symbolically faces France. The view from the top is one of Berlin's best – the Brandenburg Gate announcing the grandly restored streets of eastern Berlin, the mid-renovation Reichstag standing like a gnarled protector at the edge of the park. Have a look, too, at the mosaics at the column's base, which show the unification of the German peoples and incidents from the Franco-Prussian War: they were removed after 1945 and taken to Paris, only to be returned when the lust for war spoils had subsided. Dotted around the Siegessäule are **statues** of other German notables, the most imposing being that of Bismarck, the "Iron Chancellor", under whom the country was united in the late nineteenth century. He's surrounded by figures symbolizing his achievements; walk around the back for the most powerful.

Around the Tiergarten

From the Siegessäule it's a long hike down to the Brandenburg Gate and Reichstag, and most visitors take the #100 bus from the city centre. If you do come this way, it's worth looking out for **Schloss Bellevue**, an eighteenth-century building that was once a guesthouse for the Third Reich and is today the Berlin home of the Federal President – and only visitable when he's not in residence. Further east, on John-Foster-Dulles-Allee, sits the upturned banana of the **Kongresshalle**, an exhibition centre whose concept couldn't be matched by available technology: its roof collapsed in 1980, and it has since been rebuilt and reopened as the Haus der **Kulturen der Welt**, a venue for theatre, music, performance art and exhibitions from the Third World and Far East (see "Clubs and live venues" in Listings). South from here, on the north side of Strasse des 17 Juni, is the **Soviet War Memorial** to the Red Army troops who died in the Battle of Berlin. Built from the marble of Hitler's destroyed Berlin HQ, the Reich's Chancellery, it's flanked by two tanks that were supposedly the first to reach the city.

On the southeast side of the park, the Tiergarten Museum Complex offers a variety of cultural delights (see p.56). Few visitors venture north into **Wedding**, an industrial/working-class residential suburb whose charms are few, despite its prewar fame as a socialist heartland known as "Red Wedding". But it's worth pushing north from the park for the **Hamburger Bahnhof** at Invalidenstr. 50–51 (Tues–Fri 9am–5pm, Sat & Sun 10am–5pm; DM8, concessions DM4, free first Sun of each month; S-Bahn line #3 to Lehrter Stadtbahnhof or bus #248). Like the Anhalter Bahnhof to the south (see p.122), the Hamburger station was damaged in the war, though it had ceased functioning as a station as early as 1906. Fortunately, it didn't suffer its twin's fate in postwar redevelopment, and is today the home of the new **Museum for Contemporary Art**. The collection here represents a thorough survey of postwar art: Rauschenberg, Twombly, Warhol, Beuys, Lichtenstein, right on up to Keith Haring and Donald Judd. And the old railway station makes a spacious, effective setting, particularly the main hall, where large sculptures by Judd, Anselm Kiefer and Richard Long, among others, are displayed. It's well worth a visit, though there are disappointingly few surprises. When you need a break, there's a good bookstore and café on the premises.

The Reichstag – and the legacy of the Wall

CENTRAL BERLIN

Strasse des 17 Juni comes to an end at the Brandenburg Gate, but it's better to start exploring a little further north – at the **Reichstag**.

Built in the late nineteenth century to house the German parliament, familiar from flickering newsreels as it burned in 1933, and

---

The Reichstag in flames

Debate as to who actually started the fire that gutted the Reichstag in 1933 has resumed in recent years. In a show trial, Göring, as Minister of the Interior for the State of Prussia, successfully accused an educationally sub-normal partially-sighted Communist Dutch bricklayer, **Marius van der Lubbe**, of arson; he was executed the following year. It's equally likely that members of the SA, the precursors of the SS, began the fire to allow draconian measures to be brought in against the Nazis' enemies. By an emergency decree on the day after the fire, the basic civil rights guaranteed by the Weimar constitution were suspended and the death penalty was introduced for a range of political offences.

The
Reichstag

The Reichstag in polypropylene

In 1995, after some twenty years of lobbying, wrangling and debate, the conceptual artist **Christo** and his wife Jeanne-Claude realized their long-held dream of wrapping up the Reichstag. For two weeks in June and July, the historic building was packaged in 100,000 square metres of shiny-grey polypropylene and tied with deep-blue rope. Several hundred people were involved in the massive project, many of them mountain climbers employed to scramble along the sides of the building laying rope and tying knots. Some one million visitors saw the artwork, and even most detractors had to admit that it was indeed impressive. The price tag was said to be around $9 million.

the scene of Hitler's wresting of control of Germany in the same year, the Reichstag today seems lost in a sea of irony. Inscribed with the words *Dem Deutschen Volke* ("To the German People"), what was once the symbol of national unity for years stood hard by the border that underlined its division. But it's not difficult to imagine the scenes the building has witnessed: in November 1918 the German Republic was declared from a balcony here, while Karl Liebknecht was busy proclaiming a Socialist Republic down the road at what became the State Council building in eastern Berlin, thus cementing his and Rosa Luxemburg's fate.

The Reichstag is currently undergoing major renovations to prepare it to once again – and for the first time since 1933 – hold united Germany's parliament. The revamped building, its original interior completely gutted, will sport a new glass dome designed by British architect Sir Norman Foster. It will be closed until at least 1999, but it's worth a visit in the meantime to gape at a new government quarter being created more or less from scratch.

Re-establishing Berlin as the centre of parliamentary and governmental activity is a political process that some – wary of Europe's memories of two world wars and the size and latent power of the new Germany – are nervous about. In addition, neither Berlin nor Bonn nor government workers are happy about the change: Bonn loses its economic base, Berlin becomes overcrowded, and the state bureaucrats must uproot themselves and move from peaceful Bonn to the noisy metropolis. But the political momentum of reunification – and the fact that Bonn was always legally only a provisional capital – has cast these doubts and desires aside.

The Berlin Wall

Immediately behind the Reichstag, it's only just possible to make out the course of the **Berlin Wall**, which for 28 years divided the city; to the right of the entrance, a poignant series of plaques marks the names (where known) of those killed trying to swim to the West across the nearby River Spree.

The Wall – some history

After the war, Berlin was split among its conquerors, as Stalin, Roosevelt and Churchill had agreed at Yalta. Each sector was administered by the relevant country, and was supposed to exist peacefully with its neighbours under a unified city council. But almost from the outset, antagonism between the Soviet and other sectors was high. Only three years after the war ended, the Soviet forces closed down the land access corridors to the city from the Western zones in what became known as the **Berlin Blockade**: it was successfully overcome by a massive Western **airlift** of food and supplies that lasted nearly a year. This, followed by the 1953 uprising, large-scale cross-border emigration (between 1949 and 1961, the year the Wall was built, when over three million East Germans fled to the Federal Republic – almost a fifth of the population) and innumerable "incidents", led to the building of what was known in the GDR as the "anti-Fascist protection wall".

When the four powers were deciding on sectors, one of the parish maps of Greater Berlin from 1920 was used to delineate them: the Wall followed the Soviet sector boundary implacably, cutting through houses, across squares and rivers with its own cool illogicality. An oddity of the Wall was that it was built a few metres inside GDR territory; the West Berlin authorities therefore had little control over the **graffiti** that covered it. The Wall was an ever-changing mixture of colours and slogans, with occasional bursts of bitterness: "*My friends are dying behind you*"; humour: "*Why not jump over and join the Party?*"; and stupidity: "*We shoulda nuked 'em in 45*".

Over the years, at least eighty people were **killed** endeavouring to cross the Wall. Initial escape attempts were straightforward, and often successful – hollowing out furniture, ramming checkpoint barriers and simple disguise brought many people over. However, the authorities quickly rose to the challenge, and would-be escapees became more resourceful, digging tunnels, and constructing gliders, one-man submarines and hot-air balloons. By the time the Wall came down, every escape method conceivable seemed to have been used – even down to passing through Checkpoint Charlie in the stomach of a pantomime cow – and those desperate to get out of the GDR preferred the long wait and complications of applying to leave officially to the risk of being gunned down by a border guard. The guards, known as Grepos, were under instructions to shoot anyone attempting to scale the Wall, and to shoot accurately: any guard suspected of deliberately missing was court-martialled, and his family could expect severe harassment from the authorities.

When the end came, it happened so quickly that Berliners, East and West, seemed not to believe it; but within days of the announcement that citizens of the GDR were free to travel, enterprising characters were renting out hammer and chisels so that souvenir hunters could take home their own chip of the Wall. Today, especially in the city centre, it's barely possible to tell exactly where the Wall ran: odd juxtapositions of dereliction against modernity, an unexpected swathe of erstwhile "Death Strip", are in most cases all that's left of one of the most hated borders the world ever knew.

One sad postscript to the story of the Wall hit the headlines in spring 1992. Two former **border guards** were tried for the murder of Chris Gueffroy, shot dead while illegally trying to cross the border at Neukölln in February 1989. Under the GDR government the guards had been treated to a meal by their superiors and given extra holiday for their patriotic actions; under the new regime, they received sentences for murder – while those ultimately responsible, the former leaders of the GDR, evaded punishment.

For a more detailed history of the Wall and the traumas it caused, visit the Haus am Checkpoint Charlie – p.82.

The
Reichstag

Erected overnight on August 13, 1961, to cordon off the Soviet sector and corral the British, American and French sectors of the city some 200km inside the GDR, the Wall underlined the city's schizophrenia and frenzy and marked (as Berliners are fond of telling you) the city's *raison d'être* – the "stabilization of the impossible". Late in 1989 the East German government, spurred by Gorbachev's *glasnost* and confronted by a tense domestic climate, realized it could keep the impossible stable no longer. To an initially disbelieving and then jubilant Europe, travel restrictions for GDR citizens were lifted on November 9, 1989 – effectively, the Wall had ceased to matter, and pictures of Berliners, East and West, hacking away at the detested symbol filled newspapers and TV bulletins around the world. Now the Wall has almost entirely vanished, and the few sections that remain are protected from the tourist chisels by barbed wire and by its official status as an "historic landmark".

CENTRAL BERLIN

All Tiergarten sites can be reached on bus #129, #148 and #348.

The Tiergarten Museum Complex

To the west of Potsdamer Platz, the **Tiergarten Complex** (also known as the *Kulturforum*) is a recently built mixture of museums and cultural forums that could easily fill a day of your time. Along with the Dahlem museum complex and the collections on the Museum Island, it's one of Berlin's cultural focal points. With the recent completion of the Gemäldegalerie, which brings together a world-class collection of early European paintings formerly split between museums in the east and west, this complex has finally achieved the prominent status intended for it when construction began in a still-divided city.

The Neue Nationalgalerie

By far the finest building here – architecturally speaking – is the **Neue Nationalgalerie**, Potsdamer Str. 50 (Tues–Fri 9am–5pm, Sat & Sun 10am–5pm; DM4, concessions DM2, free first Sun of each month), a black-rimmed glass box that seems almost suspended above the ground, its clarity of line and detail having all the intelligent simplicity of the Parthenon. Designed by Mies van der Rohe in 1965, the upper section is used for temporary exhibits, often of contemporary art, while the underground galleries contain paintings from the beginning of the twentieth century onwards. Included among the permanent collection are the paintings of the "Brücke" group, such as Ernst Kirchner and Karl Schmidt-Rottluff. **Kirchner** spent time in Berlin before World War I, and his *Potsdamer Platz* dates from 1914, though it might as well be in another country instead of just down the road. The galleries move on to the portraits and Berlin cityscapes of **Grosz** and **Dix**, notably Grosz's *Gray Day* and Dix's *Maler Family*. Cubism is represented by work from **Braque**, **Gris** and **Picasso** (though the latter is seen in greater number and to better effect in the Berggruen Collection in

Charlottenburg; see p.142). There are also pieces by, among others, Klee, Max Beckmann and Lyonel Feininger.

The Gemäldegalerie

The real jewel of the Tiergarten Complex is the newly opened **Gemäldegalerie** (Picture Gallery; Tues–Fri 9am–5pm, Sat & Sun 10am–5pm; DM8, concessions DM4, free first Sun of each month), which holds a stupendous collection of early European paintings. Originally housed in the prewar Kaiser-Friedrich Museum, the gallery's paintings were stashed in various places throughout the city for safekeeping during the war years, with the result that after the division of Berlin the collection was split between the Bode Museum in the east and the Dahlem complex in the west. The gallery's holdings have just been reunited for the first time in fifty years in a new custom-built structure.

Arranged in chronological order, and subdivided by region, the nine hundred paintings on display begin on the north side of the building with **German works** of the middle ages and Renaissance. Highlights include the large *Passion Altar* of 1437, made in the workshop of the great Ulm sculptor Hans Multscher; its exaggerated gestures and facial distortions mark it out as an ancient precursor of Expressionist painting. An interesting contrast is offered by the far more subtle *Solomon before the Queen of Sheba*, painted in the same year by Konrad Witz, while the exquisite *Nativity* by Martin Schongauer is the most important surviving panel by the father-figure of the German Renaissance.

These apart, the best works here are by Albrecht Altdorfer, one of the first fully realized German landscape painters, and Albrecht Dürer – among others, *Portrait of a Young Venetian Woman* and *Praying Maria* – with an impressive group of works by Dürer's eccentric pupil Hans Baldung, notably an exotic *Adoration of the Magi* triptych. Holbein the Younger is represented by several superbly observed portraits, the most celebrated being *The Danzig Merchant Georg Gisze*, with a still-life background that's a real tour-de-force of artistic virtuosity. Notable among the many examples of Cranach are his tongue-in-cheek *The Fountain of Youth*, and his free reinterpretation of Bosch's famous triptych *The Garden of Earthly Delights*.

The Netherlandish section

A lighter, less crude treatment of religious subjects is apparent in the **Netherlandish section**. Particularly illustrative is Jan van Eyck's beautifully lit *Madonna in the Church*, crammed with architectural detail and with the Virgin lifted in the perspective for gentle emphasis. Petrus Christus is thought to have been a pupil of van Eyck, and certainly knew his work, as *The Virgin and Child with St Barbara and a Carthusian Monk* reveals: in the background are tiny Flemish houses and street scenes, the artist carefully locating the event in his native Bruges. Dieric Bouts' figures tend to be stiff and rather formalized, but his *Christ in the House of Simon the Pharisee* is filled with gesture, expression and carefully drawn detail.

Also on show are some pieces by Rogier van der Weyden, which show the development of the Eyckian technique to a warmer, much more emotional treatment of religious subjects. The figures in his *Bladelin Altarpiece* reveal a delicacy of poise and an approachable humanity that was to greatly influence German painting in the fifteenth century. Albert van Ouwater was also influential, although his *Raising of Lazarus* is the only complete work to have survived; it's a daring picture, the richly dressed merchants on the right contrasting strongly with the simplicity of the Holy Family on the left. Geertgen tot Sint Jans was Ouwater's pupil, though his *St John the Baptist* is quite different from his master's painting – the saint sits almost comically impassive against a rich backdrop of intricately constructed landscape. Two other major paintings nearby are both by Hugo van der Goes: the *Adoration of the Shepherds* (painted when the artist was in the first throes of madness) has the scene unveiled by two characters representing the prophets, while the shepherds stumble into the frame. The *Adoration of the Magi* – also known as the *Monforte Altarpiece* – has a superbly drawn realism that marks a new development in Netherlandish art, carrying precision over into a large-scale work with a deftly executed, complex perspective. The small altarpiece *Triptych with the Adoration of the Magi* by Joos van Cleve reveals how these techniques were absorbed by Goes' successors. The collection then moves into the sixteenth century and the works of Jan Gossaert, Quentin Massys and Bruegel the Elder, whose *Netherlandish Proverbs* is an amusing, if hard-to-grasp, illustration of over a hundred sixteenth-century proverbs and maxims – a key and English translation help you pick out a man armed to the teeth, banging his head against a brick wall and casting pearls before swine.

The Dutch and Flemish collections

The next section reveals the gallery's second strength in the **Dutch and Flemish collections**. This contains the large portraits of Van Dyck and the fleshy canvases of Rubens, as well as a fine group of Dutch interiors. The paintings of Vermeer are the most easily identifiable, though his *Woman with a Pearl Necklace* is not one of his greater works. Better is *Man and Woman Drinking Wine*, which displays his usual technique of placing furniture obliquely in the centre of the canvas, the scene illuminated by window light. De Hooch used a similar technique in *Woman Weighing Gold*, though more complex, both compositionally and morally, is his *The Mother*, a masterly example of Dutch interior painting at its finest. Other rooms trace the development of Dutch art through the works of Maes, Terborch, Dou, Jan Steen and Frans Hals.

The highpoint of this section, hung in a large octagonal room, are the paintings of **Rembrandt**, perhaps the largest collection of his work in the world. The most famous picture here, *The Man in the Golden Helmet*, was recently proved to be the work of his studio rather than the artist himself, though this does little to detract from the elegance and power of the portrait, its reflective sorrow relieved by the bright helmet. Other (verified) works include a 1634 *Self-Portrait*, painted at the height of the artist's wealth and fame; a *Portrait of Saskia*, Rembrandt's wife, painted in the year of her death; a beautifully warm and loving *Portrait of Hendrickje Stoffels*, the artist's later, common-law wife, and numerous other religious paintings. Following this room are paintings by **French artists** – including a rare fifteenth-century panel painting, Jean Fouquet's *Etienne Chevalier and St Stephen*, which shows the Treasurer of France accompanied by his patron saint – and **English portraits** of the eighteenth century.

Italian paintings

The galleries on the museum's southern side contain **Italian paintings** from the Renaissance to the eighteenth century. This collection is particularly strong on works from the Florentine Renaissance: Fra Filippo Lippi's *The Adoration in the Forest* is a mystical image of unusual grace and beauty, rightly one of the most admired paintings of the period. Also much prized is the gorgeously colourful *Adoration of the Magi* by Domenico Veneziano, which perfectly captures the full regal splendour of the subject. Correggio's playfully suggestive *Leda with the Swan* is a good example of the Classical preoccupations of the period; its subject so offended an eighteenth-century religious fanatic that he hacked it to pieces. There's work here, too, by Giotto, Verrocchio, Masaccio, Mantegna, Raphael and Titian, and, most importantly, by Botticeli, including *Virgin and Child with the Two St Johns*, *Portrait of a Young Woman* and *St Sebastian*.

Other noteworthy painters represented in the museum include Goya, Caravaggio (*Cupid Victorious*, heavy with symbolism and homoeroticism), Poussin (the important *Self-Portrait*), Claude and Canaletto.

The Philharmonie

North of the Nationalgalerie the **Matthäikirche** (Matthias Church) stands in lonely isolation on a barren landscape that now forms a car park for the **Philharmonie**, home of the Berlin Philharmonic and, until he retired and subsequently died in 1989, its renowned conductor **Herbert von Karajan** (see overleaf). Looking at the gold-clad ugliness of the building, designed in the 1960s by Hans Scharoun, and bearing in mind von Karajan's famously short temper with artists, it's easy to see how it got its nickname among Berliners of "Karajan's circus". Should you wish to reserve a seat the box office is open Monday to Friday from 3.30 to 6pm, Saturday and Sunday 11am to 2pm (☎25 48 81 32): the chances

For more on classical music and the performing arts, see "The arts" in Listings.

The Tiergarten Museum Complex

Herbert von Karajan (1908–89)

The success of Austrian conductor **Herbert von Karajan** in the postwar years obscured a murky past that included a close association with the Nazi party. Exactly what this association was is unclear, though his orga-nizing of concerts for the Führer – including an occasion when he had the audience seating arranged in the form of a swastika – is well documented, and in later years few of the world's great Jewish soloists ever performed or recorded with him.

From the 1960s to the 1980s von Karajan ruled the Berlin Philharmonic with a rigid discipline that alienated many who worked under him, but proved fabulously successful in the field of popularizing classical music. Under the Deutsche Grammophon label, they recorded just about every-thing that had a chance of selling, all in the highly polished von Karajan style – a style as distinctive (and to some as likeable) as that of Mantovani.

of getting a ticket for major concerts under the orchestra's current conductor, Claudio Abbado, are slim unless you've booked months in advance, but it's worth trying your luck for other performances under guest conductors.

The Musikinstrumenten museum

Continuing the musical theme, the **Musikinstrumenten museum** (Tues–Fri 9am–5pm, Sat & Sun 10am–5pm; DM4, concessions DM2, free on first Sun of each month) at Tiergartenstr. 1, just below the Philharmonie, comes as something of a disappointment. Its collec-tion of (mostly European) keyboards, wind and string instruments from the fifteenth century to the present day is comprehensive and impressively laid out, but it's all strictly look-don't-touch stuff, with guards vigilant for the slightest tinkle. Content yourself with the pre-recorded tapes that give a taste of the weird and wonderful sounds of the instruments.

Two museums and a library

Much better is the **Kunstgewerbemuseum** (Museum of Applied Arts; Tues–Fri 9am–5pm, Sat & Sun 10am–5pm; DM4, concessions DM2, free first Sun of each month) at Matthäikirchplatz 10, an encyclope-dic but seldom dull collection of European arts and crafts. The top floor contains the Renaissance, Baroque and Rococo pieces (won-derful silver and ceramics), along with *Jugendstil* and Art Deco objects, particularly furniture. The first floor holds the Middle Ages to Early Renaissance collections, with some sumptuous gold pieces. The highlights are Lüneburg's municipal silver and the treasures from the Stiftskirche in Enger and, in the basement, a small but great assembly of Bauhaus furniture, glittering contemporary jewellery, and a display on the evolution of product design.

The **Kupferstichkabinett** (Engraving Cabinet; times and prices as above) at Matthäikirchplatz 4 holds an extensive collection of

European medieval and Renaissance prints, drawings and engravings, many kept under protective lighting. Founded by William Humboldt in 1831, the collection includes Botticelli's exquisite drawings for Dante's *Divine Comedy* (until recently divided between the Altes Museum and the Dahlem museum complex). The museum organizes exhibitions on all aspects of print-making, drawing and related design.

Lastly, the **Staatsbibliothek** (Mon–Fri 9am–9pm, Sat 9am–5pm; free), across Potsdamer Strasse from the other buildings, has over three and a half million books, occasional exhibitions, a small concert hall, a reasonable café and a wide selection of British newspapers. As the final building to be designed by Hans Scharoun, and the most popular of his works among his fans, the *Staabi*'s most recent claim to fame came when it was used as an important backdrop in Wim Wenders' poetic film elegy to the city, *Wings of Desire*.

Chapter 3

Unter den Linden and around

U nter den Linden and the surrounding streets formed the show-piece quarter of Hohenzollern Berlin, capital of Brandenburg-Prussia and later the German Empire. Berlin had been a relative backwater until the seventeenth century, but with the rise of Prussia architects were commissioned to create the trappings of a capital city – churches, theatres, libraries, palaces and an opera house – which were all set down here. Safe **Baroque** and **Neoclassical** styles predominate, and there are no great flights of architectural fancy. These buildings were meant to project an image of solidity, permanence and power, perhaps to allay the latent insecurity of Brandenburg-Prussia as a relatively late arrival on the European stage.

Almost every one of these symbols of Hohenzollern might was left gutted by the bombing and shelling of World War II. Paradoxically, it was the postwar Communist regime that resurrected them from the wartime rubble to adorn the capital of the German Democratic Republic. The result was a pleasing re-creation of the old city, though one of the motives behind this restoration was to import a sense of historical continuity to the East German state by tacitly linking it with Prussia. Whether anyone outside the Politbüro really bought into this particular conceit is doubtful, but central East Berlin always compared favourably with the haphazard, soulless jumble of central West Berlin.

So successful has the **restoration** been that, looking at these magnificent eighteenth- and nineteenth-century buildings, it's difficult to believe that as recently as the 1960s large patches of the centre lay in ruins. Like archeologists trying to picture a whole vase from a single fragment, the builders took a facade, or just a small fraction of one, and set about re-creating the whole. And even though much of what can be seen today is an imitation, it's often easy to suspend one's disbelief and imagine an unbroken continuity.

The rejuvenation is still going on. This is most notable on the Gendarmenmarkt, a few blocks to the south, where as recently as ten years ago the twin Neoclassical churches that grace the square were bombed-out shells. Now restoration of the area is complete and Gendarmenmarkt has been returned to its position as one of Berlin's most striking corners.

It's in the area south of Unter den Linden that the forest of building cranes dominating the Berlin skyline is at its thickest, with huge building projects, particularly along **Friedrichstrasse** and around **Potsdamer Platz**, poised to transform this part of the city. By the time the proposed schemes are completed this part of town will, without doubt, have been transformed beyond all recognition for anyone who knew the pre-*Wende* city.

Unter den Linden

CENTRAL BERLIN

Unter den Linden itself is Berlin's grandest boulevard, rolling due east from the Brandenburg Gate towards Alexanderplatz. Once the main east–west axis of Imperial Berlin and site of many of the city's foreign embassies, it has been revitalized since 1989, reassuming its old role as one of Berlin's most important streets. The street – "beneath the lime trees" – was named after the trees that border its central island. The first saplings were planted by the Great Elector during the seventeenth century to line the route that ran from his palace to the hunting grounds in the Tiergarten. The original trees were replaced by crude Nazi totem-poles during the 1930s, and the present generation dates from a period of postwar planting.

Until 1989 the western extremity of Unter den Linden marked the end of the road for East Berliners: a low barrier a hundred metres or so short of the Brandenburg Gate cut it off from Charlottenburger Chaussee (today known as Strasse des 17 Juni), its prewar continuation through the Tiergarten to the city's West End. From this vantage point it was possible to view the Brandenburg Gate, beyond which the discreet presence of armed border guards and the sterile white concrete of the Wall signalled the frontier with West Berlin. During this period Unter den Linden was reduced to little more than a grandiose blind alley, lined by infrequently visited embassies that gave it a strangely decorative feel. Now, however, traffic is heavier as tourists compete for pavement space with civil servants and businesspeople, and the embassies have been joined by the offices of international companies and expensive stores. Federal ministries have also opened here in preparation for the full transfer of government to Berlin from Bonn early next century.

From the Brandenburg Gate to Bebelplatz

At the head of Unter den Linden is the **Brandenburg Gate** (*Brandenburger Tor*), another of those Berlin buildings dense with meaning and historical associations. Originally built as a city gate-

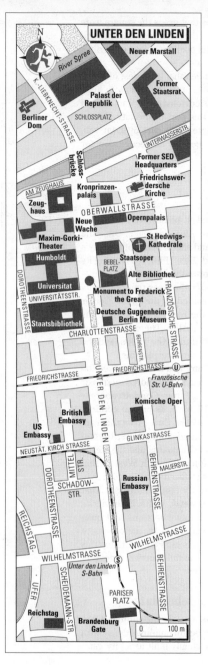

River Spree

K.-LIEBKNECHT-STRASSE

Neuer Marstall

Former Staatsrat

Palast der Republik

SCHLOSSPLATZ

Berliner Dom

UNTERWASSERSTR.

Schloss-brücke

Former SED Headquarters

AM ZEUGHAUS

Kronprinzen-palais

Friedrichswer-dersche Kirche

Zeug-haus

OBERWALLSTRASSE

Neue Wache

Opernpalais

Maxim-Gorki-Theater

St Hedwigs-Kathedrale

Humboldt

BEBEL-PLATZ

Staatsoper

DOROTHEENSTRASSE

Universität

UNIVERSITÄTSSTR.

Alte Bibliothek

Monument to Frederick the Great

FRANZÖSISCHE STRASSE

Staatsbibliothek

Deutsche Guggenheim Berlin Museum

CHARLOTTENSTRASSE

BEHRENSTR.

FRIEDRICHSTRASSE

FRIEDRICHSTRASSE

UNTER DEN LINDEN

Französische Str. U-Bahn

Komische Oper

British Embassy

US Embassy

GLINKASTRASSE

NEUSTÄT. KIRCH STRASSE

MITTEL-STR.

BEHRENSTRASSE

MAUERSTR.

SCHADOW-STR.

Russian Embassy

DOROTHEENSTRASSE

REICHSTAG

WILHELMSTRASSE

Unter den Linden S-Bahn

WILHELMSTRASSE

BEHRENSTRASSE

SCHEIDEMANNSTR.

UFER

PARISER PLATZ

Reichstag

Brandenburg Gate

0   100 m

cum-triumphal arch in 1791, it was designed by Carl Gotthard Langhans and modelled after the Propylaea, the entrance to the Acropolis in Athens. The Gate became, like the Reichstag later, a symbol of German unity, looking out to the Siegessäule and guarding the city's grandest thoroughfare. In 1806 Napoleon marched under the arch and took home with him the **Quadriga**, the horse-drawn chariot that tops the Gate. It was returned a few years later, and the revolutionaries of 1848 and 1918 met under its gilded form; later the Gate was a favoured rallying point for the Nazis' torch-lit marches.

After the building of the Wall placed the Gate in the Eastern sector, nearby observation posts (now dismantled) became the place for visiting politicians to look over from the West in what was a handy photo-opportunity – the view was apparently emotive enough to reduce Margaret Thatcher to tears. With the opening of a border crossing here just before Christmas 1989, the east–west axis of the city was symbolically re-created and the post-Wall mood of eagerness for unification was strengthened. When the GDR authorities rebuilt the Quadriga following wartime damage, they removed the Prussian Iron Cross from the Goddess of Victory's laurel wreath, which topped her staff, on the grounds that it was "symbolic of Prussian–German militarism". When the border was reopened, the Iron Cross was replaced. Yet, despite the recent jubilation, it's easy to see why some, mindful of historical precedent, still view the Gate with a frisson of unease.

The Brandenburg Gate has been partly reopened to traffic, with buses and taxis (but not private cars) allowed to pass between its massive pillars. On

---

A chip off the Eastern bloc

If you're looking for the standard souvenir, a chip of the Berlin Wall,
you'll find that Wall shards are hard to come by these days. Be warned that
the pieces sold on the street by the Brandenburg Gate and Checkpoint
Charlie are almost never the real thing. Despite official-looking "certificates of authentication" often given with a purchase, the only way you can
be sure of getting the real thing is to look for a pale aggregate of flint, pebbles and other hard stones.

Pariser Platz, the square just to the east, symmetrical ornamental
gardens have been restored according to prewar plans, though most
of the passing tourists are more interested in the numerous street
stalls selling Soviet and GDR ephemera.

On the southeast corner of the Platz, the legendary **Adlon Hotel**,
once one of Europe's grandest hotels, has been rebuilt. The original
was host to luminaries from Charlie Chaplin to Lawrence of Arabia
and Kaiser Wilhelm II, and was regarded throughout the continent as
the acme of luxury and style. The building was destroyed in the closing days of the war, and this new version, patterned closely after its
predecessor – the lobby fountain, for example, was salvaged from
the original – attempts the same heights of opulence. Even if you
can't afford a drink here, let alone a room, have a look at the lobby
and imagine a time when Berlin was the cultural capital of Europe.

The Russian Embassy to the Friedrichstrasse intersection

Among the first buildings you'll see as you head east down Unter den
Linden from Pariser Platz is the massive **Russian Embassy** which
rears up on the right. Built in 1950 on the site of the prewar (originally Tsarist) embassy, it's an example of the much-maligned
Zuckerbäckerstil or "wedding-cake style" characteristic of Stalin-
era Soviet architecture, and was the first postwar building to be
erected on Unter den Linden. *Zuckerbäckerstil* is a kind of blunted,
monumental Classicism, and Berlin has a number of such buildings,
the most spectacular being those along Karl-Marx-Allee (see p.163).

The next block along from the embassy is a row of shops which also
includes the box office for the **Komische Oper**, one of Berlin's leading
opera companies. The actual entrance to the theatre itself is on the
street behind at Behrenstr. 55–57, and though the building doesn't
look like much from the outside, the interior is a wonderful 1890s frenzy of red plush, gilt and statuary (see "The arts" in Listings). Back on
Unter den Linden at no. 39, a couple of doors along from the Komische
Oper box office, is a **Meissen porcelain shop** – just the place if you
want to blow your life's savings on a six-cup coffee service.

Unter den Linden hits **Friedrichstrasse** at the next junction;
before the war this was one of the busiest crossroads in the city, a

focal point for cafés and hotels, including the famous *Café Kranzler*. Like most of the rest of Weimar Berlin the café vanished in the debris of the war, although it was later re-established on the Kurfürstendamm in the west of the city.

The Deutsche Guggenheim Berlin Museum

At the southeast corner of Unter den Linden and Charlottenstrasse is the recently opened German branch of New York's **Guggenheim Museum** (daily 11am–8pm; DM8, concessions DM5). It's a far cry from the museum's architectural landmarks in New York and Bilbao. Housed in a former bank building, this exhibition space shows rotating exhibitions focusing on top-drawer modern painters and important schools and movements. The galleries are modest in size, but comfortably laid-out and well-lit. There's a small museum shop and a sleek, quiet café on site.

The Staatsbibliothek and monument to Frederick the Great

A little further along Unter den Linden on the northern side is the **Staatsbibliothek zu Berlin** (Mon 2pm–9pm, Tues–Fri 9am–9pm, Sat 9am–5pm; free; tours every first Sat of the month at 10.30am), the former Prussian (and later GDR) state library, now twinned with the Staabi on Potsdamer Strasse (see p.61). It's a typically grandiose edifice dating from the turn of the century, with a facade extensively patched up after wartime shrapnel damage, and is now mainly the haunt of Humboldt University students. Visitors who don't feel like delving into the volumes within can sit in the ivy-clad courtyard by the fountain and have a drink or snack at the small café. As you do so, admire a GDR-era sculpture showing a member of the proletariat apparently reading a didactic Brecht poem on a relief at the other side of the fountain. The subject of the poem is the way in which the workers and soldiers who carry out the orders of kings and emperors are forgotten while the rulers themselves live on as historical figures.

Back on Unter den Linden is a statue commemorating just such a historical figure. Christian Rauch's verdigris-coated equestrian **monument to Frederick the Great** dates from the nineteenth century and shows Frederick astride a charger. Around the plinth, about a quarter of the size of the monarch, are representations of his generals, mostly on foot and conferring animatedly. Frederick was the enlightened despot who laid the foundations of Prussian power.

For more on the life of Frederick the Great, see "Park Sanssouci", p.194.

After the war, *Der alte Fritz*, as the king was popularly known, was removed from Unter den Linden and only restored to its city centre site in 1981 after a long exile in Potsdam. Its reinstatement reflected an odd revaluation by Erich Honecker's GDR of the pre-socialist past. No longer were figures like Frederick the Great, Blücher, Scharnhorst *et al* to be reviled as imperialistic militarists, but were to be accorded the status of historic figures worthy of com-memoration. Even Bismarck, the Iron Chancellor of Wilhelmine Germany, was recognized as having "in his *Junker* way played a pro-gressive historical role".

The Humboldt Universität

Frederick the Great's monument is the vanguard of a whole host of historic buildings, survivors of nineteenth-century Berlin that were described by Christopher Isherwood as "so pompous, so very cor-rect", and have been restored over the last 45 years or so from the postwar rubble. On the left-hand side of the street is the **Humboldt Universität**, a restrained Neoclassical building from 1748, original-ly built as a palace for Frederick the Great's brother. In 1809 the philologist, writer and diplomat Wilhelm Humboldt founded a school here that was to become the University of Berlin, and later be renamed in his honour. Flanking the entrance gate are statues of Wilhelm and his brother Alexander, famous for his exploration of Central and South America. Wilhelm is contemplating the passing traffic, book in hand, and Alexander is sitting on a globe above a ded-ication to the "second discoverer of Cuba" from the University of Havana. Alumni of the Humboldt Universität include Karl Marx, Friedrich Engels and Karl Liebknecht, the socialist leader and pro-claimer of the first German republic who was murdered in 1919 (see p.86). The philologists Jacob and Wilhelm Grimm (better known as the Brothers Grimm) and Albert Einstein are some of the better-known former staff members.

You don't need student ID to eat in the uni-versity mensa (turn left out of the main entrance hall and continue down the corridor).

Bebelplatz and around

Directly opposite the university is **Bebelplatz**, formerly Opernplatz, the scene on May 11, 1933, of the infamous *Büchverbrennung*, the burning of books that conflicted with Nazi ideology. On the orders of Hitler's propaganda minister, Joseph Goebbels, thousands of books went up in smoke, including the works of "un-German" authors like Erich Maria Remarque, Thomas Mann, Heinrich Mann, Stefan Zweig and Erich Kästner, along with volumes by countless foreign writers, H.G. Wells and Ernest Hemingway among them. The most fitting comment on this episode was made with accidental foresight by the Jewish poet Heinrich Heine during the previous century: "Where they start by burning books, they'll end by burning people." A recent and intriguing memorial to the bookburning, "The Empty Library", in fact incorporates these words on a plaque. Go to the middle of Bebelplatz and look through the glass pane set in the ground.

Bebelplatz was originally conceived by Frederick the Great as a tribute to the grandeur of ancient Rome and a monument to the greater glory of himself. He and the architect **Georg Wenzeslaus von Knobelsdorff** drew up plans for what was to be known as the Forum Fridericianum, a space that would recall the great open squares of Classical Rome. It never fulfilled such lofty ambitions, and instead exhibits a rather humble and unimpressive mien.

The Alte Bibliothek and Staatsoper

On the western side of the square is the **Alte Bibliothek**, a former royal library known colloquially as the **Kommode** ("chest of drawers"), thanks to its curved Baroque facade. The design of the Kommode, which was built between 1775 and 1780, was based on that of the Michaelertrakt in Vienna's Hofburg. Lenin spent some time here poring over dusty tomes while waiting for the Russian Revolution, and despite the fact that only the building's facade survived the war, it's been immaculately restored. Knobelsdorff's Neoclassical **Staatsoper**, on the eastern side of the square, looks a little plain opposite the Kommode, though it represented the pinnacle of the architect's career and was Berlin's first theatre. The building is best viewed from Unter den Linden, where an imposing portico marks the main entrance. Just under two centuries after its construction it became the first major building to fall victim to World War II bombing, on the night of April 9–10, 1941. The Nazi authorities restored it for its bicentenary in 1943, but on February 3, 1945, it was gutted once again. Like virtually everything else around here it has been totally reconstructed and is now one of Berlin's leading opera houses (see "The arts" in Listings).

Sankt-Hedwigs-Kathedrale

Just behind is another Knobelsdorff creation, the stylistically incongruous **Sankt-Hedwigs-Kathedrale**, which was built as a place of worship for the city's Catholic minority in 1747 and is still in use. According to popular legend it owes its circular shape and domed profile to Frederick the Great's demand that it be built in the form of an upturned teacup. This probably stems from the fact that the monarch "advised" Knobelsdorff, but the truth is that the building's shape was inspired by the Pantheon in Rome. Reduced to a shell on March 2, 1943, the cathedral was not reconstructed until 1963, a restoration that left it with a slightly altered dome and a modernized interior.

The interior, past the hazy biblical reliefs of the entrance portico, is perhaps the most unusual aspect of the whole building. The greatest feature of the vast main hall is the split-level double altar – the upper one is used on Sundays and special occasions, while the sunken altar in the crypt, reached by a flight of broad stairs, is used for weekday masses. All this is complemented by the stainless steel pipes of the ethereal-sounding organ above the entrance and 1970s-style globe-lamps hanging from the ceiling. If you've survived the combined effects of all this, the crypt with its eight grotto-like side chapels and near-abstract charcoal drawings is a further attraction.

The Opernpalais and Kronprinzenpalais

Back on Unter den Linden, just east of the Staatsoper, is a lawn dotted with **statues of Prussian generals**. Scharnhorst stands at the front, while Yorck, Blücher and Gneisenau bring up the rear. Blücher, whose timely intervention turned the day at Waterloo, looks most warlike, with his foot resting on a cannon barrel and a sabre in his hand.

Next door to this martial grouping is the eighteenth-century **Opernpalais**, a Baroque palace known as the Prinzessinpalais (Princess's Palace) before the war, in memory of its role as a swanky town residence for the three daughters of Friedrich Wilhelm III. It's now home to a couple of pricey restaurants and the genteel *Operncafé* (see "Cafés and bars" in Listings). There's outdoor seat-

---

Karl Friedrich Schinkel (1781–1841)

Karl Friedrich Schinkel was an incredibly prolific architect who quite literally transformed nineteenth-century Berlin, creating some of the city's most famous Neoclassical buildings. His first ever design, the **Pomonatempel** in Potsdam (see p.203), was completed while he was still a nineteen-year-old student in Berlin. Despite this auspicious beginning, his architectural career did not take off immediately and for a while he worked as a landscape artist and set-decorator for the theatre, later turning his hand to set-design (an activity which he pursued even after he had established himself as an architect). Towards the end of the first decade of the nineteenth century he began submitting architectural designs for the great public works of the time, and, in 1810, he secured a job with the administration of Prussian buildings.

In 1815 he was given a position in the new Public Works Department, an appointment which marked the beginning of the most productive phase of his career. During the years between 1815 and 1830, when he was made head of the department, he designed some of his most famous buildings. Constructions like the Grecian-style **Neue Wache** (see p.71), the elegant **Schauspielhaus** (see p.79), and the **Altes Museum** (p.91) with its striking Doric columns were just what were needed to enhance the ever-expanding capital of Brandenburg-Prussia. Other creations from this period include the **War Memorial Cross** in Kreuzberg (see p.124) and the **Friedrichwerdersche Kirche** (see overleaf), both inspired by Neo-Gothic styles that were all the rage in England at the time. Later in his career Schinkel experimented with other architectural forms, a phase marked by the **Romanesque** Charlottenhof and Römischer Bäder in Potsdam (see p.200).

By virtue of his own designs and the role he played in shaping Brandenburg-Prussia's building policy, Schinkel remains, without doubt, one of the most influential German architects of the nineteenth century. Even the Iron Cross (along with the swastika, the most emotive of German military symbols) was designed by him. Nearly every town in Brandenburg has a building that Schinkel had, at the very least, some involvement in; and a lasting testimony to his importance is the fact that even the identity of late twentieth-century Berlin is in part defined by his works.

---

ing in summer, though the overall effect of the surroundings is
diminished by a garish fast-food/ice-cream stand tacked onto the
facade of the palace.

The Opernpalais is really a wing of its neighbour opposite, the
Kronprinzenpalais. Originally built in 1663 and given a Baroque
face-lift in 1732, this started life as a residence for Prussian crown
princes, but was converted into a national art gallery after 1919,
becoming a leading venue for modern art exhibitions. In 1933 the
Nazis closed it, declaring hundreds of Expressionist and contemporary works housed here to be examples of "*entartete Kunst*" or
"degenerate art". Most of these were either sold off abroad or
destroyed, and a number were bought at knock-down prices by leading Nazis, Göring among them.

To the immediate east of the Kronprinzenpalais is a grassy field,
until a few years ago the site of the former **GDR foreign ministry**. A
forgettable wedge of East German modernism empty since reunification, it was happily torn down by the government. It occupied the
former site of Karl Friedrich Schinkel's architectural school. This
was reckoned to be one of his finest creations and Schinkel even
moved in here, occupying a top-floor apartment until his death in
1841. Inevitably, wartime bombing took its toll and in 1962 the
remains were demolished in a departure from the GDR's usual policy of restoring the city's monuments wherever possible. It's been
proposed that Schinkel's *Bauakademie* be rebuilt to stand side by
side with a new foreign ministry – though at the time of writing the
government had only agreed to stump up for the ministry.

The Friedrichwerdersche Kirche and Jungfernbrücke

Karl Friedrich Schinkel was the man who, more than anyone, gave
nineteenth-century Berlin its distinctive Neoclassical stamp, and
behind the field that once housed his *Bauakademie* is the architect's **Friedrichwerdersche Kirche**, on Am Werderschen Markt,
which houses the **Schinkel Museum** (Tues–Sun 9am–5pm; DM4,
concessions DM2). The church itself is a rather plain Neo-Gothic
affair, a stylistic departure for Schinkel, who was infatuated with the
Classical styles he had encountered on trips to Italy. The inspiration
for the Friedrichwerdersche Kirche came from churches Schinkel
had seen on a visit to England in 1826.

The Schinkel Museum was opened in 1987 when postwar restoration of the building was completed to coincide with Berlin's 750th
anniversary. A display in the church's upper gallery gives a full run-
down of Schinkel's achievements, setting his work in the context of
the times, and also details the history of the church. On the ground
floor is a jumble of German Neoclassical statuary from the nineteenth century, including a representation of Schinkel himself.

In the shadow of the Friedrichwerdersche Kirche is a kitsch-looking version of Berlin's bear mascot in red tufa: mother bear watches

over her cubs atop a rather feeble fountain. The forbidding-looking building opposite the church is the former **SED Headquarters**, one-time nerve centre of the East German Communist party. Heading down Unterwasserstrasse, running alongside the Spree east of the ex-SED Headquarters, leads to the **Jungfernbrücke**, Berlin's oldest surviving bridge. It's actually a drawbridge and the creaky-looking winding gear is still used to raise it and allow passing boats by.

The Neue Wache and around

Schinkel's most famous surviving creation, the **Neue Wache**, is on Unter den Linden opposite the Opernpalais. Built between 1816 and 1818 as a guardhouse for the royal watch, it resembles a stylized Roman temple and served as a sort of Neoclassical police station until 1918. In 1930–31 it was converted into a memorial to the military dead of World War I, and in 1957 the GDR government extended this concept to include those killed by the Nazis, dedicating the building as a "Memorial to the Victims of Fascism and Militarism".

These days it serves as the "Central Memorial of the Federal Republic of Germany", and inside it a granite slab covers the tombs of an unknown soldier and an unknown concentration camp victim. At the head of this memorial stone is a statue, depicting a mother clutching her dying son, dedicated to the "victims of war and tyranny". Until 1990 one of East Berlin's better-known ironies was played out in front of the Neue Wache with the regular changing of the *Nationale Volksarmee* (National People's Army – the GDR army) honour guard, a much-photographed goose-stepping ritual that ended with the demise of the East German state.

Berlin's most spectacular war memorial – to Soviet troops killed liberating the city – is also on the eastern side of town, in the suburb of Treptow, see p.167.

The Zeughaus

Across Hinter den Giesshaus, opposite the Neue Wache, is one of eastern Berlin's finest Baroque buildings, the old Prussian Arsenal or **Zeughaus**, which now houses the **Deutsches Historisches Museum**, Unter den Linden 2 (daily except Wed 10am–6pm; free). The museum's permanent exhibition, "Pictures and Objects from German History" is an engrossing if cursory presentation, well worth a visit. A concise guide in English is available (DM9.80). There's always one or more temporary exhibitions on display as well.

The original plans for the Zeughaus were drawn up by François Blondel, but the building was completed by Andreas Schlüter, who was responsible for many of the decorative elements, notably the walls of the Schlüterhof, the museum's inner courtyard, which are lined by reliefs depicting the contorted faces of dying warriors. These are vivid, realistic depictions of agony and anguish, with nothing heroic about them; death is shown as cutting everyone down to size, and none are spared its indignities. On a more cheerful note, outdoor classical concerts are an occasional summer attraction in the Schlüterhof.

There was much excitement at the Zeughaus on June 14, 1848, when, during the revolutionary upheavals, the people of Berlin stormed the building looking for arms. A number of citizens were killed, and no weapons were found, but the incident gave the authorities an excuse to bring troops into the city and ban various democratic newspapers and organizations. Just over thirty years later the Zeughaus was turned into a museum devoted to the exploits of the Prussian army, and from 1953, though heavily damaged, the building was given over to the nascent *Museum für Deutsche Geschichte*, offering the GDR's version of German history. The highly political and subjective nature of its content was to cause problems for the directors and staff of the museum after the *Wende* and, despite attempts to redress the balance with a special exhibition about German victims of Stalinist persecution during the period, it was closed down just after reunification.

Just behind the Neue Wache is the **Maxim-Gorki-Theater** (see "The arts" in Listings), a one-time singing academy converted into a theatre after World War II. The grand-looking building just to the east is **Palais am Festungsgrab**, a building that's had a chequered career. Originally built during the eighteenth century as a palace for a royal gentleman of the bedchamber, it later served as a residence for Prussian finance ministers, and during GDR days it was the *Zentrale Haus der Deutsch-Sowjetischen Freundschaft* or "Central House of German-Soviet Friendship". Today it houses the **Museum Mitte von Berlin** (Wed & Thurs 1–5pm, Fri 1–8pm, Sat 11am–8pm, Sun 11am–5pm; free), a modest local history museum, and the *Tadschikische Teestube*, a tearoom serving Russian specialities (see "Restaurants" in Listings).

South of Unter den Linden

CENTRAL BERLIN

The network of streets south of Unter den Linden, cut in two by the north–south axis of Friedrichstrasse, is easy to explore on foot. On the western side of Friedrichstrasse the main points of interest are along Wilhelmstrasse, Berlin's prewar *Regierungsviertel* or "government quarter". Just southwest of here is **Potsdamer Platz**, which was the city's busiest corner until pulverized by the war and then effectively erased from the Berlin landscape by the building of the Wall. It's now the site of a huge construction project that hopes to return the area to its earlier importance. The area between Wilhelmstrasse and Potsdamer Platz was the site of **Hitler's Chancellory and bunker**, where the final mad chapter of the Third Reich unfolded, and though little now remains, trying to figure out what was where can be a compelling activity.

More tangible evidence of the past survives in the grid-like street pattern of Friedrichstadt on the other side of Friedrichstrasse, one of a number of seventeenth-century city extensions that took Berlin

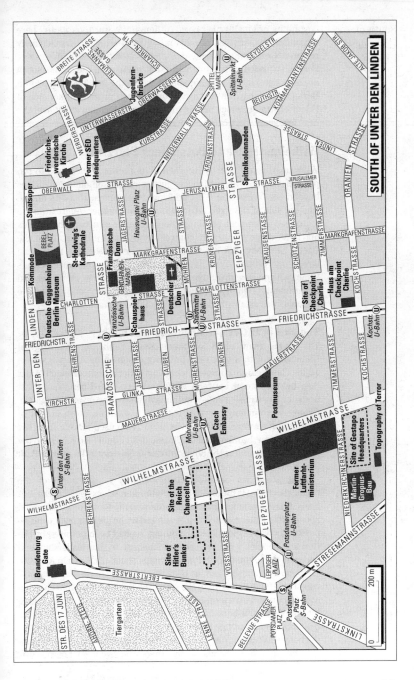

Map labels (clockwise/by area):

BREITE STRASSE
NEUMANNS GASSE
SCHARRENSTR.
Jugenfern-brücke
OBERWASSERSTR.
Spittelmarkt
U-Bahn
SEYDELSTR.
KOMMANDANTENSTRASSE
ALTE JAKOB STR.
UNTERWASSERSTR.
WERDERSCHE STRASSE
KURSTRASSE
NIEDERWALL STRASSE
BEUTHSTR.
Friedrichs-werdersche Kirche
Former SED Headquarters
Spittelkolonnaden
LINDEN STRASSE
Staatsoper
OBERWALL
STRASSE
KRONENSTRASSE
JERUSALEMER STRASSE
ORANIEN STRASSE
Kommode
BEBEL-PLATZ
Deutsche Guggenheim Berlin Museum
St-Hedwig's Kathedrale
Französische Dom
JÄGERSTRASSE
Hausvogtei Platz U-Bahn
JERUSALEMER STRASSE
STRASSE
MARKGRAFENSTRASSE
LINDEN
CHARLOTTEN
STRASSE
GENDARMEN-MARKT
Französische U-Bahn
Schauspiel-haus
Deutscher Dom
MOHREN STRASSE
CHARLOTTENSTRASSE
KRONEN STRASSE
LEIPZIGER STRASSE
KRAUSENSTRASSE
SCHÜTZEN STRASSE
ZIMMER STRASSE
KOCHSTRASSE
Site of Checkpoint Charlie
Haus am Checkpoint Charlie
FRIEDRICHSTR.
BEHRENSTRASSE
FRIEDRICH- STRASSE
Stadtmitte U-Bahn
FRIEDRICHSTRASSE
Kochstr. U-Bahn
UNTER DEN
KIRCHSTR.
FRANZÖSISCHE STRASSE
JÄGLINKA STRASSE
TAUBEN STRASSE
MOHRENSTRASSE
KRONEN STRASSE
MAUERSTRASSE
ZIMMERSTRASSE
KOCHSTRASSE
GLINKA STRASSE
MAUERSTRASSE
Mohrenstr. U-Bahn
Czech Embassy
Postmuseum
WILHELMSTRASSE
Topography of Terror
Unter den Linden S-Bahn
WILHELMSTRASSE
Site of the Reich Chancellery
LEIPZIGER STRASSE
Former Luftfahrt-ministerium
NIEDERKICHNERSTRASSE
Site of Gestapo Headquarters
Martin-Gropius-Bau
BEHRENSTRASSE
VOSSTRASSE
Potsdamer Platz U-Bahn
STRESEMANNSTRASSE
Brandenburg Gate
Site of Hitler's Bunker
LEIPZIGER PLATZ
Potsdamer platz U-Bahn
Potsdamer Platz S-Bahn
LINKSTRASSE
STR. DES 17 JUNI
HOFJÄGER STEIG
EBERTSTRASSE
LENNE STRASSE
BELLEVUE STRASSE
POTSDAMER PLATZ
Tiergarten
0   200 m

beyond its original walled core. Although the war took its toll here too, much has survived or been rebuilt, including the immaculately restored **Gendarmenmarkt**, one of the architectural highlights of Berlin. An added element of interest to wandering the streets south of Unter den Linden is being able to watch the new post-unification Berlin taking shape in extensive construction projects either side of Friedrichstrasse, which are set to have a transforming effect over the next few years, particularly around Potsdamer Platz.

Wilhelmstrasse to Potsdamer Platz

Wilhelmstrasse (recently returned to its prewar name) used to run parallel to the Wall, which lay just a couple of hundred metres beyond the late-period GDR housing development that sits on the western side of the street like a beached ocean liner. Apart from the marooned apartment building, the only other structure that stands out is an apparent airport control tower that turns out to be the **Czech Embassy**. But it's really what you can't see that makes the street interesting; from 1871 onwards it was Imperial Berlin's Whitehall and Downing Street rolled into one, lined by ministries and government buildings, including the Chancellory and, after the Republic was established in 1918, the Presidential Palace.

The site of Hitler's Chancellory and bunker

The Nazis remodelled Wilhelmstrasse, replacing the original Chancellory with a vast **new building** designed by Albert Speer in 1938. This gigantic complex, including Hitler's underground bunker (see below), stood between Wilhelmstrasse and Ebertstrasse just north of Vosstrasse. Today nothing remains, for, even though the Chancellory building survived the war, it was torn down in a fit of conquering revenge by the Soviet army, who used marble from the site to fashion the memorial on Strasse des 17 Juni (see p.53) and the huge war memorial at the Soviet military cemetery in Treptower Park (see p.167).

Just above An der Kolonnade (slightly to the north of the Chancellory site) is the site of **Hitler's bunker**, where the Führer spent his last days, issuing meaningless orders as the Battle of Berlin raged above. Here Hitler married Eva Braun and wrote his final testament: he personally was responsible for nothing; he had been betrayed by the German people, who had proved unequal to his leadership and deserved the future he could now envisage ahead of them. On April 30, 1945, he shot himself, and his body was hurriedly burned by loyal officers. In a 1992 postscript to the story, the KGB released film showing a gaunt corpse with a toothbrush moustache, allegedly Hitler, claiming that the dictator's body had in fact survived destruction in the war's final days and fallen into Soviet hands. Subsequently, so the tale went, the body was transported to Russia where it exerted a near-obsessional fascination for Stalin and many others who saw it. The corpse was

The uprising of June 1953

On June 16 and 17, 1953, Leipziger Strasse was the focal point of a nation-wide uprising against the GDR's Communist government. General dissat-isfaction with economic and political conditions in the eastern half of the city came to a head when building workers (the traditional proletarian heroes of GDR mythology) constructing the prestigious Stalinallee project went on strike, protesting at having to work longer hours for the same pay. On June 16 they marched on the *Haus der Ministerien*, which was at that time the seat of the GDR government. Here they demanded to speak to GDR President Otto Grotewohl and SED General Secretary Walter Ulbricht. These two declined to make an appearance, so speakers from the crowd got up to demand the dissolution of the government and free elec-tions. Thanks to western radio broadcasts, the news rapidly spread across the country, and in the morning of the following day, a wave of strikes and demonstrations took place throughout the GDR. Tools were abandoned, and traffic in East Berlin came to a standstill as 100,000 demonstrators marched on the *Haus der Ministerien* once again: clashes with the police followed as demonstrators attacked SED party offices and state food stores. The GDR authorities proved unequal to the situation, and at 1pm the Soviet military commandant of the city declared a state of emergency. It's estimated that several hundred people died as Soviet tanks rolled in to restore order. Afterwards, Bertolt Brecht sardonically suggested that the GDR government should "dissolve the people, and elect another".

ferried around various secret locations until the 1970s, when it was finally destroyed on the orders of Leonid Brezhnev. Details were pre-dictably sketchy and, given the obvious hard currency-spinning poten-tial of such a sensational revelation, it's hard not to suspect a dollar-making scam on the part of the former Soviet spy service.

For several years after reunification there was debate about what to do with the remains of the bunker. Some said they should be pre-served as a memorial; others claimed that they would become a shrine for rightists and neo-Nazi groups and should be destroyed. Finally it was decided to leave the bunker buried and unmarked. The large office buildings now going up on Potsdamer Platz and Leipziger Platz will soon obscure the site entirely.

Göring's Luftfahrtministerium

One relic of the Nazi past that has survived very much intact is Hermann Göring's **Luftfahrtministerium**, or air ministry, a fortress-like structure on the southwest side of the Leipziger Strasse–Wilhelmstrasse junction. Göring promised Berliners that not a single bomb would fall on the city during the war; if this were to happen, the *Reichsmarshal* said, he would change his name to Meyer – a common Jewish surname. Ironically, the air ministry was one of the few buildings to emerge more or less unscathed from the bombing and Red Army shelling. After the establishment of the GDR it became the SED regime's *Haus der Ministerien* (House of

Ministries), and was the venue for a mass demonstration on June 16, 1953 (see box on p.75), that was to be a prelude for a general but short-lived uprising against the Communist government the next day. There's a historical irony of sorts in the fact that the building became, for a number of years after reunification, the headquarters of the *Treuhandanstalt*, the agency responsible for the privatization of the former GDR's economy. Now it awaits the arrival of the government from Bonn, when it will house the Finance Ministry.

Potsdamer Platz and around

West of Göring's ministry, Leipziger Strasse runs into **Leipziger Platz**, which lies on former "Death-Strip" territory. Long an empty, derelict place, it's now the site of furious building as office towers and retail space surround this centrally located plot.

Potsdamer Platz

Beyond here is **Potsdamer Platz**, said to have been the busiest square in Europe in prewar days, and rapidly heading that way again since being reopened in the aftermath of November 9, 1989. Before

---

The future face of Potsdamer Platz

The **redevelopment of Potsdamer Platz** and the surrounding area has involved some grandiose projects and high-level jockeying. First off the mark when it came to parcelling up what had suddenly become one of Europe's most valuable vacant lots were Daimler-Benz, who snapped up the stretch south of the square between Alte Potsdamer Strasse and the Landwehrkanal. Sony moved into a triangular plot to the north of Potsdamer Strasse, and Asea Brown Boven bought up a sliver along the eastern side. Daimler-Benz put Renzo Piano, the Italian architect behind the Pompidou Centre in Paris, in charge of the redevelopment of their patch. His vast scheme calls for a series of 35-metre-high office blocks punctuated by three 85-metre skyscrapers that will redefine the skyline of this relatively flat city. Among the offices and residential space are restaurants, a Grand Hyatt hotel, a theatre, a casino, a huge 3-D cinema, and other urban amenities. For their smaller plot, Sony brought in Helmut Jahn, who has designed seven buildings around an immense circular arena. Here plans call for a film museum, with a "Marlene Dietrich Collection", and yet another 3-D cinema.

Much of the Daimler-Benz quarter is already completed, but the redevelopment project, said to be Europe's largest, will continue for a few years more. It's well worth taking a look, from the viewing deck (DM2) atop the Info Box, a temporary structure set up on the building site to promote and explain the gargantuan undertaking as well as the planning and building of the new government quarter nearby. Although the exhibition inside the Info Box is a fairly heavy-handed paean to corporate wondrousness, it does deliver lots of information and features some high-tech videos and computer games. There's also a bookstore with a great selection of material on the city.

---

the war the stores, bars and clubs here pulsed with life day and night, and the colossal redevelopment now taking place looks set to restore it to its erstwhile prominence (see below).

The war left Potsdamer Platz severely battered, though it soon regained some of its vitality in the first chaotic postwar years as a black market centre at the junction of the Soviet, American and British occupation sectors. Later, West Berliners watched from their side of the dividing line as the Soviets put down the East Berlin uprising of 1953. During the rest of the decade the Cold War was played out here in words, with the Western authorities relaying their version of the news to East Berliners by means of an electronic newsboard – countered by an Eastern billboard exhorting West Berliners to shop in cheap East Berlin stores. This ended with the coming of the Wall, which finally put a physical seal on the ideological division of Potsdamer Platz. On the Eastern side all the buildings (which were mostly war vintage wrecks) were razed to give the GDR's border guards a clear field of fire, while in the West only a couple of battered survivors, including the hulk of the *Hotel Esplanade*, once one of the city's finest, were left as a reminder of the way things used to be. For many years tourists were able to gaze out at the East from a viewing platform here, and ponder the sight of prewar tramlines disappearing at the base of the Wall.

South and east from Potsdamer Platz

Wending a way through the construction along Leipziger Strasse and then south down Stresemannstrasse will take you to Niederkirchnerstrasse, where, slightly to the east, is one of the few remaining stretches of the Wall. Protected from souvenir hunters, it's now illegal to chip a bit off.

The Martin-Gropius-Bau and the Topography of Terror

The magnificently restored building on the southern side of Niederkirchnerstrasse is the **Martin-Gropius-Bau**, whose main entrance is at Stresemannstr. 8 (Tues–Sun 10am–8pm; main collections DM6, concessions DM4, though times and prices for temporary exhibitions vary; bus #248, #341 & #129; S-Bahn Anhalter Bahnhof). Designed in 1877 by Martin Gropius, a pupil of Schinkel and the uncle of Bauhaus guru Walter (see p.130), the Gropius-Bau was, until its destruction in the war, home of the museum of applied art. In recent years it has been rebuilt and refurbished, and now houses the **Berlinische Galerie**, which exhibits a continuous collection entitled "Art in Berlin" (from 1870 onwards) and changing exhibitions of art, photography and architecture. Also contained in the building on a temporary basis are the main sections of the **Jewish Museum** (Tues–Sun 10am–8pm), with a frightening display on the war years, and large collections of German **applied and fine art**. The *Gropius Restaurant* serves vegetarian snacks and meals (see

"Restaurants" in Listings) and is a useful stopping-off point and necessary pick-me-up before tackling an adjacent exhibition, **The Topography of Terror** (Tues–Sun 10am–6pm; free). This is housed in a temporary structure a little way from the Gropius-Bau, for nothing is left of the buildings that once stood here: the Reich Security offices, including the headquarters of the Gestapo and SS. In buildings along here Himmler planned the Final Solution, the deportation and genocide of European Jews, and organized the Gestapo, the feared secret police. The exhibition is contained in what were once the cellars of the Gestapo headquarters, which stood at Prinz-Albrecht-Str. 8 (now Niederkirchnerstrasse), where important prisoners were interrogated and tortured. The staff of the SS were based in the former *Hotel Prinz Albrecht* next door, and just around the corner in the *Prinz-Albrecht-Palais* (opposite the entrance to Kochstrasse) was the SS security service headquarters, where extensive records of all "enemies of the state", a category that included Jews and homosexuals, were kept. Though the photos here tell their own story, you'll need the English translation (DM2) or the glossy guidebook (DM10) for the main text of the exhibits.

See also the Jewish Museum on p.123; and the note on p.154 on The Wannsee Conference.

The ruins of the Reich Security offices were destroyed after the war and the wasteland they once occupied, the empty space behind the Topography of Terror exhibit, is currently in the initial stages of development into larger facilities for a permanent museum. Until this opens, it's possible to follow a numbered series of noticeboards with photographs and English texts that indicate the sites of the most important Nazi buildings in the area and reveal just how massive a machine the Nazi organization became.

From here it's a ten-minute walk (or two stops on the #129 bus) down Wilhelmstrasse, along Kochstrasse and up Friedrichstrasse to the site of Checkpoint Charlie – see p.81.

Gendarmenmarkt and around

To the east of Friedrichstrasse is **Gendarmenmarkt** (reached from Unter den Linden via Charlottenstrasse; bus #147 & #257; U-Bahnhof Stadtmitte), a square whose present appearance belies the fact that its historic buildings were almost obliterated during the war. It's now one of the most successfully restored parts of the city, but rebuilding lasted until well into the 1980s, and it's only really in the last few years that the area has re-emerged as one of Berlin's most attractive corners. Gendarmenmarkt's origins are prosaic. It was originally home to Berlin's main market until the Gendarme regiment, who gave the square its name (recently re-adopted after a long GDR-era hiatus as Platz der Akademie), set up their stables on the site. With the departure of the military, Gendarmenmarkt was transformed at the behest of Frederick the Great, who ordered an architectural revamp of the two churches that stood here, in an attempt to mimic the Piazza del Popolo in Rome.

The Französischer Dom

The results are impressive, and are at their most eye-catching in the Französischer Dom at the northern end of the square. Originally built as a simple place of worship for Berlin's influential Huguenot community at the beginning of the eighteenth century, the building was transformed by the addition of a Baroque tower, turning it into one of Berlin's most appealing churches.

The tower (see below) is purely decorative and not actually consecrated, but it's so striking that a lot of visitors don't actually notice the church proper, the **Französischen Friedrichstadt Kirche** (French Church in Friedrichstadt; Tues–Sat noon–5pm, Sun 11am–5pm), which is so modest in appearance that it looks more like an ancillary building for the tower. The main entrance to the church is at the western end of the Dom, facing Charlottenstrasse. The church, reconsecrated in 1983 after years of restoration work, has a simple hall-like interior with few decorative features and only a plain table as an altar.

The Hugenottenmuseum and Dom Tower

At the base of the tower next door is the entrance to the **Hugenottenmuseum** (Wed–Sat noon–5pm, Sun 11am–5pm; DM2, concessions DM1), detailing the history of the Huguenots in France and Brandenburg. There are sections dealing with the theological background of the Reformation in France, the Revocation of the Edict of Nantes leading to the flight of the Huguenots from their native country, their settling in Berlin, and the influence of the new arrivals on trade, science and literature. The museum also has a short section on the destruction and rebuilding of the Dom.

A longish spiral of steps leads up to the Dom **tower**, which was built some eighty years after the church and only finally put to rights after wartime damage in 1987. Here you'll find the smart *Turmstuben* **restaurant** (see "Restaurants" in Listings) and a balcony (daily 9am–7pm; DM3, concessions DM2) running around the outside that offers good views of the surrounding construction sites. Another attraction are the tower bells, which ring out automatically every day at noon, 4pm and 7pm – a near deafening experience if you happen to be on the balcony at the time. At other times during the week concerts are performed by bell-ringers – ask for details.

The Deutscher Dom and the Schauspielhaus

At the southern end of the square, the **Deutscher Dom**, built for the city's Lutheran community, is the stylistic twin of the Französischer Dom. Until quite recently the Deutscher Dom was a scaffolding-shrouded wreck, and restoration, prolonged by a recent fire, has only just been completed. The Dom now hosts the interesting "Questions on German History" exhibit formerly housed in the Reichstag, which chronicles the political and cultural movements and events that have

characterized the last two hunded years of German history.
Unfortunately, the commentary is in German, and an English-language guidebook is not yet available.

Just to the southwest of the Dom, along Friedrichstrasse, con-
tractors are working on the **Friedrichstadt Passagen**, a huge development that, though still partially vacant, promises to bring shopping galleries, restaurants, offices, flats and "culture" to this historic
corner of the city.

Culture, however, is already well established here in Schinkel's
Neoclassical **Schauspielhaus** (now renamed Konzerthaus Berlin),
between the two churches. Dating from 1817, it was built around the
ruins of Langhans's burned-out National Theatre, retaining the latter's exterior walls and portico columns. A broad sweep of steps
leads up to the main entrance and into an interior of incredible opulence, where chandeliers, marble, gilded plasterwork and pastel-
hued wall paintings all compete for attention. Gutted during a raid in
1943, the building suffered further damage during heavy fighting as
the Russians attempted to drive out SS troops who had dug in here.
Reopened in October 1984, it's now the home of the Berlin
Symphony Orchestra (see "Live music" in "The arts" section of
Listings). At Christmas 1989 Leonard Bernstein conducted a performance of Beethoven's Ninth Symphony here to celebrate the *Wende*,
with the word *Freiheit* (Freedom) substituted for *Freude* (Joy) in
Schiller's choral finale.

A **statue of Schiller** stands outside the Schauspielhaus. It was
repositioned here in 1988, having been removed by the Nazis over
fifty years earlier, returned to what was then East Berlin from the
West in exchange for reliefs originally from the Pfaueninsel (see
p.153) and a statue from a Tiergarten villa. Outside Germany,
Friedrich Schiller (1759–1805) is best known for the *Ode to Joy* that
provides the words to the final movements of Beethoven's Ninth
Symphony, but in his homeland he is venerated as one of the greatest German poets and dramatists of the Enlightenment. His works,
from early *Sturm und Drang* dramas like *Die Räuber* ("The
Thieves") to later historical plays like *Maria Stuart*, were primarily
concerned with freedom – political, moral and personal – which was
probably the main reason why the Nazis were so quick to bundle him
off Gendarmenmarkt.

Leipziger Strasse and around

From Gendarmenmarkt, Charlottenstrasse continues south to
Leipziger Strasse, once a main Berlin shopping street running from
Alexanderplatz to Potsdamer Platz. For many years Leipziger
Strasse was a lifeless housing and commercial development dating
from the early 1970s "big is beautiful" phase of East Berlin town
planning. The buildings on the south side of the street are higher
than those on the north side – at this height they conveniently block

off the huge offices of the late **Axel Springer**, extreme right-wing newspaper and publishing magnate (the newspaper *Bild* was his most notorious creation) just over the erstwhile border, which the wily old media mogul had built here to cause maximum irritation to the GDR authorities.

Until the late nineteenth century Leipziger Strasse was a quiet residential area, but by the turn of the century it had become one of Berlin's foremost shopping streets, with the establishment of Tietz and Wertheim's department stores, and a host of smaller operations and restaurants, including the celebrated Kempinski's. World War II put paid to all that (all three above-mentioned concerns were Jewish owned and run and were confiscated by the Nazis), relegating the street's commercial glory to the history books. Leipziger Strasse is now once again a main route leading from the heart of Berlin towards the city's West End, as thundering traffic attests; and once redevelopment of Potsdamer Platz is finished it seems likely that Leipziger Strasse will reassume its old importance.

The Spittelkolonnaden and around

Virtually nothing remains of prewar Leipziger Strasse. The only apparent survivor, the Spittelkolonnaden, a semicircular colonnade on the right towards its eastern end, on the site of what used to be Donhoffplatz, turns out to be a copy of part of an eighteenth-century structure formerly on the opposite side of the street. In front of this replica is another copy – this time of a **milepost** that once stood in the vicinity. A little further along is the **Spittelmarkt**, which marks the site of a medieval hospital. To the left of the street is the **Spindlerbrunnen**, a chocolate-coloured nineteenth-century fountain that was erected here in 1891. It survived the war by virtue of the fact that it was removed to the grounds of a suburban hospital in 1927 and only returned to its old site in 1980.

The postal ministry

Towards the western end of Leipziger Strasse, at the junction with Mauerstrasse, is the former Imperial **postal ministry** (a prime example of late nineteenth-century bureaucratic Baroque). It's undergoing restoration until autumn 1999, when it will reopen as a postal and communications museum. Until then, the city's Museum für Post und Kommunikation is located in Schöneberg (see p.136).

Checkpoint Charlie and around

A couple of hundred metres south of the Leipziger Strasse-Friedrichstrasse intersection is the site of **Checkpoint Charlie**, one of the most famous names associated with Cold War-era Berlin. This allied military post on Friedrichstrasse marked the border between East and West Berlin until July 1990, when it was declared redundant and removed for later reassembly in a West German museum.

South of Unter den Linden

While it stood it was one of Berlin's more celebrated landmarks and the building lent its name informally to the adjacent GDR border crossing (official title *Grenzübergang Friedrichstrasse*), which, with its dramatic "YOU ARE NOW LEAVING THE AMERICAN SEC-TOR" signs and unsmiling border guards, used to be the archetypal movie-style Iron Curtain crossing. In the Cold War years it was the scene of repeated border incidents, including a stand-off between American and Soviet forces in October 1961, which culminated in tanks from both sides growling at each other for a few days.

The site of the border crossing itself is hardly recognizable now. The extensive **border installations** were torn down in 1991, having stood derelict since the spring of the previous year, and in their place was an impromptu coach park. A high-profile complex of office buildings and retail shops called the American Business Center – part of it designed by American architect Philip Johnson – is now going up. All that remains of the border crossing is a former guard tower, now designated a historic monument.

The Museum Haus am Checkpoint Charlie

For tangible evidence of the trauma of the Wall, head for the **Museum Haus am Checkpoint Charlie** at Friedrichstr. 44 (daily 9am–10pm; DM7.50, concessions DM4.50; nearest U-Bahn Kochstrasse or bus #129). Here the history of the Wall is told in photos of escape tunnels and with the home-made aircraft and convert-ed cars by which people attempted, succeeded, and sometimes trag-ically failed to break through the border. Films document the stories of some of the eighty people murdered by the East German border guards, and there's a section on human rights behind the Iron Curtain, but it's a scruffy, rather dated collection, and not quite the harrowing experience that some visitors seem to expect. For more details, pick up a copy of *It Happened at the Wall* or *Berlin – From Frontline Town to the Bridge of Europe*, both on sale here.

CENTRAL BERLIN

North of Unter den Linden

Heading **north of Unter den Linden** along **Friedrichstrasse** itself takes you towards Bahnhof Friedrichstrasse, once the biggest border crossing point for East Berlin-bound travellers. Before the war, Friedrichstrasse was a well-known prostitutes' haunt, lined by cafés, bars and restaurants. Nazi puritanism dealt the first blow to this thriving *Vergnügungsviertel* (Pleasure Quarter), and their work was finished by Allied bombers, which effectively razed the street. The destruction caused by bombing widened Friedrichstrasse con-siderably, turning what had once been a narrow, slightly claustro-phobic street into a broad, desolate road that offered many visitors a first, uninspiring impression of East Berlin. Friedrichstrasse has now slipped back into its north–south axis role, though the stretch above the train station still seems lifeless when compared to the frantic development going on south of Unter den Linden.

Around Bahnhof Friedrichstrasse

Just before the train station on Friedrichstrasse is a symbol of Honecker-era East Berlin in the shape of the Japanese-built **Internationales Handelszentrum**, a 93.5-metre-high piece of self-consciously modernist architecture whose main purpose was to show that West Berlin didn't have a monopoly on thrusting, commercial dynamism. Renovation is now modernizing the station, once a tangle of checkpoints and guard posts. Under the tracks to the east of the station, beside the Handelszentrum, is a delightful antiques market with a fascinating assemblage of old art, jewellery, books and curios.

Bahnhof Friedrichstrasse

Before the *Wende*, **Bahnhof Friedrichstrasse**, as one of the main border crossing points for western visitors to East Berlin, was probably the most heavily guarded train station in Europe. There was always a regular flow of mainline and S-Bahn traffic between Friedrichstrasse and Zoo Station in West Berlin (except during the Berlin Blockade of 1948–49, see p.125), but until late 1989 the East German government did all it could to keep its own citizens from joining it. Customs and passport controls and, more discreetly, armed guards separated westbound platforms from the rest of the station.

Two bodies were found here in the 1970s, during renovations: rumour had it that one was the missing Nazi leader Martin Bormann, but there has since been neither confirmation or denial.

The Tränenpalast

Between Bahnhof Friedrichstrasse itself and the River Spree is a glass and concrete construction that was, until 1990, the **border crossing entrance** for westbound travellers, with an estimated eight million people passing through its doors each year. Known as the Tränenpalast or "Palace of Tears", this is now a venue for musical productions, such as *Grease*; but during the days when the Berlin Wall was a very real barrier, visitors and tourists – and occasionally East German citizens who had been granted exit visas – queued inside to get through passport and customs controls before travelling by U- or S-Bahn to West Berlin.

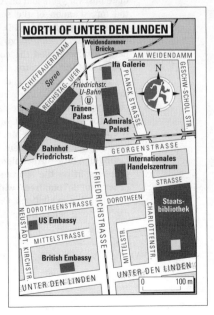

NORTH OF UNTER DEN LINDEN

Weidendammer Brücke
AM WEIDENDAMM
Ifa Galerie
SCHIFFBAUERDAMM
Spree
REICHSTAG-UFER
Friedrichstr. U-Bahn
Tränen-Palast
Admirals-Palast
PLANCK STRASSE
GESCHW-SCHOLL STR
N
Bahnhof Friedrichstr.
GEORGENSTRASSE
Internationales Handelszentrum
FRIEDRICHSTRASSE
STRASSE
DOROTHEENSTRASSE
NEUSTADT. KIRCHSTR
US Embassy
MITTELSTRASSE
British Embassy
UNTER DEN LINDEN
DOROTHEEN
MITTELSTR.
CHARLOTTENSTR.
Staats-bibliothek
UNTER DEN LINDEN
0   100 m

Visitors to the East had to return to the West by midnight, and the functional entrance to the Tränenpalast was the scene of many a poignant farewell as people took leave of relatives, friends and lovers here. Within, a few reminders of its old role survive, including a cubicle with blackened glass windows overlooking the main hall, from which border guards watched those leaving the country.

Between the wars the site now occupied by the Tränenpalast was an unsightly vacant lot and, before the Nazis came to power, an architectural competition was held in search of a suitable design for a building to fill it. Some incredibly imaginative – and improbable – proposals were submitted, many of which were way ahead of their time. One entrant was Mies van der Rohe, who proposed an immense, tricornered glass and steel tower. History overtook the various proposals and the space remained unused until the construction of the Wall set the seal on the division of Berlin.

North of the station

Back on Friedrichstrasse, just north of the rail bridge, on the right at no. 101, is the *Jugendstil* **Admiralspalast**, a rare prewar survivor originally built as a variety theatre in 1910. Amid the predominantly concrete architecture of the immediate area, its partly gilded facade, divided by fluted columns and inset with bas-reliefs, comes as a real surprise. As one of the few buildings in the area to have survived the bombing, it became an important political meeting hall in the immediate postwar years and on April 22 and 23, 1946, was the venue for the forced union of the social democratic SPD with the prewar Communist party, the KPD. This resulted in the birth of the SED (*Sozialistische Einheitspartei Deutschlands*), the GDR Communist party that controlled the country until March 1990. The building houses *Die Distel* theatre, a satirical cabaret whose occasionally daring performances highlighted the paradoxes and frustrations of the pre-*Wende* GDR and provided Western journalists with good intro paragraphs for state-of-the-nation pieces in the autumn of 1989.

Across the courtyard of the Admiralspalast, another ex-East German institution, the **Metropol Theater**, still purveys indifferent musical light entertainment (for details on both, see "The arts" in Listings). A little further along Friedrichstrasse at no. 103, it's worth dropping in on the spartan-looking **Ifa Galerie Friedrichstrasse** (Tues–Sun 2–7pm; free), which has occasionally interesting art and photographic exhibitions. Catch it while it's still there, as it surely can't be long before this prime site is grabbed by some developer.

Chapter 4

Schlossplatz and the Museum Island

A
t the eastern end of Unter den Linden the Schlossbrücke leads onto **Schlossplatz** and the island in the middle of the River Spree that formed the core of the medieval twin town of Berlin-Cölln. By virtue of its defensive position, this island later became the site of the Hohenzollern *Residenz* – location of the fortress-cum-palace and church of the family who controlled Berlin and Brandenburg from the fifteenth century onwards. Centred roughly around present-day Schlossplatz, this was originally a martial, fortified affair, as much for protection from the perennially rebellious Berliners as from outside enemies, but over the years domestic stability resulted in the reshaping of the *Residenz* on a slightly more decorative basis. With the consolidation of their authority during the nineteenth century and the rise of Brandenburg-Prussia to great power, the Hohenzollerns decided it was time to add a museum quarter to their increasingly bombastic capital. This was duly done, over eighty years or so, on the northern tongue of the mid-Spree island, an area which became known as the Museuminsel or **Museum Island**.

Schlossplatz and around

Schlossplatz (known as Marx-Engels-Platz until 1994) is reached from Unter den Linden via Schinkel's **Schlossbrücke**. When it was opened on November 28, 1823, the bridge was not fully completed, lacking among other things a fixed balustrade, and twenty-two people drowned when temporary wooden barriers collapsed. Eventually cast-iron balustrades were installed, featuring graceful dolphin, merman and sea-horse motifs designed by Schinkel. The very pristine-looking Classical statues of warriors and winged figures lining each side of the bridge represent scenes from ancient Greek mythology and earned the bridge the popular epithet of *Puppenbrücke* or

CENTRAL BERLIN

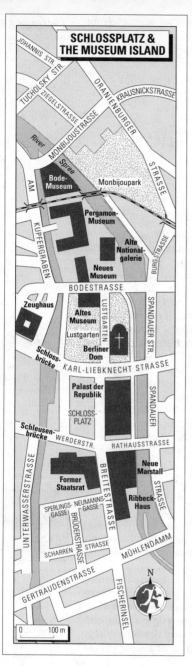

SCHLOSSPLATZ & THE MUSEUM ISLAND

"Puppet Bridge". Once wartime bombing started they were removed for safekeeping; after the division of the city they ended up in West Berlin, and were only returned to the East in 1981.

Schlossplatz

Beyond the bridge is **Schlossplatz** itself, former site of the Berliner Schloss, the old Imperial Palace, the remains of which were demolished by the Communists after the war, and which, along with the Berliner Dom (see p.88), formed the Imperial *Residenz*. Work began on the palace in 1443 and the Hohenzollern family were to live there for nearly half a millennium. Over the centuries the Schloss was constantly extended and reshaped, the first major overhaul coming in the sixteenth century when it was transformed from a fortress into a Renaissance palace. Later it received a Baroque restyling, and subsequently virtually every German architect of note, including Schlüter, Schinkel and Schadow, was given the opportunity to add to it. For centuries the Schloss dominated the heart of Berlin, and until the 1930s no city centre building was allowed to stand any higher.

On November 9, 1918, the end of the Hohenzollern era came when Karl Liebknecht proclaimed a "Free Socialist Republic" from one of the palace balconies (now preserved in the facade of the Staatsrat building, see opposite), following the abdication of the Kaiser. Almost simultaneously the Social Democrat Phillip Scheidemann was proclaiming a democratic German republic from the Reichstag, and it was in fact the latter that prevailed, ushering in the pathologically unstable Weimar Republic of the 1920s.

After the war the Schloss, as a symbol of the still recent Imperial past, was an embarrassment to the SED authorities and they ordered the dynamiting of its ruins in 1950, despite the fact that it was

art works are reshuffled and galleries renovated, the Alte
nalgalerie and the Bodemuseum are **closed**. Parts of the Alte
nalgalerie collection can now be seen at the Altes Museum.

ng the museums

to the Pergamonmuseum is DM8, concessions DM4, and entry
on the first Sunday of every month. For the Altes Museum, the
aries depending upon the exhibition. Exhibits throughout the
m Island are not labelled in English, although some museums
vide cassettes and information sheets. Note that all the muse-
e **closed** on Monday.

Pergamonmuseum

rgamonmuseum (Tues–Sun 9am–5pm) is accessible from
ofergraben on the south bank of the River Spree. It's a mas-
ucture, built in the early part of this century in the style of a
nian temple, to house the treasure trove of the German arche-
s who were busy plundering the ancient world, packaging it
sending it back to Berlin. Cassette recorders with tapes in
, available in the foyer, give a useful introduction to the col-
and help to place them in historical context.

ment of Antiquities

seum is divided into three sections, the most important of
he **Department of Antiquities** on the main floor, contains
amon Altar. A huge structure dedicated to Zeus and Athena,
om 180 to 160 BC, it was unearthed at Bergama in western
by the archeologist Carl Humann and brought to Berlin in
he **frieze** shows a battle between the gods and giants and is
dously forceful piece of work, with powerfully depicted fig-
thing in a mass of sinew and muscle. The section also con-
er pieces of Hellenistic and Classical architecture, including
storey **market gate** from the Turkish town of Miletus. Built
omans in 120 AD, the gate was destroyed by an earthquake
r a thousand years later and brought to Berlin in fragmen-
for reconstruction during the nineteenth century.

ldle Eastern Section

le Eastern Section, also on the main floor, has items going
r thousand years to Babylonian times. The collection
he enormous **Ishtar Gate**, the **Processional Way** and the
the **Throne Room** from Babylon, all of which date from the
ebuchadnezzar II in the sixth century BC. While it's impos-
o be awed by the size and remarkable state of preservation
p-blue enamelled bricks of the Babylon finds, it's as well to
that much of what you see is a mock-up, built around the

no more badly damaged than a number of other structures subsequently rebuilt. Today the Berliner Schloss can only be appreciated
in photographs and there is, predictably, great nostalgia for it, with
some even calling for it to be re-created – despite the fact that its
piecemeal construction and bombastic architectural style made it a
rather unattractive building. Notwithstanding, during the summers
of 1993 and 1994 the pro-Schloss lobby erected a spectacular scaf-
folding and canvas replica of the building here, to mobilize public
support for their aims. Tepid response and a lack of money have put
the project on the back burner.

The Palast der Republik

It was no coincidence that the GDR authorities chose the space formerly occupied by the Schloss for their **Palast der Republik**, which
was built on the southeastern side of Schlossplatz during the early
1970s to house the *Volkskammer*, the GDR's parliament.
Irreverently dubbed *Ballast der Republik*, this huge angular building with its bronzed, reflecting windows was completed in less than
a thousand days, and was a source of great pride to the Honecker
regime. As well as the former *Volkskammer*, it also housed an entertainment complex, including restaurants, cafés, a theatre and a bowling alley. The interior is a masterpiece of tastelessness and the hundreds of lamps hanging from the ceiling of the main foyer gave rise
to its other nickname, *Erichs Lampenladen* – "Erich's lamp shop".
Shortly before unification an asbestos hazard was discovered in the
building, and following October 3, 1990, it was closed indefinitely.
Today it stands empty, an unmissable reminder of the old GDR and
an embarrassment to the new Germany, its future – indeed its existence – uncertain.

The Staatsrat and Neue Marstall

A slightly less jarring reminder of the GDR is the former **Staatsrat** or
State Council on the southern side of Schlossplatz, an early 1960s
building with some stylistic affinities to the *Zuckerbäcker* architecture of the Stalin era. It's enhanced by the inclusion in its facade of a
big chunk of the Berliner Schloss, notably the balcony from which
Karl Liebknecht proclaimed the German revolution in 1918.
Immediately to the east of the Staatsrat is the **Neue Marstall**, an
unimaginative turn-of-the-century construction, built to house the
hundreds of royal coaches and horses used to ferry the royal household around the city.

From this building revolutionary sailors and Spartacists beat off
government forces during the November Revolution of 1918, when
the building was headquarters of the revolutionary committee. A
couple of plaques commemorate this deed of rebellious derring-do
and Liebknecht's proclamation of the Socialist republic. One shows
Liebknecht apparently suspended above a cheering crowd of sailors

and civilians, while the other, to the left of the entrance, has the head of Marx hovering over some excited but purposeful-looking members of the proletariat. These days the building houses Berlin's city library with occasionally interesting art and history exhibitions on the ground floor. Just behind the Neue Marstall, at Breite Str. 25, is the delicately gabled **Ribbeckhaus**, a late Renaissance palace from the seventeenth century that's one of the city's oldest surviving buildings.

The Berliner Dom

On the northern side of Karl-Liebknecht-Strasse, opposite the Palast der Republik, is a hulking symbol of Imperial Germany that managed to survive the GDR era. The **Berliner Dom** (Mon–Sat 9am–7.30pm, Sun noon–5pm; DM5, concessions DM3) was built at the turn of the century on the site of a more modest cathedral, as a grand royal church for the Hohenzollern family. Fussily ornate with a huge dome flanked by four smaller ones, its appearance was meant to echo that of St Peter's in Rome, but somehow it comes across as little more than a dowdy Neo-Baroque imitation.

The Berliner Dom served the House of Hohenzollern as a family church until 1918, and its vault houses ninety sarcophagi containing the remains of various members of the line. The building was badly damaged during the war, but has undergone a long period of reconstruction, leaving it looking like a simpler version of its prewar self, with various ornamental cupolas missing from the newly rounded-off domes.

The main entrance leads into the extravagantly overstated **Predigtkirche**, the octagonal main body of the church. From the marbled pillars of the hall to the delicate plasterwork and gilt of the cupola, there's a sense that it's all meant to reflect Hohenzollern power rather than serve as a place of worship. As if to confirm this impression six opulent Hohenzollern sarcophagi, including those of Great Elector Wilhelm I, and his second wife, Dorothea, are housed in galleries at the northern and southern ends of the Predigtkirche. The spiritual underpinnings of the society they ruled are less ostentatiously represented by statues of Luther, Melanchthon, Calvin and Zwingli, along with four German princes favourable to the Reformation, in the cornices above the pillars in the main hall.

For an overhead view of all this, head for the **Kaiserliches Treppenhaus** (Imperial Staircase), a grandiose marble staircase at the southwest corner of the building, which leads past pleasantly washed-out paintings of biblical scenes to a balcony looking out onto the Predigtkirche. Here you'll also find a small exhibition on the history of the building. To the south of the Predigtkirche is the restored **Tauf- and Traukirche**. On first sight this appears to be a marbled souvenir shop, but it is in fact a side chapel used for baptism and confirmation ceremonies.

The Lustgarten

Adjacent to the Dom is the **Lust** the Great Elector, and later tu Friedrich Wilhelm I, Prussia's " attempt to transform the city int fighters under the Jewish Com anti-Communist exhibition that cost them their lives. It is com square which, despite the inscr with the Soviet Union", still att end of the square, at the foot Museum (see p.91), is what lo was carved from a huge gla Fürstenwalde, just outside Berl for passing tourists.

The Museum Isl

Northwest of Schlossplatz, exte is an area known as the **Museu** eastern Berlin's most importar the **Altes Museum**, the **Alte Na** Their origins go back to 181 decided Berlin needed a museu lection of royal treasures. He c Spree-side marsh and commiss able building – the Altes Museu

Things really started to ta archeologists began plundering Asia Minor. The booty brought Carl Richard Lepsius during th to become a huge collection, house it at the behest of King I tury the Imperial haul was au Turkey by Heinrich Sch Pergamonmuseum was constr

During World War II the c away in bunkers and mine sha in the confusion of 1945 and t difficult to recover the scatter others ended up in museums ii peared to the East with the Re pieces were tracked down and was returned to the Museum Berlin tourist draw.

Unification has brought t bringing together long-divide

The nearest U- and S-Bahn station to the Museum Island is Friedrichstrasse; buses #100, #157 and #348 also pass nearby.

The
Museum
Island

original finds. Look out for the weird mythical creatures that adorn the Ishtar Gate, and check the small model of the whole structure to get some idea of its enormous scale.

The Islamic Section

Pride of place in the museum's **Islamic Section** goes to the relief-decorated facade of a Jordanian **Prince's Palace** at Mshatta, from 743 AD, presented to Kaiser Wilhelm II by the Sultan of Turkey. On a slightly more modest scale is a thirteenth-century **prayer niche** decorated with turquoise, black and gold tiles, from a mosque in Asia Minor. Also worth seeking out is the **Aleppo Room**, a reception chamber with carved wooden wall decorations, reassembled in Berlin after being removed from a merchant's house in present-day Syria. The section is also home to a host of smaller but no less impressive exhibits from Arabia and Persia, including carpets, ceramics, leatherwork, and wooden and ivory carvings.

The Alte Nationalgalerie

Roughly behind the Pergamonmuseum and Neues Museum (see overleaf) is the **Alte Nationalgalerie** (entrance on Bodestrasse), a slightly exaggerated example of post-Schinkel Neoclassicism that normally contains the nineteenth-century section of Berlin's state art collection. The main body of the museum is a colonnaded, temple-like structure raised above the lower block where the main entrance is situated. A double flight of stairs leads up either side of the entrance to an equestrian statue of King Friedrich Wilhelm IV, commemorating his role in expanding the Museum Island during the mid-nineteenth century.

The museum is closed for renovations until 2001. Highlights from its collection are currently on display at the neighbouring Altes Museum. It's worth taking a peek at the building, though, a grandiose interpretation of a Corinthian temple, built in 1876 and placed atop a huge pediment fronted by a statue of its royal patron, Friedrich Wilhelm IV. Subtle it's not. There's a pleasant little lawn in front punctuated by several sculptures, including *Centaur and Nymph* by Reinhold Begas, dating from around 1888, and Louis Tuaillon's 1895 *Amazon*.

The Altes Museum

At the head of the Lustgarten the **Altes Museum** (Tues–Sun 9am–5pm; entrance fee varies according to exhibition; rotunda free) is perhaps Schinkel's most impressive surviving work with an 87-metre-high facade fronted by an eighteen-column Ionic colonnade. Along with Schauspielhaus (see p.80), this is one of Berlin's most striking Neoclassical buildings. Originally opened as a home for the royal collection of paintings in 1830, the Altes Museum is now host to changing special exhibitions – check tourist information or the press for details.

While the Alte Nationalgalerie is being renovated, highlights from its collection of nineteenth-century art can be seen here on a rotating basis. Particularly noteworthy are several works of the "German Romans", mid-nineteenth-century artists like Anselm Feuerbach and Arnold Böcklin, who spent much of their working lives in Italy. Böcklin's mortality-obsessed **Romanticism** is particularly eye-catching, with paintings like *The Isle of the Dead* and *Self-Portrait with Death Playing the Fiddle* striking a note of melancholy grandeur. The broad canvases of Adoph von Menzel strike a rather different note. Though chiefly known during his lifetime for his detailed depictions of court life under Frederick the Great, it's his interpretations of Berlin on the verge of the industrial age, such as *The Iron Foundry* and *The Berlin-Potsdam Railway*, that make more interesting viewing today. Also on hand are a handful of **Impressionist** works by Van Gogh, Degas, Monet and Cézanne.

One floor below is a new permanent installation of objects from the *Antikensammlung*, small scupture and pottery from the city's famed Greek and Roman collections. The collection of Greek vases is considered to be among the finest in the world.

The Bodemuseum

At the northeastern tip of the Museumsinsel is the **Bodemuseum**, housed in an intimidating, turn-of-the-century Neo-Baroque building. It is also presently **closed** (until the end of 2000) as part of the large-scale renovation and reorganization of Berlin's collections. When restored, the impressive building will house the *Skulpturensammlung*, an excellent, chiefly German collection of sculpture particularly authoritative in its sections detailing the Middle Ages – including work by the masters Tilman Riemenschneider, Nicolaus Gerhaert, Michael Erhart and Hans Multscher. Also finding a home here will be the Museum für Spaetantike und Byzantinische Kunst, with an extensive range of objects, mainly religious in nature, from the pre-medieval eastern Mediterranean. Later on, sometime around 2004, it is planned that the Aegyptisches Museum, with its famous bust of Nefertiti, will end up here as well.

The Neues Museum

Between the Altes Museum and the Pergamonmuseum is the **Neues Museum**, originally built to house the Egyptian Collection. Bombed out in the war, the building stood gutted and empty until 1990, and at the time of writing was being rebuilt to house the Bodemuseum's Egyptian section and other collections from Charlottenburg (see p.143).

Alexanderplatz and around

Alexanderplatz, dominated by a huge TV tower and furnished almost exclusively in concrete, is an unmistakeable product of the old East Germany. During East Berlin's forty-year existence, while Unter den Linden was allowed to represent the glories of past Berlin, Alexanderplatz and its environs were meant to represent the glories of a modern socialist capital city. It's hard to imagine, though, that the concrete giganticism of the GDR era will wear as well as the efforts of Schinkel and his contemporaries. This is one part of town where there's little point in trying to spot what remains of prewar Berlin by looking at old photos. Elsewhere at least a few buildings have made it through to the postwar period, but around Alexanderplatz there's almost no trace of the buildings that stood here before 1945. Whole streets have vanished – the open area around the base of the TV tower, for example, used to be a dense network of inner-city streets – and today only a few survivors like the Marienkirche and Rotes Rathaus remain standing amid the modernity.

This is not to say that Alexanderplatz is worth passing up. If you can let your sensibilities take a back seat, it's worth exploring not

---

The Berlin that never was

As you survey what has replaced the destroyed city centre around Alexanderplatz, ponder on a couple of paths that history nearly took: one school of thought considered that Berlin in 1945 was simply not worth rebuilding, and proposed to build a **new Berlin** from scratch, 60km away, as had been done at Stalingrad. More disturbing, though, was the wartime plan by the Allies to drop **anthrax bombs** on the city, which would have killed all the inhabitants but left the buildings standing. Had this happened, it would now be possible (presumably having donned protective gear) to wander the streets of a ghost city, completely unchanged since the day the bomb dropped.

ALEXANDERPLATZ AND AROUND

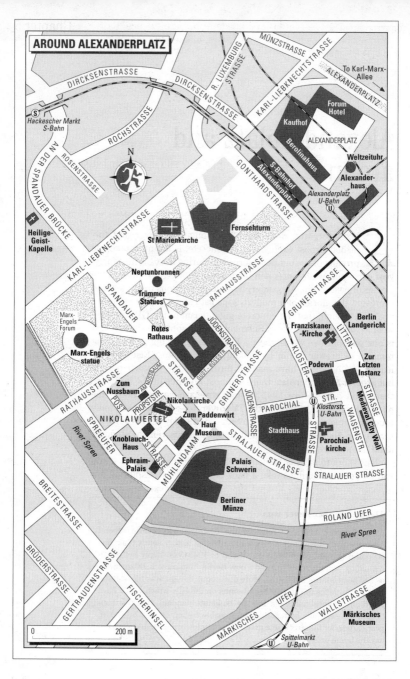

AROUND ALEXANDERPLATZ

MÜNZSTRASSE

DIRCKSENSTRASSE

R. LUXEMBURG STRASSE

KARL-LIEBKNECHTSTRASSE

ALEXANDERPLATZ

To Karl-Marx-Allee

DIRCKSENSTRASSE

ROCHSTRASSE

Hackescher Markt S-Bahn

AN DER SPANDAUER BRÜCKE

ROSENSTRASSE

N

Forum Hotel

Kaufhof

Berolinahaus

ALEXANDERPLATZ

S.Bahnhof Alexanderplatz

Weltzeituhr

Alexander-haus

Alexanderplatz U-Bahn

GONTHARDSTRASSE

Heilige-Geist-Kapelle

KARL-LIEBKNECHTSTRASSE

St Marienkirche

Fernsehturm

RATHAUSSTRASSE

SPANDAUER

Neptunbrunnen

Trümmer Statues

Marx-Engels Forum

Rotes Rathaus

JUDENSTRASSE

GRUNERSTRASSE

LITTEN-

Berlin Landgericht

Franziskaner-Kirche

Marx-Engels statue

STRASSE

GUST. BOSSSTR.

GRUNERSTRASSE

Podewil

KLOSTER

Zur Letzten Instanz

STRASSE

Medieval City Wall

RATHAUSSTRASSE

Zum Nussbaum

AM NUSSBAUM

PROPSTSTR.

POST.

Nikolaikirche

JUDENSTRASSE

PAROCHIAL

STR.

Klosterstr. U-Bahn

WAISENSTR.

SPREEUFER

River Spree

NIKOLAIVIERTEL

Zum Paddenwirt

Hauf Museum

STRALAUER STRASSE

Stadthaus

STRASSE

Parochial-kirche

Knoblauch-Haus

STRASSE

MÜHLENDAMM

Palais Schwerin

Ephraim-Palais

STRALAUER STRASSE

Berliner Münze

ROLAND UFER

River Spree

BREITESTRASSE

BRUDERSTRASSE

GERTRAUDENSTRASSE

FISCHERINSEL

MÄRKISCHES UFER

WALLSTRASSE

Märkisches Museum

Spittelmarkt U-Bahn

0   200 m

only the area's handful of historic buildings but also the ugly East German creations that have their own place in Berlin's architectural chronology.

If it all gets too much, relief from the concrete is on hand in the nearby **Nikolaiviertel**, an attempt to re-create the destroyed medieval heart of Berlin; and also in the area to the immediate east, which has a clutch of secluded old buildings and a stretch of Berlin's first wall – built to keep people out rather than in. Also close by are a few interesting museums, detailing the history of the city itself.

Marx-Engels-Forum to Alexanderplatz

CENTRAL BERLIN

Despite its apparent concrete aridity, this area has some rewarding corners. Most of the attractions are of GDR vintage, foremost among them being the gargantuan TV tower or **Fernsehturm** and Alexanderplatz itself. Surprisingly, one or two older landmarks have managed to cling to life amid the brutalist modernity, including the city's oldest church, the medieval **Marienkirche**, and the nineteenth-century **Rathaus**, now once again seat of Berlin's civic administration. The route to Alexanderplatz from Schlossplatz leads up **Karl-Liebknecht-Strasse**, a busy street of shops and restaurants.

Around the Marx-Engels-Forum

On the right-hand side, opposite the *Radisson Plaza Hotel*, is the **Marx-Engels-Forum**, a severely well-ordered patch of city-centre greenery. At its heart sits a lumpen bronze representation of the founders of the "scientific world view of the working class", as pre-*Wende* guidebooks used to refer to Karl Marx and Friedrich Engels. Facing the monument are six steel pillars bearing photogravure images of uplifting scenes from Soviet and East German life and events from various revolutionary struggles. These have been partly vandalized, and someone has made a determined effort to scratch out the face of Erich Honecker on one of them. Nearby are some blurred bronze reliefs of men and women doing nothing in particular, and between the Marx-Engels statue and the Palast der Republik are similarly unclear stone reliefs showing muscular men writing furiously.

Heilige-Geist-Kapelle and Hackescher Markt Station

Just beyond the *Radisson Plaza Hotel*, it's worth taking a quick walk north along Spandauer Strasse, once one of the city's more important streets, though almost all its historic buildings were destroyed during the war. One of the few exceptions, a little way along on the left, is the quaintly incongruous fourteenth-century **Heilige-Geist-Kapelle**. Today this red-brick Gothic edifice is dwarfed by a larger, newer building (originally a trade school, now part of Humboldt Universität) that was grafted onto it at the turn of the century. In many ways it's a miracle the chapel is still standing: during the course of the last six hundred years, it has survived a huge city fire in 1380, the enormously destructive explosion of a nearby gunpowder magazine in 1720, and, above all, wartime bombing. At the moment the chapel is being used as a mensa but restoration of the interior is in the offing.

At its northern end Spandauer Strasse turns into An der Spandauer Brücke. Nearby is **Hackescher Markt S-Bahn station**, a nineteenth-century construction retaining its original red-tile facade, with mosaic decorative elements and rounded windows typical of the period. It's now a protected building and its architectural features are best appreciated by walking through the station itself and taking a look at the northern facade. The station has undergone several name changes this century. Until recently it was called S-Bahnhof Marx-Engels-Platz and before the war it was known as *Bahnhof Börse* or "Stock Exchange Station", thanks to its proximity to Berlin's long since vanished commodities market. The Stock Exchange, which stood behind the Humboldt University building on Spandauer Strasse (the site is now occupied by the *Radisson Plaza Hotel*), was gutted during the war and suffered an unlikely fate: it was demolished and its granite blocks were used to build the panorama wall of East Berlin's zoo, behind the polar bear enclosure (see p.51).

The Neptunbrunnen

Returning to Karl-Liebknecht-Strasse, head east past the Hungarian and Polish cultural centres (full of folksy tack). Roughly opposite these, on the other side of the street, is a large open space on which stands the **Neptunbrunnen**, an extravagantly imaginative fountain incorporating a statue of a trident-wielding Neptune sitting on a shell. A serpent, seal and alligator spray the god of the sea with water, and he is supported by strange fish and eel-draped aquatic centaurs with webbed feet instead of hooves. Around the rim of the fountain sit four female courtiers, symbolizing what were at the time the four most important German rivers: the Rhine, the Vistula, the Oder and the Elbe. The statue was built in 1891 and originally positioned on the Schlossplatz.

The Marienkirche

To the north of the Neptunbrunnen is the **Marienkirche** (Mon–Thurs 10am–noon & 1–5pm, Sat & Sun noon–5pm; bus #100 & #157), Berlin's oldest parish church, once hemmed in by buildings and now standing oddly isolated in the shadow of the huge Fernsehturm (see opposite). The Gothic nave in stone and brick dates back to about 1270, but the tower is more recent, having been added in 1466, with the verdigris-coated upper section tacked on towards the end of the eighteenth century by the designer of the Brandenburg Gate, Carl

Gotthard Langhans. This uncontrived combination of architectural styles somehow makes the Marienkirche one of Berlin's most appealing churches, its simplicity a reminder of the city's village origins.

The interior is an excellent place to escape the increasingly frenetic streetlife of the area and listen to a free organ recital (Sat 4.30pm). Near the main entrance at the western end of the church is a small cross erected by the citizens of Berlin and Cölln as penance to the Pope, after a mob immolated a papal representative on a nearby marketplace. There are five holes in the cross and, according to tradition, during the Middle Ages convicted criminals wishing to prove their innocence could do so by inserting the fingers of one hand into the holes simultaneously – not too many escaped punishment, though, as the feat is virtually an anatomical impossibility. Just inside the entrance, look out for the fifteenth-century *Totentanz*, a 22-metre frieze showing the dance of death. It's very faded, but accompanied by a representation of what it should look like, with Death shown as a shroud-clad mummy popping up between people from all levels of society.

The vaulted nave is plain and white but enlivened by some opulent decorative touches. Foremost among these is Andreas Schlüter's magnificent **pulpit**, its canopy dripping with cherubs and backed by a cloud from which gilded sunrays radiate. Complementing this are the white marble altar with a huge triptych altarpiece and the eighteenth-century organ, a riot of gilded filigree and yet more cherubs, topped by a sunburst.

The Fernsehturm

The Marienkirche, like every other building in the vicinity, is overshadowed by the gigantic **Fernsehturm** or TV tower just to the east (daily 9am–1am; DM8; U- & S-Bahn Alexanderplatz, bus #100, #142, #157 & #257). This 365-metre transmitter is the second highest structure in Europe and dominates the eastern Berlin skyline like a displaced satellite sitting on top of a huge factory chimney. It was built during the isolationist 1960s, a period when the east part of the city was largely inaccessible to West Germans, and intended as a highly visible symbol of the permanence of East Berlin and the German Democratic Republic. Its construction was watched with dismay and derision by West Berliners (and many people in the East), but after completion in 1969 the tower soon became a popular stopoff on the East Berlin tourist circuit.

These days, having outlasted the regime that conceived it, the Fernsehturm has become part of the scenery, and though few would champion it on the grounds of architectural merit, it does have a certain retro appeal. It also makes an unmissable orientation point, and there's a tremendous **view** (40km on a rare clear day, although the summit is often shrouded in cloud) from the observation platform – reached by a very fast lift. Above the observation platform is the

Tele-Café (see "Cafés and bars" in Listings), whose main attraction is that it revolves on its own axis twice an hour.

When the sun shines on the globe of the tower, the reflected light forms a cross visible even in western Berlin, much to the reported chagrin of the old GDR authorities and amusement of Berliners, who call it the "pope's revenge". If you want to go up, bear in mind that there are sometimes long queues (the evening is your best bet). At the foot of the tower is a jumble of cafés, restaurants and exhibition halls, welded together by a series of walkways, and with abundant surfaces of sloping concrete that are a boon for local skateboarders.

The Rotes Rathaus

Across Rathausstrasse from the Neptunbrunnen is a rare survivor of Hohenzollern-era Berlin in the shape of the **Rotes Rathaus**, Berlin's "Red Town Hall". So called because of the colour of its bricks rather than its politics, the Rotes Rathaus has a solid angularity that contrasts sharply with the finicky grandeur of contemporaries like the Dom (see p.88). This is perhaps because it's a symbol of the civic rather than the Imperial Berlin of the time: a city in the throes of rapid commercial expansion and industrial growth. The building has lost some of its impact now that it's been hemmed in by new structures, but it remains a grandiose, almost Venetian-looking structure – look out for the intricate bas-relief in terracotta, illustrating episodes from the history of Berlin, that runs around the building at first-floor level. The Rathaus was badly knocked around in 1945, but made a good comeback following restoration during the 1950s. During GDR days it was headquarters of the East Berlin city administration (West Berlin was administered from Schöneberg town hall, see p.136), but since October 1991 it's been the seat of the united Berlin government.

The reconstruction of the Rathaus and thousands of other Berlin buildings is largely due to the *Trümmerfrauen* or "Rubble Women", who set to work in 1945 clearing up the 100 million tons of rubble created by wartime bombing and shelling. Their deeds are commemorated by the **statue** of a robust-looking woman facing the eastern entrance to the Rathaus on Rathausstrasse. Women of all ages carried out the bulk of the early rebuilding work, since most of Berlin's adult male population was dead, disabled or being held in PoW camps by the Allies. Despite this, the male contribution to the work is also marked by a statue of a man looking wistfully towards his *Trümmerfrau* counterpart from the western end of the Rathaus.

From the Rathaus the pedestrianized Rathausstrasse leads northeast up towards Alexanderplatz, past a series of largely missable shops and cafés, a legacy of the old regime's efforts to jazz up the city centre. At the end of the street the arched canopy of **S-Bahnhof Alexanderplatz** rises above *Imbiss* stands and street stalls. The station is one of the few buildings around here bearing any resemblance to its prewar appearance (though it's actually a 1960s rebuild).

Following the war and the bloody Battle of Berlin, healthy adult men were virtually eradicated in the city. Today Berlin has a visibly high number of elderly single and widowed women.

Alexanderplatz

Just to the southeast of the station entrance, Rathausstrasse passes
under the rail tracks onto **Alexanderplatz** itself, a huge, windswept,
pedestrianized plaza surrounded by high-rises. Alexanderplatz has
long been an important business and traffic centre. During the eighteenth century routes to all parts of Germany radiated out from here,
and a cattle and wool market stood on the site. It acquired its present
name after the Russian tsar Alexander I visited Berlin in 1805, and
was made famous beyond the city by Alfred Döblin's unreadable
novel of life in the Weimar era, *Berlin Alexanderplatz* (subsequently filmed by Fassbinder). Today, in addition to the S-Bahn line
running overhead, three underground lines cross beneath the Platz
and various bus routes converge on the area, making it one of central Berlin's busiest corners.

The route onto "Alex" leads through a gap between a couple of
prewar survivors: the **Alexanderhaus** and the **Berolinahaus**, two
buildings designed at the beginning of the 1930s by the architect and
designer Peter Behrens, whose ideas influenced the founders of the
Bauhaus. These two buildings, which house respectively various
shops and offices and the central Berlin district council, are the only
Alexanderplatz buildings not to have been destroyed in the war.
Today Behrens's buildings, once the tallest in the area, have been put
in the shade by the ugly *Forum Hotel* and various other local high-
rises. At the centre of things is the sorry-looking **Brunnen der
Völkerfreundschaft** (Friendship of the Peoples Fountain), which
used to be a hangout for prostitutes. A more renowned monument is
the **Weltzeituhr** (World Clock) in front of the Alexanderhaus.
Central Berlin's best-known rendezvous point, it tells the time in different cities throughout the world, and looks like a product of the
same architectural school responsible for the Fernsehturm.

Despite its drab contemporary appearance, Alexanderplatz has
figured prominently in city upheavals ever since revolutionaries
(including the writer Theodor Fontane) set up barricades here in
1848. In 1872 it was the site of a demonstration by an army of homeless women and children, and half a century later, during the revolution of 1918, sailors occupied the Alexanderplatz police headquarters (a feared local landmark that lay just to the southeast of the Platz
– a plaque marks the spot) and freed the prisoners. More recently,
Alexanderplatz was the focal point of the million-strong city-wide
demonstration of November 4, 1989, which formed a prelude to the
events of November 9. Hundreds of thousands of people crammed
into the square to hear opposition leaders speak. Veteran writer
Stefan Heym summed up the mood in his speech to the crowd:
"Power belongs not to one, not to a few, not to the party and not to
the state. The whole people must have a share."

Before the war, Alexanderplatz was one of the city's main shopping centres with two expensive department stores in the vicinity:

Hermann Tietz, a Neo-Baroque palace between the Berolinahaus and what is now the *Forum Hotel*, and Wertheim, the biggest department store in Germany, which stood on the opposite side of the S-Bahn tracks to the Alexanderhaus. Both were Jewish-owned until "Aryanized" by the Nazis. The Kaufhof department store facing the fountain was, as Centrum, one of the best-stocked shops in East Germany, though these days it's just another run-of-the-mill big store. Today commercial life on Alexanderplatz seems to happen more at street level, with clusters of stalls jostling for space around the edges of the plaza.

Throughout its existence the face of Alexanderplatz has undergone many transformations. A major reshaping at the end of the 1920s cleaned up what had turned into a rather sleazy corner of the city, and during the early 1960s the GDR-era city authorities decided to realize their vision of what a modern, socialist metropolis should look like by giving the then still war-damaged area the form it retains today. Further major changes are afoot and over the next decade or so Alexanderplatz looks set to be transformed into a US-style "downtown", dominated by a dozen or so high-rise office and apartment buildings.

Along Karl-Marx-Allee

From Alexanderplatz, a short walk takes you southeast down **Karl-Marx-Allee** towards the district of Friedrichshain. The section of Karl-Marx-Allee running between Alexanderplatz and Strausberger Platz went up during the early to mid-1960s and is predictably stark and angular; this is where the GDR Politbüro and Eastern Bloc dignitaries took the salute during the military parades held every year to mark the GDR's anniversary. The last such occasion was on October 7, 1989, when Mikhail Gorbachev warned that "Life punishes those who arrive late" – a pointed reference to the East German leadership's rejection of his liberalization plans. It was already too late for Honecker and his Politbüro though, and the event sparked a series of demonstrations across the country that led to the downfall of the SED regime and subsequent collapse of the GDR. From Strausberger Platz onwards, where the district of Friedrichshain begins, the architecture recalls an earlier era and things get more interesting (see p.162).

Nikolaiviertel and around

CENTRAL BERLIN

Slightly to the southwest of the Rotes Rathaus lies the **Nikolaiviertel**, a recent development that attempts to re-create the old prewar heart of Berlin on the site of the city's **medieval** core, which was razed overnight on June 16, 1944.

To the east of here, in a quiet quarter cut off from the rest of the city centre by the speeding traffic of Grunerstrasse, a few historic buildings and one of the city's oldest *Gaststätten* survive. It's also worth heading south across the River Spree, to where a couple of museums, including the Märkisches Museum, have some excellent material on the history of the city.

Nikolaiviertel and around

The Nikolaiviertel

The compact network of streets that forms the **Nikolaiviertel** was a radical architectural departure for the old-style GDR. No longer, it seems, did the city planners feel compelled to build enormous monuments to the concrete-pourer's art; most of the Nikolaiviertel buildings are no more than four or five storeys high, and a concerted effort was made to inject a bit of vernacular individuality into the designs. One or two original buildings aside, the Nikolaiviertel consists partly of exact replicas of historic Berlin buildings that didn't make it through to the postwar era and partly of stylized buildings not based on anything in particular, but with a vaguely "old Berlin" feel. Sometimes it doesn't quite come off, and in places the use of typical East German *Plattenbau* construction techniques, with prefabricated pillars and gables, isn't too convincing, but all in all the Nikolaiviertel represents a commendable effort to get away from the monumentalism of earlier postwar construction projects. It also represents an attempt to attract big-spending tourists, with a series of expensive restaurants, cafés and *Gaststätten* (see "Cafés and bars" and "Restaurants" in Listings).

The nearest U-Bahn station to the Nikolaiviertel is Klosterstrasse; buses #142 and #257 also pass nearby.

Around the Nikolaikirche

At the centre of it all, on Nikolaikirchplatz, just off Propststrasse, is the Gothic **Nikolaikirche** (Tues–Sun 10am–6pm; DM3, concessions DM1), a thirteenth-century church, restored to its twin-towered pre-war glory. The Nikolaikirche is one of the city's oldest churches and it was from here on November 2, 1539, that news of the Reformation was proclaimed to the citizens of Berlin. The distinctive needle-like spires date from a nineteenth-century restoration of the church, or rather their design does – the building was thoroughly wrecked during the war, and what you see today is largely a rebuild, as extensive patches of lighter, obviously modern masonry show.

The church is now a museum (part of the Märkisches Museum, see p.104) housing an exhibition about the "historical development of Berlin from its founding until 1648". It's all slightly dull and not terribly informative but worth looking in on briefly, if only for a couple of models that give a graphic picture of how the city developed from a couple of tiny riverside villages into a respectable fifteenth-century town that incorporated the Marienkirche, Nikolaikirche and an early version of the Schloss. There are also a few interesting pre-war photographs of the Nikolaiviertel area, and an odd assortment of pots, armour and jewellery from medieval Berlin. Highlight of the collection is the *Spandau Madonna*, a thirteenth-century statue carved out of sandstone with great attention to detail.

Some of the **best Nikolaiviertel houses** are around the
Nikolaikirche, along Propststrasse and on the southern side of
Nikolaikirchplatz, behind the church itself. The last are particularly
convincing – it's hard to believe that these pastel-facaded townhouses are fakes dating back only as far as the beginning of the 1980s.

*For details of
Zum
Nussbaum and
other eating
places in this
area, see
"Cafés and
bars" and
"Restaurants"
in Listings.*

For a little light relief head for *Zum Nussbaum* on the corner of
Propststrasse and Am Nussbaum, a handily located copy of a celebrated sixteenth-century *Gaststätte* that stood on the nearby
Fischerinsel until destroyed during the bombing. The original is said
to have been the local haunt of Berlin artists Heinrich Zille and Otto
Nagel, and the replica is a faithful copy, right down to the walnut tree
in the tiny garden. It's a little touristy but still a good place for a beer,
particularly in summer if you can get a table outside.

Propststrasse runs all the way down to the River Spree and a
rather clichéd statue of **St George and the Dragon**. Before here a
right turn into Poststrasse will take you past the Gerichtslaube,
another Nikolaiviertel replica, this time of Berlin's medieval courthouse. The original was dismantled in 1870 in order to create the
space needed for the building of the Rotes Rathaus, and was
removed to the grounds of Schloss Babelsberg in Potsdam where it
can still be seen (see p.206). The copy houses a couple of pricey
tourist restaurants.

The Knoblauch-Haus

A left turn at the Propststrasse–Poststrasse intersection is more
rewarding, leading to the **Knoblauch-Haus**, Poststr. 23 (Tues–Sun
10am–6pm; DM2, concessions DM1), a Neoclassical townhouse
built in 1759 and a rare survivor of the war. It was home to the patri-
cian Knoblauch family, who played an important role in the commercial and cultural life of eighteenth- and nineteenth-century
Berlin, and now contains an exhibition about their activities. While
the careers of Eduard Knoblauch, Berlin's first freelance architect,
and Armand Knoblauch, founder of a major city brewery, are interesting up to a point, the real appeal here is the interior of the house
itself, furnished in the grand-bourgeois style of the times, which
gives a good impression of upper middle-class life in Hohenzollern-
era Berlin. The ground floor and vaulted basement of the Knoblauch-
Haus are home to the *Historische Weinstuben* (see "Restaurants" in
Listings), a reconstruction of a nineteenth-century wine-restaurant
once favoured by the playwrights Gerhart Hauptmann, August
Strindberg and Henrik Ibsen.

The Ephraim-Palais

There's another relic of Berlin bourgeois highlife at the southern end
of Poststrasse, where the elegant Rococo facade of the **Ephraim-
Palais**, Poststr. 16 (Tues–Sun 10am–6pm; DM2, concessions DM1),
curves round onto Mühlendamm. A rebuild of an eighteenth-century

merchant's mansion, this building now houses a museum of Berlin-related art from the seventeenth to the beginning of the nineteenth centuries, with numerous pictures, prints and maps giving a good impression of how the city looked in its glory days.

The Ephraim-Palais was built by Veitel Heine Ephraim, court jeweller and mint master to Frederick the Great, and all-round wheeler dealer. He owed his lavish lifestyle primarily to the fact that he steadily reduced the silver content of the Prussian *thaler*. This earned a great deal of money for Frederick and Ephraim himself but ruined the purchasing power of the currency. Ephraim's palace housed a museum of sport from 1925 to 1934, before being dismantled in 1935 as part of a road-broadening scheme; much of the facade, however, was preserved and later turned up in West Berlin, whence it was returned to be incorporated into the 1980s rebuild.

The Hanf Museum

Nearby, in another reconstructed Berlin house, is the **Hanf Museum**, Mühlendamm 5 (Hemp Museum; Tues–Fri 10am–8pm, Sat & Sun noon–8pm; DM5), Germany's only museum dedicated to cannabis. It's somewhat amateurish, filled with an odd assortment of glass cases and ill-framed exhibits, but there is a surprisingly large amount of information about the history, uses and cultural significance of the notorious plant. Devotees may find it interesting, but all exhibits are in German. A small shop offers pipes, pamphlets, reggae tapes and the like, and there's a café in the basement. Alternatively, next door is *Zur Rippe*, an old-style *Gaststätte* where you can slake your thirst and dine on traditional Berlin specialities like *Eisbein* (see "Cafés and bars" in Listings).

Around the Molkenmarkt

The area where Mühlendamm meets Stralauer Strasse is known as the **Molkenmarkt**, one of the oldest public spaces in Berlin. The two pompous and dull buildings on the southern side of Mühlendamm are the **Berliner Münze** (Berlin Mint) and the former **Palais Schwerin** (built for Otto Schwerin, a minister of Friedrich I of Prussia). The latter is completely missable and the only redeeming feature of the former is a replica of a frieze depicting coining techniques by Gottfried Schadow, designer of the Brandenburg Gate Quadriga.

The Stadthaus and around

Bypass them both and head for Jüdenstrasse – "Jews' Street" – running north from Stralauer Strasse in the shadow of the domed **Stadthaus**. Reminiscent of the Französischer Dom but dating from as recently as 1911, this building is a relic of the area's days as an administrative district of Wilhelmine Berlin and now houses federal government offices. The area around Jüdenstrasse was Berlin's original ghetto, a role that ended when the Jews were driven out of Brandenburg in 1573. When the Jews were allowed back into Berlin in 1671 they settled mainly around what is now Oranienburger Strasse (see p.113).

A right turn midway along Jüdenstrasse leads into Parochialstrasse, where the first stone of Communist control over postwar eastern Berlin was laid at **Parochialstrasse 1**. The building hosted the opening meeting of Berlin's post-Nazi town council, headed by future SED chief Walter Ulbricht, even as fighting still raged a little to the west. Ulbricht and his comrades had been specially flown in from Soviet exile to sow the seeds for a future Communist civil administration and moved in here, having been unable to set up shop in the still-burning Rotes Rathaus. Further along the street is the **Parochialkirche**, a Baroque church that dates back to the sixteenth century. The bare brick interior (legacy of the usual wartime gutting) is a venue for changing art exhibitions (free) of the worthy-but-boring kind usually found in churches.

Around Klosterstrasse

On the northeastern side of the Parochialstrasse–Klosterstrasse (named after a long-vanished local monastery) junction is **Podewil**, an eighteenth-century residence that's now home to an arts centre and pleasant café (see "Cafés and bars" and "Clubs and live venues" in Listings). Not far away at the top of Klosterstrasse is the gutted thirteenth-century **Franziskaner-Kirche**, destroyed by a land mine in 1945 and left a ruin as a warning against war and Fascism. Behind here, at Littenstr. 14–15, is the **Berlin Landgericht**, a courthouse whose Neo-Baroque facade conceals a wonderful *Jugendstil* interior of strange interlocking stairwells that seem to owe their structure to organic processes rather than the work of an architect. A rather more functional piece of Berlin architectural history can be seen towards the southern end of Littenstrasse in the shape of a fragment of Berlin's medieval Stadtmauer or city wall. If you're thirsty or hungry, try Berlin's oldest pub, *Zur letzten Instanz* (see "Cafés and bars" in Listings) on nearby Waisenstrasse.

South of the Spree

From Klosterstrasse it's a short U-Bahn hop to Märkisches Museum station on the **southern side of the Spree** (you can also walk via the Fischerinsel, a shoddy GDR-era showpiece housing development), where you'll find the Märkisches Museum, an institution dating from before reunification. There is little else in the neighbourhood to attract attention. East of the museum, old factories and large industrial yards line the banks of the Spree. Southwards lies a swath of residential buildings.

The Märkisches Museum

Looking like a red-brick Neo-Gothic cathedral, the **Märkisches Museum**, Am Köllnischen Park 5 (Tues–Sun 10am–6pm; DM3, concessions DM1; nearest U-Bahn Märkisches Museum or bus #147j or #240), is one of central Berlin's better museums, covering the history of Berlin and the Mark Brandenburg. The oldest exhibit is a seventh-millennium BC **deer mask** in the pre- and early history section on the ground floor, probably used for ritual purposes by a Middle Stone Age hunter. It's the earliest relic of human settlement in the Brandenburg area, but being little more than a pair of antlers, is not terribly exciting to look at. More rewarding are the maps, prints, photos and models in the section about the development of Berlin from 1648 to 1815, on the same floor, which make for endless spot-the-difference poring. The Berlin historical theme continues on the next floor up, bringing you bang up to date with coverage of the events of 1989. This section also covers the applied arts in endless displays of glassware, porcelain and the like – delve according to taste – while other rooms cover the performing arts with a fascinating display of manuscripts, set models and information about the leading lights of the Berlin theatre scene during the nineteenth century.

On the second floor is the art section, with scores of fine paintings ranging from the seventeenth century to the present day by way of artists as diverse as Adolph von Menzel and Otto Dix. Equally interesting is the display on **Heinrich Zille**, the Berlin artist who produced earthy satirical drawings of Berlin life around the turn of the century. A **statue** outside shows him sketching in the street with a passer-by peering over his shoulder. Behind the museum is a leafy park with a **bearpit**, home to a couple of sleepy brown bears.

Nearby, at Märkisches Ufer 10, is the Baroque **Ermeler Haus**, an eighteenth-century mansion transplanted here from nearby Breite Strasse – these days it houses a couple of decent restaurants (see "Restaurants" in Listings).

Chapter 6

The Scheunenviertel and around

T he **Scheunenviertel** is the name commonly given to the north-ern periphery of central Berlin, a crescent-shaped area running roughly from Weidendammer Brücke (which crosses the River Spree just north of Bahnhof Friedrichstrasse) to Rosa-Luxemburg-

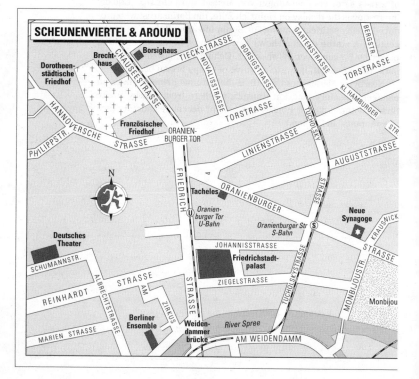

Platz. Since the *Wende* this has emerged as one of the most intriguing parts of the unified city, its appeal based on both its history as Berlin's prewar **Jewish quarter** and a contemporary nightlife boom that makes it one of Berlin's essential after-hours destinations.

The district has its origins in the Spandauer Vorstadt, one of a number of suburbs built beyond Berlin's walled centre during the seventeenth century. *Scheunenviertel*, meaning "barn quarter", originally just described what is now Rosa-Luxemburg-Platz and its environs, where barns were built following a decree that flammable hay and straw could no longer be stored in the city centre. However, the term has since become common usage to describe most of the area covered in this chapter.

The Jews moved in after they were permitted to return to Berlin in 1671, following the expulsion orders a century before. From that point on the area became a refuge for Jews fleeing persecution and pogroms in eastern Europe and Russia, and by the nineteenth century the Scheunenviertel was the cultural and spiritual centre of Berlin's by now well-established and influential Jewish community.

The melting-pot atmosphere made the area an ideal refuge for those at odds with the Prussian and later the Imperial German estab-

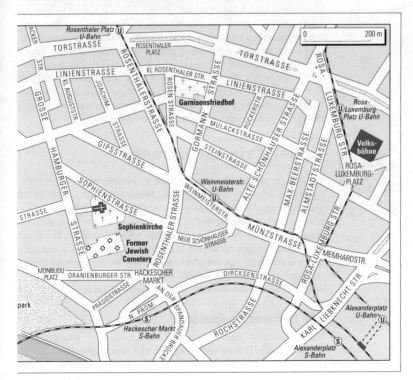

lishment, and it became a notorious centre of revolutionary and criminal activity. In fact the authorities were constantly trying to find ways to justify pulling it down. At one point they refused to put down cobblestones in the heart of the Scheunenviertel for fear that the inhabitants would rip them up and use them to build barricades.

The Scheunenviertel's vibrant nature also attracted **artists** and **writers** who created their own bohemian enclave here, and during the 1920s local bars and dives numbered personalities like Bertolt Brecht, Marlene Dietrich and the actor Gustav Gründgens among their patrons. During these years the Scheunenviertel became a regular battleground for the street gangs of the left and right, who had their own *Kneipen* and meeting halls in the area.

Deportation of the Jews under the Nazis did much to take the soul out of the Scheunenviertel and this was followed in the GDR-era by a general shutting down of what little business-life remained. From the 1950s until the *Wende* the quarter was little more than a network of decrepit prewar streets punctuated by the occasional slab of GDR-era housing. Few visitors strayed here from Unter den Linden, and apart from a couple of pockets of restoration the area was allowed to decay quietly – forgotten almost as much by the authorities as by visitors to East Berlin. Today the Scheunenviertel is undergoing a dramatic revival, with renovation projects putting the infrastructure to rights and **new bars** and **cafés** appearing almost every week. All this, coupled with unexpected discoveries among the brightly painted squatted houses in the backstreets, makes it one of the most rewarding corners of the city to explore.

For the visitor the main points of interest are on and around the neat triangle formed by Oranienburger Strasse, Auguststrasse and Grosse Hamburger Strasse – the focus of Jewish settlement and now the centre of a rapidly expanding café and gallery scene.

Upper Friedrichstrasse

These days the streets around **Upper Friedrichstrasse**, across the Spree just north of Bahnhof Friedrichstrasse, are home largely to shops and apartments, belying the fact that this is where the industrial revolution first hit Berlin. The main attractions have artistic associations, like the Berliner Ensemble, where Brecht worked upon his postwar return to Berlin; and the nearby Deutsches Theater, which is shaping up as one of the city's, if not the country's, best contemporary theatres. The **Brecht** connection also takes in the playwright's home and workplace and, not far away, his grave.

The Berliner Ensemble

Friedrichstrasse runs north via the handsome wrought-iron Weidendammer Brücke into central Berlin's theatreland. Immediately to the left on Bertolt-Brecht-Platz is the **Berliner Ensemble** theatre (see "The arts" in Listings), generally thought of as Berlin's "Brecht theatre", complete with a statue of the man himself in front. The theatre is currently trying to disassociate itself from the legacy of the GDR days, when its stock in trade was slightly lacklustre productions of Brecht's work, performed in ritualistic tribute to one of the few world-renowned German writers East Germany could claim as its own.

The building, which dates from the early 1890s, is rather austere from the outside but boasts an opulent Neo-Baroque interior. Originally known as the Theater am Schiffbauerdamm (after the street on which it stands), the Brecht connection goes back to the 1920s: on August 31, 1928, the world premiere of his *Dreigroschenoper* ("The Threepenny Opera") was staged here, the first of 250 consecutive performances. After spending much of the Nazi era in American exile, Brecht returned in 1949 with his wife, Helene Weigel, to take over direction of the theatre, marking his return by painting a still-visible red cross through the coat of arms on the royal box.

The Deutsches Theater

A few streets to the northwest at Schumannstr. 13a (turn right by the war-era bunker on Reinhardtstrasse) is the elegant **Deutsches Theater** (see "The arts" in Listings), founded in 1883. In 1905 Max Reinhardt, who was to dominate the theatre scene for nearly three decades, took over as director (moving on from the Theater am Schiffbauerdamm); and in 1922 a young and unknown Marlene Dietrich made her stage debut here. A couple of years later Bertolt Brecht arrived from Munich and began his energetic conquest of Berlin's theatre world. In time for its 1983 centenary, millions were spent on restoring the interior to its turn-of-the-century splendour; and in contrast to the Berliner Ensemble, the Deutsches Theater is going from strength to strength, and is now widely regarded as one of the city's best.

At its western end Reinhardtstrasse passes under a low S-Bahn bridge, which was bricked off by the Wall until 1989. Now that there are no more guards lurking in the shadows, you can walk through onto a patch of apparent wasteland which, for over 28 years, was part of the *Todesstreife* or "Death Strip" of the Wall fortifications. To the south is the Spree and an impressive view of the Reichstag on the opposite bank, while to the west looms a huge construction site, building for the bureaucrats of the national government when they move from Bonn sometime around 1999.

Around Oranienburger Tor

Returning to the junction of Reinhardtstrasse and Friedrichstrasse, the clumsy GDR-era Jugendstil pastiche of the **Friedrichstadt Palast** theatre (again, see "The arts" in Listings) rears up opposite; it's perfect if you're into scantily clad revues, but otherwise you should give it a miss. Things start to get more interesting a little further to the

Upper Friedrich-strasse

north along Friedrichstrasse, around **Oranienburger Tor**. During the nineteenth century this area was the location of one of Berlin's densest concentrations of heavy industry. Development had begun during the 1820s with the establishment of a steam-engine factory and iron foundry in Chausseestrasse. In 1837 August Borsig built his first factory, and by the 1870s his successors were churning out hundreds of steam engines and railway locomotives each year.

Other industrial concerns were also drawn to the area, earning it the nickname *Feuerland* – "Fireland". However, by the end of the century most had outgrown their roots and relocated en masse at the edges of the rapidly expanding city. A reminder of the past, and of Borsig's local influence, is the **Borsighaus** at Chausseestr. 9. Once the central administration block of the Borsig factories, this sandstone building, its facade richly decorated with bronze figures, looks like a displaced country residence.

Bertolt Brecht (1898–1956)

Bertolt Brecht is widely regarded as one of the leading German dramatists of the twentieth century. Born in Augsburg, the son of a paper-mill manager, he studied medicine, mainly to avoid full military service in World War I. Working as an army medical orderly in 1918, his experiences helped shape his passionate anti-militarism. Soon he drifted away from medicine onto the fringes of the theatrical world, eventually winding up as a dramaturg at the Munich Kammerspiele in 1921. Increasingly he was drawn to Berlin, and a few years later took up a similar position at the Deutsches Theater under Erwin Piscator, where he began his speedy ascent to the heights of German theatre. Brecht's earliest plays were anarchic semi-Expressionistic pieces: his first work, *Baal*, depicted life as an intensely sensual yet ultimately futile and doomed experience. Although his work attracted the attention of the critics and his first-performed play, *Trommeln in der Nacht* ("Drums in the Night"), won the prestigious Kleist prize in 1922, it wasn't until the premiere of the *Dreigroschenoper* ("The Threepenny Opera") co-written with the composer Kurt Weill, six years later, that Brecht's real breakthrough came.

The *Dreigroschenoper* marked the beginning of a new phase in Brecht's work. A couple of years earlier he had embraced Marxism, an ideological step that had a profound effect on his literary output, leading him to espouse a didactic "epic" form of theatre. The aim was to provoke the audience, perhaps even move them to revolutionary activity. To this end he developed the technique of **Verfremdung** ("alienation") to create a sense of distance between spectators and the action unfolding before them. By using effects such as obviously fake scenery, monotone lighting, and jarring music to expose the sham sentimentality of love songs, he hoped constantly to remind the audience that what they were doing was watching a play – in order to make them judge, rather than be drawn into, the action on stage. The result was a series of works that were pretty heavy-going, though the opera *Aufstieg und Fall der Stadt Mahagonny* ("Rise and Fall of the City of Mahagonny") and *Die Heilige Johanna der Schlachthöfe* ("St Joan of the Stockyards") from this period are reasonably accessible.

The Dorotheenstädtische Friedhof

Roughly opposite here is the **Dorotheenstädtische Friedhof**
(daily: April–Sept 8am–7pm; Oct–March 8am–4pm; U-Bahn
Oranienburger Tor, bus #140, trams #1 & #13), eastern Berlin's
VIP cemetery. Here you'll find the graves of Bertolt Brecht and
Helene Weigel; the architect Karl Friedrich Schinkel, his last rest-
ing place topped by an appropriately florid monument; John
Heartfield, the Dada luminary and inter-war photomontage expo-
nent, under a headstone decorated with a runic H; the philosopher
Georg Hegel, whose ideas influenced Marx; the author Heinrich
Mann, and many other Berlin worthies. A leaflet detailing who lies
where is available from the cemetery administration offices (on the
right at the end of the entrance alley) for DM2. The
Dorotheenstädtische Friedhof also encloses the **Französischer**

In 1933, unsurprisingly, Brecht went into exile, eventually ending up in
the States. His years away from Germany were among his most productive.
During this time he wrote some of his greatest parable-plays, works that
benefited from a tempering of the writer's more overt didactic intent:
Leben des Galilei ("The Life of Galileo"), *Der gute Mensch von Sezuan*
("The Good Woman of Szechuan"), *Mutter Courage und ihre Kinder*
("Mother Courage and her Children"), *Der Kaukasische Kreidekreis*
("The Caucasian Chalk Circle"). The political message was still very much
present in his work, but somehow the dynamic and lyrical force of his writing meant that it was often largely lost on his audience – at the Zürich premiere of *Mutter Courage* in 1941, Brecht was dismayed to learn that the
audience in fact identified with his heroine, whom he had intended to serve
as an unsympathetic symbol of the senselessness of wartime sacrifice.

In America Brecht had tried to make a living as a Hollywood scriptwriter,
though not with much success – only one film made it to the screen,
Hangmen Also Die, directed by another German-in-exile, Fritz Lang. In
1947 Brecht came before the Committee for Un-American Activities, but
was able to defend himself without implicating any of his friends. Returning
to Europe, he finally settled in East Berlin in 1949, after a brief period in
Switzerland. His decision to try his luck in the Soviet-dominated Eastern sector of Germany was influenced by the offer of the chance to take over at the
Theater am Schiffbauerdamm, the theatre where the *Dreigroschenoper* had
been premiered more than twenty years earlier. However, before heading
east, Brecht first took the precaution of gaining Austrian citizenship and
lodging the copyright of his works with a West German publisher.

The remainder of Brecht's life was largely devoted to the running of
what was now known as the *Berliner Ensemble* and facing up to his own
role in the fledgling GDR. The workers' uprising of 1953 prompted a private ironic outpouring (see p.75), but did not prevent him from accepting
the Stalin Peace Prize the following year. Two years later Brecht died, and
though he never did break with the workers' and peasants' state, it's interesting to reflect on what might have happened had he lived a few years
longer.

Friedhof (entrance on Chausseestrasse), originally built to serve Berlin's Huguenot community and now rather overgrown.

The Brecht-Haus

Just past the Dorotheenstädtische Friedhof entrance is the **Brecht-Haus**, Chausseestr. 125 (tours every 30min Tues–Fri 10–11.30am & also Thurs 5–6.30pm & Sat 9.30am–1.30pm; afternoon tours can be booked by calling ☎2 82 99 16; DM4, concessions DM2; U-Bahn Oranienburger Tor, bus #157, trams #1 & #13), final home and workplace of Brecht and Helene Weigel, his wife and collaborator. The guided tours take in the seven simply furnished rooms – an absolute must for Brecht fans, but not so fascinating if you're only casually acquainted with his works. The Brecht-Haus also has a Bertolt Brecht **archive** (Tues–Fri 8am–4pm) and the basement is home to the *Kellerrestaurant im Brechthaus* (see "Restaurants" in Listings), which dishes up Viennese specialities, supposedly according to Weigel's recipes.

A little way past the Brecht-Haus is a supermarket, behind which survives a brutalist **pillar commemorating the Spartakusbund**, the breakaway anti-war faction of the SPD formed by Karl Liebknecht in 1916, which later evolved into the KPD, Germany's Communist party. The inscription, a quote from Liebknecht, says, "Spartakus means the fire and spirit, the heart and soul, the will and deed of the revolution of the proletariat". The modern-day proletariat, however, seems more interested in the special offers available next door than this relic of its revolutionary past.

Museum für Naturkunde

Returning to Friedrichstrasse and heading northwest, a left turn into Invalidenstrasse leads to the **Museum für Naturkunde** at no. 43 (Tues–Sun 9.30am–5pm; DM5, concessions DM2.50; U-Bahn Zinnowitzer Strasse, bus #157, #245 or #340), one of the world's largest natural history museums. The museum's origins go back to 1716 though the present building, and the nucleus of the collection it houses, date from the 1880s.

High point of the sixteen-room display (exhibits are not labelled in English) is the reconstructed Brachiosaurus skeleton in the main hall. The museum is also home to the fossil remains of an Archaeopteryx, the oldest known bird. Elsewhere, amid the endless glass cases containing stuffed animals, fossils, and insects pinned on card, the rooms devoted to the evolution of vertebrates and the ape family stand out, as does the interesting if slightly ghoulish section on how the numerous stuffed animals were "prepared for exhibition", as the commentary delicately puts it. The museum also boasts a vast mineralogy collection including a number of meteorites.

Oranienburger Strasse and east

CENTRAL BERLIN

The area around Oranienburger Strasse, which runs southeast from Friedrichstrasse just below Oranienburger Tor, is the start of the Scheunenviertel proper and heart of Berlin's prewar **Jewish district**. Although Berlin's Jewish population numbers only around twelve thousand today, it has an enduring symbol in the shape of the Neue Synagoge, which over the last couple of years has been restored and is now a museum. With the opening of a number of Jewish cafés and a cultural centre, Oranienburger Strasse has regained a little of its pre-Nazi identity.

A few streets away on Grosse Hamburger Strasse are further reminders of Jewish Berlin, although here the past is recalled more by the absence of certain landmarks than by their presence. Just behind Grosse Hamburger Strasse, Sophienstrasse ranks as one of Berlin's best-restored nineteenth-century streets, taking its name from the nearby Sophienkirche, the city's finest Baroque church.

Oranienburger Strasse

Until 1989 **Oranienburger Strasse** was one of central Berlin's more desolate streets, but since the *Wende* it has become a major **bar/café-crawling strip**, with a host of stylish watering holes both here and on the surrounding streets. In fact, the pace of development around here has been so rapid that Oranienburger Strasse is as much a trendy tourist haunt as part of the new eastern Berlin *Szene* (see p.156). The run-down buildings of former East Berlin and the prostitutes soliciting passing motorists under the eyes of the police provide a frisson of excitement for large numbers of western German and foreign visitors.

The revitalization of Oranienburger Strasse began with **Tacheles**, a group of young international artists who took over a gutted building on the southern side of the street, just beyond the Oranienburger Tor junction, in early 1990. The exterior is usually festooned with works-in-progress, and the building has become home and workplace to an ever-changing band of painters, sculptors, kindred spirits and hangers-on. Inside is a café/bar (see "Cafés and bars " in Listings) and regular gigs and events take place here (see "Clubs and live venues" in Listings). The place has come a long way since its anarchic beginnings; it's now something of an institution, much to the disappointment of those involved in the early days, who inevitably claim the new-look *Tacheles* with its plate-glass windows is not the place it once was.

The *Tacheles* building itself has an interesting past, reflecting the history of the city in which it stands. Built in 1907, it was one of the first ferro-concrete structures in Europe, originally housing the Friedrichstrassepassagen shopping centre, then between the wars the AEG's exhibition hall for all its electrical products. From 1934 onwards the building was used by the SS and the Deutsche

Kristallnacht and Berlin's Jews

Kristallnacht, so called after the sound of breaking glass as Jewish businesses and institutions were wrecked, marked an intensification of Nazi
attacks on the Jews. The murder of Ernst vom Rath, a German official in
Paris, by Herschel Grynszpan, a young German-Jewish refugee protesting
at his parents' forced deportation to Poland with ten thousand other Jews,
gave the Nazis the excuse they had been waiting for to unleash a general
pogrom on German Jews. (Ironically, vom Rath was an anti-Nazi whom
Grynszpan had mistaken for his intended target, the German ambassador.)
At a party meeting on November 9, 1938, Nazi propaganda minister
Joseph Goebbels, having broken the news of the assassination, ordered
Reinhard Heydrich, chief of the Reich's Security Head Office, to organize
"spontaneous" anti-Jewish demonstrations. Heydrich directed the police
to ensure that attacks on the German Jewish community, mainly instigated by SA men in civilian clothes, were not hindered. *Kristallnacht* resulted in the deaths of at least 36 Jews and the destruction of 23 of the city's
29 synagogues, with hundreds of shops and businesses wrecked. After the
attacks the Nazi government fined the German Jewish community one billion marks, ostensibly to pay for the damage, and enacted new laws con-
fiscating Jewish property.

 Kristallnacht was the violent public culmination of a process of state-
backed persecution of German Jews that had started when the Nazis
assumed power in 1933. The first step was the SA-enforced boycott of
Jewish shops, businesses, and medical and legal practices that began on
April 1 of that year. A series of laws passed in the years that followed
banned Jews from most of the professions, and in September 1935 the
Nürnberg laws effectively deprived Jews of their German citizenship,
introducing apartheid-like classifications of "racial purity". There was a

Arbeitsfront, a Nazi labour organization. After the war it housed a
cinema and work space for art students before suffering partial
demolition and standing vacant for many years until the *Tacheles*
collective moved in. Change is afoot though: the ground on which
the building stands has been put up for sale by the city and a Cologne
developer is the likely buyer. They have, however, pledged to build
around *Tacheles* and its home, though it's hard to imagine that the
still anarchic spirit of the place will survive such an incorporation.

 A little way along from *Tacheles*, on the opposite side of the street,
is an important-looking building that turns out to be a nineteenth-century post office administration building. It's built in the mock-Moorish
style so favoured by Berlin civic architects during the last century.
They decked out everything from stations to breweries in alternating
bands of orange and yellow brick, with generously arched doorways
and windows and fanciful turrets with decorative cupolas.

The Neue Synagoge and around

Before the war Oranienburger Strasse and its immediate environs
were at the heart of Berlin's main **Jewish quarter**. During the initial

brief respite in 1936 when Berlin hosted the Olympic Games and the Nazis, wishing to show an acceptable face to the outside world, eased up on overt anti-Semitism, but by the following year large-scale expropriation of Jewish businesses had begun. After *Kristallnacht* all remaining Jewish businesses were forcibly "Aryanized", effectively excluding Jews from German economic life. With the outbreak of war in September 1939, Jews were forced to observe a night-time curfew and were forbidden to own radios. Forced transport of Jews to the east (mainly occupied Poland) began as early as February 1940, and September 1941 saw the introduction of a law requiring Jews to wear the yellow Star of David, heralding the beginning of mass deportations.

In January 1942, the **Wannsee Conference** held in a western suburb of Berlin (see p.154) discussed the *Endlösung* or "Final Solution" to the "Jewish Question", drawing up plans for the removal of all Jews to the east and, implicitly, their eventual extermination. As the Final Solution began to be put into effect, daily life for Berlin's Jews grew ever more unbearable: in April they were banned from public transport, and in September their food rations were reduced. By the beginning of 1943 the only Jews remaining legally in Berlin were highly skilled workers in the city's armaments factories, and in February deportation orders began to be enforced for this group, too. Most Berlin Jews were sent to Auschwitz and Theresienstadt concentration camps, and only a handful survived the gas chambers. By the end of the war Berlin's 160,564 Jewish population (1933 figure) had been reduced to about 6500; 1400 survived as "U-boats", hidden by gentile families at great personal risk, and the rest had somehow managed to evade the final round-ups, usually as a result of having irreplaceable skills vital to the war effort.

waves of Jewish immigration from the seventeenth century onwards the area was a densely populated and desperately poor ghetto, but by the nineteenth century Berlin's Jews had achieved a high degree of prosperity and assimilation. This was reflected in the building of the grand **Neue Synagoge**, to a design by Eduard Knoblauch, halfway down Oranienburger Strasse just off the corner of Krausnickstrasse. The synagogue was inaugurated in the presence of Bismarck in 1866, a gesture of official recognition which, coming at a time when Jews in Russia were still enduring officially sanctioned pogroms, must have made many Jews feel that their position in German society was finally secure. It was perhaps the acceptance that they had enjoyed in Wilhelmine Germany that contributed to the sense of disbelief many Jews felt at the rise of Nazism during the 1920s and 1930s.

Like the post office building near the *Tacheles*, the Neue Synagoge was built in mock-Moorish style, with the conspicuous addition of a bulbous gilt and turquoise dome. It was Berlin's central synagogue for over sixty years, serving also as a venue for concerts, including one in 1930 by Albert Einstein in his lesser-known role as a violinist. A Jewish museum was opened next door on January 24,

1933, just six days before the Nazi takeover. Neither museum nor synagogue survived the Third Reich: both were damaged on *Kristallnacht* (see pp.114–115). The synagogue wasn't actually destroyed thanks to the intervention of the local police chief who chased off SA arsonists and called the fire brigade to extinguish the flames. It remained in use as a place of worship until 1940 when it was handed over to the *Wehrmacht*, who used it as a warehouse until it was gutted by bombs on the night of November 22, 1943.

After the war the synagogue remained a ruin and in 1958 the main hall, which was thought to be on the verge of collapse, was demolished, leaving only the building's facade and entrance rooms intact. For many years these stood here largely forgotten, a plaque on the shattered frontage exhorting the few passers-by to: "*Vergesst es nie*" – "Never forget". The Jewish community pressed for what was left to be turned into a museum, but the authorities did not respond until 1988, when it was decided to resurrect the shell as a "centre for the promotion and preservation of Jewish culture".

A new plaque was affixed to the building amid much official pomp and ceremony on November 9, 1988, the fiftieth anniversary of *Kristallnacht*, and work began on restoration of the facade and the reconstruction of the gilded dome. In 1995, the extensive renovation work was completed and the building was reopened as a museum and cultural centre, officially called **Centrum Judaicum – Neue Synagoge** (Mon–Thurs & Sun 10am–6pm, Fri 10am–2pm; entry free except for special exhibitions). Inside there are two permanent exhibitions: one on the history and restoration of the synagogue itself, and another on the Jewish life and culture that could once be found in the surrounding area. Already the synagogue's dome, visible from far and wide, has become a Berlin landmark once again.

The offices next door to the synagogue at Oranienburger Strasse 28–29 are the **headquarters** of Berlin's Jewish community (Mon–Thurs 9am–4.30pm, Fri 9am–1.30pm), and it's worth dropping in to pick up literature about the synagogue and a map (English-language versions of both available) showing important Jewish sites in the city past and present. In order to get in (the offices and the museum share an entrance) you'll have to pass through airport-type magnetic detectors – a sad reflection of the continuing threat to Jewish institutions from terrorist attack and the homegrown far right.

See "Cafés and bars" in Listings for more details.

There's a clutch of **cafés and bars** in the vicinity of the synagogue on Oranienburger Strasse, including the kosher vegetarian *Oren* next door, full of city intellectuals in wire-rimmed glasses, *Café Silberstein* with its famous crazy chairs, and the studenty cellar-bar *Assel* further down the street.

Towards the southern end of Oranienburger Strasse is **Monbijoupark**, once the grounds of a Rococo royal palace, reduced to rubble by the war and, like so many Hohenzollern relics, never rebuilt. Today this park contains an open-air swimming pool for children (see

"Children's Berlin" in Listings) and it makes an unexpected and shady refuge from the unrelentingly urban landscape of the area. A foot-bridge at its southwestern corner links it to the Museuminsel.

Oranien-
burger
Strasse and
east

Auguststrasse

Auguststrasse, which branches off from Oranienburger Strasse opposite the *Tacheles*, is another street that's undergone a breath-taking transformation since 1989, and is now the centre of a thriving arts scene. The galleries on and around Auguststrasse attract artists from all around the world and feature some of the most interesting and controversial work you're likely to see in Berlin. The city authorities have provided an enviable level of financial support. In June 1992 they stumped up for the "37 Rooms Exhibition" in which the whole of Auguststrasse was turned into a giant gallery, an event widely viewed as having given artistic life on the street an air of legitimacy.

A good starting point is *Galerie EIGEN + Art*, Auguststr. 26, an excellent place to pick up information about what's going on in other venues along the street.

Around Grosse Hamburger Strasse

At the eastern end of Oranienburger Strasse, a left turn leads into Grosse Hamburger Strasse, site of some poignant reminders of the area's Jewish past. It also offers access to one of Berlin's prettiest churches and an attractive restored street.

The Jewish Cemetery and around

On the immediate right, just into Grosse Hamburger Strasse, is the location of Berlin's oldest **Jewish cemetery**, established in 1672, and the first **Jewish old people's home** to be founded in the city. The Nazis used the building as a detention centre for Jews, and 55,000 people were held here before being shipped off to the camps. A memorial tablet, on which people have placed pebbles as a mark of respect, and a sculpted group of haggard-looking figures representing deportees, mark the spot where the home stood.

The grassed-over open space behind is the site of the cemetery itself. In 1943 the Gestapo smashed most of the headstones and dug up the remains of those buried here, using gravestones to shore up a trench they had excavated through the site. A few cracked headstones with Hebrew inscriptions line the graveyard walls. The only freestanding monument was erected after the war to commemorate Moses Mendelssohn, the philosopher and German Enlightenment figure. Also adorned with pebbles, it's on the spot where he is thought to have been buried, with an inscription in German on one side and in Hebrew on the other. Just to the north of the cemetery at **Grosse Hamburger Str. 27** is a former Jewish boys' school, recently reopened as a Jewish sec-

Wartime scars

Like the old houses around Grosse Hamburger Strasse, nearly all buildings that remain from the war show the damage inflicted during the Battle of Berlin: take a look at Friedrichstrasse below Kochstrasse, or almost anywhere in Prenzlauer Berg (see Chapter 9), and you'll see scores of bullet and shell marks.

ondary school for both sexes. Above its entrance a still-visible sign from prewar days reads, in German, "Jewish Community Boys' School". On the facade a plaque pays homage to Mendelssohn, who was a founder of Berlin's first Jewish school here in 1778, and who, until 1938, was commemorated by a bust in the school garden.

On the other side of the street is the **Missing House**, a unique and effective monument to the wartime destruction of Berlin. A gap in the tenements marks where house number 15–16 stood until destroyed by a direct hit during an air raid. In the autumn of 1990 the French artist Christian Boltanski put plaques on the side walls of the surviving buildings on either side as part of an installation, recalling the names, dates and professions of the former inhabitants of the vanished house.

The Sophienkirche

Continuing north along the street, past turn-of-the-century Neo-Baroque apartment buildings with shrapnel-pitted facades, brings you to the entrance gateway of the **Sophienkirche** on the right-hand side.

Dating back to 1712, this is one of the city's finest Baroque churches, and was the only central Berlin church to survive the war more or less undamaged. Its clear, simple lines come as a welcome change after the monumental Neoclassicism and fussy Gothic revivalism of so much of Berlin's architecture. The church's seventy-metre-high tiered tower is one of the area's most prominent landmarks and was added during the 1730s.

The ground on which the church was built was a gift from the Jewish community to the Protestant community, who at the time were slightly financially embarrassed. The church itself was paid for by Princess Sophie Louise, in order to provide a parish church for the neighbourhood, then an outlying area known as the *Spandauer Vorstadt*. The interior, in washed-out shades of green and grey, is a simple but pleasing affair, and you can't help but feel that this is one church where restoration could only have a detrimental effect. The one note of aesthetic exuberance is a pulpit with a crown-like canopy, set on a spiral pillar, which makes it look exactly like a chalice.

Sophienstrasse

Just beyond the Sophienkirche, a sharp turn to the right takes you into **Sophienstrasse**, first settled at the end of the seventeenth century and once the Spandauer Vorstadt's main street.

During the 1980s the street was extensively restored and its buildings now house a mix of retailers and arts and crafts workshops. In places, however, the restoration is only skin deep and the pastel frontages of the old apartment houses conceal squalid, crumbling courtyards. House no. 11 dates back to 1780, and the vaguely Gothic-looking **Handwerkervereinshaus** at Sophienstr. 18 used to be the headquarters of the old Craftsmens' Guild. Until the founding of the German Social Democrat Party (SPD), this had been the main focus of the Berlin workers' movement, and thereafter its headquarters continued to play an important role as a frequent venue for political meetings, including the first public gathering of the *Spartakusbund* (Spartacus League), the breakaway anti-war faction of the SPD that later evolved into the KPD (Communist Party of Germany) on November 14, 1918.

At Sophienstr. 21, a doorway leads to the **Sophie-Gips Höfen**, a recently renovated retail and office complex that houses *Barcomi's Delicatessen* and the *Speed Bar*, two trendy establishments representative of the current climate of the neighbourhood. Further down, just past the *Sophienclub* at no. 8 (see "Clubs and live venues" in Listings), is a narrow passageway leading into the **Häckesche Höfe**, a series of nine courtyards built between 1905 and 1907 to house businesses, flats and places of entertainment. Restored to their former Art Deco glory, the courtyards bustle with crowds visiting the several cafés, stores, and theatres within. It's one of the main draws of the neighbourhood, and is definitely worth a look-in. The last courtyard of all, decorated with blue mosaic tiles, is home to the **Chamaleon Varieté**, a venue at the forefront of the revival of the city's inter-war cabaret tradition (see "The arts" in Listings).

North and east of Sophienstrasse

North of Sophienstrasse are a couple of lesser-known attractions, worth seeking out if you've developed a taste for wandering the backstreets of central Berlin. East of Sophienstrasse, between Alte Schönhauser Strasse and Karl-Liebknecht-Strasse, is the traditional heart of the old Scheunenviertel quarter, and one-time centre of the city's scrap-iron and rag-and-bone trades.

The Garnisonsfriedhof and Volkspark am Weinberg

The leafy **Garnisonsfriedhof** on Kleine Rosenthaler Strasse is a neglected military cemetery dating from the eighteenth century, full of rusting cast-iron crosses with near-obliterated inscriptions commemorating the officers and men of the Prussian army. Also here is the rather grander tomb of Adolph von Lützow, a general who found fame during the Napoleonic Wars, contrasting sharply with the overgrown wooden crosses commemorating victims of the Battle of Berlin, hidden away in a far corner. Information about the history of the cemetery is available from the administration offices near the entrance, which also house a small exhibition. There's more inner-city greenery a few streets to the northwest in the **Volkspark am Weinberg**, a sloping park on the site of a former vineyard at the corner of Brunnenstrasse and Veteranenstrasse.

The Volksbühne and Karl-Liebknecht-Haus

On Rosa-Luxemburg-Platz the most prominent landmark is the **Volksbühne** theatre, built in 1913 with money raised by public subscription. Under the directorship of the ubiquitous Max Reinhardt, it became Berlin's people's theatre and, daringly for that time, put on plays by Hauptmann, Strindberg and Ibsen. Erwin Piscator continued the revolutionary tradition from 1924 to 1927, and immediately after the war in September 1945 a production of Lessing's plea for tolerance, *Nathan the Wise*, was put on here. The theatre was officially reopened in 1954 and became one of the ex-GDR capital's best theatres. These days it's still one of the most exciting and innovative theatres in the city, under director Frank Castorf (see "The arts" in Listings).

Nearby, at Weydingerstr. 14 and Kleine Alexanderstr. 28, is the **Karl-Liebknecht-Haus**, the former KPD central committee headquarters, which also housed the editorial offices of the Communist newspaper *Rote Fahne* ("Red Flag"). From the late 1920s onwards this was an important centre of resistance to the increasingly powerful Nazis: 100,000 pro-Communist workers demonstrated here on January 25, 1933, just a few days before Hitler came to power. After the Reichstag fire in February 1933 the KPD was broken up and its headquarters ransacked.

A couple of nearby streets, Almstadtstrasse and Mulackstrasse, though fairly unremarkable today, were important parts of the Scheunenviertel scene during its heyday. Almstadtstrasse, formerly known as Grenadierstrasse, became a magnet for Jewish migrants from eastern Europe and Russia at the end of the nineteenth century and it was here that a bustling street market grew up, echoing the *Schtetl* districts where Jewish traders did business in eastern European and Russian towns. During the inflationary period of 1923–4 the street gained notoriety as a black-market centre, with dealers trading illegally in everything from currency to precious stones. These days the main landmark is the **Galerie Weisser Elefant** at no. 11, an independent art gallery that's been here since before the *Wende*.

Mulackstrasse was home to a famous Scheunenviertel *Gaststätte*, the *Mulack-Ritz*, whose clientele encompassed pimps, prostitutes and small-time gangsters, as well as artists and actors. The establishment survived until the general closing down enforced by the GDR authorities in the 1960s, though the interior has been preserved in the Gründerzeitmuseum in Mahlsdorf (see p.174).

Chapter 7

South of the centre

D irectly south of the Tiergarten and the centre lie the *Bezirke*, or districts of **Schöneberg** and **Kreuzberg** respectively. Both are, in the main, residential: by day, Kreuzberg is the more unkempt and less immediately likeable of the two; Schöneberg is more middle class and less ethnically mixed. If you've taken pension accommodation or found a private room via the tourist office, chances are that you'll end up in one of these areas, and while not crammed with things to see, both have their attractions. **Nightlife** in both is excellent, with the bars and clubs around Schöneberg's Nollendorfplatz being the place where smart people (and particularly smart gay people) hang out; Kreuzberg's reputation

SOUTH OF THE CENTRE

NOLLENDORF PLATZ · LEIPZIGER STR. · **Gropius Bau** · Wittenberg Platz U-Bahn · Nollendorfplatz U-Bahn · POTSDAMER STR. · Gleisdreieck U-Bahn · **Anhalter Bahn** · WILHELM STR. · LINDENSTR. · ORANIEN STR. · **Berlin Museum** · Moritzplatz U-Bahn · STRASSE · MANTEUFFEL STR. · GITSCHINER STR. · PRINZEN STR. · STRASSE · KOTTBUSSER · WIENER STR. · **Deutsches Technikmuseum Berlin** · Kleistpark · K R E U Z B E R G · URBAN · GNEISENAUSTR. · Südstern U-Bahn · DAMM · PANNIERSTR. · LUTHERSTRASSE · Kleistpark U-Bahn · Yorkstr. U-Bahn · KATZBACHSTR. · **Victoria-park** · Platz der Luftbrücke U-Bahn · HASENHEIDE · KARL-MARX STRASSE · SONNENALLEE · GRUNEWALD · STRASSE · KOLONNENSTR. · DUDENSTR. · BOELCKESTRASSE · TEMPELHOFER · PLATZ DER LUFTBRÜCKE · Volkspark Hasenheide · HERMANNSTRASSE · **Rathaus Schöneburg** · HAUPT · SACHSENDAMM · MANTEUFFELSTR. · Tempelhof Airport · RHEINSTRASSE · GRAZER DAMM · ALBOIN STR. · SCHÖNE BGR. STR. · DAMM · GERMANIA-STRASSE · S C H Ö N E B E R G · OBERLANDSTR. · SILBERSTEIN · STRASSE · TEILESTRASSE · **SOUTH OF THE CENTRE** · N · 0 · 1 km as home to some of the city's more avant-garde nightspots still rings true, even if it's no longer at the cutting edge of Berlin's *Szene**.

Kreuzberg

The area directly south of Berlin's centre, bounded to the east by the River Spree and to the south by the *Bezirk* of Tempelhof, is **KREUZBERG**, famed for its large immigrant community and self-styled "alternative" inhabitants, nightlife and goings on. Effectively there are two Kreuzbergs: the **west**, the area bounded by Friedrichstrasse, Viktoriapark and Südstern, is a richer, fancier, more sedate area than its neighbour to the **east**, which is sometimes referred to as **SO 36** after its old postal code. East Kreuzberg is western Berlin's "happening" quarter, a mix of punks and old hippies, and the place to hang out and hit the raucous nightspots. Throughout the 1970s and 1980s, this was where the youth of the Federal Republic came to get involved in alternative politics and (until the loophole was abolished; see box opposite) avoid national service. Though there's precious little in the way of things to see, next to Prenzlauer Berg (see p.156) it's the city's liveliest neighbourhood.

West Kreuzberg

First the west. It's only a short walk south, cutting down Stresemannstrasse, from the Gropius-Bau (see p.77) to the remains of the **Anhalter Bahnhof**, a sad reminder of misguided civic action that some would term civic vandalism. The Anhalter Bahnhof was once one of the city's (and Europe's) great rail termini, forming Berlin's gateway to the south. Completed in 1870, it received only mild damage during World War II and was left roofless but substantial in 1945. Despite attempts to preserve it as a future museum building, it was blown up in 1952 – essentially because someone had put in a good offer for the bricks. Now only a fragment of the facade stands, giving a hint at past glories. The patch of land that the station once covered is today a park, and now sports the tents of the *Tempodrom*, a popular venue for concerts of touring bands and world music (see "Clubs and live venues" in Listings).

The S-Bahn

If you look to one side of the Anhalter Bahnhof, you'll see a blunt and featureless building, a fortified bunker-storehouse built during the war and one of a handful of Nazi buildings that remain in the city. The National Socialists also excavated the stretch of the **S-Bahn**, that runs underground south of the Anhalter Bahnhof and heads north below

---

* The term *Szene* ("the scene") is commonly used to refer to the happening places of the moment, and to those people who see themselves as the movers and shakers in current trends and fashions.

How Berliners avoided national service

Because of Berlin's erstwhile position as an "occupied" city, it was the only place in Germany where permanent residence meant that the compulsory eighteen months' **national service**, which all males between the ages of 18 and 32 are obliged to do, could be avoided. Throughout the 1960s, 1970s and 1980s, especially when anti-war feelings were running high, the city thus became a haven for those who refused to do their service. With unification, the anomaly was abolished – and many of those who thought they'd escaped doing their stint found themselves called up.

Potsdamer Platz to Bahnhof Friedrichstrasse. It was built in 1935 and supposed to be ready in time for the 1936 Olympics; however, the furious pace at which it was excavated meant that safety measures were skimped: when part of the tunnel between Potsdamer Platz and the Brandenburg Gate collapsed, nineteen workers were killed, and the line was only finally completed in 1939. The tunnel passes under the River Spree, the Landwehrkanal and the U-Bahn line #2, which, during the war, sheltered Berliners from bombing raids. When on May 2, 1945, it was thought that the Soviets were preparing to use the S- and U-Bahn systems to send shock troops directly into the city centre, the Nazis blew up the bulkheads where the tunnel passes under the Landwehrkanal, flooding the tunnel and the local U-Bahn system. As a result, many civilians sheltering in the U-Bahn died horrific deaths, drowning in the choking muddy waters that surged through the tunnels.

Across the road from the ruins of the Anhalter Bahnhof, the **Deutschlandhaus**, Stresemannstr. 90 (Mon–Fri 9am–7pm, Sat & Sun 2–6pm; free; bus #129, #341) does its patriotic bit for the "lost" Germany, with exhibits on east German culture and towns now in Poland that were once German.

The Berlin Museum

A brisk twenty-minute walk east from here, through streets levelled during wartime bombing, takes you to another Kreuzberg high spot, the **Berlin Museum** at Lindenstr. 14, which attempts to show the history and development of the city through paintings, prints and crafts. Currently, though, it's closed, awaiting the opening of a major extension that will hold all of the **Jewish Museum** for the first time. Of 60,000 Jews remaining in the city in 1939, 50,000 died in the concentration camps, and the museum here, scheduled for opening in 1999, is intended to be a memorial as much as a collection of artefacts from everyday Jewish life in Berlin.

The Deutsches Technikmuseum Berlin

An easier approach to the area is to catch the U-Bahn to Möckernbrücke station on line #1 or #7, an enjoyable above-ground ride through old warehouses and towering postwar redevelopment.

Kreuzberg

Walking south from the station, over the Landwehrkanal and turning right along Tempelhofer Ufer, you pass one of the decaying but still ornate **public toilets** erected in the early years of this century: gents can pop in for a Bismarckian moment of relief. Characteristically dark green in colour, these conveniences were usually erected in places affording easy access to the city's canals, in a fairly primitive attempt at sanitation. A little further on, at Trebbiner Str. 9, is the **Deutsches Technikmuseum Berlin** (German Technology Museum of Berlin; Tues–Fri 9am–5.30pm, Sat & Sun 10am-6pm; DM5, concessions DM2; U-Bahn Möckernbrücke, bus #129 and #248), one of the city's most entertaining museums and a children's and button-pushers' delight. The technology section has plenty of experiments, antiquated machinery and computers to play with, alongside some elegant old cars and planes. The transport museum, a superb collection of ancient steam trains and carriages, is even more impressive; the polished behemoths have been brought to rest in what was once a workshop of the old Anhalter Bahnhof.

The Deutsches Technikmuseum Berlin will absorb children's interest for hours – see "Children's Activities" in Listings for more ideas.

The Viktoriapark and around

Reaching the **Viktoriapark** (the "Kreuzberg", as it's popularly known) from here means a half-hour's walk, retracing your steps to the U-Bahn and heading south down Grossbeerenstrasse. On the slopes of a hill, the park is one of the city's most likeable, a relaxed ramble of trees and green space with a pretty brook running down the middle. To one side is the *Golgotha Café* and disco (see "Cafés and bars" in Listings), packed on summer evenings; on another side is what claims to be Germany's northernmost vineyard; and atop the hill is the **Cross** (though it's more of a Neoclassical spire) from which Kreuzberg gets its name, designed by Schinkel to commemorate the Napoleonic Wars. The view is a good one, too, made all the more pleasant by the wafting aromas from the Schultheiss brewery on the southern slopes.

The well-restored streets around the hill, along with Yorckstrasse to the north, have a scattering of cafés, their tone and clientele reflecting the residents of the neighbourhood, who are on the whole slightly older than those of East Kreuzberg. Between Hagelbergerstrasse and Yorckstrasse, the **Riehmer's Hofgarten** is an impressive turn-of-the-century bourgeois residential building, though the steel and glass *Yorck Cinema* doesn't fit well in the ensemble.

Chamissoplatz also has one of Berlin's few remaining Wihelmine pissoirs; see above for a description.

East of the park, the area around **Bergmannstrasse**, filled with Trödelläden (junk shops, though with a few antiques), is worth a wander, as is **Chamissoplatz** for its well-preserved, tidily balconied nineteenth-century houses and watertower.

These buildings are among the few that housed working-class families at the end of the last century to have survived in what was West Berlin: restoring them to their original design has been painstaking, and though the area is now thoroughly gentrified, there's no denying that it's a pleasant place to live. About halfway along Bergmannstrasse the **Marheineke market hall** has a little of everything, including some real bargains amid the dross. Keep walking and you reach the eighteenth- and nineteenth-century **cemeteries** along the eastern stretches of Bergmannstrasse. They're full of forgotten Berlin worthies, the only name of any real note being Gustav Stresemann, Chancellor and Foreign Minister in the Weimar years – he's in Luisenstädtischen Kirchhof, the most southeasterly of the four cemeteries here.

Kreuzberg

Just to the west, intersecting Bergmannstrasse, is Mehringdamm, location of the Schwules Museum (Gay Museum) at Mehringdamm 61: see p.35.

Tempelhof Airport

South and east of the Viktoriapark, the housing fades away to the flatlands containing **Tempelhof Airport** (not actually in Kreuzberg but in the neighbouring *Bezirk* of Tempelhof). The airport was built in the 1920s and was once Germany's largest; the eagles that decorate the buildings actually predate the Nazis, which may explain their survival. A huge bronze eagle that surmounted the building was removed in the 1960s, ostensibly to make way for a radar installation (the eagle's head can still be seen at the entrance to the airport), but

---

The Berlin Blockade (1948–49)

The **Berlin Blockade** was the result of an escalation in tensions between East and West in the late 1940s. These came to a head when the Western zone introduced the Deutschmark as currency in June 1948: the Soviets demanded that their own Ostmark be accepted as Berlin's currency, a move that was rejected by the city's parliament. Moscow's answer to this was an attempt to bring West Berlin to its knees by severing all road and rail links to the Western zones and cutting off the power provided by plants on the Eastern side. West Berlin had to "import" almost all of its food and fuel: when the Soviets pulled the plugs, the city had only a month's supply of food and ten days' of coal.

Rather than use military force, it was decided to try and supply the city by air: the Soviets, it was gambled, would not dare risk an international incident – possibly even war – by shooting down Western aircraft. The airlift thus began on June 26, 1948, and at its height nine months later, planes were landing or taking off every thirty seconds and bringing 8000 tons of supplies to the city each day.

The Soviets called off the Blockade in May 1949, but they had been defeated in more ways than one. For the occupying British and American forces, the propaganda value was enormous: aircrews who a few years previously had been dropping bombs on the city now provided its life line. Photographs of the "candy bomber" – a USAF captain who dropped chocolate bars and sweets from his plane on small parachutes for the city's children – went around the world. No longer were the occupiers seen as enemies, but rather as allies against the Soviet threat. The Blockade considerably eased the birth pangs of the Federal Republic, which took place the same year.

you can't help thinking that its removal probably had more to do with its being an ugly reminder of the Nazi past. Until recently the airport was used only for visiting dignitaries and the military, but today it handles only a light load of domestic flights. Sadly, the airport is scheduled to close in a few years' time; what will become of the land is a matter for heated debate.

It was to Tempelhof that the Allies flew in supplies to beat the **Berlin Blockade** of 1948–49 (see box on previous page) – an act that was to strengthen anti-Soviet feeling among West Berliners and increase the popularity of the occupying forces. At the height of the airlift a plane landed here every minute and the **Luftbrückendenkmal**, a memorial at the entrance to the airport, commemorates the seventy airmen and eight ground crew who died in crashes while attempting to land. The memorial represents the three air corridors used, and forms half of a bridge: the other half, "joined by air", is in Frankfurt. Inside the airport a small exhibition shows photographs of its building and the Blockade – mostly publicity shots of gleaming USAF pilots and scruffy kids, with little on the role of Tempelhof in the war years.

Other than the airport there's little to detain you here. The **Polizeihistorische Sammlung** at Platz der Luftbrücke 6 (Police History Collection; Mon–Wed 9.30am–11.30am & 1–3pm, Thurs & Fri by appointment; free; U-Bahn Platz der Luftbrücke, bus #104, #119, #184 or #341) is worth dipping into for its nineteenth-century uniforms and illustrations intended to help police determine "typical criminal types".

East Kreuzberg: "SO 36"

In the 1830s, Berlin's industries started recruiting peasants from the outlying countryside to work in their factories and machine shops. It was to the small village of Kreuzberg that many came, to work in the east of the city and live in buildings that were thrown up by speculators as low-rent accommodation. Kreuzberg was thus established as a solidly working-class area and, in time, a suburb of Greater Berlin. Siemens, the electrical engineering giant, began life in one of Kreuzberg's rear courtyards. In the 1930s local trade unionists and workers fought street battles with the Nazis, and during the war it was one of the very few areas to avoid total destruction, and among the quickest to revive in the 1950s. When the Wall was built in 1961, things changed: Kreuzberg became an eastern outpost of West Berlin, severed from its natural hinterland in the East. Families moved out, houses were boarded up, and Kreuzberg began to die. At the same time, the city, deprived of cheap East Berlin labour to work in its factories, began to look further afield for the migratory workers who have come to be known as *Gastarbeiter*. Turks began to move to the city in large numbers, in time bringing their families and Islamic customs; few landlords welcomed the new workers, who gradually began to found a community in the area with the cheapest rentable property: Kreuzberg.

Throughout the 1960s and 1970s, Kreuzberg developed as West Berlin's Turkish enclave, with other *Gastarbeiter* from Yugoslavia, Greece, Spain and Italy joining them. Along, too, came the radicals, students and dropouts of the 1968 generation – attracted to the city because of the national service loophole (see box on p.123), and to Kreuzberg because it offered vast potential for **squatting**. The ruling that pre-1950s-built apartments were subject to rent restrictions meant that speculators often allowed them to fall into disrepair so that they could erect new buildings and charge whatever rent they pleased: squatters who maintained and developed these old apartments thus saved some of the city's old architecture.

In the 1980s Kreuzberg became the focus and point of reference for squatters throughout the Federal Republic, and the Social Democratic city government adopted a liberal approach to them, offering subsidies to well-organized squats and giving them some security of tenure. Projects like the **Mehringhof**, an adult education centre and home for alternative industries and arts (actually just in west Kreuzberg at Gneisenaustr. 2), flourished.

All went well until the Christian Democrats took over the city. Using arguments over the role of city property – many of the buildings here are owned by the government – and the growing problems of crime and drug dealing, the right-wing Minister of the Interior ordered the riot police to enter Kreuzberg and forcibly close down the squats. There were riots in the streets, demonstrations all over the city, and intense political protest, which reached its peak with the death of a fifteen-year-old boy who was hit by a bus during a demonstration. Activists called a strike and the city government had to back down.

Over the last half decade, the squatter movement has died a natural death. The city government occasionally clears out a building, but generally the squatters themselves haved moved on or up of their own volition, and less than a handful of squats remains. The Turks and other immigrant communities are thriving; and slowly, though perhaps inevitably, signs of gentrification are appearing, as astute Berliners (with an eye to their political profiles) move to the area. To say you lived in Kreuzberg was, until the Wall came down, a way of making a statement. At one time, if you wanted to gauge the political temperature of West Berlin, you had only to see what was happening on the streets here. In 1988, Kreuzberg constituted enough of a threat for the authorities to seal off the area during the annual conference of the IMF. Despite the provocation, things – perhaps surprisingly – remained calm. With the end of the Wall only the occasional uprising still occurs, usually on or around May Day, and the atmosphere is more subdued and less political than it was pre-*Wende*. It remains to be seen to what extent activists here will again turn their attention away from local matters towards national issues.

You don't, however, need any interest in revolution or city machinations to enjoy Kreuzberg. The **nightlife** here is among the city's wildest (see "Clubs and live venues" in Listings), and it's an enjoyable area to wander through by day, stopping off at one of the innumerable Turkish snack bars for a kebab, breakfasting on a 9am vodka-and-beer special at a café (see "Cafés and bars" in Listings), or just taking in the feel of the place – which is much like an Istanbul market in an eastern bloc housing development.

Around Oranienstrasse

Catching U-Bahn line #1 (unkindly named the "Istanbul Express" in this stretch) to **Kottbusser Tor** or Schlesisches Tor stations is a good introduction to eastern Kreuzberg.

The area around Kottbusser Tor is typical: a scruffy, earthy shambles of Turkish street vendors and cafés, the air filled with the aromas of southeast European cooking. Cutting through Dresdener Strasse, past the *Babylon Cinema* (a venue, incidentally, that often shows films in English; see "The arts" in Listings), takes you to Kreuzberg's main strip, **Oranienstrasse**, which from Moritzplatz east is lined with café-bars, art galleries and clothes shops, and in a way forms an "alternative" Kurfürstendamm.

South of Kottbusser Tor U-Bahn, it's less than ten minutes' walk down Kottbusser Damm to the Landwehrkanal. Turning left here and walking along Paul-Lincke-Ufer in an eastward direction elicits a peculiar mix of emotions, with the beauty of the natural surroundings long muted by the derelict, deserted factories of eastern Berlin on the other side of the Wall – the sense of despondency that the separation brought is only slowly dissipating. One thing that shakes off the blues is the food **market** that brings Maybachufer, on the opposite side of the canal, alive in a myriad of colours and a babble of noise and excitement on Tuesday and Friday afternoons.

Around the Schlesisches Tor

Schlesisches Tor is only ten minutes' walk, or a few stops away from Treptower Park and the remarkable memorial to Soviet troops killed in the Battle of Berlin – see p.167 for details.

Around the **Schlesisches Tor** (the "Silesian Gate", which gave the station its name, was the former entrance to the city for immigrants from Silesia) things are more residential, although for years the nearness of the Wall heightened the tension of the area. The River Spree here was in GDR territory, a strange situation for those residents of West Berlin whose apartments backed directly on to it. In the midst of the desolate buildings close by, a post-modernist construction swathed in grey and designed by the Portuguese architect Alvaro Siza bears the emblem – courtesy of the local punks – "Bonjour Tristesse". At night the areas around both the Schlesisches Tor and the Kottbusser Tor seem a little sharper, darkness giving them an edge of danger and a sense of concealed, forbidden pleasures.

The Landwehrkanal runs south of Oranienstrasse, and below that the broad path of Hasenheide-Gneisenaustrasse, marking the transition from east to west Kreuzberg. Around the Südstern (which has a convenient U-Bahn station) is another clutch of café-bars, and Gneisenaustrasse has some good restaurants; but the flavour of east Kreuzberg has gone, and things feel (and are) a lot tamer.

Schöneberg

Like Kreuzberg, **SCHÖNEBERG** was once a separate suburb, one that was swallowed up by Greater Berlin as the city expanded in the late eighteenth and nineteenth centuries. Blown to pieces during the war, it's now a mostly middle-class residential area, stretching below the Tiergarten and sandwiched between Kreuzberg to the east and Wilmersdorf to the west. Things to see are few, but what is here is both fascinating and moving.

The Bauhaus Archive

Although Schöneberg officially begins south of Kurfürstenstrasse, on the edge of the Tiergarten at Klingelhöferstr. 14 is the **Bauhaus**

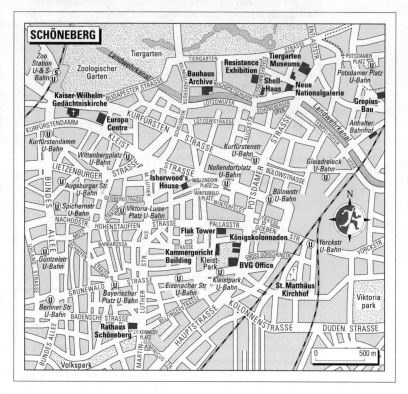

Schöneberg **Archive** (daily except Tues 10am–5pm; DM5, concessions DM2.50; bus #129 to Lützowplatz). The Bauhaus school of design, crafts and architecture was founded in 1919 in Weimar by Walter Gropius. It moved to Dessau in 1925 and then to Berlin, to be closed by the Nazis in 1933. The influence of Bauhaus has been tremendous, and you do get some idea of this from the small collection here. Marcel Breuer's seminal chair is still (with minor variations) in production today, and former Bauhaus director Mies van

---

The Bauhaus

Bauhaus, a German word whose literal meaning is "building-house", has become a generic term for the aesthetically functional design style that grew out of the art and design philosophy developed at the Dessau school. The origins of the Bauhaus movement lie in the *Novembergruppe*, a grouping of artists founded in 1918 by the Expressionist painter Max Pechstein with the aim of utilizing art for revolutionary purposes. Members included Bertolt Brecht and Kurt Weill, Emil Nolde, Eric Mendelssohn and the architect **Walter Gropius**. In 1919 Gropius was invited by the new republican government of Germany to oversee the amalgamation of the School of Arts and Crafts and the Academy of Fine Arts in Weimar into the *Staatliche Bauhaus Weimar*. It was hoped that this new institution would break down the barriers between art and craft, creating a new form of applied art. It attracted over two hundred students who studied typography, furniture design, ceramics, wood-, glass- and metal-working under exponents like Paul Klee, Wassily Kandinsky and Lazlo Moholy-Nagy.

Financial problems and opposition from the conservative administration in Weimar eventually forced Gropius to relocate to Dessau, chosen after the town authorities offered financial and material support and because it was home to a number of modern industrial concerns, notably an aeroplane factory and a chemical works. Dessau's *Bauhausgebäude*, designed by Gropius and inaugurated on December 4, 1926, is one of the classic buildings of modern times – a forerunner of architectural styles that would not come into their own until the 1950s and 1960s.

Towards the end of the 1920s the staff and students of the Bauhaus school became increasingly embroiled in the political battles of the time. As a result, Gropius was pressurized into resigning by the authorities and replaced by the Swiss architect Hannes Meyer. He, in turn, was dismissed in 1930 because of the increasingly left-wing orientation of the school. His successor **Ludwig Mies van der Rohe** tried to establish an apolitical atmosphere, but throughout the early 1930s Nazi members of Dessau town council called for an end to subsidies for the Bauhaus. Their efforts finally succeeded in the summer of 1932, forcing the school to close down. The Bauhaus relocated to the more liberal atmosphere of Berlin, setting themselves up in a disused telephone factory in Birkbuschstrasse, in the Steglitz district. However, after the Nazis came to power, police harassment reached such a pitch that on July 20, 1933, van der Rohe took the decision to shut up shop for good. He and many of his staff and students subsequently went into exile in the United States.

der Rohe's designs and models for buildings show how the modernist Bauhaus style has changed the face of today's cities. There's work, too, by Kandinsky, Moholy-Nagy, Schlemmer and Klee, all of whom worked at the Bauhaus. The building, incidentally, was designed by Gropius himself.

The diplomatic district

East of the Archive, Reichspietschufer, which in the late 1930s was the centre of Berlin's **diplomatic district**, follows the leafy course of the Landwehrkanal towards the Neue Nationalgalerie. The next left turn off Reichspietschufer, **Stauffenbergstrasse**, takes its name from one of the instigators of the July Bomb Plot to assassinate Hitler, **Count Claus Schenk von Stauffenberg**. Stauffenberg (see overleaf) was chief of staff at the German Army Office that once stood on this street, formerly known as Bendlerstrasse; today, the site of the building where he worked and died is occupied by the permanent exhibition **Resistance to National Socialism**, Stauffenbergstr. 13–14 (Mon–Fri 9am–6pm, Sat & Sun 9am–1pm; free; bus #129), a well-mounted collection of photos and documents covering the surprisingly wide range of groups opposed to the Third Reich. This absorbing exhibition is a little off the beaten track, though translation of the main exhibits makes it highly accessible.

The Shell-Haus

On the corner of Reichspietschufer and Stauffenbergstrasse, the **Shell-Haus** – now known as the Bewag building – is one of Berlin's great edifices that substantially survived World War II. A procession of tiered levels, this office building was designed by Emil Fahrenkamp in 1931 and was a leading piece of modernist architecture. Have a look at James Stirling's blue and pink monstrosity of a residential building, just to the east, if you're in any doubt about the Shell-Haus's credentials.

Down Potsdamer Strasse

Potsdamer Strasse itself leads south into Schöneberg proper, quickly becoming a broad, untidy strip of Turkish cafés, restaurants and wholesalers. By night the junction of Potsdamer Strasse and Kurfürstenstrasse is a gathering place for the city's heroin addicts and dealers: conspiratorial little groups form and quickly disperse, deals having been done. It's fairly unpleasant, but not perhaps as bad as the prostitution that goes on further along Kurfürstenstrasse. Since unification prostitution here has escalated enormously, with women from the former GDR finding it the easiest (in some cases the only) way of making money. Many of the women are also drug addicts, which accounts for the dealing on the street corner.

Schöneberg

The July Bomb Plot

The **July Bomb Plot** that took place in the summer of 1944 at Hitler's Polish HQ, the "Wolf's Lair" in Rastenburg, was the assassination attempt that came closest to success. The plot, led by **Count Claus Schenk von Stauffenberg**, an aristocratic officer and member of the General Staff, had gained the support of several high-ranking members of the German army. Sickened by atrocities on the eastern front, and rapidly realizing that the Wehrmacht was fighting a war that could not possibly be won, von Stauffenberg and his fellow conspirators decided to kill the Führer, seize control of army headquarters on Bendlerstrasse and sue for peace with the Allies. Germany was on the precipice of total destruction by the Allies: only such a desperate act, reasoned the plotters, could save the Fatherland.

On July 20, Stauffenberg was summoned to the Wolf's Lair to brief Hitler on troop movements on the eastern front. In his briefcase was a small bomb, packed with high explosive: once triggered, it would explode in under ten minutes. As Stauffenberg approached the specially built conference hut, he triggered the device. Taking his place a few feet from Hitler, Stauffenberg positioned the briefcase under the table, leaning it against one of the table's stout legs, no more than six feet away from the Führer. Five minutes before the bomb exploded, the Count quietly slipped from the room unnoticed by the generals and advisers, who were absorbed in listening to a report on the central Russian front. One of the officers moved closer to the table to get a better look at the campaign maps and, finding the briefcase in the way of his feet under the table, picked it up and moved it to the other side of the table leg. Now, the very solid support of the table leg lay between the briefcase and Hitler.

At 12.42pm the bomb went off. Stauffenberg, watching the hut from a few hundred yards away, was shocked by the force of the explosion. It was, he said, as if the hut had been hit by a 155mm shell; there was no doubt that the Führer, along with everyone else in the room, was dead.

Stauffenberg hurried off to a waiting plane and made his way to Berlin to join the other conspirators. Meanwhile, back in the wreckage of the conference hut, Hitler and the survivors staggered out into the daylight: four people had been killed or were dying from their wounds, including Colonel Brandt, who had moved Stauffenberg's briefcase and thus unwittingly saved the Führer's life. Hitler himself, despite being badly shaken, suffered no more than a perforated eardrum and minor injuries. After being attended to, he prepared himself for a meeting with Mussolini later that afternoon.

It quickly became apparent what had happened, and the hunt for Stauffenberg was on. Hitler issued orders to the SS in Berlin to summarily execute anyone who was slightly suspect, and dispatched Himmler to the city to quell the rebellion.

A little further south on Potsdamer Strasse is the *Begine* café (no. 139) – part of a cluster of women's groups here and about the only thing on the street to which even money can't buy access for men.

The Sportpalast

Continuing south, it's worth turning off Potsdamer Strasse at Pallasstrasse and heading west for a block. This was the site of the

Back in the military Supreme Command headquarters in Bendlerstrasse, the conspiracy was in chaos. Word reached Stauffenberg and the two main army conspirators, generals Beck and Witzleben, that the Führer was still alive. They had already lost hours of essential time by failing to issue the carefully planned order to mobilize their sympathizers in the city and elsewhere, and had even failed to carry out the obvious precaution of severing all communications out of the city. After a few hours of tragicomic scenes as the conspirators tried to persuade high-ranking officials to join them, the Bendlerstrasse HQ was surrounded by SS troops, and it was announced that the Führer would broadcast to the nation later that evening. The coup was over.

The conspirators were gathered together, given paper to write farewell messages to their wives, taken to the courtyard of the HQ and, under the orders of one General Fromm, shot by firing squad. Stauffenberg's last words were "Long live our sacred Germany!"

Fromm had known about the plot almost from the beginning, but had refused to join it. By executing the leaders he hoped to save his own skin – and, it must be added, save them from the torturers of the SS.

Hitler's ruthless revenge on the conspirators was without parallel even in the bloody annals of the Third Reich. All the colleagues, friends and immediate relatives of Stauffenberg and the other conspirators were rounded up, tortured and taken before the "People's Court" (the building where the court convened, the Kammergericht building, still stands – see below), where they were humiliated and given more or less automatic death sentences, most of which were brutally carried out at **Plötzensee prison** to the northwest of the city centre (see p.144). Many of those executed knew nothing of the plot and were found guilty merely by association. As the bloodlust grew, the Nazi party used the plot as a pretext for settling old scores, and eradicated anyone who had the slightest hint of anything less than total dedication to the Führer. General Fromm, who had ordered the execution of the Bendlerstrasse conspirators, was among those tried, found guilty of cowardice and shot by firing squad. Those whose names were blurted under torture were quickly arrested, the most notable being Field Marshal Rommel, who, because of his popularity, was given the choice of a trial in the People's Court – or suicide and a state funeral.

The July Bomb Plot caused the deaths of at least five thousand people, including some of Germany's most brilliant military thinkers and almost all of those who would have been best qualified to run the postwar German government. Within six months the country lay in ruins as the Allies advanced; had events at Rastenburg been only a little different, the entire course of the war – and European history – would have been altered incalculably.

famed **Sportpalast**, a sports centre that was the main venue for Nazi rallies in the 1930s. Hitler delivered some of his most famous speeches in the Sportpalast: most of the old newsreels showing the Führer working himself up into an oratorical fever were filmed here, and it was also the place where Goebbels asked the German people if they wanted "total war" – the affirmative reply failing to comprehend the force of destruction that would be unleashed on the city.

The Sportpalast was demolished in 1974 to make way for the huge and undistinguished apartment building that straddles the road. Just before this, on the south side of the road, is one of the city's remaining **flak towers**. Several of these were built to defend the city from Allied raids: the largest, the Tiergarten tower, was severely damaged by bombing (the raid also destroyed the best of the city's collection of Egyptian ceramics, which had been stored in the tower for safekeeping). After the war, the Pallasstrasse tower proved impervious to demolition attempts, and the lower levels, which had been air-raid shelters, were used by NATO troops to store food and provisions in case of a Soviet invasion. Ironically, from the Cold War years until recently, supplies that were reaching the end of their shelf-life were sold off – usually on the cheap to the Soviet Union.

Around the Kleistpark

South of Pallasstrasse is the **Kleistpark**, (summer 7am–8pm; winter 7am–4pm), which, fronted by the **Königskolonnaden**, a colonnade from 1780 that originally stood on Alexanderplatz gives this stretch of Potsdamer Strasse a touch of dignity: on a misty morning you might be fooled into thinking you were in Paris. The **Kammergericht building** behind the park was once the Supreme Court of Justice. Here the Nazi courts under the infamous Judge Freisler held the "People's Court" following the July Bomb Plot, as well as show trials of their political opponents, a prelude to the inevitable executions – which often took place in Plötzensee prison (see p.144). Freisler met his unlamented end here in the final few weeks of the war: on his way from the courtroom a bomb from an American aircraft fell on the building, dislodging a beam that crushed Freisler's skull. Today much restored, only 30 of the building's 486 rooms are in use, formerly as a meeting place of the Allied Air Control, which oversaw safety in the air corridors leading to the city. Until the meetings came to an end with unification, a place was always set for Soviet representatives – even though they ceased to attend meetings in 1948. The building is now used by NATO.

Over Potsdamer Strasse from the Kleistpark, at the end of Grossgörschenstrasse, lies the **Sankt-Matthäus-Kirchhof**, a dark, brick-built church whose graveyard contains the bodies of the Brothers Grimm, united in death as they were in copyright. The bodies of Stauffenberg and his co-conspirators were also buried here following the July Bomb Plot, only to be exhumed a few days later and burned by Nazi thugs.

Around Nollendorfplatz

Back in the middle of Potsdamer Strasse, it's a short detour west along Bulow Strasse to **Nollendorfplatz**. In the Weimar Berlin of the 1920s and early 1930s, Nollendorfplatz was the centre of the city's large **gay and lesbian community**. Even by contemporary standards, Berlin's gay scene in those days was prodigious: there were around forty gay bars on and near this square alone, and gay life in the city was open, fashionable and well organized, with its own newspapers, community associations and art. The city's theatres were filled with plays exploring gay themes, homosexuality in the Prussian army was little short of institutionalized, and gay bars, nightclubs and brothels proudly advertised their attractions – there were even gay working men's clubs. All this happened at a time when the rest of Europe was smothered under a welter of homophobia and repression, when to be "discovered" as a homosexual or lesbian meant total social ostracism. Under the Third Reich, homosexuality was quickly and brutally outlawed: gays and lesbians were rounded up and taken to concentration camps, branded for their "perversion" by being forced to wear (respectively) pink or black triangles. (The black triangle represented "antisocial" offenders: in an attempt to ignore the existence of lesbianism, lesbians were arrested on pretexts such as swearing at the Führer's name. As homosexuality was, at the time, still illegal in Allied countries, no Nazis were tried for crimes against gays or lesbians at Nürnberg.) A red granite plaque in the shape of a triangle at Nollendorfplatz U-Bahn station commemorates the thousands of men and women who were murdered in the camps. Today, the area around Nollendorfplatz remains the focus of western Berlin's gay nightlife and especially its bars (see "Gay Cafés and bars" in Listings).

As well as its first-rate nightlife, Nollendorfplatz holds a couple of offbeat attractions by day. Walk past the proto-Deco **Metropol disco** (see "Clubs and live venues" in Listings), and down Maassenstrasse, which leads on to Nollendorfstrasse, where at no. 17 stands the building in which **Christopher Isherwood** lived during his years in prewar Berlin, a time that was to be elegantly recounted in perhaps the most famous collection of stories about the city ever written – *Goodbye to Berlin*:

> *From my window, the deep solemn massive street. Cellar shops where lamps burn all day, under the shadow of top-heavy balconied façades, dirty plaster frontages embossed with scroll work and heraldic devices. The whole district is like this: street leading into street of houses like shabby monumental safes crammed with the tarnished valuables and secondhand furniture of a bankrupt middle class.*

Schöneberg has since been reborn as a fancy, even chic neighbourhood; the would-be Isherwoods of the moment hang out in East Kreuzberg, or Prenzlauer Berg (see p.156) in eastern Berlin. At night, this part of Schöneberg, particularly the area around **Winterfeldtplatz**, is good for eating and especially drinking: tidily bohemian, less sniffy than Savignyplatz (see p.50), and much more middle-of-the-road than East Kreuzberg. On Wednesday and

Schöneberg

Saturday mornings the square holds an excellent **market** – see "Shopping" in Listings.

West of Nollendorfplatz, the **Museum für Post und Kommunikation** at An der Urania 15 (Tues–Sun 9am–5pm; U-Bahn Nollendorfplatz, bus #100, #119, #129 or #219), takes as its less than fascinating theme the history of the Prussian post office, with a collection of stamps new and old and a description of the Berlin postal system. One for raving philatelists only.

Rathaus Schöneberg

Schöneberg's most famous attraction actually has the least to see: the **Rathaus Schöneberg** on Martin-Luther-Strasse, the penultimate stop on U-Bahn line #4. Built just before World War I, the Rathaus became the seat of the West Berlin parliament and senate after the last war, and it was outside here in 1963 that **John F. Kennedy** made his celebrated speech on the Cold War political situation, just a few months after the Cuban missile crisis:

> *There are many people in the world who really don't understand, or say they don't, what is the great issue between the free world and the Communist world. Let them come to Berlin. There are some who say that Communism is the wave of the future. Let them come to Berlin. And there are some who say in Europe and elsewhere we can work with the Communists. Let them come to Berlin. And there are even a few who say it is true that Communism is an evil system, but it permits us to make economic progress. Lässt sie nach Berlin kommen. Let them come to Berlin . . . All free men, wherever they may live, are citizens of Berlin, and, therefore, as a free man, I take pride in the words "Ich bin ein Berliner".*

Rousing stuff. But what the president hadn't realized as he read from his phonetically written text was that he had actually said "I am a small doughnut", since *Berliner* is the local name for jam doughnuts. So popular has this subtext become that it's possible to buy little plastic doughnuts bearing the historic words. The day after Kennedy was assassinated, the square in front of the Rathaus was given his name – a move apparently instigated by the city's students, among whom the president was highly popular.

If you've time and interest you can climb the Rathaus tower (daily 10am–5pm) and see the replica **Liberty bell** donated to the city by the US in 1950, though it's more pleasant, and certainly less strenuous, to take a stroll in the small **Volkspark**, a thin ribbon of greenery that runs southwest from here.

Chapter 8

West of the centre

W hile there's more than enough to detain you in Berlin's centre, the **western suburbs** hold a disparate group of attractions of considerable cultural and historical interest. **Schloss Charlottenburg** is the prettiest point here – Berlin's pocket Versailles – with fine collections of paintings inside and wanderable gardens out. The most important target, though, is the **Dahlem museum complex**: a huge conglomeration of collections with something to please almost everyone. The **Olympic Stadium** and **Plötzensee Prison Memorial** are strong reminders of the 1930s and wartime Berlin.

Further west still are the lakes and woodlands of the **Grunewald** – the city's very own eco-friendly play pen. Once you're out of the claustrophobic city, the verdant **countryside** and **lakes** come as a surprise, a reminder of Berlin's position in Mitteleuropa – and of the fact that one-third of the city is greenery and parkland. Thanks to the efficient U- and S-Bahn systems it's possible to reach Berlin's western edges in under three-quarters of an hour, making the contrast between inner-city excitement and rural relaxation all the stronger.

Charlottenburg: the Schloss and museums

The district of **CHARLOTTENBURG** stretches north and west of the centre of town, reaching as far south as the forests of the Grunewald. The most significant attraction here, one that needs half a day at least to cover, is the **Schloss Charlottenburg and museum complex** on Spandauer Damm; while you can round off a day here with a visit to one of the other museums across the way, notably the **Ägyptisches Museum**. If, however, museums aren't to your taste, there are few better ways to idle away a morning in Berlin, or take a break from sightseeing, than to explore the surrounding **Schloss Gardens**. Unfortunately, there's no U-Bahn station near the Schloss; the near-

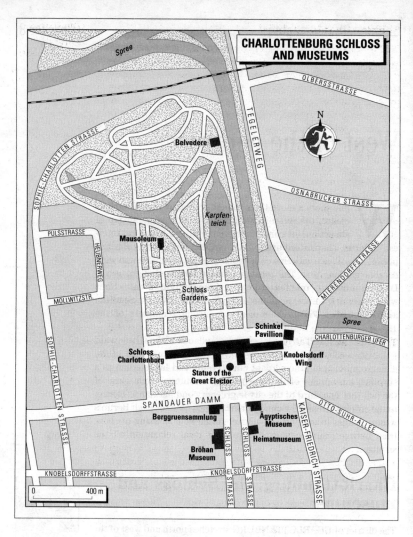

CHARLOTTENBURG SCHLOSS AND MUSEUMS

Spree

OLBERSSTRASSE

TEGELERWEG

N

SOPHIE-CHARLOTTEN STRASSE

Belvedere

OSNABRUCKER STRASSE

PULSSTRASSE

HEUNERWEG

*Karpfen-
teich*

Mausoleum

MIERENDORFFSTRASSE

MOLLWITZSTR.

Schloss
Gardens

Spree

Schinkel
Pavillion

CHARLOTTENBURGER UFER

SOPHIE-CHARLOTTEN STRASSE

Schloss
Charlottenburg

Knobelsdorff
Wing

Statue of the
Great Elector

SPANDAUER DAMM

OTTO-SUHR-ALLEE

Berggruensammlung

Ägyptisches
Museum

KAISER-FRIEDRICH-STRASSE

SCHLOSS STRASSE

SCHLOSS STRASSE

Heimatmuseum

Bröhan
Museum

KNOBELSDORFFSTRASSE

KNOBELSDORFFSTRASSE

KAISER-FRIEDRICH-STRASSE

0   400 m

est bus routes are the #X21, #X26, #109, #110 and #145. The Schloss is open Tuesday to Friday from 9am to 5pm, and Saturday and Sunday from 10am to 5pm; combined tickets, which are the best value and include entrance to all other Schloss buildings, cost DM15, concessions DM10; entry costs for individual galleries and buildings are given in the text.

Continuing westwards, Charlottenburg breaks out into open country and forest, with the Olympic stadium and tower the main draws (see p.145).

Schloss Charlottenburg

Schloss Charlottenburg comes as a surprise after the unrelieved modernity of the city streets. Commissioned as a country house by the future Queen Sophie Charlotte in 1695 (she also gave her name to the district), the Schloss was expanded and added to throughout the eighteenth and early nineteenth centuries to provide a summer residence for the Prussian kings, the master builder Karl Friedrich Schinkel providing the final touches. Approaching the sandy elaborateness of the Schloss through the main courtyard, you're confronted with Andreas Schlüter's **statue** of Friedrich Wilhelm, the Great Elector, cast as a single piece in 1700. It's in superb condition, despite (or perhaps because of) spending the war years sunk at the bottom of the Tegeler See for safekeeping. Immediately behind is the entrance to the Schloss. To view its central section, which includes the restored residential quarters, you're obliged to go on the conducted **tour** that's in German only, which makes it worth buying the detailed (English) guidebook before you start. The tour (DM8, concessions DM4) is a traipse through increasingly sumptuous chambers and bedrooms, filled with gilt and carving. Look out for the **porcelain room**, packed to the ceiling with china, and the **chapel**, which includes a portrait of Sophie Charlotte as the Virgin ascending to heaven.

The Knobelsdorff Wing

It's just as well to remember that much of the Schloss is in fact a fake, a reconstruction of the buildings following wartime damage. This is most apparent in the **Knobelsdorff Wing** to the right of the Schloss entrance as you face it; the upper rooms, such as the elegantly designed Golden Gallery, are too breathlessly perfect, the result of intensive restoration. Better is the adjacent White Hall, whose destroyed eighteenth-century ceiling painting has been replaced by a witty contemporary pastiche. Next door, the Concert Room contains a superb collection of works by **Watteau**, including one of his greatest paintings, *The Embarcation for Cythera*, a delicate Rococo frippery tinged with sympathy and sadness. Also here is his *The Shop Sign*, painted for an art dealer in 1720.

The Galerie der Romantik

Downstairs, the Knobelsdorff Wing currently contains the **Galerie der Romantik** (Tues–Fri 9am–5pm, Sat & Sun 10am–5pm; DM5, concessions DM4, free first Sun of each month), a collection of nineteenth-century paintings from the German Romantics, Classical and Biedermeier movements. Most dramatic are the works of **Caspar David Friedrich**, all of which express a powerful elemental and religious approach to landscape. This is particularly evident in *Morning in the Riesengebirge* and *Der Watzmann*, where it seems as if some massive, primeval force is about to leap forth from the earth.

Typical of the brooding and drama of his Romantic sensibility is the *Monastery Among Oak Trees* of 1809, perhaps the best known of his works. In the next room, *Moonrise at Sea* reveals something of Friedrich's philosophy: initially a straightforward seascape, on closer study the painting unfolds its deeper meaning: the moon that illuminates the scene and guides the ships represents Christ; the rock on which the figures sit is a symbol of the constancy of Christian faith.

This room also contains works by **Karl Friedrich Schinkel**, the architect responsible for the war memorial in Kreuzberg and, more notably, the Neoclassical design of the Altes Museum and many other buildings standing today in eastern Berlin. His paintings are meticulously drawn Gothic fantasies, often with sea settings. *Gothic Church on a Seaside Bluff* is the most moodily dramatic and didactic in purpose: the medieval knights in the foreground stand next to a prayer tablet – Schinkel believed that a rekindling of medieval piety would bring about the moral regeneration of the German nation. His *Medieval City on a River*, painted shortly after the end of France's domination of Schinkel's native Prussia, is even more overt in its religious and political overtones. The unfinished spire of the cathedral is topped by a flag bearing the imperial eagle; the king, at first barely noticeable beneath the cathedral, is returning home in triumph; and the storm clouds, symbol of French dominance, are clearing. Look out, too, for the topographical paintings of **Eduard Gaertner**, which show the Berlin of the early nineteenth century – and reveal just how good a restoration job the GDR authorities made of Unter den Linden. Check out Gaertner's 1853 painting of that name for evidence.

The Museum für Vor- und Frühgeschichte

The western wing of the Schloss once sided an orangerie (much depleted after the war) and the **gallery** there now houses major exhibitions. Also in the west wing is the **Museum für Vor- und Frühgeschichte** (Museum of Pre- and Early History; Mon–Thurs 9am–5pm, Sat & Sun 10am–5pm; DM4, concessions DM2, free first Sun of each month), an unexciting collection of archeological finds from the Berlin area, along with general European prehistoric finds. There are, though, some interesting pieces from the Schliemann excavations of Troy, though the best finds (some represented here in reproductions) remain in Russia, carted away as spoils of war.

Around the Schloss Gardens

Laid out in the French style in 1697, the **Schloss Gardens** (usually open daily 9am–5pm, till 9pm in the summer months – check at the Schloss complex) were transformed into an English-style landscaped park in the early nineteenth century; after severe damage in the war, they were mostly restored to their Baroque form. Though it's possible to buy a map in the Schloss, it's easy enough to wander through the garden to the lake and on to the grounds behind, which do indeed have the feel of an English park. Places to head for are the **Schinkel Pavilion**, on the far eastern side (Tues–Sun 10am–5pm; DM3, concessions DM2), designed by the architect for Friedrich Wilhelm III, and where the king preferred to live, away from the excesses of the Schloss. Square and simple, it today houses Schinkel's drawings and plans. Deeper into the gardens, on the north side of the lake, is the **Belvedere** (Tues–Sun 10am–5pm; DM3, concessions DM2), built as a teahouse in 1788 and today housing a missable collection of Berlin porcelain.

On the western side of the gardens a long tree-lined avenue leads to the hushed and shadowy **Mausoleum** (April–Oct Tues–Sun 10am–5pm; Nov–March Tues–Fri noon–4pm, Sat & Sun noon–5pm; DM2, concessions DM1), where Friedrich Wilhelm III is buried, his sarcophagus, carved with his image, making him seem a good deal younger than his seventy years. Friedrich Wilhelm had commissioned the mausoleum to be built thirty years earlier for his wife, Queen Luise, whose own delicate sarcophagus depicts her not dead but sleeping. Later burials here include Kaiser Wilhelm I, looking every inch a Prussian king.

Other museums

Though you could happily spend a whole day wandering around the Schloss and its gardens, just across the way another group of excellent museums beckons. These in themselves could easily take an afternoon of your time; it's best to come on Sunday when all are open – preferably on the first Sunday of the month, when most are free.

The Ägyptisches Museum

The best of the museums opposite the Schloss is the **Ägyptisches Museum** (Schlossstr. 70; Mon–Fri 9am–5pm, Sat & Sun 10am–5pm; DM8, concessions DM4, free first Sun of each month), the result of innumerable German excavations in Egypt from the early part of the century. The museum's pride and joy is the *Bust of Nefertiti* on the first floor, a treasure that has become a symbol for the city as a cultural capital. There's no questioning its beauty – the queen has a perfect bone structure and gracefully sculpted lips – and the history of the piece is equally interesting. Created around 1350 BC, the bust probably never left the studio in Akhetaten in which it was created, acting as a model for other portraits of the queen (its use as a model explains why the left eye was never drawn in). When the studio was deserted, the bust was left there, to be discovered some 3000 years later in 1912. In the last few days of the war, the bust was "removed" from the Soviet sector of Berlin, and until recently wrangles continued over its return. Elsewhere in the museum, atmospheric lighting focuses attention on the exhibits, which are of a uniformly high standard. Look out for the Expressionistic, almost Futuristic *Berlin*

Green Head of the Ptolemaic period, and the Kalabsha Monumental Gate, given to the museum by the Egyptian government in 1973.

The Heimatmuseum Charlottenburg and the Berggruen Collection

Immediately south of the Ägyptisches Museum at Schlossstr. 69, the **Heimatmuseum Charlottenburg** (Tues–Fri 10am–5pm, Sun 11am–5pm; free) isn't anything special except for a few photos of Charlottenburg from the Weimar and wartime eras. Across Schlossstrasse, however, is a wonderful new museum, the **Berggruen Collection: Picasso and His Age** (Tues–Fri 9am–5pm, Sat & Sun 10am–5pm; DM8, concessions DM4, free first Sun of each month). Heinz Berggruen, a young Jew forced to flee Berlin in 1936, wound up as an art dealer in Paris, where he got to know Picasso and his circle and assembled a collection of personal favourites. In 1996 the city gave him this building to show off, in a comfortable, uncrowded setting, dozens of his Picassos. The Picassos, most of them rarely seen before, steal the show, of course, but the collection also boasts a handful of Cezannes and Giacomettis and a pair of Van Goghs – all highly recommendable.

The Bröhan-Museum

Just south of the Berggruen Collection, the **Bröhan-Museum** at Schlossstr. 1a (Tues–Sun 10am–6pm; DM5, concessions DM3) houses a great collection of Art Deco and *Jugendstil* ceramics and furniture, laid out in period rooms dedicated to a particular designer and hung with contemporary paintings – worthiest of which are the pastels of Willy Jaeckel and the resolutely modern works of Jean Lambert-Rucki. Small, compact and easily taken in, the Bröhan forms a likeable alternative to the more extensive Ägyptisches Museum or the Schloss collections.

Dahlem: the museum complex

The suburb of **Dahlem** lies to the southwest of central Berlin in the district of Zehlendorf, a neat village-like enclave that feels a world away from the technoflash city centre. Mostly residential, it's home to the Free University, the better-off bourgeoisie and a group of museums that's the most important on the western side of the city.

To reach the museums, take U-Bahn line #1 to Dahlem-Dorf and follow the signs; the main block is on Arnimallee.

Housed in a large building, the **Dahlem museum complex** can be overpowering if you try and do too much too quickly: it's wiser to make a couple of trips here, taking time out to visit the Botanical Gardens nearby (detailed on p.144). If you are pushed for time, the musts are the Museum for Indian Art and the South Seas Ethnographic Collection. The museums are open from Monday to Friday 9am to 5pm, Saturday and Sunday 10am to 5pm. Admission

There has of late been a major restructuring at several of the city's museums as eastern and western collections are reunited and rearranged. Most
important of these changes include: The Gemäldegalerie (Picture Gallery)
of European art formerly in Dahlem has been reunited with the smaller collection from the Bodemuseum and is now housed in a new museum in the
Kulturforum south of the Tiergarten. The Skulpturensammlung (Sculpture
Collection) and the Museum für Spätantike und Byzantinische Kunst
(Museum for Late Antique and Byzantine Art) from Dahlem have been
moved to the Bodemuseum, but due to renovations will not be on display
until 2000. The Alte Nationalgalerie is closed until 2001; highlights of its
collection can be seen at the Altes Museum, which is also now housing
selections from the old Antikensammlung, the city's excellent collection of
Greek and Roman sculpture and vases.

to all the collections is DM8, concessions DM4; on the first Sunday
of the month entry is free. Almost all the major exhibits here are
labelled in English.

The recent transfer of the Gemäldegalerie (Picture Gallery) from
the Dahlem complex to the Tiergarten Complex in the Mitte district
(see p.143) has removed the star attraction here. But it has brought
some of the other fine collections, which were undeservedly overshadowed by the famous paintings of the Picture Gallery, into the light.

The **ethnographic** sections of the Dahlem museum complex –
rich and extensive collections from Asia, the Pacific and South Sea
islands of Melanesia and Polynesia – are imaginatively and strikingly
laid out. In particular, look out for the group of sailing boats from the
South Sea islands, dramatically lit and eminently touchable. Equally
imposing is a wall of masks from South Asia and an exhibit of huts
from Polynesia, Micronesia, New Guinea and New Zealand. But many
of the smaller pieces, such as bronzes from Benin and carved figures
from Central America, are also captivating.

The **Museum for Indian Art** is another standout. It is the largest
collection in the country, with an especially good Nepalese section.
Other collections within the museum include Asian, East Asian and
Islamic art – dip in according to your tastes.

Folk art and the Geheimes Staatsarchiv

At Im Winkel 6, a short signposted walk directly north from the main
complex, is the **Museum für Volkskunde** (Museum of Folklore;
Tues–Fri 9am–5pm, Sat & Sun 10am–5pm; free), a static and rather
dull collection of furniture, tools and costumes from the sixteenth
century onwards. Of much more specialized interest, the **Geheimes
Staatsarchiv**, in the next street to the west (Secret State Archive;
Archivstr. 12–14; reading room Mon & Thurs 1–9pm, Tues, Wed &
Fri 9am–5pm), holds the once-secret Prussian State Archive, a mass
of state documents, records and files now chiefly used as a resource
for academic study.

The Dorfkirche St Annen and Domäne Dahlem

Further west (turn left out of the U-Bahn station and continue along Königin-Luise-Strasse to no. 49) is the **Domäne Dahlem** (Mon & Thurs–Sun 10am–6pm; DM3, concessions DM1.5), a working farm and handicrafts centre that attempts to show the skills and crafts of the nineteenth century. The old estate house has a few odds and ends, most interesting of which are the thirteenth-century swastikas, but the collection of agricultural instruments in an outbuilding is better, with some good turn-of-the-century inducements to farmers from grain manufacturers. Elsewhere are demonstrations of woodcarving, wool and cotton spinning and various other farm crafts, but it's best to come at the weekend, when some of the old agricultural machinery is fired up and the animals are paraded round. Phone up first to see what's on: ☎8 32 50 00.

A little further down Königin-Luise-Strasse, at no. 55, is the **Dorfkirche St Annen**, a pretty little brick-built church that dates back to 1220. If it's open (officially Mon, Wed & Sat 2–5pm, but seemingly random), pop in for a glimpse of the Baroque pulpit and gallery, and carved wooden altar. If not, content yourself with the old gravestones.

The Botanical Gardens

Finally, as an escape from cultural overload, catch a #183 bus east to the **Botanical Gardens** (Königin-Luise-Str. 6–8; daily: March 9am–5pm; April, Sept & Oct 9am–7pm; May–Aug 9am–8pm, Nov–Feb 9am–4pm; Greenhouses summer 9am–5.15pm, winter 9am–3.15pm; DM6, concessions DM3; also bus #101 from the city centre) where you'll find palatial, sticky hothouses sprouting every plant you've ever wondered about (some 18,000 species), enticingly laid out gardens and an uninspiring **Botanical Museum** (Tues–Sun 10am–5pm; free).

The Plötzensee Prison Memorial

Berlin sometimes has the feel of a city that has tried, unsuccessfully, to sweep its past under the carpet of the present. When concrete reminders of the Third Reich can be seen, their presence in today's postwar city becomes all the more powerful. Nowhere is this more true than in the buildings where the Nazi powers brought dissidents and political opponents for imprisonment and execution – what is today the **Plötzensee Prison Memorial**.

Plötzensee stands in the northwest of the city, on the border between the boroughs of Charlottenburg and Wedding. To get there, take bus #123 from Tiergarten S-Bahn station to the beginning of Saatwinkler Damm (ask for the "Gedenkstatte Plötzensee" stop; the journey takes 30min), and walk away from the canal along the wall-sided path of Hüttigpfad.

The former prison buildings have been refurbished as a juvenile detention centre, and the memorial consists of the buildings where the executions took place. Over 2500 people were hanged or guillotined here between 1933 and 1945, usually those sentenced in the Supreme Court of Justice in the city. Following the July Bomb Plot (see pp.132–133), 89 of the 200 people condemned were executed here in the space of a few days. Hitler ordered the hangings to be carried out with piano wire, so that the victims would slowly strangle rather than die from broken necks, and spent his evenings watching movie footage of the executions. Today the execution chamber has been restored to its wartime condition: on occasion, victims were hanged eight at a time, and the hanging beam, complete with hooks, still stands. Though decked with wreaths and flowers, the atmosphere in the chamber is chilling, and in a further reminder of Nazi atrocities an urn in the courtyard contains soil from each of the concentration camps. Perhaps more than at any other wartime site in Berlin, it is at Plötzensee that the horror of senseless, brutal murder is most palpably felt. The memorial is open daily from March to September 8am–6pm, October and February 8.30am–5.30pm, November and January 8.30am–4.30pm and December 8.30am–4pm.

The
Plötzensee
Prison
Memorial

The Maria Regina Martyrum church

Ask at the memorial and you'll be given a map that shows you how to reach the church of **Maria Regina Martyrum** at Heckerdamm 230, a purposefully sombre memorial church dedicated to those who died in the Nazi years (alternatively, you can hop back on the #123 bus and save yourself the 3.5km walk). Completed in 1963, the church's brutally plain exterior is surrounded by a wide courtyard whose wall's are flanked by abstract *Stations of the Cross* modelled in bronze. The interior is a plain concrete shoebox, adorned only with an abstract altarpiece that fills the entire eastern wall. It's a strikingly unusual design, and one that has stood the test of time well.

Points west: the Funkturm, Olympic Stadium and beyond

To reach the **Funkturm**, the skeletal transmission mast that lies to the west of Charlottenburg, it's an easy matter of catching U-Bahn line #2 to Kaiserdamm, then travelling one stop south on bus #204, or catching bus #149 from Zoo Station. The Funkturm was built in 1928 as a radio and, eventually, a TV transmitter. One of Dr Goebbels's lesser-known achievements was to create the world's first regular TV service in 1941. Transmitted from the Funkturm, the weekly programme could only be received in Berlin; the service continued until just a few months before the end of the war. Today the Funkturm only serves police and taxi frequencies, but the mast

Points west:
the
Funkturm,
Olympic
Stadium
and beyond

remains popular with Berliners for the toe-curling views from its 126-metre-high **observation platform** (daily 11.30am–11pm; DM6, concessions DM3). With the aluminium-clad monolith of the **International Congress Centre** immediately below, it's possible to look out across deserted, overgrown S-Bahn tracks to the gleaming city in the distance – a sight equally mesmerizing at night.

The Olympic Stadium

To reach the **Olympic Stadium** (daily 8am–sunset; DM1, concessions DM0.50) from the Funkturm, catch the U-Bahn line #2 three stops westwards to the Olympia-Stadion (Ost) station. From there, it's a fifteen-minute signposted walk to the stadium itself. If you take the (less convenient) #149 bus up Heerstrasse, you cross **Theodor-Heuss-Platz**, a huge square formerly known as Adolf-Hitler-Platz: in the centre of the square is an eternal flame that used to be dedicated to the reunification of East and West Germany – and which is still, rather oddly, alight. The #218 bus, starting at Theodor-Heuss-Platz, goes slightly nearer the stadium entrance than the #149.

Built for the 1936 Olympic Games, the Olympic Stadium is one of the few Fascist-era buildings left intact in the city, and remains very much in use. Whatever your feelings about it, the building is still impressive, the huge Neoclassical space a deliberate rejection of the modernist architecture then prevalent elsewhere.

*For more on
what goes on
in the stadium
today, see
"Sport" in
Listings.*

It's possible to walk around inside the stadium: as you come in at the main (eastern) entrance, the sheer size of the stadium comes as a surprise, since the seating falls away below ground level to reveal a much deeper auditorium than you'd imagined. Walk around to the western side, where the Olympic flame was kept and where medal winners are listed on the walls, and it's easy to see how this monumental architecture, and the massive sculptures dotting the grounds outside, some of which are still extant, could inspire the crowds. During the Olympics, Berliners were kept up-to-date with commentary on the games, interspersed with stirring music, from hundreds of loudspeakers that ran all the way from the Museum Island via Unter den Linden and the Brandenburg Gate, through the Tiergarten and out to the stadium. Standing here, looking back out to the city, you realize what an achievement this was.

Around the Olympic Stadium

The area in which the stadium stands was under the control of the British: the army had its HQ and hospital nearby, and the fields around were used for drilling teenage recruits into shape. This meant that much of the stadium's environs were out of bounds, and probably explains its survival – the British being less eager to demolish interesting structures than the other Allies. Now, with the British army merely a memory, the land around the stadium is one of the most attractive and sought-after pieces of real estate in the city.

If you cut south and west around the stadium, down the road named after Jesse Owens, and take a right onto Passenheimer Strasse, you reach the **Glockenturm** or bell tower (April–Oct daily 9am–6pm; DM4, concessions DM1.50), the spot where Hitler would enter the stadium each morning, state business permitting. Rebuilt after wartime damage, it's chiefly interesting for the stupendous view it gives, not only over the stadium but also north to the natural amphitheatre that forms the Waldbühne, an open-air concert site (see "Clubs and live venues" in Listings), and across the beginnings of the Grunewald to the south. Also easy to spot is the **Teufelsberg** (Devil's Mountain), a massive mound that's topped with a faintly terrifying fairytale castle that used to be a US signals and radar

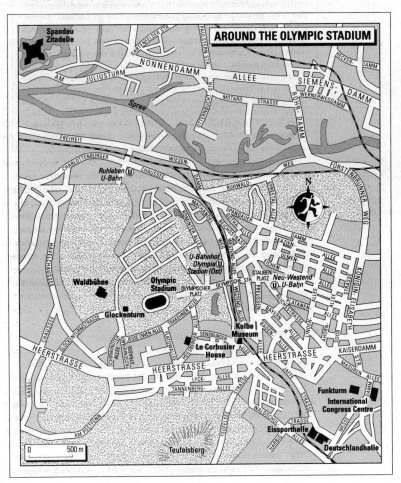

Points west: the Funkturm, Olympic Stadium and beyond

The 1936 Olympic Games

Hitler used the international attention the 1936 Olympics attracted to show the "New Order" in Germany in the best possible light. Anti-Semitic propaganda and posters were suppressed in the city, German half-Jewish competitors were allowed to compete, and when (for the first time in the history of the games) the Olympic flame was relayed from Athens, the newsreels and the world saw the road lined with thousands wearing swastikas and waving Nazi flags. To the outside world, it seemed that the new Germany was rich, content, and firmly behind the Führer.

Though the games themselves were stage-managed with considerable brilliance – a fact recorded in Leni Riefenstahl's poetic and frighteningly beautiful film of the events, *Olympia* – not everything went according to official National Socialist doctrine. Black American athletes did supremely well in the games, **Jesse Owens** alone winning four gold medals, disproving the Nazi theory that blacks were "subhuman" and the Aryan race all-powerful. But eventually Germany won the most gold, silver and bronze medals (there's a memorial at the western end of the stadium), and the games were deemed a great success.

At the medal ceremony Hitler did not shake Owens's hand, not, as is usually stated, because of any racist reasons (though they were undoubtedly there), but because, as patron of the games, he had been told that he must either congratulate all the medal winners (which would have been impractical) or none. Owens must have been even more upset when he got back to the States, since President Roosevelt also refused to shake his hand.

base, built to listen in to eastern bloc radio signals; no longer needed, it's scheduled to be dismantled – though no one seems in a hurry. The mountain itself is artificial: at the end of the war, the mass of debris that was once Berlin was carted to several sites around the city, most of the work being carried out by women known as *Trümmerfrauen* – "rubble women". Beneath the poplars, maples and ski runs lies the old Berlin, about 25 million cubic metres of it, presumably awaiting the attention of some future archeologist. In the meantime, it's popular as a place for weekend kite flying, and skiing and tobogganing in winter (see "Children's Berlin" in Listings).

Le Corbusier house and Georg-Kolbe-Museum

If you're a fan of the French architect Le Corbusier, you may want to make a pilgrimage to the **Le Corbusier house**, between Flatowallee, the street leading directly south of the stadium, and Heilsberger Allee. Built as part of the International Building exhibition in 1957, it contains more than five hundred apartments, shops and its own post office and cinema. Once heralded as a modernist vision of the ideal living environment, it now seems similar to all the other depressing concrete boxes thrown up in the 1960s. More interesting is the **Georg-Kolbe-Museum** at Sensburger Allee 25 (Tues–Sun 10am–5pm; DM5, concessions DM3; bus #149). Kolbe, a sculptor who died in 1947, never achieved the eminence of his contemporary Ernst Barlach – a judgement that perhaps seems reasonable when you view some of the 180 bronze figures and numerous drawings in what was the artist's home.

Spandau

SPANDAU, situated on the confluence of the Spree and Havel rivers, about 10km as the crow flies northwest of the city centre, is Berlin's oldest suburb – it was granted a town charter in 1232, and managed to escape the worst of the wartime bombing, preserving a couple of old streets and an ancient moated fort, the **Zitadelle**. But the word Spandau immediately brings to mind the name of its jail's most famous – indeed in later years only – prisoner, **Rudolf Hess**.

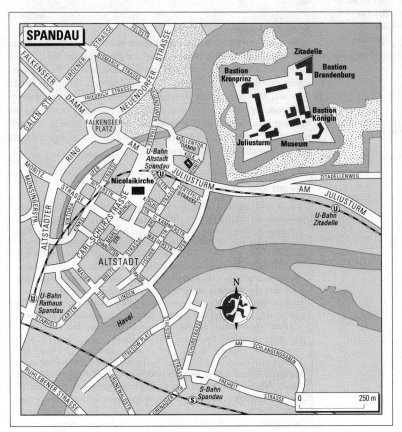

Spandau

To get to the Zitadelle take U-Bahn line #7 to Zitadelle station or bus #133. Spandau town is a ten-minute walk from the Zitadelle or one stop further on the U-Bahn to Altstadt Spandau.

The Zitadelle

However, there's little connection between Hess and Spandau itself. The jail, 4km away from the centre on Wilhelmstrasse, was demolished to make way for a supermarket for the British armed forces, and the chief reason to come here today is to escape the city centre, wander Spandau's village-like streets, and to visit the **Zitadelle** at Am Juliusturm (Tues–Fri 9am–5pm, Sat & Sun 10am–5pm; DM1.50, concessions DM1), a fort established in the twelfth century to defend the town. Postcard-pretty from the outside, with its moat and russet walls built during the Renaissance by an Italian architect, it is explorable, if not totally engrossing. There's a small *Heimatmuseum*, a pricey *bürgerlich* restaurant and the **Juliusturm**, from which there's a good view over the ramshackle Zitadelle interior and the surrounding countryside. If nothing else, it's a pleasant spot to picnic away a hot summer's day.

Spandau town

Aside from the Zitadelle, **Spandau town** is of minor interest, at its best around its church (where there's a good *Konditorei*), in the playful sculptures of its modern marketplace, and in the restored street called **Kolk** (turn right off Am Juliusturm, opposite Breite Strasse). Also here is the **Brauhaus**, a nineteenth-century brewery that produces beer to a medieval recipe, and has tours explaining the brewing process. It's also possible in the summer months to catch **boats** from Spandau to Tegel, Wannsee and elsewhere; call the main private operators for details, see p.18.

Rudolf Hess (1894–1987)

Rudolf Hess marched in the Munich Beer Hall *Putsch* of 1923 and was subsequently imprisoned with Hitler in Landsberg jail, where he took the dictation of *Mein Kampf*. For a time he was the deputy leader of the Nazi party, second only to the Führer himself. He flew to Scotland in 1941, ostensibly in an attempt to sue for peace with King George VI and ally Great Britain with Germany against the Soviet Union. Perhaps because there seems no sane reason why Hess, who was immediately arrested and held until the Nürnberg trials, should have attempted his flight, various sources have claimed that the man held in jail until his suicide in 1987 was not actually Hess – and that it would have been impossible for a 93-year-old man to have hanged himself on a short piece of lamp flex. The basis of this story came from the doctor who examined Hess's corpse; he could find no trace of the serious wounds Hess had acquired in World War I. But it's recently been proved that Hess could indeed have killed himself using the lamp flex, and diligent research in archives in Munich has revealed that Hess's wartime wounds were in fact minor enough to have healed over the years – so putting to rest a colourful (and headline-grabbing) piece of conspiracy theory.

Woodlands and lakes: the Grunewald, Havel and Wannsee

Few people associate Berlin with walks through dense woodland or swimming from crowded beaches, though that's just what the **Grunewald** forests and the Havel lakes have to offer. The Grunewald is 32 square kilometres of mixed woodland between the suburbs of Dahlem and Wilmersdorf, and the Havel lakes to the west; it's popular with Berliners for its bracing air and walks. Seventy percent of the Grunewald was cut down in the postwar years for badly needed fuel, and subsequent replanting has replaced pine and birch with oak and ash, making it all the more popular.

Jagdschloss Grunewald

One possible starting point is the **Jagdschloss Grunewald** (Tues–Sun: April–Sept 10am–6pm; March & Oct 10am–5pm; Nov–Feb 10am–4pm; DM4, concessions DM2; buses #111, #115 and, most usefully, #183 from the city centre), a royal hunting lodge built in the sixteenth century and enlarged by Friedrichs I and II. Today it's a museum housing old furniture and Dutch and German painting, including works by Cranach the Elder and Rubens; there's a small hunting museum in the outbuildings. Really it's more fun to wander around outside than see the collections: it's refreshing to walk by the nearby lake, the **Grunewaldsee**, and concerts are held here on summer evenings (usually starting at 6pm; see *Zitty* or *Tip* magazine for details).

In the middle of the western side of the forest, right next to the Havel, is the **Grunewaldturm** (daily 10am–dusk; DM2) which was built at the end of the nineteenth century as a memorial to Kaiser Wilhelm I: the 55-metre-high tower has a restaurant and views out across the lakes.

The Brücke Museum and the AVUS

Just southeast of the Jagdschloss, the **Brücke Museum** at Bussardsteig 9 (Mon & Wed–Sun 11am–5pm; DM7, concessions DM3), houses a collection of works by the group known as *Die Brücke* (The Bridge), who worked in Dresden and Berlin from 1905 to 1913, and whose work was banned by the Nazis. The big names are Kirchner, Heckel and Schmidt-Rottluff, who painted Expressionist cityscapes and had a large influence on later artists. Many of their works were destroyed during the war, making this collection all the more interesting.

Jagdschloss and the Brücke Museum can also be reached by walking, if you have a good map and a stout pair of legs, from the Grunewald S-Bahn station. It was from here, from October 1941 onwards, that the city's **Jewish population** was rounded up and

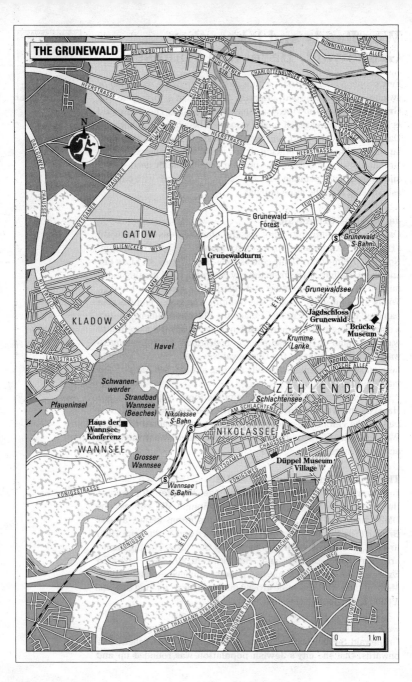

THE GRUNEWALD

loaded onto freight trains, to be taken to the death camps in the east. Previous round-ups in the city centre had offended some Berliners' sensibilities: here in the woods, the Jews were out of sight and out of mind.

Glance at a map of the Grunewald and you'll see a broad, ruler-straight road that runs down to Dreilinden. Known as the AVUS, this once formed part of a prewar motor racing circuit; today it fills a not dissimilar function, as motorists, bored with the 80km/h speed limit on the entry roads into the city, take out their frustration as soon as they hit straight road. Formerly without a speed limit, the AVUS now has a 100km/h maximum, introduced in 1990 after much environmental pressure.

Strandbad Wannsee

An alternative approach to the Grunewald, and to the start of a strip of **beaches**, is to take the S-Bahn, lines #1, #3 or #7, to Nikolassee Station, from where it's a ten-minute walk or a quick bus ride to **Strandbad Wannsee**, a kilometre-long strip of pale sand that's the largest inland beach in Europe, and one which is packed as soon as the sun comes out. From here it's easy to wander into the forests, or, more adventurously, catch one of several **ferries** that leave a little way from the S-Bahn station (ask there for directions).

From Strandbad Wannsee, it's possible to sail across the lake to Kladow on the F10 (your S-Bahn ticket is valid, otherwise it's DM3.60); south to Potsdam and north to Spandau by other seasonal (or private) services; and to the **Pfaueninsel** (Peacock Island; daily: April & Sept 8am–6pm; May–Aug 8am–8pm; March & Oct 9am–5pm; Nov–Feb 10am–4pm; ferry DM2). The attractions here include a mini-Schloss, built by Friedrich Wilhelm II for his mistress and today containing a small **museum** (April–Sept Tues–Sun 10am–5pm; Oct Tues–Sun 10am–4pm; DM4, concessions DM2). Most enjoyable, though, are the gardens, landscaped by Peter Lenné, the original designer of the Tiergarten. No cars are allowed on the island (nor, incidentally, are dogs, ghetto-blasters or smoking), which has been designated a conservation zone and is home to a flock of peacocks. The Pfaueninsel was a favourite party venue for the Nazis: in the 1930s, Joseph Goebbels, Minister of Propaganda, hosted a massive "Italian evening" here for over a thousand guests, including many famous German film stars and celebrities of the day.

Several boat companies run trips around the Grunewald lakes: see "Getting around" in Basics for more details.

Between April and mid-October, *Stern und Kreisschiffahrt* (☎8 03 87 50) runs a four-hour tour that takes in the whole length of the lake systems connecting Wannsee to Tegel; it's worth contacting them for details of special and seasonal trips.

Museumsdorf Düppel

Otherwise, the Grunewald area is ideal for walking. Targets include the **Museumsdorf Düppel** (Düppel Museum Village; 6km to the east of Wannsee U-Bahn at Clauertstr. 11; May–Sept Sun 10am–5pm, occasionally Thurs 3–7pm; phone to confirm ☎8 02 66 71; DM3; bus #115), a reconstructed medieval country village, with demonstrations of contemporary handicrafts and farming techniques; and the surrounding, little-visited **Düppel Forest**.

The Wannsee villa

While it can't be described as the most enjoyable of sights, the one place that should on no account be missed on a trip here is the house overlooking the lake, where on January 20, 1942, the fate of European Jewry was decided: the **Wannsee villa** at Am Grossen Wannsee 56–58 (Mon–Fri 10am–6pm, Sat & Sun 2–6pm; free). To

---

The Wannsee Conference

The conference at the **Wannsee villa** on January 20, 1942, was held at the instigation of Reinhard Heydrich, Chief of Reich Security Head Office and second only to Himmler. Göring had ordered Heydrich to submit plans for the rounding up, deportation and destruction of the Jews in Reich territory. Heydrich summoned SS and government officials, including Adolf Eichmann and Roland Freisler, later to gain infamy as the judge at the Volksgerichthof. Eichmann kept a complete set of minutes of the meeting, and these documents, discovered after the war, were to play an important part in the later Nürnberg trials of war criminals.

The problem Heydrich delineated was that Poland, France and the USSR contained ten million Jews: the "Final Solution" to the "Jewish Question" was that these people should be taken to camps and worked to death. Those who survived should be executed, since, under Nazi principles of natural selection, they would be the toughest, and in Heydrich's words could be "regarded as the germ cell of a new Jewish development". In these early stages the systematic killing machines like Auschwitz and Bergen-Belsen were not yet envisaged. More discussion was spent on how the Jews should be rounded up: great deception was to be used to prevent panic and revolt, and the pretence that Jews were being moved for "resettlement" was extremely important. Heydrich charged Eichmann with this task, a job that would eventually cost him his life when he was sentenced to death for war crimes in Israel in 1960.

At no time during the conference were the words "murder" or "killing" used, only careful euphemisms to shield the enormity of what was being planned. Reading through the minutes (copies are kept in the villa's library), it's difficult not to be shocked by the matter-of-fact manner in which the day's business was discussed, the way in which German politeness and efficiency absorb and absolve all concerned. When sterilization was suggested as one "solution" it was rejected as "unethical" by a doctor present; and there was much self-congratulation as various officials described their areas as "Judenfrei".

Heydrich himself died following an assassination attempt in Prague: some of the others present did not survive the war either, but, in contrast to the millions who were destroyed by their organizational genius, many of the Wannsee delegation lived on to gain a pension from the German state.

---

get here, take the S-Bahn to Wannsee, then catch a #114 bus (about a 5-min journey) and get off at "Haus der Wannsee-Konferenz".

The villa, which is entered through strong security gates, contains an exhibition showing the entire process of the Holocaust, from segregation and persecution to the deportation and eventual murder of the Jews from Germany and all the lands the Third Reich conquered. Each room examines a different part of the process, and there's an English-language translation of the exhibits available from the ticket desk. Inevitably, it's deeply moving: many of the photographs and accounts are horrific, and the events they describe seem part of a world far removed from the quiet suburban backwater of Wannsee – which, in a way, underlines the tragedy. Particularly disturbing is the photograph of four generations of a single family – babe-in-arms, young mother, her older mother and ancient great-grandmother – moments before their executions.

The room where the conference took place is kept as it was, with documents from the meeting on the table and photographs of participants ranged around the walls, their biographies showing that most lived on to comfortable old age. Even fifty years after the event, to stand in the room where the decision was taken to coldly and systematically annihilate six million people brings a shiver of fear and rage. The vast scale of the Holocaust sometimes makes it hard to grasp the full enormity of the crime: looking into the faces of the guilty, and then of those they destroyed, brings across the evil in a very real way.

The villa also has a library containing reference material such as autobiographies, first-hand accounts, slides, newspapers and much else concerning the Holocaust and the rise of neo-Fascist groups.

Chapter 9

East of the centre

The suburbs on the **eastern** side of Berlin contrast starkly with those to the west. The legacy of the GDR era is apparent from the run-down appearance of many areas and the proliferation of construction and renovation projects aimed at ironing out the remaining differences between the two halves of the city. There's much to see, including some decidedly offbeat attractions, and the subtly different atmosphere of the eastern districts or *Bezirke* makes visiting these areas an important part of understanding the true identity of Berlin.

Your first goal should be the streets of **Prenzlauer Berg**, a part working-class, part bohemian district that fans out northeast of the city centre, and has long been a centre of "alternative" culture and lifestyle. This area is also home to some of the best cafés, bars and nightlife in the eastern part of the city. **Friedrichshain**, immediately to the east of the centre, has some fascinating examples of GDR architecture, and one of the city's oldest and best parks. If you've enough time, head out southeast to **Treptow** and its massive Soviet war memorial and riverside parks, and to **Lichtenberg**, with eastern Berlin's sprawling zoo, and, nearby, the building where the German army surrendered to the Soviets at the end of World War II.

Moving north away from the inner city, **Pankow**, once home to the GDR capital's elite, and the tidy district of **Weissensee**, where you'll find the city's largest Jewish cemetery, offer a break from urban grime. For a real escape from the city, head south for the lakes and woods around **Köpenick**, which are surprisingly unspoiled. All of the places described in this chapter are easily reached by S- and U-Bahn, tram or bus, and are as much an essential part of Berlin's identity as the better-known sights.

Prenzlauer Berg

The old working-class district of **PRENZLAUER BERG** radiates out from the city centre in a network of tenement-lined cobbled streets, and is rapidly usurping Kreuzberg's role as home of the Berlin *Szene*.

But then, even in GDR days it was a uniquely vibrant and exciting corner of East Berlin, home to large numbers of artists and young people seeking an alternative lifestyle who chose to live here on the edge of established East German society (literally as well as figuratively – the western boundary of Prenzlauer Berg was marked by the Berlin Wall). Given the all-embracing nature of the state, this was not as easy as in "alternative" West Berlin, since in the GDR even minor acts of nonconformism, or actions that wouldn't have been regarded as out of the ordinary at all in the West, like organizing an unofficial art exhibition or concert, could result in a run-in with the police or attract the unwelcome attentions of the *Stasi*.

Since 1989 countless new bars and galleries have opened, particularly in the streets around Kollwitzplatz, thriving partly because the area's original inhabitants have been joined by an influx of people

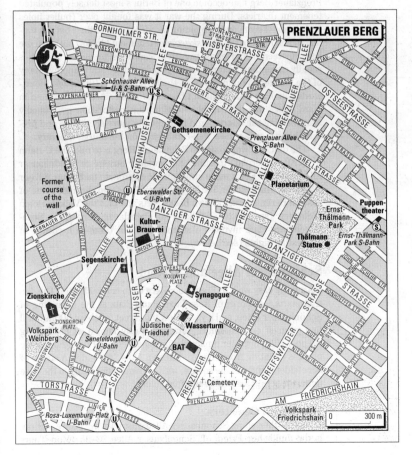

(often students) drawn from the west by cheap accommodation and **squatting** opportunities, though with many buildings being reclaimed by their original owners, the days for breaking into the squat scene are over. Most of the new bars aren't dramatically different from those of western Berlin, but they have a sense of freshness, and are less jaded and established than the equivalent Kreuzberg and Schöneberg haunts.

Historically, Prenzlauer Berg is a relatively new *Bezirk*. It's set on a gently sloping hill that served as a wooded hunting ground for the local aristocracy until the first farmers moved in towards the end of the eighteenth century, clearing the trees and building windmills to take advantage of the exposed position. For the next fifty years or so the area was rural, lying outside the city limits. Industrialization resulted in an explosion of building, and by the turn of the century Prenzlauer Berg had become one of Berlin's most densely populated tenement districts. During the war it was fought over (bullet holes and shrapnel scars on the building facades testify to this) but not flattened, and most of the *Mietskaserne* (tenement blocks) put up in the late nineteenth and early twentieth centuries to house the city's rapidly expanding factory worker population are still standing. Many of the blackened buildings, with their overgrown *Hinterhöfe* (courtyards), look as if they haven't been renovated since the war, and in many cases this is probably so. However, restoration is gradually transforming the district, and many of the more accessible and presentable streets are now well-established on the tourist itinerary.

The quickest way to **get to Prenzlauer Berg** is to take the U-Bahn from Alexanderplatz to either Eberswalder Strasse or Schönhauser Allee stations. For a more atmospheric approach, take tram #13 or #53 from Hackescher Markt, which will take you through some of eastern Berlin's lesser known backstreets and past the Volkspark am Weinberg (see p.120). Walking to Prenzlauer Berg from Rosa-Luxemburg-Platz involves a steepish hill but takes in a couple of interesting sights (see below).

Schönhauser Allee and around

It's a fairly easy walk to Prenzlauer Berg from central Berlin. The district starts just north of Rosa-Luxemburg-Platz at the beginning of **Schönhauser Allee**, and if you follow this street for about 600m you'll find yourself on **Senefelderplatz**, previously known as Pfefferberg (Pepper Hill), but later renamed after the inventor of the lithographic process (printing from engraved stone), Alois Senefelder. A statue of Senefelder stands on the square, with his name appearing on the base in mirror script, as on a lithographic block.

The Jewish Cemetery

A little further along Schönhauser Allee, just past the police station, is the **Jüdischer Friedhof**, Schönhauser Allee 23–25 (Mon–Thurs

8am–4pm, Fri 8am–1pm; male visitors are requested to keep their heads covered), Prenzlauer Berg's Jewish cemetery, which opened when space ran out at the Grosse Hamburger Strasse cemetery. Over twenty thousand people are buried here, but for most this last resting place is an anonymous one; in 1943 many of the gravestones were smashed and a couple of years later the trees under which they had stood were used by the SS to hang deserters found hiding in the cemetery during the final days of war. Today many of the stones have been restored and repositioned, and a memorial stone near the cemetery entrance entreats visitors: "You stand here in silence, but when you turn away do not remain silent."

Along and around Schönhauser Allee

Further along Schönhauser Allee, on the left near the junction with Wörtherstrasse, is the confused **Segnerkirche**, a bizarre mix of Gothic and neo-Renaissance styles. About 500m or so north of here is Eberswalder Strasse U-Bahn station, and the busy junction of Schönhauser Allee, Danziger Strasse, Kastanienallee and Eberswalder Strasse. Beyond the junction, **Schönhauser Allee** assumes its true identity as Prenzlauer Berg's main drag, an old-fashioned shopping street which, thanks to its cobbled streets and narrow shop facades, still retains a vaguely pre-*Wende* (or perhaps even prewar) feel. This effect is enhanced by the U-Bahn, which runs overground and becomes an elevated railway. Supported by ornate steel pillars, it leaves much of Schönhauser Allee in the shadows and was nicknamed the *Magistratschirm* or "municipal umbrella" at the time of its construction.

Schönhauser Allee extends northwards for a couple of kilometres towards Pankow, lined by shops and street stalls. Just to the southeast of Schönhauser Allee U-Bahn station, at the intersection of Stargarder Strasse and Greifenhagener Strasse, is the **Gethsemanekirche**, which was a focal point for reformist activities during the summer 1989 exodus from the GDR, and in the months leading up to the *Wende*. Given the peaceful nature of Schönhauser Allee today, it's hard to imagine that on October 7, 1989, the police were beating nonviolent demonstrators here, during the anti-government street protests that followed the celebrations of the GDR's fortieth anniversary. Just over a month later, however, the nightmare was over, and it was in Prenzlauer Berg that ordinary East Germans first experienced the reality of the passing of the old order. At 9.15pm on November 9, 1989, a couple walked through the nearby Bornholmer Strasse border crossing into West Berlin, becoming the first East Berliners to take advantage of the opening of the Wall (see "*Die Wende* to the present" in Contexts).

These days, however, it's in the maze of run-down streets east of Schönhauser Allee that Prenzlauer Berg's real attractions lie. Here, you'll find some of the best **cafés** and **bars** in the eastern part of

Nightlife in Prenzlauer Berg

Since the *Wende* numerous new bars and cafés have opened here. The most accessible concentrations are around the junction of Knaackstrasse and Rykestrasse (in the shadow of the nineteenth-century water tower), and along Husemannstrasse and Sredzkistrasse. These tend on the whole to attract visitors from the western part of the city and hip tourists, so if you're looking to meet locals rather than other visitors, delve deeper into the district and head for streets like Lychener Strasse and Dunckerstrasse, on the other side of Danziger Strasse. See "Cafés and bars" in Listings.

Berlin (see box above). The area is best explored by turning into Sredzkistrasse from Schönhauser Allee: on the left is the former **Schultheiss Brauerei**, an 1890s brewery built in the pseudo-Byzantine style much favoured by Berlin's architects during the late nineteenth century. The grounds of the former brewery have been transformed into the **KulturBrauerei**, a cultural centre with an alternative slant. Passing through the entrance around the corner at Knaackstrasse 97, you'll discover an inner courtyard of clubs, galleries and studios amidst artefacts of the original brewery, where there's almost always something – cultural, political or just entertaining – going on. Of particular interest here is the **Sammlung Industrielle Gestaltung** (Collection of Industrial Design; Wed–Sun 2–9pm; entry free). This museum presents a fascinating permanent display of furniture, porcelain and appliances from the former East Germany, and changing exhibitions on aspects of East German design and architecture.

Kollwitzplatz and around

A right turn from Sredzkistrasse into Knaackstrasse leads to **Kollwitzplatz**, focal point for Prenzlauer Berg's main sights. It is named after the artist **Käthe Kollwitz**, who lived in nearby Weissenburgerstrasse (now called Kollwitzstrasse) from 1891 to 1943. Her work embraced political and pacifist themes and can be best appreciated in the Käthe Kollwitz museum in the West End (see p.50). There's also an unflattering statue of Kollwitz in the little park on the square.

Along Husemannstrasse

Running north from Kollwitzplatz is **Husemannstrasse**, a nineteenth-century tenement street that was restored to its former glory in late GDR days and turned into a kind of living museum in an attempt to recall the grandeur of old Berlin. Since the *Wende*, restoration projects have gradually transformed neighbouring streets too, covering raddled facades with fresh stucco and installing new wrought-iron balconies.

Husemannstrasse is now home to a lively restaurant and bar scene, anchored by the well-known and well-regarded *Restauration 1900*, which was established long before the Wall came down (see "Restaurants" in Listings).

South of Kollwitzplatz

A left turn at the southern corner of Kollwitzplatz will land you on Knaackstrasse, where, after 50m or so, the huge red-brick **Wasserturm** (water tower) looms over the surrounding streets. Built in 1875 on the site of a pre-industrial windmill, the tower has been designated an historic monument and converted into apartments with room plans that follow the circular shape of the building. After the Nazis came to power the SA turned the basement into a torture chamber, and later the bodies of 28 of their victims were found in the underground pipe network. A memorial stone on Knaackstrasse commemorates them: "On this spot in 1933 decent German resistance fighters became the victims of Fascist murderers. Honour the dead by striving for a peaceful world." Before the construction of the Wasserturm, Prenzlauer Berg's water requirements had been provided by the slim tower at the southern end of the square. Before that people had had to lug their water up from city centre wells, and open sewers had taken their waste back downhill to the Spree, with the unsurprising result that disease was rife. The immediate vicinity of the Wasserturm, a fairly quiet area until a couple of years ago, is now home to a number of conspicuously stylish new cafés and bars.

From Knaackstrasse, a left turn into Rykestrasse brings you to eastern Berlin's only functioning **synagogue**, an ornate edifice in the courtyard of house no. 53. Originally built in 1904–5, this survived both *Kristallnacht* and use as a stables by the SA. It was designated a "Temple of Peace" in 1953 but today, poignantly, its capacity exceeds the Jewish population of the eastern part of the city.

On the southwestern side of the water tower is Belforter Strasse, where at no. 15 you'll find the **BAT** or **Studiotheater der Hochschule für Schauspielkunst Ernst Busch**, which is part of the School of Dramatic Art (see "The arts" in Listings). At the end of Belforter Strasse, cross Prenzlauer Allee into Heinrich-Roller-Strasse, which leads down to Greifswalder Strasse. On the right is a venerable and overgrown cemetery dating back to the early nineteenth century (access from Greifswalder Strasse), with some elaborate tombstones and vaults. Many of the memorials bear shrapnel and bullet scars, an indication of just how intense the fighting during the Battle for Berlin must have been; even the city's graveyards were fought for inch by inch. **Greifswalder Strasse** itself is a main route out of the city and looks very neat with its freshly painted facades. In pre-*Wende* days traffic came to a standstill along the side streets a couple of times a day as a convoy of black Citroëns and Volvos sped by, whisking high-ranking government members (notably Erich

Honecker himself) from the Palast der Republik to their homes in the now infamous lakeside town of Wandlitz to the north of Berlin. But behind the immaculate facades, the *Hinterhöfe* of Greifswalder Strasse are just as run-down as those in the backstreets.

Ernst-Thälmann-Park and around

At the northeastern end of Greifswalder Strasse is another example of former GDR civic window-dressing in the shape of the **Ernst-Thälmann-Park** (walkable from the Heinrich-Roller-Strasse and Greifswalder Strasse intersection or, if you're feeling lazy, take tram #2, #3 or #4, or bus #257). This is a model housing development, set in a small park and fronted by a gigantic marble sculpture of the head and clenched fist of Ernst Thälmann, the pre-1933 Communist leader who was imprisoned and later murdered by the Nazis. Floodlit and guarded round the clock by police in pre-*Wende* days, his likeness is now daubed with graffiti, and the concrete terrace on which it stands is favoured by local skateboarders. About four thousand people, mostly from the ex-GDR elite, live here in high-rise buildings with restaurants, shops, nurseries and a swimming pool all immediately at hand.

Behind the Ernst-Thälmann-Park on Prenzlauer Allee is the silver-domed **Zeiss Planetarium** (Mon & Tues 10am–noon, Wed & Sat 10am–noon & 1.30–9pm, Thurs & Fri 6–10pm, Sun 1.30–6pm; DM8, concessions DM6), with a missable German-only display on the evolution of the universe. Nearby is Prenzlauer Allee's distinctive, yellow-brick 1890s S-Bahn station, one of the best-looking in the city, and just northeast of here, between Sültstrasse and Sodtkestrasse, is the so-called **Flamensiedlung**, a model housing development built in 1929–30 according to plans by the architect Bruno Taut. With his associate Franz Hillinger, Taut wanted to create mass housing that broke away from the tenement-house concept. Basing their design on work already done in Holland, they diffused the angularity of their apartment blocks with corner windows and balconies, and left open areas between them to a create an environment far removed from the gloom of the tenement *Hinterhof*.

Friedrichshain

Spreading out east from the city centre, **FRIEDRICHSHAIN** is mainly residential in the north, but given over to extensive goods yards and moribund industry around the Hauptbahnhof and down towards the River Spree in the south. Friedrichshain's longest-established attractions are the Stalinist architecture of **Karl-Marx-Allee**, and the **Volkspark Friedrichshain**, resting place of the victims of the 1848 revolution. Since 1989 these attractions have been augmented by a museum in the former **headquarters** of the Stasi, and the **East Side gallery**, a surviving stretch of Wall that has been transformed into a unique open-air art gallery.

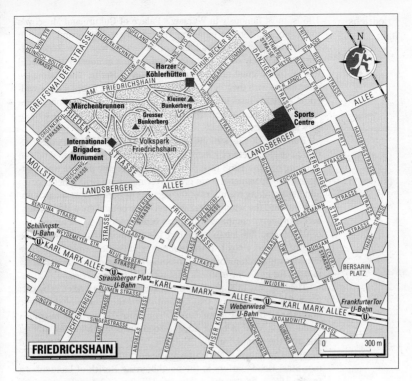

Karl-Marx-Allee

Heading east along **Karl-Marx-Allee** from Strausberger Platz, the prefabricated blocks of the 1960s give way to the *Zuckerbäckerstil* (wedding-cake style) of the previous decade (see below). In September 1951, work began on a scheme to turn Karl-Marx-Allee, then known as Stalinallee, into "Germany's first socialist street", providing modern flats that would be "palaces for the people". The first foundation stone of what was to become an ornate high-rise apartment building, the **Hochhaus an der Weberwiese**, was laid at Marchlewskistr. 25, just south of Weberwiese U-Bahn station. Over the next few years similar buildings were constructed from Strausberger Platz to the Frankfurter Tor U-Bahn station, which marked the eastern limit of the old Stalinallee. At **Strausberger Platz** itself, huge twin-tiered towers flank the route into central Berlin, while 1500m further east two similarly grandiose structures at Rathaus Friedrichshain, topped by ecclesiastical-looking domes, stand on the site of an earlier customs gate.

These buildings epitomize the *Zuckerbäckerstil*, a mutated Classicism that was repeated across the Soviet bloc throughout the

1950s, most famously in Warsaw's Palace of Culture and Moscow's university and foreign ministry. Though the style was and is much derided in the west, the buildings of Stalinallee were a well-thought-out and relatively soundly constructed attempt at housing that would live up to the great architectural tradition of Berlin. The Stalinallee apartments with their central heating and parquet floors also provided an enviable level of comfort at a time when most Berliners were crowded into bomb-shattered tenement blocks or makeshift temporary housing.

Ironically, it was striking workers from the Stalinallee construction project, angered by increased work norms, who sparked off the uprising of June 1953 (see p.75). Later, when the project was completed, the apartments were given over mainly to SED functionaries and high-ranking members of the security services. Most tenants are now old and the whole street was recently bought by a Wiesbaden-based property company which has begun much-needed renovation of the blocks. The inhabitants have been assured that no one will be thrown out but many fear that sooner or later the former Stalinallee housing will be transformed into upmarket apartments conveniently located for city-centre offices, institutions and ministries.

The best way to appreciate the scale of Karl-Marx-Allee is by car; it's worth taking a taxi trip up and down the length of this huge boulevard. Beyond Frankfurter Tor, Karl-Marx-Allee becomes Frankfurter Allee, a bleak arterial road lined by high-rises, rolling out into the suburbs in the direction of Frankfurt an der Oder and Poland. The only real attraction anywhere along its length is the former Stasi Headquarters in the neighbouring Bezirk of Lichtenberg (see p.168) – to get there take the U-Bahn to Magdalenenstrasse station.

Volkspark Friedrichshain

Fifteen minutes' walk north of Karl-Marx-Allee is **Volkspark Friedrichshain**, one of the city's oldest and largest parks (and a well-known gay cruising area). At the western entrance to the park, where Friedenstrasse and Am Friedrichshain meet, is the **Märchenbrunnen** (Fairytale Fountain), a Neo-Baroque arcade and fountain with statues of characters from Brothers Grimm stories. Intended as a gift to tenement-dwelling workers, it was put up in 1913 at the instigation of Social Democratic members of the city council, in direct contravention of the Kaiser's wishes.

A detour to a monument and a graveyard

A few hundred metres to the southeast of the Märchenbrunnen is the **Gedenkstätte für die Deutschen Interbrigadisten**, a monument to the German members of the International Brigades who fought against the Fascists in Spain in the Spanish Civil War. Of the five thousand Germans (including many leading Communists) who went to Spain, only two thousand returned. There's another monument to the east of here (just off Landsberger Allee), this time to victims of an upheaval closer to home. The **Friedhof der Märzgefallenen** is where many of the 183 Berliners killed by the soldiers of King Friedrich Wilhelm IV during the Revolution of March 1848 were buried, their interment attended by eighty thousand of their fellow citizens. Only a few of the original gravestones survive, but the dead of 1848 have been joined by 33 of those killed in the November Revolution of 1918, commemorated by a statue of a *Rote Matrose* or "Red Sailor" at the cemetery entrance, reflecting the role played in the revolution by Imperial navy sailors.

The Bunkerbergs

The final resting place of the revolutionaries is overshadowed by the **Grosser Bunkerberg** and **Kleiner Bunkerberg**, two artificial hills created when a million cubic metres of rubble from bombed-out Berlin were dumped over a couple of wartime bunkers. In between the two is a small, tree-shaded lake, and nearby you'll find the kind of worthy sporting amenities and giant outdoor chess sets that keep many Germans amused during their free hours. Set on a grassy slope a little to the east is a **monument** commemorating the joint fight of the Polish army and German resistance against the Nazis. Given the feelings most Germans and Poles have for each other, the sentiments expressed seem rather unconvincing, though so far it's escaped the attentions of graffiti artists. A path snakes down from here to the not-so-worthy *Harzer Köhlerhütten*, a fake charcoal-burners' village with beer and food counters where Germans with a more anti-social bent like to drink, eat *Bockwurst* and threaten each other with physical violence.

In the area to the immediate east of the park Ordnung reasserts itself in the shape of the **Sport und Erholungszentrum**, Landsberger Allee 77, a big modern leisure centre with several swimming pools, a wave machine, an ice- and roller-skating rink, a sauna, a bowling alley and various cafés (see "Sport" in Listings). The entrance is near the junction of Danziger Strasse and Landsberger Allee.

The East Side Gallery

The **East Side Gallery** is a surviving stretch of Wall that has been turned into an open-air art gallery. Running along Mühlenstrasse, between the Hauptbahnhof and the Oberbaumbrücke in the south of the district, it's been daubed with various political/satirical images, some imaginative, some trite and some impenetrable. One of the most telling images shows Brezhnev and Honecker locked in a fraternal bear-hug, with the inscription, "God, help me survive this deadly love." The gallery can also be reached from the Kreuzberg side over a pedestrian bridge just north of Schlesisches Tor U-Bahn station, or even glimpsed from a subway car as the train crosses the recently reopened Oberbaumbrücke spanning the Spree River.

Treptow

TREPTOW stretches out 8km southeast from the city centre between the River Spree and what used to be the border with West Berlin. It's a mainly residential district with a few industrial pockets, and the major attraction for visitors is the large Spree-side park with its huge and sobering Soviet war memorial. The area is best reached from Treptower Park S-Bahn station, or by buses #166, #167, #177 and #265.

Treptower Park

As Berlin expanded rapidly during the nineteenth century, **Treptower Park** was one of the places where the city's tenement-dwellers could let off steam, and by 1908 there were thirty-odd dance halls and restaurants here. Later, during the inter-war years, the park became a well-known assembly point for revolutionary workers

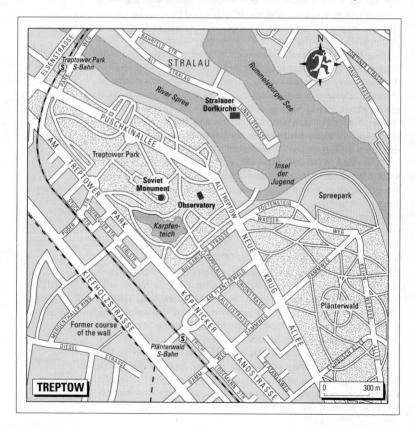

about to embark on demonstrations or go off to do battle with the Brownshirts. Today, things are very different, since it's here that many of the Soviet casualties from the Battle of Berlin are buried.

The Soviet Memorial

At the heart of the park, the **Sowjetisches Ehrenmal** commemorates the Soviet Union's 305,000 estimated casualties during the Battle of Berlin in April and May 1945 and is the burial place of 5000 of them. It's best approached from the arched entrance on the south side of Puschkinallee. A little way to the south of here is a sculpture of a grieving woman representing the Motherland, to the left of which a broad concourse slopes up towards a viewing point flanked by two vast triangles of red granite, fashioned from stone bought from Sweden by the Nazis to furnish Berlin with projected victory monuments. From the viewing point the vista is dominated by a vast symbolic statue, a typical Soviet piece of gigantism using marble from Hitler's Chancellory. Over eleven metres high, and set on top of a hill modelled on a *kurgan* or traditional warriors' grave of the Don region, it shows an idealized Russian soldier clutching a saved child and resting his sword on a shattered swastika. Inside the plinth is a memorial crypt with a mosaic in true Socialist Realist style, showing Soviet citizens (soldiers, mother, worker, peasant, and what looks like an old age pensioner) honouring the dead. In the long sunken park area that leads up to the statue are the mass graves of the Red Army troops, lined by sculpted frescoes of stylized scenes from the Great Patriotic War.

In January 1990 the monument hit the headlines briefly when it was defaced, allegedly by neo-Nazis, despite the fact that the place was guarded around the clock. Many East Berliners suspected a put-up job, engineered by the still-Communist government or its supporters, ostensibly to combat rising neo-Nazism. Until the *Wende* most of the visitors to the monument were Soviet citizens who came here by the busload to pay their respects, but since the beginning of the 1990s increasing numbers of former West Berliners have discovered the place, and it's become a popular Sunday promenade destination for the space-starved inhabitants of Neukölln and Kreuzberg. It remains an important part of the Berlin cityscape, its sheer scale imparting a sense of the Soviet Union's colossal losses during World War II, losses that shaped postwar Soviet defence and foreign policy, and explain as much as anything why history unfolded as it did in postwar Berlin.

One of the interesting things about the memorial is the complete lack of any religious iconography – eschewed by the Soviet state. It shows that grandiose memorials needn't depend on pious objects in order to have spiritual power.

Around the rest of the park

The rest of the park conceals a couple of low-key attractions, including the **Karpfenteich**, a large carp pool just south of the memorial, and, a little to the east of here, the **Archenhold Sternwarte** (shows at Wed 6pm, Sat & Sun 3pm; DM6, concessions DM4), an observatory with the longest refracting telescope in the world.

The park continues north of Puschkinallee, where you'll also find the *Eierschale-Zenner* (see "Cafés and bars" in Listings), a riverside *Gaststätte* whose origins go back to the eighteenth century. Just to the east is the **Insel der Jugend**, a small island in the Spree reached via the **Abteibrücke**, an ornamental footbridge built by French prisoners of war in 1916 to link the island to the mainland. The end of Treptow's summer festival is marked by a firework display from this bridge, an event known as *Treptow in Flammen* or "Treptow in Flames". The island was originally the location of an abbey, but now the main attraction is Die Insel, a tower-like clubhouse that houses a café, cinema and gallery and is a regular venue for club nights and gigs, with occasional outdoor raves in summer (see "Clubs and live venues" in Listings).

Just southeast of the Insel der Jugend is the **Spreepark**, a funfair featuring the usual rides, *Bockwurst* stands and a big wheel. It's all part of the Plänterwald woods, which cover a couple of square kilometres and offer good, untaxing strolling. Just to the southwest of Neue Krug is the *Plänterwald*, a largish *Gaststätte* that makes a good place to interrupt your wanderings.

Gartenstadt Falkenberg

About 8km away, at the southeastern edge of Treptow, is the **Gartenstadt Falkenberg**, a settlement of model housing designed by Bruno Taut in response to slum conditions in the city-centre tenements. To get there, take the S-Bahn to Grünau station, whence it's a short walk southwest along Bruno-Taut-Strasse to the houses on the western end of that street and Akazienhof. The best examples are along Akazienhof: pastel-painted, cottage-like dwellings that must have seemed paradise to their first inhabitants, newly escaped from the filth and industry of the inner *Bezirke*. A plaque at Akazienhof used to state, without irony: "Many of the founder members [of the settlement] were active opponents of war and Fascism. Their ideals have become reality in the German Democratic Republic."

Lichtenberg and Marzahn

North of Treptow is the *Bezirk* of **Lichtenberg**, a sprawling working-class district, part prefabricated postwar mass dwellings and part traditional tenement blocks, with heavy concentrations of industry in the north and south. Until the mid-nineteenth century Lichtenberg was little more than a country town and popular Sunday-outing destination for Berliners. With industrialization, however, the familiar Berlin tenements sprang up and the area's rustic past was soon forgotten. In these post-unification days Lichtenberg has been hard hit by the collapse of the old order, with unemployment running high. A nasty side-effect of all this is a reputation for mindless, often racially motivated violence, making it a place to avoid at night. By day, however, head here for the excellent **zoo** in Friedrichsfelde, in the eastern sector of the *Bezirk*. Of more esoteric appeal are the memorial to various figures from the socialist past in Lichtenberg proper, and the museum in Karlshorst, in the building where the *Wehrmacht* surrendered to the Soviet armed forces in 1945.

East and north of Lichtenberg is Marzahn, a mid-1970s satellite town which is not perhaps the most obvious sightseeing destination. Silo-like apartment blocks and soulless shopping precincts stretch for miles out towards the edge of the city in what has to be one of the most desolate of the city's **Bezirke**. However, this *is* Berlin for tens of thousands of Berliners, and is worth a look for this reason alone.

Lichtenberg

There's not much to write home about in **LICHTENBERG** proper. The only real reason to come here is to visit the former headquarters of the *Stasi*, the GDR's all-pervasive secret police, which has been turned into a slightly ghoulish tourist attraction, just a couple of minutes' walk from Magdalenenstrasse U-Bahn station.

The Stasi headquarters and around

The former **Stasi headquarters** is a huge complex bounded by Frankfurter Allee, Ruschestrasse, Normannenstrasse and Magdalenenstrasse – an area approximately the size of London's Whitehall – with another slightly smaller complex a few streets to the north. From here East Germany's infamous *Staatssicherheitsdienst* (state security service) kept tabs on everything that happened in the GDR. It was its job to ensure the security of the country's borders, carry out surveillance operations on foreign diplomats, businesspeople and journalists, and monitor domestic and foreign media. It was, however, in surveillance of East Germany's own population that the organization truly excelled. Very little happened in the GDR without the *Stasi* knowing about it; files were kept on millions of innocent citizens and insidious operations were orchestrated against dissidents, real and imagined.

Part of the building from which all this was controlled now houses a museum with an unwieldy title, the **Forschungs- und Gedenkstätte Normannenstrasse** (Normannenstrasse Research – and Memorial – Centre, Ruschestr. 59, Haus 1 (Tues–Fri 11am–6pm, Sat & Sun 2–6pm; DM5; U-Bahn Magdalenenstr.), covering the GDR political system and the way in which the massive surveillance apparatus of the *Stasi* helped maintain it. Walking along the bare, red-carpeted corridors and looking at the busts of Lenin and Felix Dzerzhinsky – founder of the Soviet *Cheka*, forerunner of the KGB and model for the *Stasi* – it all seems to belong to a much more distant past, rather than an era which came to an end only at the beginning of 1990. But then the obsessively neat office and apartment of **Erich Mielke**, the

The Stasi

The **Stasi** was the so-called "Schild und Schwert" – "sword and shield" – of the German Democratic Republic. It had around 85,000 full-time employees, all of whom held military ranks, and in 1989, the final year of its existence, its budget was about £1 billion. Though the *Stasi* was also responsible for external espionage and counter-espionage, it's thought that about 95 percent of its budget was spent on spying on the East German people. The *Stasi* mounted what was probably the most comprehensive and long-lasting surveillance of its own population by any state: phones were tapped, mail intercepted, people followed, photographed and filmed. Much of the surveillance legwork was done by a 180,000-strong army of *Informeller Mitarbeiter* or *IM* ("unofficial co-workers"). These were, in effect, paid informers, and every factory, school, institute and military unit had at least one person in this category among its personnel. Most people in the GDR reckoned that their circle of friends and acquaintances would also include at least one *IM*.

The *Informeller Mitarbeiter* gathered material for the exhaustive files the GDR kept on about six million of its citizens (out of a total population of 16 million). As well as detailing anti-regime activities or comments, these files also recorded things like drinking habits, debts and sexual preferences – all useful material for possible blackmail. When details of some files emerged, the level of banality was scarcely believable – the most minute movements of subjects under observation were recorded, right down to visits to the bathroom and walks with the family dog. *Stasi*-chief Mielke felt that everyone was a potential enemy of the state and that it was thus of vital importance to know everything about everyone.

One result of this obsessive information gathering was that the *Stasi* was always well informed about the true state of affairs in the GDR. During 1989, according to Mielke, in an interview carried out in his jail cell with the news magazine *Spiegel*, the *Stasi* kept the government closely informed about the growing crisis. It was fully aware of popular discontent

Minister of State Security who oversaw Stasi operations from 1957 to October 1989, somehow makes it all the more immediate. Everything is just as he left it: white and black telephones stand on the varnished wooden desk as though awaiting incoming calls, and Mielke's white dress uniform hangs in a wardrobe. The only vaguely personal touch are the clay animal figures made by kindergarten children, so incongruous that the effect is almost grotesque.

On the floor above Mielke's offices various rooms are devoted to different aspects of the history of the Stasi and the GDR. Unfortunately, the commentary is in German only, which makes much of it rather difficult to figure out. However, the displays of *Stasi* surveillance apparatus, most of it surprisingly primitive, speak for themselves. The extensive array of bugging devices and cameras reveals the absurd lengths the GDR went to in order to keep tabs on what its citizens were doing – included in the display are watering cans and plant pots concealing toylike cameras. You'll also find a about shortages, crumbling infrastructure, poor working conditions, and anger at the totalitarian nature of the regime, and reported its findings assiduously and impartially. It all made no difference in the end though; when the GDR finally went under the *Stasi* went with it, though not without a struggle.

On November 17, 1989, the Ministry for State Security was officially turned into the supposedly government-accountable Office for State Security. However, the first thing this ostensibly new organization did was order the destruction of *Stasi* files, an act which generated widespread popular outrage. In January 1990 the GDR government proposed a reorganization of its security service to counter an alleged neo-Nazi threat (not quite as absurd now as it seemed to many at the time). By now public patience was at an end and on January 15 the *Stasi* HQ was attacked by a mob. No one was lynched, though in the confusion some files were destroyed, but it was obvious that the *Stasi* as a cohesive organization was finished. Its operatives did their best to disappear and cover their tracks. Over the following months the press carried a number of gleeful articles about *Stasi* operatives living in reduced circumstances, including one about a former colonel now working as a toilet cleaner, but many people suspect that a shadowy Mafia-like organization remains, a kind of spies' old boys' network, providing contacts for jobs and information.

And the story is by no means over. At the beginning of 1991 former citizens of the GDR were given the right to apply to see their *Stasi* files. Tens of thousands availed themselves of the opportunity to find out what the *Stasi* had recorded about them, and more importantly who had provided the information. Apart from a few well-publicized cases involving former dissidents, few have actually seen their files yet. The sheer volume of material involved has inevitably meant delays in processing it all, but there's also almost certainly a desire on the part of the German government to slow down the process – in the hope that people will be less inclined to seek rough justice against those who informed on them once a few years have gone by.

couple of rooms stuffed with medals, badges, flags and other items of GDR kitsch. For German-speakers the sections on political terror during the Stalin years and forced resettlement from border zones throw light on otherwise little-known aspects of GDR history.

Elsewhere in Lichtenberg

A rather sinister-looking **Rathaus** looms over Möllendorffstrasse a few streets to the west, and just north of here, marooned amid the traffic, is an improbably rustic **Dorfkirche**, dating back to Lichtenberg's village origins. The stone walls date from the original thirteenth-century structure, but the rest is more modern, the spire having been tacked on as recently as 1965. The only other attraction in Lichtenberg itself is the **Gedenkstätte der Sozialisten** or "Memorial to the Socialists", a kilometre or so northeast of Lichtenberg U- and S-Bahn station, at the end of Gudrunstrasse, and perhaps only for die-hard fans of GDR arcana. Its centrepiece is a four-metre chunk of red porphyry bearing

Lichtenberg and Marzahn

the inscription *Die Toten mahnen uns* – "The dead remind us", commemorating the GDR's socialist hall of fame from Karl Liebknecht and Rosa Luxemburg onwards. A tablet bears a list of names that reads like the street directory of virtually any town in pre-*Wende* East Germany, recording the esoteric cult-figures of the workers' and peasants' state in alphabetical order, and until 1989 the East Berlin public were cajoled and coerced into attending hundred-thousand-strong mass demonstrations here. The whole thing actually replaced a much more interesting Mies van der Rohe-designed memorial that stood here from 1926 until the Nazis destroyed it in 1935. Altogether much more uncompromising, featuring a huge star and hammer and sickle, the original memorial caused problems for van der Rohe when he came before Joseph McCarthy's Un-American Activities Committee in 1951. The Gedenkstätte is also the burial place of Walter Ulbricht, the man who took the decision to build the Wall, and Wilhelm Pieck, the first president of the GDR.

The Tierpark

To reach Lichtenberg's sprawling **Tierpark** or zoo (daily 9am–sunset or 7pm at the latest; DM12, concessions DM6) in Friedrichsfelde, take the U-Bahn to Tierpark station (the zoo entrances are on the eastern side of Am Tierpark). The Tierpark ranks as one of the largest zoos in Europe and a thorough exploration of its wooded grounds could easily absorb the better part of a day. It's an ideal destination for families, though some visitors may balk at the traditional nature of the place and the fact that some of the animals are kept in very small cages. However, others have much more space to roam around and virtually every species imaginable, from alpaca to wisent, can be found here, including rare Przewalski horses, which have been bred in the zoo in great numbers over the years, bringing the breed back from the edge of extinction.

Hidden away in the grounds of the zoo, just beyond an enclosure of lumbering pelicans, is **Schloss Friedrichsfelde** (Tues–Sun 10am–6pm; DM3.50, concessions DM2.50), a Baroque palace housing an exhibition of eighteenth- and nineteenth-century interior decor. Theodor Fontane described it as the Schloss Charlottenburg of the East, but he was exaggerating – the best thing about it are its pretty ornamental grounds.

Karlshorst

From the Tierpark, a stroll south down Am Tierpark, bearing left along Treskowerallee for about a kilometre, will bring you to **Karlshorst** (alternatively take the S-Bahn from Alexanderplatz, changing at Ostkreuz). For many years you were more likely to hear Russian than German spoken on the streets around here, as the area was effectively a Russian quarter, thanks to the presence of large numbers of Soviet soldiers and their dependants. The Russians accepted the unconditional surrender of the German armed forces in a *Wehrmacht* engineer's school here on May 8, 1945, and went on to establish their Berlin headquarters nearby. For many years after Karlshorst was a closed area, fenced off and under armed guard, out of bounds to ordinary East Germans. Later, they were allowed back into parts of the area, but Karlshorst retained an exclusive cachet, its villas given over to the elite of GDR society – scientists and writers – or used as foreign embassy residences.

The Russians finally left in the summer of 1994 but a reminder of their presence endures in the shape of the **Museum Berlin-Karlshorst** in Rheinsteinstrasse (corner of Zwieseler Str., Tues–Sun 10am–6pm; free), the building where the German surrender was signed. Under the Russians this museum was officially known as the "Museum of the Unconditional Surrender of Fascist Germany in the Great Patriotic War 1941–45". Since then it has been renamed and rearranged to suit post-Cold War sensibilities. It features an exhibition on the long and tumultuous German-Russian relationship, obviously focusing on the treaty that ended the war.

Another unusual Karlshorst attraction is the **Trabrennbahn Karlshorst**, Treskowerallee 129, where you can enjoy a day at the races Berlin-style, watching trap- and dog racing – most events take place at the weekend. The racetrack is to the left of Treskowerallee, just south of the S-Bahn bridge.

Marzahn

To see the real legacy of East Berlin – **MARZAHN** – it's probably best to go by day and preferably not looking too much like a tourist, as the area has a reputation for violence. It's in such places as Marzahn, all across the former GDR, that people are bearing the economic brunt of reunification's downside – unemployment, *Kurzarbeit* or "short-time working", and low wages – and where you'll see the worst effects caused by the collapse of a state that, for all its faults, ensured a certain level of social security for its citizens. Ironically, Marzahn was one of the GDR's model new towns of the 1970s, part of Honecker's efforts to solve his country's endemic housing shortage by providing modern apartments in purpose-built blocks with shopping facilities and social amenities to hand. But like similar developments in Western countries, it never quite worked out according to plan, with the usual crime and drugs (in this case alcohol and prescribed tranquillizers) surfacing.

Springpfuhl to Marzahner Promenade

Most of Marzahn dates from the 1970s, when it was built with an attendant industrial zone just to the west. Over 150,000 people live in a six-kilometre by two-kilometre strip of high-rise developments stretching from Springpfuhl in the south to Ahrensfelde in the north. For a brief taste, head for the **Wohngebiet am Springpfuhl**

(Springpfuhl S-Bahn station), a representative development between Märkische Allee and Allee der Kosmonauten. There's little to do other than wander, trying to take in the immensity of it all, amid the blocks and windblown shopping precincts.

To the north of here is Alt-Marzahn (tram #18 for four stops from Helene-Weigel-Platz), where something of the area's village past survives. Admittedly it's not a very pleasant past; from 1866 the fields of the area were used as *Rieselfelder*, specially designated for the disposal of Berlin's sewage. Despite this malodorous development, Marzahn acquired a **Dorfkirche** in Neo-Gothic style a few years later, built by Schinkel's pupil Friedrich August Stüler. While you're here check out the worthwhile **Berliner Dorfmuseum**, Alt-Marzahn 31 (Tues–Sun 10am–6pm; DM2, concessions DM1), the "Berlin Village Museum", centred around a typical nineteenth-century farmhouse, complete with barn, cow-stall and lots of archaic implements. From Alt-Marzahn, head for **Marzahner Promenade** (bus #192 for three stops), which is more or less in the middle of things, and from where endless blocks stretch out north and south. By now you'll probably want to leave it all behind, and the S-Bahn, located at the southeastern end of the promenade, will whisk you back into town from S-Bahnhof Marzahn.

The Gründerzeitmuseum Mahlsdorf

Alternatively, take tram #62 from Mahlsdorf's S-Bahn station two stops south along Honower Damm, or walk for about ten minutes. The suburb of **Mahlsdorf** (in the neighbouring *Bezirk* of Hellersdorf), about 5km southeast of Marzahn, is no cultural centre, but it does boast one of the city's most notable museums, the excellent **Gründerzeitmuseum Mahlsdorf**, Hultschiner Damm 333 (Wed & Sun 10am–6pm; DM7, concessions DM5), a collection of furniture and household gear from 1880–1900, the period known as the Gründerzeit or "foundation time" when the newly united Germany was at its Imperial peak. The founder of the museum, Lothar Berfelde (better known in Germany as a writer under his pseudonym, Charlotte von Mahlsdorf), got the collection together during GDR days when such an undertaking was by no means an easy task, creating a representative *Gründerzeit* apartment by taking the complete contents of rooms and relocating them in this eighteenth-century manorhouse. Depending on your tastes the result is either exquisite or over-the-top, but either way the museum is fascinating and certainly worth the long haul out to the suburbs. In the basement are furnishings from the *Mulack-Ritz*, a famous turn-of-the-century Berlin *Kneipe* that originally stood on Mulackstrasse in the Scheunenviertel (see p.120). Lothar Berfelde was awarded the *Bundesverdienstkreuz*, Germany's equivalent of the OBE, in the summer of 1992 for his services to the preservation of the city's cultural and social heritage; he is, incidentally, one of Berlin's better-known transvestites.

Pankow and Weissensee

Pankow, the northernmost eastern Berlin *Bezirk* before the city gives way to open countryside, has a slightly different atmosphere to other Berlin suburbs. It has an almost village-like feel, contrasting sharply with the grime and decay of inner-city *Bezirke* like Prenzlauer Berg, and though there's not much in the way of sights, its broad streets and parks make for an hour or two's pleasant strolling. The neighbouring *Bezirk* of **Weissensee** is also largely residential, though as home to Germany's largest Jewish cemetery its attractions are perhaps a little more tangible than those of Pankow.

Pankow

PANKOW was always more than just another East Berlin suburb. For years its villas and well-maintained flats were home mainly to members of the upper reaches of East Berlin society: state-approved artists and writers, scientists, East Berlin resident diplomats and the *Parteibonzen* (party bigwigs) of the old regime. Up until the 1960s the area was perceived in the West as being the real centre of power

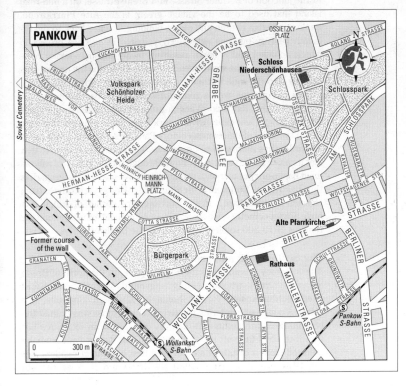

in the old GDR; Schloss Niederschönhausen, an eighteenth-century palace on the edge of the *Bezirk*, was the official residence of the GDR's first president, Wilhelm Pieck, and later of SED General Secretary Walter Ulbricht, the man who took the decision to build the Wall. The name of the suburb was also appropriated by one of the ex-GDR's best-known rock bands, in a satirical dig at the social hierarchy of the workers' and peasants' state.

Pankow's main street is **Breite Strasse**, best reached by taking the S-Bahn to Pankow station. Between Schönhauser Allee and Pankow the train passes through what used to be the *Todesstreifen* or "Death Strip", which separated East Berliners from the Wall proper. Though you'd hardly know it now, until November 9, 1989, this was the closest most East Berliners were ever likely to get to the West. From Pankow station it's a short walk north along Berliner Strasse to Breite Strasse. Alternatively, tram #53 from Hackescher Markt will take you directly there, clattering through the streets of Prenzlauer Berg.

Breite Strasse and around

At the junction of Berliner Strasse and Breite Strasse, on a mid-road island that used to be the village green, is the **Alte Pfarrkirche**, Pankow's parish church and oldest building. It dates back to the fifteenth century but was extensively restored in 1832, a project in which Schinkel had a hand, resulting in an unusual-looking Neo-Gothic jumble. At the western end of Breite Strasse is the turn-of-the-century Neo-Baroque **Rathaus**, a red-brick affair of fanciful gables, towers and cupolas, with a good *Ratskeller* in its basement.

Beyond the Rathaus, Wilhelm-Kuhr-Strasse leads to the neat **Bürgerpark**, a one-time private park with an impressive entrance portal symbolic of nineteenth-century Pankow's status as a villa quarter for Berlin's more well-to-do citizens. The Panke, a small river that lent its name to the settlement, flows through the park, and its willow-lined banks are popular with promenaders. West of the Bürgerpark is the heath-like **Volkspark Schönholzer Heide** (entrance from Herman-Hesse-Strasse), in the northwestern corner of which is a huge **Soviet cemetery**, where dozens of communal graves contain the remains of 13,200 soldiers killed during the Battle of Berlin.

The Schlosspark and around

A less gloomy possibility is the **Schlosspark**, to the north of Breite Strasse, in whose leafy grounds lurks **Schloss Niederschönhausen**, former home of Elisabeth Christine, the estranged wife of Frederick the Great. The Schloss was built at the beginning of the eighteenth century and given an extensive but run-of-the-mill face-lift in 1764. During GDR days it could only be admired from a distance, as it served first as official residence of the GDR president, from 1949 to 1960, and then as the old

regime's most prestigious state guesthouse; these days you're free
to wander the slightly dreary grounds from 9am until 7pm (9pm in
summer). A few streets to the north of the park on Platanenstrasse
is Pankow's most unusual building, the **Maria-Magdalenenkirche**,
an Expressionist church from 1930, with a bizarre slab of a tower
topped by three giant crucifixes.

Weissensee

WEISSENSEE, directly to the east of Pankow, is a predominantly
middle-class area with a slightly sleepy atmosphere, hinting at the
open countryside only a few kilometres away. The main attraction
here is Berlin's largest Jewish cemetery, another indicator of the
high profile of the all-but-vanished Jewish community. Tram #2, #3
or #4 from Hackescher Markt stops near the junction of Berliner
Allee and Pistoriusstrasse.

The Jewish Cemetery

The **Jüdischer Friedhof Weissensee** (Mon–Thurs & Sun 8am–5pm, Fri
8am–3pm) lies at the end of Herbert-Baum-Strasse (named after the
Jewish resistance hero executed for his part in an attack on a Nazi propaganda exhibition in the Lustgarten in 1942, see p.89), ten minutes
south of Berliner Strasse. Opened in 1880, when the Schönhauser Allee
cemetery had finally been filled to capacity, this is one of Europe's
largest Jewish cemeteries, and certainly the biggest in Germany.

*At the
entrance to the
cemetery a
sign requests
that male vis-
tors cover
their heads
before enter-
ing; this you
are firmly
expected to do.
You may bor-
row a skullcap
from the ceme-
tery office to
the right.*

Immediately beyond the entrance is a memorial "to our murdered
brothers and sisters 1933–45" from Berlin's Jewish community. It
takes the form of a circle of tablets bearing the names of all the large
concentration camps. Like many memorials to the war years in the
city, it's a poignant monument to the horrors that occurred, and suc-
ceeds in being less inflated and militaristic than many others. Nearby
is a memorial to Herbert Baum.

Beyond here are the cemetery administration buildings (information about the cemetery is available from here), constructed in similar mock-Moorish style to the synagogue on Oranienburger Strasse.
The cemetery itself stretches back from the entrance for about a kilometre: row upon row of headstones, with the occasional extravagant
family monument in between, a muted roll call of families systematically wiped out by the Final Solution.

A handful of well-tended postwar graves near the administration
buildings are, paradoxically, symbols of survival, witness to the fact
that a few thousand Berlin Jews did escape the Holocaust and that
the city still has a small Jewish community of around ten thousand
people.

The Weisser See and around

Back on Berliner Allee, it's only a few minutes' walk to the shady
park containing the **Weisser See**, the lake that gives the district its

name. Near the park entrance is a **monument** commemorating the struggle against Fascism. The Communist authorities tried to foster a tradition whereby newly engaged couples would lay flowers at the memorial, but this is an activity that has declined drastically in popularity since 1989. In the park itself it's possible to rent boats on the lake (which features a fairly unspectacular fountain), and there's an open-air stage and a *Gaststätte* nearby. Adjacent to the lake is an open-air swimming pool, which is fed by an underground spring. To the north of the park, off Radrennbahnstrasse, is the **Radrennbahn Weissensee**, an open-air cycle track where rock concerts are occasionally held. In the old days the SED administration brought in biggish-name Western acts like James Brown and ZZ Top at great expense, as a sop to the nation's disaffected youth. The initial impetus for this came after young people clashed with police who had attempted to move them on from streets near the Wall in the city centre, where they had been listening to a Eurythmics concert going on just over the border in West Berlin.

Along Pistoriusstrasse

After Berliner Allee, Weissensee's main street is the mostly residential **Pistoriusstrasse**, which branches off northwest from the former just before the Weisser See itself. Roughly halfway along it is Pistoriusplatz, site of a weekend market and prelude to another Berlin architectural experiment, the **Gemeindeforum Kreuzpfuhl**, which lies just to the right of the street, set around a small lake called the **Kreuzpfuhl**. It looks like no other development in the city, benefiting heavily from its position on the tree-lined lake shore, and is perhaps the most aesthetically successful of the many attempts to break away from the dreadful housing conditions of the *Mietskaserne*. These four-storey apartment blocks with their decorative red-brick facades and distinctive gabled roofs were built in 1908 and have been officially designated a "valuable monument of social history".

Köpenick and around

Köpenick is one of eastern Berlin's more pleasant *Bezirke*, located on the banks of the River Spree towards the southeast edge of the city, and easily reached by S-Bahn from Alexanderplatz (via Ostkreuz). The town of Köpenick is a slow-moving little place, but ideal to visit as an escape from the city centre. It also makes a convenient base for exploring Berlin's southeastern lakes, in particular the Müggelsee, with its appealing shoreline towns of Friedrichshagen and Rahnsdorf. Also easily accessible are the Müggelberge, Berlin's 150-metre "mountains", and the towns of Grünau and Schmöckwitz on the banks of the Lange See, which gives access to the Zeuthener See and Krossinsee.

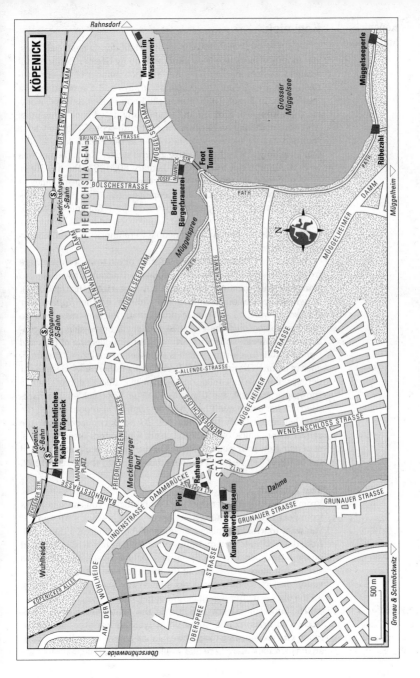

Köpenick

KÖPENICK itself was a town in its own right during medieval times, and though it has since been swallowed up by Greater Berlin, it still retains a distinct identity. The presence of a number of major factories in the area meant that Köpenick always had a reputation as a "red" town. In March 1920, during the Kapp *Putsch* attempt, workers from Köpenick took on and temporarily drove back army units who were marching on Berlin in support of the coup. The army later returned, but its success was short-lived as the *Putsch* foundered – thanks mainly to a highly effective general strike. This militancy was to continue into the Nazi era: on January 30, 1933, the day Hitler came to power, the red flag could be seen flying from the chimney of the brewery in the suburb of Friedrichshagen. This defiance was punished during the *Köpenicker Blutwoche* ("Köpenick Week of Blood") in June, during which the SA swooped on Social Democrats and Communists. Five hundred people were imprisoned and ninety-one murdered.

At the heart of Köpenick is the Altstadt or old town. To walk there from the S-Bahn station, follow Borgamannstrasse to Mandrellaplatz, location of Köpenick's **Amtsgericht** (District Court), in whose execution chamber the victims of the *Köpenicker Blutwoche* were killed. From Mandrellaplatz, Puchanstrasse leads to Am Generalshof and the entrance to a small Spree-side park containing the **Mecklenburger Dorf**, an open-air collection of bars and *Imbiss* stands in a setting which is supposed to conjure up the ambience of a north German village. In reality it's rather tacky, despite (or perhaps because of) folkloric touches like thatched roofs and a showpiece windmill, but this doesn't deter Köpenick's more hardened drinkers, who quaff here with determined abandon. Behind the Mecklenburger Dorf, the Platz des 23 April commemorates the arrival in Köpenick of the Soviet army – liberators or conquerors, depending on your point of view. On the Platz a sculpted clenched fist on top of a stone tablet honours those killed by the Nazis in 1933.

The Altstadt

From the Mecklenburger Dorf the Dammbrücke (you can rent boats from near here) leads across the Spree into Köpenick's **Altstadt** (if you want to avoid the places mentioned above, there's a direct link from the S-Bahn station on tram #60 or #62, or bus #169). Situated on an island between the Spree and Dahme rivers, the Altstadt's streets run more or less true to the medieval town plan. A big renovation project, already some years underway, has been smartening up the old town after a long period of neglect.

The most prominent building is the turn-of-the-century Neo-Gothic **Rathaus** on Alt Köpenick, a typically over-the-top gabled affair with an imposing clock tower. Eight years before World War I, an incident took place here that would capture the imagination of the world's press and provide the inspiration for a play that would make Köpenick famous far beyond the city limits of Berlin. On October 16, 1906, an unemployed shoemaker named **Wilhelm Voigt**, who had spent some time in prison, disguised himself as an army officer and commandeered a troop of soldiers. He marched them to the Köpenick Rathaus and, with their assistance, requisitioned the contents of the municipal safe. Having ordered his detachment to take Köpenick's mayor and book-keeper to the Neue Wache guardhouse in the city centre, he disappeared. Although Voigt was soon caught, the story was seized on abroad as an example of the Prussian propensity to blindly follow anyone wearing uniform. Later, the playwright Carl Zuckmeyer turned Voigt's exploits into a play, *Der Hauptmann von Köpenick* (The Captain of Köpenick). The robbery is re-enacted every summer in the second half of June during the Köpenick summer festival.

In **Grünstrasse** and **Böttcherstrasse** are a number of typical nineteenth-century *Bürgerhäuser* with restored facades, and given the sometimes down-at-heel nature of the Altstadt it's not hard to picture this area as it must have been a century or so ago.

The Schloss

At the southern end of the Altstadt island a footbridge leads to the Schlossinsel, site of Köpenick's Baroque **Schloss**, which is more of a fortified manor house dating back to the seventeenth century. The Schloss houses the **Kunstgewerbemuseum** (Museum of Applied Art; Tues–Sun 9am–5pm; DM4, concessions DM2). Despite an extensive selection of porcelain, glass, textiles, leather, jewellery, tin, iron, gold and silver work from the Middle Ages through to the present day, it's all rather dull, perhaps because of its stuffy layout and the presence of eagle-eyed attendants on the lookout for infringements of the regulations. Highpoint is the treasury, with an opulent hoard of gold and silver, including the eleventh-century *Giselaschmuck*. Also impressive is the *Berliner Silberbuffet*, a set of silver tableware made for the Brandenburg prince who was to become Friedrich I, Prussia's first king. There's a disappointingly small *Jugendstil* section, and a collection of uninspiring contemporary work. Occasional concerts are held in the Schloss concert hall and in the seventeenth-century chapel at weekends.

The Kietz

Just to the southeast of the Altstadt is the **Kietz**, a cobbled street of fishing cottages whose origins go back to the early thirteenth century. The houses, with their painted shutters and whitewashed facades, back onto the **Frauentog**, a bay that separates the Schlossinsel from the mainland, where Köpenick's fishermen used to cast their nets. As in the Altstadt, renovation over the past several years has brightened up most of the cottages, and it's a pleasant stroll along the street.

FEZ Wuhlheide and Oberschöneweide

From Köpenick Altstadt, you can take tram #67 a few stops north-west to the **Freizeit- und Erholungszentrum (FEZ) Wuhlheide** (Mon–Fri 10am–5pm, Sat & Sun 10am–6pm; free), a large amuse-ment park for children which takes up a sizeable chunk of the Wuhlheide woods. It's all a bit worthy, with workshops, open-air stages and sports facilities, but the main attraction seems to be the seven-kilometre-long **Berliner Parkeisenbahn**, a narrow-gauge rail line operated by children. For details on what's going on drop in at the information centre in the **FEZ-Palast** at the heart of it all.

For architecture fans **Oberschöneweide**, a little to the west of the FEZ, boasts some impressive modernist buildings designed by the architect Peter Behrens during the early part of the century. The first, opposite the FEZ itself at An der Wuhlheide 192–194, is a boathouse which used to be owned by AEG, and there are a couple of Behrens' factory buildings at Wilhelminenhofstr. 83–85 (on the route of trams #26 or #61). Nearby, Zeppelinstr. 11–71, Roedernstr. 8–14b and Fontanestr. 8a–12c are all examples of Behrens-designed residential housing.

The Grosser Müggelsee and around

From Luisenhain, opposite the Rathaus in Köpenick Altstadt, it's possible to take a *Stern und Kreisschiffahrt* boat trip around the nearby **Grosser Müggelsee**, one of Berlin's main lakes, just a few kilometres east of Köpenick itself. Although the lake lies within the city limits of Berlin, the atmosphere of suburbs like Friedrichshagen and Rahnsdorf is distinctly small-town, and wandering the shores of the lake and the surrounding woods is a welcome relief from pound-ing Berlin's relentless urban streets. Beware, though: the Müggelsee area gets very crowded at all times of the year – in summer people swarm here for sun and sailing, and in winter to ice skate.

Friedrichshagen and the Müggelsee shore

Another way of reaching the Grosser Müggelsee is to take the S-Bahn to **FRIEDRICHSHAGEN**, a small town founded in 1753 as a settle-ment for Bohemian cotton spinners who, as a condition of their being allowed to live here, were required by law to plant mulberry trees for the rearing of silkworms. Leading down from the S-Bahn station is Friedrichshagen's main drag, **Bölschestrasse**, where a number of single-storey houses survive from the original eighteenth-century settlement, dwarfed by later nineteenth-century blocks, and a few vestigial mulberry trees still cling to life at the roadside. About halfway down this otherwise attractive street the **Christophoruskirche**, a gloomy Neo-Gothic church in red brick, puts a Lutheran damper on things.

To get away from it, make for the lake, which is reached via Josef-Nawrocki-Strasse, passing the extensive buildings of the **Berliner**

Bürgerbrauerei, from whose chimney the red flag flew provocative-
ly the day Hitler was sworn in as chancellor. Following the road
around leads to a small park at the point where the Spree flows into
the Grosser Müggelsee. Here there's a cruise-ship pier and a foot
tunnel that takes you under the river. At the other side a path through
the woods follows the lakeshore to the *Gaststätten* at Rübezahl and
then **Müggelseeperle** (both of these can be reached on the cruise
boats that run out here from the city – see "Getting around" in
Basics). The *Rübezahl Gaststätte* is a real architectural eyesore,
looking like a transplant from Alexanderplatz, and the food isn't
much better, but stopping off for a quick drink entails no major gas-
tronomic risks (see "Cafés and bars" in Listings).

Halfway between Friedrichshagen and Rahnsdorf is the **Museum
im Wasserwerk**, Müggelseedamm 307 (mid-March to mid-Nov
Wed–Fri 10am–4pm, Sat & Sun 10am–5pm; DM4, concessions
DM2), an old waterworks building that's been turned into a museum
detailing the history of Berlin's water supply. Take tram #60 for six
stops from Friedrichshagen S-Bahn station.

The Müggelberge

A little to the south of the *Rübezahl* is the main road and the bus
stop from where bus #169 runs to Köpenick S-Bahn station.
Opposite the bus stop is a path leading through the woods up to the
summit of the **Müggelberge**. Around about the halfway mark is the
Teufelsee (Devil's Lake), a small pool with a glass-smooth surface,
which acts as a focus for various nature trails. More information on
these, and on the flora and fauna of the area, can be obtained at the
nearby **Lehrkabinett** information centre (May–Sept Wed–Fri
10am–4pm, Sat & Sun 10am–5pm; Oct–April Wed, Thurs, Sat & Sun
10am–4pm). Pushing on and up through the woods leads to the
Müggelturm, a functional-looking observation tower offering great
views of the lake and woods, plus a café, bar and restaurant (see
"Cafés and bars" in Listings). Incidentally, both the Teufelsee and
Müggelturm are accessible by car and bike (if you've got the stami-
na) along reasonably well-surfaced tracks from the main road. Also
accessible by car, but more pleasantly reached on foot, are the
Schmetterlingshorst and the *Marienlust*, a couple of *Gaststätten*
on the shore of the Langer See about 500m south of the Müggelturm
(see "Cafés and bars" in Listings).

Rahnsdorf

At the east end of the Grosser Müggelsee, the little town of **RAHNS-
DORF** can be reached by S-Bahn or by tram #61 from
Friedrichshagen. Rahnsdorf itself is one of eastern Berlin's more
delightful hidden corners, a sprawl of tree-shaded lakeside houses
with an old fishing village at its core. Head for **Dorfstrasse**, a cobbled street at the southern end of the village (bus #161 from the S-

Bahn station for six stops, then follow the signs for *Altes Fischerdorf* or ask directions), lined by fishermen's cottages and centred around a small parish church. The best way to explore Rahnsdorf is to simply wander the lakeside and soak up the atmosphere. Just off Fürstenwalder Damm, on the western edge of town, there's an *FKK* (*Freikörperkultur*) **nudist beach** for hardy souls.

Grünau

Another possible local destination is **GRÜNAU** on the River Dahme, just to the south of Köpenick (tram #68 runs directly from Köpenick, and there's an S-Bahn station). There isn't a great deal in terms of sights, but you could do worse than go for a walk along the quiet banks of the Langer See, as the Dahme is called beyond Grünau.

The Langer See itself is a watersports centre, and the **Strandbad Grünau**, a beach of sorts, lies just outside town, with numerous *Gaststätten* nearby. To reach it, head along Regattastrasse past the **Regattatribüne**, starting point for boat races along this stretch and venue for part of the 1936 Olympics.

Schmöckwitz

Tram #68 passes through the tranquil villa settlement of Karolinenhof to **SCHMÖCKWITZ**, which has been inhabited since prehistoric times. Again, there aren't any real sights, but you can spend a pleasant hour or two wandering through the **Schmöckwitzer Werder**, a woodland area occupying a finger of land several kilometres square between the Zeuthener See and Krossinsee, southeast of Schmöckwitz. On the shores of the Krossinsee (and accessible by occasional buses from Schmöckwitz) are a couple of decent **campsites** (see "Accommodation" in Listings).

Chapter 10

Potsdam and Sanssouci

"**T**he first fine day should be devoted to Potsdam, without which a complete impression of Berlin can scarcely be obtained," claims the prewar Baedeker, a nod to the fact that **Potsdam**, although not officially part of Berlin, was the natural completion of the Hohenzollern city, forming a unity with Charlottenburg and the old centre along Unter den Linden.

Above all, Potsdam means **Sanssouci**, Frederick the Great's splendid landscaped park of architectural treasures, including Schloss Sanssouci, the king's palace retreat. There is, however, much more to Potsdam; in the town itself, despite the depredations of Allied bombing and insensitive, politically motivated GDR planners, much of the historic centre remains intact, with grandiose city gates and an eighteenth-century **Baroque quarter** recalling the atmosphere of a *Residenzstadt* or royal residence. Other sights include **Cecilienhof**, where the fate of postwar Europe was sealed at the Potsdam conference; **Russische Kolonie Alexandrowka**, a nineteenth-century Russian colony of timber houses overlooked by an Orthodox chapel; the **Pfingstberg**, with its forlorn Jewish cemetery and ruined Belvedere; another Schloss across the River Havel in **Babelsberg**, which also boasts a film studio prominent in the history of German cinema; and myriad smaller attractions in between.

Despite the fact that it lies just to the southwest of Berlin, until 1990 it was difficult to reach Potsdam: visa regulations made visiting a complicated affair and many people left it off their itineraries. Since the withering away of the border, however, the town has enjoyed an enormous influx of visitors from the west. Although Potsdam makes for a good day out from the city, you'll probably find that you need two or three days to take everything in, so practical details and listings are included in this chapter.

The telephone code for Potsdam is ☎0331.

Potsdam

Like most towns in the Berlin area, **POTSDAM**'s origins are Slavonic and its first documented mention was as *Poztupimi* during the tenth century, making it older than Berlin by a couple of hundred years. In 1160 a castle was built here, marking the first step in the town's gradual transformation from fishing backwater, though for the next couple of centuries it remained a relatively sleepy place.

Under the Hohenzollerns, Potsdam became a **royal residence** and **garrison town**, roles which it enjoyed right up until the abdication of Kaiser Wilhelm II in 1918. World War II left Potsdam badly damaged: on April 14, 1945, a bombing raid killed four thousand people and reduced the town centre to ruins, destroying many fine Baroque buildings (the raid was so heavy that it could be heard and seen from Bernau, over 40km to the northeast). Immediately after the war, Potsdam was chosen by the victorious Allies as the venue for a conference where, on

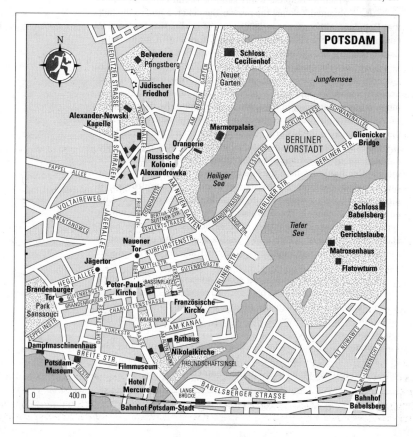

August 2, 1945, the division of Germany and Europe was confirmed. Subsequently, under the SED regime, it was decided to demolish the ruins of much of the old town and undertake extensive modern building programmes in pursuit of a "new, socialist Potsdam". These account for the unattractive and confused appearance of the eastern half of the town centre, and although attempts were made to preserve the architectural integrity of the town during the 1980s, the Communists always felt ill at ease with its historical role and Imperial associations.

With the opening of the border in 1989, Potsdam's links with the rest of Berlin were once again revived. But reminders of the immediate past remain: until the summer of 1994 the grim red-brick *Uhlan* barracks that ring the town were occupied by Russian soldiers. With the departure of the Russians an important vestige of Potsdam's GDR-era identity has vanished and a further step on the road to post-Communist normalization has been completed. The troops' presence had lent an anachronistic edge of Cold War exotica to the town, but few locals were sorry to see them depart.

Arrival, information and accommodation

Visiting Potsdam couldn't be easier. There are excellent transport links from Berlin, and the local tourist office can arrange accommodation in either private rooms or hotels (due to the large volume of visitors, local accommodation is harder to come by in summer).

If you can't make it here under your own steam (though it's easy enough) there are plenty of organized day trips run from the city – see Basics.

There are direct S-Bahn links (lines #3 and #7) from Berlin's Bahnhof Friedrichstrasse to **S-Bahnhof Potsdam-Stadt**, from where it's just a few minutes' walk north across the Lange Brücke into the centre of town. Coming in by road from western Berlin, bus #116 from S-Bahnhof Wannsee will deposit you on the Potsdam side of the **Glienicker Bridge**, just east of the centre. From here you can catch tram #93 to the **Platz der Einheit** in the centre of town. A more atmospheric approach is provided by the cruise-boats from Wannsee (see p.153).

Just south of the Platz der Einheit is Potsdam's **tourist information office**, at Friedrich-Ebert-Str. 5 (April–Oct Mon–Fri 9am–8pm, Sat 10am–6pm, Sun 10am–4pm; Nov–March Mon–Fri 10am–6pm, Sat & Sun 10am–2pm; ☎27 55 80). It's well equipped with maps and will book rooms in private accommodation.

Accommodation

Ideally, you should spend at least a couple of days in Potsdam. If you're on a budget the best bet is to book a **private room** (around DM50 single or DM100 double per night) through the tourist office (see above). Potsdam also has a couple of **campsites**. For information, call the tourist office or the German Camping Club, in Berlin on ☎03 02 18 60 71.

For details of accommodation price codes see "Accommodation" in Listings.

Am Jägertor, Hegelallee 11 ☎2 18 34. A comfortable, mid-sized hotel close to Sanssouci and central Potsdam. ③

art'otel potsdam, Zeppelinstr. 136 ☎9 81 50. A bright and colourful new luxury hotel, part of it within an historic building. ⑥

Babelsberg, Stahnsdorfer Str. 68 ☎7 88 89. An old-fashioned, value-for-money hotel on the Babelsberg side of the Havel. ①

Hotel Schloss Cecilienhof, Im neuen Garten ☎3 70 50. Housed in a wing of Schloss Cecilienhof, this is the place to head for if you want a little luxury. ⑤

Hotel Mercure Potsdam, Lange Brücke ☎46 31. A typical GDR-era plush hotel in the heart of town. ⑤

Hotel Zum Hummer, Im Park Babelsberg 2 ☎61 95 49. A good-value place, pleasantly located in Babelsberg Park. ③

The Altstadt

Platz der Einheit (formerly Wilhelmplatz) makes a good starting point for any exploration of the Altstadt, although only a few non-concrete buildings survive in its immediate vicinity, hinting at a world long since vanished. The fancy-looking building at the southeast corner of the square is a Neo-Baroque post office, to the immediate north of which stood the Wilhelm III Synagoge until it was wrecked on *Kristallnacht*, and later completely demolished – a plaque marks the spot. Southeast of the post office Am alten Markt branches off Am Kanal, leading to the Nikolaikirche. This stately domed building, its Neoclassical lines at odds with its surroundings, will probably have attracted your attention already if you've come into town from the S-Bahn station. It was originally built according to plans drawn up by Schinkel, and the impact of its exterior is echoed within – the walls are decorated with paintings of New Testament scenes and the effect of the dome is, if anything, more impressive than from the outside. Much of what can be seen, however, is a restoration, as the church was very badly damaged during the war.

Diagonally opposite the Nikolaikirche is another survivor, Potsdam's former Rathaus, which was built in Palladian Classical style during the mid-eighteenth century, when it must have represented something of a departure for Brandenburg's municipal architecture. Until 1875 the circular Rathaus tower, on top of which a gilded Atlas supports the globe, served as the town jail. The Rathaus lost its town-hall function in 1885, and was taken over by a bank, which remained there until the bombs came. Under the old authorities the building became a *Kulturhaus* or arts centre, a role it retains – inside you'll find a theatre, a couple of galleries and a number of cafés. The obelisk in front of the Rathaus was designed by Knobelsdorff and in its original form bore four reliefs depicting the Great Elector and his successors. When it was re-erected during the 1970s these were replaced with reliefs of architects whose work did much to shape Potsdam: Schinkel, Knobelsdorff, Gontard and Persius.

East of the Platz der Einheit only a few ailing eighteenth-century townhouses survive on Am Kanal, although this area is the oldest part of Potsdam: at the southern end of Fischerstrasse is the site of what was once the Slavonic island settlement of *Poztupimi*, the fore-runner of the modern town. Just to the southeast lies the **Freundschafts Insel**, a leafy mid-Havel island that makes a good place to take a break from street-pounding, with its ornamental garden and boat rental facilities.

West of the Platz der Einheit

Slightly more tangible vestiges of old Potsdam survive in a few of the streets west of the Platz der Einheit. **Yorckstrasse** boasts a number of fine – albeit slightly run-down – **Baroque houses**, as does **Wilhelm-Staab-Strasse**. The **Neuer Markt** quarter, just to the south of Yorckstrasse, also has a couple of good-looking survivors, including some improbably grand (but decrepit) eighteenth-century coaching stables with an entrance in the form of a triumphal arch, which are now home to a haulage firm. At Am neuen Markt 1 is the **Kabinetthaus**, a small mansion that was the birthplace of Friedrich Wilhelm II, the only member of the Hohenzollern family actually born in Potsdam.

The large modern building to the immediate west of the Nikolaikirche is a teacher training institute on whose ground floor you'll find Potsdam's **tourist information office** (entrance in Friedrich-Ebert-Strasse – see p.187). This uniformly dull colossus forms a neat ensemble, representative of the high-rise chicken-coop school of GDR architecture, with the startlingly unattractive and even more gargantuan *Hotel Mercure Potsdam* opposite.

The hotel stands on the site of the **Stadtschloss**, a Baroque residence built at the behest of the Great Elector between 1662 and 1669. It was reduced to a bare, roofless shell in 1945 and the demolition of its skeletal remains in 1960 removed the last vestiges of what, judging by prewar photographs, was a not unappealing building, although a number of its statues were recently discovered languishing in a local wood. Like the royal palace in eastern Berlin, the Stadtschloss, with its Hohenzollern connections, was an embarrassment to the Communist authorities – so they quite simply erased it.

The Marstall and around

A little to the west across Breite Strasse is the former palace **Marstall** or royal stables, the oldest town-centre survivor. Originally built as an orangerie towards the end of the eighteenth century and converted into a stables by that scourge of frivolity, Friedrich Wilhelm I, the building owes its subsequent appearance to Knobelsdorff, who extended and prettified it during the eighteenth century. Today the Marstall houses Potsdam's **Filmmuseum**, Schlossstr. 1 (Tues–Fri 10am–5pm, Sat & Sun 10am–6pm; DM4, concessions DM2).

This makes for an interesting hour or so's visit. Drawing on material from the UFA studios in nearby Babelsberg (later DEFA, the GDR state film company), the museum presents both a technical and artistic history of German film from 1895 to 1980, with some particularly fascinating material concerning the genres of the immediate postwar period. There's a vaguely hands-on feel, with a few visitor-operated Bioscopes and numerous screens playing clips. The museum **cinema** is the best in Potsdam and there's also a good **café**.

A little to the west of the Marstall, a prefabricated office building occupies the site of the **Garnisonkirche**, Potsdam's Baroque garrison church, last resting place of many prominent members of the Hohenzollern family. On March 23, 1933, the Reichstag was reconvened here following the fire and the subsequent elections that had given the Nazis a small majority (see p.53). The building was later wrecked during the bombing, and its burnt-out shell finally demolished in 1968, despite protest from both home and abroad – another victim of the old regime's discomfort with relics of the Prussian and Imperial German past. The elimination of the Garnisonkirche and Schloss transformed this part of the town, destroying its atmosphere – it's hard to imagine that the bleak Breite Strasse was the main promenade of the prewar town.

Also vanished from the town plan is the **Stadtkanal** or city canal, tree-lined remnant of a fortification system that once ran around the core of old Potsdam, following modern Dortustrasse, turning east into Yorckstrasse, and then running the length of Am Kanal. An address here was highly desirable, despite the stench from the stagnant waters, but in 1972 public hygiene won the day and the canal was filled in. Just west of the point where Breite Strasse intersects with Dortustrasse is the **Militärwaisenhaus**, a late eighteenth-century military orphanage that looks positively palatial, despite the fact that it's obviously lost its dome. The present building replaced an earlier half-timbered one and its main purpose was to provide a home for the illegitimate offspring of grenadiers and local girls.

A little further along is the **Potsdam-Museum**, Breite Str. 8–12 (Tues–Sun & first Mon of each month 9am–5pm; DM4, concessions DM2, free first Mon of each month), which details Potsdam's civic history in uninspiring fashion. The museum building was constructed in 1769 with the architecture of Whitehall in London as its model, at the instigation of Friedrich II. An annexe to the museum is housed at Breite Str. 13.

From here it's worth making a quick detour down **Kiezstrasse**, where a number of eighteenth-century Rococo houses have been beautifully restored, including no. 4 which houses *Der Froschkasten*, a traditional, and recommended, *Kneipe*. The nearby high-rises on the Neustädter Havelbucht don't compare very favourably, but do hide in their midst the **Dampfmaschinenhaus** (guided tours mid-May to mid-Oct Sat & Sun 10am–noon & 1–5pm; DM4), which ranks as the most imaginative pump-house in Germany. At first sight it looks like a mosque, and that's what the architect, Ludwig Persius, intended when he built it at the beginning of the 1840s. The chimney takes the form of a minaret, and the striped stonework and tiling look wildly incongruous. The pump originally supplied water to a reservoir on the Ruinenberg hill near Sanssouci.

The Baroque quarter and the Holländisches Viertel

North of the Platz der Einheit, the area bounded by Schopenhauerstrasse, Hegelallee, Hebbelstrasse and Charlottenstrasse is Potsdam's **Baroque quarter**, built between 1732 and 1742 on the orders of Friedrich Wilhelm I. **Bassinplatz**, though disfigured by a huge modern bus station, offers the best introduction to this episode of Potsdam's architectural history. At the southeastern corner of the square is the **Französische Kirche**, completed according to plans by Knobelsdorff in 1753, in imitation of the Pantheon in Rome, a recurring theme in German architecture of the period. At its western end, Bassinplatz is graced by the nineteenth-century **Peter-Pauls-Kirche**, a replica of the campanile of San Zeno Maggiore in Verona, and the first large Catholic church to be built in the town.

The main concentration of ornate Baroque houses, built with slight variations in detail to avoid monotony, lies to the west of here, on and around **Brandenburger Strasse**, Potsdam's pedestrianized main shopping street. The whole quarter was intended as a settlement for tradespeople in the then rapidly expanding town. Some 584 houses were built in all, and this area, unlike the Altstadt, survived the war substantially intact. Turning into Lindenstrasse from Brandenburger Strasse, the Dutch-style former **Kommandantehaus**, at Lindenstr. 54–55, is a building with uncomfortably recent historical associations. Until the *Wende* it served as a *Stasi* detention centre, known as the "Lindenhotel": it was handed over to the embryonic political opposition groups in November 1989; enquire within about guided tours.

It's worth taking a quick look at the western reaches of Gutenbergstrasse, where some of the buildings have been allowed to decay until little more than shells remain. This area is, incidentally, the focus of Potsdam's **squat scene**. To the north and west of the Baroque quarter are the most impressive of Potsdam's three surviving town gates – the **Jägertor** or "Hunter's Gate" (at the end of Lindenstrasse), surmounted by a sculpture of a stag succumbing to a pack of baying hounds, and the **Brandenburger Tor** (at the western end of Brandenburger Strasse), a triumphal arch built by Gontard in 1733, with a playfulness lacking in its Berlin namesake.

The Holländisches Viertel
Just to the north of Bassinplatz is the **Holländisches Viertel** or "Dutch quarter", the best-known and most appealing part of Friedrich Wilhelm I's town extension. In the area bounded by

Gutenbergstrasse, Kurfürstenstrasse, Friedrich-Ebert-Strasse and Hebbbelstrasse are 134 gabled, red-brick houses put up by Dutch builders for the immigrants from Holland who were invited to work in Potsdam by the king. In fact, not many Dutch took up the invitation, and many of those who did returned home when the promised employment dried up following Friedrich Wilhelm's death, allowing Germans to move into their houses.

Under the old regime it was decided to renovate the quarter, which even at the time of its building was recognized as one of the most attractive in the town. Restoration work has so far been only a partial success: modern builders lacked the skills to restore the carved gables, and bad planning meant that in some cases inhabitants were moved out but work was never started. As a result, a few of the houses look derelict, but some excellent restored examples can be found along **Mittelstrasse**, particularly at the junction with Benkertstrasse. Mittelstrasse seems to be shaping up for a chi-chi future, with a number of new shops and cafés staking tentative claims on some of Potsdam's most sought-after real estate. Finally, at the top of Friedrich-Ebert-Strasse, at the northwestern corner of the Holländisches Viertel, is the **Nauener Tor**, a stylistically messy-looking town gate inspired by English architectural trends of the mid-eighteenth century.

Eating, drinking and nightlife

Eating and drinking pose few problems in Potsdam. There's a reasonable array of **restaurants**, and most places are pleasant enough, though few would gain any stars in a gourmet's guide to the Berlin area. In town, the major and most convenient concentration of possibilities is along Brandenburger Strasse, although it pays to go a little further afield.

Restaurants

Hafthorn, Friedrich-Ebert-Strasse 90 ☎2 80 08 20. Large and lively restaurant offering Swabian specialities for surprisingly little money.

Kleines Schloss, Park Babelsberg ☎70 51 56. A traditionally minded lakeside place far from the hubbub of the city. Standard German dishes. Wed–Sun 11am–9pm.

Luise Restaurant, Luisenplatz 6 ☎29 27 97. Mid-priced German and Continental food in casual surroundings. The perfect place to eat before tackling Sanssouci, just up the road.

Restaurant Pegasus, Schlossstr. 14 ☎29 15 06. Good but expensive German cuisine, and the floorshow may give you indigestion.

Schloss Cecilienhof in Schloss Cecilienhof ☎3 70 50. The poshest and, not surprisingly, most expensive restaurant in Potsdam. Offers dishes allegedly served up to Churchill, Stalin and Truman during the Potsdam conference, but the high prices do not always guarantee the quality of the food.

Terrassenrestaurant-Minsk, Max-Planck-Str. 10, am Brauhausberg ☎29 36 36. This ugly-looking modern establishment on the Babelsberg side of the

Havel serves surprisingly good pseudo-Byelorussian cuisine. Clear views across to Potsdam are an additional attraction.

Waage, am Neuen Markt 12 ☎2 70 96 75. Inventive dishes with local ingredients. A little on the pricey side.

Zum Laubenpieper, am Pfingstberg 25 ☎294 311. Rustic restaurant offering huge servings of old-fashioned German food. Hilltop beer garden open during the summer.

Cafés and bars

As in the rest of the former GDR, you're best catered for in **bars and cafés**, many of which have excellent, though usually simple, food menus.

Babette, Brandenburger Str. 71 ☎29 16 48. Pleasant little café, also open as a cocktail bar Wed–Sun until 1am.

Café Gallerie 0815, Friedrich-Ebert-Str. 118 ☎29 34 73. A combined café-gallery with a young crowd – could be a way into the Potsdam *Szene*.

Café im Filmmuseum, Schlossstr. 1 ☎2 70 20 41. One of Potsdam's best cafés, and a good place to take a break after visiting the museum.

Drachenhaus, Maulbeerallee ☎29 15 94. A pleasant and genteel little café in the grounds of Schloss Sanssouci itself, housed in a pagoda-style building once used by royal vintners. You can also eat well here.

Froschkasten, Kiezstr. 4 ☎29 13 15. One of the best and oldest bars in Potsdam, a *Kneipe* that also serves good food.

Kultur im Denkmal e.V, Mittelstr. 18 ☎2 80 47 25. An arty but friendly café, bar and gallery in a venerable Dutch house. One of the best in town. Cheap food with an outdoor barbecue in summer.

La Madeleine, Lindenstr. 9 ☎2 70 54 00. A small creperie featuring over 30 variations – some decidedly odd – of the French speciality.

Langer Kerl, Brandenburger Str. 37; ☎29 68 78. Straightforward beer joint in an eighteenth-century townhouse. Closed Sun & Mon, and usually shut by 7pm.

Matschkes Galerie Café, Alleestrasse 10 ☎2 70 12 10. A quiet, leafy courtyard provides a wonderfully restful spot to enjoy authentic Russian cuisine.

Die Rebe, Feuerbachstr. 1 ☎96 48 47. A very pleasant wine-*Kneipe* serving food, just southwest of the Brandenburger Tor. Open until midnight but closed Sun & Mon.

Seerose, Breite Str. 24 ☎97 41 17. Housed in a bizarre-looking modern building, this popular bar offers good views across the Neustädter Havelbucht.

Souterrain, Allee nach Sanssouci 4 ☎90 38 74. Away from the centre on the road to Sanssouci, this lively café-bar is worth dropping into.

Nightlife

For **nightlife** the best bet is the *Lindenpark*, Stahnsdorfer Str. 76–78 (☎7 89 90), over in Babelsberg, with regular "alternative" discos and live bands – the club is entered via an old double-decker bus that has been rammed through the wall. *Fabrik*, Gutenbergstr. 105, in the centre of town is also an alternative venue for gigs and events, and *Waschhaus*, Schiffbauergasse 1, just off Berliner Strasse on the way into town from the Glienicker Brücke, stages dance-music-oriented, ravey events. For German-speakers the Hans-Otto-Theater, Zimmerstr. 10 (☎2 30 38), is Potsdam's main **theatre**, with a programme worth investigating. The town also boasts a **cabaret**, the Kabarett "Am Obelisk", Schopenhauerstr. 27 (☎2 17 38).

Listings

Bike rental Fahrad Bels, Röhrenstr. 4 (Mon–Fri 10am–6pm, Sat 9am–2pm ☎62 21 13).

Boat rental on the Freundschaftsinsel, and at Grosse Fischer 11;☎61 90 26.

Boat trips Weisse Flotte, Lange Brücke ☎2 75 92 10. Tickets and information May–Sept daily 8–11am & 11.30am–5.45pm; April & Oct daily 10am–3.30pm. Regular sailings to Wannsee, Caputh, Werder, Ferch and Templin.

Car rental Babelsberger Autovermietung, Babelsberger Str. 29 ☎2 70 37 00; Ahrens & Merkle, Grünstr. 25 ☎70 77 13.

Gay info Homosexuellen-Integrations-Projekt, Berliner Str. 49 ☎2 20 65.

Lost property Friedrich-Ebert-Str. 79–81 ☎2 89 15 87.

Petrol stations Horstweg 2, Babelsberg (24hr); Potsdamerstr. 164.

Police Henning-von-Treskow-Str. 9–13 ☎2 83 02.

Post office Main post office: Am Kanal 16–18 ☎3 80.

Public transport information Johannsenstr. 12–17 ☎2 37 52 75; train info ☎03 01 94 19.

Swimming Indoor pools at Am Brauhausberg, Max-Planck-Strasse (☎24 46 91) and Puschkinallee 16 (☎2 70 15 21). For outdoor bathing head for the beaches at Caputh and Templin (also for naturists) and at Glindow.

Taxis ☎29 22 31. Taxi ranks at Am Bassinplatz, the Hauptbahnhof, Potsdam-West and Drewitz stations, Rathaus Babelsberg and Friedrich-Wolf-Strasse.

Women's centre Frauenzentrum, Zeppelinstr. 189 (☎29 14 75), with café on Fri & Sat.

Park Sanssouci

There's a colour map of Park Sanssouci at the end of this book.

Park Sanssouci, Frederick the Great's fabled retreat, stretches out for two kilometres west of Potsdam town centre, and its gardens and palaces are what draw most visitors to the town. In 1744 Frederick ordered the construction of a residence where he would be able to live "without cares" – "sans souci" in the French spoken in court. The task was entrusted to the architect Georg von Knobelsdorff, who had already proved himself on other projects in Potsdam and Berlin. **Schloss Sanssouci**, on a hill overlooking the town, took three years to complete, while the extensive parklands to the west – the **Rehgarten** – were laid out over the following five years. As a finishing touch Frederick ordered the construction of the **Neues Palais** at the western end of the park, to mark the end of the Seven Years' War. Over the following 150 years or so, numerous additions were made, including the Orangerie and the laying of Jubiläumstrasse (now known as Maulbeerallee) just south of the **Orangerie** in 1913. The park is at its most beautiful in spring, when the trees are in leaf and the flowers in bloom, but these days it's usually overrun by visitors. To avoid the crowds, visit on a weekday, preferably outside summer, when you'll be better able to appreciate the place.

Schloss Sanssouci

To approach **Schloss Sanssouci** as Frederick the Great might have done, make for the eighteenth-century **obelisk** on Schopenhauerstrasse, which marks the main entrance to the park. Beyond, Hauptallee runs through the ornate Knobelsdorff-designed **Obelisk-Portal** – two clusters of pillars flanked by the goddesses Flora and Pomona – to the **Grosse Fontäne**, the biggest of the park's many fountains, around which stand a host of Classical statues, notably those of Venus and Mercury. The approach to the Schloss itself leads up through the Weinbergterrassen, whose terraced ranks of vines are among the northernmost in Germany.

Frederick had very definite ideas about what he wanted and worked closely with Knobelsdorff on the design of his palace, which was to be a place where the king, who had no great love for his capital, Berlin, or his wife Elizabeth Christine, could escape both. It's a surprisingly modest one-storey Baroque affair, topped by an oxidized green dome and ornamental statues, looking out over the vine terraces towards the high-rises of the Neustädter Havelbucht. Frederick loved the Schloss so much that he intended to be buried here, and had a **tomb** excavated for himself in front of the eastern wing, near the graves of his Italian greyhounds, animals whose company he preferred to that of human beings during the last, increasingly eccentric years of his life. When he died, however, his nephew Friedrich Wilhelm II had him interred in the Garnisonkirche in Potsdam itself, next to the father Frederick hated. Towards the end of World War II, the remains of Frederick and his father were exhumed and eventually taken to Schloss Hohenzollern in Swabia for safekeeping from the approaching Soviet army. Only in August 1991, after reunification, were the remains returned and buried with much pomp at the site Frederick had chosen. He lies there now, his last resting place marked by a simple stone bearing the terse inscription "*Friedrich der Grosse*".

Schloss Sanssouci opening times and prices

The Schloss can only be visited as part of a **guided tour**. These take place every twenty minutes and tickets for the whole day go on sale at 9am – get there as early as possible as demand is high.

The Schloss is open Tues–Sun: April–Oct 9am–5pm; Feb & March 9am–4pm; Nov–Jan 9am–3pm (closed 12.30–1pm); DM10, concessions DM5.

The interior

Inside, the Schloss is a frenzy of Rococo, spread through the twelve rooms where Frederick lived and entertained his guests – a process that usually entailed quarrelling with them. The most eye-catching rooms are the opulent **Marmorsaal** (Marble Hall) and the **Konzertzimmer** (Concert Room), where the flute-playing king forced eminent musicians to play his own works on concert evenings. Frederick's favourite haunt was his library where, surrounded by his two thousand volumes – mainly French translations of the classics and a sprinkling of contemporary French writings – he could oversee the work on his tomb. One of Frederick's most celebrated house guests was Voltaire, who lived here from 1750 to 1753, acting as a kind of private tutor to the king, finally leaving when he'd had enough of Frederick's bizarre behaviour, damning the king's

---

Frederick the Great

Frederick (1740–1786) had the great misfortune to be born the son of Friedrich Wilhelm I, Brandenburg-Prussia's "Soldier King", a stern militarist whose attitude to his children seems to have been much the same as his attitude to the conscripts in his army. Frederick was subjected to a strict and unforgiving regime from the earliest age. His education included the Lutheran catechism and military drill but precious little else, certainly no hint of the arts or humanities.

Frederick's interest in the latter emerged despite his father's best efforts, leading to conflict between the king and the young crown prince. Friedrich Wilhelm I's odious treatment of his son – he frequently thrashed him and forced him to kiss his boots in public – éventually prompted Frederick to try to flee the country in 1730, enlisting the aid of two friends, Hans Hermann von Katte and Karl Christoph von Keith. At the last moment von Keith hesitated, betraying the conspiracy before escaping himself. Frederick and Katte (with whom the prince had a very close, possibly homosexual, relationship) were arrested and stripped of rank and privileges. Both were court-martialled; Katte was sentenced to two years' imprisonment but the court declared itself unable to sit in judgement over a crown prince.

At this point the old king intervened to drastic effect. Katte was sentenced to death and Frederick was forced to watch his beheading from his cell, having been led to understand that he too was under sentence of death. When news of his shattered state was conveyed to the king by a priest, the monarch, having achieved his intended effect, granted Frederick a conditional pardon.

As penance and a test of his remorse Frederick had to serve in his father's civil administration pending restitution of rank and freedom. There was a marked improvement in his circumstances when in 1733 he was sent to the north Brandenburg town of Rheinsberg where, away from his father's hypercritical eyes, he was able to renew his interest in the arts. Only an arranged marriage to Elizabeth Christine, daughter of the Duke of Brunswick-Bevern, blighted what had become a relatively idyllic existence.

In 1740 the king died and Frederick acceded to the throne, much to the delight of the populace, who had been worn down by Friedrich Wilhelm I's

---

intellect with faint praise and accusing him of treating "the whole world as slaves". In revenge Frederick ordered that Voltaire's former room be decorated with carvings of apes and parrots.

The **Damenflügel**, the west wing of the Schloss (mid-May to mid-Oct Sat & Sun only 10am–5pm; DM3) was added in 1840, and its thirteen rooms housed ladies and gentlemen of the court. Nearby on the terrace is a wrought-iron summerhouse protecting a weatherbeaten copy of a Classical statue, while just to the south an eighteenth-century sculpture of Cleopatra looks over the graves of Frederick's horses.

Around the Schloss

East of Schloss Sanssouci, overlooking the ornamental Holländischer Garten or Dutch Garden, is the **Bildergalerie** (mid-May to mid-Oct

---

austere style of rule. Initially Frederick lived up to early expectations, abolishing torture and censorship, establishing ostensible freedom of worship, and recalling exiled scholars. With the aid of Voltaire he published his **Antimachiavel**, a treatise expounding a princely ethic based on virtue, justice and responsibility. However, Frederick inclined towards enlightened despotism, and as his rule progressed he introduced increasingly unpopular measures such as the establishment of state monopolies for certain commodities. His first notably un-progressive act, however – the invasion of and subsequent annexation of Silesia – came in 1740 at the very beginning of his reign.

In 1756 Austria, Saxony, France and Russia, alarmed at the growing strength of Prussia, began squaring up for the **Seven Years' War**. Frederick struck first, attacking Saxony and, though initially successful, was later beaten at the Battle of Kolin. Encouraged, the French invaded Prussia and, though able to beat them back, Frederick could not prevent military defeat at the Battle of Kunersdorf, after which the Russian army occupied Berlin. With British aid Frederick was able to push out the invaders, gaining important victories in 1760 and 1761, but eventually the war fizzled out with all sides exhausted, and a general peace was concluded in 1763.

Frederick's 1740–1745 acquisitions were confirmed, the Habsburg hold on the now crumbling Holy Roman Empire had been lessened and Prussia was the leading German state. The remaining 23 years of Frederick's reign were a period of reconstruction, marked by increasing eccentricity on the part of the monarch, who during this period came to be known as **Der alte Fritz** ("Old Fritz"). He retreated to Schloss Sanssouci and, in the company of Voltaire, honed his francophile tendencies while overseeing the upkeep of his army (and extraction of punitive taxes from his people to finance it).

In 1772 he successfully secured a chunk of Poland for Prussia during the First Partition of that country and in 1777 launched his final military action, an unsuccessful campaign against Bavaria. When he died in 1786, he was, like his father, not mourned.

10am–noon & 12.30–5pm; DM4, concessions DM2), a restrained Baroque creation, which, it's claimed, was the first building in Europe to be erected specifically as a museum. Unfortunately, wartime destruction and looting scattered the contents, but a new collection was put together after the war, comprising paintings from around the GDR that had survived, including Caravaggio's wonderful *Incredulity of St Thomas* and several works by Rubens and Van Dyck.

Just to the right of the Holländischer Garten is the **Neptungrotte**, a Knobelsdorff-designed architectural oddity: a grotto with a Rococo entrance and a ring of empty statue pediments in front. The statues, representing Moorish figures, are currently in Schloss Sanssouci awaiting renovation.

The Neue Kammern and gardens

On the opposite side of the Schloss, from a point near the Cleopatra statue, steps lead down to the **Neue Kammern** (mid-May to mid-Oct Tues–Sun 10am–5pm; DM4, concessions DM2), the architectural twin of the Bildergalerie, originally used as an orangerie and later as a guesthouse. Immediately to the west of the Neue Kammern is the prim **Sizilianischer Garten** or Sicilian Garden, crammed with coniferous trees and subtropical plants, complementing the **Nordischer Garten**, another ornamental garden just to the north, whose most interesting feature is the strange-looking **Felsentor** or Rock Gate, a gateway fashioned out of uncut stones and topped by a lumpen-looking eagle with outstretched wings.

Frederick was prepared to go to some lengths to achieve the desired carefree rural ambience for Sanssouci and retained an old wooden windmill as an ornament just north of the Neue Kammern. Four years after his death, this was replaced by a rustic-looking stone construction, the **Historische Mühle**, which is now a restaurant.

The Ruinenberg

The **Ruinenberg**, rising to the north of Schloss Sanssouci, looks like a cluster of Classical ruins, but in fact these fragments are artificial, designed to render a little more interesting a small reservoir built during the eighteenth century to feed the fountains in the park. However, it was a long time before this reservoir fulfilled its purpose, as attempts to fill it with water from the Havel proved fruitless. It worked briefly in 1754 when Frederick the Great (in a characteristic fit of manic inventiveness) allowed it to be filled with snow. When the snow melted the locks were opened and water coursed through the system, giving the fountains in the park a few minutes' life. It wasn't until the building of the mosque-shaped pump-house in the town centre that the problem was solved.

The Orangerie

From the western corner of the Sizilianischer Garten, **Maulbeerallee** (Mulberry Alley), a road open to traffic, cuts through the park to the ascent to the **Orangerie** (open for special exhibitions only; DM5, concessions DM2).

This Italianate Renaissance-style structure with its belvedere towers is perhaps the most visually impressive building in the park, and is certainly more outwardly imposing than the Schloss. A series of terraces, with curved retaining walls sporting water spouts in the shape of lions' heads, lead up to the sandy-coloured building, whose slightly down-at-heel appearance lends it added character.

It was built at the behest of Friedrich IV and, like the Friedenskirche, inspired by the architecture seen on his travels in Italy. The facade is lined with allegorical statues set in niches, depicting figures like "Industry" holding a cog wheel. The western wing of the building is still used for its original purpose, as a refuge for tropical plants in winter, and during the summer it's possible to ascend the western tower, from where there are great views of the Neues Palais and depressing vistas of Potsdam's high-rises to the east. The Orangerie also houses a gallery, the Raphaelsaal, with copies of paintings looted by Napoleon. Part of the Orangerie is given over to private flats, occupied by members of the park staff – which must be just about the best address in Potsdam.

Below the Orangerie, south of Maulbeerallee, is the Jubiläumsterrasse with a large goldfish-inhabited pool, beyond which are statues of Mercury and an equestrian Frederick the Great, a replica of the bronze one on Unter den Linden (which incidentally stood for many years in Potsdam).

The Belvedere, Drachenhaus and around

From the western wing of the Orangerie, the arrow-straight **Krimlindenallee**, lined with lime trees, leads up towards a ruined Rococo **Belvedere**, the last building to be built under Frederick the Great. It was the only building in the whole park to suffer serious war damage, and is presently undergoing restoration. A couple of hundred metres short of the belvedere a path branches off to the left, leading to the **Drachenhaus**, a one-time vintner's house built in the style of a Chinese pagoda for the small vineyard nearby. Today there's a genteel café inside, an ideal point to interrupt your wanderings. Southwest of the Drachenhaus, a pathway leads across the park to the **Spielfestung**, the toy fort to end all toy forts, which was built for the sons of Wilhelm II, and even armed with miniature Krupp cannons. Returning to the path, follow it to the **Antikentempel**, originally built in 1768 to house part of the art collection of Frederick the Great. This domed rotunda is now the last resting place of a number of members of the Hohenzollern family, including the Empress Auguste Victoria, and Hermine, the woman Wilhelm II married in exile, who came to be known as the "last Empress".

The Neues Palais

To the west through the trees rises the **Neues Palais** (daily except Tues: April–Oct 9am–12.45pm & 1.15–5pm; Feb & March closes

4pm; Nov–Jan closes 3pm; DM8, concessions DM4), another massive Rococo extravaganza from Frederick the Great's time, built between 1763 and 1769 to reaffirm the might of Prussia and its king after the Seven Years' War. At the centre of the palace is a huge green-weathered dome, topped by a gilded crown. It must have been the Neues Palais that inspired Lewis Carroll to note in his diary when visiting the town: "The amount of art lavished on the whole region of Potsdam is marvellous; some of the tops of the palaces were like forests of statues." The Classical figures adorning the roof were specially mass-produced by a team of sculptors to adorn Frederick's new creation.

The main entrance to the palace is in the western facade, approached via gates flanked by stone sentry boxes. Theoretically you have to join a guided tour, but once inside you can pretty much take things at your own pace. The interior is predictably opulent, though a couple of highlights stand out: the vast and startling **Grottensaal** on the ground floor, decorated entirely with shells and semiprecious stones to form images of lizards and dragons, and the equally huge **Marmorsaal**, with its beautiful floor of patterned marble slabs. The southern wing contains Frederick's apartments and the theatre where the king enjoyed Italian opera and French plays. A francophile to the point of near mania, Frederick believed that the Germans were philistines incapable of producing great art. It was said that he'd "rather a horse sang him an aria, than allow a German in his opera". The last Imperial resident of the Neues Palais was Kaiser Wilhelm II, who packed sixty train carriages with the contents of the palace when he and his family fled in November 1918, following the revolution and abdication. Facing the Neues Palais entrance are the **Communs**, a couple of pointless Rococo fantasies joined by a curved colonnade. They look grandiose, but their purpose was mundane: they were built for the serving and maintenance staff of the palace.

The Rehgarten and Charlottenhof

From the Neues Palais, Ökonomieweg leads east through the **Rehgarten** or Deer Garden, the former court hunting ground (and still home to a few deer), where you'll find the slightly kitsch-looking **Chinesisches Teehaus** (daily except Fri: mid-May to mid-Oct 9am–noon & 12.30–5pm; DM2, concessions DM1), a kind of Rococo pagoda housing a small museum of Chinese and Meissen porcelain and surrounded by eerily lifelike statues of Oriental figures.

The broad expanse of rough parkland to the south of Ökonomieweg is **Charlottenhof**, a park created by Friedrich Wilhelm III as a Christmas present for his son, and today one of Sanssouci's quieter corners. A path leads over a bridge past a small farm building to the **Römische Bäder** (daily except Thurs: mid-May to mid-Oct 10am–noon & 12.30–5pm; DM7.50, includes entry to Schloss Charlottenhof), built by Schinkel and Persius in convincing imitation of a Roman villa.

Across the lawns to the south is **Schloss Charlottenhof** (daily except Wed: mid-May to mid-Oct 10am–12.30pm & 1–5pm; DM7.50, includes entry to Römische Bäder), another Roman-style building, once again designed by Schinkel and Persius for Friedrich IV. Though designated a palace it is, in reality, little more than a glorified villa, but its interior, unlike most Sanssouci buildings, is original. The effect is impressive: the hallway is bathed in blue light filtered through coloured glass decorated with stars, a prelude to the **Kupferstichzimmer**, or print room, whose walls are now covered in copies of Italian Renaissance paintings. Immediately east of Schloss Charlottenhof is the **Dichterhain** (Poets' Grove), an open space dotted with busts of Goethe, Schiller and Herder, among others. West of here through the woods and across a racetrack-shaped clearing called the **Hippodrom** is the **Fasanerie**, another Italian-style edifice built between 1842 and 1844.

The Grünes Gitter and around

At the southeastern corner of Sanssouci is the **Grünes Gitter** or Green Gateway entrance to the grounds, where there's an **information kiosk** with a few leaflets about the park and its environs. Immediately to the north of here is the Italianate **Friedenskirche** (mid-May to mid-Oct daily 10am–6pm), designed by Persius for Friedrich Wilhelm IV and completed in 1850. With its 39-metre campanile and lakeside setting, it conjures up the southern European atmosphere that Friedrich Wilhelm was striving to create when he ordered the construction of the church using the St Clemente Basilica in Rome as a model, with the design centered on the magnificent Byzantine apse mosaic that was brought here from Murano. Adjoining the church is a domed Hohenzollern mausoleum containing the tombs of Friedrich Wilhelm IV and his wife Elizabeth, and Friedrich III and his wife Victoria. Directly to the west of the Friedenskirche is the **Marly-Garten**, once the kitchen garden of Friedrich I, who named it, with intentional irony, after Louis XIV's luxurious Marly park.

North of the centre

Heading north from the Nauener Tor along Friedrich-Ebert-Strasse will bring you to some of Potsdam's most fascinating, yet least-known, corners. The beginnings are inauspicious – on the left is a mid-nineteenth-century Italianate villa, once the residence of a royal gardener, behind which the former district headquarters of the *Stasi* rise up, while the Neo-Baroque affair a little to the north is a turn-of-the-century local government office.

Alexandrowka

However, after about fifteen minutes' walking you'll reach **Russische Kolonie Alexandrowka**, a settlement of Russian-style wooden houses, built for a group of Russian military musicians who found themselves marooned here after the Napoleonic Wars. Its incongruity makes it one of the most intriguing sights in town, a collection of two-storey dwellings with steeply pitched roofs laid out in the form of a St Andrew's cross. The buildings are in fact half-timbered, but plank cladding gives them the look of birch-log cabins.

Their inhabitants were originally prisoners of war, among five hundred captured when the Prussians were fighting with the French in Kurland (part of modern Latvia). Sixty-two of these men were selected to form a Russian choir for the entertainment of the troops, and after the Prussians joined forces with the Russians to combat Napoleon's armies, their services were retained. At the end of the Napoleonic Wars they were stationed in Potsdam, consumed by homesickness but forbidden to return to Russia.

Eventually, in 1826, Friedrich Wilhelm III gave the order that houses should be built for these men and their families. Eight houses were constructed on the arms of the cross, four more at the semi-circular linking roads at each end, with an overseer's residence in the middle. The names of the original occupants and subsequent inhabitants (a few of them descendants of the Russians, even today) are carved into the housefronts. Some of the oldest inscriptions are in Cyrillic script.

For many years this whole area was the focus of the Russian presence in Potsdam. The Red Army occupied huge barrack buildings along Voltaireweg and Pappelallee, formerly the property of the *Wehrmacht* and before that the Imperial German army, while Soviet officers and their families lived in the nearby flats.

The Alexander Newski Kapelle

Directly to the north of the settlement is the **Kapelle des heiligen Alexander Newski**, a church built for the Russians in 1829, set on top of the closely wooded Kapellenberg hill. Access is either by scrambling up the hillside, or via a track branching to the right off Nedlitzer Strasse, which leads to a rudimentary car park. The chapel is a fragment of Russia transplanted to Brandenburg: a compact building in pink stucco edged with white, topped by a central onion-domed tower, with smaller domes at each corner.

The chapel is usually accessible at weekends, but if there's anyone about during the week it's often possible to take a look around. The interior is festooned with icons, many of them gifts from the Tsarina Alexandra, who started life as Princess Charlotte of Prussia. The priest's wife oversees a little stall selling replica icons and holy medals, and often plays Russian Orthodox choir tapes, which enhance the already ethereal effect.

The first service held here, in 1829, was attended by Tsar Nicholas I, and the chapel remained in use for well over a century, boosted by the arrival in Berlin of thousands of Russian emigrés after the Russian Revolution of 1917. During the 1960s the chapel lost its priest, but in 1986 the patriarchate of Moscow sent a new one, and regular church services are held for Potsdam's handful of Orthodox families.

The Pfingstberg

Immediately to the north of the Kapellenberg is the wooded **Pfingstberg**, another little-known Potsdam curiosity which, like the Russian settlement and the Kapellenberg, has been rediscovered over the past few years. At the foot of the Pfingstberg is the walled **Jüdischer Friedhof** or Jewish cemetery. Only organized visits are possible, every Sunday at 10am – enquire at the tourist office in town for details. The cemetery was given by the town to Potsdam's growing Jewish population in 1763 – until then they had had to bury their dead in Berlin. As recently as 1933 the Jewish community of Potsdam numbered several hundred, of whom just two returned after the war.

From the cemetery the path leads on up the hill to the ruined nineteenth-century **Belvedere**, a vast and improbable-looking edifice, built to plans drawn up from Friedrich Wilhelm IV's sketches of the folly-like castles constructed in Italy during the Renaissance. As the name suggests, this unusual building was erected as a kind of viewing terrace for the royal inhabitants of nineteenth-century Potsdam and their guests. Its walkways and towers give great views of Potsdam itself, and of the landscape north as far as Spandau and Charlottenburg, and west as far as the town of Brandenburg.

Unfortunately, it's almost impossible to enjoy them today. Although virtually undamaged by the war, the belvedere was allowed to collapse into ruin by the pre-*Wende* city authorities, because (according to some Potsdamers) it afforded such good views of the border and West Berlin. The small building just to the southeast of the belvedere is the **Pomonatempel**, Schinkel's first-ever finished building, constructed in 1800 when he was a nineteen-year-old student of architecture. The neat Neoclassical temple, fronted by a four-columned portico, has recently been renovated after years of neglect, though the building remains closed.

The Neuer Garten

To the east of the Pfingstberg is the **Neuer Garten**, another large park complex, which includes Schloss Cecilienhof, venue of the Potsdam conference in 1945. The main entrance is at the eastern end of Alleestrasse, beyond which a road snakes through the park. A couple of hundred metres east of the road, overlooking the Heiliger See, stands the **Marmorpalais** or Marble Palace (mid-July to mid-Oct daily except Tues 10am–5pm; mid-Oct to mid-July Sat & Sun 10am–3pm; DM6, concessions DM3) built for Friedrich Wilhelm II, who died a premature death here in 1797, allegedly as a consequence of his dissolute lifestyle. In more recent years it was home to the GDR's main military museum, and until 1990 visitors were greeted by the incongruous sight of a Mig 17 parked in the palace grounds. It has recently been restored to an approximation of its original royal condition and the sumptuous rooms can be seen once again.

Schloss Cecilienhof

Towards the end of the road through the wooded grounds of the Neuer Garten is **Schloss Cecilienhof** (Tues–Sun 9am–5pm; DM8, concessions DM4), which looks like a mock-Elizabethan mansion transplanted from the English Home Counties. Building work on this, the last palace to be commissioned by the Hohenzollerns, began in 1913 and was completed in 1917, the war having evidently done nothing to change the architectural style. Cecilienhof would only rate a mention in passing, were it not for the fact that the **Potsdam conference**, confirming the decisions made earlier that year at Yalta about the postwar European order, was held here from July 17 to August 2, 1945. The conference was as much symbolic as anything else, providing a chance for Truman, Stalin and Churchill (replaced mid-conference by Clement Attlee) to show the world that they had truly won the war by meeting in the heart of the ruined Reich.

Centre of attraction within is the **Konferenzsaal** or conference chamber, where the Allied delegates worked out the details of the division of Europe, and which resembles the assembly hall of a British minor public school. Everything has been left pretty much as it was in 1945, with the huge round table specially made in Moscow for the conference still in place, despite the fact that in July 1990, there was an arson attack on the hall. The fire brigade arrived within a few minutes and extinguished the fire, but not before considerable damage had been done. A remarkably quick restoration job has left few traces of what happened. It's still not known who was responsible for the attack but local *Faschos* – neo-Fascists – are thought to be the most likely culprits.

It's also possible to visit the delegates' workrooms, furnished in varying degrees of chintziness. The study of the Soviet delegation is about the most tasteless, but the British room (with a bronze stag at bay in the fireplace and furniture that looks like it was bought as a job lot from a defunct presbytery) comes a close second. Cecilienhof has been used as a hotel since 1960 and there's an expensive restaurant which is also only for the deep of pocket (for information, see "Accommodation" on p.187 and "Restaurants" on p.192).

A walk along the lake shore to the north of the Schloss is interesting simply because before the *Wende* it was impossible. Until 1990 the view north of the Schloss was cut off by a strip of impassable white concrete and signs warned that this was a border area.

The Berliner Vorstadt and Glienicker Brücke

On the opposite shore of the Heiliger See to the Neuer Garten is the **Berliner Vorstadt**, formerly an elegant Potsdam suburb, whose crumbling villas were given over to various party and social institutions under the SED regime. Here, too, were numerous Imperial army barracks, housing elite units like the Garde du Corps and Hussars, which until the summer of 1994 were in Russian hands. At the end of Berliner Strasse, leading back to Berlin, is the **Glienicker Brücke**, the famous spy-swap bridge which inspired many a Cold War film scene. Here, in 1962, U-2 pilot Gary Powers was traded for a Soviet agent, while more recently, in 1986, Jewish dissident Anatoly Scharansky was freed into the West by the Soviet authorities in an early manifestation of Gorbachev's *glasnost*. The bridge was reopened to normal traffic at the beginning of 1990, and today there are few reminders of the era when people living in the immediate vicinity needed special permits simply to come and go from their own homes.

Babelsberg

On the eastern bank of the Havel is the town of **BABELSBERG**, now officially part of the Potsdam administrative district. Crossing the Lange Brücke from Potsdam, it's hard not to notice a square tower rising up out of the trees atop the **Brauhausberg** hill on the Babelsberg side. This is the former local SED headquarters or **"Kreml"** (Kremlin), to give it its local nickname. Originally built as a military college at the turn of the century, it later served as a state archive building – a dark oval patch on the side of the tower marks where the SED symbol used to be.

The Telegrafenberg and the Einsteinturm

Like Potsdam, Babelsberg has a few secrets ripe for rediscovery. Above the Lange Brücke, Albert-Einstein-Strasse leads up onto the **Telegrafenberg**. This was the site chosen in 1832 for a telegraph station, one of a whole network positioned between Berlin and Koblenz to relay messages by means of mechanical signal arms. Just over forty years later, when the mechanical system had been rendered obsolete, it was decided to build an astronomical observatory here. The complex still stands, finished in the orange- and yellow-striped brickwork typical of the late nineteenth century.

Beyond the observatory, a path leads to the nearby **Einsteinturm**, a twenty-metre-high observatory tower designed by Erich Mendelsohn in 1920. An unrepentedly phallic piece of Expressionist architecture, it looks like an element from a Dali dreamscape and is the most remarkable modern building in the Potsdam area. Experiments testing the Theory of Relativity were car-

ried out here in the presence of Einstein, and scientific work continues here today with research into the sun's magnetic field.

On the eastern side of the Telegrafenberg are a couple of musts
for cemetery fans: the **Neuer Friedhof**, laid out in 1866 according to
plans drawn up by the architect Lenné, and, below it on the other
side of Heinrich-Mann-Allee, the eighteenth-century **Alte Friedhof**
with its Classical mausoleum and numerous overgrown monuments,
including one to Eleonore Prochaska, who joined the Prussian army
in 1813 disguised as a man, successfully fooling her comrades, and
later fell in the war against Napoleon.

Nowawes and Park Babelsberg

From the junction of Heinrich-Mann-Allee and Friedrich-Engels-
Strasse, buses #601, #619 and #692 follow the latter to the centre of
Babelsberg. Alighting just north of Lutherplatz, it's a short walk south
across this square to **Neuendorfer Anger**, once the heart of the old
town, with now only the shell of the **Neuendorfer Dorfkirche** as a
reminder. Follow Karl-Liebknecht-Strasse northwards; on either side
of the road is an area known as **Nowawes**, where single-storey cottages survive from a settlement of Protestant Czech weavers founded
by Friedrich Wilhelm II. The name *Nowawes* came from *Nowa Ves*,
Czech for Neuendorf – "new village" – and the streets either side of
Karl-Liebknecht-Strasse today have names like Spindelallee and
Jutestrasse, bearing witness to the trades once plied here. A right turn
onto Weberplatz brings you to the pretty eighteenth-century
Friedrichskirche, one of the most appealing buildings in Nowawes.

Between Alt Nowawes and the Tiefer See is the **Park Babelsberg**,
Potsdam's third great park complex, designed by Lenné, and
neglected by most visitors in favour of Sanssouci. The main entrance
is at the end of **Allee nach Glienicke**, the northern extension of Alt
Nowawes, although until 1989 this was closed because of the proximity of the border fortifications. A roadway leads through the hilly,
roughly wooded park to **Schloss Babelsberg** (Wed–Sun 9am–5pm;
DM4, concessions DM2), a Neo-Gothic architectural extravaganza
built by Schinkel at the behest of Prince Wilhelm, brother of
Friedrich Wilhelm IV, and inspired by England's Windsor Castle. A
couple of nineteenth-century architectural oddities lurk in the park:
the **Flatowturm**, an improbable-looking Neo-Gothic guesthouse and
lookout tower, and the **Matrosenhaus**, a bizarrely styled gabled
house built for the men who crewed the royal boats and barges of the
Hohenzollerns. The park is also home to the thirteenth-century
Gerichtslaube, Berlin's Gothic courthouse building, brought here in
1872 after the Rotes Rathaus had displaced it.

The Babelsberg Film Studios and Jagdschloss Stern

Babelsberg has a couple of other curiosities. At the eastern end of
town, served by buses #601, #603, #690 and #692 from the cen-

tre, are the **Babelsberg Film Studios**, August-Bebel-Str. 26–53 (entrance on Grossbeeren Str.; Mar–Oct daily 10am–6pm; DM25, concessions DM18), a huge complex, originally founded in 1917. As the UFA film studios, during the 1920s this was the heart of the German film industry and rivalled Hollywood as a centre of cinematic innovation. Films produced during the heyday of UFA included Robert Wiene's Expressionist masterpiece *Das Kabinett des Dr Caligari* ("The Cabinet of Dr Caligari"), Fritz Lang's *Metropolis* and *Der Blaue Engel* ("The Blue Angel") starring the young Marlene Dietrich. Under the Nazis the anti-Semitic *Jud Süss* was filmed here in 1940, followed a few years later by the special effect-laden colour epic *Münchhausen*. Later, as the DEFA studios, it was the heavily subsidized centre of the East German film industry, which didn't last much longer than the GDR itself after the *Wende*. These days Babelsberg has reinvented itself as the "Film Experience Park", and visitors can wander through the costume and props departments and watch technicians going through the motions of shooting film scenes for their benefit. It's also possible to visit the hangar-like studio where Fritz Lang may have filmed *Metropolis* (no one is quite sure of the exact location) and admire a reproduction of his Futuristic set.

If you have the time or the inclination for yet another royal leftover, take the bus as far as the stop just before Steinstrasse on the eastern edge of town, then follow Jagdhaus Strasse on foot to the **Jagdschloss Stern** (mid-May to mid-Oct Sat & Sun 9am–5pm; DM3, concessions DM1.50), a former royal hunting lodge in gabled Dutch style, built in 1732 by Friedrich Wilhelm I. The Schloss is quite plain, a reflection of the soldier king's preferences, and comes as a surprise after the splendour of Potsdam's other royal palaces. East of the Schloss, well-signposted trails lead through the wooded **Parforceheide**, a one-time hunting ground of the king.

Berlin: Listings

Chapter 11

Accommodation

It isn't easy or cheap to get a room for the night in Berlin. For anything other than **private rooms**, it's essential to book at least three months in advance, particularly for budget places on the western side of the city. Remember, too, that the city's **hotels** fill completely during important trade fairs and festivals, and at Easter and Christmas; summer weekends are also problematic. At the bottom end of the market, most of the city's **hostels** are fully booked weeks in advance, and there's no **campsite** anywhere near the city centre – indeed, although things are improving, Berlin's lack of low-budget accommodation has forced the city authorities into setting up a large tent out of the centre, *Übernachtung im Zelt*, specifically for young travellers (see "Camping" on pp.220–221).

On the plus side, **Berlin Tourismus Marketing** has a seemingly inexhaustible supply of private rooms at moderate prices; most hostels, hotels and pensions include breakfast in their rates; and the the accommodation agencies known as **Mitwohnzentralen** can almost always find somewhere at reasonably short notice – especially if you're after a long-term stay.

The hotel and pension listings that follow are our pick of what the city has to offer; remember that prices can change (usually upwards) and standards can drop, and always ask for the cheapest room.

Private rooms

Private rooms offer the best and, at around DM50 per person per night, the most cost-effective solution to finding somewhere to stay. There is also quite a lot of privacy – often you'll barely see your host. The only disadvantage is that they can be located away from the city centre action in residential suburbs, both eastern and western.

Private accommodation in the city is organized through Berlin Tourismus Marketing free of charge (see p.216 for details). Although you can choose

The tourist office leaflets Jugendgästehäuser und Campingplätze and Berlin Hotels und Pensionen (also available from German National Tourist Offices, see p.22) have useful lists of hotels and pensions.

See "Hotels and Pensions" for details of Berlin Tourismus Marketing advance booking service.

Berlin Tourismus Marketing offices

Main office: Europa Center (entrance on Budapester Str.), Tiergarten ☎25 00 25, fax 25 00 24 24. Mon–Sat 8am–10pm, Sun 9am–9pm.

Tegel airport (main hall, left luggage office) ☎41 01 34 26. Daily 5am–10.30pm.

Brandenburg Gate Daily 9.30am–6pm.

Info-Point Dresdener Bank, Unter den Linden 17, Mitte. Mon, Wed & Fri 8.30am–2pm, Tues & Thurs also open 3.30–6pm.

Info-Point KaDeWe, Wittenbergplatz, Charlottenburg. Mon–Fri 9.30am–8pm, Sat 9am–4pm.

Accommodation

whereabouts you'd like to stay, at busy times it's pretty much a lucky dip as to where you'll end up, and most of the rooms are on the western side. Rooms cost upwards of DM60 single, DM100 double per night, including breakfast, and are are usually of a good standard: clean and simple, often self-contained. You may be politely requested to return to your room by a reasonable hour – and you should certainly inform the owner if you intend to stay out until the early morning.

Mitwohnzentralen

Mitwohnzentralen are agencies that can find just about any type of room, and for any length of time – from a week in a bedroom in a shared flat to an entire luxury apartment for six months. In the summer, plenty of places become available for rent while people are away on holiday, and your chances of finding something immediately are high. But where the *Mitwohnzentralen* come into their own is in arranging **longer-term stays**. Monthly charges for a self-contained apartment start at DM650, about half to two-thirds of that if you're prepared to share kitchen and bathroom facilities; agency fees are usually one percent of the annual rent per month. **Shorter stays** will work out a little more expensive than the pro rata rate, and the shortest period of time a *Mitwohnzentrale* will book a room for is usually one week. But, considering this works out to roughly DM40–50 per person per night, it clearly represents the best cost-cutting option except for the cheapest hostel beds or private rooms. Almost all *Mitwohnzentralen* will take advance bookings by phone, and vary only in the number of places they have on their files – and in some cases, their degree of efficiency.

Agentur Wohnwitz, Holsteinische Str. 55, Wilmersdorf ☎8 61 82 22 (Mon–Fri 10am–7pm, Sat 11am–2pm). Friendly and fairly central, specializing in inner-city rooms. Also has women-only apartments.

Casa Nostra, Winterfeldtstr. 46, Schöneberg ☎2 35 51 20 (Mon–Fri

10am–8pm, Sat 11am–3pm). Rooms not only in Berlin but throughout Europe.

Mitwohnzentrale Kreuzberg, Mehringdamm 72, Kreuzberg ☎7 86 20 03 (Mon–Fri 10am–7pm). As the name suggests, its rooms tend to be in the Kreuzberg/eastern part of the city only, and therefore cheaper.

Mitwohnzentrale Ku'damm Eck, Joachimstaler Str. 17, Charlottenburg ☎1 94 45 (Mon–Fri 9am–6pm, Sat 11am–2pm). Biggest of the Mitwohnzentralen and an easy walk from Zoo Station. Also has women-only apartments.

Mitwohnagentur Streicher, Immanuelkirchstr. 8, Prenzlauer Berg ☎4 41 66 22 (Mon–Fri 11am–2pm & 3pm–6pm). Helpful agency with rooms and apartments all over the eastern part of the city. English spoken.

Zeitraum Mitwohnzentrale, Horstweg 7, Charlottenburg ☎3 25 61 81 (Mon–Fri 10am–1pm & 3–7pm). Well-organized agency which specializes in providing accommodation for budget travellers. Rooms from DM30 a night, even less if you are a student and book ahead. Also has some dormitory-type accommodation for DM20 a night.

Youth hostels

Berlin's **youth hostels** are used extensively by school and sporting parties, and rooms tend to be booked well in advance: it's essential to phone through first.

IYHF hostels

All require an **IYHF card** which can be bought from your own national association (see box opposite), or the organization's Berlin offices at Tempelhofer Ufer 32, Kreuzberg (☎2 62 31 24; nearest U-Bahn Möckernbrücke). All hostels have a midnight curfew (frustrating in this insomniac city) and include bedding and a spartan breakfast in the price.

Jugendgästehaus, Kluckstr. 3, Tiergarten ☎2 61 10 97. Bus #129, direction Oranienplatz. Most central of the IYHF hostels, handy for the Tiergarten muse-

Youth hostel associations

Australia
**Australian Youth Hostels
Association**, 422 Kent St, Sydney
☎ 02/9261 1111 (and in major cities
throughout the country)

Canada
**Hostelling International/Canadian
Hostelling Association**, Room 400,
205 Catherine St Ottawa ON K2P 1C3
☎ 613/237-7884 or 1-800/663-5777

England and Wales
Youth Hostel Association (YHA),
Trevelyan House, 8 St Stephen's Hill,
St Albans, Herts AL1 2DY
☎ 01727/855215
*London membership desk and booking
office*: 14 Southampton St, London WC2
7HY ☎ 0171/836 1036

Ireland
**Youth Hostel Association of
Northern Ireland**, 22 Donegall Rd,
Belfast BT12 5JN ☎ 01232/324 733
An Oige, 61 Mountjoy St, Dublin 7 ☎
01/830 4555

New Zealand
**Youth Hostels Association of New
Zealand**, PO Box 436, Christchurch 1
☎ 03/799 970

Scotland
Scottish Youth Hostel Association, 7
Glebe Crescent, Stirling FK8 2JA
☎ 01786/451181

US
**Hostelling International-American
Youth Hostels (HI-AYH)**, 733 15th St
NW, Suite 840, PO Box 37613,
Washington DC 20005 ☎ 202/783-6161

---

ums, but very solidly booked. DM31 for those under 27, DM40 others; key deposit DM15. Lockout 9am–noon.

Jugendherberge Ernst Reuter,
Hermsdorfer Damm 48–50, Reinickendorf ☎ 4 04 16 10. U-Bahn line #6 to Alt-Tegel, then bus #125 towards Frohnau. Situated so far from town that it's the least popular of the hostels and therefore least likely to fill up in summer: worth bearing in mind as an emergency option. Under-27s DM25, others DM32; key deposit DM10.

Jugendherberge Wannsee, Badeweg 1, Zehlendorf ☎ 8 03 20 34. S-Bahn lines #1, #3 or #7 to Nikolassee. Very pleasantly located, with plenty of woodland walks on hand near the beaches of the Wannsee lakes, but far from the city centre – and with a curfew that renders it useless if you're enjoying the nightlife. DM31 for under-27s, DM40 others; key deposit DM20.

Other hostels

Bahnhofsmission, Zoo Station, Charlottenburg ☎ 3 13 80 88. Church-run

mission with limited accommodation for train travellers (you may need to show your ticket) for one night only. No risk that you'd want to stay any longer, mind, since the rooms are windowless and dingy and the atmosphere starchily puritan. DM20 per person for a four-bedded cell with a meagre breakfast; rise and shine by 6am. A desperate option, worth it only if you're penniless or arrive in town very late.

Circus Hostel, Am Zirkus 2-3, Mitte ☎ 28 39 14 33. U-Bahn line #6, S-Bahn Friedrichstr. New hostel in tip-top shape, with a friendly staff and a good location on the edge of the historic centre of town. Singles DM38, doubles DM30, DM25 per bed in a five-bed room (breakfast not included). No curfew.

Jugendgästehaus am Zoo,
Hardenbergerstr. 9a, Charlottenburg ☎ 3 12 94 10. U- and S-Bahn Zoologischer Garten. An excellent location and extremely popular. Singles DM47, doubles DM85, four people in a room DM35. No curfew.

**Jugendgästehause Deutsche
Schreberjugend**, Franz-Künstler-Str. 10,

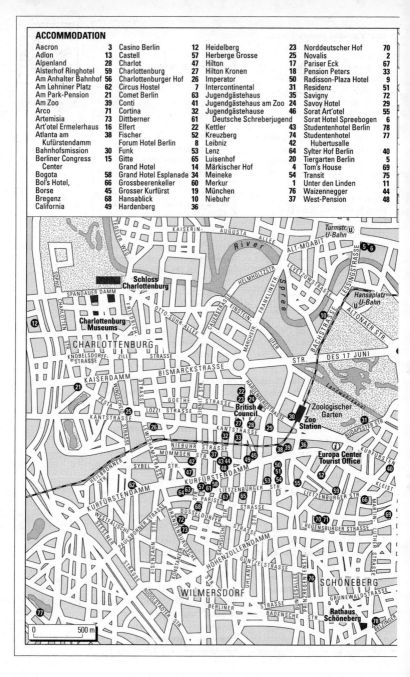

ACCOMMODATION

Aacron	3	Casino Berlin	12	Heidelberg	23	Norddeutscher Hof	70
Adlon	13	Castell	57	Herberge Grosse	25	Novalis	2
Alpenland	28	Charlot	47	Hilton	17	Pariser Eck	67
Alsterhof Ringhotel	59	Charlottenburg	27	Hilton Kronen	18	Pension Peters	33
Am Anhalter Bahnhof	56	Charlottenburger Hof	26	Imperator	50	Radisson-Plaza Hotel	9
Am Lehniner Platz	62	Circus Hostel	7	Intercontinental	31	Residenz	51
Am Park-Pension	21	Comet Berlin	63	Jugendgästehaus	35	Savigny	72
Am Zoo	39	Conti	41	Jugendgästehaus am Zoo	24	Savoy Hotel	29
Arco	71	Cortina	32	Jugendgästehause	46	Sorat Art'otel	55
Artemisia	73	Dittberner	61	Deutsche Schreberjugend		Sorat Hotel Spreebogen	6
Art'otel Ermelerhaus	16	Elfert	22	Kettler	43	Studentenhotel Berlin	78
Atlanta am		Fischer	52	Kreuzberg	74	Studentenhotel	77
Kufürstendamm	38	Forum Hotel Berlin	8	Leibniz	42	Hubertusalle	
Bahnhofsmission	30	Funk	53	Lenz	64	Sylter Hof Berlin	40
Berliner Congress		Gitte	65	Luisenhof	20	Tiergarten Berlin	5
Center	15	Grand Hotel	14	Märkischer Hof	4	Tom's House	69
Bogota	58	Grand Hotel Esplanade	34	Meineke	54	Transit	75
Bol's Hotel,	66	Grossbeerenkeller	60	Merkur	1	Unter den Linden	11
Borse	45	Grosser Kurfürst	19	München	76	Waizennegger	44
Bregenz	68	Hansablick	10	Niebuhr	37	West-Pension	48
California	49	Hardenberg	36				

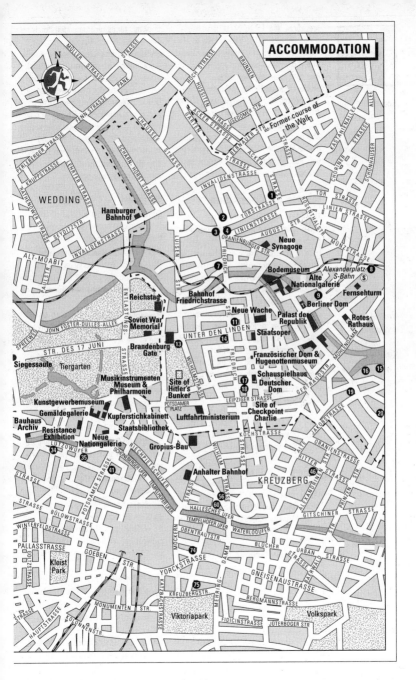

ACCOMMODATION

N

ACCOMMODATION

MÜLLER STRASSE
PANK
HOCH STRASSE
HUSSITEN
BRUNNEN
PHILBERGER STRASSE
FENN STRASSE
CHAUSSEE STRASSE
GARTEN
ACKER STRASSE
USEDOM STR.
BERNAUER STR.
ACKER STR.
Former course of
the Wall
KASTANIENALLEE
SCHÖNHAUSER
ALLEE

RATHENOWER STR.
KRUPPSTRASSE
LEHRTER STRASSE
SCHMIDT-HORST-STRASSE
INVALIDENSTRASSE
TORSTRASSE
TOR STRASSE
CHORINER
SCHÖNHAUSER

WEDDING
SEYDLITZSTR.
INVALIDENSTRASSE
LINIENSTRASSE
ROSENTHALER STR

**Hamburger
Bahnhof**
LUISEN STR.
FRIEDRICH STR.
LINIENSTRASSE
AUGUST
**Neue
Synagoge**
MÜNZSTRASSE
LINIEN STRASSE

ALT-MOABIT
PAULSTR.
ORANIENBURGER STR
Bodemuseum
Alexanderplatz
S-Bahn
**Alte
Nationalgalerie**
Fernsehturm

ENTLASTUNGS
Reichstag
**Bahnhof
Friedrichstrasse**
Neue Wache
Berliner Dom
**Rotes
Rathaus**

SPREEWEG
JOHN FOSTER-DULLES-ALLEE
STR. DES 17 JUNI
**Soviet War
Memorial**
STRASSE
**Brandenburg
Gate**
UNTER DEN LINDEN
**Palast der
Republik**
Staatsoper

Siegessäule
Tiergarten
WILHELM STRASSE
FRIEDRICH STR.
**Französischer Dom &
Hugenottenmuseum**

**Musikinstrumenten
Museum &
Philharmonie**
**Site of
Hitler's
Bunker**
POTSDAMER
PLATZ
Schauspielhaus
**Deutscher
Dom**
LEIPZIGER STRASSE
GENDARMEN STR.

Kunstgewerbemuseum
Gemäldegalerie
Kupferstichkabinett
Luftfahrtministerium
**Site of
Checkpoint
Charlie**
JAKOBSTRASSE

**Bauhaus
Archiv**
**Resistance
Exhibition**
**Neue
Nationalgalerie**
Staatsbibliothek
KOCHSTRASSE
ORANIENSTRASSE
ALTE JAKOBSTR.
RITTER STR
PRINZEN STR

LÜTZOWUFER
34
35
Gropius-Bau
WILHELM STR.
46

STRASSE
POTSDAMER STRASSE
REICHPIETSCHUFER
SCHÖNEBERGER UFER
TEMPELHOFER UFER
41
Anhalter Bahnhof
KREUZBERG

STRASSE
BÜLOWSTRASSE
56
HALLESCHES UFER
TEMPELHOFER UFER
WATERLOOUFER
GITSCHINER STRASSE

WINTERFELDTSTRASSE
PALLASSTRASSE
GOLTZSTRASSE
GOEBEN STR
MÖCKERN STR.
OBENTRAUTSTR.
BLÜCHER STR.
URBAN STRASSE
BÄRWALD STR.

**Kleist
Park**
YORCKSTRASSE
74
DAMM STR.
MEHRING
GNEISENAUSTRASSE

STRASSE
BOULONNERSTR
MONUMENTEN STR
KATZBACHSTRASSE
KREUZBERGSTR.
75
BERGMANNSTRASSE

HAUPTSTR
Viktoriapark
FIDICINSTRASSE
JÜTERBOGER STR.
Volkspark

Accommodation

Kreuzberg ☎6 15 10 07. U-Bahn line #1 to Hallesches Tor. Easy access to hot spots in both eastern and western areas of the city. Doubles or triples DM37, including breakfast. No curfew.

Studentenhotel Berlin, Meiningerstr. 10, Schöneberg ☎784 6720. Buses #104 or #146 to Rathaus Schöneberg, or Bayerishcher Platz U-Bahn. Dormitory accommodation at the relaxed edge of the city's action. Doubles DM41 per person, including breakfast. No curfew; key deposit DM20.

Hotels and pensions

The following listings indicate some of Berlin's best value **hotels and pensions**. Broadly, a pension is smaller than a hotel, and usually cheaper, although the categories are not strictly applied. Also there are "Hotel–Pensions", which may be either or both, so it's not worth taking too much notice of the labels (they have been omitted here). The codes below indicate **prices** for the cheapest available double room in high season. The bulk of our recommendations fall in categories ② to ⑥. Bear in mind that many of the more upmarket hotels slash their tariffs at the weekend when the business types have gone home, and that many of the cheaper places will also have more expensive rooms. If you're in a group or arrive out of season, it's often possible to get a price lower than we've quoted.

If our listings don't come up with what you want, or you arrive without making a booking, the Europa-Center **Berlin Tourismus Marketing** office listed on p.211 takes same-day personal

Most of the accommodation options listed are marked on the map on p.000.

bookings for its recommended hotels. This service is free. Obviously, though, the cheaper vacancies disappear first, so if you want a bargain you should book in advance. This can only be done by calling or faxing the office direct, telling staff roughly where you want to stay and how much you're prepared to pay. You can also send for Berlin Tourismus Marketing's authoritative *Hotels und Pensionen* booklet, which gives details (though not descriptions) of all recommended hotels and pensions.

Tiergarten

Conti, Potsdamer Str. 67 ☎2 61 29 99. Not the nicest neighbourhood, but clean basic rooms and bargain prices. ①

Grand Hotel Esplanade, Lützowufer 15 ☎25 47 80. Top-class hotel with full facilities and *Harry's* New York-style cocktail bar on the ground floor. Great choice if you're not paying. ⑦

Hansablick, Flotowstr. 6 ☎3 90 48 00. A short hop from the Tiergarten, this is one of the few "alternative" hotels in town, being run by a collective. ⑤

Intercontinental, Budapester Str. 2 ☎2 60 20. Plush modern stopover for high-powered businesspeople and visiting rock stars. Among its legion attractions are a fully equipped health studio, sauna and pool. Absolute luxury. ⑦

Sorat Hotel Spreebogen, Alt-Moabit 99 ☎3 99 20. A spirited hotel housed in a former dairy, but its position across the Spree River means it's isolated from most of the action. ⑥

Tiergarten Berlin, Alt-Moabit 89 ☎39 98 96 00. A slick modern complex in a rather seedy part of town, but handy for public transport; S-Bahn Turmstrasse is a couple of minutes by foot. ⑤

Charlottenburg

Alpenland, Carmerstr. 8 ☎3 12 39 70. Unpretentious and well situated. The broad price range means an equally wide range of clientele. ②–⑤

Am Lehniner Platz, Damaschkestr. 4 ☎3 23 51 00. Tiny and economical pension

---

Accommodation price codes

①	Up to DM100
②	DM100–120
③	DM120–140
④	DM140–170
⑤	DM170–260
⑥	DM260–340
⑦	DM340–450 and above

in the middle of an area that's lively at night. Four-bedded room available, plus single (DM45) and double (DM120) options. ③

Am Park-Pension, Sophie-Charlotten-Str. 57 ☎3 21 34 85. Small, cosy pension, located next to Lietzensee, one of the city's more romantic lakes, an area awash with weeping willows and total peace and quiet. ②

Am Zoo, Kurfürstendamm 25 ☎88 43 70. A gleaming gold foyer ushers you into a swish and plush hotel smack bang in the centre of town. ⑥

Atlanta am Kufürstendamm, Fasanenstr. 74 ☎8 81 80 49. Centrally located, but rather overpriced. ⑤

Bogota, Schlüterstr. 45 ☎8 81 50 01. Pleasant luxury at affordable prices. Ask about the interesting history of the hotel's name. ③

Borse, Kurfürstendamm 34 ☎8 81 30 21. Located on the city's busiest shopping street and near west Berlin's nightlife. ④

California, Kurfürstendamm 35 ☎88 01 20. While it's right in the centre of Ku'damm's shops, and fairly slick (there's a chunk of the Wall in the lobby), this is fairly pricey for what you get. ⑤

Casino Berlin, Königin-Elisabeth-Str. 47a ☎30 30 90. 24-roomed hotel with cable TV. ④

Castell, Wielandstr. 24 ☎8 82 71 81. While the cheaper rooms don't have shower and toilet en suite, this is still an attractively priced and well-placed option if you're aiming to explore Ku'damm's shops. ②–④

Charlot, Giesebrechtstr. 17 ☎3 23 40 51. Neatly restored *Jungendstil* building that's efficiently run by friendly staff. Near Adenauerplatz and good value for this area. ③–⑤

Charlottenburg, Grolmannstr. 32–33 ☎8 81 52 54. Another small pension off the Savignyplatz. Cheap and functional. ②

Cortina, Kantstr. 140 ☎3 13 90 59. Reasonable rooms in a good area, with breakfast included. Ideal for exploring the West End and Savignyplatz. ①

Dittberner, Wielandstr. 26 ☎8 84 69 50. Old-fashioned finery in comfortable surroundings and at affordable prices. ④

Elfert, Knesebeckstr. 13–14 ☎3 12 12 36. Pension with pleasant, comfortable decor in a location that's central by both day and night. ②

Fischer, Nürnberger Str. 24A ☎2 18 68 08. Small and very basic pension, but central and cheap, with deals on single, triple and quad rooms. A 15min walk from Zoo Station. ①

Funk, Fasanenstr. 69 ☎8 82 71 93. Interesting re-creation of a prewar flat, with furniture and objects from the 1920s and 1930s, when it was the home of Danish silent movie star Asta Nielsen. This, plus its location and price, makes it a good bargain. ③

Hardenberg, Joachimstaler Str. 39–40 ☎8 82 30 71. Smack in the city centre, on a busy main street filled with tourists – not for those who value peace and quiet. ⑤

Heidelberg, Knesebeckstr. 15 ☎3 13 01 03. Central hotel in an area good for bars and on a street noted for its bookshops. ④

Herberge Grosse, Kantstr. 71 ☎3 24 81 38. A small pension perched high on the fourth floor above busy Kantstrasse. Rooms are a bargain, although the breakfast buffet costs extra. ①

Imperator, Meinekestr. 5 ☎8 81 41 81. Great-value central, intimate hotel, situated on one of the most exclusive yet friendly streets in the city. Though it only has 20 beds, rooms are spacious and stylishly decorated, and all but two have showers. Recommended. ③

Kettler, Bleibtreustr. 19 ☎8 83 49 49. A tiny and charming pension on a lively, café-lined street. ③

Leibniz, Leibnizstr. 59 ☎3 23 84 95. Only double rooms available, but children under 11 can stay free. Rather noisy location. ②

Meineke, Meinekestr. 10 ☎88 28 11. Old-fashioned, typical Berlin hotel, with an amiable atmosphere, a minute's walk from the Ku'damm. ⑤

Accommodation

Accommodation

Niebuhr, Niebuhrstr. 74 ☎3 24 95 95. Clean and fresh pension in a quiet back-street location that's within spitting distance of the Ku'damm and Kantstrasse. Breakfast is served in your room at whatever time you desire. Popular with gay guests. ④

Pension Peters, Kantstr. 146 ☎3 12 22 78. Spare and inexpensive pension with facilities for children. ③

Residenz, Meinekestr. 9 ☎88 44 30. Situated in a quiet street off the Ku'damm, with an ambience often lacking in the larger hotel chains. ⑥

Savoy Hotel, Fasanenstr. 9–10 ☎31 10 30. Luxury hotel with a traditional, old-world atmosphere. ⑥

Sorat Art'otel, Joachimstalerstr. 29 ☎88 44 70. Light, airy and minimalist, popular with passing celebrities. ⑤

Waizennegger, Mommsenstr. 6 ☎8 81 45 28. Cosy little place (6 rooms) with a likeable intimacy and management. On the minus side, it's on the edge of Savignyplatz's action. ③

West-Pension, Kurfürstendamm 48 ☎8 81 80 57. Great value for money along one of the city's busiest streets; offers conference and disabled facilities. Has its own garage. ③

Wilmersdorf

Artemisia, Brandenburgische Str. 18 ☎8 73 89 05. The sole women-only hotel in the city , with a roof garden and exhibitions. Singles DM100, doubles DM169. Fills up quickly, so book well in advance. ⑤

Alsterhof Ringhotel, Augsburgerstr. 5 ☎21 24 20. A pleasant modern hotel with warm interior decor. Central, but far enough away from the bustle of the Ku'damm. Pool, solarium and sauna. ⑥

Bregenz, Bregenzer Str. 5 ☎8 81 43 07. Small, family-run set-up, a 10min walk from Kurfürstendamm. Kids welcome. ①

Comet Berlin, Kurfüstendamm 175 ☎8 80 41 70. Centrally located along Berlin's main shopping street and, considering its position, good value for money. ④

Gitte, Pfalzburger Str. 87 ☎8 81 84 27. Quiet pension, yet centrally located, only 10min from the hustle and bustle of Kurfürstendamm. ④

Lenz, Xantener Str. 8 ☎8 81 51 58. Medium-sized hotel in the city's West End, located along a quiet, leafy side street. A 5min walk from U-Bahn Adenauerplatz. ⑤

München, Güntzelstr. 62 ☎8 57 91 20. A straightforward, unpretentious pension with light, bright modern decor, friendly management and prices that make it a highly recommendable bargain. ①

Pariser Eck, Pariser Str. 19 ☎8 81 21 45 or 8 83 63 35. Adequate pension in a pleasant, leafy backstreet. A ten-minute walk from the Ku'damm and with some classy cafés nearby. ①

Savigny, Brandenburgische Str. 21 ☎8 81 30 01. Just 10min south of Adenauerplatz, with decent facilities. ③

Studentenhotel Hubertusalle, Delbrückstr. 24 ☎8 91 97 18. Open March–Oct. While the building resembles an ugly college hall of residence, the *Studentenhotel* is right by the Hubertus lake, which makes it pleasant in summer. Its popularity with student groups means you need to book way in advance. ①

Mitte

Aacron, Friedrichstr. 124 ☎2 82 93 52. About as central as you're likely to get at this price. The pension rooms are spartan but bearable. ①

Adlon, Unter den Linden 77 ☎2 26 10. The jewel of Berlin's prewar luxury hotels has been re-created in all its excessive splendour. Prices fit for a kaiser. ⑦

Art'otel Ermelerhaus, Wallstr. 70–73 ☎24 06 20. Smart, lively hotel with quirky decor and lots of modern art. ⑤

Berliner Congress Center, Märkisches Ufer 54 ☎2 75 80. Primarily a conference centre but its comfortable if slightly dull rooms are available to individuals too. ⑤

Forum Hotel Berlin, Alexanderplatz ☎2 38 90. A big, ugly block dominating Alexanderplatz, but its 900 en-suite rooms are pleasant enough in a bland way, with unbeatable views over the city. ⑥

Grand Hotel, Friedrichstr. 158–164 ☎2 02 70. Fully living up to its name, a traditional-style hotel with a little more atmosphere than some of its rivals. ⑦

Grosser Kurfürst, Neue Ross-Str. 11 ☎24 60 00. Recently renovated and brought up to west Berlin luxury standards. ⑤

Hilton, Mohrenstr. 30 ☎2 02 30. Luxurious, expensive and not much different to any other *Hilton* hotel in the world; the place to head if you enjoy being completely insulated from the outside world when you visit a city. Features sauna, swimming pool and squash court. ⑦

Hilton Kronen, Mohrenstr. 30 ☎2 02 30. In the same building as the *Hilton*; a slightly cheaper though still very upmarket establishment, modelled along the same lines as its parent. ⑤

Kastanienhof, Kastanienallee 65–66 ☎44 30 50. Well-appointed rooms at reasonable prices. Away from the centre of things but handy for the nightlife of nearby Prenzlauer Berg. ④

Luisenhof, Köpenicker Str. 92 ☎2 41 59 06. A rarity among more expensive Mitte hotels, in that it's not a GDR-era ferro-concrete construction. This nineteenth-century coaching company building has been well restored inside and out and is one of the best options in this price range. ⑤

Märkischer Hof, Linienstr. 133 ☎2 82 71 55. Centrally located, a stone's throw from Oranienburger Strasse and within easy strolling distance of Unter den Linden. Comfortable rooms with TV, mini-bar etc. Most rooms have showers. ④

Merkur, Torstr. 156 ☎2 82 82 97. Fairly comfortable rooms within easy walking distance of city-centre attractions and local nightlife. Most rooms have showers. ③

Novalis, Novalisstr. 5 ☎2 82 40 08. Quiet, small hotel not far from Oranienburger Tor S-Bahn station. Rooms have shower and WC. ④

Radisson-Plaza Hotel, Karl-Liebknecht-Str. 5 ☎2 38 28. A grand luxury hotel with every conceivable facility and extra. ⑦

Unter den Linden, Unter den Linden 14 ☎23 81 10. Simply furnished but comfortable mid-range place at the junction of Friedrichstrasse and Unter den Linden. ⑤

Western suburbs

Am Anhalter Bahnhof, Stresemannstr. 36, Kreuzberg ☎2 51 03 42. Ideally placed between the two centres of Berlin (the Ku'damm and Alexanderplatz), although don't expect peace and quiet – the building faces a major throughfare. ②

Die Fabrik, Schlesische Str. 18, Kreuzberg ☎6 11 71 16. A hip and inexpensive pension in a converted factory building that appeals to backpackers and other young travellers. Three- and four-bed rooms. ①

Estrel Residence & Congress Hotel, Sonnenallee 225, Neukölln ☎6 83 10. Claims to be the largest hotel in the country, with 1125 rooms. In the middle of nowhere, this complex is intended for business travellers and conventioneers and is unlikely to appeal to anyone else. ④

Grossbeerenkeller, Grossbeerenstr. 90, Kreuzberg ☎7 42 49 84. Pleasant family-run pension that's better known for its ancient bar of the same name in the cellar (see p.250). ②

Humboldt Mühle Sorat, An der Mühle 5–9, Reinickendorf ☎43 90 40. Modern yet pleasant hotel housed in a former windmill. ⑤

Igel, Friederikestr. 33–34, Reinickendorf ☎4 36 00 10. Quiet green location, almost on the shores of Lake Havel and far from the centre in Reinickendorf. For those with their own transport. ⑤

Korso am Flughafen, Tempelhoferdamm 2, Tempelhof ☎7 85 70 77. Conveniently placed if you need to use Tempelhof airport, and not too far from Kreuzberg's nightlife. ①

Kreuzberg, Grossbeerenstr. 64, Kreuzberg ☎2 51 13 62. Close to Kreuzberg hill at

Accommodation

the smarter end of that neighbourhood. This pension offers very basic amenities at basic prices. Communal bathrooms, no lift, no phones; but with double rooms starting at DM95, who's complaining? ①

Norddeutscher Hof, Geisbergstr. 30, Schöneberg ☎2 35 14 80. Situated in the middle of Berlin's four-star hotel district, this hotel is cheap, cheerful and basic. ②

Schöneberg, Hauptstr. 135, Schöneberg ☎7 81 88 30. Highly recommended pension that borders leafy surburban Friedenau to the south of the city centre. Has some no-smoking rooms. ⑤

Sylter Hof Berlin, Kurfürstenstr. 116, Schöneberg ☎2 12 00. Rather unexciting hotel complex, but handy for exploring Kreuzberg and the east of the city. ⑤

Transit, Hagelbergerstr. 53–54, Kreuzberg ☎7 85 50 51. Recently renovated converted factory in a quiet courtyard that attracts a young clientele. ②

Eastern Suburbs

Am Weissen See, Parkstr. 78, Weissensee ☎9 78 90 10. Tiny pension out in leafy Weissensee, but with reasonable public transport access to the centre. ③

BCA Hotel Lichtenberg, Rhinstr. 159, Lichtenberg ☎54 93 50. A medium-sized hotel located in a rather dreary neighbourhood, but not far from east Berlin's Tierpark zoo. ⑤

Gästehäuser Schloss Niederschönhausen, Tschaikowskistr. 1, Pankow ☎47 47 16 61. Former GDR state guesthouse in the grounds of Schloss Niederschönhausen. The rooms are comfortable enough, though the building itself is hideous. ⑤

Greifswald, Greifswalder Str. 211, Prenzlauer Berg ☎4 42 78 88. Located in an unremarkable neighbourhood, but quite near Alexanderplatz and the nightlife along Oranienburger Strasse. ④

Touristenhaus Grünau, Dahmestr. 6, Lichtenberg ☎6 76 98 08. A bit hostel-like (only a handful of rooms have en-suite WCs and bathrooms) but pleasantly situated on the banks of the Langer See out in Grünau. ①

Lesbian and gay accommodation

Bed & Breakfast Berlin (☎ 6 93 84 66) will arrange gay-friendly private rooms or apartments from DM35 up, while **Man-O-Meter Information und Treffpunkt für Schwule** (☎2 15 16 66) runs a gay accommodation service. For other options, you might check out the classified adverts in the monthly magazine *Siegessäule* (see p.34).

There are no hotels or pensions in Berlin specifically for **lesbians**; however, there is one women-only hotel, the *Artemisia* (see "Wilmersdorf", p.218 for details). Listed below are some hotels popular with gay men:

Arco, Geisbergstr. 30, Charlottenburg ☎218 2128. Popular with an international gay/straight crowd. ②

Bol's Hotel, Fuggerstr. 33, Charlottenburg ☎2 17 70 28. Inexpensive hotel located above the famous hardcore Connection club. ①

Charlottenburger Hof, Stuttgarter Platz 14, Charlottenburg ☎32 90 70. Centrally located hotel above the 24-hour *Café Voltaire*. ③

Niebuhr, Niebuhrstr. 74 ☎3 24 95 95 (see under "Charlottenburg", on p.218).

Le Moustache, Gartenstr. 4, Mitte ☎2 81 72 77. Gay hotel next door to the leather bar of the same name (see p.258). Price includes entry to adjacent swimming pool, Stadtbad Mitte. ①

Tom's House, Eisenacher Str. 10, Schöneberg ☎2 18 55 44. Clean and friendly gay hotel, popular with those into leather. ④

Camping

None of Berlin's **campsites** is close to the centre: each requires time and effort to reach, and, unlike many other European cities, there's no specifically youth-designated site. All the campsites are inexpensive (prices are a uniform DM7 per tent plus DM9 per person per night), well run and, with one exception, open year-round. If you're intending to camp with a group it's recommended that you contact the **Deutscher Camping Club e.V.**, Geisberger Str. 11, 10777 Berlin (☎2 18 60 71), to make a prior reservation.

"The Tent" (*Übernachtung im Zelt*) is a valuable addition to the city's high-summer accommodation options. Set up by the authorities in response to the lack of budget accommodation for backpackers – in an attempt to prevent them from dossing around Zoo Station – it is an inexpensive and useful alternative, especially if you haven't prebooked and arrive at a busy time. See the listing below and ask at any of the tourist offices (see p.211) for the latest information.

If you are looking to cut costs, and intend to stay for a while, bear in mind that a *Mitwohnzentrale* flat may work out almost as cheap once you've added the cost of travel. Further afield, the Brandenburg region that surrounds Berlin has innumerable sites: the various tourist offices should be able to give you a complete list.

Camping Dreilinden, Albrechts Teerofen, Zehlendorf ☎8 05 12 01; open March–Oct. U-Bahn to Oskar-Helene-Heim then a #118 bus in the direction of Kohlhasenbrück, and get off at the Katchenweg stop. Close to the former border in the southwest of the city, the site is 2.5km from the nearest bus stop, so inadvisable unless you have transport. Free showers and a small restaurant.

Camping Kladow, Krampnitzer Weg 111–117, Spandau ☎3 65 27 97. U-Bahn to Rathaus Spandau, then #134 bus to Kladow; at the southern end of Kladower Damm (Alt-Kladow stop), change to the #234, get off when the bus swings off Krampnitzer Weg and walk west to the end of the road. Friendly campsite on the western side of the Havel Lake, with the best facilities of all the sites, including a free crèche, bar, restaurant, shop and showers (DM0.50). Six-week maximum stay.

Camping Kohlhasenbrück, Neue Kreis Str. 36, Zehlendorf ☎8 05 17 37. A 10-min walk from S-Bahnhof Griebmitzsee. Has all the basic facilities (showers, laundry etc), a children's playground and a restaurant.

Camping Krossinsee, Wernsdorfer Str. 45, Köpenick ☎6 75 86 87. From S-Bahn Grünar take tram #68 to Schmöckwitz; here, catch bus #463 to the site. The only site in the erstwhile GDR, *Krossinsee* is pleasantly located in the woods just outside the southeastern suburb of Schmöckwitz, and offers easy access to local lakes.

Übernachtung im Zelt–Jugendcamp Fliestal, Waidmannsluster Damm/Ziekowstrasse, Reinickendorf ☎4 33 86 40; open July–Aug. "The Tent" is 35min from Friedrichstrasse U-Bahnhof. First take U-Bahn #6, direction Alt-Tegel, to the end of the line; it's then a short hop on bus #222, direction Alt-Lübars. Only those aged between 14 and 26 (which you will be asked to prove) are admitted. You'll be provided with a sleeping mat and blanket. Basic facilities; DM10 per night.

Accommodation

Chapter 12

Restaurants

Berlin has all the possibilities you'd expect from a major European capital city, with virtually every imaginable type of cuisine represented: indeed, the national cuisine takes a back seat to Greek, Turkish, Balkan, Indian and Italian food. The more established and sure-footed restaurants are in the west, but in the last couple of years the eastern districts of the city have experienced a restaurant boom. Generally speaking, these eastern establishments cater to a young and savvy crowd and emphasize nouvelle and ethnic menus. Particularly in Mitte and Prenzlauer Berg, there are now plenty of choices and excellent food to be had. Still, it's new ground: restaurants and chefs come and go quickly and many places are still finding their stride.

*Berlin's **cafés** are detailed in Chapter 13.*

Restaurant eating in Berlin need not be expensive: a sit-down meal starts at around DM12, and drinks aren't hiked up much more than you'd pay in a bar. **Prices** quoted are for a single main course without starter, dessert or drink. When it comes to **tipping**, add around ten to fifteen percent to the bill. By law, all restaurants are obliged to display their menu and prices by the door, as well as indicating which is their *Ruhetag/e* (closing day/s).

Where to eat

Not surprisingly, the places around the Ku'damm and Europa Center tend to be overpriced, and for the best-value food, you need to head a little way

from the city centre. It's worth noting that Italian, Yugoslav or – especially – Greek eateries often provide the best bargains, while if you're *really* on a budget, there's rock-bottom eating at the city's *Imbiss* and student *Mensa* restaurants.

German restaurants, on the other hand, are generally expensive, and the only places really worth going to are those out from the city centre, where wild game is served up (at equally wild prices). The *Gaststätte*, or traditional German eating place, is occasionally seen in a sort of kitsch version meant to appeal to the upper working classes, or in a run-down insalubrious version in the former East Berlin. Both are to be strenuously avoided.

What to eat

To enjoy traditional **German cuisine**, it does help if you share the national penchant for solid, fatty food accompanied by compensatingly healthy fresh vegetables and salad.

The **pig** is the staple of the German menu – it's prepared in umpteen different ways, and just about every part of it is eaten. Sausages are the country's most popular snack, while *Kassler Rippen* (smoked and pickled pork chops) and *Eisbein* (pig's trotters) are Berlin favourites – although the fatty *Eisbein* tend to be more of a winter speciality, as is *Boulette*, a sort of German hamburger. *Königsberger Klopse* (meat dumplings in a caper- and lemon-flavoured sauce) can also be found on many menus.

Unusual things are done with **potatoes**, too: try *Kartoffelpuffer* (flour and potatoes mixed into a pancake) or *Pellkartoffeln mit Quark und Leinöl*, a stomach-churning combination of baked potatoes, low-fat cheese and linseed oil that's best digested with lashings of beer or schnapps.

Where they exist at all, **desserts** in Berlin's German restaurants are something of an anti-climax. *Rote Grütze* (mixed soft berries eaten hot or cold with vanilla sauce) is one of the few distinctive dishes. Otherwise it's the usual selection of fresh and stewed fruits, cheeses and ice creams; if you have a sweet tooth, best head for a café that serves one of the delicious cakes or gateaux of which Germans are so fond (see Chapter 13).

A recent reaction against heavy traditional cooking is **Neue Deutsche Küche**, the German equivalent of nouvelle cuisine. While not as minimalistic as the French or Californian versions, like any food trend it tends to be expensive – particularly so for the quantity you get. The places we recommend are, of course, exceptions.

Snacks and budget eating

For cheap, on-the-hoof snacks, head for one of the ubiquitous **Imbiss** stands found on street corners, where for a few marks you can fill up on *Currywurst* – curry-flavoured sausages that originated in Berlin – and French fries. Chinese and Greek *Imbiss* stands have recently become popular, selling Greek döner kebabs, known as gyros, in a puffy pittaish bread, generally with a tsatziki-type sauce, which are great value at DM3–6.

Otherwise, **fast-food places** and **burger bars** are everywhere, especially around Zoo Station in the centre. Takeaway pizzas are a major boon if you're on a tight budget, with prices as low as DM1.75 for a square of cheese, tomato and salami pizza. The city's large Turkish community, particularly in and around Kreuzberg, means that kebab places are also common.

Around lunchtime in the main shopping areas, such as those around Wilmersdorferstrasse and Walter-Schreiber-Platz U-Bahns, it's worth trying some of the **fish shops**, which sell rolls with a good variety of fishy fillings. A few **bakeries** in these places also sell filled bread rolls for around DM3.

For something more substantial but not that much more expensive, **Imbiss** restaurants – a step up from the *Imbiss* street stall – charge between DM7 and DM12 for a meal, handy if you just want to refuel for a few Marks. Alternatively, at lunchtime, head for either of the city's **Mensas**, officially for university students only but usually open to anyone who broadly fits that description. In either case, make sure you head for the *Bargeld* (cash) queue. Some of the *Imbiss* places listed below offer limited seating.

Ashoka-Imbiss, Grolmanstr. 51, Charlottenburg (off Savignyplatz). About the best of the lot, dishing up good portions of tremendous-value Indian food, with vegetarian options. Daily 10am–2am.

Bagels & Bialys, Rosenthaler Str. 46–48, Mitte. Tiny stand-up place for bagels

Restaurants

*Most restaurants are usually able to rustle up something for **vegetarians**, though a small number of specifically vegetarian restaurants provide a welcome relief from salads; see p.236.*

Restaurants

FOOD GLOSSARY

Basics

Frühstück	breakfast
Mittagessen	lunch
Abendessen	supper, dinner
Messer	knife
Gabel	fork
Löffel	spoon
Speisekarte	menu
Teller	plate
Tasse	cup
Glas	glass
Vorspeise	starter
Hauptgericht	main course
Nachspeise	dessert
Brot	bread
Brötchen	bread roll
Butter	butter
Butterbrot	sandwich
Belegtes Brot	open sandwich
Marmelade	jam
Honig	honey
Käse	cheese
Fleisch	meat
Fisch	fish
Ei	egg
Gemüse	vegetables
Obst	fruit
Joghurt	yoghurt
Zucker	sugar
Pfeffer	pepper
Salz	salt
Öl	oil
Essig	vinegar
Senf	mustard
Sosse	sauce
Reis	rice
Spätzle	shredded pasta
Maultaschen	form of ravioli
Rechnung	bill
Trinkgeld	tip

Soups and starters

Suppe	soup
Erbsensuppe	pea soup
Linsensuppe	lentil soup
Bohnensuppe	bean soup
Zwiebelsuppe	onion soup
Gulaschsuppe	thick soup in imitation of goulash
Leberknödelsuppe	clear soup with liver dumplings
Fleischsuppe	clear soup with meat dumplings
Ochsenschwanzsuppe	oxtail soup
Flädlesuppe, Pfannkuchensuppe	clear soup with pancake strips
Hühnersuppe	chicken soup
Leberpastete	liver paté
Lachsbrot	smoked salmon on bread
Melone mit Schinken	melon and ham
Grüner Salat	mixed green salad
Gurkensalat	cucumber salad
Fleischsalat	sausage and onion salad
Schnittlauchbrot	chives on bread
Sülze	jellied meat loaf

Meat and Poultry

Aufschnitt	slices of cold sausage
Bockwurst	chunky boiled sausage
Bratwurst	grilled sausage
Broiler	chicken
Currywurst	sausage served with piquant sauce
Eisbein	pigs' trotters
Ente	duck
Fasan	pheasant
Frikadelle	meatball
Froschschenkel	frogs' legs
Gans	goose
Geschnetzeltes	shredded meat, usually served with rice
Gyros	kebab
Hackbraten	mincemeat roast
Hackfleisch	mincemeat
Hammelfleisch	mutton
Hase	hare
Herz	heart
Hirn	brains
Hirsch, Reh	venison
Huhn, Hähnchen	chicken
Innereien	innards
Jägerschnitzel	cutlet in wine and mushroom sauce
Kaninchen	rabbit

Kassler Rippen	smoked and pickled pork chops
Kotelett	cutlet (cheapest cut)
Krautwickerl	cabbage leaves filled with mincemeat
Lamm	lamb
Leber	liver
Leberkäse	baked meatloaf
Lunge	lungs
Nieren	kidneys
Ochsenschwanz	oxtail
Rahmschnitzel	cutlet in cream sauce
Rindfleisch	beef
Sauerbraten	braised pickled beef
Saure Lunge	pickled lungs
Schaschlik	diced meat with piquant sauce
Schinken	ham
Schnecke	snail
Schnitzel Natur	uncoated cutlet
Schweinebraten	roast pork
Schweinefleisch	pork
Speck	bacon
Truthahn	turkey
Wiener Schnitzel	thin cutlet in breadcumbs
Wienerwurst	boiled pork sausage
Wild	wild game
Wildschwein	wild boar
Wurst	sausage
Zigeunerschnitzel	cutlet in paprika sauce
Zunge	tongue

Fish

Aal	eel
Forelle	trout
Hecht	pike
Hering, Matjes	herring
Hummer	lobster
Kabeljau	cod
Karpfen	carp
Kaviar	caviar
Krabben	crab
Lachs	salmon
Makrele	mackerel
Muscheln	mussels
Rotbarsch	rosefish
Sardinen	sardines
Schellfisch	haddock
Scholle	plaice
Schwertfisch	swordfish
Seezunge	sole
Scampi	scampi
Thunfisch	tuna
Tintenfisch	squid
Zander	pike-perch

Vegetables

Blumenkohl	cauliflower
Bohnen	beans
Bratkartoffeln	fried potatoes
Champignons	button mushrooms
Erbsen	peas
Grüne Bohnen	green beans
Gurke	cucumber
Karotten, Möhren	carrots
Kartoffelbrei	mashed potatoes
Kartoffelpuree	creamed potatoes
Kartoffelsalat	potato salad
Knoblauch	garlic
Knödel, Kloss	dumpling
Kopfsalat	lettuce
Lauch	leeks
Maiskolben	corn on the cob
Paprika	green or red peppers
Pellkartoffeln	jacket potatoes
Pilze	mushrooms
Pommes frites	chips/French fries
Salzkartoffeln	boiled potatoes
Reibekuchen	potato cake
Rosenkohl	brussels sprouts
Rote Rübe	beetroot
Rotkohl	red cabbage
Rübe	turnip
Salat	salad
Sauerkraut	pickled cabbage
Spargel	asparagus
Tomaten	tomatoes
Weisskohl	white cabbage
Zwiebeln	onions

Fruit

Ananas	pineapple
Apfel	apple
Aprikose	apricot
Banane	banana
Birne	pear

Restaurants

Fruit *continued*

Brombeeren	blackberries
Datteln	dates
Erdbeeren	strawberries
Feigen	figs
Himbeeren	raspberries
Johannisbeeren	redcurrants
Kirschen	cherries
Kompott	stewed fruit or mousse
Mandarine	tangerine
Melone	melon
Obstsalat	fruit salad
Orange	orange
Pampelmuse	grapefruit
Pfirsich	peach
Pflaumen	plums
Rosinen	raisins
Schwarze Johannisbeeren	blackcurrants
Trauben	grapes
Zitrone	lemon

Cheeses and desserts

Emmentaler	Swiss Emmental
Käseplatte	mixed selection of cheeses
Schafskäse	sheep's cheese
Weichkäse	cream cheese
Ziegenkäse	goat's cheese
Apfelstrudel mit Sahne	apple strudel with fresh cream
Berliner	jam doughnut
Dampfnudeln	large yeast dumplings served hot with vanilla sauce
Eis	ice cream
Gebäck	pastries

Kaiserschmarrn	shredded pancake served with powdered sugar, jam & raisins
Käsekuchen	cheesecake
Keks	biscuit
Pfannkuchen	doughnut
Nüsse	nuts
Nusskuchen	nut cake
Obstkuchen	fruitcake
Schokolade	chocolate
Schwarzwälder Kirschtorte	Black Forest gateau
Torte	gateau, tart

Common terms

Art	in the style of
Blau	rare
Eingelegte	pickled
Frisch	fresh
Gebacken	baked
Gebraten	fried, roasted
Gedämpft	steamed
Gefüllt	stuffed
Gegrillt	grilled
Gekocht	cooked
Geräuchert	smoked
Gut bürgerliche	traditional German
Küche	cooking
Hausgemacht	home-made
Heiss	hot
Kalt	cold
Spiess	skewered
Topf (Eintopf)	stew, casserole
Vom heissen Stein	raw meats you cook yourself on a red-hot stone

(flown in from New York!) and döner kebabs.

Baharat Falafel, Winterfeldtstr. 14, Schöneberg. The best falafels this side of Baghdad – to the swaying and rippling of a (German) belly dancer. DM5 and up; open till 2am.

Beef Schnell House, Sonnenalle/Reuterstr., Neukölln. Excellent Chinese *Imbiss*, owned and run by an English-speaking Cantonese

chef. All dishes are under DM10; the speciality is the duck.

Bio Insel, Friedrichstr. 67 (in the Friedrichstadt Passagen), Mitte. One of several snack places in the food court of the upscale *Friedrichstadt Passagen* shopping mall, the food here is surprisingly good and fresh.

Brooklyn, Oranienstr. 176, Kreuzberg. Great American-style hero sandwiches, wonderful cheesecake and brownies, and all of it cheap. DM5–10.

Café Marché, Kurfürstendamm 14–16, Charlottenburg. Part of chain run by Mövenpick, a well-established Swiss catering company. Rather like a glorified canteen, it features a help-yourself buffet, with daily specials. There are always lots of salads, vegetarian dishes, exotic fruit juices and great cakes.

Croissant Imbiss, Wittenbergplatz U-Bahn, Schöneberg. The aroma hits you almost as soon as you get off the train, and makes the pure butter croissants in all guises irresistible. Great for breakfast; standing only. Mon–Fri 6am–6pm.

Die Tofuerei, Krefelderstr. 2, Tiergarten. As the name suggests, a vegetarian *Imbiss* (though the premises once contained a butcher's shop) with tasty and imaginative daily specials. Closes at 6pm and all day Sun.

Einhorn, Mommsenstr. 2, Charlottenburg. Vegetarian wholefood at its best, in a friendly and relaxed atmosphere – though it's standing only and closes at 6.30pm daily (4pm on Sat). DM6–9.

Ernst-Reuter-Platz Mensa, Ernst-Reuter-Platz, Charlottenburg. Small mensa of the nearby Technical University, with limited choice of meals. Around DM3, ISIC required. Mon–Fri 11.15am–2.30pm.

Fressco, Oranienburger Str. 48-49, Mitte & Stresemannstr. 34, Kreuzberg. Clean, well-lighted places featuring quiches, sandwiches, pasta and Italian nibbles. Tables at the Kreuzberg location, stand-up counters only in Mitte, and a no-smoking policy at both. Daily noon–1am.

Habibi, Goltzstr. 24, Schöneberg. Amiable late-night falafel shop with seating. DM3.50 upwards. Open through to 3am.

Humboldt-Mensa, Humboldt-Universität, Unter den Linden, Mitte. If you're doing Unter den Linden and money's tight, then it's worth popping in here to fill up on the cheap. No ID needed.

Imbiss Konnopke, Schönhauser Allee/Kastanienallee, Prenzlauer Berg. Beneath the S-Bahn arches, a Prenzlauer Berg legend that serves what's claimed to be the best *Currywurst* in the city.

Imbiss 195, Wilmersdorf. *Imbiss*-eating deluxe style. Scoff some of the city's tastiest *Wurst*, acompanied by a bottle of Dom Perignon. Open till 5am.

Lotus, Pestalozzistr. 29, Charlottenburg. Healthfood shop with vegetarian meals and salads to eat in or take out.

Mai Thai, Zossener Str. 13, Kreuzberg. Inexpensive, undecorated Thai fast food restaurant. Quality uneven.

Mensa of the Free University, Habelschwerdter Allee, at the junction with Thielallee, Dahlem (nearest U-Bahn #2 to Dahlem-Dorf). Only worth considering if you're spending the day at the Dahlem museums. Around DM3, ISIC advisable. Mon–Fri noon–2pm.

Nachtigall Imbiss, Ohlauerstr. 10, Kreuzberg. Arab specialities, including the delicious *Schwarma* kebab – lamb and houmous in pitta bread. Good salads for vegetarians.

Naturkost am Mehringdamm, Mehringdamm 47, Kreuzberg. Tasty vegetarian stand-up *Imbiss* featuring daily specials: salads, soups, quiches, lasagne, etc. Open during normal office hours.

Nordsee, Karl-Liebknecht Str. 6, Mitte. This seafood shop has a takeaway counter offering inexpensive fish sandwiches and seafood salads. A great respite from hamburgers and döner kebabs.

Orientalischer Imbiss, Mehringdamm 63, Kreuzberg. Arab *Schwarma* specialities: spiced lamb, chickpea puree and salad in pitta bread. Other delicacies include marinated sheeps' tongues with tabouli.

Pagode, Bergmannstr. 88, Kreuzberg. Inexpensive Thai meals with a high reputation among Berlin's *Imbiss* aficionados.

Rani Indischer Imbiss, Goltzstr. 32, Schöneberg. Another budget-priced Indian, ideal for cheap eats when exploring the bars of Winterfeldtplatz. Noon–midnight.

Safran-Falafel, Knaackstr. 14, Prenzlauer Berg. Where trendy bars appear falafel takeways are sure to follow – Prenzlauer

Restaurants

Restaurants

Berg's first, offering an extensive vegetarian menu.

Sesam, Gneisenaustr. 22, Kreuzberg. Falafel, houmous, tabouli and *Schwarma* all in pitta bread and all at budget prices. Great for stand-up snacks.

Solomon Bagels, Joachimsthaler Str. 13. A small, smart stand-up place, featuring hand-baked bagels and fresh tasty toppings. Almost like New York.

Sushi, Emserstr. 25, Wilmersdorf. Japanese food fans flock to this little snack bar, where the sushi is authentic, fresh and very cheap.

Tex-Mex, Georgenstr. 198, Mitte. A kitschy little place with chile, tacos and the like. Inexpensive, but not what you'd get in Mexico City.

Tibet Haus, Zossener Str. 19, Kreuzberg. A long menu, with lots of vegetarian options, from the country on top of the world. Cheap and very good.

Toni's Snack, Wörtherstr. 26, Prenzlauer Berg. Great-value pizza, pasta dishes, vegetarian döners and, for jaded palates, Bulgarian specialities. Until 6pm.

Tori Katsu, Winterfeldtstr. 7, Shöneberg. Wide selection of Japanese dishes and sushi at knock-down prices.

TU Mensa, Hardenbergstr. 34, Charlottenburg. Meals around DM4; buy your meal ticket before getting your food. Inferior to the Free University mensa, but much more central. Mon–Fri 11.15am–2.30pm.

Vietnam Imbiss, Damaschkestr. 30, Charlottenburg. Popular little *Imbiss* serving inexpensive Vietnamese dishes. Closed Sat & Sun.

Restaurants

The prices quoted below are for main courses, exclusive of starters, drinks or tips. Where you may need to book, we've included the phone number. Don't forget that many of the cafés and bars listed in the following chapter can be excellent (and inexpensive) choices for food, especially breakfast (see p.239).

Chinese, Japanese and Vietnamese

Cat Food, Körterstr. 8, Kreuzberg. Small and stylish sushi bar that's become a neighbourhood favourite. DM12–20.

Good Friends, Kantstr./Schlüterstr., Charlottenburg ☎3 13 26 59. One of the few Berlin Chinese restaurants to offer Peking Duck (24hrs' notice required) and the like. If your written Chinese is up to scratch, try ordering some authentic tastes from the ideogrammed menu. Always busy, evening bookings recommended. DM15–25.

Ho Lin Wah, Kurfürstendamm 218, Charlottenburg. The former Chinese embassy transformed into a Chinese restaurant. Something of an oddity.

Kyoto, Wilmersdorfer Str. 94, Charlottenburg. Excellent Japanese locale with sushi to your heart's content. Snooty service at times. DM15–25.

Mao Thai, Wörther Str. 30, Prenzlauer Berg ☎4 41 92 61. A bit expensive but the food is excellent and the service unfailingly polite. Dishes up to DM30.

Sabu, Salzburger Str. 19, Schöneberg ☎7 87 44 83. Sophisticated but pricey-place with some of the best Japanese food in town. DM16–35.

Sapporo-Kan, Schlüterstr. 52, Charlottenburg. Admire the wax culinary creations in the window, then eat the real thing inside. Japanese restaurant that's a popular lunchtime spot. DM10–20.

Vietnam, Suarezstr. 61, Charlottenburg. One of the city's most popular Vietnamese restaurants, quietly situated in a street of junk shops. Meals are broadly similar to Chinese, but spicier. DM10–30.

Wang Hoo, Wilmersdorfer Str. 75, Charlottenburg. Soothing surroundings draw a thirty-something crowd. Delicious DM35 set menu.

Eastern European

Café Haus Ungarn, Karl-Leibknecht.Str. 9, Mitte. A hold-over from GDR days, the food here is nothing to write home about, but it's one of the last places you can experience the old pre-unification ambience. DM8–15.

Samowar, Luisenplatz 3, Charlottenburg. Expensive but exquisite Russian cooking, a stone's throw away from Schloss Charlottenburg. DM23 and up.

Tadschikische Teestuben, Palais am Festungsgraben, Mitte ☎20 31 92 62. More famous for its tea specialities, but also serves up tasty Russian and Tadzhik dishes, the latter mainly involving lamb. The intricately decorated interior is a protected monument. DM15–30.

Zlata Praha, Meinekestr. 4, Charlottenburg. Classy Czech restaurant with nouveau-riche clientele. DM20–30.

French

Astir's, Grolmanstr. 56, Charlottenburg ☎3 13 63 20. Brightly decorated French bistro, kitted out Parisian style with checked cloths, chrome bar and tiled floors. Good portions of classic staples, as well as three-course prix fixe menu for under DM30.

Borchardt, Französischer Str. 47, Mitte ☎20 38 71 17. A re-creation of an elegant prewar restaurant of the same name, and widely considered one of the top restaurants in the city. DM22-40.

Café Einstein, Kurfürstenstr. 58, Tiergarten. Elegant literary café (see "Cafés and bars") with pricey French-style food served in a lovely tree-filled garden.

Le Canard, Knesebeckstr. 88, Charlottenburg ☎312 2645. Old, sleepy, much-favoured French restaurant, smack in the centre of town. Often fully booked for business lunches, so call ahead. Main courses cost around DM20. The two-course DM16.50 lunch is worth sampling.

Cour Carrée, Savignyplatz 5, Charlottenburg. Deservedly popular French restaurant with *fin-de-siècle* decor and garden seating. DM15–25.

Epikur, Prinzregentenstr. 53, Schöneberg ☎8 54 61 40. Excellent French bistro with a solid variety of country cuisine on offer. DM20 and up.

Französischer Hof, am Gendarmenmarkt, Jägerstr. 36, Mitte ☎2 04 35 70. The decor is typical of the last days of the GDR – expensive-looking but bland. Still, you can enjoy a superb view of the

Schauspielhaus and the Französischer Dom, the French specialities are better than average and there's a good wine list. DM10–60. Open until midnight.

Kolk, Hoher Steinweg 7, Spandau ☎3 33 88 79. Excellent French food with the usual German slant: slightly formal, slightly expensive (DM25–37) but worth it for the best food in Spandau.

Paris Bar, Kantstr. 152, Charlottenburg ☎3 13 80 52. This was once the city's most famous meeting place for artists, writers and intellectuals. Now high prices (DM30 plus) mean that it's wholly the preserve of the moneyed middle classes. The food is French/Viennese in style and the service immaculate.

Paris-Moskau, Alt-Moabit 141, Alt-Moabit ☎3 94 20 81. Housed in the former train station stopoff on the Paris to Moscow line, this popular French restaurant manages to be elegant without being too snooty. DM30 and up.

Publique, Yorckstr. 62, Kreuzberg ☎7 86 94 69. Friendly café-cum-restaurant serving tasty inexpensive food till 2am. Plenty of fish dishes and a set menu.

Reinhards, Kurfürstendamm 190, Charlottenburg. After making a killing in former East Berlin just after the Wall came down, *Reinhards* moved to the Kurfürstendamm. But all that's on offer here is lukewarm food at inflated prices and under-30s arranging supper parties on their mobiles. DM20–35.

St. Germain, Damaschkestr. 20, Charlottenburg. Trendy French bistro, heavy on sauces, but with hard to find dishes – in Berlin, anyway – like Cassoulet and Confit de Canard, and a weekly Couscous special. Closed Sun. DM25–35.

Storch, Wartburgstr. 54, Schöneberg ☎7 84 20 59. Rustic eatery serving cuisine from the Alsace region in what was once – they claim – a brothel. The excellent food, a mix of French and German, is served at long communal tables, so don't come for an intimate chat. All main dishes under DM30; bookings advisable, though none taken after 8pm.

Restaurants

Restaurants

Theodors, Theodor-Heuss-Platz 10, Charlottenburg ☎3 02 57 70. Elegant mosaic interior along the lines of a Parisian brasserie. The usual French fare, though the veg are cooked and presented à l'Allemande. One of the best choices for this part of town. DM25–35.

Ty Breizh, Kantstr. 75, Charlottenburg ☎3 23 99 32. Chaotic place serving up mounds of traditional northern French cuisine, including crepes. The colourful owner adds to the fun. DM17.

Traditional German

Alexander Bräu, Hausbrauerei am Alex, Karl Liebknecht Str. 13, Mitte. A "brew house" which makes its own quite tasty beer, accompanied by traditional German dishes. Touristy but not uncomfortably so. DM12–17.

Ambrosius, Einemstr. 14, Tiergarten. Large portions of cheap grub at Berlin's answer to the working men's caff. Popular for its *Eisbein* (boiled pork knuckle) – a dish that's guaranteed to spoil the day of any vegetarian. DM8–12

Austria, Bergmannstr. 30, Kreuzberg. Dark rustic surrounds and solid wood tables give the place a rather dour atmosphere, and miss the intended *gemütlichkeit* (bourgeois) mark, but the locals stay all night and the Austrian-style food is tasty and filling. DM18–30.

Ax-Bax, Leibnizstr. 34, Charlottenburg. Limited menu of Viennese dishes, with good cakes and desserts. Favourite stomping ground for arts and film people. DM15–25.

Britzer Mühle, Buckower Damm 130, Neukölln ☎6 04 10 05. Freshly prepared, meaty German fare in one of Berlin's few remaining traditional eating houses out in the middle of nowhere. The building forms part of a non-working windmill complex, and has scenic outdoor eating in summer. Booking essential.

Ermeler Haus, Märkisches Ufer 10, Mitte. Inside this Spree-side building check out the *Raabediele*, an unpretentious basement restaurant where you can get well-priced traditional dishes in slightly folksy

surroundings for DM15–25. On the first floor you'll find a pricier and less congenial wine restaurant (DM15–35).

Ephraim Palais, Spreeufer 1, Mitte ☎2 42 51 08. Trad German cuisine in the plush surroundings of this rebuilt eighteenth-century mansion. DM15–30.

Fridericus, Opernpalais, Unter den Linden 5, Mitte ☎20 26 83. Regional specialities in the city centre, with the accent on fish. It's all competently prepared and served and attracts a steady flow of tourists and businesspeople.

Henne, Leuschnerdamm 25, Kreuzberg ☎6 14 77 30. Pub-style restaurant with the best chicken in Berlin. The interior here is original – it hasn't been changed, the owners claim, since 1905. Reservations essential. DM9–15.

Historische Weinstuben, Poststr. 23, Mitte. A reasonable little wine restaurant in the basement of the Knoblauch-Haus in the Nikolaiviertel. DM8–20.

Kartoffelhaus No. 1, Richardplatz 20, Neukölln ☎6 85 90 41. Variations on that German staple, the potato. Soups, *Kartoffelklösschen* (stodgy potato dumplings), baked potatoes and *Kartoffelpuffer* (sweet or savoury type of potato pancakes). Portions are large.

Kellerrestaurant im Brechthaus, Chausseestr. 125, Mitte ☎2 82 38 48. Atmospheric restaurant, decorated with Brecht memorabilia, including models of his stage sets, in the basement of Brecht's old house. Viennese specialities – from recipes supposedly dreamed up by Brecht's wife Helene Weigel – make this one of the few good places in the area, so it gets crowded. DM15–25

Kleine Markthalle, Legiendamm 32, Kreuzberg. Wonderful crispy chicken in a basic, old-fashioned bar and restaurant. Similar to its better-known neighbour *Henne*, but easier to get into.

Koller, Paul-Lincke-Ufer 44a, Kreuzberg. Just off the scenic Landwehr Canal, this cosy place serves heaps of Austrian food at quite reasonable prices. DM16–28.

Königin Luise, Opernpalais, Unter den Linden 5, Mitte ☎20 26 83. High-class

German cuisine in an Opernpalais place catering mainly for visitors and the business-expenses crowd.

Offenbach-Stuben, Stubbenkammerstr. 8, Prenzlauer Berg ☎4 45 85 02. A near-legend even in GDR days and one of the best places in Prenzlauer Berg, with all kinds of unexpected specialities on the menu. Theatrical decor and intimate seating niches great for late-night conversation. Booking essential.

Ratskeller Köpenick, Alt Köpenick 21, Köpenick. Always a handy standby for decent, value-for-money food. DM7–22.

Ratskeller Pankow, Breite Strasse, Pankow. Reasonably priced, and a cut above the average *Ratskeller*. DM8–23.

Riehmers, Hagelberger Str. 9, Kreuzberg. Excellent husband-and-wife-run restaurant with a comfortable ambience and outstanding food and service. Outdoor seating in summer in the historic *Riehmer's Hofgarten*. DM18–35.

Rosenstübchen, Husemannstr. 2, Prenzlauer Berg. Attempts a vaguely nineteenth-century atmosphere – slightly kitsch but not unpleasant, and very popular with its mainly middle-aged clientele, for whom the extensive wine list is a big attraction. DM6–19. Wed–Sun only, until midnight.

Tegernseer Tönnchen, Berliner Str. 118, Charlottenburg. Bavarian cuisine – which means enormous dishes of *Wurst* and *Schnitzel* washed down with pitchers of beer. Excellent value at DM10–17.

Tiergartenquelle, Stadtbahnbogen 482, Tiergarten (underneath the arches at S-Bahn Tiergarten). A boozy, smoky corner of the Tiergarten that delights because of its mammoth portions of traditional stodge at knockdown prices. DM8–15.

Trio, Klausener Platz 14, Charlottenburg ☎3 21 77 82. A well-kept secret in the middle of town: gourmet eating starting at DM50 for two courses. The house cocktail depends on the time of year: in July, for example, it's *Himbeerbowle* – raspberries and Sekt. Booking essential; closed Wed.

Weltrestaurant Markthalle, Pücklerstr. 34, Kreuzberg. Spacious restaurant with long communal tables offering German food in hearty portions. Popular with a young crowd, perhaps because the *Q-Club* disco resides in the basement. DM15–25.

Zitadellen Schänke, Am Juliusturm, Spandau Zitadelle, Spandau ☎3 34 21 06. Witches' lair-effect in a cellar serving sumptuous portions of good *Bürgerlich* food. Can be a bit overpowering both gastronomically and socially, but the scenic surroundings go some way to make up for it. Set seven-course meal DM68; booking necessary.

German – Neue Deutsche Küche

Altes Zollhaus, Carl-Herz-Ufer 30, Kreuzberg ☎6 92 33 00. Very classy place in an old half-timbered building overlooking a canal. Several set menus, starting at about DM65.

Café Jolesch, Muskauerstr. 1, Kreuzberg. Noisy , smoky and very popular Austrian restaurant with great food and divine desserts. DM28. No credit cards.

Deininger, Friesenstr. 13, Kreuzberg. Bar-cum-café serving inventive, cheap bistro meals. Vegetarians are well catered for, and salad fans have a choice of ten homemade dressings. DM12–25.

Diekmanns, Meinekestr. 7, Charlottenburg. Housed in a former *Tante Emma Laden*, with much of the original decor. Good large portions. From DM22.

Florian, Grolmanstr. 52, Charlottenburg. Leading light of the new German cuisine movement in Berlin, this is as much a place to be seen as to eat in. The food, similar to French *nouvelle cuisine*, is light, flavourful – and expensive. DM20 and up.

Franzmann, Goltzstr. 32, Schöneberg ☎2 16 35 14. Elegant but unpretentious restaurant serving immaculate *Neue Deutsche Küche* with French overtones.

Frühsammers Restaurant an der Rehweise, Matterhornstr. 101, Zehlendorf ☎8 03 27 20. Part of a trend among the city's more elite restaurants: traditional German cooking revamped and refined. Expect some interesting sausage creations from one of Berlin's leading chefs. Not cheap, mind. From DM28.

Restaurants

Restaurants

Gugelhof, Knaackstr. 37, Prenzlauer Berg. Inventive German, French and Alsatian food, beautifully presented. DM18–28.

Kulisse, Friesenstr. 14, Kreuzberg. Swabian specialities. Reasonably priced, but imagination sometime exceeds skill here. From DM15.

Medici, Lausitzer Str. 25, Kreuzberg ☎6 18 68 26. New German cuisine in stylish surroundings. Trendy, so book ahead. Under DM30. Fri–Wed 7pm–1am.

Merz, Schöneberger Ufer 65, Tiergarten ☎2 61 38 82. Classic dining in opulent surroundings, with an excellent choice of wines. A longstanding favourite, and deservedly so, though prices are high. Around DM35. Thurs–Sun 7pm–1am.

Restauration 1900, Husemannstr. 1, Prenzlauer Berg ☎4 42 24 94. Another Prenzlauer Berg culinary highlight, serving traditional German dishes that spring a few surprises.

Slobo's, Heimstr. 8, Kreuzberg ☎6 93 09 00. One of Berlin's smallest restaurants, on the border of Kreuzberg and Neukölln, creating imaginative dishes with a French/German slant. Average DM25. Booking advised. Closed Wed.

Turmstuben, Französischer Dom, Gendarmenmarkt, Mitte ☎2 29 93 13. In the tower of the Französischer Dom, this classy restaurant was the culinary flagship of the new-look East Berlin the authorities were trying to create in the years leading up to the *Wende*. The food is good and best enjoyed in one of the upstairs niches; book if possible, as it can get crowded in the evenings. DM10–30. Open noon–midnight.

Van Loon, Carl-Herz-Ufer 5, Kreuzberg ☎6 92 62 93. A converted pleasure cruiser moored on the Landwehrkanal, with great fish dishes and on-deck eating (weather permitting). Average DM22.

Wirtshaus Schildhorn, Strasse am Schildhorn 4a, Grunewald ☎3 05 31 11. Housed in an attractive old *Wirtshaus* (a traditional inn) on the edge of Lake Havel, this is an ideal spot if you've spent the day exploring the area. DM23 and up.

Greek

Akropolis, Wielandstr. 38, Charlottenburg. Taped Greek Communist songs accompany the moussaka in a tranquil locale. More expensive than the average Greek restaurant. DM12–20.

Athener Grill, Kurfürstendamm 156, Charlottenburg. Ordinary Greek fast-food place that's heavy on grease but handy for late nights. DM5–12; closes 6am.

Boikos, Grossgörschenstr. 6, Shöneberg. *Nouvelle cuisine* restaurant that lightens up the often heavy Greek repertoire.

Dionysos, Schöneberger Ufer 47, Tiergarten. Slightly pricey for a Greek place, but much better value than any of the cafés in the surrounding Tiergarten museums. DM8–20.

Fou Fou, Görlitzer Str. 63, Kreuzberg ☎6 17 59 71. Fish, inventive twists on traditional dishes, and a merciful absence of the usual blue-and-white decor have made this attractive restaurant a popular choice with a young trendy crowd. Best to book ahead. DM16–35.

Skales, Rosenthaler Str. 13, Mitte ☎2 83 30 06. Trendy Greek place in the Scheunenviertel. The food is fairly pedestrian but it's more a place to be seen than anything else.

Taverna Labrys, Wielandstr. 26, Charlottenburg. Run-of-the mill fare made exemplary by the use of top-quality ingredients, and on offer at very reasonable prices.

Terzo Mondo, Grolmanstr. 28, Charlottenburg. Raucous bar and restaurant with live music, owned by the Greek star of *Lindenstrasse*, one of German TV's most popular soap operas. Open till 4am daily.

To Steki, Kantstr. 22, Charlottenburg. Conveniently close to the bars of Savignyplatz, but recent reports state that its formerly excellent standards have plummeted. Inexpensive (DM7–15).

Zorbas, Zossener Str. 25, Kreuzberg ☎6 91 94 34. The most likeable of several Greek places in the neighbourhood (off Gneisenaustrasse in west Kreuzberg), and popular with the Greek locals, always a good sign. DM8–20; open till late.

Indian

Bombay Palast, Yorckstr. 60, Kreuzberg. A much-needed addition to Indian dining in Kreuzberg. Authentic, decoratively presented dishes (fiery, if you ask them) for DM15 and under.

Golden Temple, Rankestr. 23, Charlottenburg. Friendly restaurant serving up not-so-spicy Indian food and lots of vegetarian dishes. DM10–25.

Khan Mongolian Barbecue Restaurant, Budapester Str. 11–13, Charlottenburg. The Mongolian barbecue hits Berlin: choose your food and grill away.

India-Haus, Feurigstr. 38, Schöneberg. Solid quality Indian, with first-rate veggie options. From DM12.

India-Palace, Leibnizstr. 35, Charlottenburg. Huge variety and low prices (DM10–14). One of the few places in Berlin to do a halfway decent Chicken Tikka.

Kalkutta, Bleibtreustr. 17, Charlottenburg. Arguably the finest Indian restaurant in Berlin. DM20 and up.

Kashmir Palace, Marburger Str. 14, Charlottenburg. Upmarket Indian (DM20-plus) with authentic northern Indian cuisine.

Maharadscha, Fuggerstr. 21, Schöneberg. Though the ambience is that of a German farmhouse, the food is pure Indian. DM10–15.

Italian

Al Dente, Greifswalder Str. 24, Prenzlauer Berg. Traditional Italian food in simple, light surroundings. Great for a hearty meal on cold winter nights. DM20-24.

Amore, Pichelsdorfer Str. 121, Spandau ☎3 31 18 56. Remarkably good pizzas (from DM8 up), charmingly served. All pizzas and pasta DM6 at lunchtime.

Ana e Bruno, Sophie-Charlotte-Str. 101, Charlottenburg ☎3 25 71 10. One of the city's finest Italian restaurants with superb regional food made from the freshest ingredients. Interestingly, no dishes are on the menu more than once a year. Not cheap (4 courses cost around DM100). Booking essential; Tues–Sat.

Anselmo, Damaschkestr. 17, Wilmersdorf. High-tech ultra-modern decor sets the scene for this top-range Italian eatery. Popular with Berlin's beautiful people.

Aroma, Hochkirchstr. 8, Schönberg ☎7 82 58 21. Well above average, inexpensive Italian with photo gallery and Italian films on Tues nights. One of the best options in this part of town, and it's advisable to book after 8pm. DM8–18.

Bar Centrale, Yorckstr. 82, Kreuzberg. Chic Italian locale, popular with alternative types transforming themselves into yuppies, and exiled Italians. DM10–25.

Blumenladen, Bahnhofstr. 4a, part of S-Bahn Friedenau, Steglitz ☎8 52 09 09. Crisp, clean Italian located in a former flower shop – hence the name – away from the bustle of the city, with an interesting choice of food and a good wine list. Booking advisable. DM12–25.

Café Tucci, Grolmanstr. 52, Charlottenburg. Italian bar-restaurant with the emphasis on simple but fresh Italian delights. Great desserts. Always full. DM14–25.

Candela, Grunewaldstr. 81, Schöneberg. Solid Italian food at reasonable prices, with service top of the range.

Canta Maggio, Alte Schönhauser Str. 4, Mitte. Wonderful classic Italian food has made this new Scheunenviertel place deservedly popular. The service can be idiosyncratic, however. DM15–25.

Ciao-Ciao, Kurfürstendamm 156, Wilmersdorf. Chi-chi Ku'damm trattoria offering excellent, authentic Italian cooking, with patio eating in summer. Above average prices.

Don Camillo, Schlossstr. 7, Charlottenburg. Particularly renowned for its fish, this is one of the best Italians in the city, with a delightful garden terrace. Prices, though, are steep at DM35 and up; go if someone else is footing the bill . . .

Esquina, Danziger Str./Dunckerstr., Prenzlauer Berg. Laid-back, fashionable pizzeria serving smple pizzas from DM5.50.

Restaurants

Restaurants

Chamisso, Willibald-Alexis-Str. 25, Kreuzberg ☎6 91 56 42. Long-established *Szene* eating spot, with Italian (and French) food on the menu, including good pasta. DM15–25. Booking advisable.

La Cascina, Delbrückstr. 28, Zehlendorf. Quality Italian restaurant beloved of the Berlin film crowd. Pricey (DM28 and up).

Giallo E Blu, Fasanenstr. 76–77, Charlottenburg ☎8 85 12 10. Elegant, expensive and worth it if you're flush. Fresh fish is a speciality, pizza with lobster a favourite. DM22–35.

Gorgonzola Club, Dresdener Str. 121, Kreuzberg ☎6 15 64 73. Classy pizzas and freshly made pasta – choose any sauce with any pasta – in a rustic, fun atmosphere that's also, unfortunately, often very smoky.

Il Calice Enoiteca, Giesebrechtstr. 19, Charlottenburg. An upmarket wine bar serving superb wines and an unusual array of antipasti to Berlin's more bourgeois middle classes.

Milano, Clayallee 327, Zehlendorf ☎8 02 72 63. Outstanding restaurant with exemplary food and service. Best budget bet are the pizzas. Booking advisable. DM15 and up.

Osteria No. 1, Kreuzbergstr. 71, Kreuzberg ☎7 86 91 62. Classy, inexpensive and therefore highly popular Italian run by a collective. Booking essential; DM10–20.

Oxymoron, Hackescher Höfe, Rosenthaler Str. 40/41, Mitte ☎28 39 18 85. Restaurant by day, club by night. The Tuesday "Pasta Opera" lets you eat and dance simultaneously. DM14-20.

Parlamento, Bergmannstr. 3, Kreuzberg ☎6 94 77 45. Back-to-basics restaurant, with generous portions of hearty country cuisine and Italian football on the bar's TV set. DM18–24.

Petite Europa, Langenscheidtstr. 1, Schöneberg ☎7 81 29 64. Unpretentious neighbourhood place with an informal, lively atmosphere. A good selection for vegetarians. Usually full.

La Riva, Spreeufer 2, Mitte ☎2 42 51 83. Pricey Tuscan cuisine in the Nikolaiviertel. DM14–35. Open until midnight.

Tartuffel, Körtestr. 15, Kreuzberg ☎6 93 74 80. Large sprawling restaurant serving an intriguing selection of dishes featuring the humble potato. A main course will leave you with change from DM20.

Zagato, Bergmannstr. 27. Tiny local joint, with basic but delicious recipes and very low prices. The surly service is part of the attraction. DM10–18.

XII Apostoli, Bleibtreustr. 49, opposite S-Bahn Savignyplatz, Charlottenburg (☎3 12 14 33) and Georgenstr. 177–180, Mitte (☎2 01 02 22). This de luxe pizzeria has been packing them in since the moment it opened, with out-of-the-ordinary toppings like smoked salmon and cream cheese and five types of calzone. The new Mitte branch, under the railroad tracks by Frierichstrasse station, is just as popular, and offers a piano bar to boot.

Mexican, Latin American and Caribbean

Carib, Motzstr. 31, Schöneberg. Classic Caribbean cuisine and friendly service from the Jamaican owner. DM14–22.

La Batea, Krummer Str. 42, Charlottenburg. Unexceptional Latin American food in a convivial atmosphere with frequent live music. DM10–18.

La Estancia, Bundesallee 45, Wilmersdorf. Very good value for money Latin American restaurant, patronized mainly by environmentally and politically conscious Berliners. DM12–18.

El Parron, Carmerstr. 17, Charlottenburg. Solid Latin American food, and good fun when patrons leave their tables to tango. DM15–30.

Lone Star Taqueria, Bergmannstr. 11, Kreuzberg. A variety of tacos, as the name implies, but lots more, including powerful Margaritas. One of the better of the city's Tex-Mex joints.

Los Cucarachas, Oranienburger Str. 38, Mitte. Very popular and spirited place that fills up just about every night. Burritos and tacos from the Mexican side of the border; hamburgers and fried chicken from the Texas side.

Tres Kilos, Marheinekeplatz 3, Kreuzberg ☎6 93 60 44. Upmarket Tex-Mex place just by the covered market, and popular with the bright young things who've taken over the Chamissoplatz neighbourhood. Brain-stewing cocktails; main courses from DM16.

Middle Eastern and Egyptian

Amun, Möckenstr. 73a, Kreuzberg. Egyptian specialities in a relaxing atmosphere that, save for a picture or two of Nefertiti, avoids the usual Egyptian kitsch. Occasional bellydancing.

Der Ägypter, Kantstr. 26, Charlottenburg. Egyptian falafel-type meals. Spicy, filling and an adventurous alternative to the safe bets around Savignyplatz. Good vegetarian selections. DM14–20. The Egyptian jewellery shop next door, run by the same owners, is worth a look.

Diyar, Dresdener Str. 9, Kreuzberg. Lively, crowded venue offering Turkish staples alongside many vegetarian options. If drinking only, head for the cushioned area where you can sip supine.

Foyer, Uhlandstr. 28, Charlottenburg ☎8 81 42 68. Tiny Turkish restaurant, tucked away in a *Hinterhof* off the Kurfürstendamm. A small menu ensures freshness, although non-meat eaters may be unlucky. DM15–20; closed Sun.

Hitit, Knobelsdorffstr. 35, Charlottenburg. The proof that Turkish cuisine offers much more than döner kebabs with an equal mix of meat and vegetarian choices. DM10–18.

Istanbul, Knesebeckstr. 77, Charlottenburg. Arabian-nights-type interior and equally fairytale prices. DM15 and up.

Merhaba, Hasenheide 39, Kreuzberg. Highly rated Turkish restaurant that's usually packed with locals. A selection of the starters here can be more interesting than a main course. DM18–29.

Restaurant am Nil, Kaiserdamm 114, Charlottenburg (near Sophie-Charlotte-Platz). Moderately priced Egyptian with easy-going service. DM14–30.

Sondo, Husemannstr. 10, Prenzlauer Berg ☎4 42 07 24. While döner stands have proliferated across the eastern part of the city, it's taken a bit longer for upmarket Turkish cuisine to arrive. Judging by the Anatolian specialities dished up here it's been worth the wait. Up to DM25.

Tabuna, Alt-Moabit 59, Tiergarten ☎3 90 70 40. Israeli restaurant with, the owner claims, the only Tabuna oven in Europe. Unique or not, it delivers up warm and delicate pitta bread like you've never had before. DM16–35.

Spanish and Portuguese

Andaluz, Katzbachstr. 30, Kreuzberg. Tapas bar with requisite whitewashed walls and Spanish tiles. Fortunately, the food outshines the decor. DM15–20.

El Bodegon, Schlüterstr. 61, Charlottenburg. Old established Spanish eatery, complete with musicians serenading the tables. DM18.

Borriquito, Wielandstr. 6, Charlottenburg. Lively, noisy Spanish restaurant that's open till 5am daily. DM18 and up.

Carpe Diem, Savigny Passage 577, Charlottenburg. Trendy tapas bar underneath the arches near S-Bahn Savignyplatz in an upmarket shopping area. Open Tues–Sat.

Casa Portuguesa, Helmholtzstr. 15, Charlottenburg. Small, rustic family-run Portuguese, with well-above-average food, musicians some evenings and the freshest of fish. It's in the middle of nowhere, so hop on bus #101, direction Waldstrasse, Alt-Moabit. Around DM20.

Don Juan, Wielandstr. 37, Charlottenburg ☎3 24 79 93. Very traditional Spanish restaurant, strong on meat dishes, but with accommodating chef who can turn your requests into reality.

Litfass, Sybelstr. 49, Charlottenburg. Don't be put off by the bunker-like exterior; great portions of Portuguese food and particularly tasty seafood. DM15–22.

Lusiada, Kurfürstendamm 132a, Wilmersdorf ☎8 91 58 69. Boisterous Portuguese place renowned for its fish dishes. DM20 and under.

Restaurants

Restaurants

Yosoy, Rosenthaler Str. 37, Mitte.
Inexpensive tapas bar perfectly placed for
before-drinking or after-clubbing dinners.

Thai and Indonesian

Mao Thai, Wörther Str. 30, Prenzlauer
Berg ☎4 41 92 61. Fabulously popular
Thai outpost in the former east, serving
meals that are fresh, delicate and delicious. DM15–25.

Edd's Thailändisches Restaurant,
Goebenstr. 20–21, Schöneberg ☎2 15
52 94. Huge portions of superbly cooked
fresh Thai food make this a popular place
any day of the week. All the duck and
fish dishes are worth sampling. DM15–25.
Booking essential; closed Wed.

Mahachai, Schlüterstr. 60, Charlottenburg
☎3 13 08 79. Smart Thai eatery, decked
out in Indonesian style and popular with
large groups and businesspeople.

Samâdhi, Goethestr. 6, Charlottenburg
☎3 13 10 67. Tofu, coconut milk and
chilli are the main ingredients at this
Indonesian, which turns run-of-the-mill

vegetarian dishes into something worth
crossing town for.

Sarod's Thai Restaurant, Friesenstr. 22,
Kreuzberg ☎6 94 21 84. A Thai-run
restaurant offering some spectacular and
imaginative dishes. Try the *Ente VIP* –
duck cooked in coconut milk and green
curry paste. Interesting vegetarian options.

Sawaddi, Bülowstr. 9, Schöneberg ☎2
16 57 52. Thai through and through, but
rather pricey, starting at DM20. If you feel
like a change, opt for the table without
seats, and eat traditional Thai-style.

Tuk-Tuk, Grossgörschenstr. 2,
Schöneberg ☎7 81 15 88. Amiable
Indonesian near Kleistpark U-Bahn.
Enquire about the heat of your dish
before ordering. Booking advisable at
weekends. DM10–25.

Vegetarian

Beth Café, Tucholskystr. 40, Mitte. Small
and spare vegetarian kosher café featuring Israeli and traditional eastern
European specialities. DM10–22.

Berlin ohne Speck – a guide for vegetarians

In the 1930s, Berlin had over thirty vegetarian restaurants, and while the city
can't field anything like that amount
today, it's still the best place to be in a
country that seems to sustain itself
exclusively on dead pig. You'll have no
problem finding something in the listings here: otherwise you should generally steer clear of German restaurants
whether traditional or Neue Deutsche
Küche – lard and beef stock are used
ubiquitously, and there's an unwritten
convention that no meal is really complete until sprinkled with small pieces
of Speck (bacon). Refuse your plain
omelette because it's been so garnished
and you'll be treated with incredulity.

Thankfully, the city's cosmopolitan
spread of cuisines means that choosing
an Italian, Indian or Thai option will
usually yield something without meat on
the menu, and most upmarket cafés have

a flesh-free option. If you're on a budget,
head for one of our vegetarian *Imbiss*
listings rather than an *Eckkneipe*, where
you stand as much chance of getting
something meat-free as you do of being
thrown out for swearing.

Useful phrases

Remember to be forceful and insistent:
to many Germans, small bits of bacon,
ham or lard just don't count as meat.

Ich bin Vegetarier. I am a vegeterian.

Ich esse keinen Fleisch oder Fisch. I
don't eat meat or fish.

*Ich möchte keinen Speck oder keine
Fleischbrühe essen*. I cannot eat bacon
or meat stock.

Gibt's Fleisch drin? Has it got any meat
in it?

Gibt's was ohne Fleisch? Do you have
anything without meat in it?

Blue Gout, Anramer Str. 38, Mitte ☎4 48 58 40. Wonderful hideaway in a courtyard serving elegant food made from organic ingredients. DM18–30.

Derya, Chaussestr. 116, Mitte. A rarity: not only does *Derya* offer hard-to-find Turkish vegetarian food, but it also boasts, in the middle of the city, a large and peaceful beer garden. DM12–20.

Abendmahl, Muskauerstr. 9, Kreuzberg ☎6 12 51 70. A magnificent restaurant in every respect: excellent food (especially the soups – try the *Kürbis* or pumpkin), a busy but congenial atmosphere and reasonable (DM20–30) prices. One of Berlin's most enjoyable choices.

Café Oren, Oranienburger Str. 28, Mitte ☎2 82 82 28. Next door to the Oranienburger Strasse synagogue, offering light vegetarian (and kosher-esque) dishes in a stylish interior.

Hakuin, Martin-Luther-Str. 1, Schöneberg ☎2 18 20 27. Excellent Japanese vegetarian-macrobiotic à la Zen. DM30–50; best to book. Quiet and no smoking.

Restaurant V, Lausitzer Platz 12, Kreuzberg. Wholefood locale run by a collective. Rather unenterprising compared to some of the city's other restaurants. DM13–18.

Samâdhi, Goethestr. 6, Charlottenburg ☎3 13 10 67. Indonesian vegetarian. See opposite.

Thürnagel, Gneisenaustr. 57, Kreuzberg ☎6 91 48 00. Small, smart, convivial place in west Kreuzberg. DM10–20.

Zenit, Liebenwalder Str. 2, Wedding. Vegetarian German food, dumplings, *Käsespätzle* and the like, in a far-flung neighbourhood. DM8–18.

Others

Afrika Nah, Mainzer Str. 17, Neukölln ☎6 21 89 59. A clash of colours and styles greets you in this culinary high spot in the middle of Neukölln, which serves up platefuls of yam – and plantain – based rice dishes. Closed Mon.

Arche Noah, Fasanenstr. 79, Charlottenburg. Wonderful kosher delights in a good atmosphere. DM16–30.

Café Nola, Dortmunderstr. 9, Tiergarten ☎3 99 69 69. An unusual location for an exceptional restaurant that specializes in Californian-style chargrilled dishes and pungent reduced-fruit sauces.

Hard Rock Café, Meinekestr. 21, Charlottenburg. Loud, cold – the air conditioning is always on full – and totally packaged, the only thing that distinguishes it from other HRCs across Europe is its unusually high prices.

Jimmy's Diner, Pariser Str./Sächsisches Str., Wilmersdorf. One of the few authentic American-style diners in Germany. Popular with an under-30s crowd, who visit for chilled American beer and real hamburgers. Food is served until the *very* early hours.

Katschkol, Pestalozzistr. 84, Charlottenburg ☎3 12 34 72. Berlin's only Afghani restaurant, offering food with Indian and Persian overtones, the emphasis being on vegetarian combinations.

Kopenhagen, Kurfürstendamm 203, Charlottenburg. Danish and pricey for what you get. DM20 and up. Full of German businessmen and old ladies.

Outback, Damaschkestr. 17, Schöneberg ☎3 23 20 48. Kitschy Australian restaurant. If you have a hankering for ostrich burgers or kangaroo steak, this is the place to go.

Tomasa, Motzstr. 60, Schöneberg. Known locally for its breakfasts, this 1970s-style café is recommended for its wide-ranging menu that's a jumble of European cuisines. Menu available in English.

Zur Nolle, Georgenstrasse, In den S-Bahnbogen 203, Mitte. Pleasant restaurant in the railway arches beneath Bahnhof Friedrichstrasse. The reliable menu, featuring the likes of spaghetti bolognaise and fillet of salmon, makes it popular with business lunchers. DM10–25.

Restaurants

Several of the city's dirt-cheap Imbiss restaurants are vegetarian; see p.223 for reviews.

Chapter 13

Cafés and bars

Nowhere in Berlin is more than a stone's throw from a **bar**. The basic, no-frills drinking hole known as a *Kneipe* is found on street corners throughout the city and identifiable by its general gloom and all-male clientele. *Kneipen* are the cheapest places to drink (a small beer costs around DM3) and can be fun if the regulars decide to befriend you. Unaccompanied women should bear in mind that such befriending may have unwanted overtones; as a rule, local women do not frequent these places, choosing instead to head for more mixed and more upmarket bars – often referred to as *Szene* ("Scene") hang-outs – where pose (or self-conscious lack of it) is all – and cafés that make up the bulk of our listings. While the trendier-looking bars are more expensive, few are outrageously so; and, given their tendency to cluster, it's easy to bar-hop until you find a favourite. Almost all the better bars serve food, too, and this can be a bargain – though beware the most chic places, where that interesting-looking item on the menu turns out to be a plate of asparagus tips for DM30.

You'll find that most bars stay open later than elsewhere in Germany: it's quite feasible to drink **around the clock** here, the result of a law that requires bars to close for just an hour a day for cleaning In reality, most bars open at lunchtime and close at between 1 and 5am.

However, if you feel you just can't take the pace of nonstop drinking, help

is at hand. Berlin also has an established **café scene**, with hundreds of coffee houses acting as additional social hangouts. And if you can't decide whether to drink or not, many places operate as dual-functioning café-bars, so you can change your mind as the evening wears on.

Afternoon is traditionally time for *Kaffee und Kuchen* (coffee and cakes) in one of the self-consciously elegant (and, therefore, ultra-expensive) cafés in the city centre. Although indelibly associated with Austria, they're just as popular an institution in Germany. Serving various types of coffee with cream cakes, pastries or handmade chocolates, they're the ideal place to head should your mid-afternoon blood sugar level need pepping up.

Finally, if **breakfast** (Frühstück) isn't provided with your accommodation, it can be bought at certain cafés (listed opposite), many of which continue to serve breakfast throughout the afternoon and into the evening. Prices start at around DM5 for a basic bread, eggs and jam affair, rising to DM25-plus for more exotic, champagne-swigging delights. Several cafés also have eat-as-much-as-you-like buffets for a reasonable set price.

Typically, you'll be offered a small platter of **cold meats** (usually sausage-based) and **cheeses**, along with a selection of marmalades, jams and honey, and, occasionally, muesli or another cereal. You're generally given a variety of **breads**, one of the most distinctive features of German cuisine. Both brown and

Breakfast cafés

The following cafés are our choices for breakfast, whichever area of the city you happen to find yourself in. See listings for full reviews.

Cafés and bars

SCHEUNENVIERTEL
Schokoladen, Ackerstr. 169–170.
Strandbad Mitte, Kleine Hamburger Str. 16.

PRENZLAUER BERG
Café Anita Wronski, Knaackstr. 26-28.
Café Westphal, Kollwitzstr. 63.

KREUZBERG
Café am Ufer, Paul-Lincke-Ufer 43.
Café Fontane, Fontanepromenade 1.
Café Stresemann, Stresemannstr. 90.
Café Übersee, Paul–Lincke-Ufer 44.
Golgotha, Viktoriapark.
Milagro, Bergmannstr. 12.
Rampenlicht, Körtestr. 33.

SCHÖNEBERG
Café Leising, Hauptstr. 85.
Tomasa, Motzstr. 60.
S-Bahn Café, S-Bahn Friedenau, Bahnhofstr. 4C, Friedrichshain.

AROUND NOLLENDORFPLATZ AND WINTERFELDPLATZ
Café Berio, Maassenstr. 7.
Café Einstein, Kurfürstenstr. 58.
Café M, Goltzstr. 34.
Café Savarin, Kulmerstr. 17.

Café Sidney, corner of Maasenstr. and Winterfeldtstr.
Café Swing, corner of Kleiststr. and Motzstr.
Klang 3 ("Café Drei Klang"), Goltzstr. 51.
Mediencafé Strada, Potsdamer Str. 131.

SAVIGNYPLATZ AND AROUND
Café au Lait, Kantstr. 110.
Café Bleibtreu, Bleibtreustr. 45.
Café Savigny, Grolmanstr. 53
Filmbühne am Steinplatz, corner of Hardenbergstr. and Steinplatz.
Rosalinde, Knesebeckstr 156.
Schwarzes Café, Kantstr. 148.
Schell, Knesebeckstr. 22.
Zillemarkt, Bleibtreustr. 48.

CHARLOTTENBURG AND THE WEST
Café Hardenberg, Hardenbergstr. 10, Charlottenburg.
Café Knobelsdorff, Knobelsdorffstr. 38, Charlottenburg.
Café Rix, Karl-Marx-Str. 141, Neukölln.
Café Solo, Pariser Str. 19, Wilmersdorf.
Kronenbourg Café, Pfalzburgerstr. 11, Wilmersdorf.
Wintergarten, inside the *Literaturhaus*, Fasanenstr. 23, Charlottenburg.

If finances are tight, best bet for a stand-up morning snack is in one of the bakeries (Bäckerei), where coffee and cake will set you back a couple of marks.

white rolls are popular, often baked with caraway, coriander, poppy or sesame seeds. The rich-tasting black rye bread, known as *Pumpernickel*, is a particular favourite, as is the salted *Bretzel*, which tastes nothing like any foreign imitation.

Coffee (usually freshly brewed) is the normal accompaniment, though **tea** – whether plain or herbal – and **hot chocolate** are common alternatives. A glass of **fruit juice** – almost invariably orange – is sometimes included as well.

Beer

For serious **beer drinkers**, Germany is the ultimate paradise. Wherever you go, you can be sure of getting a product made locally, often brewed in a distinctive style. The country boasts around forty percent of the world's breweries, with some 800 (about half the total) in Bavaria alone. It was in this province in 1516 that the *Reinheitsgebot* ("Purity Law") was formulated, laying down stringent standards of production, including a ban on chemical substitutes. This has been rigorously adhered to ever since (even in products made for export), and was also taken up by the rest of the country, but only for beers made for the domestic market. It was not so scrupulously adhered to by the Communists, but has since been reintroduced in those east German breweries that survived closure. Unfortunately, the

Cafés and bars

law has fallen foul of the EU bureaucrats, who deem it a restriction on trade, since very few foreign beers meet the criteria laid down (and so could not be imported). Though the law is now unenforceable, thankfully it hasn't forced the Germans into lowering their own standards, the entire brewing industry having reaffirmed its commitment to the *Reinheitsgebot*. All in all, the current outlook is very rosy: although the odd brewery bites the dust each year, there has been a revival of long-forgotten techniques, often put into practice in new small *Hausbrauereien*.

More generally, there's an encouraging continuation of old-fashioned **top-fermented** brewing styles. Until last century, all beers were made this way, but the interaction of the yeasts with a hot atmosphere meant that brewing had to be suspended during the summer. It was the Germans who discovered that the yeast sank to the foot of the container when stored under icy conditions; thereafter, brewing took on a more scientific nature, and yeast strains were bred so that beer could be bottom-fermented,

thus allowing its production all year round. While the *Reinheitsgebot* has ensured that bottom-fermented German brews are of a high standard, the technique has been a major factor in the insipidity of so much beer in other countries, including Britain. The top-fermentation process, on the other hand, allows for a far greater individuality in the taste (often characterized by a distinct fruitiness), and can, of course, now be used throughout the year, thanks to modern temperature controls. All wheat beers use this process.

Berlin beer specialities include *Berliner Weisse*, a top-fermented "young beer" that's only just fermented and still quite watery and sour, and must be drunk with a shot of fruity syrup or *Schuss*. Ask for it *mit grün* and you get a dash of woodruff, creating a greeny brew that tastes like liquid silage; *mit rot* is a raspberry-flavoured drink that works wonders at breakfast time.

Wine

Many people's knowledge of German **wine** starts and ends with *Liebfraumilch*, the medium sweet easy-drinking wine.

Wine categories

TAFELWEIN

Tafelwein can be a blend of wines from any EU country; *Deutscher Tafelwein* must be 100 percent German. *Landwein* is a superior *Tafelwein*, equivalent to the French *Vin de Pays* and medium dry. Like all German wines, *Tafelwein* can be *trocken* (dry) or *halb-trocken* (medium dry).

QUALITÄTSWEIN

There are two basic subdivisions of *Qualitätswein*: **Qba** (*Qualitätswein eines bestimmten Anbaugebietes*) and **Qmp** (*Qualitätswein mit Prädikat*). "Qba" wines come from eleven delimited regions and must pass an official tasting and analysis. "Qmp" wines are further divided into six grades:

Kabinett The first and lightest style.

Spätlese Must come from late-picked grapes, which results in riper flavours.

Auslese Made from a selected bunch of grapes, making a concentrated medium-sweet wine. If labelled as a *Trocken*, the wine will have lots of body and weight.

Beerenauslese Wine made from late-harvested, individually picked grapes. A rare wine, made only in the very best years, and extremely sweet.

Trockenbeerenauslese Trocken here means dry in the sense that the grapes have been left on the vine until some of the water content has evaporated. As with *Beerenauslese*, each grape will have been individually picked. This is a very rare wine which is intensely sweet and concentrated.

Eiswein Literally "ice wine", this is made from *Beerenauslese* grapes – a hard frost freezes the water content of the grape, concentrating the juice. *Eiswein* is remarkably fresh, due to its high acidity.

Drinks glossary

Wasser	water
Sprudel, Selters	sparkling mineral water
Milch	milk
Milchshake	milkshake
Kaffee	coffee
Kaffee mit Milch	coffee with milk
Tee	tea
Zitronentee	lemon tea
Kräutertee, Pflanzentee	herbal tea
Kakao	cocoa
Trinkschokolade	drinking chocolate
Apfelsaft	apple juice
Traubensaft	grape juice
Orangensaft	orange juice
Tomatensaft	tomato juice
Zitronenlimonade	lemonade
Bier	beer
Weisswein	white wine
Rotwein	red wine
Roséwein	rosé wine
Sekt	sparkling wine
Glühwein	hot mulled wine
Apfelwein	apple wine
Herrengedeck	cocktail of beer and Sekt
Weinbrand	brandy
Korn	rye spirit
Likör	liqueur
Grog	hot rum

Cafés and bars

Sadly, its success has obscured the quality of other German wines, especially those made from the *Riesling* grape, and it's worth noting that the *Liebfraumilch* drunk in Germany tastes nothing like the bilge swilled abroad.

The vast majority of German wine is white since the northern climate doesn't ripen red grapes regularly. If after a week or so you're pining for a glass of red, try a *Spätburgunder* (the *Pinot Noir* of Burgundy).

First step in any exploration of German wine should be to understand what's on the label: the predilection for Gothic script and gloomy martial crests makes this an uninviting prospect, but the division of categories is intelligent and helpful – if at first a little complex.

Like most EU wine, German wine is divided into two broad categories: *Tafelwein* ("table wine", for which read "cheap plonk") and *Qualitätswein* ("quality wine"), equivalent to the French *Apellation Controllée*. For a detailed rundown on wine categories, see the box opposite.

Cafés and bars

Berlin's café and bar scene is focused on a number of distinct areas. Both drinking and eating are generally best done away from the obvious tourist strips like Unter den Linden and Kufürstendamm, where standards tend to be lower and prices higher. Since 1990, the **former east** has really come into its own, with **Scheunenviertel**, just north of the city centre, and the inner-city district of **Prenzlauer Berg** – former East Berlin's hidden heart, and now synonymous with alternative-tinged good times – today boast the city's most eclectic possibilities, hip tourist strips with new bars and cafés springing up all the time. To some extent their appeal is based on the novelty value of their being in the east – most are not intrinsically better than their counterparts in the west – but they have a subtle edge that makes traditional

Cafés and bars

Kreuzberg and Schöneberg haunts seem a little tired. However, a lot of west and east Berliners still tend to stick to their own parts of the city – and some east-erners resent the way the aforemen-tioned districts have been effectively colonized by westerners, especially at the weekends.

Scheunenviertel apart, the rest of **Mitte**, Berlin's centre and for many years the showpiece core of the GDR capital, has a lively scene, with a number of repro old-Berlin bars worth seeking out.

Meanwhile, the institutionalized anar-chy of **Kreuzberg** – for so long *the* area to be after hours – is starting to feel slightly shopworn. Despite all this, it remains a good place to get plastered and it would be quite easy to spend a few weeks bar-crawling here before you even began to exhaust the possibilities. Local drinkers include political activist types waxing nostalgic for the days of regular street showdowns with the *Polizei*, punks so lost in time they still think the UK Subs are a great band, and members of the various post-punk tribes wearing their baseball caps and skate-gear with pride. Adjacent **Schöneberg** tends to be a little smarter and a little more sedate; you'll find a scattering of slick cafés alongside corner *Kneipen*, but none of the extremities of its neigh-bour.

Cafés and bars – a warning

The ever-changing face of Berlin makes it impossible to guarantee the accuracy of the listings that fol-low. Yesterday's rough-and-ready squatter hangout can be trans-formed into a smooth café-bistro in a matter of months, and once-hip places can slide into obscurity, or even disappear altogether, just as speedily. Equally, new cafés and bars open all the time. Our listings, therefore, should only form a base to your own wanderings and discov-eries: let us know of any you make.

The area around **Nollendorfplatz** and **Winterfeldplatz** attracts an older, less image-conscious crowd. If you haven't visited the city before and are looking for a gentle introduction to Berlin nightlife, this makes a good place to start. It's also an area with plenty of **gay bars**, which are listed on p.257.

One part of town that hasn't been too badly affected by the loss of busi-ness to the east is **Savignyplatz**, the haunt of Berlin's conspicuous goodtimers – gilded youth in designer casualwear, and their older siblings, well-dressed dri-vers of flash cars. It is possible to have a good time around here but there is a distinct element of "see and be seen" to it all which can be trying.

For a change of pace, it's worth heading out to some of the **suburban places**, particularly the *Gartenlokalen*, beer-restaurants with outdoor seating, along the shores of the city's lakes.

Scheunenviertel

Assel, Oranienburger Str. 61. The student regulars in this simply furnished cellar bar compete for space at the candlelit tables with passing tourists. The service can be offhand but it's worth dropping in, not least for the cheap food. Open until 3am.

Aufsturz, Oranienburger Str. 67. Not as hip as some of the local hangouts but comes into its own on those occasional broiling summer days, thanks to outdoor seating on the shady side of the street. An additional attraction is the extensive range of bottled beers, taking in every-thing from erstwhile GDR premium beer *Radeberger* to cherry-flavoured Belgian arcana.

Barcomi's, Sophienstr. 21. Spacious and relaxing New York-style coffee house and deli, notable for its authentic bagels, delicious muffins and sinful brownies.

Beth Café, Tucholskystr. 40. Run by a small orthodox Jewish congregation, a slightly snooty place for would-be intel-lectuals to size each other up over the tops of their wire-framed specs.

Café Aedes East, Hackescher Höfe,

Rosenthaler Str. 40-41. A slick, high-tech place – lots of polished metal and halogen lighting – that attracts a high-brow crowd of students and their professors.

Café CC, Rosenthaler Str. 39. This cinema-themed café – East German film posters and cinematic lights as decor – attracts a slightly serious, studenty crowd. It's cheapish and pleasant, but perhaps not the place for a raucous night out.

Café Ici, Auguststr. 61. By day pipe-smoking aesthetes sit composing poetry amid the venerable furnishings of this pleasantly soporific café-gallery, and though things tend to liven up a bit in the evening it's a good place to escape the Scheunenviertel crowds. Open until 3am.

Café Orange, Oranienburger Str. 32. Everything about this arty café, from the opera filtering out of the speakers to the soft wooden furnishings, radiates contrived good taste and a certain preciousness. Be careful not to laugh too loudly – you could be asked to leave for disturbing the barman's concentration. The food (DM10–24) is reasonable, though the ineffectual salads may leave you lusting for *Bockwurst* and chips.

Café Oren, Oranienburger Str. 28. This place, more than any other, is a symbol of the staggering transformation that's occurred around Oranienburger Strasse over the past few years. Watching the earnest diners discuss *Kultur* over vegetarian kosher-style dishes, it's hard to believe that until a few years ago the only possibilities in this neck of the woods were workers' beer joints. Open until 1am.

Café Silberstein, Oranienburger Str. 27. Great place, usually packed to the gills with party people, and celebrated for its weird welded chairs (for sale). Arriving late when everybody's well-oiled and starting to let their hair down a bit makes it easier to get to know people. Mutates into a club from 11pm at weekends (see p.261).

Café Zapata, Oranienburger Str. 54-56. Part of the *Tacheles* multimedia extrava-ganza. The addition of plate-glass windows and permanent fixtures and fittings have toned this once wild place down a little, but it's still fairly shambolic, attracting a lot of *Szene* tourists from all over Europe. Regular live music.

Edwin Café & Patisserie, Grosse Hamburger Str. 15. Not really part of the Scheunenviertel scene, but a handy place for a coffee-and-cake break if you're exploring the area around the Sophienkirche.

Eimer, Rosenthaler Str. 68. Determinedly alternative café that was one of the first to open post-*Wende*. Worth investigating for gigs and events, though you won't feel too welcome if your face and clothes don't fit.

Hackbarths, Auguststr. 49a. Dominated by a huge triangular bar that seems to fill the whole place, this one attracts a very mixed crowd, intellectual but still up for a good time. Good food, including excellent quiche. Open until 3am.

Mendelssohn, Oranienburger Str. 39. Self-conscious and trendy, with decent enough food and a cheery crowd of mostly tourists.

Meilenstein, Oranienburger Str. 7. Can't quite decide whether it's part of the local *Szene* or just a normal café. Nevertheless, it's not a bad place and the food is cheap. The lentil soup (*Linsensuppe*) is a meal in itself – try it with vinegar, like the locals do. Open 9am–5am.

Obst und Gemüse, Oranienburger Str. 48. Always crowded, always chaotic, in many ways this is the quintessential Oranienburger Strasse bar. You can wait a while to get served but, as the place attracts quite a lot of tourists, at least you'll be waiting in company.

The Pips, Auguststr. 84. Sophisticated cocktail bar and dance club that's very much in vogue at the moment. Fills up fast and stays that way through the night.

Roter Salon, Rosa-Luxemburg-Platz. Part of the Volksbühne theatre, with lurid red decor and chintzy furniture giving it the

Cafés and bars

Most of the bars in Scheunenviertel centre around Oranienburger Strasse.

Cafés and bars

feel of a 1950s brothel. Readings, concerts and club nights are held here, otherwise it's undervisited and worth dropping in on. Exhibitionists may enjoy the fact that you can sit on the stage.

Schokoladen, Ackerstr. 169–170. The spartan, bare-brick interior of this former chocolate factory is a hangover from its time as a squatted building in the early post-*Wende* days. Now a venue for occasional theatrical and art events, and with live music on Sat. Beer is cheap and there's free chocolate on the bar. Breakfast served Sat & Sun from 8am.

Sophie, Grosse Hamburger Str. 37. A distinctly untrendy old-style pub serving wine, beer and food amid the nineteenth-century facades of Sophienstrasse. Low-key but OK for a quick drink and a bite to eat. Open until 1am.

Speed, Gipsstr. 12. Slick and polished bar and restaurant that attracts art lovers and club goers with deep pockets. Doesn't really get going until late.

Strandbad Mitte, Kleine Hamburger Str. 16. At the end of a small street off the

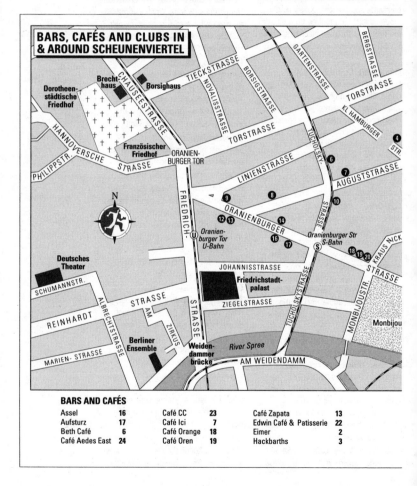

BARS AND CAFÉS

Assel	16	Café CC	23	Café Zapata	13
Aufsturz	17	Café Ici	7	Edwin Café & Patisserie	22
Beth Café	6	Café Orange	18	Eimer	2
Café Aedes East	24	Café Oren	19	Hackbarths	3

beaten tourist track, this inviting café and bar makes a good retreat when it all becomes too much. Excellent breakfasts served 9am–4pm.

Village Voice, Ackerstr. 1a. Read while sipping espresso in an environment inspired by the bookshop/cafés of the US.

Zosch, Tucholskystr. 30. Alternative but, as long as you're not wearing an Armani suit, you don't have to be. Run by a Turk and an east Berliner, it started as a squat and is now a good tip for gigs

and club nights in the cellar. Usually open until 5am.

Mitte

Café Clara 90, Dorotheenstr. 90 (second courtyard). Office workers and tourists pop in for drinks and snacks by day, while readings and the like draw a more arty crowd at night. A bit gloomy and sterile but there's not much else in the area.

Café Einstein, Unter den Linden 42. A new branch of the popular Kurfürstenstrasse Viennese-style café, but

Cafés and bars

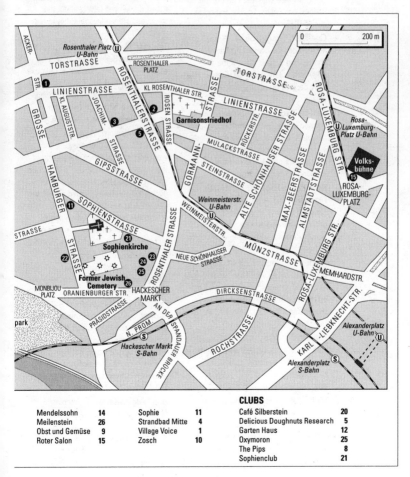

Mendelssohn	14	Sophie	11	
Meilenstein	26	Strandbad Mitte	4	
Obst und Gemüse	9	Village Voice	1	
Roter Salon	15	Zosch	10	

CLUBS

Café Silberstein	20
Delicious Doughnuts Research	5
Garten Haus	12
Oxymoron	25
The Pips	8
Sophienclub	21

Cafés and bars

this small outlet can match neither the pomp nor flair of the original.

Café Mosaik, Rathausstr. 5. Part of the rather tired row of retail outlets on the southern side of Alexanderplatz, this small and boxy café is low on personality, but serves up a decent breakfast.

Café Möhring, Jägerstr./Charlottenstr. Handy for *Kaffee und Kuchen* near the Gendarmenmarkt, though a little noisy at the moment thanks to all the surrounding construction projects.

Café Podewil, Klosterstr./Parochialstr. A quiet, airy little café that's part of the Podewil arts centre. Snacks and pasta dishes DM5–10.

Café-Rosé, Leipziger Str. 30. A small café not far from the site of Checkpoint Charlie, and a good place if the *Café Adler* (see p.250) is too full. Great coffee, tasty pastries and home-made ice cream.

Café im Zeughaus, Unter den Linden 2. Located in the German History Museum, this place offers surprisingly good and inexpensive quiches, pastas, and the like. And it's one of the very few non-smoking cafés in the city.

Denk Bar im Haus der Demokratie, Friedrichstr. 165. A buzzing and cheap café that belongs to a building of non-profit groups and advocacy organizations. Talk tends to be deep and impassioned.

Friederich's, Mauerstr. 83–84. Bright, open-plan bistro, with New German-style lunch and dinner specials and an interesting wine selection. Attracts office workers and the east German entrepreneur keen to impress.

Kaffeestube, Poststr. 19. A Nikolaiviertel café that tries to evoke the atmosphere of a turn-of-the-century coffee house. Breakfast is DM7.

Kilkenny Irish Pub, Im S-Bahnhof Hackescher Markt. Three pubs in one in the S-Bahnhof. *Guiness*, *Kilkenny*, Irish whiskey. The menu includes Irish stew (DM7) and that well-known Irish dish *tzatziki*. Popular with expat construction workers.

Kisch Kaffee, Unter den Linden 60. First café after the Brandenburg Gate, and a good place to limber up for Unter den Linden sights.

Operncafé, Opernpalais, Unter den Linden 5. In a former royal palace, this elegant café is a deliberate attempt to evoke the atmosphere of Imperial Berlin for Unter den Linden wanderers. Coffee and amazing cakes make it a recommended stopping-off point. Daily 9am–midnight.

Oscar Wilde Irish Pub, Friedrichstr. 112a. Generic Irish bar with all the usual attractions – *Guinness*, *Kilkenny* etc. Expats get all dewy-eyed talking about the stews and French fries, but they're not cheap (DM8–20).

Tele-café, Alexanderplatz. This café, 207 metres above Berlin in the upper reaches of the TV tower, turns on its own axis once an hour and you can enjoy a wonderful panoramic view of the city while tucking into a pricey ice cream. An essential Berlin tourist experience.

Zur letzten Instanz, Waisenstr. 14–16. One of the city's oldest *Kneipen*, with a wonderful old-fashioned interior, including a classic tiled oven, and a great beer garden. Reasonably priced traditional dishes, all with legal-themed names like *Zeugen-Aussage* ("Eyewitness account"), a reminder of the days when people used to drop in on the way to the nearby courthouse. Open until 1am Mon–Sat.

Zum Nussbaum, Probststr./Am Nussbaum. In the heart of the Nikolaiviertel, a convincing copy of a pre-war bar destroyed in an air raid. The original stood on the Fischerinsel and was favoured by the artists Heinrich Zille and Otto Nagel, and though the replica verges on the expensive and flirts dangerously with olde worlde kitsch, it's a good place to soak up a bit of ersatz old-Berlin ambience. *Kneipe* specialities like *Eisbein* and *Kassler Rippchen* (DM8–20).

Zum Paddenwirt, Nikolaikirchplatz 6. Another pseudo-old Berlin *Speisegaststätte*. On Sunday mornings you can enjoy the old German tradition of *Frühschoppen* – drinking, while playing cards or dice. Food DM6–15.

Zur Rippe, Poststr./Mühlendamm. Another Nikolaiviertel *Kneipe* in old Berlin style. Food DM5–17.

Prenzlauer Berg

Akba Lounge, Sredzkistr. 64. Very popular, so the narrow bar gets uncomfortably crowded very fast. The adjoining club plays house and acid music.

Babel, Käthe-Niederkirchner-Str. 2. A wildly decorated place well worth investigating, particularly in summer when the courtyard is open for al fresco drinking.

Bar Berlin, Oderberger Str. 38. New and hip cocktail bar, a bit too self-conscious but with vegetarian food at fair prices.

Bla-Bla, Sredzkistr. 19a. The occasionally slow service is a reflection of the laid-back nature of the place – just sink down into the deep, comfortable sofas amid the flea-market decor and take it easy. Good mixed drinks and snacks. Open late, but sometimes operates a

Cafés and bars

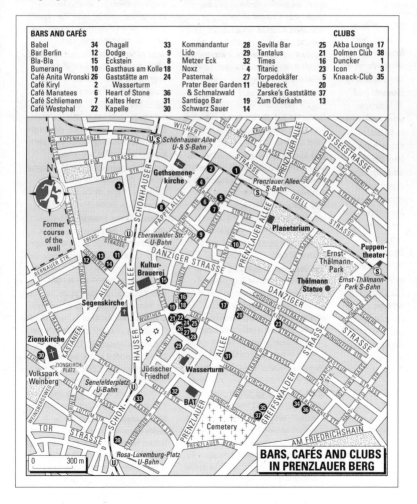

BARS AND CAFÉS

Babel	34	Chagall	33	Kommandantur	28	Sevilla Bar	25
Bar Berlin	12	Dodge	9	Lido	29	Tantalus	21
Bla-Bla	15	Eckstein	8	Metzer Eck	32	Times	16
Bumerang	10	Gasthaus am Kolle	18	Noxz	4	Titanic	23
Café Anita Wronski	26	Gaststätte am		Pasternak	27	Torpedokäfer	5
Café Kiryl	2	Wasserturm	24	Prater Beer Garden	11	Uebereck	20
Café Manatees	6	Heart of Stone	36	& Schmalzwald		Zarske's Gaststätte	37
Café Schliemann	7	Kaltes Herz	31	Santiago Bar	19	Zum Oderkahn	13
Café Westphal	22	Kapelle	30	Schwarz Sauer	14		

CLUBS

Akba Lounge	17
Dolmen Club	38
Duncker	1
Icon	3
Knaack-Club	35

BARS, CAFÉS AND CLUBS IN PRENZLAUER BERG

0 — 300 m

Cafés and bars

At the time of writing, places around the Wasserturm at the junction of Knaack- and Rykestrasse were reckoned to be the domain mainly of visitors and outsiders. If you really want to meet the locals, head for the northern side of Danziger Strasse and side streets like Lychener Strasse, Dunckerstrasse and Stargarder Strasse.

"members only" policy in the small hours.

Bumerang, Stubbenkammerstr. 6. The windows of this slightly decrepit little bar are filled with potted plants and there's an aquarium above the door. Inside, woolly alternative characters gather, nodding along to the occasional live music performances. Good-value snacks.

Café ACUD, Veteranenstr. 21. Live rock, blues and, occasionally, acid-jazz sounds, along with cheap beer, are what draws the punters to this scruffy bar spread over a couple of floors.

Café Anita Wronski, Knaackstr. 26–28. This smart Wasserturm café-bar is an excellent place to start local wanderings, though it can get very crowded. Great breakfasts 10am–3pm.

Café Kiryl, Lychener Str. 73. Arty bar that's a good place for whisky fans. Connected with the alternative publishing house and record label housed in the same building.

Café Manatees, Lychener Str. 64. A new bar catering to a somewhat younger crowd. The distinguishing feature here is a Sunday breakfast that starts at 5am.

Café Schliemann, Schliemannstr. 21. A fairly alternative hangout – if at first you don't get in, it's probably not worth persisting. Holds occasional exhibitions. Open until 6am.

Café Westphal, Kollwitzstr. 64. One of the original Prenzlauer Berg squatted cafés, this one is now almost part of the establishment. Its rough-hewn chic attracts lots of po-faced *Szene*-types, but you can still have a good time here. Excellent-value breakfasts served up Sat & Sun 10am–3pm. Food DM5–15.

Chagall, Kollwitzstr. 2. A little piece of Russia in the heart of Berlin: a comfortable café serving up Russian specialities such as *pelmeni* and *soljanka* to the sounds of balalaikas. A healthy selection of vodkas, of course.

Dodge, Dunckerstr. 80. Popular despite its airbrushed decor. More of a place for locals really, though you won't be made to feel unwelcome. Food DM6–15.

Eckstein, Pappelallee 73. The long frontage and glass doors give this place an airy feel and in fine weather you can sit outdoors. Attracts a trendily bespectacled public who don't seem unduly bothered by the slow service.

Gasthaus am Kolle, Wörtherstr. 35. Cheerful and reasonably cheap little spot on Kollwitzplatz, with a good selection of ice cream.

Gaststätte am Wasserturm, Knaackstr./Rykestr. Former basic beer bar transformed into yet another fashionable-looking watering hole. The clientele is more mixed than usual, though, and there's a reasonably imaginative menu.

Heart of Stone, Käthe-Niederkirchner Str. 34. Dedicated to the music and trappings of the Rolling Stones, and the crowd here is just what you'd expect.

Kaltes Herz, Prenzlauer Allee 32. Despite the name – cold heart – this is a warm and snug café of dark wood, candlelight and cheap and filling food. A nice place to linger over coffee and a book.

Kapelle, Zionskirchplatz 22–24. Designer decay in the shadow of the hulking Zionkirche. A little off the beaten track but worth the detour. Snacks available.

Kommandantur, Knaackstr. 20. Subtly different from the places on nearby Kollwitzplatz, perhaps because it's supposed to be an *Ossi* hangout. Fairly spartan and the music is loud – it also gets hellishly overcrowded late at night.

Lido, Knaackstr. 28. Right in the thick of the Wasserturm scene, this genial place is just as comfortable as its neighbours, though less crowded and often cheaper.

Metzer Eck, Metzer Str. 33. Founded in 1913, this *Kneipe* was a well-known *Szene* haunt during GDR times, as the signed celebrity photos that adorn the walls attest. Its old-fashioned feel makes a change from the slicker, newer places.

Noxz, Lychener Str./Stargarder Str. A starkly decorated bar popular with local techno fans. A good place to pick up flyers and word-of-mouth information about some of the more underground club events.

Pasternak, Knaackstr. 22–24. An under-stated establishment that recalls the cafés and restaurants founded by Berlin's large Russian emigré community during the 1920s. There's a good selection of Russian dishes, including *borscht, pel-meni* and *blinis*, and an extensive range of vodkas. Popular with discreetly afflu-ent west Berliners. Open noon–2am.

Prater, Kastanienallee 7–9. A traditional beer garden, built in the last century and recently renovated. In summer you can swig beer, feast on *bratwurst*, pig's feet or other native food, and listen to German rock from the 1970s. A true Berlin experience.

Times, Husemannstr. 10. The kitchen here is open until 6am – handy if you're on a long pub crawl in the neighbourhood.

Santiago Bar, Wörther Str. 36. Light, colourful bar with tasty Latin American snacks and meals. Across the street from Kollwitzplatz.

Schmalzwald, Kasanienallee 7–9. This chaotic, kitschy bar, tucked inside the *Berliner Prater* beer garden, has become something of a nightlife legend. Evenings here are often punctuated by avant garde concerts, eccentric fashion shows, or other funky diversions. Recommended.

Schwarz Sauer, Kastanienallee 13–14. A trendy little café with pavement seating. Food (pasta etc) up to DM15.

Sevilla Bar, Rykestr. 54. A little north of the action around the Wassertum, this narrow little cocktail bar gets missed by most tourists, meaning you can enjoy the cocktails and tapas in relative peace.

Tantalus, Knaackstr. 26. Popular little bar near the Wasserturm. Apart from the fact that the punters are packed in more tightly, there's not much to distinguish it from the competition.

Titanic, Winsstr. 30/Christburger Str. From moustached *Ossis* in stone-washed den-ims to students with lopsided haircuts, everyone seems to gravitate to this busy, friendly bar.

Torpedokäfer, Dunckerstr. 69. A vast cockroach mosaic is the first thing to catch your eye in this arty bar. You can buy the works on display, though you'd need to secure a bank loan first. Simple pasta and salad dishes up to DM8.

Uebereck, Prenzlauer Allee/Christburger Str. A long narrow bar with a big silver heating duct running through it. It's all a bit subdued and the emphasis seems to be on events and exhibitions rather than having a good time and meeting people.

Zarske's Gaststätte, Greifswalder Str. 228. A basic working-class bar that opens at 7am on weekdays. Just the place if you can't face reality after a night on the tiles.

Zum Oderkahn, Oderberger Str. 11. A genuine old Berlin *Kneipe* with the kind of atmosphere that encourages impromptu marathon drinking sessions. Early, secret meetings of the opposition group Neues Forum were held here. Simple dishes like soup and *Bockwurst* from DM3.

Kreuzberg

Ankerklause, Kottbusser Brücke/Maybachufer. A sleepy, nautically-themed pub overlooking a bucolic canal has been transformed into a hip, techno-filled bar. Extremely trendy at time of writing and packed by 11pm.

Arcanoa, Zossener Str. 48. A dark, loud punk hangout with a bar made of mar-ble tombstones. Upstairs are several rooms with large chairs where the previ-ous night's customers can often be found sleeping it off.

Atlantic, Bergmannstr. 100. Upmarket and chic, this is Kreuzberg's attempt at a New York bar.

Bar, Skalitzerstr. 64, corner with Wrangelstr. Normally packed, chiefly because the bar staff are apt to forget to measure the drinks.

Barcomi's, Bergmannstr. 21. American-style coffee house with exotic blends accompanied by bagels, brownies and other American baked goods. Scattered copies of the *New Yorker* as well.

Bar Centrale, Yorckstr. 82. See p.233.

Bar Zyankali, Grossbeerenstr. 64. Weird cellar bar furnished on the "living room as

Cafés and
bars

Cafés and bars

acid nightmare" theme. Dimly lit and not that cheap, but good fun for this area.

Bierhimmel, Oranienstr. 183. Candlelit bar with a cosy 1950s cocktail lounge out back. Great atmosphere, and a second home to many locals. Cocktail bar open Wed–Sun from 10pm..

Café Adler, Friedrichstr. 206, Kreuzberg. Small café whose popularity came from its position by the site of Checkpoint Charlie. Serves breakfast and other meals.

Café Alibi, Oranienstr. 166. Largish murky café-bar that forms part of the Oranienstrasse *Szene*.

Café am Ufer, Paul-Lincke-Ufer 43. Good views of the Landwehrkanal if you sit outside and of the frequent fights if you stay inside. Nevertheless a fun place, with all-you-can-eat breakfasts for DM10 at weekends from 10am.

Café Anfall, Gneisenaustr. 64. Sharp, punk-filled bar that looks as if it were thrown together from local junkshops. Music at maximum distortion level.

Café Fontane, Fontanepromenade 1. Slick bar next to Südstern U-Bahn – rather synthetic and out of place. A bit of a teenies hangout. Breakfasts 9am–5pm.

Café Jedermann, Dieffenbachstr. 18. A modern update of a traditional bar, good if you like this sort of thing.

Café LebensArt, Mehringdamm 40. A very traditional kind of café, with a long glass counter of wonderful cakes and cookies in front, and several smoky rooms for breakfast and lunch in back.

Café LoLo, Grossbeerenstr. 57a. A small café featuring occasional jazz programmes and peopled with lots of English-speakers. Part of *Riehmer's Hofgarten*, an elaborately designed, turn-of-the-century residential apartment block.

Café Ritz, Monumentenstr. 29. Pleasant neighbourhood joint without pretension, and with sidewalk seating in summer.

Café Stresemann, Stresemannstr. 90. Large, traditional Berliner *Kneipe*-style café at the Anhalter Bahnhof. Breakfast 10am–4pm.

Café Übersee, Paul-Lincke-Ufer 44. Great location by the canal and a slightly upmarket atmosphere for the area; but beware the 10pm curfew, if drinking outside on balmy summer nights. Breakfast served 10am–2pm.

Debut, Cuvrystr. 29, corner with Görlitzer Str. Very black, very loud, very Kreuzberg.

Die Rote Harfe, Oranienstr. 13. Extreme left-wing ideologists knock back some of the cheapest beer around, while the upstairs eating area looks bizarrely like an old English tearoom.

Enzian, Yorckstr. 77. Wonderfully tacky and lively bar said to be the hangout for one of the country's most popular home-grown bands, Die Toten Hosen.

espede, Stresemannstr. 28. Sleek, austere café located in the Berlin headquarters of the Social Democratic Party. Good international menu, a little pricey.

Ex, Mehringhof, Gneisenaustr. 2a. Low prices and occasional live music in the bar of the famous alternative Mehringhof collective, with outside drinking on the cobbled Hinterhof (courtyard) in summer.

Futura Café Bar, Adalbertstr./Waldemarstr. Cosy corner café-bar, deep in Kreuzberg 36, popular with locals.

Golgotha, Viktoriapark. Enormous open-air café (summer only), perched near the top of Kreuzberg's hill. Hugely popular. Breakfast served 11am–3pm.

Grossbeerenkeller, Grossbeerenstr. 90. Old-fashioned wood-panelled cellar bar, strewn with nineteenth-century knick-knacks and photos of famous German actors and celebrities.

Heidelberger Krug, Arndtstr. 15. Another favourite meeting place for Kreuzberg's self-styled intelligentsia.

O-Bar (aka Oranien-Bar), Oranienstr. 168. Famed gay-friendly Kreuzberg watering hole. The interior is half-plastered (as are most of the clientele), giving it a sort of post-nuclear chic. See p.258.

Kap Horn, Hornstr. 4. Decoration here consists of a few old fishing nets and a plastic lobster or two. Still, this little bar on a quiet side street makes a relaxing break. A front garden is open in summer.

Kloster, Skalitzerstr. 76. Loud and raucous night bar with a religious icon theme, located close to the former border by the Oberbaumbrücke. Self-service and fun.

Locus, Marheinekeplatz 4. Somewhat sober decor, with a small plaza open in summer. Mexican food.

Madonna, Wiener Str. 22. Grimy paint job, a sparse interior, and waning popularity, this is nevertheless one of western Berlin's "in" places. Loud music.

Malheur, Gneisenaustr. 17. Packed (though not uncomfortably so) at most times with the broadest mix possible. Gets going after midnight.

Max und Moritz, Oranienstr. 162. Old-fashioned bar-restaurant that, while a world away from the *Szene* places down the street, still packs in a youthful crowd.

Milagro, Bergmannstr. 12. A bar that's become popular for its imaginative food and huge breakfasts (9am–4pm). *Kloster* beer on tap.

Minicafé, Spreewaldplatz 14. Tiny and unavoidably intimate.

Myslivska, Schlesische Str. 35. Small, under-decorated place that doesn't really get going until the wee hours, when it pumps out techno and trip-hop.

Rampenlicht, Körtestr. 33. Centrally placed bar-café, a little way north from the Südstern. Good breakfasts (9am–4pm); can get packed at weekends.

Sale e Tabacci, Kochstr. 18. Authentic and beautiful Italian café where patrons spend hours over espresso and cigarettes.

Turandot, Bergmannstr. 93. A well-known, down-at-heel local joint, attracting a mix of students and old hippies.

Wiener Blut, Wiener Str. 14. A sort of compact version of *Madonna*, up the road (see above). Buoyant, spirited atmosphere. Cocktail night Thurs.

Wirtschaftswunder, Yorckstr. 81. Popular Fifties rock 'n' roll theme bar with authentic furniture and a long cocktail list.

Wunderbar, Körtestr. 38. Large and animated bar with pool room and youthful, varied punters. Perfect for the first drink of the evening when arriving at Südstern U-Bahn, just across the street.

Yorckschlösschen, Yorckstr. 15. Firmly entrenched hippy and alternative crowd; rather like an English pub. Live music Sun.

Zaubergarten, Paul-Lincke-Ufer 11. Prettily located garden pub. Specializes in pizzas.

Zum Alten, Dresdener Str. 17. Once a haunt of Kreuzberg's smack heads, now much cleaned up but still fairly stoned. The spirit of 1976 lives on . . .

Schöneberg

Amadeus, Hauptstr. 158. Relaxed, low-key coffee bar/café.

Café Leising, Hauptstr. 85. Minimalist bar decorated with abstract art. Imaginative food, good breakfasts Sat & Sun 10am–3pm.

E&M Leydicke, Mansteinstr. 4. Claims to be the oldest *Kneipe* in western Berlin, and quite aged in feel, though some of the decorations look suspiciously recent. Geared towards tourists.

Ex 'n' Pop, Mansteinstr. 14. Part-run by musician Nick Cave, this neighbourhood bar comes alive on Thursday when anyone looking for fifteen minutes of fame can get up on stage and strut their stuff. Open from 8pm.

Feinbäckerei, Vorbergstr. 2. Good wine in a former bakery, with Swabian (South German) snacks on offer.

Forum-Café, Akazienstr. 19. Perfectly normal café with rather comical aspirations to being a literary centre for budding writers and poets to declaim their works. Easy amusement if you can stifle the sniggers.

Graffiti, Naumannstr. 3. The scrawlings here have gone but the name's remained the same. Cheap.

Hudsons, Elssholzstr. 10. American-style cocktail bar, glistening in pink and gold, which attracts a primarily gay crowd. Offers a huge selection of liquors, and is said by many to serve up the city's best cocktails. Ring for entry. Sun–Thurs only.

Kleisther, Hauptstr. 5. Large and always crowded with Schöneberg's more style-conscious alternative types. Open till 3am-ish.

Kumpelnest 3000, Lützowstr. 23. Carpeted walls and a mock-Baroque effect attract a

Cafés and bars

Cafés and bars

rough-and-ready crew of under-30s to this erstwhile brothel. Gets going around 2am. Fine fun, and the best place in the area. Normally standing room only.

Leuchtturm, Crellestr. 41. Another homage to 1968. Strictly for nostalgites.

Malustra, Martin-Luther-Str. 42. Smoky student bar in an area otherwise lacking in drinking possibilities.

Matzis, Sponholzstr./Baumeisterstr. Popular beer garden with good food – try the *Käse Spätzle* (cheese noodles). Always full.

Monte Video, Viktoria-Luise-Platz 6. Hopping place that's been popular for years, though neither the food nor ambience is particularly distinctive. In summer a little porch opens onto picturesque Viktoria-Luise-Platz.

N N Train, Haupstr. 162. Two subway cars converted into a long, thin cocktail bar. Inside it's bouyant and not as kitschy as you'd think.

Pinguin Club, Wartburgstr. 54. Tiny and cheerful bar with 1950s and 1960s America supplying its theme and background music. Well worth a visit.

Rossli Bar, Eisenacher Str. 80. Late-night bar with weird fibreglass decor. Try the *Bolk Stoff* beer, if only for the label. Open till 8am.

S-Bahn Café, S-Bahn Friedenau, Bahnhofstr. 4c. One of the city's smallest bars, collectively run, with a likeable cobbled patio. Breakfasts 10am–4pm.

Tomasa, Motzstr. 60. Rather tacky 1970s-style interior design, but excellent food including breakfast (10am–4pm).

Toronto, Crellestr. 17. Classy wood-panelled café spilling onto a large leafy plaza. Perfect on a fine summer day.

Zoulou Club, Hauptstr. 5. Compact, little-known bar packed after 11pm with Schönebergers. Rather wonderful, in a low-key sort of way.

Around Nollendorfplatz and Winterfeldtplatz

Bar am Lützowplatz, Lützowplatz 7. Distinguished in having the longest bar in the city, this also has Berlin's best selection of whiskies (63) and a superb range of moderately priced cocktails. A dangerously great bar.

Bei Spatz, Kurfürstenstr. 56. Spruced-up corner *Kneipe* with a rustic feel to match the low prices. Huge plates of German food also available.

Café Belmundo, Winterfeldtstr. 36. Relative peace – despite the shrieking colour scheme – in one of the busiest nighttime areas. Great coffee and snacks.

Café Berio, Maassenstr. 7. Quiet (except during the Wed and Sat market) and civilized bar for those who prefer conversation to music. Breakfast served 8am–midnight.

Café Einstein, Kurfürstenstr. 58. Housed in a seemingly ancient German villa, this is about as close as you'll get to the ambience of the prewar Berlin *Kaffeehaus*, with international newspapers and breakfast served 10am–2pm. Occasional live music, and a good garden. Expensive, though, and a little snooty.

Café Lure, Kyffhäuserstr./Barbarossastr. Classic alternative crowd; not terribly exciting.

Café Lux, Goltzstr. 35. A desirable alternative to the shrill atmosphere of the *Café M* a few doors away. Open (and usually packed) till late.

Café M, Goltzstr. 34. Though littered with tatty plastic chairs and precious little else, *M* is Berlin's most favoured rendezvous for self-styled creative types and the conventionally unconventional. The cool thing to drink is *Flensburger Pils*, from the bottle. Usually packed, even for its famous breakfasts (9am–3pm).

Café Savarin, Kulmerstr. 17. Chiefly popular for its breakfast (noon–4pm), homemade quiches and pastries. The back room is preferable, decked out like your great aunt's parlour.

Café Savo, Goltzstr. 3. Low-key bar and café, with a warm muted-red interior and mosaic floor and a mock-1950s bar. Good-value snacks.

Café Sidney, Maassenstr./Winterfeldtstr. Big and brash modern meeting place, especially for breakfast (9am–2pm) on Sat. Always crowded.

Café Swing, Kleiststr./Motzstr. Plasticky and noisy modern café a little way from *Metropol*. Convivial new-wave atmosphere, with live music, especially on Mon and Thurs. Breakfast 10.30am–5am.

Café Winterfeldt, Winterfeldtstr. 37. Sparsely decorated with a narrow drinking area, but a relaxing alternative – when it's not full.

Domina, Winterfeldtstr. 20. Tiny cellar bar that gets lively in the early hours. Small dance floor.

Fischlabor, Frankenstr. 13. Offbeat night bar that's very popular with a mixed crowd.

Green Door, Winterfeldtstr. 50. Somewhat snooty cocktail bar, attracting a well-dressed crowd of young professionals and party-goers. Once you're past the pretension, though, the place can be fun, and they mix an awfully good cocktail.

Irish Pub, Eisenacher Str. 6. Gregarious Irish-run bar, popular with expats. Draught *Guinness*.

Karakus, Kurfürstenstr. 9. Wild and wacky night bar run by Brazilians. The ceiling is full of pink plastic flowers, the bar full of lethal cocktails, the dance floor full of writhing bodies. Good fun.

Klang 3 ("Café Drei Klang"), Goltzstr. 51. Small, friendly bar that seems unsure of which crowd it's trying to attract. Good snacks and breakfasts (10am–2pm).

Mediencafé Strada, Potsdamer Str. 131. Self-styled café for media types (the offices of *Tip* magazine are nearby), with a few foreign newspapers thrown in for effect. Imaginative food, including breakfasts (10am–3pm).

Metropol, Nollendorfplatz 5. Warehouse-sized Art Deco dance hall (for which see "Clubs and live venues"), with a downstairs bar fine for vegging out in front of the enormous TV screen. Popular with all-nighters and transvestites.

Mister Hu, Goltzstr. 39. Cool blue cocktail bar with a great offering of drinks and some of the city's best bartenders.

Nollywood, Motzstr. 8. Said to be a hangout for actors and directors, but you won't find Wim Wenders here. Does

sumptuous breakfasts and an American-style Sunday brunch.

Mutter, Hohenstaufenstr. 4. Large café and bar of indirect lighting and loud music. Quite popular and usually crowded. Sushi available.

Screwy Club, Frankenstr. 2. The speciality here is frozen drinks, and the place tends to draw a younger set that enjoys such novelties.

Sexton, Winterfeldtstr. 35. Dimly lit hellhole of hard rock and denims. Low on the trendiness scale, but always full.

Slumberland, Goltzstr. 24. The gimmicks here are sand on the floor and a tropical theme. Laid-back, likeable, and one of the better bars in this area.

Savignyplatz and around

Aschinger, Kurfürstendamm 26. Old-fashioned underground *Bierkeller*. Catering for tourists, but nonetheless pleasant enough to fill up on unusual beers and traditional German food.

Café Aedes, Savignypassage. Austere café-bar attached to an art gallery, also beneath the arches of Savignyplatz S-Bahn; can get very smoky.

Café au Lait, Kantstr. 110. Small, quirky bar-restaurant with a relaxed atmosphere and Latin American music. Breakfast from 10am.

Café Bleibtreu, Bleibtreustr. 45. One of Savignyplatz's more disreputable cafés. Pleasantly down-at-heel, and cheap. Breakfast 9.30am–3.30pm.

Café Hardenberg, Hardenbergstr. 10. Large, old-fashioned café with excellent, cheap food that draws in local students. Breakfast served 9am–midnight.

Café Savigny, Grolmanstr. 53. Bright, sharp café, with superb coffee, on the edge of Savignyplatz, catering to an arty/media crowd. Mildly gay. Breakfast 10am–4pm.

CUT, Knesebeckstr. 16. Over 300 cocktails in a black cocoon, and certainly a cut above the rest pricewise.

Dicke Wirtin, Carmerstr. 9. Noisy, boozy and popular place, more for the 1970s rock crew than anyone else. Excellent bowls of filling stew for under DM8.

Cafés and bars

Cafés and bars

Dralles, Schlüterstr. 69. Notably pricier than other bars in the area, this is the place to see and be seen: the 1950s decor is chic and understated, the clientele aspires likewise. Go beautiful and loaded, or not at all . . .

Filmbühne am Steinplatz, Hardenbergstr./Steinplatz. One of the least pretentious and more original cafés in Berlin, most of which is contained within a cleverly designed conservatory. Breakfast served from 10am.

Galerie Bremer, Fasanenstr. 37. Gallery with a cocktail bar that's a meeting point for actors and artists of every age and bent. Closed Mon.

Hegel, Savignyplatz 2. Tiny café on the southeastern side of Savignyplatz that attracts an older crowd. Gregarious fun when someone starts up on the piano.

Le Bar, Grolmanstr. 52. Cocktails and pose value in one of the most up and coming parts of town. From 9pm onwards.

Lubitsch, Bleibtreustr. 47. Slick bistro-style café, a bit on the expensive side, and very popular with the business class.

Paris Bar, Kantstr. 152. More famous for its restaurant (see p.229), this was once the local of the city's actors and film crowd, though today it seems to live on a long-dead reputation. Middle-aged, sedate and very expensive. Go if you're not paying.

Rosalinde, Knesebeckstr. 16. Upmarket café with an unusual variety of breakfasts, served 9.30am–noon: the *Fitness Frühstück* (muesli, fresh fruit and nuts) does the trick after a rough night out, and there's hot food until 2am.

Rost, Knesebeckstr. 29. Cosy new addition to the Savignyplatz bar scene. Great snacks, popular with the theatre crowd.

Schwarzes Café, Kantstr. 148. Kantstrasse's best young, chic hangout, with a relaxed atmosphere, good music and food (like all-day breakfast and a "Black special" of black coffee, a Sobranie Black Russian cigarette and black bread). Dated perhaps, but still a

classic. Open 24hr (closed Tues 8am–8pm).

Schell, Knesebeckstr. 22. The archetypal Berlin posing parlour, the air thick with the sipping of Perrier and the rustle of Filofaxes. Vegetarian food and good breakfasts (9am–2pm).

Strüdel, Grunewaldstr. 21. A cosy, dimly lit bar, specializing in unusual export bottled beers. Slightly off the beaten track, and therefore never totally packed.

Wirtshaus Wuppke, Schlüterstr. 21. Old-fashioned *Kneipe* without the sleaze.

Zillemarkt, Bleibtreustr. 48. Wonderful if shabby bar that attempts a *fin-de-siècle* feel. Unpretentious and fun, and a good place to start Savignyplatz explorations – it's by the S-Bahn. Breakfast 10am–4pm.

Zwiebelfisch, Savignyplatz 7. Corner bar for would-be arty/intellectual types. Jazz, earnest debate and good cheap grub.

Charlottenburg and western Berlin

Aue, Berliner Str. 48, Wilmersdorf. Unprepossessing old Berlin pub established in 1909, and peopled by regulars who've been drinking here almost as long.

Berlin Bar, Uhlandstr. 145, Wilmersdorf. Narrow enough to be cosy, expensive enough to make a treat, but cute nevertheless and valued for its intimacy.

Blisse 14, Blissestr. 14, Wilmersdorf. Café-bar designed especially, but not exclusively, for disabled people. A good meeting place.

Café Arc, Fasanenstr. 81a, Charlottenburg. Intimate café in an arch under the elevated train tracks. Predominantly but not exclusively gay.

Café Knobelsdorff, Knobelsdorffstr. 38, Charlottenburg. Charming café with Viennese specialities and popular breakfasts (8am–4pm).

Café Melanie, Rheinstr. 43, Steglitz. One of the few decent places in the area. Good coffee and late opening (till around 4am) are the other bonuses.

Café am Neuen See, Lichtensteinallee 1. Smack in the middle of the Tiergarten park, this upmarket venue has slick Italian food in a beautiful lakeside setting. Summer outdoor eating is especially pleasant.

Café New York, Olivaer Platz 15, Charlottenburg. Clean-cut, pop-loving teenagers' hangout.

Café Rix, Karl-Marx-Str. 141, Neukölln. Part of a cultural complex that's housed in an old dance hall in Neukölln. Pleasant summer seating in a cobbled courtyard, and reasonably priced food, including breakfast (noon–4pm).

Café Sino, Flensburger Str. 7, Tiergarten. Cellar bar with a cosy real fire in winter and a small patio for summer. Home-made food.

Café Solo, Pariser Str. 19, Charlottenburg. Fine example of the classy bars dotted along this street. Breakfast 10am–4pm.

Caracas Bar, Kurfürstenstr. 9, Tiergarten. Tropical-style cellar bar adorned with plastic flowers and party lights. Things don't get going until early in the morning, when nightbirds fly in for a last raucous round after a long night's partying.

Champussy, Uhlandstr. 171, Charlottenburg. Champagne-only bar, where the booze flows freely and everyone pretends they don't care about the bill. Attracts exactly who you'd expect.

Coxx Café, Nürnberger Str. 17, Charlottenburg. A great find in an area awash with bland tourist drinking holes. Mixed gay/straight crowd, snack lunches and home-made cakes.

Dicker Wirt, Danckelmannstr. 43. Very typical neighbourhood pub, full of smoke and besotted regulars. Serves up a particularly good chile con carne, though.

Felsenkeller, Akazienstr. 2., Schöneberg. An unpretentious old bar recently discovered by a young hip crowd. Unchanged by the experience, it continues to dish up beer and cheap bar food.

Frische Brise, Holsteinische Str. 40, Wilmersdorf. Young and old from every conceivable profession mingle in all that a good pub should be.

Galerie Café, Am Bundesplatz 8, Wilmersdorf. Alcohol-free café with art on the walls and a garden. Pleasant and unhurried.

Harry's New York Bar, Lützowufer 15 in the *Hotel Esplanade*, Tiergarten. Ritzy piano bar shoehorned into a narrow space in a luxury hotel. Frequented by businesspeople and conventioneers.

Holst am Zoo, Joachimstaler Str. 1, Charlottenburg (in the arcade southwest of Zoo Station). *The* bar for football fans: walls plastered with pictures of favourite teams and assorted ephemera.

Jimmy's Diner, Pariser Str./Sächsische Str., Charlottenburg. A real American diner with a replica 1950s interior. Serves American food through to 4am, 6am at weekends.

Kastanie, Schlossstr. 22, Charlottenburg. Amiable bar near Schloss Charlottenburg that's best on summer evenings for its small beer garden.

Khan, Pariser Str. 20, Charlottenburg. The decor – with one or two minor adjustments – has remained faithful to the bar's origins in the 1960s students' movement.

Kleine Orangerie, Spandauer Damm 20. Bustling café and beer garden across the street from Schloss Charlottenberg. A perfect place to rest up before or after tackling the palace.

Kleine Weltlaterne, Nestorstr. 22, Wilmersdorf. Local artists' hangout, with hardcore regulars – so you might feel left out – but almost the only option in an area full of car showrooms.

Klo, Leibnizstr. 57, Charlottenburg. This one you'll love or hate. A theme bar based on or around things lavatorial (drinks are served in urine sample bottles). If you share the German fascination for anything related to peeing you'll wet yourself laughing; otherwise it's pricey and a bit tacky. Entry DM0.25.

Kronenbourg Café, Pfalzburgerstr. 11, Charlottenburg. Friendly, classy café serving interesting German dishes at affordable prices. Breakfast noon–4pm.

Lentz, Stuttgarter Platz 20, Charlottenburg. Furrow-browed intellectuals and artists on the pick-up. Outdoor seating in summer.

L'Escargot, Brüsseler Str. 39, Wedding. Often described as the only reason to

Cafés and bars

Cafés and bars

travel to the suburb of Wedding, this has fabulous and cheap food, imaginatively presented. Many vegetarian options.

Loretta am Wannsee, Kronprinzessinweg 260, Zehlendorf. Popular bar near Wannsee S-Bahn station, with an inviting tree-lined beer garden.

Loretta im Garten, Lietzenburger Str. 89, Charlottenburg. Though angled mainly at the tourist market, this large beer garden can be fun if you're in the right mood.

Luise, Königin-Luise-Str. 40, Zehlendorf. A smaller and more convivial beer garden, just a stone's throw from the Dahlem museums. Usually packed with students from the nearby Free University.

Luisenbräu, Luisenplatz 1, Charlottenburg. Large bar that brews its own (you can see it happening), within sight of Schloss Charlottenburg. Popular with locals and almost a German cliché for its muscular bar staff carrying large numbers of frothing mugs. Beer is served in 0.2 litre glasses "so that it's always fresh".

Mey's, Pfalzburgerstr. 83, Charlottenburg. Pleasant, unpretentious cocktail bar with great service and drinks.

Nussbaum, Bundesplatz 6. Traditionally-minded Berlin pub and beer garden with over a dozen beers on tap and home-made northern German specialities.

Rixdörfer Bräuhaus, Glasower Str. 27, Neukölln. Actually part of a brewery, this bar is crammed full of knick-knacks and beer-related paraphernalia, and is Berlin's closest relative to the British village pub.

Sabine II, Siemenswerder Weg 4, Spandau. This permanently moored yacht on Lake Havel provides the setting for a fun-packed night, since its sequestered location allows revellers to make as much noise as they like. Access by boat also possible. Closed Tues.

Saftladen 2, Wegenerstr. 1, Wilmersdorf. When the booze gets too much, come here, where alcohol-free drinks – some of them quite inventive – are the speciality.

SPQR, Kantstr. 32, Charlottenburg. A small, gently lit bar with an attractively

intimate ambience, and some of the best bar food in town. Fresh fish on Friday. Opens 6pm.

Strassenbahn, Laubacher Str. 29, Wilmersdorf. Once a train station, now a popular *Szene* hangout. Good breakfasts.

UFA-Café, Viktoriastr. 13, Tempelhof. Amazingly cheap bar/café in the middle of the huge UFA cultural complex.

Wintergarten, Fasanenstr. 23, Charlottenburg. Part of the *Literaturhaus*, an institution given over to poetry readings and other bookish events, this has a beautifully renovated interior and a peaceful garden. Moderate prices. Breakfasts from 10am.

Wirtshaus Moorlake, Moorlakenweg 1, Zehlendorf; take bus #216 to the Moorlake stop. An easy-going café by the side of the Havel, whose genial beer garden escapes the hordes.

Zur Weissen Maus, Ludwigkirchplatz 12, Charlottenburg. Chic 1920s-style bar with reproductions of Otto Dix and Max Beckmann reflected in the mass of mirrors. Popular with older artists and has good, if expensive, cocktails. Opens around 10pm.

The eastern suburbs

Café Liebig, Regattastr. 158, Köpenick. Not far from Grünau S-Bahn station, this Jugendstil café makes a good starting point for a stroll along the banks of the Langer See.

Drittes Ohr, Matternstr. 14, Friedrichshain. Bluesy music bar for the over-thirty crowd. Sit amid old signs and musical instruments, have a go on the billiards table and think about growing a beard.

Eierschale-Zenner, Alt-Treptow 14–17, Treptow. Opel Manta owners limbering up for serious drink-drive sessions do a lot to spoil the ambience of this Spreeside Gaststätte after dark. However, it's worth dropping in during the daytime.

Geierwally's, Prenzlauer Promenade 3, Weissensee. Relax on plush sofas and admire the supermarket trolleys welded into the bar in this alternative hangout.

Marienlust, Am Langen See, Köpenick. A big old *Gartenlokal* overlooking the Langer See, with outdoor seating and decent fish dishes. DM8–25. Wed–Sun 11am–6pm.

Müggelseeklause, Müggelseedamm/Bruno-Wille-Str., Köpenick. A stone's throw from the Müggelsee in Friedrichshagen, and with a bit of old Berlin panache. Art exhibitions are put on here too. Closed Mon.

Müggelseeperle, Am grossen Müggelsee, Köpenick. A good place to interrupt wanderings along the Müggelsee. Outdoor seating, food DM7–25.

Müggelturm, In den Müggelbergen, Köpenick. The restaurant in the viewing tower on top of the Müggelberge won't win any prizes for its basic pork and spuds cuisine, but it makes a good target if you're indulging in some city-edge wandering. DM8–20. May–Sept until 7pm (10pm weekends), Oct–April until 6pm (7pm weekends).

Neu-Helgoland, An der Müggelspree/Oderheimer Str., Köpenick. In the little town of Müggelheim, this one heaves with day-trippers in summer. Open until 11pm.

Rübezahl, Am grossen Müggelsee, Köpenick. Unreliable food and hideous Alexanderplatz-style architecture, but a good place for a beer looking out over the Müggelsee. Closes at 6pm.

Schmetterlingshorst, Am langen See, Köpenick. Lakeside pork and potatoes cuisine with lashings of beer. DM7–14.

Thaerkocher, Thaerstr. 39, Friedrichshain. Join the laid-back crowd of Friedrichshain locals who come here for cheap beer, billiards and bluesy sounds.

Zur Fähre, Müggelseedamm 162, Köpenick. Old-style *Gaststätte* with outdoor seating. Closed Sun.

Gay cafés and bars

The most concentrated area of **gay bars** is between Wittenbergplatz and Nollendorfplatz, south of Kleiststrasse. For more detailed listings, pick up a copy of *Berlin von Hinten* (DM22.80) or

Siegessäule (free), available from most bars, and see also "Gay and lesbian Berlin" in Basics. As you'd expect, the majority of gay bars are on the western side of the city.

Altberliner Bierstuben, Saarbrücker Str. 17, Prenzlauer Berg. A bar with a dual identity, dishing up meat and two veg Berlin specialities to locals during the day, and mutating into a discreet gay bar at night.

Andreas' Kneipe, Ansbacher Str. 29, Schöneberg. A favourite among Berliners for the last thirty years, and a good place to begin wanderings in the Wittenbergplatz area.

Berlin Connection, Martin-Luther-Str. 19, Schöneberg. Modern café-bistro, strewn with palms and mirrors, which attracts a young to late-30s crowd. Second corner bar, and terrace in summer.

Besenkammer, Rathausstr. 1 (under the Alexanderplatz S-Bahn arches), Mitte. Tiny bar just off Alexanderplatz. Not particularly stylish but you won't have any trouble getting to know people. Open 24hr.

Blue Boy Bar, Eisenacher Str. 3, Schöneberg. Tiny, convivial and relaxed bar, far less raucous than many that surround it. Open till 6am.

Burgfrieden, Wichertstr. 69, Prenzlauer Berg. A well-known haunt that's been going since the 1960s, with a 35-plus crowd that takes in everyone from leathermen to transvestites and all points in between. Two bars, one serving beer, the other cocktails.

Café Anal, Muskauer Str. 15, Kreuzberg. Long-established alternative bar in east Kreuzberg and a second home for gay punks. Gets lively after 11pm.

Café am Senefelderplatz, Schönhauser Allee 173, Prenzlauer Berg. Relaxed, long-established East Berlin gay and lesbian hangout with discos every Fri. Various snack dishes, including excellent chips.

Café Sundstrom, Mehringdamm 61, Kreuzberg. Small and pleasant café that's low-key and comfortable.

Café PositHiv, Alvensleberstr. 26, Schöneberg. Quiet self-help café run by

Cafés and bars

Cafés and bars

and for PWAs and men and women who are HIV positive. Tues–Sun 3pm onwards.

Chapeau Claque, Bergstr. 25, Mitte. Arty bar liberally decorated with found objects – everything from puppets to antique commodes. Regular venue for literary readings and operatic evenings. Attracts customers of all ages.

Club 70 Berlin, Eberstr. 58, Schöneberg. Bar and pension, but welcomes non-residents. It's also something of a cultural centre, running day-trips and activities. Popular with over-40s; bar closed Mon.

Club Trommel, Thomasstr. 53, Neukölln. Gaudy, kitsch bar in the southeast of the city. Discos at weekends.

Dandy Club, Urbanstr. 64, Kreuzberg. Ring the doorbell to enter. Dark, naughty and famous for its "underwear" parties on the first and third Fridays of the month, for which there's a DM10 cover charge.

Flair, Nachodstr. 5, Wilmersdorf. Perhaps the most important facet of *Flair* is that it's only closed for one hour a day (usually 5–6am). It also boasts a summer terrace and decent food.

Fledermaus, Joachimstaler Str. 17–19, Charlottenburg. Bar and coffee shop popular with tourists as well as locals; one of the city's most relaxing gay bars, open till 5am.

Flipflop, Kulmerstr. 20a. Imaginatively decorated bar/cocktail lounge that attracts a diverse clientele. Popular for its Sunday brunch, served from noon till 4pm.

Hafen, Motzstr. 19, Schöneberg; adjacent to *Tom's Bar* (see opposite). Longtime popular cruising bar for 20 to 30-year-olds. Always packed, open till late.

Kleine Philharmonie, Schaperstr. 14, Charlottenburg. Shoebox-sized place packed with antiques and umbrellas. Marvellous proprietress, unavoidably intimate. Closed Sun.

Knast, Fuggerstr. 34, Schöneberg. If you're in Berlin for the S&M leather action, look no further. Wicked leather bar in prison-like surroundings: service is from behind a grill and handcuffs line the walls.

Lenz, Eisenacherstr. 3, Schöneberg. Straightforward, likeable *Szene* bar that attracts a goodlooking crowd. Specializes in cocktails (125 on its list) and whiskies (80-plus).

Le Moustache, Gartenstr. 4, Mitte. Popular leather bar in the tiled surroundings of an old butcher's shop. Average, but there are few other gay haunts in this part of town. Open from 8pm though usually gets going around 11pm. Closed Mon. Has a pension attached (see p.220).

O-Bar/Oranien-Bar, Oranienstr. 168, Kreuzberg. While the name changes, this popular gay haunt has long been a favourite of passing straights bar-hopping along Oranienstrasse. Occasional discos.

Pick ab!, Greifenhagener Str. 16, Prenzlauer Berg. As the name suggests, this place is anything but restrained. "Porn videos will be shown", they claim, and there's a dark room at the back. Fri & Sat 11pm until dawn or thereabouts.

Schall und Rauch, Gleimstr. 23, Prenzlauer Berg. Tasteful designer elegance in this hip young bar. A place to see and be seen – and eat, thanks to an imaginative and ever-changing menu.

Schoppenstube, Schönhauser Allee 44, Prenzlauer Berg. The best-known gay place in the east. In reality this is two very different bars: a pleasant wine bar upstairs, and a steamy, cruiser's haven downstairs. Knock for entry and if the doorman likes the look of you you're in.

Scheune, Motzstr. 25, Schöneberg. Very popular leather club with regular theme parties for devotees of rubber, uniforms or sheer nakedness. Darkroom, baths and other accoutrements.

Sonderbar, Käthe-Niederkirchner-Str. 34, Prenzlauer Berg. Weekend pre-club rendezvous and chill-out bar. Fifty-five different cocktails on offer.

Stiller Don, Erich-Weinert-Str. 67, Prenzlauer Berg. A gay place that makes an accessible intro to the scene in the former east. More like a slightly intellectual neighbourhood bar with a clientele that runs right across the age spectrum. Cheap and recommended.

Tom's Bar, Motzstr. 19, Schöneberg. Dark, sweaty and wicked cruising bar with a large back room. Possibly Berlin's most popular gay bar, and a great place to finish off an evening.

Tunnel Bar, Schlesische Str. 32, Kreuzberg. New bar and dance club for a younger crowd. Thurs men only.

Twilight Zone, Welserstr. 24, corner with Fuggerstr., Schöneberg. Candlelit basement bar underneath *Connection* disco. On Wed, Thurs and Sun it's leather, rubber or uniforms only. Fairly macho/heavy. Closed Mon & Tues.

Women's cafés and bars

Many of Berlin's **women-only** bars have a strong lesbian following, though straight women are welcome everywhere.

Begine, Potsdamer Str. 139, Schöneberg (women only). Stylishly decorated bar-bistro/gallery with inexpensive food. Hosts films, readings and concerts. See also "Women's Berlin" in Basics.

Café Seidenfaden, Dircksenstr. 47, Mitte. Alcohol-free café, open only until 9pm.

La Chiantina, Paul-Lincke-Ufer 44, Kreuzberg. Pleasant women-run restaurant with exhibitions.

Die Zwei, Am Wasserturm, Spandauer Damm, Spandau. The city's tackiest best, a determinedly (non-exclusive) lesbian bar, popular particularly among older women, with music from Marlene via Iron Butterfly to Madonna.

Dinelo, Vorbergstr. 10, Schöneberg. Traditional, comfortable bar with pool table. Salads and hefty German dishes, DM8–17. Closed Mon; women only.

Frauen und Kindercafé, in the EWA e.V Frauenzentrum, Prenzlauer Allee 6,

Prenzlauer Berg. An airy café-gallery with a children's play area. Offers advice, discussion and events.

Futuro, Adalberstr. 79, Kreuzberg. Popular with lesbians and gay men.

Hofgarten, Regensburger Str. 5, Kreuzberg. Classy and friendly bar for men and women, with a strong feminist following.

Lärm und Lust, Oranienstr. 189 (to the right of the rear courtyard, 3rd floor), Kreuzberg. Women musicians' collective and occasional cabaret with a diverse programme. Open sessions Fri.

Pour Elle, Kalckreuthstr. 10 , Schöneberg. Intimate disco-bar frequented by the more conservative sort of (generally older) lesbian. Pricey. Closed Mon; women only except Wed.

Roses, Oranienstr. 187, Kreuzberg. Gay bar but with a strong lesbian presence. Currently one of the locales of choice.

Schoko-Café, Mariannenstr. 6, on Heinrichplatz, Kreuzberg. Very alternative converted warehouse housing a health-conscious café and offering information on the many activities organized by the Schokofabrik collective. Cliquey atmosphere that's a little intimidating if you're new to the place. The women-only Turkish baths next door are open from September to the end of May (see "Women's Berlin" in Basics). Closed Sat.

SO 36, Oranienstr. 190, Kreuzberg. Outrageous gay disco with a rotating programme of parties and events, often for lesbians. Every third Friday in the month sees the Jane Bond Party for "women, lesbians, drag queens and other feminimities".

Whistle Stop, Knaackstr. 94, Prenzlauer Berg. Attractive, low-key lesbian bar and café.

Zufall, Pfalzburger Str. 10, Wilmersdorf. Non-exclusive bar-cum-disco, a focal point for Berlin's showier characters.

Cafés and bars

Chapter 14

Clubs and live venues

Nothing brought you so much face to face with the pathological distortion of Germany's post-war mentality as the weird nightlife of Berlin. Its grotesqueness destroyed for many of us younger men all the illusions about sex that some people retain throughout their whole lives. One year in Berlin revealed more of the perversions in which man's lower nature can indulge than a normal lifetime spent elsewhere.

R. Landauer, describing Weimar Berlin in *Seven*.

Many of the venues listed below are marked on the maps on pp.244–245 and p.247.

Since the time of the Weimar Republic, and even through the lean postwar years, Berlin has had a reputation for having some of the best – and steamiest – nightlife in Europe, an image fuelled by the cartoons of George Grosz and films like *Cabaret*. Today the big draw is the **clubs** that have grown up out of the city's techno (or, as the locals call it, "*tekhno*") scene. In a remarkably short space of time these places, many housed in abandoned buildings on or around the former no-go area of the East-West border strip, have spawned a scene that ranks among the most exciting in Europe.

If manic dance music is not your thing, then the city also has a wide range of more traditional clubs and discos, ranging from slick hangouts for the trendy to raucous punky dives.

Musically there's much of appeal here: venues cover a breadth of tastes and are rarely expensive. As ever, it's the tension the city seems to generate that gives the nightlife its colour.

Two of the city's venues are unclassifiable: the *Waldbühne* is a large outdoor amphitheatre on the Hollywood

Bowl model, just west of the Olympic Stadium. It presents everything from opera to movies to rock – unbeatable in summer. The *Tempodrom*, two tents in Kreuzberg at the Anhalter Bahnhof, hosts concerts and circuses in the larger tent, cabaret and intimate performances in the smaller.

Clubs and discos

Berlin's clubs and discos are smaller, cheaper and less exclusive than their counterparts in London or New York – and fewer in number. You don't need much nous to work out that the places along the Ku'damm are tourist rip-offs: the real all-night sweats take place in the newer **dance-music clubs** that have opened up, mainly in the former East Berlin, where glitz is out and raving is in. For the slightly older, post-punk crowd, Schöneberg and Kreuzberg tend to be where it's happening. Don't bother turning up until midnight at the earliest, since few places get going much before then. Admission is often free – when you do pay, it shouldn't be much more than DM15. Some of the ravey places have strict door policies, but if you look the part and speak English you'll probably get in. Like most cities, Berlin's turnover in nightspots is rapid: expect the following listings to have changed at least slightly by the time you arrive – this applies particularly to the newer places in what used to be East Berlin. Some of the longer established venues (many of these are former Socialist Youth organization clubhouses) in the east also put on **live gigs**.

For the latest information on Berlin nightlife happenings, check the listings magazines *Tip* and *Zitty*, and look out for posters and flyers. Two free leaflets, *Flyer* and *guide*, list parties and clubs. Both can be picked up in record shops, clubs and *Szene* bars and cafés.

Abraxas, Kantstr. 134, Charlottenburg ☎3 12 94 93. Hot and sweaty dance floor, specializing in salsa and Latin American sounds. Not pretentious, just lots of fun. Tues–Sun 10pm–5am. Free during the week, DM10 Fri & Sat.

Akba Lounge, Sredzkistr. 64, Prenzlauer Berg ☎4 41 14 63. Anything from soul to German pop gets played in this tight but friendly club. Thurs–Sat from 11pm. DM10.

Ankerklause, Kottbusser Damm/Maybachufer, Kreuzberg ☎6 93 56 49. A little café, perched by the Landwehr canal, turns into a funk and soul club by night. Very trendy and very crowded. From 11pm. DM5.

Big Eden, Kurfürstendamm 202, Charlottenburg ☎8 82 61 20. Enormous tourist trap disco, also popular with teenagers – check out the dance floor first on the video monitors outside. It's free for everyone Sun–Thurs, and for women all the time: but drinks are expensive. Not recommended in the slightest. Sun–Fri 7pm–4am, Sat 7pm–7am.

Blue Note, Courbièrestr. 13, Schöneberg ☎2 18 72 48. Eclectic mix of rock, Latin and (chiefly) jazz sounds. Small dance floor, best after midnight. Tues–Sun 10pm–5am. DM6 on Fri & Sat.

Boudoir, Brunnerstr. 192 (in back courtyard), Mitte ☎6 13 44 97. Almost an institution, this funky little club plays

disco and 1970s music for an uninhibited audience. Sat from 10pm. DM10.

bronx, Wiener Str. 34, Kreuzberg ☎6 11 84 45. All the 1970s rock'n'roll standards in a long-running venue for longhairs and stoners. Nightly from 10pm; DM5.

Café Silberstein, Oranienburger Str. 27, Mitte ☎2 81 28 01. Café-bar by day (see p.243), club from around 11pm at weekends. Once the sound system is cranked up, things really get going. House, jungle etc. Free.

Club Banana, Fasanenstrasse 81 (S-Bahn arch 558), Charlottenberg. ☎3 13 37 73. Small but always crowded club with a mainly gay audience. Thurs is usually women-only. Nightly from 10pm.

Connection, Fuggerstr. 83, Schöneberg ☎2 18 14 32. Very popular gay disco, attracting a largely leather-clad crowd. Fri & Sat from 10pm.

Cosmopolitan Club, Oranienstr. 39, Kreuzberg ☎6 14 35 73. Small but lively split-level bar/disco in the centre of the Kreuzberg action; musically, there's something for everyone, especially devotees of funk and rap. Nightly except Tues, 11pm onwards.

Delicious Doughnuts Research, Rosenthaler Str. 9, Mitte ☎2 83 30 21. Beautiful party people (or those who'd like to be) grooving to acid jazz and funk beats. There's a bar at the front and a sweaty dance floor at the back.

Die Insel, Alt-Treptow 6, Treptow ☎5 34 88 51. Reliable venue for thrashy/punky gigs and club nights, with occasional outdoor raves in summer, plus a cinema and gallery. On a Spree island that's part of Treptower Park. Fri & Sat from 10pm.

Dolmen Club, Schönhauser Allee 6–7, Mitte ☎4 40 60 26. Despite the strange Druid-inspired interior, this basement club is a popular rendezvous for hip-hop fans. Fri & Sat from 11pm.

Duncker, Dunckerstr. 64, Prenzlauer Berg ☎4 45 95 09. Indie, industrial and unashamedly Goth sounds. Open most nights after 10pm.

El Barrio, Potsdamer Str. 84, Tiergarten ☎2 62 18 53. An irresistable salsa/lam-

Clubs and
live venues

Clubs and live venues

bada disco precedes weekend bands (see also "Live Venues").

Far Out, Kurfürstendamm 156, Wilmersdorf (near Lehniner Platz) ☎32 00 07 23. Formerly a Bhagwan disco, now a friendly nightspot for a mix of off-beat conservatives and tourists. Gets crowded. Tues–Thurs 10pm–3am, Fri & Sat 10pm–6am. DM6.

Fou-Na-Na, Bachstr. (S-Bahn arch 475, Tiergarten ☎3 91 24 42. Reggae sounds underneath the arches of the S-Bahn lines. Tues–Sun from 11pm; DM10.

Garten Haus, Oranienburger Str. 53–56, Mitte ☎2 81 61 19. In back of the *Tacheles* art centre, a war-time barrack features funk, soul and ambient music. Thurs, Fri & Sat from 10pm.

Golgotha, in the Viktoriapark, Kreuzberg ☎7 85 24 53. Kreuzberg's popular hill-side café (see p.250) hosts a daily al fresco disco from 10pm April–Sept: good fun on warm evenings.

Huxley's Junior, Hasenheide 108–114, Kreuzberg ☎6 27 93 20. Hip-hop and funky rock for the skateboarding crew on Fri & Sat, reggae on Sun. "Twisted Kicks" on Thurs is a nostalgist's delight with punk and proto-punk sounds of the last twenty years or so. Thurs, Fri & Sat from midnight; DM5. Sun from 10pm; free.

Icon, Cantianstr. 15, Prenzlauer Berg (no phone). Big and trendy techno and house club.

Knaack-Club, Greifswalder Str. 224, Prenzlauer Berg ☎4 42 70 60. Rock (David Byrne to Nirvana) in the cellar and dance on the first floor of a big old club building in a Prenzlauer Berg courtyard, drawing a young, mainly east Berlin crowd. Nightly from 10pm. DM3–10.

Lime Club, Dircksenstr. 105, Mitte ☎2 81 45 85. In an archway under the ele-vated subway tracks, this unassuming club features trance, house and a little disco. Very in at the moment. Fri–Sun from 11pm. DM10–20.

Madow, Pariser Str. 23, Charlottenburg ☎8 83 92 60. Big unpretentious disco, for a no-nonsense boogie in a friendly atmos-phere. Wed–Sun from 10pm. DM10.

Metropol, Nollendorfplatz 5, Schöneberg ☎2 16 41 22. Berlin's largest disco, housed in a marvellous Art Deco building but otherwise rather ordinary. The odd live band. Fri & Sat 10pm–4am; DM10–15.

MS Sansouci, Gröbenufer/Oberbaumbrücke, Kreuzberg ☎6 11 12 52. Very trendy party boat with trip-hop and other cutting-edge sounds. As much a place to be seen as to dance. Thurs & Fri from 11pm; DM10.

Oxymoron, 40/41 Rosenthaler Str. (in the Hackesche Höfe), Mitte ☎28 39 18 85. House and trip-hop in a big space in the Art Deco *Hackesche Höfe* retail complex. An Italian restaurant by day (see p.234). Fri–Sun 10pm–4am.

The Pip's, Augustrasse 84, Mitte ☎2 82 45 12. Trendy bar offering a minuscule dance floor with a good mix of funk, soul, trip-hop, and occasionally Latin. Tues–Sun from 10pm; free.

Q-Club, Pücklerstr. 34 (in the basement of Weltrestaurant Markthalle), Kreuzberg ☎6 11 30 02. Jazz and funk at week-ends, caberet and other happenings in the week. Nightly from 10pm; DM7–12.

Salsa, Wielandstr. 13, Charlottenburg ☎3 24 16 42. Exuberant Latin American disco with floor shows and dance lessons thrown in. DM6–12.

Schleusenkrug, Müller-Breslau Strasse/Landwehrkanal, Tiergarten ☎3 13 99 09. An old-fashioned pub recently transformed into a hip bar and café with techno and house played Fri & Sat from 10pm. DM5–15.

Schnabelbar, Oranienstr. 31, Kreuzberg ☎6 15 85 34. Though the dance floor's small this Kreuzberg bar is packed for hip-hop on Sat, jazz-funk on Sun and different DJs each Fri. The rest of the week there's a changing mix of house, world music, reggae and trip-hop. Nightly 10pm–5am; DM5–10.

Sophienclub, Sophienstr. 6, Mitte ☎2 82 45 52. This intimate (read crowded) cen-tral club does different nights for different tastes, taking in soul, funk, house and indie. Nightly from 9pm. DM5.

S036, Oranienstr. 190, Kreuzberg ☎6 15 26 01. Perennial punk, post-punk and thrash venue. Spirit of 76. Nightly from 10pm; DM6–10.

Tanzpalast, Kantstr. 162, Charlottenburg ☎8 83 83 64. An old-style dance hall where gentlemen are expected to ask ladies for the pleasure. Nostalgic, but not for everyone – dress smart. Wed–Mon from 8pm.

Trash, Oranienstr. 40, Kreuzberg ☎6 14 23 28. Current home of Berlin youth's weirder elements. Black walls, black clothes, tattoos and hard rock sounds. Tues–Sun 11pm onwards.

Tresor/Globus, Leipziger Str. 126a, Mitte. A key player in the burgeoning of Berlin's dance music scene since 1990, though the regulars claim that it's not as good as it used to be. Nevertheless trouser-shaking techno in the steamy basement and slightly mellower house and hip-hop beats upstairs still attract clubbers from all over Europe. Wed and weekends 11pm until dawn; DM10.

90° ("Neunzig Grad"), Dennewitzstr. 37, Kreuzberg ☎2 62 89 84. One of the former West's better clubs, at the far eastern end of Kurfürstenstrasse. Wed–Sat hip-hop, ragamuffin, soul and funk are on the turntables, while Sun is gay night (but not exclusively so) with house and garage. Wed–Sun from 11pm, action starts around 2am; DM10–15.

Live music

The way to find out exactly what's on and where is by checking the listings magazines *Tip*, *Zitty*, *Prinz* and *Berlin Programm*, or on the innumerable fly posters about town.

Major venues

The following are the sort of places you can expect to find international super-groups playing. Book well in advance for anything even vaguely popular. Invariably you can't buy tickets from the places

themselves, but need to go to one of the ticket offices listed on p.267.

Arena, Eichenstr. 4, Treptow ☎5 33 73 33. Located almost in the middle of nowhere, this medium-sized hall usually offers rappers, teenie groups and other popular bands for a young audience.

Deutschlandhalle, Messedamm 26, Charlottenburg ☎3 03 81. Like the *Eissporthalle* below, part of the Congress Centre, west of the city. Zero atmosphere, biggish name bands.

Die Halle, An der Industriebahn 12–16, Weissensee ☎9 66 91 06. A former factory building in the eastern suburb of Weissensee that plays host to medium-sized bands.

Eissporthalle, Jafféstr. 1, Charlottenburg ☎30 38 44 44. Another large site. The *Sommergarten im Messegelände* nearby (around the Funkturm) has, as the name suggests, outdoor concerts in summer.

Huxley's Neue Welt, Hasenheide 108–114, Kreuzberg ☎6 27 93 20. One of the top venues for touring bands.

ICC Berlin, Messedamm 26, Charlottenburg ☎3 03 81. Vast, soulless hall for trade fairs that often hosts gigs.

Waldbühne, Glockenturmstr./ Passenheimer Str., Charlottenburg ☎3 04 06 76. Open-air spot in a natural amphitheatre near the Olympic Stadium that features movies, bands, classical concerts, and other entertainments. Great fun on summer evenings, but arrive early as it often gets crowded.

Smaller venues

Remember that many bars and cafés often have live music: skim through *Zitty*, *Tip* and *Prinz* magazines for up-to-the-minute listings.

Acud, Veteranenstr. 21, Mitte ☎44 35 94 97. Rock and blues are the mainstay of this no-frills venue, though from time to time acid-jazz gets a look in. There's also a gallery and movie theatre tucked inside.

A-Trane, Bleibtreustr./Pestalozzistr., Charlottenburg ☎3 13 25 50. Up-and-

Clubs and live venues

Clubs and live venues

coming and well-known jazz artists in a comfortable, intimate setting. Weekends from 10pm; DM15.

Badenscher Hof, Badensche Str. 29, Schöneberg ☎8 61 00 80. Lively café-restaurant that draws in the Schöneberg crowd for its frequent jazz concerts, the best of which are at weekends.

b-flat, Rosenthaler Str. 13, Mitte ☎2 80 63 49. Small jazz club with live groups on weekends and a serious audience – don't talk during sets. From 10pm. Entry varies.

Café Swing, Motzstr./Kleiststr., off Nollendorfplatz ☎2 16 61 37. A tiny club, but one offering free concerts on Mon and Thurs at around midnight or 1am. Anything is possible, from avant-garde performance art to straight rock-'n'roll. See also "Cafés and bars" p.253.

Checkpoint, Leipziger Str. 55, Mitte ☎2 08 29 95. A multimedia cultural centre staging off-the-wall events – film shows, theatre, gigs – with a cheap bar. DM9–10.

Eierschale Dahlem, Podbielskiallee 50, Zehlendorf ☎8 32 70 97. Lively venue with large beer garden in summer. Always packed towards the end of the week. Music most nights, often appalling but with free disco before and after the bands. Free.

Eierschale Zenner, Alt-Treptow 14–17, ☎5 33 73 70. A large and popular beer garden by the shore of the Spree river, with oldies and other summery music.

El Barrio, Potsdamer Str. 84, Tiergarten ☎2 62 18 53. Berlin's best venue for salsa and South American sounds. Also has a great disco. DM10 upwards.

Flöz, Nassauische Str. 37, Wilmersdorf ☎8 61 10 00. Basement club that's the meeting point for Berlin's jazz musicians and a testing ground for the city's new bands. Also offers occasional salsa and cabaret. Can be wild.

Haus der Kulturen der Welt, John-Foster-Dulles-Allee 10, Tiergarten ☎39 78 71 75. Bus #100. The city's number one venue for world music. Always worth checking out (see *Tip* or *Zitty*).

Hochschule der Künste, Hardenbergstr. 33, Charlottenburg ☎3 13 70 07. Part of Berlin's art school, and a venue for bands, media performances and dance troupes – particularly with a South American theme.

Knaack, Greifswalderstr. 224, Prenzlauer Berg ☎4 42 70 60. Mostly local rock bands you're unlikely to have heard of, plus the odd visiting band you probably won't have heard of either.

K.O.B., Potsdamer Str. 157, Schöneberg ☎2 15 20 60. A pub in a (now legally) squatted house, which at weekends hosts interesting groups at low prices (DM5). R&B, jazz and psychedelic sounds play here, but the favourites are local anarcho- and fun-punk bands.

Kulturbrauerei, Knaackstr. 97, Prenzlauer Berg ☎4 41 92 69. Sharing space in a nineteenth-century brewery with an arts and cultural centre, this club offers local and mid-level bands.

The Loft, part of the *Metropol*, Nollendorfplatz 5, ☎7 86 50 23. Features a whole range of independent artists, with a view to innovation and introducing new music. Also organizes larger concerts in the *Metropol* itself.

Podewil, Klosterstr. 68–70, Mitte ☎24 74 96. Jazz, world music and occasional classical concerts. Less lively than some other venues but dedicated to the music.

Quasimodo, Kantstr. 12a, Charlottenburg ☎3 12 80 86. Berlin's best jazz spot, with nightly programmes starting at 10pm. A high-quality mix of international, usually American, stars and up-and-coming names. Small, with a good atmosphere. Often free on weekdays.

Metropol, Nollendorfplatz 5, Schöneberg ☎2 16 41 22. Well-known, if not mega, names play frequently in this large dance space.

Saalbau Neukölln, Karl-Marx-Str. 141, Neukölln ☎68 09 37 79. Part of Neukölln's attempt to up its cultural offerings. Live music – both classical and contemporary – literary and poetry recitals, and dance. Interesting location in a 1930s ballroom, with a good café, *Rix*, attached (see p.255).

Tacheles, Oranienburger Str. 53–56, Mitte ☎ 2 81 61 19. Concerts from around 10pm. The performers are likely to be pretty eclectic, ranging from guitar bands to industrial noise merchants.

Tempodrom, behind the facade of the Anhalter Bahnhof, Kreuzberg. Two tents, the larger hosting contemporary bands of middling fame. Hosts a free music festival each summer.

Tränenpalast, Reichstagsufer 17, Mitte ☎ 2 38 62 11. A former waiting room at the border between east and west is now a medium-sized hall featuring rock, soul and jazz.

Clubs and live venues

Chapter 15

The arts

When Berlin was a divided city, the federal government poured in subsidies for all kinds of **art**: the annual sum given to the city by the government (DM550 million) was over half the federal budget for culture for the entire United States. Now, in the mood of glum post-unification realism, things are very different: the plugs have been pulled on almost all subsidies, and orchestras and theatres are being forced to look elsewhere for funding; don't be surprised if some of the companies in these listings are no more by the time you reach the city.

Which is not to say that all is black in Berlin: there are high quality dance groups performing everything from classical ballet to contemporary experimental works, and scores of mainstream and arthouse cinemas. The art gallery scene is thriving, and the city still has one of the world's finest **symphony orchestras**. Unification has left it with a "doubling" of facilities, three magnificent opera houses and one of the liveliest arts scenes of any European city. Berlin's reputation as a leader of the avant-garde is reflected in the number of small, often experimental theatre groups working here. The scene is active, though it's worth remembering that many **theatre companies** take a break in July and August.

Ticket agencies and offices

Ticket offices or **Theaterkassen** are usually the easiest (and occasionally the

only) way of buying tickets for all major music, theatre and dance events in both western and eastern Berlin. Open during working hours (or longer), they charge a hefty commission (up to 17 percent) on the ticket price. The first place to try, especially for fringe-type theatre, less popular classical concerts and dance, is *Hekticket* (see box opposite for details), which sells half-price tickets, and charges only DM2 commission on tickets for the same day's performance.

Classical music

For years classical music in Berlin meant one man and one orchestra: Herbert von Karajan and the Berlin Philharmonic. Since his death in 1989, the **Philharmonie**, under conductor Claudio Abbado, has had its former supremacy questioned by the rise of the excellent **Deutsches Sinfonie Orchester** under Vladimir Ashkenazy. And, as elsewhere in the arts, cutbacks in state and senate funding have brought about a more cautious and conservative atmosphere in the classical music world.

The Philharmonie and Deutsche Sinfonie Orchester are by no means the only options. Many smaller orchestras play at sites in and around the city, and museums and historic buildings often host chamber concerts and recitals. It's possible to pick up inexpensive tickets for many performances from Hekticket (see above). As ever, see *Zitty* and *Tip* for listings. For opera venues, see the following section.

Ticket offices

Note that most offices do not take credit cards.

Berlin Ticket
Potsdamer Str. 96, Schöneberg ☎23 08 82 30.

Box office
Nollendorfplatz 7, Schöneberg ☎2 15 54 63.

Europa Center
Tauentzienstr. 9, Charlottenburg ☎2 64 11 38.

Hekticket
Rathausstr. 1, Mitte ☎24 31 24 31.

KaDeWe
Tauentzienstr. 21, Schöneberg ☎2 17 77 54.

Kant-Kasse
Krumme Str. 55, Charlottenburg ☎3 13 45 54.

Karstadt
Schlossstr. 7–10, Steglitz ☎7 92 28 00.

Telecard
Birchbuschstr. 14, Steglitz ☎8 34 40 73. *Accepts most credit cards.*

Theaterkasse Centrum
Meinekestr. 25, Charlottenburg ☎8 82 76 11.

Ticket Counter
Europa Center, Tauentzienstr. 9, Charlottenburg ☎2 64 11 38.

Ticket Hotline
☎8 09 90 90.
Credit card bookings only.

Wertheim
Kurfürstendamm 231, Charlottenburg ☎8 82 25 00.

Wildbad-Kiosk
Rankestr. 1, Charlottenburg ☎8 81 45 07.

The arts

Orchestras and venues

Berlin Sinfonie Orchester. Founded in 1952 and based in the Konzerthaus, this used to be eastern Berlin's main symphony orchestra. In the summer it puts on concerts every Thursday at 7.30pm in the Schlüterhof at the Museum für Deutsche Geschichte, Unter den Linden 2, which always attract a good crowd. Currently under the directorship of Michael Schønvandt.

Deutsche Oper Berlin, Bismarckstr. 35, Charlottenburg; box office ☎3 43 84 01 (Mon–Sat 11am–6pm). Formerly West Berlin's premier opera house, built in 1961 after the Wall cut access to the Staatsoper. Still the city's most prestigious venue in terms of visiting performers. Often has Wagner. Tickets DM20–200.

Deutsche Sinfonie Orchester. Shares the Konzerthaus with the Berlin Sinfonie Orchester and, under conductor Vladimir Ashkenazy, has stolen much of the Berlin Philharmonie's limelight over the last few years.

Staatsoper, Unter den Linden 5–7, Mitte; box office ☎20 35 45 55 (Mon–Sat 10am–8pm, Sun 2–8pm). The city's oldest and grandest music venue, built for Frederick the Great in 1742 to a design by Knobelsdorff. While little remains from that time (the building was bombed out in 1941, rebuilt, destroyed again in 1945 and rebuilt to the current specifications in 1955), the interior is all you'd expect a grand opera house to be.

During the GDR years, political isolation meant that performers didn't match the glamour of the venue. The appointment of Daniel Barenboim as musical director is a clear attempt to bring the Staatsoper to the forefront of the international opera scene. Though there's still some way to go, the Staatsoper has come on leaps and bounds. Chamber music performances take place in the Apollo Saal and tickets for most operas are around DM12–115.

Komische Oper, Behrenstr. 55–57, Mitte; box office at Unter den Linden 41 ☎20 26 03 60 (Mon–Sat 11am–7pm, Sun 1pm to 90min before performance). Less traditional than the Staatsoper, but a reliable venue for well-staged operatic productions, under the direction of Harry

The arts

Kupfer. Expert cutting-edge interpretation of modern works alongside the usual fare – and tickets at half the price of the Deutsche Oper.

Konzerthaus Berlin (Schauspielhaus), Gendarmenmarkt, Mitte; box office ☎ 2 03 09 21 01 (Mon–Sat noon–8pm, Sun and hols noon–4pm). A super venue, not only for performances by the resident Deutsche Sinfonie and Berlin Sinfonie orchestras, but also visiting musicians, orchestras and ensembles. Two concert spaces occupy the Schinkel-designed building: the Grosser Konzertsaal for orchestras and the Kammermusiksaal (not to be confused with that of the same name in the Philharmonie) for smaller groups and chamber orchestras. Look out for performances on the Konzerthaus's famed organ.

Philharmonie, Matthäikirchstr. 1, Tiergarten; box office ☎ 2 61 43 83 (Mon–Fri 3.30–6pm, Sat & Sun 11am–2pm). Home to the world-famous Berlin Philharmonic, Hamns Scharoun's indescribably ugly building is acoustically near-perfect – though you'll have to be near-loaded (financially) to enjoy it. Chances of getting a bargain seat are slim, and you should phone ahead for any concerts featuring the orchestra and its star conductor, Claudio Abbado. The Philharmonie also contains the smaller **Kammermusiksaal** for more intimate performances, and your best chance of getting a ticket is when guest orchestras are playing. Generally expect to pay around DM120; some half-price tickets for students available 30min before performances.

Urania, An der Urania 17, Shöneberg ☎ 22 18 90 91. Has a wide-ranging programme and reasonably priced seats.

Theatre

Sad to say, the mainstream **civic and private theatres** in Berlin are, on the whole, dull, unadventurous, and expensive – though it's often possible to cut costs by buying student standby tickets. You'll find little in English save for the work of small, roving theatre groups. And

in recent years, many professional people have left the birthplace of experimental theatre and returned to Munich and the lure of the film business.

Nevertheless, Berlin's reputation as Germany's **Theaterstadt** still holds firm for the thousands of eager young Germans who flock to the city every year, rent a space, and stage their work. The city is still a major venue for **experimental work**, and if your German is up to it, a number of groups are worth the ticket price; check under "Off-Theater" in *Tip* or *Zitty* for up-to-the-minute listings. Groups that have the word *Freie* in their name indicate that they're not dependent on city or state subsidies, which often impose creative constraints on a group's output.

You can get **tickets** for almost all theatre performances other than "Free" theatre at the ticket offices listed in the box on p.267; you'll pay between DM15 and DM80.

Civic and private theatres

Berliner Ensemble, Bertolt-Brecht-Platz 1, Mitte ☎ 2 82 77 12. Recently privatized, but Brecht's old theatre now seems a little adrift. Brecht still forms the staple fare here, though thankfully the productions are a little livelier than in GDR days. There are also occasional experimental productions on the Probebühne (rehearsal stage).

Deutsches Theater, Schumannstr. 13a, Mitte ☎ 28 44 12 21. Good, solid productions taking in everything from Schiller to Mamet make this one of Berlin's best theatres. Invariably sold out. Also includes a second theatre, the Kammerspiele des Deutschen Theaters, and Die Baracke, an experimental stage.

Friedrichstadt Palast, Friedrichstr. 107, Mitte ☎ 23 26 24 74. All-singing, all-dancing revues with much flesh on display draw the crowds here.

Hansa-Theater, Alt-Moabit 48, Tiergarten ☎ 3 91 44 60. Traditional and folk theatre.

Hebbel Theater, Stresemannstr. 29, Kreuzberg ☎ 25 90 04 27. Hosts short runs of European (and American) theatre and dance. Often interesting.

Komödie, Kurfürstendamm 206, Wilmersdorf ☎ 47 02 10 10. Period and contemporary comedies. Allied with the Theater am Kurfürstendamm.

Maxim-Gorki-Theater, Am Festungsgraben 2, Mitte ☎ 20 22 11 15. Consistently good productions of modern works like Tabori's *Mein Kampf* and Schaffer's *Amadeus*. More experimental works are staged on the Studiobühne.

Schaubühne am Lehniner Platz, Kurfürstendamm 153, Wilmersdorf ☎ 89 00 23. State-of-the-art theatre that hosts performances of the classics and some experimental pieces. Its high reputation means booking ahead is advisable.

Schiller-Theater, Bismarckstr. 110, Charlottenburg ☎ 31 11 31 11. Once renowned for cutting-edge productions, the *Schiller* was privatized some years ago and has since maintained itself with mainstream Broadway productions, often in English.

Schlosspark Theater, Schlossstr. 48, Charlottenburg ☎ 7 93 15 15. Interesting if mainstream theatre, with large local following.

Theater am Kurfürstendamm, Kurfürstendamm 206, Wilmersdorf ☎ 47 02 10 10. Run-of-the-mill plays and comedies of little interest to non-German-speakers.

Theater des Westens, Kantstr. 12, Charlottenburg ☎ 8 82 28 88. Musicals and light opera, the occasional Broadway-style show. Beautiful turn-of-the-century building, often sold out.

Volksbühne, Rosa-Luxemburg-Platz, Mitte ☎ 2 47 67 72. Under director Frank Castorf, this has become one of Berlin's most adventurous and interesting theatres. Castorf has gone all out to bring in young audiences with the result that performances are often highly provocative – nudity and throwing things at the audience crop up fairly regularly and there's a statistically high chance of witnessing a partial audience walkout. Recommended.

Experimental and free theatre groups

Ballhaus Naunynstrasse, Naunynstr. 27, Kreuzberg ☎ 25 88 66 44. Former ballroom fully refurbished in 1950s style. Repertoire of events includes mixed-media performances, dance and fringe theatre.

BAT (Studiotheater der Hochschule für Schauspielkunst), Belforter Str. 15, Prenzlauer Berg ☎ 4 42 79 96. Originally a "workers' and students' theatre", founded in 1975, this one can usually be relied on to come up with challenging experimental offerings, including theatre student graduation projects. A meeting point for everyone interested in theatre.

Berliner Figurentheater, Yorckstr. 59, Kreuzberg ☎ 7 86 98 15. Experimental puppet theatre group dealing with topical issues; constantly innovative. Superbly crafted dolls.

Freunde der Italienischen Oper, Fidicinstr. 40, Kreuzberg ☎ 6 91 12 11. Tiny courtyard theatre specializing in fringe productions performed in English.

Grips-Theater, Altonaer Str. 22, Steglitz ☎ 3 91 40 04. First-rate children's/young people's theatre; usually all improvised, occasional English performances. Booking recommended.

Neuköllner Oper, Karl-Marx-Str. 131, Neukölln ☎ 68 89 07 77. Opera and musicals, often obscure or unknown.

Out to Lunch Theatre Group, ☎ 8 91 37 25. Fringe theatre group formed by American and English actors, who perform a mixed bag of plays. Phone for venues.

Schiller-Theater-Werkstatt, Bismarckstr. 110, Charlottenburg ☎ 3 12 65 05. The experimental group of the Schiller Theater.

Theater der Freien Volksbühne, Schaperstr. 24, Wilmersdorf ☎ 8 84 20 80. Struggling to get by without the subsidies it once enjoyed, but still presenting serious drama.

Theater 89, Torstr. 216, Mitte ☎ 2 82 46 56. A small venue putting on modern works in classic style.

The arts

The arts

UFA-Fabrik, Viktoriastr. 10–18, Tempelhof ☎75 50 30. The most famous, and most efficiently run, cultural factory, with just about every aspect of the performing arts on offer. It acts as an umbrella group for all kinds of performances – theatre, dance, music and film – and it's always worth checking what's on.

Dance and cabaret

Though there are few **dance groups** in the city, those that exist are of a high quality: you can expect to see plenty of original, oddball and unusual performances.

In the 1920s and 1930s, Berlin had a rich and intense **cabaret scene**: hundreds of small clubs presented acts that were often deeply satirical and political. When the Nazis came to power these quickly disappeared, to be replaced by anodyne entertainments in line with Party views. Sadly, the cabaret scene has never recovered: most of what's on show today is either semi-clad titillation for tourists or that most German of predilections, the drag show. However, a few places are worth trying, notably the **Chamäleon Variete**, which plays host to some very eclectic acts. Check out the *Mitternachtshow* ("Midnight Show") on Friday and Saturday. Be warned that most cabaret venues make their money by charging very high prices at the bar; entrance is usually around DM30.

Dance

Deutsche Oper Berlin, see "Civic and private theatres". Classical ballet and opera and, to a lesser extent, contemporary work. Mainstream programme lacking in innovation.

Die Etage, Hasenheide 54, Kreuzberg ☎6 91 20 95. Contemporary dance and mime; also runs dance classes.

Hebbel Theater, see "Civic and private theatres". Featuring *Tanz in Winter* and *Tanz in August*, two three-week festivals of contemporary dance.

Komische Oper, see "Classical music". Modern ballet and experimental works.

Staatsoper, see "Classical music". Ballet and dance under the direction of Michael Denar, formerly of the Paris opera.

Tanzfabrik Berlin, Möckernstr. 68, Kreuzberg ☎7 86 58 61. Experimental and contemporary works, usually fresh and exciting. This is also Berlin's biggest contemporary dance school.

Cabaret venues: interesting

Bar Jeder Vernunft, Scharperstr. 24, Wilmersdorf ☎8 83 15 82. Currently the city's best, younger and hipper than most.

BKA (Berliner Kabarett Anstalt), Mehringdamm 32, Kreuzberg ☎2 51 01 12. Politically-tinged shows.

Chamäleon Variete, Rosenthaler Str. 40–41, Mitte ☎2 82 71 18. Very lively, with jugglers, acrobats and the like.

Die Distel, Friedrichstr. 101 (in the Admiralspalast), Mitte ☎2 04 47 04.

Hackesches Hof Theater, Rosenthaler Str. 40/41, Mitte ☎2 83 25 87. Musical theatre.

Meringhof Theater, Gneisenaustr. 2a, Kreuzberg ☎6 91 50 99.

Scheinbar Variete, Monumentenstr. 9, Schöneberg ☎7 84 55 39

Cabaret venues: touristy

Kartoon, Französische Str. 24, Mitte ☎2 04 47 56.

Klimperkasten, Otto-Suhr-Allee 102, Charlottenburg ☎7 85 64 77.

La Vie en Rose, Flughafen Tempelhof, Kreuzberg ☎69 51 30 00. Transvestite variety shows and some magic.

Stachelschweine, Europa Center, Charlottenburg ☎2 61 47 95.

Wintergarden, Potsdamer Str. 96, Tiergarten ☎23 08 82 30. An attempt to re-create the Berlin of the 1920s, with live acts from all over the world – cabaret, musicians, dance, mime, etc. Very expensive.

Wühlmäuse, Nürnberger Str. 33, Wilmersdorf ☎2 13 70 47.

Film

When the all-night drinking starts to get too much, it's always possible to veg out in front of the silver screen. The cinemas along the Ku'damm and around the Gedächtniskirche show major international releases, with ticket prices from DM12 to DM20; two days a week, usually Tuesday and Wednesday are designated *Kinotag*, when prices are reduced to around DM6. Language can be a problem: if a film is listed as **OF** or **OV** (*Originalfassung*) it's in its original language; **OmU** (*Originalfassung mit Untertiteln*) indicates German subtitles. Otherwise, the film will have been dubbed into German. You may very occasionally see films listed as **OmE** – original with English subtitles.

A host of **smaller cinemas** show arthouse and independently made movies, and some of the more interesting places are listed below. *Tip* and *Zitty* have listings of all the films showing each week: their daily listings are of "off-Ku'damm" cinemas; the big city cinemas are listed separately under "Ku'damm-Kinos".

Should you be here in February, the **Berlin International Film Festival** dominates the city's cultural life. Second only to Cannes in European terms, it has increasingly showcased east German and East European films alongside important releases from around the world. For details of screenings, see the listings magazines, call the Berliner Festspiele, Budapester Str. 50, Tiergarten (☎25 48 90), or enquire at Berlin Tourismus Marketing in the Europa Center. For season tickets for the festival, take two passport-size photos and DM200–300 to the **Berlinale Shop**, Budapester Str. 50, Tiergarten (☎25 48 91 00).

Cinemas

Arsenal, Welserstr. 25, Schöneberg ☎2 18 68 48. Specializes in retrospectives and series, with a second screen showing experimental work.

Babylon, Dresdener Str. 126, Kreuzberg ☎61 60 96 93. New films in English, with and without subtitles.

Babylon Mitte, Rosa-Luxemburg-Str. 30, Mitte ☎2 42 50 76. Central Berlin's best repertory cinema, and also home to a cinematic art museum. Occasional films with English subtitles.

Berliner Kinomuseum, Grossbeerenstr. 57, Kreuzberg. A shoebox of a place where an eccentric film buff presents classic silent movies from his collection.

Capitol-Dahlem, Thielallee 36, Zehlendorf ☎8 31 64 17. First-run films, but usually dubbed versions.

Checkpoint, Leipziger Str. 55, Mitte ☎2 08 29 95. Classic arthouse fare like *Two Lane Blacktop* combined with the latest cinematic causes célèbres (anything involving Tarantino etc).

Cinema Walter-Screiber-Platz, Bundesallee 111, Schöneberg ☎8 52 30 04. Screens works by and for women.

Colosseum, Schönhauser Allee 123, Prenzlauer Berg. Local cinema in Prenzlauer Berg which occasionally comes up with interesting offerings.

Cosima, Sieglinderstr. 10, Schöneberg ☎8 53 33 55. Tends to show one film for long periods.

Eiszeit-Kino, Zeughofstr. 20, Kreuzberg ☎6 11 60 16. Tiny cinema tucked away in a *Hinterhof*, specializing in retrospectives and alternative films.

International, Karl-Marx-Allee 33/Schillingstr., Mitte ☎24 75 60 11. A big, comfortable modern cinema showing new releases.

Kino in der Brotfabrik, Prenzlauer Promenade 3, Weissensee ☎4 71 40 02. Weissensee arthouse cinema. Worth checking out.

Kosmos, Karl-Marx-Allee 131a, Friedrichshain ☎4 22 47 44. One of eastern Berlin's biggest cinemas, usually showing mainstream releases.

Kurbel I, II & III, Giesebrechtstr. 4, Charlottenburg ☎8 83 53 25. Shows the latest commercial releases, often with the German-dubbed version running next door.

Lupe 1, Kurfürstendamm 202, Charlottenburg ☎8 83 61 06. Very occasional English-language releases.

The arts

The arts

Video rental

The average Berlin video store has the usual schlock-horror selection along with Hollywood hits, all clumsily dubbed into German. For English-language video, you'll need to visit one of the following shops. All will require ID, and it's best to go with a friend registered at a Berlin address. Expect to pay around DM7 per night per video.

British Council, Hardenbergstr. 20, Charlottenburg ☎31 10 99 10. Classic British films, plus the "Best of" the BBC on tape.

Incredibly Strange, Eisenacher Str. 115, Schöneberg ☎2 15 17 70. 2500 titles, with lots of weird and wonderful stuff.

Videodrom, Mittenwalder Str. 11, Kreuzberg ☎6 92 88 04. Berlin's largest selection of English-language movies, with over 3500 titles.

Moviemento I, Kottbusser Damm 22, Kreuzberg ☎6 92 47 85. Excellent late-night programme, often double bills.

Notausgang, Vorberstr. 1, Schöneberg ☎7 81 26 82. Mainly Hollywood classics shown in the original, ie without titles or dubbing. Ernst Lubitsch, the great emigré director, was born nearby — and has a seat for every show.

Odeon, Hauptstr. 116, Schöneberg ☎78 70 40 19. If you're after English-language releases, the Odeon will have them first.

Regenbogenkino, Lausitzerstr. 22, Kreuzberg ☎611 9875. Alternative Kreuzberg cinema, running occasional English retrospectives.

Sputnik-Südstern, Hasenheide 54, Kreuzberg ☎6 94 11 47. Best of the three Sputnik cinemas, even though it's claustrophobic in summer.

Thalia 2, Kaiser-Wilhelm-Str. 71, Steglitz ☎7 74 34 40. Films in English.

Xenon, Kolonnenstr. 5, Schöneberg ☎7 82 88 50. Often screens English-language independent films.

Zeughaus-Kino, Unter den Linden 2, Mitte ☎21 50 20. Cinema in the Zeughaus which often unearths fascinating films from the pre- and postwar years.

Art and design

Broadly speaking, the Berlin art scene falls into three main areas: the **Kurfürstendamm** and surrounding streets for the expensive, more established galleries; **Kreuzberg** for the "off" galleries, where younger and usually lesser-known artists have a chance to show their work; and **Auguststrasse**, the latest, and most up-and-coming strip. A useful and comprehensive source of information about what's on in the city's galleries is the English/German monthly magazine *artery berlin* (DM3.50). The quarterly *Berliner Kunstblatt* has selective listings. *Zitty* or *Tip* (under "Galerien" in "Ausstellungen") are also worth checking for up-to-the-minute details. Most galleries are open from about 2 to 7pm and close on Monday. It's pretty easy to gatecrash openings.

Each district of western Berlin has a **Kunstamt**, an office set up by the council to promote art in the community. It's worth checking your nearest *Kunstamt* – listed in the phone book – to see if there's anyone interesting exhibiting.

Galleries

Aktions Galerie, Grosse Präsidentenstr. 10, Mitte ☎28 59 96 50. Experimental and conceptual art and happenings, generally outrageous.

Muncipal art galleries

Several public galleries also exhibit contemporary/twentieth-century art – for more details, see the following:

The arts

DAAD Galerie, Kurfürstenstr. 58, Tiergarten ☎ 2 02 20 80 26. Exhibits pieces by artists who are working in the city on scholarships awarded by the Deutsche Akademischer Austausch Dienst (German Academic Exchange Service). Daily 12.30–7pm.

Dogenhaus Galerie, Auguststr. 63 (in the courtyard), Mitte ☎ 2 83 37 65. Concentrating on artists from the former East Germany (chiefly Berlin, Leipzig and Chemnitz) and often featuring unusual sculptures. Wed–Fri 2–7pm, Sat noon–5pm.

EIGEN+ART, Auguststr. 26, Mitte ☎ 2 80 66 05. Run by Gerd Harry Lybke, who opened the first private gallery in the GDR back in the 1980s, this is one of the most important Auguststrasse galleries. Though originally a showcase for east German talent, the programme now covers painting, installations and photography by (predominantly young) international artists. Tues–Fri 2–7pm, Sat 11am–5pm.

Fine Art Rafael Vostell, Knesebeckstr. 30, Charlottenburg ☎ 8 85 22 80. International artists of the 1960s with a mix of young Berlin painters. Mon–Fri 11am–7pm, Sat 11am–4pm.

Galerie am Chamissoplatz, Chamissoplatz 6, Kreuzberg ☎ 69 40 12 45. Politically oriented art, on the site of a former bakery in the heart of Kreuzberg. Tues–Fri 1–6pm, Sat & Sun 3–6pm.

Galerie Anselm Dreher, Pfalzburgerstr. 80, Wilmersdorf ☎ 8 83 52 49. Top avant-garde gallery. Tues–Fri 2–6.30pm, Sat 11am–2pm.

Galerie Argus Fotokunst, Marienstr. 25, Mitte ☎ 2 83 30 49. Interesting, often provocative fine art and documentary photographs. Wed–Sun 3–6pm.

Galerie Bodo Niemann, Rosenthaler Str. 40/41 (Hackescher Höfe) ☎ 2 85 83 12. Berlin city life in the 1920s is the theme of this gallery. Tues–Fri 1–7pm, Sat noon–6pm.

Galerie Bremer, Fasanenstr. 37, Wilmersdorf ☎ 8 81 49 08. One of the first places to show work banned by the Nazi regime. Also has a good cocktail bar. Tues–Fri noon–6pm.

Galerie Brusberg, Kurfürstendamm 213, Charlottenburg ☎ 8 82 76 82. Excellent contemporary figurative work and sculpture. Tues–Fri 10am–6.30pm, Sat 10am–2pm.

Galerie Eva Poll, Lützowplatz 7, Tiergarten ☎ 2 61 70 91. Contemporary art, with an emphasis on international figurative work. Mon 10am–1pm, Tues–Fri 11am–6.30pm, Sat 11am–3pm.

Galerie Fahnemann, Unter den Linden 42, Mitte ☎ 8 83 98 97. More high-quality avant-garde art. Tues–Fri noon–6pm, Sat noon–2pm.

Galerie Franck + Schulte, Mommsenstr. 56, Charlottenburg ☎ 3 24 00 44. Well-presented photographic exhibitions and installations, frequently featuring established artists from America. Mon–Fri 11am–6pm, Sat 11am–3pm.

Galerie Georg Nothelfer, Uhlandstr. 184, Charlottenburg ☎ 8 81 44 05. Renowned contemporary art gallery. Tues–Fri 2–6.30pm, Sat 10am–2pm.

Galerie Klaus Fischer, Motzstr. 9, Schöneberg ☎ 2 15 82 73. Graphics and prints, including work done in collaboration with writers and poets. By appointment only.

Galerie Kyra Maralt, Leibnizstr. 60, Charlottenburg ☎ 3 24 78 23. Avant-garde paintings and photos. Tues–Fri 1–7pm, Sat noon–4pm.

Galerie Nierendorf, Hardenbergstr. 19, Charlottenburg ☎ 8 32 50 13. Mainly German Expressionism. Closed by the Nazis in 1936, Karl Nierendorf's gallery was one of the first to exhibit Die Brücke group, Dix, Kirchner and Kandinsky. Tues–Fri 11am–6pm.

Galerie O Zwei, Oderberger Str. 2, Prenzlauer Berg ☎ 4 40 71 36. Resolutely uncommercial with a programme that includes installations, performance and stunts – like printing money that could be spent only in certain local bars on a certain day (and which declined in worth during that day). Tues–Fri 1–7pm.

The arts

Galerie Pels-Leusden, in der Villa Grisebach, Fasanenstr. 25, Charlottenburg ☎8 85 91 50. Renowned gallery, one of the oldest in Berlin. Specializes in classical-modern and contemporary art. Mon–Fri 10am–6.30pm, Sat 10am–2pm.

Galerie Sophien-Edition, Sophienstr. 24, Mitte ☎2 82 82 33. Small space in a back courtyard, featuring work by young artists. Wed–Sun noon–6pm.

Galerie Springer, Fasanenstr. 13, Charlottenburg ☎3 12 70 63. Top-class contemporary stuff. One of the galleries foremost in establishing the art scene in Berlin after World War II. Mon–Fri 2–7pm, Sat 11am–2pm.

Galerie Unwahr, Kleine Hamburger Str. 16, Mitte ☎6 11 55 10. Low-budget operation that attempts to bring unusual artists from abroad, particularly eastern Europe, to the attention of a wider public. Wed–Sun 4–7pm.

Galerie Wohnmaschine, Tucholskystr. 36, Mitte ☎30 87 20 15. Young gallery-owner Friedrich Loock opened his first gallery in his flat (he's one of the few people involved in the Scheunenviertel art scene who actually comes from the area) and now specializes in promoting the works of young, predominantly Berlin artists. Tues–Fri 2–7pm, Sat noon–5pm.

ifa Gallerie, Dorotheenstr. 72, Mitte ☎2 08 07 64. Promotes international cultural awareness with exhibitions by foreign artists, often from developing countries. Daily except Mon 2–7pm.

Kunst-Werke Berlin, Auguststr. 69, Mitte ☎2 81 73 25. Flagship gallery, heavily subsidized by the senate. Varies from has-been American artists carpet-bagging their way into the city arts scene to astute reflections on contemporary Berlin. Daily except Mon 2–6pm.

museumsakademie berlin, Rosenthaler Str. 39, Mitte ☎30 87 25 80. In a back courtyard, second floor; shows mainly young Berlin artists. Tues–Sat 2–7pm.

Petersen Galerie, Herderstr. 5, Charlottenburg ☎3 13 45 08. Indefinable mix of action art and "happenings". Mon–Fri 2–7pm, Sat 11am–2pm.

Raab Galerie, Potsdamer Str. 58, Tiergarten ☎2 61 92 17. Avant-garde and contemporary art; popular meeting place for the art "in" crowd. Mon–Fri 10am–7pm, Sat 10am–4pm.

Wewerka Gallerie, Homeyerstr. 32, Pankow ☎4 82 66 62. Prominent city gallery. Mon–Fri 9am–5pm.

Zwinger Gallerie, Gipsstr. 3, Mitte ☎28 59 89 07. One of the city's most important galleries, presenting a mixture of the avant-garde and conventional. Tues–Fri 2–7pm, Sat 11am–2pm.

Chapter 16

Children's Berlin

Berlin isn't most people's first choice when it comes to travelling with **kids**, but there's enough to keep them occupied during the day and, should you need them, baby-sitting and child-minding services are good. **Attitudes** to young children in Berlin strike the outsider as oddly ambivalent. While the city has a large number of single-parent families and excellent social service provisions for them, Berliners aren't too tolerant of kids in "adult" places, such as restaurants or bars; and though the city consists of a higher proportion of lakes, parks and woodland than any other European capital, there's little in them directly geared to entertaining children. If you're bringing kids, be prepared to do Berlin versions of the obvious things – zoos, museums and shops – rather than anything unique to the city. On a day-to-day basis, check the listings in *Tip* (under *Kindertheater* – "childrens' theatre"), *Zitty* (under *Kinder*) and *Prinz* for details of what's on.

Baby-sitting services

If you're planning a long stay in Berlin and need a **baby-sitter**, you could try placing a small ad on the noticeboard at the British Council, Hardenbergstr. 20, Charlottenburg (☎31 10 99 10); the charge is DM5 per month. The Amerika Haus, Hardenbergstr. 22–24, Charlottenburg ☎31 10 73), offers a similar service. There's an **emergency**

service available through Hekticket (☎24 31 24 31): call and mention the area you're in and, for no extra charge, you'll have a sitter. Other Berlin baby-sitting services include Heinzelmännchen der Freien Universität Berlin, Unter den Eichen 96, Steglitz (☎8 31 60 71; reservations for sitters taken Mon, Tues & Thurs 7am–6pm, Wed & Fri 7am–5pm); and TUSMA der Technischen Universität Berlin, Hardenbergstr. 35, Charlottenburg (☎3 15 93 40; reservations taken Mon–Fri 7am–7pm, Sat 8am–1pm). Rates are approximately DM13 per hour.

Parks and activities

With over a third of Berlin being forest or parkland, often with playgrounds dotted around, there's no shortage of spaces for children to go and let off steam. The most central and obvious choice is the **Tiergarten** northeast of Zoo Station, though this is rather tame compared to the rambling expanses of the **Grunewald** (S-Bahn Grunewald). In both parks paddle and rowing boats can be rented; bikes too at Grunewald S-Bahn station. The Grunewald borders the **Wannsee** lake, and it's fun to take the ferry over to the **Pfaueninsel** (Peacock Island), where there's a castle and plenty of strutting peacocks; see p.153 for details. **Freizeitpark Tegel** (U-Bahn Tegel, walk to the lake, then turn right) has playgrounds, trampolines, table tennis and paddle boats. The **Teufelsberg** (Devil's Mountain; bus

Children's Berlin

#149 to Preussenallee stop then walk for 20min south down Teufelsseechaussee), a large hill to the west of the city, is the place to go kite-flying at weekends. On the southeastern edge of the city, the woods around the **Grosser Müggelsee** (S-Bahn to Friedrichshagen) offer lakeside walking trails, and there's also a good nature trail around the **Teufelsee** (S-Bahn to Köpenick, bus #169 for five stops), just south of the Müggelsee.

Playgrounds and pools

Of the city's sports facilities, probably of most interest to kids is the **blub Badeparadies**, a slick indoor and outdoor pool complex at Buschkrugalle 64, Neukölln (☎6 06 60 60; U-Bahn Grenz Allee; Mon–Sat 10am–11pm, Sun & hols 9am–11pm; for 4hr, adults DM21, children up to 12 DM16). It's a bit of a trek out, and expensive to boot, but worth it for the waterfalls, whirlpools, 12-metre chute and wave machine, to name but a few facilities. There's a similar complex in the eastern suburb of Friedrichshain: the **SEZ-Sport und Erholungszentrum**, Landsberger Allee 77, Friedrichshain (☎42 18 20; tram #5 or #15 from Hackescher Markt). In summer there's also a small outdoor pool for children in the city centre Monbijoupark, the **Kinderbad Monbijou**, Oranienburger Str. 79, Mitte (☎2 82 86 52).

Excursions and trips

For views of Berlin from on high (in ascending order of terror), try the **Siegessäule** (not for little legs; see p.52), the **Fernsehturm** (p.97), and the **Funkturm** (p.145). Also, the **Müggelturm** (p.183) offers mildly hair-raising views of the woods and lakes at the southeastern edge of the city. Older children might appreciate a visit to the **Planetarium am Insulaner**, Munsterdamm 86, Steglitz (S-Bahn Priesterweg; guided tours Tues, Thurs & Fri 9pm; Sat 6pm & 9pm; Sun 4.30pm, 6pm & 8pm; adults DM7.50, children DM5).

Circuses and funfairs

The UFA-Zirkus at the UFA-Fabrik, Viktoriastr. 10, Tempelhof (☎75 50 30), is a residential **circus** offering an inventive alternative to the usual lions-and-clowns stuff. Circus troupes visit the city regularly during the summer months. To find out where and when, contact the Zirkusdirektorenverband, Xantener Str. 9, Wilmersdorf (☎8 81 46 60).

Small **funfairs** can be found almost year-round in Berlin on the small patches of park that dot the city. Check with the tourist office in the Europa Center for locations.

The Zoo and children's farms

The **Zoo**, Hardenbergplatz 8, Charlottenburg (☎2 61 11 01; daily 9am–6pm; DM11, children 3–15 DM5.50), near the train station of the same name, has an array of exotic animals in surroundings that attempt to mimic their natural habitat. Of most interest to kids will be the monkeys, orangutans and gorillas, the hippo house, the nocturnal rooms (a darkened area where varieties of gerbil-type creatures do their thing), pony and horse and trap rides around the zoo, and a playground. The **Aquarium** nearby, at Budapester Str. 32, Tiergarten (☎2 61 11 01); daily 9am–6pm, last Sat in month & public holidays until 10pm; DM11, children 3–15 DM5.50; combined tickets with zoo DM18/9), is also well worth the money, though probably best seen on a separate trip from the zoo. The huge **Tierpark**, Am Tierpark 125, Lichtenberg (☎51 53 10); U-Bahn Tierpark, trams #26 & #27, buses #194 & #296; open daily 9am to dusk – last entrance 4pm Oct–April; DM11, children DM4), in the eastern suburb of Friedrichsfelde, is worth a day out in itself – this sprawling zoo will be enough to exhaust even the most demanding child.

Educationally oriented **Kinder-bauern-höfen**, or children's farms, can be fun without knowing the language: they're to be found at Domäne Dahlem (see "Museums" for details), Wiener Str. 59,

Kreuzberg (U-Bahn Görlitzer Bahnhof or bus #129 then follow footpath; summer Mon, Tues, Thurs & Fri 10am–7pm, Sat & Sun noon–7pm; closes at 5pm during winter months); and in the UFA-Fabrik, Viktoriastr. 13–18, Tempelhof (U-Bahn Ullsteinstrasse; open daily from 10am). At the eastern end of town is **the FEZ Wühlheide**, An der Wühlheide, Köpenick (☎ 53 07 14 23), a large recreation park, packed with play- and activity-areas for kids of all ages (S-Bahn to Wühlheide; Mon–Fri 10am–5pm, Sat 1–5pm, Sun 10am–5pm) and including a popular narrow-gauge railway.

Museums

Almost all museums give a discount for children; the following are the most interesting in terms of special areas for kids, interactive exhibits, and fun things to do.

Dahlem Junior Museum, Arnimallee, Zehlendorf (near U-Bahn Dahlem-Dorf ☎ 8 30 14 34). Part of the Dahlem museum complex. Plenty for the kids to touch, especially in the ethnographic sections of the main museum, where boats and huts from the South Seas are just waiting to be climbed on and crawled into. Tues–Sun 9am–5pm; free.

Deutsches Technikmuseum Berlin, Trebbiner Str. 9, Kreuzberg ☎ 25 48 40 (U-Bahn Möckernbrücke, buses #129 & #248). Lots of gadgets to experiment with, plus a great collection of old steam trains and carriages. Highly diverting; the perfect thing for a wet afternoon. See p.123. Tues–Fri 9am–5.30pm, Sat & Sun 10am–6pm; DM5, children DM2.

Domäne Dahlem, Königin-Luise-Str. 49, Zehlendorf ☎ 8 32 50 00 (U-Bahn Dahlem-Dorf). This working farm and craft museum has plenty to entertain kids besides farmyard animals, especially at weekends when craft fairs are held here, and there are games and shows especially for children. Phone ahead to see what's on. Mon & Wed–Sun 10am–6pm; DM3, children DM1.50.

Düppel Museum Village, Clauertstr. 11,

Zehlendorf ☎ 8 02 66 71 (bus #115). Reconstruction of a medieval country village, with demonstrations of the handicrafts and farming methods of those times. Better for older children. May to mid-Oct Thurs 3–7pm, Sun 10am–5pm; DM3.

Museum for Natural History, Invalidenstr. 43, Mitte ☎ 20 93 85 91 (U-Bahn Zinnowitzer Str., trams #6, #8, #50, buses #157 & #245). The main attraction here is the gigantic Brachiosaurus skeleton, and once that's been admired the rest of the display is a bit of an anticlimax. However, it should keep animal-crazy kids happy for an hour or so. Tues–Sun 9.30am–5pm; DM5, children DM2.50.

Teddy-museum, Kurfürstendamm Karree (first floor), Charlottenburg ☎ 8 91 59 02. A collection of 5000 teddy bears and associated ephemera. Wed–Fri 3–6pm; free.

Wilmersdorf Community Gallery – Children's Gallery, Hohenzollerndamm 176, Wilmersdorf ☎ 86 41 39 10. Plenty of free material with which children can paint, draw and build, plus films of their choice. Mon–Fri 10am–5pm, Sun 11am–5pm. The local history museum next door has exhibitions on how the young and old of Wilmersdorf used to live (Mon, Wed & Fri 10am–2pm, Tues & Thurs 2–6pm; free).

Theatres and cinemas

Most cinemas show **children's films** during the school holidays but these are likely to be German-language only. The one time you're likely to catch English language kids' films is during the Berlin Film Festival in February (see p.271), which always offers a *Kinderprogramm* – children's programme. Berlin supports an astonishing number of **puppet theatres**, most of which put on worthwhile performances which kids don't need a knowledge of German to enjoy. For details of children's films and theatre performances, check the listings magazines or call the venues.

Children's Berlin

Children's Berlin

Berliner Figuren Theater, Yorckstr. 59, Kreuzberg ☎7 86 98 15. Constantly innovative puppet theatre with superbly crafted dolls.

Berliner Kino Museum, Grossbeerenstr. 57, Kreuzberg (no phone). Tiny place with old cinema furniture. Often shows silent comedies with Laurel & Hardy and the like.

Figurentheater Grashüpfer, Puschkinallee 16a, Treptow ☎53 69 51 50. Audience participation plays and puppetry for younger children.

Fliegendes Theater Berlin, Hasenheide 54, Kreuzberg ☎6 92 21 00. Puppet theatre for kids of 4 and over.

Grips, Altonaer Str. 22, Tiergarten ☎3 91 40 04. Top-class children's/young people's theatre; usually all improvised. German-speaking only.

Homunkulus Figurentheater, Florastr. 16, Pankow ☎4 85 40 46. Innovative puppet theatre.

Klecks, Schinkestr. 8–9, Neukölln ☎6 93 77 31. Puppet theatre aimed specifically at the 3- to 8-year-old age group.

LesArt, Weinmeisterstr. 5, Mitte ☎2 82 97 47. Plays and events for children of all ages.

Narrenspiegel, Hauptstr. 50, Schöneberg ☎7 81 45 49. Children's theatre presenting fairy tales and original productions.

Puppentheater Berlin, Haubachstr. 26, Charlottenburg ☎3 42 19 50.

Puppentheater Firlefanz, Sophienstr. 10, Mitte ☎2 83 35 60. Scheunenviertel puppet theatre.

Puppentheater Regina Wagner, Schönwalderstr. 33, Wedding ☎3 35 37 94.

Schaubude, Greifswalderstr. 81–84, Prenzlauer Berg ☎4 23 43 14. Beautiful, often elaborate puppets and settings in original productions.

Zaubertheater Igor Jedlin, Roscherstr. 7, Charlottenburg ☎3 23 37 77. Jedlin's one-man magic shows have been a hit for years.

Shops

There's a fair but not overwhelming selection of children's shops in Berlin, with an emphasis on wooden toys, ecological themes and multicultural education. Plastic pistols and toy soldiers are definitely out of favour and hard to find. For a full list of shops, see Chapter 18.

Anagramm, Mehringdamm 50, Kreuzberg ☎7 85 95 10. Neighbourhood bookstore with an excellent children's section and a reading corner.

Baby-Korb, Bundesallee 17, Wilmersdorf ☎8 83 30 07. Accessories and European designer clothes; middle price range.

British Bookshop, Mauer Str. 83–84, Mitte ☎2 38 46 80. Great selection of books for toddlers and pre-school children through to teenagers, all in English.

Die Schlange, Elberfelder Str. 6, Tiergarten ☎39 1 99 63. Snakes!

Elephant's Knot Meinekestr. 3, Charlottenburg ☎8 83 38 97. Designer kids' clothing including items from the current Moschino-influenced look on the Italian fashion scene.

Fliegender Hamburger, Torstr. 98, Mitte ☎2 82 22 67. Model trains and accessories.

Grober Unfug, Zossener Str. 32, Kreuzberg ☎69 40 14 90. Large display of international comics. See also p.284.

H+M, Kurfürstendamm 234 Charlottenburg ☎8 82 38 44. Now young fans of grown-ups' clothing store *H+M* (see p.287) have a branch all to themselves. This former turn-of-the-century café stocks a wide range of designs.

Jonglerie, Hasenheide 54, Kreuzberg ☎6 91 87 69. Magic tricks, balloons, and toys.

Kinderboutique Cinderella, Kurfürstendamm 46, Charlottenburg ☎8 81 28 63. Ralph Lauren for kids, and other top-notch designers.

Pre-Natal, Tauentzienstr. 1, Schöneberg. ☎2 11 73 40. Smart kiddies' clothing up to five years. Not cheap, but not a rip-off either considering the prominent location.

Speilbrett, Körtestr. 27, Kreuzberg ☎6 92 42 50. Picture books, games and puzzles.

Spiel-Vogel-Werner, Uhlandstr. 137, Wilmersdorf ☎8 73 23 77. Toys, games and model-making equipment.

Stiefelchen, Kurfüstendamm 51, Charlottenberg ☎8 81 29 43. Pricey but classy children's shoes.

Übermuth, Mommsenstr. 64, Charlottenburg ☎8 81 39 50. Charming children's wear, cute without being cutesy. Not cheap.

Vogel Spielwaren, Uhlandstr. 137, Wilmersdorf ☎8 73 23 77. Toys, games and model-making equipment.

Vom Winde Verweht, Eisenacher Str. 81, Schöneberg ☎78 70 36 36. Kites – the place to come before heading off for the Teufelsberg hill. Mon–Fri 2–6.30pm, Sat 10am–1pm.

Werken, Speilen, Schenken, Florastr./Schlossstr., Charlottenburg ☎7 90 80 90. Large store of games and hobby wares, with a kids' book section.

Wundertüte, Stuttgarter Platz 5, Neukölln ☎3 23 40 54. New and secondhand kids' clothes and accessories.

Zauberkönig, Hermannstr. 84, Neukölln ☎6 21 40 82. Illusions and tricks for magicians and their apprentices.

Zinnsoldaten, Skalitzerstr. 81, Kreuzberg ☎6 18 38 15. Enormous selection of tin soldiers and figures. Mon–Fri 4–6pm, Sat 11am–1pm.

Children's Berlin

Chapter 17

Sport

While Berliners go in for healthy eating in a big way, they're not famous for being fitness fanatics – they need all their energy for the frenetic nightlife. But there is a surprising variety of **participatory sports** available in the city, in case you feel like flexing all your muscles and not just those in your right arm. Sports **facilities** are fine if you're participating, not so hot if you're watching. There's only one city **soccer team**, BSC Hertha, who play in the Zweite Bundesliga (second division) at the Olympic Stadium, and sporting events are rarely at an international level. The only exception is the annual **International Women's Tennis Tournament**, in May, a highly popular event, with tickets at around DM35. For details, contact the Rot–Weiss Tennisclub, Gottfried-Von-Cramm-Weg 47–55, Wilmersdorf (☎89 57 55 21).

For a complete rundown of all annual sporting events, visit the **Landessportbund Berlin e.V**, Jesse-Owens-Allee 1–2, Charlottenburg (☎30 00 20), where you can pick up a copy of the yearly *Freizeitsports Kalender*, which has full details of both spectator and participatory sports.

Boat rental and ice skating

Paddle and rowing boats are a pleasant, if rather strenuous, way of enjoying Berlin's lakes during the summer. Try Strandbad Wannsee, the Neuer See in Tiergarten, or the quieter Schlachtensee. For other waterborne trips, see "Getting around", in Basics.

Some of the city lakes are also good for **ice skating**, but if they haven't frozen over and you're forced indoors, there are rinks at **Eissporthalle Berlin**, Jafféstrasse, Charlottenburg, an indoor rink with a disco on Monday evenings during the winter from 7.30 to 9.45pm (☎3 03 80; DM8), and **Eisstadion Berlin-Wilmersdorf**, Fritz-Wilding-Strasse 9, Wilmersdorf (☎8 24 10 12; DM6, children DM3), an outdoor rink with a limited skating time of up to two hours.

Fishing

There's plenty of choice of fishing spots in Berlin: for detailed information and the necessary visitor's fishing licence (*Fischereischein*), contact the **Fischereiamt beim Senator für Stadtentwicklung und Umweltschutz**, Havelchaussee 149, Charlottenburg (☎3 00 69 90), which can also advise on the best places to rent the necessary equipment.

Jogging

The most convenient but crowded spot is around the Tiergarten, just behind Zoo Station. Alternatively, it's worth trekking up to the area just south of the *Tempodrom*, where some very pretty and quiet wooded glades surround a small stream. The lakes around the city are also popular with joggers: try Schlachtensee, Krumme Lanke or Grunewaldsee.

If you're into long-distance running, a trip around Grunewald lake should be more of a challenge, or there's always the **Berlin Marathon** on the last weekend in September. This starts on Strasse des 17 Juni and ends nearly 50km later, after passing through Dahlem and along the Kurfürstendamm, back at the Kaiser-Wilhelm Memorial Church. To enter, write to **SCM Berlin**, Alt-Moabit 29, 10559 Berlin (☎3 92 11 02): closing date for entries is one month before the marathon. The SCM can also supply details on numerous other meetings, including the 10km race along the Kurfürstendamm in July.

Roller skating and skateboarding

Apart from zooming around Breitscheidplatz or the outskirts of the Alte Nationalgalerie, try:

Rollerhaus, Miraustr. 62–80, Wittenau ☎43 55 13 94. Huge skater's paradise wtih rink, ramps, pipes and more. Skate rentals available. Mon–Thurs 3–11pm, Fri 3pm–midnight, Sat 11am–midnight, Sun 11am–10pm. Adults DM8, children under 18 DM5.

Skate in, Schichauweg 48, Lichtenrade ☎7 21 50 70. Two halls, one for laps and disco, another, with ramps and pipes, for hot-dogging. Mon–Thurs & Sun 10am–10pm, Fri & Sat 10am–2am. Adults DM10, children under 18 DM8.

Z.B. Stadion Wilmersdorf, Fritz-Wilding-Str. 9, Wilmersdorf ☎8 24 10 12. Outdoor rink May–Sept Tues–Fri 9am–4pm.

Skiing

Believe it or not, there are five **ski slopes** in Berlin and, in the case of heavy snowfalls, skiing lessons on the Teufelsberg take place both day and night. Contact the **Skiverband Berlin e.V.im Landessportbund Berlin**, Bismarckallee 2, Wilmersdorf (☎8 91 97 98); for more information. You can rent skis from *Ski-sport-stadl*, Lützowstr. 104, Tiergarten (☎2 61 58 05).

Swimming pools

Most districts throughout the city have both indoor and outdoor **swimming pools** (not necessarily in the same place). Details of all opening times, prices, special offers and activities are listed in a biannual pamphlet issued by the Berlin Senate called *Öffnungszeiten der Städtischen Bäder Berlins*, and available from the tourist office and all swimming pools. Many pools have special women- or families-only days or evenings. Watch out too for **Warmbädetag**, when the water is warmer than usual – and admission usually more expensive.

Bad am Spreewaldplatz, Wiener Str. 59h, Kreuzberg ☎6 12 70 57. Popular indoor pool complete with sauna and wave machine. Tues–Fri 8am–9pm, Sat & Sun 1–9pm; Tues & Thurs women only, Wed men only, Fri, Sat & Sun mixed.

blub baderparadis, Buschkrugallee 64, Neukölln ☎6 06 60 60 (U-Bahn Grenz Allee). Magnificent indoor and outdoor pool with wave machine, 120-metre chute, whirlpools, waterfalls, sauna and fitness centre. 10am–11pm daily; for 4hr, DM21, children up to 12 DM16.

Freibad Halensee, Königsallee 5a, Wilmersdorf ☎8 91 17 03. Lakeside pool.

Freibad Friedrichshagen, Müggelseedamm 216, Köpenick ☎6 45 57 56. Outdoor swimming in the Müggelsee lakes, including a nudist section.

Olympia-Schwimmstadion, Olympischer Platz (Osttor), Charlottenburg ☎30 06 34 40. Outdoor pool, part of the Olympic Stadium complex.

Schwimhalle Fischerinsel, Fischerinsel 11, Mitte ☎2 01 39 85. GDR-era modern pool that's a convenient place for a dip if you're staying in the city centre.

SEZ (Sport- und Erholungszentrum), Landsberger Allee 77, Friedrichshain ☎42 18 20. Sports centre that has a superb pool complex with wave machine, fountains, high diving, saunas and a "polar bear pool". Also has an ice rink, a bowling alley and many other facilities. Entry varies for different facilities; swimming pool DM10.

Sport

Sport

Sommerbad Neukölln, Columbiadamm 169–190, Neukölln ☎68 09 27 75. Outdoor pool, open from May to mid-Sept.

Stadtbad Charlottenburg (Alte Halle), Krumme Str. 10, Charlottenburg ☎34 30 32 41. A delightful, old-fashioned tiled pool with sauna, which is relatively unknown and as a result seldom crowded. Women only Mon & Thurs. Mon–Sat from 7am, Wed from noon, irregular closing time.

Stadtbad Mitte, Gartenstr. 5, Mitte ☎30 88 09 10. Centrally located old-fashioned pool.

Stadtbad Neukölln, Ganghoferstr. 5, Neukölln ☎68 09 26 53. Swim and relax in a setting resembling a Hungarian spa. Two pools (one heated, one cool) decorated with fountains and mosaic tiles, encased in a maze of archways and colonnades. Sauna and steamroom available. Mon 2–6pm, Tues–Fri 7–8am & 2–9pm, Sat 8am–5pm.

Stadtbad Wilmersdorf, Mecklenburgische Str. 80, Wilmersdorf ☎8 21 02 60. Indoor pool with solarium, easily accessible from the city centre. Mon & Sat 7am–7pm, Tues–Fri 7am–9.40pm.

Strandbad Wannsee, Wannseebadweg 25, Zehlendorf ☎8 03 56 12. Outdoor pool with beach nearby, lots of activities in the summer and usually packed. May–Sept daily 7am–8pm.

Tennis

Apart from private clubs, some parks have **tennis courts**, notably the **Freizeitpark Tegel**, Reinickendorf (next to Tegeler See; ☎4 34 66 66). This is open from mid-April to mid-October (Mon–Fri 8am–4pm). Courts cost DM18 per hour from 4pm to 9pm, bookable up to six days in advance.

Tobogganing

A favourite winter pastime in Berlin – and not just for children. The **Teufelsberg**, and to the north of the city, the **Freizeitpark Lübars**, have the most hair-raising slopes, or for more nervous souls there's the **Rodelbahn Goethepark**, Transvaalstrasse, Wedding, and the **Rodelbahn Humboldthain**, Gustav-Meyer-Allee, Wedding. The **Senatsverwaltung für Stadtentwicklung, Umweltschutz und Technologie**, Am Köllnischen Park 3, Kreuzberg (☎32 47 10), has details of the best tobogganing spots.

Chapter 18

Shopping

Berlin isn't exactly a shopper's paradise, but there's an interesting selection of quirky specialist shops and earthy markets, and it's an excellent place to buy secondhand clothes. Glitz and dazzle are the prerogatives of **Wittenbergplatz** and the **Kurfürstendamm**, with its two miles of luxury galleries, antique shops and designer clothes shops, while the areas around **U-Bahns Wilmersdorfer Strasse**, **Walter-Schreiber-Platz** and **Hermannplatz** are good for chain-store clothes and all-purpose shopping. Ethnic foods and the "alternative" businesses are mostly in **East Kreuzberg**, with a more upmarket alternative scene in **Charlottenburg**. The big chains seem to have made it a matter of pride to open up branches in the eastern part of the city – something that, after the initial flush of euphoria, many are now regretting in the current economic climate. Eventually its shops will seem little different from those in the west, but at the moment what's on offer seems distinctly overpriced. The following listings, therefore, concentrate on western Berlin.

Normal **shop opening hours** are Monday to Friday 9am to 8pm, and Saturday 9am to 4pm. Smaller shops outside of the major shopping districts tend to close earlier: 6pm on weekdays and 2pm on Saturdays. Except for the larger places, **credit cards** are not widely accepted.

Books, magazines and prints

Although it's not the most exciting place in the world for books, Berlin is an ideal city for leisurely, unharassed browsing, with one bookshop, *Marga Schoeller*, even providing a few chairs for the purpose. There are quite a few places to find **English-language books**, most of them situated in or around Knesebeckstrasse, the street with Berlin's highest concentration of bookstores.

English-language/general

Autorenbuchhandlung, Carmerstr. 10, Charlottenburg ☎31 01 51. Some English-language books; regular readings by (non-English) authors.

Books in Berlin, Goethestr. 69, Charlottenberg ☎3 13 12 33. Small bookstore with a good selection of English-language history and popular fiction.

British Bookshop, Mauerstr. 83–84, Mitte ☎2 38 46 80. Berlin's best and biggest English-language bookstore, with a good selection of books on and about the city, as well as daily and Sunday papers, magazines and literature on cassette. Often organizes readings and other happenings.

Buchexpress, Habelschwerdter Allee 4, Zehlendorf ☎8 31 40 04. Specializes in English and American literature.

Fair Exchange, Dieffenbachstr. 58, Kreuzberg ☎6 94 46 75. Secondhand bookshop that specializes in English literature. Part-exchange possible.

Shopping

Children's bookstores are covered in Chapter 16; see pp.278–279.

Hugendubel, Tauentzienstr. 213, Charlottenburg ☎21 40 60. Huge general bookstore with a smattering of English-language books among its large stock.

Kiepert, Hardenbergstr. 4–5, Charlottenburg ☎31 18 80. Sprawling over the corner into Knesebeckstrasse, *Kiepert* has an excellent selection of books under every major subject heading, with a particularly good travel department and a limited but well-chosen assortment of English-language books. Branches at Friedrichstr. 63, Mitte ☎2 08 25 11 and Georgenstr. 2, Mitte ☎2 03 99 60.

Marga Schoeller, Knesebeckstr. 33–34, Charlottenburg ☎8 81 11 12. Rather eccentric shop assistants will point you to a good array of English fiction and non-fiction (this is the best place for esoteric topics in English) and then wrap up your purchases prettily on request.

Prinz Eisenherz, Bleibtreustr. 52 Charlottenburg ☎3 13 99 36. Primarily a gay bookshop, stocking a well-chosen selection of English and American authors. Also has author readings and book signing sessions. Friendly and helpful service.

Ringelnatz, Zossener Str. 15, Kreuzberg ☎6 92 45 01. Good all-rounder.

Discount/secondhand

Antiquariat Skowronska Thomas, Schustehrusstr. 28, Charlottenburg ☎3 41 58 33. A little of everything.

Buch- und Kunstantiquariat Tode, Dudenstr. 36, Kreuzberg ☎7 86 51 86. Deep in the back of the cellar is a good selection of old Penguins and literature.

Bücherhalle Buchhandlung, Hauptstr. 154, Schöneberg ☎7 81 56 69. Large, well-kept selection.

Knesebeck 11, Knesebeckstr. 11, Charlottenburg ☎3 12 28 36. General bookstore with a section of secondhand books, but also a good venue to scout for more unusual titles. Provides a quick and efficient mail order service.

Art and architecture

Bücherbogen am Savignyplatz, Stadtbahnbogen 593–594, Charlottenburg ☎3 12 19 32. Situated under the S-Bahn arches, a nevertheless airy and spacious setting for specialist art, architecture, film and photography books.

Kiepert, Hardenbergstr. 4–5, Charlottenburg ☎31 18 80. Art books at knock-down prices, usually on display on the street outside.

Kunstbuchhandlung Galerie 2000, Knesebeckstr. 56–58, Charlottenburg ☎8 83 84 67. Mainly photography; some art books and art exhibition catalogues.

Comics and science fiction

Grober Unfug, Zossener Str. 32, Kreuzberg ☎69 10 14 90. Large display of international comics, plus gimmicky T-shirts on sale. Prides itself on being the number-one place for cartoon enquiries. Often has exhibitions of cartoonists' work in the small gallery upstairs.

Modern Graphics, Oranienstr. 22, Kreuzberg ☎6 15 88 10. Small, serious shop stuffed with sci-fi comics, cards, and posters.

Videodrom Basement, Fürbringer Str. 24, Kreuzberg ☎6 94 90 10. Science fiction and subculture books, comics and videos.

Gay, feminist and radical

Lilith Frauenbuchladen, Knesebeckstr. 86–87, Charlottenburg ☎3 12 31 02. Selection of fiction by feminist writers, some in English; records and international newspapers.

Prinz Eisenherz Buchladen GmbH, Bleibtreustr. 52, Charlottenburg ☎3 13 99 36. Large selection of gay fiction and non-fiction, mainly in English.

Schwarze Risse, Gneisenaustr. 2a (in back courtyard), Kreuzberg ☎6 92 87 79. Radical bookstore located in the Mehringhof complex, home to several left and alternative shops and organizations.

Spiritual

Adhara, Pestalozzistr. 35, Charlottenburg ☎3 12 24 62. Cosy and friendly mind, body and spirit bookshop.

Daulat, Wrangelstr. 11, Steglitz ☎7 91
18 68. Books, body oils, crystals and
other esoterica.

Dharma, Akazienstr. 17, Schöneberg ☎7
84 50 80. Books with a slant towards
occultism and Oriental philosophies, with
a few in English.

Kristall Buchhandlung, Weimarer Str. 16,
Charlottenburg ☎3 13 87 93. Large,
well-stocked shop with a good variety of
titles, several in English.

Theatre and film

Bücherbogen am Savignyplatz,
Stadtbahnbogen 593–594,
Charlottenburg ☎3 12 19 32. See "Art
and architecture".

Kiepert, Hardenbergstr. 4–5,
Charlottenburg ☎31 18 80. See
"English-language/general".

Kommedia Medienbuchladen,
Potsdamer Str. 131, Tiergarten ☎2 16
13 69. Every aspect of media and communications.

Travel

British Bookshop, Mauerstr. 83–84, Mitte
☎2 38 46 80. See "Children's Berlin",
p.278 and "English-language/general"
p.283.

Buchhandlung Schropp, Lauterstr.
14–15, Steglitz. ☎8 59 49 11. Specialist
travel book and map store, with a large
well-chosen selection. Also stocks
detailed cycling maps of Berlin and
Germany.

Kiepert, Hardenbergstr. 4–5,
Charlottenburg ☎3 11 00 90. See
"English-language/general".

Newspapers and magazines

The majority of places selling international
newspapers and magazines are, as you
might expect, clustered around the Zoo
Station area, the best stocked being
Internationale Presse, Joachimstalerstr. 1,
Charlottenburg, open daily until midnight,
which has every London-printed morning
newspaper by 1pm. Also open late and
well laid-out for browsing is the selection
at **Ku'damm Karree**, Kurfürstendam 206–9,
Charlottenburg. Alternatively, there's a **kiosk**

on the corner of Joachimstalerstrasse and
the Kurfürstendamm, or try the store on
the first floor of the **Europa Center**, open
daily until 10pm. The new branch of
Internationale Presse, just inside the main
entrance to Zoo Station, also has a wide
selection of newspapers and magazines.
See also "Information and maps" in Basics.

Shopping

Posters, prints and cards

Ararat, Bergmannstr. 99a, Kreuzberg ☎6
93 5080. Huge selection of cards,
posters and prints.

Scenario, Savigny Passage (next to S-
Bahn Savignyplatz), Charlottenburg ☎3
12 91 99. Everything from run-of-the-mill
postcards to hand-painted greetings
cards. Part gift shop also, this shop is
great for browsing and not expensive.

CDs, records and tapes

Berlin doesn't have a large number of general record stores but there are plenty of
smaller shops dedicated to just one style.

Canzone Importschallplatten, Savigny
Passage S-Bahnbogen 583,
Charlottenburg ☎3 12 40 27. For lovers
of Latin American and Oriental sounds.
Expect some unusual finds, and a
superb CD selection.

City Music, Kurfürstendamm 11,
Charlottenburg ☎88 55 01 30. A small-
er, though equally central, version of
WOM (see overleaf).

Down-Beat, Dresdener Str. 19, Kreuzberg
☎61 60 93 26. Reggae, soul, R&B and
jazz, with some rare items.

Gelbe Musik, Schaperstr. 11,
Charlottenburg ☎2 11 39 62. Avant-
garde place thats's not so much a record
shop as a music gallery.

Groove Records, Pücklerstr. 36,
Kreuzberg ☎6 18 86 39. New wave.

Hard Wax, Paul-Lincke-Ufer 44a,
Kreuzberg ☎61 13 01 11. Premier
dance music specialist. Techno, trance:
you name it, they should have it. And if
they haven't, they'll get it for you.

Jazzcock, Fürbringer Str. 17, Kreuzberg
☎6 93 61 33. Over 5000 jazz titles;
specialists in European avant-garde.

Shopping

Mr Dead & Mrs Free, Bülowstr 5, Schöneberg ☎2 15 14 49. Primarily rock records on independent labels. And a great name.

Musicland, Klosterstr. 12, Spandau ☎3 32 20 72. Fine selection of hits ancient and modern, with many discounted items.

Rockers, Weinerstr. 20, Kreuzberg ☎6 18 27 12. Punk, metal, and hip-hop with a good selection of collectibles.

Soundgarden, Hauptstr. 9, Schöneberg ☎7 87 58 91. Buys and sells LPs and CDs modern and mainstream.

Soundman-Shop, Urbanstr. 112, Kreuzberg ☎6 93 47 58. Everything for your Walkman.

WOM, Augsburger Str. 35–41 (behind *Wertheim* on the Ku'damm), Charlottenburg ☎8 85 75 40, and at *Forum Steglitz*, Schlossstr. 1, Steglitz ☎7 91 80 83. Huge choice of records.

Clothes

Although they like to think of themselves as such, Berliners aren't exactly trendsetters: the punks look like pale imitations of their London cousins, hippy fashion has never really left town, and black from head to toe seems to be the sartorial standby for everyone from fourteen to to forty. Having said that, it's possible to pick up superb **bargains** at the many **secondhand** clothes stores (usually open Mon–Fri 11am–8pm, Sat 11am–4pm): you'll find unusual (and trendy) items here at very low prices. Easier access to the discarded wardrobes of the East has brought many odd items of official uniform and clothing since the Wall fell.

The main shopping areas at Wilmersdorferstrasse U-Bahn, Wilmersdorf, and Walter-Schreiber-Platz U-Bahn, Steglitz, have plenty of inexpensive name-brand styles. The Ku'damm and Friedrichstrasse boast the designer clothes shops, but unless you're very rich and very conservative, these aren't worth the time. A couple of exceptions are leather outlets, which have both cheap and good quality jackets, and, though you won't make any great savings, the excellent and stylish shoe shops.

Secondhand

More upmarket and designer secondhand clothing (Jill Sander, Yves Saint Laurent, etc) can be found by perusing Mommsenstrasse, starting at the Knesebeckstrasse end, in Charlottenburg.

Checkpoint, Mehringdamm 57, Kreuzberg ☎6 94 43 44. Funky club wear and other brightly coloured youth fashions. Shoes too.

Colours, Bergmanstr. 102 Hinterhof, Kreuzberg ☎6 94 33 48. Kin to *Made in Berlin* (see below), but with a wider range of clothes.

Garage, Ahornstr. 2, Schöneberg ☎2 11 27 60 (Mon–Sat noon–9pm). Largest secondhand clothes store in Europe; good for jackets, coats and jeans. Prices are according to weight (the clothes', not yours).

Global Textil, Mehringdamm 25, Kreuzberg ☎6 94 77 35. Small shop with conservative men's and women's fashions.

Made in Berlin, Potsdamer Str. 106, Tiergarten ☎2 62 24 31. Excellent selection of shirts, dresses and items in black: popular with the *Szene* crowd.

Second Coming, Motzstr. 15, Schöneberg. Rather a raggedy selection: hunt hard enough and you might find a bargain.

Secondo, Mommsenstr. 61, Charlottenburg ☎8 81 22 91. Exclusive designer clothes.

Textil-Basar, Hauptstr. 51, Shöneberg ☎8 59 28 29. Women's designer clothing, some leather goods.

New and designer labels

Clothes shops open, close and change hands almost as fast as bars in Berlin. To find the latest additions, wander down Bleibtreustrasse between the Ku'damm and Kantstrasse – this area is also great to browse in during the sales in January (*Winterschluss verkauf*) and July/August (*Sommerschluss verkauf*), when designer and less well-known names are on offer at knockdown prices – the length of Pestalozzistrasse (until Wilmersdorfer Strasse), Oranienstrasse, Stuttgarter Platz and Ludwigkirschstrasse, off Uhlandstrasse.

Blue Moon, Wilmersdorfer Str. 80, Wilmersdorf ☎3 23 70 88. Ultra-trendy *Szene* shop.

Boutique Soft, Bleibtreustr. 6, Charlottenburg ☎3 12 14 03. Jean Paul Gaultier, Thierry Mugler, Montana et al.

Donna Karan, Friedrichstr. 71 (in the Friedrichstadt Passagen), Mitte ☎20 94 60 10. The local branch of the wildy popular New York label.

Evento, Grolmanstr. 53–54, Charlottenburg ☎3 13 32 17. Understated linen and wool designs for women, some belts and bags. Great quality and reasonable prices.

Hallhuber, Kurfürstendamm 13, Charlottenburg ☎8 81 20 78. This store concentrates on affordable high-street fashions using natural fibres and carries its own label alongside others such as Esprit and Strenesse.

Hennes & Mauritz, Kurfürstendamm 20, Charlottenburg ☎8 82 62 99, and Tauentzienstr. 13a, Charlottenburg ☎2 13 90 92. Inexpensive, up-to-the-minute styles.

Inge Helf, Uhlandstr. 170, Charlottenburg ☎8 83 48 16. International designs and young fashions, in bigger than standard sizes.

Jean Pascale, Europa Center, Tauentzienstr. 9, Charlottenburg ☎2 62 54 90. Similar to H&M, only cheaper.

Kramberg, Kurfürstendamm 56–57, Charlottenburg ☎3 27 90 10. Stocks mainly Italian and US designs: Armani, Versace, Romeo Gigli, Donna Karan, plus Vivienne Westwood. Also sells US toiletries, exclusive to Berlin.

Levi's, Kurfürstendamm 36, Charlottenburg ☎8 85 78 10, and Schlossstr. 9, Steglitz ☎7 91 70 80. All styles of Levi's jeans stocked, along with Levi sweatshirts, T-shirts, footwear and bags. Jeans around DM140.

Lisa D., Rosenthaler Str. 40-41 (in the *Hackescher Höfe*), Mitte ☎2 82 90 61.

One of Berlin's very few local designers to have made a name for herself, Lisa D. favours fitted dresses in muted colours.

Marco Polo, Uhlandstr./Kurfürstendamm, Charlottenburg ☎8 85 48 86. Pure cotton knits, shirts, suits, wool sweaters and jeans for men and women. Slightly pricey, but quality is normally good. Some shoes. Also has a seconds shop at Kaiserdamm 7, Charlottenburg ☎3 25 61 60.

Mike's Laden, Nürnbergerstr. 53–55, Charlottenburg ☎2 18 80 20, and Rheinstr. 35, Schöneberg ☎8 52 16 21. Junior Gaultier for men, More and More and excellent (if pricey) underwear by Antiflirt. Also stocks Paul Smith and Jean Paul Gaultier.

Mientus Studio 2002, Wilmersdorfer Str. 73, Charlottenburg ☎3 23 90 77. Casual and formal up-to-the-minute menswear, ranging in price from reasonable to outrageously expensive.

Molotow, Gneisenaustr. 112, Kreuzberg ☎6 93 08 18. The best of west and east Berlin designers; middle price range.

Morgan, Friedrichstr. 67 (in the Friedrichstadt Passagen), Mitte ☎20 94 58 90. The Paris-based boutique offers its spirited, youthful clothing and accessories in this upscale shopping mall.

Nix, Auguststr. 86, Mitte ☎2 81 80 44. Unusual designs for women from a couple of young east Berliners.

Retro Mode, Langenscheidtstr. 6a, Schöneberg ☎7 84 62 55. Stylish Italian suits and shoes and, two doors down, a separate shop with leather jackets and coats.

Wicked Garden, Grunewaldstr. 71, Schöneberg ☎7 82 04 55. Extravagant and outrageous club wear.

Zeppelin, Oranienburger Str. 87, Mitte. Smart and expensive Italian clothes for men and women.

7 UP'S, Bleibtreustr. 48, Charlottenburg ☎8 83 51 08. Wonderful jackets.

Shoes

The best place to track down reasonably priced shoes is in the Wilmersdorfer Strasse U-Bahn area, where a number of

Shopping

For details of children's clothing stores, see pp.278–279 of Chapter 16.

Shopping

For serious cowboy and bike boot shopping, take a stroll along Kantstrasse from Schlüterstrasse to Wilmersdorfstrasse.

shops provide a vast selection. For something special, try the following.

Barfuss oder Lackschuh, Oranienburgerstr. 89, Mitte ☎28 39 19 91. The place to head for everything from designer shoes to (fashionable) workboots.

Luccico, Goltzstr. 34, Schöneberg, Zossenerstr. 32, Kreuzberg and Bergmannstr. 97, Kreuzberg. Wild and wacky Italian shoes, plus plainer varieties.

Roots, Kantstr. 57, Charlottenburg ☎3 23 30 21. Specializes in comfortable "earth" styles.

Saloon, Boots and Stuff, Oranienstr. 4, Kreuzberg ☎6 12 54 76. Cowboy boots and other Wild West essentials.

Schuhtick, Savignyplatz 11, Charlottenburg ☎3 15 93 80 and Tauentzienstr. 5, Schöneberg ☎2 14 09 80. Wide range of desirable shoes.

Zapato, Maassenstr. 14, Schöneberg ☎2 16 65 67. Full of interesting styles for men and women.

Underwear

As a rule, any form of underwear not bought in a supermarket – or at Hennes & Mauritz (see previous page) – is fiercely expensive in Berlin, and, from a quality point of view, not worth the extra outlay. Tights are individually sized and generally cut small – buy a couple of sizes larger for a good fit.

Femme Dessous, Fasanenstr. 31, Charlottenburg ☎8 82 53 39. Luxury lingerie from La Perla.

Fogal, Kurfürstendamm 216, Charlottenburg ☎8 81 15 16. Luxury tights and stockings for one-off occasions.

Körpernah, Maassenstr. 10, Schöneberg ☎2 15 74 71. About the only cheap and decent place in town. Well-designed French and Italian underwear; friendly service.

Rose, Rosa, Bleibtreustr. 5a, Charlottenburg ☎3 12 21 40. Hanro, Bleyle and other German brands.

Strumpfladen, Kurfürstendamm 66, Charlottenburg ☎8 83 62 54 and in Europa Center, Charlottenburg ☎2 61 20 25. Wide selection of tights, stockings and leggings.

Other accessories

Augenoptik Neumann, Gneisenaustr. 22, Kreuzberg ☎6 91 93 34. Large variety of 1950s glasses, currently all the rage here.

Fiona Bennett, Brunnenstr. 192, Mitte ☎2 82 84 92. Unique and avant garde designer hats for men and women.

Glasses, Nürnberger Str. 50–56, Schöneberg ☎2 18 24 74. Optician's set out like a cocktail bar, would you believe?

Goldpfeil, Tauentzienstr. 16, Charlottenburg ☎2 18 11 92. Exclusive bags and leather accessories.

Nine, Grolmanstr. 32, Charlottenburg ☎8 81 96 80. Superb quality leather bags backpacks, purses and shoes.

Optiker Hübner, Torstr. 119, am Rosenthaler Platz, Mitte ☎4 49 61 00. Purveyor of gimmick glasses (such as Batman and Robin style), and the "Windscreenwiper", for those rainy days.

Rio, Bleibtreustr. 52, Charlottenburg ☎3 13 31 52. Unusual decorative costume jewellers, specializing in earrings at affordable prices.

Sack & Pack, Kantstr. 48, Charlottenburg ☎3 12 15 13. Natural and black leather bags in sporty styles.

Scenario, Savigny Passage, Bogen 602, Charlottenburg ☎3 12 91 99. Upmarket gift shop, with leather goods and jewellery among its wares.

Fabrics

Adelt-Lederwar, Joachim-Friedrich Str. 41, Wilmersdorf ☎8 91 33 34. Leather.

Bramigk, Savignypassage, Charlottenburg ☎3 13 51 25. Italian cottons and silks in exquisite designs.

India art Boutique, Uhlandstr. 47, Charlottenburg ☎8 81 15 63. Oriental prints and silks at sensible prices.

Knopf Paul, Zossener Str. 10, Kreuzberg ☎6 92 12 12. Amazing range of buttons.

Schwarze Mode, Grunewaldstr. 91, Schöneberg ☎7 84 59 22. Latex.

Hair and beauty

There are plenty of places to get yourself dolled up and smelling sweet in Berlin, though note that as a rule hairdressers are closed on Monday. As well as the parfumiers listed below, there are also branches of *Parfumerie Douglas* (several on Kurfürstendamm – notably on the corner with Fasanenstr.) and *Sandra Droyerie* (Uhlandstr. and Wilmersdorfer Str., Charlottenburg), which carry an extensive range of up-to-date and established perfume lines.

HAIR

Carlo Piras, Fasanenstr. 42, Charlottenburg ☎ 8 82 11 00. Classy salon in the Italian school of hairdressing.

Heinz Schlicht, Uhlandstr./ Kurfürstendamm, Charlottenburg ☎ 8 82 73 05. A favourite among Berliners for twenty years. Service is professional but relaxed, and some of the staff are English.

Jason's Hairpower, Leibnizstr. 102, Charlottenburg ☎ 3 41 90 85. Ultra-hip and ultra-expensive hairstylist that has numbered David Bowie and Brigitte Nielsen among its customers.

Toni & Guy, Kaiser-Friedrich-Str. 1a, Charlottenburg ☎ 3 41 85 45. Local branch of the London-based hair stylists, and staffed with many English-speakers.

Udo Waltz, Kurfürstendamm 200, Charlottenburg ☎ 8 82 74 57. Hairstylist to the very rich and famous, including Annie Lennox and Claudia Schiffer. Booking advised.

Venus, Goltzstr. 38, Schöneberg ☎ 2 16 47 91. Punk and "normal" hairstyles at reasonable prices.

Vidal Sassoon, Schlüter Str. 38, Charlottenburg ☎ 8 84 50 00. After a successful run in Munich and Hamburg, this outfit has decided at long last to add Berlin to its list. From DM80. Predominantly English and American staff.

PERFUME

Belladonna, Bergmannstr. 101, Kreuzberg ☎ 6 94 37 31. Large choice of natural cosmetics.

Body Shop, Schlossstr. 25, Steglitz ☎ 7 92 25 57, also Zoo Station shopping complex, Charlottenburg. Berlin franchise of the familiar British-based concern. Daily until 9pm.

Harry Lehman, Kantstr. 106, Charlottenburg ☎ 3 24 35 82. Mix your smells then take them away, for DM5. Over fifty different brews, including one aptly named "Berlin".

Ligne de Vie, Friedrichstadt Passagen, Friedrichstr. 70, Mitte. Elegant and expensive scents in an upscale shopping complex.

Tessuti, Savigny Passage, Charlottenburg ☎ 3 13 80 16. Fashionable and rich display of natural fibres (no synthetic dyes) from Italy, with advice if needed.

Travel equipment

Bannat, Lietzenburger Str. 65, Charlottenburg ☎ 8 82 76 01. Dedicated to travel equipment.

Farradbüro Berlin, Hauptstr. 146 (next to Kleiststr. U-Bahn), Schöneberg ☎ 78 70 26 00. Every conceivable piece of equipment for bikes.

Outdoor, Bergmannstr. 108, Kreuzberg ☎ 6 93 40 80. A small but thorough store of boots, packs, jackets and travel books.

Department stores

There are no surprises inside Berlin's **department stores** and, with the exception of KaDeWe, they're only worth popping into to stock up on essentials or to buy **concert and theatre tickets** at the *Theaterkassen*. Listed below are the most central ones; check the phone book for outlying branches.

Galeries Lafayette, Französische Str. 23, Mitte ☎ 20 94 80. Branch of the upscale Paris-based department store.

Shopping

Surprisingly small, but packed with beautiful and expensive things.

Hertie, Wilmersdorfer Str. 118, Charlottenburg ☎31 10 50, and Blücherplatz 3, Kreuzberg ☎25 38 75. Not as wide a range of goods as at *Karstadt* (see below) and more expensive. The branch at Blücherplatz has a slightly better selection.

KaDeWe, Tauentzienstr. 21, Schöneberg ☎2 12 10. Content rather than flashy interior decor rules the day here. From designer labels to the extraordinarily good displays at the international delicatessen, where you can nibble on some piece of exotica or stock up on double-price El Paso taco mix, everything the consumer's heart desires can be found at this, the largest department store on the Continent.

Karstadt, Wilmersdorfer Str. 109, Charlottenburg ☎3 31 18 90, Schlossstr. 7, Steglitz ☎79 00 10, and Hermannplatz, Kreuzberg ☎6 95 50. Good basic all-rounder, classier and cheaper than *Hertie*. The branch at Hermannplatz is the best stocked.

Wertheim, Kurfürstendamm 231, Charlottenburg ☎88 00 30. A smaller and cheaper version of *KaDeWe*. Everything is beautifully laid out, with a particularly good menswear department.

Woolworth, Wilmersdorfer Str. 113, Charlottenburg ☎3 13 40 95, and Johannisthaler Chaussee 319, Neukölln ☎6 66 91 60. Good for cheap basic toiletries and essentials.

Food and drink

Of the city's **supermarket chains**, *Pennymarkt* is by far the cheapest for food and drink, although with a little less choice than the rest. *Ullrich*, on Hardenbergstrasse, underneath the railway bridge by Zoo Station, has an excellent selection of foods, wines and spirits and is very cheap despite its central position. The city's **speciality food shops** are spread throughout the town, though the majority of Turkish shops are in Kreuzberg. Health food is very popular,

particularly organically grown fruit and vegetables, and almost every neighbourhood has its own *Naturkostladen* or health-food shop, with vegetarian goodies, chemical-free beers and wines. The night shops listed in the box opposite all close before midnight, and are about a third more expensive than usual: they're particularly useful when everything else has closed for the weekend.

Bread and cakes

Freshly baked **bread** is one of the delights of Berlin, with *Vollkornbäckerei* providing wholemeal loaves fresh from their ovens. For cakes, it's hard to beat the quality and selection on offer at *KaDeWe* – you may end up paying slightly more here than elsewhere, but won't regret it.

Brendel, Grossbeerenstr. 16, Kreuzberg ☎2 16 91 55. Speciality breads, rolls, baguettes, etc.

Café Kranzler, Kurfürstendamm/ Joachimstalerstr., Charlottenburg ☎8 85 77 20. Pricey café and cake shop.

Café Möhring, am Gendarmenmarkt, Charlottenstr. 55, Mitte ☎2 03 90 22 40. One of a chain of old *Konditoreien*, some of which date back nearly a hundred years. This latest addition is the nicest.

Einhorn, Wittenbergplatz 5, Schöneberg ☎2 18 63 47. *Vollkorn* breads and cakes.

KaDeWe, Tauentzienstr. 21, Schöneberg ☎2 12 10. The sixth-floor food hall has over 400 different breads.

Leysieffers, Kurfürstendamm 218, Charlottenburg ☎8 85 74 80. Best selection of cakes, chocolates and biscuits in town.

Operncafé, Unter den Linden 5, Mitte ☎20 26 83. An amazing array of baroque extravaganzas in cakes and gateaux. Select one from the display, collect a ticket and give it to the waiter.

Weichardt, Mehlitzstr. 7, Wilmersdorf ☎8 73 80 95. Probably the best *Vollkorn* bakery in town: delicious cakes and breads.

Wiener Conditorei Kaffeehaus am Roseneck, Hollernzollerndamm 92, Zehlendorf ☎8 26 60 35. Cakes made by the *Operncafé*, on sale in Zehlendorf.

Wiener Kaffeehaus, Reichstr. 81, Charlottenburg ☎3 04 55 35. By far the most relaxing store in the Wiener chain, and a great place to linger. Open to 8pm weekday evenings.

Coffee and tea

Eduscho, Kurfürstendamm 142, Charlottenburg ☎8 92 20 87 (and branches around town). Good-quality ground coffee, and the cheapest stand-up coffee in the city.

King's Teegarden, Kurfürstendamm 217, Charlottenburg ☎8 83 70 59. Buy your tea downstairs or drink a range of brews upstairs to a background of classical music. Open all day Saturday.

Tchibo, Kurfürstendamm 11, Charlottenburg ☎8 81 11 94 (other branches around the city). The second most popular coffee shop after *Eduscho*,

---

Night shops

The following open beyond normal hours, but charge considerably for the convenience. Most **Turkish shops**, the majority being in Kreuzberg and Neukölln, are open Saturday afternoons and Sundays 1–5pm.

Edeka, in U-Bahn Schlossstrasse, Steglitz (Mon–Fri 3–10pm, Sat 1–10pm, Sun & holidays 10am–8pm).

Metro, in U-Bahn Fehrbeliner Platz 1, Wilmersdorf (daily 11am–10.30pm).

Metro, in U-Bahn Kurfürstendamm, Charlottenburg (Mon–Fri & Sun 11am–11pm, Sat 11am–midnight).

Reise Point Markt, Friedrichstrasse S- & U-Bahn, Mitte (Mon–Sat 6am–10pm, Sun 8am–10pm). Everything from videos to shaving cream, but at hugely inflated prices.

---

with the advantage that you can mix your own blend of beans from a small choice at the counter.

TeeHaus, Krumme Str. 35, Charlottenburg ☎3 13 01 31. A tea lover's paradise: teas sold loose and to suit every taste. Also English jams and natural honeys.

Tee & Tee, Kaiser-Wilhelm-Passage at Kaiser-Wilhelm-Platz 1–2, Schöneberg ☎7 81 12 30. One of a chain of small and well-stocked shops of teas and accessories.

Delicatessens and ethnic foods

Alimentari e Vini, Skalitzer Str. 23, Kreuzberg ☎6 11 49 81. A slick shop in scruffy Kreuzberg offering wines, pastas and other Italian deli items.

Aqui Espana, Kantstr. 34, Charlottenburg ☎3 12 33 15. Spanish and South American foods, though rather pricey.

Fuchs & Rabe, Schlossstr. 119, Steglitz ☎7 92 81 68. Row upon row of exotic and unusual cheeses and dishes containing cheese. Made-to-order rolls at lunchtime. Also at Ludwigskirchstr. 2, Wilmersdorf ☎8 82 39 84, for fresh home-made pasta and a good stand-up *Imbiss*.

Galeries Lafayette, Französische Str. 23, Mitte ☎20 94 80. Like the larger KaDeWe, this swank department store offers a gourmet food section with delectables from around the world.

Holland Shop, Mehringdamm 73, Kreuzberg ☎6 92 69 67. Far Eastern specialities, lots of cheap herbs and spices, flavourings and sauces.

Italian Spezialitäten, Nollendorfstr. 13, Schöneberg ☎2 16 60 50. Italian meats, cheeses and wines. The fresh pasta is a disappointment.

KaDeWe, Tauentzienstr. 21, Schöneberg ☎2 12 10. The sixth-floor food hall (*Feinschmecker Etage*) of the giant department store is a gourmet's delight: 400 types of bread, 1200 cheeses and 1400 meats, plus cafés where you can sample lots of the goodies on sale. The dough for their French bakery, *Le Notre*, is flown in from Paris daily.

Shopping

Shopping

Kolbo, Auguststr. 78, Mitte ☎2 81 31 35. Kosher food and wine, and Jewish specialities.

Ku Long, Nollendorfstr. 8, Schöneberg ☎2 16 66 98. Southeast Asian ingredients.

La Cantina, Kreuzbergstr. 76, Kreuzberg ☎7 85 87 93. Top-class Italian deli, with olive oils, fresh pasta and exotic vinegars.

Nana, Linienstr. 154, Mitte ☎2 85 96 65. Mediterranean specialities in the still re-awakening eastern side of the city.

Salumeria da Pino & Enzo, Windscheidstr. 20, Charlottenburg ☎3 24 33 18. Wines and yummy Italian delicacies. Mouthwatering nibbles available for lunch.

Sikasso, Dresdener Str. 124, Kreuzberg ☎6 14 87 29. African food and objets d'art.

Südwind, Akaziestr. 7, Charlottenburg ☎7 82 04 39. Wines and products from Tuscany. Very good value.

Fish and meats

Alternative Fleischerei, Körtestr. 20, Kreuzberg ☎6 91 64 86. Cows and chickens that weren't stuffed with chemicals and hormones before they were killed.

Fische & Geflügel, Maxstr. 17, Wilmersdorf ☎4 56 68 07. Family-run business specializing in fish and wild-fowl. A bit out of the way, but worth it.

Rogacki, Wilmersdorfer Str. 145–146, Charlottenburg ☎3 41 40 91. Great selection of fresh and smoked fish, with an eat-in *Imbiss*.

Schlemmermeyer, Schlossstr. 6, Steglitz ☎7 93 31 38. Bavarian sausage, cooked and smoked meat heaven.

Health food

Kräuter Kuhne, Tempelhofer Damm 177, Tempelhof ☎7 51 60 22. Herbal specialist, with a good selection of sweet and savoury snacks.

Lotus, Pestalozzistr. 29, Charlottenburg ☎3 13 46 33. Health-food shop with vegetarian meals and salads to eat in or take out. Closes at 4.30pm.

Mutter Erde, Behaimstr. 18, Charlottenburg ☎3 41 79 55. Large stock of everything from organic vegetables and wines to "green" household products.

Naturkost Mitte, Linienstr. 150, Mitte ☎2 85 84 33. Small shop with vegetables and other organically grown products.

Risico, Dieffenbachstr. 59, Kreuzberg ☎6 94 28 62. Health-food shop and café.

Sesammühle, Knesebeckstr. 89, Charlottenburg ☎3 12 51 99. Health foods.

UFA-Fabrik-Laden, Viktoriastr. 13, Tempelhof ☎75 50 31 51. Wholefoods and goods from developing and politically emergent countries.

Wines and spirits

Bernhard & Hess Weingeschäft, Bergmannstr. 16, Kreuzberg ☎6 92 39 12. Upmarket wines from France and Italy, plus oils and exotic vinegars.

La Cantina, Kreuzbergstr. 77, Kreuzberg ☎7 86 39 43. Italian wines.

Der Rebgarten, Bergmannstr. 112, Kreuzberg ☎6 94 55 02. Organically grown wines and juices. Open afternoons and Saturday mornings only.

Vendemmia, Akaziestr. 20, Schöneberg ☎7 84 27 28. Bulk-bought Italian wines, so good for bargains. Also sells inexpensive olive oil.

Wein & Glas Compagny, Prinzregentenstr. 2, Schöneberg ☎2 35 15 20. German and French wines (and some glasses).

Weinkeller, Gneisenaustr. 15, Kreuzberg ☎6 93 46 61. Spanish, French, Italian and German wines, and sherries and whiskies from the cask.

Weinstein, Lychener Str. 33, Prenzlauer Berg ☎4 41 18 42. Italian and French wines from the barrel, filled in the shop.

Markets

There are several food markets within each quarter of the town, too numerous to mention here; listed below is a selection of the best **flea markets** and outdoor food markets. For junk shops, Suarezstrasse in Charlottenburg, Gotzstrasse in Schöneberg and Bergmannstrasse in Kreuzberg are the places to head.

Flea markets

Antiquitäten- und Flohmarkt, Bahnhof Friedrichstrasse (under the railway arches 190–203), Mitte. Tending more towards the antique end of things with numerous little shops selling everything from books to jewellery. Not particularly cheap. Mon & Wed–Sun 11am–6pm.

Brandenburg Gate, Unter den Linden, Mitte. Russian memorabilia – fur hats for DM40, watches for DM30, loads of badges and military stuff, and dubious bits of the Wall. Don't forget to haggle. At weekends this also extends to the back of the Reichstag building in the eastern side – where you'll need to delve more deeply but the outcome is much more rewarding. A good place to stock up on unusual German Reich mark notes from the hyper-inflationary pre-Hitler period. Daily 8am–7pm.

Fehrbelliner Platz. Small flea market next to the U-Bahn station. Lots of plants and old pictures. Sat & Sun 8am–3pm.

Humboldt University, Unter den Linden, Mitte. Secondhand books, mostly in German. Daily, around 2pm onwards.

Kunst und Trödelmarkt Hackescher Markt, Dircksenstrasse. A real junk market, tucked away in the railway arches north of Alexanderplatz station. You may find something of interest among the 1960s radios and bits of GDR ephemera. Mon–Fri 10am–6pm, Sat 10am–2pm.

Marheinekeplatz Markthalle, Marheinekeplatz, Kreuzberg. Indoor market with a little of everything and some bargains. Good for fresh fruit and veg and especially fish. Mon–Sat 8am–6pm.

Strasse des 17 Juni, north side of road near Ernst-Reuter-Platz, Charlottenburg. Pleasant enough for a Sunday morning stroll, but the most expensive of the flea markets, and with horribly tourist-oriented wares. Good for embroidery and lace though. Sat & Sun 10am–5pm.

Türken-Markt, Kottbusser Damm/ Maybachufer, Neukölln. Definitely worth a visit, especially on Friday when there's a real Oriental flavour. Handy for all things Turkish, especially cheese, bread, olives and dried fruits, all at rock-bottom prices. Tues & Fri noon–6pm.

Winterfeldtmarkt, am Winterfeldtplatz, Schöneberg. Arguably the most popular market in Berlin, with brightly printed clothes, exotic smells floating in the breeze, and plenty of cafés nearby for a drink afterwards. Wed & Sat 8am–1pm.

Wittenburgplatz market, Wittenbergplatz U-Bahnhof, Schöneberg. Small market selling food and clothing. Tues & Fri 8am–1pm.

Zille-Hof, Fasanenstr. 14, Charlottenburg. Not so much a flea market as an over-grown junkshop with reproduction curios, old street signs and a miscellany of interesting junk. Not especially cheap, but good fun. Mon–Fri 8.30am–5.30pm.

Shopping

Flowers and plants

Flowers are frequently given as gifts, and are almost a prerequisite for birthdays and other special occasions. When looking for flowers, avoid the Ku'damm, where prices are steep and quality is poor, and take a look instead along some of the side streets. It's more fun choosing your own bouquet. Simply explain roughly what colours you'd like and the price you'd prefer to pay – try around DM20. The city's many open-air markets also sell interesting arrangements at affordable prices.

Art Floral, Grolmanstr. 29, Charlottenburg ☎8 83 45 84. Beautiful flowers, plants and ceramic pots from DM10.

Blumenladen, Südstern U-Bahn, Kreuzberg ☎6 91 89 24. Flowers on Sunday.

Exotic Green, Schönebergweg 2-4, Schöneberg ☎6 64 43 01. Bamboo and other indoor plants and trees.

Petit Fleur, Knesebeckstr. 88, Charlottenburg ☎3 12 93 77. Floral arrangements and plants for all occasions; also sells greetings cards and wrapping paper.

Shopping

Die Palme, Kurfürstendamm 102, Wilmersdorf ☎8 92 46 33. Exotic flowers and plants, and bonsai trees.

Crafts and antiques

Antike Uhren, Pestalozzistr. 54, Charlottenburg ☎3 23 21 36. Sells and repairs antique clocks.

Bale-Bale, Savignyplatz 6, Charlottenburg ☎3 12 90 66. Arts and crafts from India, Pakistan and Indonesia.

Casa Mano, Nikolaikirchplatz 5–7, Mitte ☎2 42 53 96. Baskets and other hand crafted gift items from far away lands.

El Condor, Kantstr. 36, Charlottenburg ☎3 13 98 28. Latin American crafts.

Dritte-Welt-Laden, inside the Gedächtniskirche, Charlottenburg ☎8 31 54 32. Non-profit organization selling handicrafts from the Third World.

Fingers, Nollendorfstrasse 35, Schöneberg ☎2 15 34 41 Weird scenes from the goldmine that was 1950s America. Ceramics, electrical household items and other odds and sods.

Jukeland, Crelle Str. 13, Schöneberg ☎7 82 33 35. For lovers of 50s paraphernalia American-style, including a selection of hugely expensive jukeboxes,

Lampen aus 100 Jahren, Mittenwalder Str. 30, Kreuzberg ☎6 92 11 15. Antique and Art Deco lamps, both sophisticated and outrageous.

Miscellaneous

For a cross-section of the weird and wonderful, Berlin is hard to beat.

Atzert-Radio, Kleiststr. 32, Schöneberg ☎2 12 98 40. Do-it-yourself radio and electronics paradise.

Bären–Luftballons, Kurfürstenstr. 31–32, Tiergarten ☎2 61 92 99. Balloons in all colours, shapes and sizes.

Foto Meyer, Viktoria-Luise- Platz 6, Schöneberg ☎2 35 09 90. Reasonably

priced cameras and darkroom equipment, plus good-quality film processing.

George Behrendt, Hauptstr. 18, Schöneberg ☎7 81 49 06. Everything for parties, including fancy-dress outfits.

Kaufhaus Schrill, Bleibtreustr. 46. Charlottenburg ☎8 82 40 48. An Aladdin's Cave of delights, from fish-shaped ties to fluorescent tutus.

Küchenladen, Knesebeckstr. 26, Charlottenburg ☎8 81 39 08. Everything for the foodie, from tortoiseshell tea-spoons to Italian cookbooks.

Münzfachgeschäft Moneta, Friedrichstr. 114, Mitte ☎2 82 67 20. An old-fashioned little shop of coins and medals.

Ostasiatica, c/o Wolfgang Bock, Gardeschützenweg 92, Steglitz ☎8 33 29 29. The ultimate in idiosyncrasy: Europe's only authorized dealer in Samurai swords.

Pfeifenmacher, Bismarckstr. 60, Charlottenburg ☎3 41 63 03. Huge selection of tobaccos and own-brand pipes made on the premises.

Souvenir Shop Boenicke, in Europa Center, Charlottenburg, ☎2 61 46 82. The place to get kitsch mementos like cuckoo clocks and beer steins.

Take Off, Langenscheidtstr. 7, Schöneberg ☎7 82 27 72. Mickey Mouse knick-knacks and presents.

Vom Winde Verweht, Eisenacher Str. 81, Schöneberg ☎78 70 36 36. Kites.

Zauberkönig, Hermannstr. 84, Neukölln ☎6 21 40 82. Illusions, tricks, and other magicians' equipment.

Zinnfiguren Kabinet, Knesebeckstr 88, Charlottenburg ☎3 13 08 02. Beautifully made model soldiers – not cheap, and certainly not toys.

Zinnsoldaten, Skalitzerstr. 81, Kreuzberg ☎6 18 38 15. Enormous selection of tin figures.

Part 4

The Contexts

The historical framework

Few cities have a history as tangible as that of Berlin. It's impossible not to be aware of the forces that have shaped the city as you walk through its streets – they have left physical reminders in the shape of shrapnel scars on buildings and, most telling of all, a huge dead swathe right through the middle of the city.

If any city embodies the twentieth century it is Berlin. Even after the darkest days of the Cold War, when agreements between the great powers put an end to the city's role as the prime focus for international tension, Berlin still somehow symbolized the postwar order. And this whole process continues. Though the space where the Wall once ran will gradually be filled, the legacy of forty years of Communist government cannot be erased overnight. The unification of Germany has raised startling problems for its capital city: today Berlin is once again the setting for world history's next instalment.

Beginnings

Archeologists reckon that people have lived around the area of modern-day Berlin for about 60,000 years. Traces of hunter-gatherer activity dating from about 8000 BC and more substantial remains of Stone Age farming settlements from 4000 BC onwards have been discovered. The Romans regarded this as barbarian territory and left no mark on the region. Although **Germanic tribes** first appeared on the scene during the fifth

and sixth centuries AD, many of them left during the great migrations of later centuries, and the vacated territories were occupied by **Slavs**. Germanic ascendancy only began in the twelfth and thirteenth centuries, when Saxon feudal barons of the Mark of Brandenburg expelled the Slavs. The **Saxons** also granted municipal charters to two humble riverside towns – where the Berlin story really begins.

The twin towns

Sited on marshlands around an island (today the Museuminsel and Fischerinsel) at the narrowest point on the River Spree, **Berlin** and **Cölln** were on a major trade route to the east, and began to prosper as municipalities. Despite many links (including a joint town hall built in 1307), they retained their separate identities throughout the fourteenth century, when both received the right to mint their own coinage and pronounce death sentences in local courts. Their admission to the powerful **Hanseatic League** of city-states in 1369 confirmed their economic and political importance. By 1391, Berlin and Cölln were virtually autonomous from the Mark of Brandenburg, which grew ever more chaotic in the early years of the fifteenth century.

Order was eventually restored by **Friedrich Hohenzollern**, burgrave of Nuremburg, whose subjugation of the province was initially welcomed by the burghers of Berlin and Cölln. However, when his son Johann attempted to treat them likewise, they forced him to withdraw to Spandau. It was only divisions within their ranks that enabled **Friedrich II**, Johann's brother, to take over the two cities. Some of the guilds offered him the keys of the gates in return for taking their part against the Berlin-Cölln magistrates. Friedrich obliged, then built a palace and instituted his own harsh rule, forbidding any further union between Berlin and Cölln.

After swiftly crushing a **rebellion** in 1448, Friedrich imposed new restrictions. To symbolize the **consolidation of Hohenzollern power**, a chain was placed around the neck of Berlin's heraldic symbol, the bear, which remained on the city's coat of arms until 1875. After the

Hohenzollerns moved their residence and court here, Berlin-Cölln assumed the character of a *Residenzstadt* (royal residence) and rapidly expanded, its old wattle and daub dwellings replaced with more substantial stone buildings – culminating in a Renaissance Schloss finished in 1540. Yet life remained hard, for despite wars involved in the Reformation, Berlin-Cölln lagged behind the great cities of western and southern Germany, and in 1576 it was ravaged by plague. The **Thirty Years' War** (1618–1648) marked a low point. After repeated plundering by Swedish troops, the twin towns had lost half their population and one third of their buildings by the end of the war.

The Great Elector

The monumental task of postwar reconstruction fell to the Mark's new ruler, Elector Friedrich **Wilhelm of Brandenburg** (1620–1688), who was barely out of his teens. Massive fortifications were constructed, besides the residences and public buildings necessary to make Berlin-Cölln a worthy capital for an Elector. (Seven Electors – three archbishops, a margrave, duke, count and king – were entitled to elect the Holy Roman Emperor.) In recognition of his achievements, Friedrich Wilhelm came to be known as the **Great Elector**. After defeating the Swedes at the Battle of Fehrbellin in 1675, the Mark of Brandenburg was acknowledged as a force to be reckoned with, and its capital grew accordingly. Recognizing the value of a cosmopolitan population, the Elector permitted Jews and South German Catholics to move here and enjoy protection as citizens.

A later wave of immigrants affected Berlin-Cölln even more profoundly. Persecuted in France, thousands of **Protestant Huguenots** sought new homes in England and Germany. The arrival of five thousand immigrants – mostly skilled craftworkers or traders – revitalized Berlin-Cölln, whose own population was only twenty thousand. French became an almost obligatory second language, indispensable for anyone looking for social and career success. Another fillip to the city's development was the completion of the **Friedrich Wilhelm Canal**, linking the Spree and the Oder, which boosted its status as an east–west trade centre.

Carrying on from where his father had left off, Friedrich III succeeded in becoming King of Prussia to boot (and thus gained the title of

Friedrich I), while Berlin continued to expand. The **Friedrichstadt and Charlottenburg quarters** and the **Zeughaus** (now the Museum für Deutsche Geschichte in eastern Berlin) were created during this period, and Andreas Schlüter revamped the Elector's palace. In 1709, Berlin-Cölln finally became a single city named **Berlin**. None of this came cheap, however. Both Berlin and the Mark Brandenburg were heavily in debt by the end of Friedrich's reign, to the point where he even resorted to alchemists in the hope of refilling his treasury.

Berlin under the Soldier King

The next chapter in the city's history belongs to Friedrich I's son, **Friedrich Wilhelm I** (1688–1740). Known as the **Soldier King** and generally reckoned to be the father of the Prussian state, he dealt with the financial chaos by enforcing spartan conditions on his subjects and firing most of the servants at court. State revenues were henceforth directed to building up his army, and culture took a back seat to parades (eventually he even banned the theatre). While the army marched and drilled, the populace had a draconian work ethic drubbed into them – Friedrich took to walking about Berlin and personally beating anyone he caught loafing.

Friedrich tried to introduce conscription but had to make an exception of Berlin when the city's able-bodied young men fled en masse to escape the army. Despite this, Berlin became a **garrison town** geared to maintaining the army: the Lustgarten park of the royal palace was transformed into a parade ground, and every house was expected to have space available for billeting troops. Much of modern Berlin's shape and character can be traced back to Friedrich – squares like **Pariser Platz** (the area in front of the Brandenburg Gate) began as parade grounds, and **Friedrichstrasse** was built to link the centre with Tempelhof parade ground. When Friedrich died after watching rehearsals for his own funeral (and thrashing a groom who made a mistake), few Berliners mourned.

Frederick the Great and the rise of Prussia

His son, Friedrich II – known to historians as **Frederick the Great** (1712–1786) and to his subjects as *"Der alte Fritz"* – enjoyed a brief honeymoon as a liberalizer, before reverting to his father's ways. Soon Prussia was drawn into a series of wars that sent Berlin taxes through the roof, while the king withdrew to Sanssouci Palace in Potsdam, where only French was spoken, leaving the Berliners to pay for his military adventurism. Friedrich's saving grace was that he liked to think of himself as a philosopher king, and Berlin's **cultural life** consequently flourished during his reign. This was thanks in part to the work of the leading figures of the German Enlightenment, like the playwright Gotthold Ephraim Lessing and the philosopher Moses Mendelssohn, both of whom enjoyed royal patronage.

It was the **rise of Prussia** that alarmed Austria, Saxony, France and Russia into starting the **Seven Years' War** in 1756. Four years later they occupied Berlin and demanded a tribute of 4 million thalers, causing City President Kirchstein to faint on the spot. This was later reduced to 1.5 million when it was discovered that the city coffers were empty. Berlin was eventually relieved by Frederick, who went on to win the war (if only by default) after Russia and France fell out. Victory confirmed Prussia's power in Central Europe, but keeping the peace meant maintaining a huge standing army.

Besides direct taxation, Frederick raised money by establishing **state monopolies** in the trade of coffee, salt and tobacco. Citizens were actually required to buy set quantities of these commodities whether they wanted them or not. This was the origin of some of Berlin's most celebrated culinary delicacies: sauerkraut, Kassler Rippchen (salted pork ribs) and pickled gherkins were all invented by people desperate to use up their accumulated salt. Popular discontent was muffled by Frederick's **secret police** and **press censorship** – two innovations that have stuck around in one form or another ever since.

Unter den Linden came into its own during Frederick's reign as grandiose new edifices like the **Alte Bibliothek** sprang up. Just off the great boulevard, the **Französischer Dom** was built to serve the needs of the Huguenot population, while the construction of Schloss Bellevue in the Tiergarten sparked off a new building boom, as the wealthy flocked into this newly fashionable area.

Decline and occupation

After Frederick's death Prussia went into a **decline**, culminating in the defeat of its once-invincible army by French revolutionaries at the Battle of Valmy in 1792. The decline went unchecked under Friedrich Wilhelm II (1744–1797), continuing into the Napoleonic era. As Bonaparte's empire spread across Europe, the Prussian court dithered, appeasing the French and trying to delay the inevitable invasion. Life in Berlin continued more or less as normal, but by August 1806 citizens were watching Prussian soldiers set off on the march westwards to engage the Napoleonic forces. On September 19, the king and queen left the city, followed a month later by Count von der Schulenburg, the city governor, who had assured Berliners that all was going well right up until he learned of Prussia's defeat at Jena and Auerstadt.

Five days later French troops marched through the **Brandenburg Gate** and Berlin was occupied. On October 27, 1806, Napoleon himself arrived to head a parade down Unter den Linden – greeted as a liberator by the Berliners, according to some accounts. **French occupation** was uneventful, interrupted only by a minor and unsuccessful military rebellion, and ending with the collapse of Napoleon's empire after his defeats in Russia and at the Battle of Leipzig in 1813.

The rebirth of Prussia

With the end of French rule, the Quadriga (the Goddess of Victory in her chariot) was restored to the Brandenburg Gate (see p.63), but the people of Berlin only gained the promise of a constitution for Prussia, which never materialized – a portent of later conflict. The real victor was the **Prussian state**, which acquired tracts of land along the Rhine, including the Ruhr, which contained the iron and coal deposits on which its military might was to be rebuilt.

The war was followed by an era of reaction and oppression, which did so much to stifle intellectual and cultural life in Berlin that the philosopher Wilhelm von Humboldt resigned from the university in protest at the new authoritarianism. Gradually this mellowed out into the **Biedermeier years**, in which Prussia's industrial fortunes began to rise, laying the foundation of its Great Power status. Berlin continued to grow: factories and railways and the first of the city's *Mietskaserne* or **tenement buildings** were constructed – foreshadowing what was to come with full industrialization.

Revolution and reaction

Berlin enjoyed more than thirty years of peace and stability after 1815, but it shared the revolutionary mood that swept Europe in **1848**. Influenced by events in France and the writings of Karl Marx (who lived here from 1837 to 1841), the Berliners demanded a say in the running of their own affairs. King Friedrich Wilhelm IV (1795–1861) refused to agree. On March 18, citizens gathered outside his palace to present their demands. The soldiers who dispersed them accidentally fired two shots and the demonstration became a **revolution**. Barricades went up and a fourteen-hour battle raged between insurgents and loyalist troops. According to eyewitness accounts, rich and poor alike joined in the rebellion. During the fighting 183 Berliners and 18 soldiers died.

Aghast at his subjects' anger, Friedrich Wilhelm IV ordered his troops to withdraw to Spandau, leaving the city in the hands of the revolutionaries, who failed to take advantage of the situation. A revolutionary parliament and citizens' militia were established, but rather than assaulting Spandau or taking other measures to consolidate the revolution, the new assembly concerned itself with protecting the royal palace from vandalism. No attempt was made to declare a republic or seize public buildings in what was turning out to be an unusually orderly – and ultimately doomed – revolution.

On March 21, the king appeared in public wearing the black, red and gold tricolour emblem of the revolution. Having failed to suppress it, he now proposed to join it, along with most of his ministers and princes. The king spoke at the university, promising nothing much but paying lip service to the idea of German unity, which impressed the assembled liberals. Order was fully restored; then in October, a Prussian army under General Wrangel entered Berlin and forced the **dissolution of parliament**. The Berliners either gave up the fight or followed millions of their fellow Germans into exile.

Suppression followed. Friedrich gave up the tricolour and turned to persecuting liberals, before going insane shortly afterwards. His brother Prince Wilhelm – who had led the troops against the barricades – became regent, and then king himself. **Otto von Bismarck** was appointed to the chancellorship (1862), despite the almost universal loathing he inspired among Berliners.

Meanwhile, Berlin itself continued to grow apace, turning into a cosmopolitan, modern industrial city. Its free press and revolutionary past exerted a liberal influence on Prussia's emasculated parliament, the **Reichstag**, to the

irritation of Bismarck and the king (who was soon to proclaim himself emperor, or Kaiser). However, Bismarck became a national hero after the Prussian victory at the **Battle of Königgrätz** (1866) had smashed Austrian military power, clearing the way for Prussia to unite – and dominate – Germany. Although militaristic nationalism caused liberalism to wither elsewhere, Berlin continued to elect liberal deputies to the Reichstag, which became the parliament of the whole nation after **German unification** in 1871.

Yet Berlin remained a maverick city. It was here that three attempts were made to kill Emperor Wilhelm I; the final one on Unter den Linden (1878) left him with thirty pieces of shrapnel in his body. While the Kaiser recovered, Bismarck used the event to justify a **crackdown on socialists**, closing newspapers and persecuting trade unionists. The growth of unionism was a direct result of relentless urbanization. Between 1890 and 1900, Berlin's population doubled to two million and thousands of tenement buildings sprang up in working-class quarters like **Wedding**. These were solidly behind the Social Democratic Party (**SPD**), whose deputies were the chief dissenters within the Reichstag.

By 1890 Wilhelm II had become Kaiser and "dropped the Pilot" (Bismarck), but the country continued to be predominantly militaristic and authoritarian. While Berlin remained defiantly liberal, it steadily acquired the attributes of a modern capital. Now an established centre for commerce and diplomacy, it boasted electric trams, an underground railway, and all the other technical innovations of the age.

World War I and its aftermath

The arms race and dual alliances that gradually polarized Europe during the 1890s and the first decade of the twentieth century led inexorably towards **World War I**. Its outbreak in 1914 was greeted with enthusiasm by civilians everywhere – only confirmed pacifists or Communists resisted the heady intoxication of patriotism. In Berlin, Kaiser Wilhelm II spoke "to all Germans" from the balcony of his palace, and shop windows across the city were festooned with national colours. Military bands played *Heil dir im Siegerkranz* ("Hail to you in the Victor's Laurel") and *Die Wacht am Rhein* ("The Watch on the Rhine') in cafés, while Berliners threw flowers to the Imperial German army or Reichswehr as it marched off to war. The political parties agreed to a truce, and even the Social Democrats voted in favour of war credits.

The General Staff's calculation that France could be knocked out before Russia fully mobilized soon proved hopelessly optimistic, and Germany found itself facing a war on two fronts – the very thing Bismarck had dreaded. As casualties mounted on the stalemated western front, and rationing and food shortages began to hit poorer civilians, **disillusionment** set in. By the summer of 1915 housewives were demonstrating in front of the Reichstag, a portent of more serious popular unrest to come. Ordinary people were beginning to see the war as an exercise staged for the benefit of the rich at the expense of the poor, who bore the brunt of the suffering. In December 1917, nineteen members of the SPD announced they could no longer support their party's backing of the war and formed an independent socialist party known as the USPD. This party joined the "International Group" of **Karl Liebknecht** and **Rosa Luxemburg** – later known as the Spartacists – which had opposed SPD support for the war since 1915. It was this grouping that was to form the nucleus of the postwar *Kommunistische Partei Deutschlands*, or **KPD**. Meanwhile, fuel, food, and even beer shortages added to growing hardships on the home front.

Defeat and revolution

With their last great offensive spent, and America joining the Allied war effort, even Germany's supreme warlord, Erich von Ludendorff, recognized that **defeat** was inevitable by the autumn of 1918. Knowing the Allies would refuse to negotiate with the old absolutist system, he declared (on September 9) a democratic, **constitutional monarchy**, whose chancellor would be responsible to the Reichstag and not the Kaiser. A government was formed under Prince Max von Baden, which agreed to extensive reforms. But it was too little, too late, for the bitter sailors and soldiers on the home front, where the contrast between privilege and poverty was most obvious. At the beginning of November the Kiel Garrison led a **naval mutiny** and revolutionary **Workers' and Soldiers' Soviets** mushroomed across Germany.

Caught up in this wave of unrest, Berliners took to the streets on November 8–9, where they were joined by soldiers stationed in the capital. Realizing that the game was up, **Kaiser Wilhelm II abdicated**. What Lenin described as a situation of "dual power" now existed. Almost at the same time as Philipp Scheidemann of the SPD declared a "**German Republic**" from the Reichstag's balcony, Karl Liebknecht was proclaiming a "Free Socialist Republic" from a balcony of the royal palace, less than a mile away. In the face of increasing confusion, SPD leader Friedrich Ebert took over as head of the government. A deal was struck with the army, which promised to protect the republic if Ebert would forestall the full-blooded social revolution demanded by the Spartacists. Ebert now became chairman of a Council of People's Delegates that ruled Berlin for nearly three months.

Between December 16 and 21, a **Congress of Workers' and Soldiers' Soviets** was held, which voted to accept a system of parliamentary democracy. However, many of the revolutionary soldiers, sailors and workers who controlled the streets favoured the establishment of Soviet-style government and refused to obey Ebert's orders. They were eventually suppressed by staunchly anti-revolutionary units of the old Imperial army, further indebting Ebert to the Prussian establishment. This itself relied heavily on the **Freikorps**: armed bands of right-wing officers and NCOs, dedicated to protecting Germany from "Bolshevism".

Things came to a head with the **Spartacist uprising** in Berlin during the first half of January 1919. This inspired lasting dread among the bourgeoisie, who applauded when the Spartacists were crushed by the militarily superior Freikorps. The torture and **murder of Liebknecht and Luxemburg** by Freikorps officers (who threw their bodies in the Landwehrkanal) was never punished once the fighting was over. This hardly augured well for the future of the **new republic**, whose National Assembly elections were held on January 19.

The Weimar Republic

The elections confirmed the SPD as the new political leaders of the country, with 38 percent of the vote; as a result, Ebert was made president, with Scheidemann as chancellor. **Weimar**, the small country town that had seen the most glorious flowering of the German Enlightenment, was chosen as the seat of government in preference to Berlin, which was tinged by its monarchic and military associations.

A **new constitution** was drawn up, hailed as the most liberal and progressive in the world. It aimed at a comprehensive system of checks and balances to ensure that power could not become too concentrated. Authority was formally vested in the people, and the state was given a quasi-federal structure to limit excessive Prussian domination. Executive authority was shared between the president (who could rule by emergency decree if necessary) and the Reich government in a highly complex arrangement. Reichstag deputies were elected by proportional representation from party lists.

While on the surface an admirable document, this constitution was hopelessly idealistic for a people so unfamiliar with democratic practice and responsibilities. No attempt was made to outlaw parties hostile to the system; this opened the way for savage attacks on the republic by extremists at both ends of the political spectrum. The use of proportional representation, without any qualifying minimum percentage of the total vote, favoured a plethora of parties promoting sectional interests. This meant that the Weimar governments were all unwieldy coalitions, whose average life was about eight months and which often pursued contradictory policies in different ministries.

Dada

World War I smashed prevailing cultural assumptions and disrupted social hierarchies. With politics in ferment, culture became another battleground. The leading exponent of the challenge to bourgeois values was the **Dada movement**, which shifted its headquarters from Zurich to Berlin in 1919. A Dada manifesto was proclaimed, followed by the First International Dada Fair (July and August), whose content aligned the movement with the forces of revolution. The right was particularly enraged by exhibits like a stuffed effigy of an army officer with a pig's head, labelled "Hanged by the Revolution", which dangled from the ceiling. All in all, it was an appropriate prelude to the new decade.

Berlin in the 1920s – the Weimar Years

The history of Berlin in the 1920s is bound up with Germany's – much of which was being dictated by the Allies. Resentment at the harsh terms imposed by the **Treaty of Versailles** led to turmoil and a wave of political violence: Matthias

Erzberger, leader of the German delegation to Versailles, was among those assassinated. On March 13, 1920, Freikorps units loyal to the right-wing politician Wolfgang Kapp marched on Berlin, unopposed by the army. The government left Berlin but returned a week later, when the **Kapp putsch** collapsed. The army had withdrawn its support after protesters called for a general strike.

The early 1920s was a bad time for Berlin. War reparations to the Allies placed a crippling burden on the German economy. As the mark began to plunge in value, the government was shocked by the **assassination of Walter Rathenau**. As foreign minister, he had just signed the Treaty of Rapallo, aimed at promoting closer economic ties with the Soviet Union, since the western powers remained intransigent. Rathenau was killed at his own house in the Grunewald by Freikorps officers. When France and Belgium occupied the Ruhr in response to alleged defaults in the reparations payments, a general strike was called across Germany in January 1923.

The combination of reparations and strikes sent the mark plummeting, causing the worst **inflation** ever known. As their savings were wiped out and literally barrowloads of paper money wasn't enough to support a family, Berliners experienced the terrors of hyper-inflation. In working-class districts, street fighting between right and left flared up. Foreigners flocked in to pay bargain prices for carpets and furs that even rich Germans could no longer afford, and fortunes were made and lost by speculators. In the midst of all this, on November 8, Berliners' attention was briefly diverted to Munich, where a motley crew of right-wing ex-army officers including General Ludendorff attempted to mount a putsch. It failed, but Berliners were to hear of one of the ringleaders again – **Adolf Hitler**.

Finally, the mark was stabilized under a new chancellor, **Gustav Stresemann**, who proved to be a supremely able politician. Having come to realize that only an economically sound Germany would have any hope of meeting reparations payments, the Allies moderated their stance. Under the Dawes Plan of 1924, loans poured into Germany, particularly from America, leading to an upsurge in the economy.

Nightlife and the arts

Economic recovery affected the social life of Berlin. For many people the centre of the city had shifted from the old Regiurungsviertel (government quarter) around Friedrichstrasse and Unter den Linden, to the cafés and bars of the Kurfürstendamm. Jazz hit the **nightclubs** in a big way, like drug abuse (mainly cocaine) and all kinds of sex. There were clubs for transvestites, clubs where you could watch nude dancing, or dance naked yourself – and usually the police didn't give a damn. This was the legendary era later to be celebrated by Isherwood and others, when Berlin was briefly the most open, tolerant city in Europe, a mecca for all those who rejected conventions and traditions.

The 1920s was also a boom time for the arts, as the Dada shockwave rippled through the decade. **George Grosz** satirized the times in savage caricatures, while **John Heartfield** used photomontage techniques to produce biting political statements. Equally striking, if less didactic, was the work of artists like **Otto Dix** and **Christian Schad**.

Producer **Max Reinhardt** continued to dominate Berlin's theatrical life, as he'd done since taking over at the Deutsches Theater in 1905. **Erwin Piscator** moved from propaganda into mainstream theatre at the Theater am Nollendorfplatz, without losing his innovative edge, and in 1928 **Bertolt Brecht**'s *Dreigroschen Oper* (*Threepenny Opera*) was staged for the first time. Appropriately, Berlin also became a centre for the very newest of the arts. Between the wars the **UFA film studios** (see p.207) at Neubabelsberg was the biggest in Europe, producing legendary films like **Fritz Lang**'s *Metropolis*, *The Cabinet of Doctor Caligari* and *The Blue Angel* (starring Berlin-born **Marlene Dietrich**).

Middle- and lowbrow tastes were catered for by endless all-singing, all-dancing **musicals**, featuring platoons of women in various states of undress. This was also the heyday of the Berlin cabaret scene, when some of its most acidic exponents were at work.

The rise of Nazism

With inflation back under control, Germany experienced a return to relative **political stability**. The 1924 elections demonstrated increased support for centre-right and republican parties. When President Ebert died (February 28, 1925) and was succeeded by the former commander of the Imperial army, **General Field Marshal von Hindenburg**, monarchists and conservatives rejoiced. Nevertheless, it was now that the extreme right began gradually gaining ground, starting in Bavaria.

The **National Socialist German Workers' Party** (NSDAP) began as a ragbag group of misfits and fanatics, whose views were an odd mixture of extreme right and left, as the party's name suggests. It was Hitler who synthesized an ideology from existing reactionary theories, modelled the Nazis on Mussolini's *Fascisti*, and took a leaf from the Communists when it came to red flags, excessive propaganda and street fighting. For this they had the thuggish, brown-shirted **SA** (*Sturmabteilung*) Stormtroopers. As long as "reds" were the victims, the authorities did little or nothing to curb SA violence. The fear of street violence – foreshadowing a return to the anarchy of the postwar years – was calculated to drive the bourgeoisie towards Nazism, which promised drastic "solutions" to Germany's ills.

The Nazis made no headway in staunchly "red" Berlin until the end of 1926, when Hitler appointed **Joseph Goebbels** as *Gauleiter* of the city's party organization. Goebbels reorganized the SA with the intention of confronting the Communists and conquering the streets of Berlin. On February 11 the following year, he rented the Pharus hall as a site for a Nazi demonstration in the predominantly Communist suburb of Wedding. A bloody brawl ensued and an **era of violence** began. Marches by the SA and the Communist *Rote Frontkämpferbund* (Red Fighters' Front) – often culminating in pitched battles – became a regular feature of street life in Berlin's working-class suburbs. The Nazis were here to stay.

Elections and unrest

In the **1928 elections** the NSDAP won 800,000 votes and gained twelve seats in the Reichstag. In May 1929 there was serious unrest in Berlin when Communist workers clashed with armed police in Wedding. Running street battles occurred and 33 civilians, many of them innocent bystanders, were killed. Fearful for their lives and property should the Communists gain ascendancy, wealthy bourgeois and the captains of finance and industry donated heavily to the Nazis.

In October 1929 Gustav Stresemann, one of Germany's few capable politicians, died. A few weeks later came the **Wall Street Crash**. All American credit ended, and international recession wiped out what was left of Germany's economic stability. By the year's end **unemployment** had

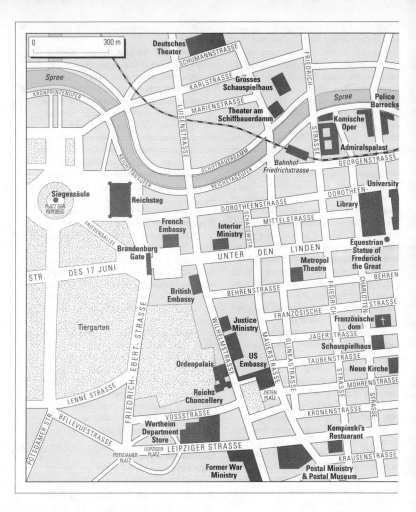

reached three million, and the poverty of the immediate postwar period had returned with a vengeance. A centrist politician, Heinrich Brüning, was appointed chancellor by Hindenburg, but failed to get any legislation passed in the Reichstag and advised Hindenburg to dissolve it, pending elections. Poverty – worsened by a state-imposed austerity programme – polarized society: gangs fought in the streets, while swastika banners and red flags hung from neighbouring tenements.

The **1930 elections** resulted in gains for the Communists, and 107 seats in the Reichstag for the Nazis. There were anti-Semitic attacks throughout Berlin as the newly elected Nazi deputies took their seats in the Reichstag on October 13. By now the parliamentary system had effectively ceased to function and Germany was being ruled by presidential decree. Financial misery and disorder showed no signs of abating, and SA uniforms became a common sight on the streets of central Berlin, where Nazi thugs attacked Jewish shops and businesses, flaunting pornographic hate-sheets like *Der Stürmer*. Their rising influence was confirmed when General

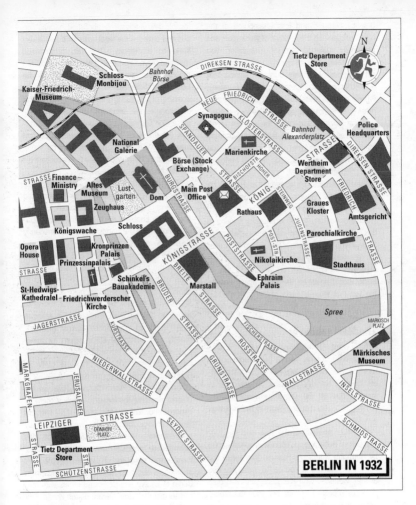

BERLIN IN 1932

Schleicher of the *Reichswehr* General Staff began to court Hitler, envisaging the Nazis as a bulwark against the left. In Berlin – with its predominantly anti-Nazi population – despair began to mount.

At the **presidential elections** of April 10, 1932, Hindenburg gained an absolute majority, but Hitler won 13.5 million votes. A month later Hindenburg dismissed Brüning for failing to control the economy and disagreeing with his speeches, replacing him with Franz von Papen. Flanked by a cabinet that the left-wing press pilloried as the "Cabinet of Barons", von Papen announced plans for "reform", amounting to a thinly disguised attempt to revive the prewar order. The July **parliamentary elections** saw street violence on an unprecedented scale and made the Nazis the largest party in the Reichstag. Despite a setback at the polls in November 1932, their strength on the streets increased – intimidating Berlin's cabarets and left-wing theatres into muted criticism or silence.

Hitler's last steps to power were assisted by conservatives who sought to use the Nazis for their own ends. First, General Schleicher (by now

Defence Minister, and less enamoured of the Nazis) engineered the removal of von Papen, and personally replaced him as chancellor. Von Papen retaliated by instigating a series of **political intrigues**. To Hindenburg he argued that Schleicher was incompetent to govern Germany, whose political mess could best be resolved by making Hitler chancellor. Von Papen reckoned that the Nazis would crush the left but reveal themselves unequal to the task of government; after a few months Hitler could be nudged aside and power would pass back into the hands of conservatives like himself.

Having come to an agreement with Hitler, he persuaded the virtually senile Hindenburg to appoint Hitler as chancellor and himself as vice chancellor (January 4, 1933). Knowing nothing of this, people were demanding the departure of Schleicher on the streets of Berlin. Two days after his resignation, they were horrified to see **Hitler sworn in as chancellor** on January 30. Life in Berlin would never be the same again, despite the fact that three-quarters of the city's electors had voted against the Nazis at the last elections.

The Nazi takeover

Hitler went immediately to the Reich's Chancellery to make his first public appearance as chancellor. Berlin thronged with Nazi supporters bearing torches, and the SA marched in strength through the *Regierungsviertel* to celebrate their victory. For anti-Nazis in Berlin, it was a nightmare come true.

The Nazi takeover of the state and the suppression of political opposition was spearheaded by **Hermann Göring**. As Prussian Minister of the Interior, he ordered the police "to make free use of their weapons wherever necessary" and built up a secret political department, soon to become notorious as the **Gestapo** (*Geheime Staatspolizei* – "secret state police"). "It's not my business to do justice; it's my business to annihilate and exterminate," boasted Göring. The pretext for an all-out assault on the Nazis' opponents was provided by the **Reichstag fire** (February 28, 1933). Whether this was really caused by the Nazis themselves, or by Marius van der Lubbe, the simple-minded Dutch Communist whom they accused, is still a subject for debate. But there's no doubt that the Nazis used the Reichstag fire to their advantage.

An **emergency decree** to "protect the people and the state" was signed by Hindenburg the fol-

lowing day. It effectively abolished habeas corpus and provided the legal basis for a permanent state of emergency. The Nazi propaganda machine played up the Red Menace. Communist offices were raided, and the head of the Communist International, Georgi Dimitrov, was accused of instigating the Reichstag fire. In this atmosphere, the **elections of March 5** took place. The Communist vote dropped by one million, but the Nazis failed to achieve an outright majority, with 43.9 percent of the vote. Nevertheless, Hitler was poised to consolidate his grip on power.

The new Reichstag was opened in the Garrison Church in Potsdam and later transferred to a Berlin opera house. Delegates were asked to approve an **Enabling Act** that would place dictatorial powers in the hands of the predominantly Nazi cabinet. By the arrest of Communist deputies and some of the SPD, and with the support of the traditional right, Hitler was only just short of the two-thirds majority he needed to abolish the Weimar Republic quite legally. The SPD salvaged some self-respect by refusing to accede to this, but the Catholic centrists failed to repeat their act of defiance against Bismarck, meekly supporting the Bill in return for minor concessions. It was passed by 441 votes to 84, hammering the final nails into the coffin of German parliamentary democracy.

On May 2, the Nazis clamped down on the unions, arresting leaders and sending them to **concentration camps**. In a series of subsequent moves opposition parties were effectively banned, and persecution of Nazi opponents was extended to embrace "active church members, freemasons, politically dissatisfied people . . . abortionists and homosexuals". An **exodus from Berlin** of known anti-Nazis and others with reason to fear the Nazis began. Bertolt Brecht, Kurt Weill, Lotte Lenya and Wassily Kandinsky all left the city, joining the likes of Albert Einstein and George Grosz in exile. The atmosphere of the city was changing irrevocably. The unemployed were drafted in labour battalions, set to work on the land or building autobahns.

On April 1, the SA launched an enforced **boycott of Jewish shops**, businesses and medical and legal practices in Berlin. Meanwhile, the Nazis put their own men into vital posts throughout local governments – in Berlin and the rest of Germany. This was the first stage of *Gleichschaltung* ("co-ordination"), whereby the machinery of state, and then society itself, would be *Nazified*. On May 11, they shocked the world by burning thousands of books that conflicted with Nazi ideology on the Opernplatz in central Berlin. After the concentration camps, the **book-burnings** (*Büchverbrennung*) remain one of the most potent symbols of Nazi brutality.

The Night of the Long Knives

In 1934 Nazi savagery was briefly turned inwards. Under **Ernst Röhm**, the SA had grown to 500,000 men and boasted of swallowing up the smaller *Reichswehr*. The SA felt cheated of the spoils of victory and muttered about a "Second Revolution". "Adolf is rotten. He's betraying all of us. He only goes around with reactionaries. . . Are we revolutionaries or aren't we?" Röhm complained. Big business, the regular army and rival Nazis like Himmler and Göring were united in their hostility towards the SA. Hitler was persuaded that Röhm and his allies were conspiring against him, and ordered a wholesale purge later known as the "**Night of the Long Knives**". On the night of June 30, the SA leaders were dragged from their boyfriends' beds in the resort of Bad Wiessee, taken to Stadelheim prison and shot in the courtyard by SS troopers; some believed this was an army coup, and died shouting "Heil Hitler!" In Berlin alone, 150 SA leaders were executed. Röhm's final words before being shot in Stadelheim prison were more appropriate: "All revolutions devour their own children."

Other victims included General Schleicher, von Papen's assistants, and the leader of the radical Nazis, Gregor Strasser. Local police and Gestapo chiefs added personal enemies to the death lists. Some of the victims had no connection with politics, like the Bavarian music critic whom the hit-squad mistook for an SA general of the same name. Aside from Hitler, Göring, and the army, the main beneficiaries of the purge were two Nazi organizations under the control of a failed chicken-farmer, **Heinrich Himmler**. His black-uniformed **SS** (*Schutzstaffel* – "Defence Staff"), originally Hitler's personal bodyguard, grew into the nucleus for a Nazi army. Meanwhile, the party's private intelligence service, the **SD** (*Sicherheitsdienst* or "Security Service"), established itself as a rival to the Gestapo and the army's *Abwehr* – military intelligence organization.

Following Hindenburg's death later that summer, Hitler merged the offices of president and chancellor and declared himself **Führer** of the German Reich. Defence Minister von Blomberg acceded to Hitler's request that all soldiers of the *Reichswehr* swear an oath of allegiance to him personally. Having assured Blomberg that the army would remain the "only bearer of arms in the nation", Hitler took the salute from the *Leibstandarte Adolf Hitler* regiment of the SS and the Hermann Göring Police Battalion – an indication of how he applied the policy of divide and rule even within the Führer state.

The Nazi impact on Berlin

In Berlin as in the rest of the Reich, **Nazi control** extended to all areas of life: the press and radio were orchestrated by Goebbels; children joined Nazi youth organizations; and every tenement building had Nazi-appointed wardens who doubled as Gestapo spies. It was even decreed that women should eschew make-up as an "un-German" artifice – one of the few edicts that wasn't taken seriously. Anti-Nazi criticism – even of the mildest kind – invited a visit from the Gestapo. Although Germans might avoid joining the NSDAP itself, it was difficult to escape the plethora of related organizations covering every aspect of life, from riding clubs and dog breeders to the "Reich Church" or "German League of Maidens". This was the second stage of *Gleichschaltung* – drawing the entire population into the Nazi net.

As the capital of the Reich, Berlin became a showcase city of banners, uniforms and parades. An image of order and dynamism, of a "new Germany" on the march, was what the Nazis tried to convey. This reached its apotheosis during the **1936 Olympics**, held at a vast purpose-built stadium in the Pichelsdorf suburb of Berlin. Hitler's expectation that the games would demonstrate Aryan racial supremacy was humiliatingly dashed when black American athlete Jesse Owens gave the greatest performance of the Olympics.

Like many previous rulers of Germany, Hitler felt uncomfortable in Berlin, probably aware that most Berliners suffered rather than supported him. He also felt the city was insufficiently grandiose for the capital of the "Thousand Year Reich", and from 1936 onwards spent much time with his favourite architect, **Albert Speer**, drawing up extensive plans for a remodelled postwar Berlin, to be called "Germania". Its main purpose would be to serve as a monument to the expected Nazi victory in the forthcoming war and as the capital of a vast empire thereafter. Hitler's millennial megalomania inspired hours of brooding on how future generations might be awed by Germania's monumental ruins – hence the need to build with the finest materials on a gigantic scale. In the meantime, he preferred to spend his time in the Berghof in Berchtesgaden.

Kristallnacht and the road to war

If the Berlin Olympics had partly glossed over the realities of Nazi brutality, *Kristallnacht* exposed them to the world. On the night of November 9–10, 1938, organized **attacks on Jewish shops and institutions** took place across Germany, an escalation in the Nazis' violent anti-Semitism. At least 36 Jews were murdered, and thousands injured; in Berlin Jews were beaten on the streets while passers-by looked on, and 23 of the city's 29 synagogues were destroyed. Many of the attacks were carried out by SA men in civilian clothes, to give the impression that these were spontaneous outbursts by German citizens. In the wake of *Kristallnacht* ("Crystal Night" – after the broken glass), new **anti-Semitic laws** were brought in, making life difficult and dangerous for German Jews, and paving the way for the greater horrors to come.

Throughout the 1930s the Nazis made **preparations for war**, expanding the army and gearing the economy for war readiness by 1940. Göring bragged of putting "guns before butter", but the real architect of the four-year plan was Hjalmar Schacht, a respected banker. It dovetailed with Hitler's foreign policy of obtaining *Lebensraum* ("living space") from neighbouring countries by intimidation. In 1936 the German army occupied the Rhineland (demilitarized under the terms of the Treaty of Versailles) to token protests from the League of Nations. The *Anschluss* (annexation) of Austria in 1938 was likewise carried off with impunity, and a few months later Britain and France agreed to the dismemberment of Czechoslovakia at Munich.

Encouraged by their pusillanimity, Hitler made new demands on Polish territory in 1939. It's probable that he believed there would be a similar collapse of will by the western powers, the more so since he had pulled off the spectacular coup of signing a non-aggression pact with his ultimate enemy, the Soviet Union, thus ensuring

that Germany could avoid a war on two fronts. But two days after the German invasion of Poland began on September 1, Britain and France declared war in defence of their treaty obligations.

World War II

The outbreak of **World War II** was greeted without enthusiasm by Berliners, despite German victories in Poland. According to American journalist and eyewitness William Shirer (see "Books"), there were few signs of patriotic fervour as the troops marched off to war through the streets of Berlin, and Hitler cancelled further parades out of pique. On October 11, there was rejoicing when a radio broadcast on the Berlin radio wavelength stated that the British government had fallen, and an immediate armistice was to be declared. Shirer noted that the Berliners showed more enthusiasm at the military parade to mark the fall of France (July 18, 1940), when German troops marched through the Brandenburg Gate for the first time since 1871. Still, he reckoned that it was the spectacle rather than martial sentiments that attracted crowds of Berliners.

Initially, Berlin suffered little from the war. Although citizens were already complaining of meagre rations, delicacies and luxury goods from occupied Europe gravitated towards the Reich's capital. What remained of the diplomatic and foreign press community, and the chic lifestyles of Nazi bigwigs, passed for high life. Open dissent seemed impossible, with Gestapo informers believed to lurk everywhere. The impact of wartime austerity was also softened by Nazi welfare organizations and a blanket of propaganda.

Air raids

Göring had publicly boasted that Germans could call him "Meyer" (a Jewish surname) if a single bomb fell on Berlin – notwithstanding which, the British RAF dropped some for the first time on August 23, 1940. A further raid on the night of August 28–29 killed ten people – the first German civilian casualties. These raids had a marked demoralizing effect on Berliners, who had counted on a swift end to the war, and Hitler had to reassure the populace in a speech at the Sportpalast. Holding up a *Baedeker* guide to Britain, he thundered that the *Luftwaffe* would raze Britain's cities to the ground one by one.

However, these early **bombing raids** caused scant real damage and it wasn't until March 1,

1943 – when defeat in the Western Desert and difficulties on the eastern front had already brought home the fact that Germany was not invincible – that Berlin suffered its first heavy raid. While the RAF bombed by night the Americans bombed by day, establishing a pattern that would reduce Berlin to ruins in relentless stages. "We can wreck Berlin from end to end if the USAAF will come in on it. It will cost us between 400 and 500 aircraft. It will cost Germany the war," the head of Bomber command, Sir Arthur "Bomber" Harris, had written to Churchill in 1943. The first buildings to go were the Staatsoper and Alte Bibliothek on Unter den Linden. On December 22 the Kaiser-Wilhelm-Gedächtniskirche was reduced to a shell. By the year's end, daily and nightly bombardments were a feature of everyday life.

During the 363 air raids until the end of the war, 75,000 tons of high-explosive or incendiary bombs had killed between 35,000 and 50,000 people and rendered 1,500,000 Berliners homeless. Yet despite the colossal destruction that filled the streets with 100 million tons of rubble, seventy percent of the city's industrial capacity was still functioning at the war's end.

Resistance against the Nazis

Anti-Nazi resistance within Germany was less overt than in occupied Europe, but it existed throughout the war, particularly in Berlin. A group of **Communist cells** run by members of the old KPD operated a clandestine information network and organized isolated acts of resistance and sabotage. But the odds against them were overwhelming, and most groups perished. More successful was the *Rote Kapelle* (Red Orchestra) headed by Harold Schulze-Boysen, a prewar Bohemian aristocrat who worked in the Air Ministry on Wilhelmstrasse, with agents in most of the military offices, supplying information to the Soviet Union. Eventually it, too, was identified and broken up by the SD and the Gestapo.

The **Kreisau Circle**, a resistance group led by Count Helmut von Moltke, and the groups around Carl Goerdeler (former mayor of Leipzig) and General Beck (ex-Chief of Staff) talked about overthrowing the Nazis and opening negotiations with the western Allies, but the most effective resistance came from **within the military**. There had been attempts on Hitler's life since 1942, but it wasn't until late 1943 and early 1944 that

enough high-ranking officers had become convinced that defeat was inevitable, and a wide network of conspirators was established. The one-armed Colonel von Stauffenberg was responsible for placing the bomb in Hitler's headquarters at Rastenberg in East Prussia, while Bendlerstrasse officers planned to use Fromm's Replacement Army to seize crucial points in Berlin.

On July 20, 1944, six weeks after the Allied invasion of Normandy, the coup was launched. Stauffenberg heard the bomb explode as he was leaving Rastenberg and signalled for the coup to go ahead. In fact, the **attempt to kill Hitler failed** through bad luck, and the conspirators botched their takeover. First they failed to cut communications between Rastenberg and Berlin, and took their time seizing buildings and arresting Nazis. Goebbels succeeded in telephoning Hitler, who spoke directly to the arrest team, ordering them to obey his Propaganda Minister. Then Goebbels set to work contacting SS and Gestapo units, and reminding army garrisons of their oath of loyalty to the Führer. The final blow came at 9pm, when Hitler broadcast on national radio, threatening to "settle accounts the way we National Socialists are accustomed to settle them".

The ringleaders were either summarily shot, or tortured into implicating others in the basement of Gestapo headquarters on Prinz-Albrecht-Strasse. Several thousand suspects were arrested and hundreds executed. Fieldmarshal Rommel was allowed to commit suicide and receive an honourable burial, but other high-ranking conspirators went before the so-called People's Court in Berlin for a public show trial (August 7–8). All were sentenced to death by the Nazi judge Ronald Freisler and hanged on meat-hooks at Plötzensee Prison, their death agonies being filmed for Hitler's private delectation. Almost all of those who would have been best qualified to lead postwar Germany had thus been killed. Freisler himself was killed by an American bomb following a later show trial.

The fate of Berlin's Jews

For Berlin's Jews (and those living elsewhere in Germany) the terror began long before the war, as a noose tightened around their right to exist. Of the 160,564 Jews in Berlin at the beginning of 1933, many left in the first year of Hitler's chancellorship, when a series of laws banned them from public office, the civil service, journalism, farming, teaching, broadcasting and acting. Still more left when the so-called **Nürnburg Laws** (September 1936) effectively deprived them of German citizenship and defined apartheid-like classifications of "racial purity". Jews who could see the writing on the wall, and had money, escaped while they could (other European countries, the US and Palestine all restricted Jewish immigration); but the majority stayed put, hoping that things would improve, or simply because they couldn't afford to emigrate. After Kristallnacht, their already beleaguered position became intolerable.

Once the war began, the Nazis embarked on outright **genocide**, corralling the Jews of Europe in ghettos, branded by their yellow stars, destined for the concentration camps and eventual extermination. Emigration and murder had reduced the Jewish population of Berlin to about 6500 by 1945. Roughly 1400 of the **survivors** were "U-Boats" who lived perpetually in hiding, usually with the help of Gentile friends; the other 5100 somehow survived in precariously legal conditions, usually by being married to non-Jews, or working as grave diggers in the Weissensee Jewish Cemetery.

The fall of Berlin

Enjoy the war while you can! The peace is going to be terrible . . .

Berlin joke shortly before the fall of the city.

By autumn 1944 it was obvious to all but the most fanatical Nazis that the end was approaching fast. Even so, Hitler would brook no talk of surrender or negotiation. Teenage boys and men in their fifties were conscripted to replace the fallen millions, as Hitler placed his faith in "miracle weapons" like the V-1 and V-2, and new offensives. A wintertime counterattack in the Ardennes temporarily checked the Allies to the west, but their advance had resumed by January 1945. Meanwhile, the Red Army had launched the largest offensive ever seen on the eastern front, 180 divisions seizing East Prussia within two weeks. The distance between the Allied forces was narrowing inexorably.

On January 27, Soviet forces crossed the Oder a hundred miles from Berlin. Only Hitler now really believed there was any hope for Germany. The Nazis threw all they could at the eastern front and mobilized the *Volkssturm*, an ill-equipped home guard of old men, boys and cripples. Thirteen- and fourteen-year-old members of the **Hitler Youth** were briefly trained in the art of using the *Panzerfaust* bazooka, then sent to fight against T-34 tanks and battle-hardened infantrymen. As thousands died at the front to buy a little time for the doomed Nazi regime, life in Berlin became a nightmare. The city was choked with refugees and terrified of the approaching Russians; it was bombed day and night, and the flash of Soviet artillery could be seen on the horizon.

Behind the lines, **flying court-martials** picked up soldiers and executed anyone suspected of "desertion" or "cowardice in the face of the enemy". On February 1, 1945, Berlin was declared *Verteidigungsbereich* (a "zone of defence") – to be defended to the last man and the last bullet. The civilian population – women, children, cripples and forced labourers – was set to work building tank traps and barricades; stretches of the U- and S-Bahn formed part of the fortifications. Goebbels trumpeted a **"fortress Berlin"**, while Hitler planned the deployment of **phantom armies**, which existed on order-of-battle charts, but hardly at all in reality.

As Berlin frantically prepared to defend itself, the Russians consolidated their strength. On April 16, at 5am Moscow time, the **Soviet offensive** began with a massive bombardment lasting 25 minutes. When the artillery fell silent, 143 searchlights spaced 200m apart along the entire front were switched on to dazzle the enemy as the Russians began their advance. Three army groups totalling over 1,500,000 men moved forward under marshals Zhukov, Konev and Rokossovsky – and there was little the vastly outnumbered Germans could do to halt them. By April 20 – Hitler's 56th birthday (celebrated with tea and cakes in the *Führerbunker*) – the Red Army was on the edge of Berlin. Next day the city centre came within range of their guns, and several people queueing outside the *Karstadt* department store on Hermannplatz were killed by shells. On April 23, Soviet troops were in the Weissensee district, just a few miles east of the centre. The Germans were offered a chance to surrender, but declined.

Hitler's birthday party was the last time the Nazi hierarchy assembled before going – or staying – to meet their respective fates. The dictator and his mistress Eva Braun chose to remain in Berlin, and Goebbels elected to join them in the

Führerbunker with his family. It was a dank, stuffy complex of reinforced concrete cells beneath the garden of the Reich Chancellery. Here Hitler brooded over Speer's architectural models of unbuilt victory memorials, subsisting on salads, herbal tisanes and regular injections of dubious substances by one Dr Morell. To hapless generals and faithful acolytes, he ranted about traitors and the unworthiness of the German Volk, declaring that the war was lost and that he would stay in the bunker to the end, after learning that General Steiner's army group had failed to stop Zhukov's advance.

The Final Days

By April 25, Berlin was completely **encircled by Soviet troops**, which met up with US forces advancing from the west. Over the next two days, the suburbs of Dahlem, Spandau, Neukölln and Gatow fell to the Russians, and the city's telephone system failed. On April 27 the Third Panzer Army was completely smashed; survivors fled west, leaving Berlin's northern flank virtually undefended. The obvious hopelessness of the situation didn't sway the top Nazis' fanatical **refusal to surrender**. Never mind that many of Berlin's defences existed only on paper, or that units were undermanned and poorly armed, with crippling shortages of fuel and ammunition. As the Red Army closed in, Goebbels called hysterically for "*rücksichtslose Bekämpfung*" – a fight without quarter – and SS execution squads worked around the clock, killing soldiers, *Volkssturm* guards or Hitler Youth who tried to stop fighting.

In the city the horrors mounted. The **civilian population** lived underground in cellars and air-raid shelters, scavenging for food wherever and whenever there was a momentary lull in the fighting. Engineers blasted canal locks, flooding the U-Bahn to prevent the Russians from advancing along it. Hundreds of civilians sheltering in the tunnels were drowned as a result (see p.122). On April 27, the Ninth Army was destroyed attempting to break out of the Russian encirclement to the south, and unoccupied Berlin had been reduced to a strip nine and a half miles long from east to west, and three miles wide from north to south, constantly under bombardment. Next the Russians captured the Tiergarten, reducing the **last pocket of resistance** to the *Regieurungsviertel*, where fighting focused on the Reichstag and Hitler's Chancellery, and on

Potsdamer Platz, only a few hundred metres from the *Führerbunker*, by now under constant shellfire.

Hitler still hoped that one of his phantom armies would relieve Berlin, but on April 28 his optimism evaporated when he heard that Himmler had been suing for unconditional surrender to the western Allies. In the early hours of the following day, he married Eva Braun, held a small champagne wedding reception, and dictated his will. As the day wore on, savage fighting continued around the Nazi-held enclave. At a final conference the commandant of Berlin, General Weidling, announced that the Russians were in the nearby Adlon Hotel, and that there was no hope of relief.

A breakout attempt was proposed, but Hitler declared that he was staying put. On the afternoon of April 30, after testing the cyanide on his pet German shepherd dog, **Hitler and Eva Braun committed suicide**: he with a revolver, she by poison. The bodies were taken to the Chancellery courtyard and doused with 200 litres of petrol; Hitler's followers gave the Nazi salute as the corpses burned to ashes. Meanwhile, Soviet troops were battling to gain control of the Reichstag, and at 11pm two Russian sergeants raised the red flag from its rooftop.

According to Hitler's will, Admiral Dönitz was appointed chancellor *in absentia*. In the early hours of May 1, Chief of Staff Krebs was sent out to parley with the Russians. After hasty consultation with Stalin, General Chuikov replied that only unconditional surrender was acceptable. When Krebs returned to the bunker, Goebbels rejected this and ordered the fighting to continue. That night he and his wife killed themselves, having first poisoned their children. The rest of the bunker occupants, with the exception of Krebs and General Burgdorf – Hitler's ADC, who committed suicide – now decided to try and break out. Weidling agreed not to surrender until the following dawn in order to give the fugitives time to **escape from the bunker** and through the railway tunnels towards northern Berlin. Of the 800 or so who tried, about 100 made it – the rest were either killed or captured. No one is sure about the fate of Hitler's deputy, Martin Bormann.

Capitulation and surrender

At 5am, Weidling offered the **capitulation of Berlin** to General Chuikov, who broadcast his surrender proclamation from loudspeaker vans around the city. At 3pm, firing in the city centre stopped, although sporadic, sometimes fierce fighting continued on the outskirts, where German troops tried to break out to the west to surrender to the British or Americans rather than the Russians. Their fears were justified, for the Soviets unleashed an **orgy of rape and looting** on the capital, lasting three days. This was Stalin's reward to his troops for having fought so long and so hard.

The **official surrender of German forces** occurred at a Wehrmacht engineers' school in the Berlin suburb of Karlshorst on May 8, 1945. Wehrmacht forces in the west had already surrendered the day before, and British, French and American delegates flew in with General Keitel, High Commander of the Armed Forces, to repeat the performance for the benefit of the Russians. Berliners had already emerged from their shelters and started to clear the dead and the rubble from the streets. Now the Red Army established field kitchens.

With the final act of surrender complete, it was time to count the cost of the Battle of Berlin. It had taken the lives of 125,000 Berliners (including 6400 suicides and 22,000 heart attacks), and innumerable German soldiers from the 93 divisions destroyed by the Red Army. The Soviets themselves had suffered some 305,000 casualties in the battle, while the city itself had been left in ruins, without even basic services.

Occupation

During the immediate postwar months, civilian rations of food, fuel and medicine were cut to the bone to support the two-million-strong **Soviet occupation forces**. Survival rations were measured in ounces per day, if forthcoming at all, and civilians had to use all their wits to stay alive. The Soviet Union had taken steps towards establishing a civilian, Communist-dominated administration even before the war was over. On April 30, a group of exiled German Communists arrived at Küstrin airfield and were taken to Berlin, where they established a temporary headquarters in Lichtenberg. Directed by **Walter Ulbricht**, the future leader of the GDR's Communist Party, they set about tracking down old Berlin party members and setting up a new **municipal administration**. In each city district, they were careful to ensure that control of education and the police went to Communists. This apparatus remained in

place even after the arrival of the British and Americans in July.

The **western occupation sectors** had been demarcated by the Allies as far back as 1943, but the troops didn't move in until July 1–4, when fifty thousand British, American and French soldiers replaced the Red Army in the western part of the city. Here, the food situation improved marginally once American supplies began to find their way through, but public health remained a huge problem. Dysentery and TB were endemic, and there were outbreaks of typhoid and paratyphoid, all exacerbated by an acute shortage of hospital beds. British and American soldiers found endless opportunities to profit from the burgeoning **black market**: trading cigarettes, alcohol, gas, NAAFI and PX supplies for antiques, jewellery, or sexual favours. With less to offer, the Russians simply demanded "*Davai chas*", and took watches at gunpoint. Huge black market centres sprang up around the Brandenburg Gate and Alexanderplatz.

From July 17 to August 3 the **Potsdam conference** took place at the Cecilienhof Palace. It was to be the last great meeting of the leaders of the Big Three wartime alliance. Churchill took the opportunity to visit the ruins of the Reich's Chancellery, followed by a mob of fascinated Germans and Russians. Mid-conference he returned to Britain to hear the results of the first postwar election – and was replaced by the newly elected Labour prime minister, Clement Attlee, who could do little but watch as Truman and Stalin settled the fate of postwar Europe and Berlin.

For Germans, the worst was yet to come. Agriculture and industry had virtually collapsed, threatening acute **shortages of food and fuel** just as winter approached. In Berlin they dug mass graves and stockpiled coffins for the expected wave of deaths, and thousands of children were evacuated to the British occupation zone in the west of the country, where conditions were less severe. To everyone's surprise the winter turned out to be uncommonly mild. Christmas 1945 was celebrated after a fashion, and mothers took their children to the first postwar Weihnachtsmarkt (Christmas fair) in the Lustgarten.

Starvation and unrest

Unfortunately the respite was only temporary, for despite the good weather, food supplies remained overstretched. In March rations were reduced drastically, and the weakened civilian population fell prey to typhus, TB and other **hunger-related diseases**; the lucky ones merely suffered enteric or skin diseases. The Allies did what they could, sending government and private relief, but even by the spring of 1947 rations remained at malnutrition levels. **Crime and prostitution** soared. In Berlin alone, two thousand people were arrested every month, many of them from juvenile gangs that roamed the ruins murdering, robbing and raping. Trains were attacked at the Berlin stations, and in the countryside bandits ambushed supply convoys heading for the city. The winter of 1946–47 was one of the coldest since records began. Wolves appeared in Berlin and people froze to death aboard trains. There were rumours of cannibalism and Berlin hospitals had to treat fifty-five thousand people for frostbite.

Meanwhile, **political developments** that were to have a lasting impact on Berlin were occurring. In March 1946, the social democratic SPD was forced into a shotgun merger with the KPD, to form the **SED** (*Sozialistische Einheitspartei Deutschlands* – "Socialist Unity Party of Germany"), or future **Communist Party** of East Germany. In the western half of the city, 71 percent of members voted against union; in East Berlin no voting was permitted, and attempts to hold ballots in the Prenzlauer Berg and Friedrichshain party offices were broken up by Russian soldiers. In October 1946, the first citywide **free elections** since 1933 were held. The SED fared badly and the SPD triumphed, much to the annoyance of the Soviet zone authorities, who abandoned free elections after this setback.

The Berlin airlift

Already the city was becoming **divided along political lines** as the wartime alliance between the western powers (France had also been allotted an occupation zone) and the Soviet Union fell apart, ushering in a new era of conflict that would all too often focus on Berlin. The Allied Control Council met for the last time on March 20, when Marshal Sokolovsky, the Soviet military governor, protested about British and American attempts to introduce economic reform in their occupation zones.

Tension mounted over the next few months as the Allies went ahead with economic reform, while the Russians demanded the right to board Berlin-bound Allied trains, and on June 16 walked out of the four-power Kommandantura that had ultimate control over Berlin. Things came to a head with the **introduction of the D-Mark** in the western zone (June 23, 1948). On that day, the Soviets presented Berlin's mayor with an ultimatum, demanding that he accept their own Ostmark as currency for the whole city. But the city's parliament voted overwhelmingly against the Soviet-backed currency.

Everyone knew that this was asking for trouble, and trouble wasn't long in coming. On the night of June 23–24, power stations in the Soviet zone cut off electricity supplies to the western half of Berlin, and road and rail links between the western part of Germany and Berlin were severed. This was the beginning of the **Berlin blockade**, the USSR's first attempt to force the western Allies out of Berlin. SPD politician Ernst Reuter, soon to be mayor of West Berlin, addressed a crowd at the Gesundbrunnen soccer field, promising that Berlin would "fight with everything we have".

There was now only one month's food and ten days' coal supply left in the city. The British and Americans realized that they had to support West Berlin, but were unwilling to use military force to push their way in overland. After some consideration it was decided to try to supply Berlin by air, as it was felt that the Soviets wouldn't dare risk intercepting Allied planes. However, there were serious doubts as to whether it was possible to sustain two million people by an airlift. The only previous attempt at a comparable scale – maintaining the German Sixth Army at Stalingrad – had been an utter failure. Berlin's needs were calculated at 4000 tons of supplies per day, yet the available aircraft could carry fewer than 500 tons.

Nevertheless, the **Berlin airlift** that began on June 26, 1948, soon gathered momentum. The Soviets maintained their blockade and made it plain that they regarded Germany as divided and Berlin as the capital of their half. America brought in huge C54 Skymaster transport planes to supplement the smaller C47s and Dakotas that the airlift began with. It soon became an around-the-clock, precision operation. By October, planes were landing every three minutes, bringing in 4760 tons of food and fuel every day. Winter was exceptionally tough. Power cuts and severe food rationing reduced living standards to the level of the immediate postwar period. The Russians made supplies available in the eastern half of the city, but relatively few West Berliners chose to take advantage of them. At municipal elections on December 7, the SPD's **Ernst Reuter** was voted in as mayor of West Berlin, becoming a kind of human symbol of its resistance.

By the spring of 1949, planes were landing or taking off every thirty seconds and shifting 8000 tons a day. At Easter, the Allies mounted a special operation to boost morale and cock a snook at the Soviets. In just twenty-four hours they flew 13,000 tons of supplies into Berlin. Shortly afterwards the Soviets gave up, lifting the blockade on May 12. The first trucks and trains to reach West Berlin received a tumultuous welcome. The airlift was continued for another four months to ensure that Berlin would be supplied should the blockade be resumed at short notice. Though it cost the lives of 48 airmen and millions of dollars, the airlift thwarted Stalin's attempt to expel the Allies from West Berlin, and dealt the Soviets a resounding propaganda defeat. It also changed most Berliners' perception of the western powers from occupiers to allies.

The birth of the two Germanys

Within six months, the political division of Germany was formalized by the creation of two rival states. First, the British, French and American zones of occupation were amalgamated to form the **Federal Republic of Germany** (May 1949); the Soviets followed suit by launching the **German Democratic Republic** on October 7. As Berlin lay deep within GDR territory, its eastern sector naturally became the official GDR capital. However, much to the disappointment of many Berliners, the Federal Republic chose Bonn as their capital. West Berlin remained under the overall control of the Allied military commandants, although it was eventually to assume the status of a Land (state) of the Federal Republic.

Although West Berlin's **economic recovery** was by no means as dramatic as that of West Germany, the city did prosper, particularly in comparison to East Berlin. The Soviets had gone in for ruthless **asset-stripping** – removing factories, rolling stock and generators to replace losses in the war-ravaged USSR – and when they eventually turned to reconstructing the GDR, the empha-

sis was put on heavy industrial production. West Berlin soon became an attractive destination for East Berliners, who were able to cross the **zonal border** more or less freely at this time. Many came to stay, while others worked in the city, benefiting from the purchasing power of the D-Mark. And those who did neither used the city to enjoy the entertainment and culture lacking in the more spartan East.

Political tension remained a fact of life in a city that had become an arena for superpower confrontations. The Soviets and GDR Communists had not abandoned the idea of driving the Allies out of Berlin, and mounted diverse operations against them; just as the Allies ran spying and sabotage operations against East Berlin. In this cradle of **Cold War espionage**, the recruitment of former Gestapo, SD or *Abwehr* operatives seemed quite justifiable to all the agencies concerned. On one side were Britain's SIS (based at the Olympic Stadium) and the American CIA, which fostered the Federal Republic's own intelligence service, the Gehlen Bureau, run by a former *Abwehr* colonel. Opposing them were the Soviet KGB and GRU (based at Karlshorst), and the GDR's own foreign espionage service and internal security police. The public side of this rumbling underground war was a number of **incidents** in 1952. An Air France plane approaching West Berlin through the air corridor was fired upon by a Russian MiG; the East German authorities blocked streets leading from West to East Berlin and expropriated property owned by West Berliners on the outskirts of the eastern sector.

The Workers' Uprising

The **death of Stalin** on March 5, 1953, raised hopes that the situation in Berlin could be eased, but these were soon dashed. In the eastern sector, the Communists unwittingly fuelled smouldering resentment by announcing a ten percent **rise in work norms** on June 16. For workers already hard-pressed to support their families, this demand to produce more or earn less was intolerable. The first to protest were building workers on block 40 of the prestigious Stalinallee construction project, who downed tools and marched on the city centre, joined by other workers and passers-by. At Strausberger Platz they swept aside Volkspolizei units who tried to stop them and headed, via Alexanderplatz, for Unter den Linden. From here, by now roughly eight thousand-strong, the **demonstration** marched to the House of Ministries, occupying Göring's former Air Ministry on Leipziger Strasse, where they demanded to speak with SED chief Walter Ulbricht and Prime Minister Otto Grotewohl, both of whom declined to appear.

Eventually three lesser ministers were sent out to speak to the demonstrators. Clearly alarmed at the scale of the demonstration, they promised to try and get the work norms lowered. But by now the crowd wanted more, and began calling for political freedom. After declaring a **general strike** for the next day, the protesters returned to Stalinallee, tearing down SED placards on the way. Grotewohl's announcement rescinding the new work norms later that day failed to halt the strike, news of which had been broadcast across the GDR by western radio stations. About 300,000 workers in 250 towns joined in, and by 7am a crowd of 100,000 people was marching through East Berlin towards the House of Ministries.

Ulbricht and Grotewohl feared for their lives and called for Russian help. When **Soviet tanks** appeared in Leipziger Strasse before noon, they found their route blocked by a vast crowd that refused to budge. The Soviet commandant, General Pavel Dibrova, warned by loudspeaker that martial law had been declared, and all violators would face summary punishment – but with little effect. Dibrova ordered his troops to move forward with the tanks following in close support, and it was at this point that the shooting started.

The crowd scattered as the first shots rang out, leaving youths to confront the T-34s with bricks and bottles. **Street fighting** raged throughout East Berlin for the rest of the day, and it wasn't until nightfall that the Soviets reasserted Communist control. At least 267 demonstrators, 116 policemen and 18 Soviet soldiers were killed during the fighting, and it's estimated that 92 civilians (including a West Berliner just passing through) were summarily shot after the **suppression of the uprising**. The western Allies did nothing to prevent this, nor the subsequent trials of "counter-revolutionaries" at which fourteen death sentences and innumerable prison terms were meted out – final confirmation that Berlin was divided.

Bertolt Brecht, who had returned to Berlin in 1949 and elected to live in the East, wrote an epitaph to this episode in a poem called "The Solution":

After the rising of 17 June
The secretary of the Writers' Union
Had leaflets distributed in Stalinallee
In which you could read that the people
Had lost the government's confidence
Which it could only regain with
Redoubled efforts. Would it in that case
Not be simpler if the Government
Dissolved the people
And elected another?

Berlin was relatively quiet for the remainder of the 1950s, but important events were taking place in **West Germany** under Chancellor Konrad Adenauer. Foremost among these was the so-called "**economic miracle**", which saw West Germany recover from the ravages of war astonishingly quickly and go on to become Europe's largest economy, which couldn't help but give a shot in the arm to the fortunes of West Berlin. On the political front, the **Hallstein doctrine** of non-recognition for the GDR reigned supreme. This was even stretched to the point of not maintaining diplomatic relations with other countries who chose to recognize the GDR. A pragmatic exception was made of the Soviet Union.

The building of the Wall

The economic disparity between East and West Germany (and their respective halves of Berlin) worsened throughout the 1950s. **Marshall Plan aid** and West German capital were transforming West Berlin into a glittering showcase for capitalism, whereas the GDR and East Berlin seemed to languish. Prospects for development in the GDR were undermined by a steady **population drain**, as mostly young and often highly skilled workers headed west for higher living standards and greater political freedom. Roughly 2,500,000 people quit the GDR during the 1950s, mostly via the open border with West Berlin, where an average of 19,000 East Germans crossed over every month. Both the GDR and Soviet governments saw this as a threat to East Germany's existence.

On November 10, 1958, Soviet leader Nikita Khrushchev demanded that the western Allies relinquish their role in the "occupation regime in Berlin, thus facilitating the normalization of the situation in the capital of the GDR". Two weeks later, Khrushchev suggested that the Allies should withdraw and Berlin should become a free city – coupled with a broad hint that if no agreement was reached within six months, a blockade would be reimposed. The Allies rejected the ultimatum, and the Kremlin allowed the deadline to pass without incident. Tripartite **negotiations** at Geneva (May–Sept 1959) failed to produce a settlement. Meanwhile, tens of thousands of East Germans continued to cross the border into West Berlin.

By 1961 Ulbricht's regime was getting desperate, and rumours that the border might be sealed began to circulate. In mid-June Ulbricht felt compelled to assure the world that no one had "the intention of building a wall". Simultaneously, however, border controls were tightened. Yet the flood of people voting with their feet continued to rise, in what West Berlin's Springer press dubbed "mass escapes . . . of avalanche proportions". It was obvious that something was about to happen.

Shortly after midnight on August 13, 1961, East German soldiers, policemen and Workers' Militia received orders to close the border with the West. At 2am, forty thousand men went into action, stringing barbed wire across streets leading into West Berlin and closing U- and S-Bahn lines to create what their commanders called "an anti-fascist protection barrier". Many Berliners were rudely evicted from their homes, while others, marginally less unfortunate, had their doors and windows blocked by bales of barbed wire and armed guards. Although the Allies reinforced patrols, they did nothing to prevent the **sealing of the border**.

Despite earlier rumours, most people in West and East Berlin were taken by surprise. Those who lived far from the border area only learned of its closure when they found all routes to West Berlin blocked. Crowds gathered and the border guards were reinforced to prevent trouble. There was little most people could do other than accept this latest development as a *fait accompli*. Others – including a few border guards – managed to take advantage of loopholes in the new barrier, and flee west. But within a few days, building workers were reinforcing the barbed wire and makeshift barricades with bricks and mortar, creating a **provisional version of the Wall**. As an additional measure, West Berliners were no longer allowed to cross the border into East Berlin.

Reaction in the West

Despite public outrage throughout West Germany and formal **diplomatic protests** from the Allies, everyone knew that to take a firmer line risked starting nuclear war. The West had to fall back on symbolic gestures: the Americans sent over General Lucius Clay, organizer of the Berlin airlift, and Vice-President Lyndon Johnson, on August 18. The **separation of families** in East Berlin to new depths and **economic problems** hit West Berlin, which was suddenly deprived of sixty thousand skilled workers who formerly commuted in from the GDR. They could only be replaced by creating special tax advantages to attract workers and businesses from the Federal Republic into West Berlin. American support for West Berlin was reaffirmed in August 1963, by President **John F. Kennedy**'s "*Ich bin ein Berliner...*" speech, but for all its rhetoric and rapturous reception, the West essentially had to accept the new status quo.

From 1961 onwards the GDR strengthened its **border fortifications**, completely sealing off West Berlin from East Berlin and the East German hinterland. The Wall became an almost impenetrable barrier – in effect two walls separated by a *Sperrgebiet* (forbidden zone) dotted with watchtowers and patrolled by soldiers and dogs. Border troops had orders to shoot to kill and often did so. Yet hundreds of successful **escapes** took place before the GDR was able to refine its techniques, and thousands of people passed over, under or through the Wall by various methods, usually involving extreme danger.

Berlin in the 1960s

The **gradual reduction of political tension** that occurred after the Wall had been standing a couple of years was partly due to improved relations between the superpowers, and mostly to local efforts. Under SPD Mayor **Willy Brandt**, talks were opened between the West Berlin Senate and the GDR government, resulting in the "**Pass Agreement**" of December 1963, whereby 730,000 West Berliners were able to pay brief visits to the East at the end of the year. Three more agreements were concluded over the next couple of years until the GDR decided to use border controls as a lever for winning **diplomatic recognition** (which the Federal Republic and its Western allies refused to give under the Hallstein doctrine). Access to West Berlin via routes through GDR territory was subject to official hindrance; on one occasion, deputies were prevented from attending a plenary session of the *Bundestag*, held in West Berlin in April 1965. New and more stringent **passport and visa controls** were levied on all travellers from June 1968 onwards.

As the direct threat to its existence receded, West Berlin society began to fragment along generational lines. Partly because Berlin residents could legally evade West German conscription, young people formed an unusually high proportion of the population. The immediate catalyst was the wave of **student unrest** in 1967–68, when initial grievances over unreformed, badly run universities soon spread to embrace wider disaffection with West Germany's materialistic culture. As in West Germany, the *APO* or **extra-parliamentary opposition** emerged as a strong and vocal force in West Berlin, criticizing what many people saw as a failed attempt to build a true democracy on the ruins of Nazi Germany. Another powerful strand was anti-Americanism, fuelled by US policy in Southeast Asia, Latin America and the Middle East. Both these viewpoints tended to bewilder and enrage older Germans.

The police reacted to street demonstrations in Berlin with a ferocity that shocked even conservatives. On June 2, 1967, a student was shot by police during a protest against a state visit by the Shah of Iran. The right-wing **Springer press** (deliberately sited just near the Wall) absolved the police, pinning all the blame on "long-haired Communists". When someone tried to kill student leader **Rudi Dutschke** (April 11, 1968), there were huge and violent demonstrations against the Springer press. Although the mass-protest movement fizzled out towards the end of the 1960s, a new and deadlier opposition would emerge in the 1970s – partly born from the West German establishment's violent response to what was initially a peaceful protest movement.

Ostpolitik and détente

The international scene and Berlin's place in it changed considerably around the turn of the decade. Both superpowers now hoped to thaw the Cold War and reach a *modus vivendi*, while elections in the Federal Republic brought to power a chancellor committed to rapprochement with the GDR. On February 27, 1969, US President Richard Nixon called for an easing of international tension during his visit to Berlin. Soon afterwards, **Four Power Talks** were held in the former Allied Control Council building in the American sector. Against a background of negotiations between West Germany and the Soviet Union, and proposals for a European security conference, the participants decided to set aside broader issues in an effort to fashion a workable agreement on the status of the divided city.

This resulted in the **Quadripartite Agreement** (September 3, 1971), followed in December by inter-German agreements regarding transit routes to West Berlin and travel and traffic regulations for West Berliners. These were largely due to the efforts of Chancellor Willy Brandt, whose **Ostpolitik** aimed at normalizing relations between the two Germanys. Treaties were signed with the Soviet Union and Poland in 1970, recognizing the validity of the Oder–Neisse line marking the Polish–German border. Finally, in 1972, the Federal Republic and the GDR signed a **Basic Treaty**. While stopping short of full recognition, it bound both states to respect each other's frontiers and *de facto* sovereignty.

In return for abandoning the Hallstein doctrine, West Germans were given access to friends and family across the border, which had been effectively denied to them (barring limited visits in the mid-1960s). However, the freedom to move from East to West was restricted to disabled people and senior citizens. This marked a concession by the new East German leader, **Erich Honecker**, who was regarded as a "liberal" when he succeeded Ulbricht in 1971. Aside from desiring access to West German know-how, markets and capital, Honecker had a personal reason for wanting closer ties: his own family lived in the Saarland.

The 1970s

During the 1970s Berlin assumed a new identity, breaking with the images and myths of the past. Thanks to the easing of Cold War tensions West Berlin was no longer a frontline city, and East Berlin lost much of its intimidating atmosphere. Throughout the decade, **West Berlin** had similar problems to those of West Germany: economic upsets triggered by the quadrupling of oil prices in 1974, and a wave of terrorism directed against the establishment. In addition, West Berlin suffered from a deteriorating stock of housing and rising unemployment – both alleviated to some extent by financial help from West Germany.

East Berlin remained relatively quiet. Under Honecker, living standards improved and there was some relaxation of the tight controls of the Ulbricht days. However, most people regarded the changes as essentially trivial, and escapes continued to be attempted, although by now the Wall was formidably deadly. In 1977 a rock concert in Alexanderplatz turned into a brief explosion of street unrest, which the authorities suppressed with deliberate brutality.

The 1980s

Throughout the 1970s and early 1980s, the Quadripartite Agreement and the inter-German treaties formed the backdrop to relations between West and East Berlin. The main irritant was the **compulsory exchange** of D-Marks for Ostmarks, which the GDR raised in value from DM6.50 to DM25 in 1980, deterring significant numbers of visitors. But on the whole, a degree of stability and normality had been achieved, enabling both cities to run smoothly on a day-to-day basis, without being the focus of international tension. Even after the partial resumption of the Cold War, following the Soviet invasion of Afghanistan in 1979, Berlin remained relatively calm. The only notable event was the shooting of an American officer on an alleged spying mission in Potsdam in the spring of 1985.

As elsewhere in West Germany, Berlin witnessed a crystallization of issues and attitudes and the flowering of new radical movements. Concern about the arms race and the environment was widespread; feminism and gay rights commanded increasing support. Left-wing and Green groups formed an **Alternative Liste** to fight elections, and a left-liberal newspaper, *Tageszeitung*, was founded. Organized squatting was the radical solution to Berlin's **housing crisis**. In 1981, the new Christian Democrat administration (elected after a financial scandal forced the SPD to step down) tried to evict the squatters from about 170 apartment buildings, and police violence sparked rioting in Schöneberg. The administration compromised by allowing some of the squatters to become legitimate tenants, which had a big effect on life in West Berlin. For the first time since the late 1960s, the social divisions that had opened up showed signs of narrowing. *Alternative Liste* delegates were elected to the

Berlin Senate for the first time in May 1981, and the same year witnessed a boom in **cultural life**, as the arts exploded into new vitality.

The **early 1980s** saw a resumption of frostiness in US–Soviet relations, which heightened concern about **nuclear weapons**. Anti-nuclear activists protested during the Berlin visit of President Ronald Reagan in June 1981. But the tension and sabre-rattling that had characterized the Cold War of the 1950s and 1960s didn't return to Berlin. In 1985 the USSR broke with its tradition of geriatric rulers when the dynamic and comparatively young **Mikhail Gorbachev** became General Secretary of the Soviet Communist Party. The West was slow to appreciate the full significance of his campaigns for *glasnost* and *perestroika*, and their initial impact on Berlin was slight. The city's status – and the division of Germany into separate states – seemed assured by the Quadripartite Agreement and the Basic Treaty.

Unfortunately, ideological hostility prevented the two halves of the city from jointly celebrating Berlin's 750th anniversary in 1987. Instead, **separate anniversary celebrations** were arranged. In East Berlin, these were preceded by a massive **urban renewal project**, in both the city centre and the inner suburbs. The SED boasted that the GDR was a mature socialist state, advancing to the front rank of European nations. It saw no need for *glasnost* or *perestroika* – indeed, it regarded them with deep suspicion.

In West Berlin, the elections of spring 1989 swept the CDU administration from power, and an **SPD/Alternative Liste coalition** took over, with Walter Momper as mayor. In Kreuzberg, demonstrations against what many regarded as an *Alternative Liste* sell-out were put down with unwarranted force, sparking running street battles. Further violence occurred on May 1, during the now-traditional annual wrecking spree by anarchists and far-leftists espousing anti-imperialist, anti-capitalist motives. For once, however, the police refrained from breaking heads, having been told to go easy by their chief.

The GDR resists Perestroika

In the East there were few visible signs of change as the decade wore on, but things were happening behind the scenes. The **Protestant Church** provided a haven for several **environmental and peace organizations**, which formed a nascent opposition. But the regime seemed as intractable as ever, dismissing Gorbachev-style reforms as inappropriate to the GDR. The most memorable rebuff was delivered by SED chief ideologist Kurt Hager, who said in April 1987, "You don't need to change the wallpaper in your apartment just because your neighbour is doing his place up." Open dissent was stamped on: in January 1988, a group of protesters who unfurled banners calling for greater freedom at the official demonstration in memory of Karl Liebknecht and Rosa Luxemburg were immediately arrested and imprisoned, later being expelled from the GDR.

Fearful of the changes sweeping the Soviet Union, Hungary and Poland, the authorities banned the Soviet magazine *Sputnik* and several Russian films from the 1960s, only now released from censorship. As a further insult to their subjects, the GDR's rulers heaped honours on the odious Romanian dictator Nicolae Ceauşescu. Although Poland and Hungary had both embarked on the road to democracy, the GDR was unmoving. SED leader Erich Honecker declared that the Wall would stand for another fifty or one hundred years if necessary, to protect "our republic from robbers". East Germans could only despair.

Few believed any more the endless lies and clichés that spanned the gap between official pronouncements and reality. The SED leadership seemed totally isolated from the mood of the people. There seemed no way out except individual attempts to escape. When Chris Gueffroy was shot dead while trying to cross the border at Neukölln on February 6, 1989, no one realized that he was to be the last person killed in such an attempt.

Something had to give, and give it did in a manner so dramatic and unpredictable that it surprised the whole world.

Die Wende to the present

1989 ranks as the most significant year in German history since 1945. In the space of twelve months a complete and unforseeable transformation (what Germans call *Die Wende*) occurred. German unification suddenly went from being a remote possibility to reality, forcing everyone to reassess the European order.

Once again Berlin was at the forefront of historical change, manifested in human terms by emotional scenes that caught the imagination of the world. When the Berlin Wall parted on November 9, 1989, it symbolized the end of an era: the Cold War was finally over, and a lifetime's dream had come true for most Germans – above all, those living in the East.

The beginning: exodus through Hungary

It was reform in another Eastern European country that made the incredible events of 1989 possible. On May 2, the Hungarian authorities began taking down the barbed wire along their border with Austria, creating a **hole in the Iron Curtain**. The event was televised worldwide, and thousands of East Germans saw it as a chance to get out. Aware that new visa laws making travel to Hungary more difficult would come into force in the autumn, they seized their chance during summer, when "holidays" provided a pretext.

It wasn't an easy option. Much of the barbed wire was still intact, and Hungarian troops patrolled the border. The lucky ones made it through the woods and swamps, evading soldiers who sometimes, but by no means always, turned a blind eye. In the early months, those who were caught were deported back to the GDR where jail awaited them. Later the Hungarians merely stamped the passports of those whom they intercepted, leaving it to the East German police to deal with them – if they returned home.

Wise to what was going on, the GDR authorities began trying to halt the increasing numbers of would-be escapees. Hungary-bound travellers were stopped and thoroughly searched. Anyone travelling light was deemed to be making a one-way trip and sent back. The same went for people carrying birth certificates and other important documents. Smart **escapers** began booking return tickets to destinations like Bulgaria, and travelling with baggage as if on a family holiday – only to make an unscheduled stop in Budapest.

The whole process was made slightly easier by the **illness of SED leader Erich Honecker**, which put him out of action from July 8 onwards. No one else seemed able to fill the ensuing power vacuum and enforce measures that would have enabled the state to check the draining away of its population. By August, some two hundred East Germans were crossing into Austria every night. Those who were caught could console themselves with the fact that the Hungarians no longer stamped their passports, leaving them free to try again. Many, unable to get through the border and rapidly running out of money, sought **refuge** in the West German embassy in Budapest. The situation was gradually reaching crisis point.

Mass escape

The first **mass exodus** happened on August 19, when seven hundred East Germans surged across the border into Austria, unhindered by Hungarian border guards. They got there under the pretext of holding a frontier peace picnic near Sopron; in fact, the whole escape was pre-arranged by the conservative *Paneuropa-Union*, with the support of the reformist Magyar politician Imre Pozsgay. On August 24, others were allowed to leave after the Red Cross stamped their documents with a "Permit de Voyage". By now some six thousand people had made it across the border and their success encouraged others to make the journey from the GDR to Hungary. By the beginning of September there were over **20,000 refugees** housed in Hungarian holiday camps and the West German embassy – which was by now overflowing.

Having considered the reactions of East and West Germany, the Hungarian government opted to please the latter, and announced on September 7 that "humanitarian measures" would take place in the next few days. This was diplomatic smooth talk for **opening the border** and allowing all the East Germans to leave. When the instruction was implemented on September 10, East German refugees heard the news at 7pm. Gyula Horn, the Hungarian foreign minister, announced: "The GDR citizens staying in this country can leave with their own, in other words GDR passports, to a country that is willing to receive them." The border opened at midnight, and 300 cars crossed over within fifteen minutes. A couple of hours later the first East German car crossed the Austro-German border at Passau. For those without transport, special buses and trains were laid on. The GDR government could only condemn what it called "an organized trade in human beings", while the West German government – from whom the Magyars hoped for investment – promised it would "not forget this independent decision by Hungary".

Other East Germans had meanwhile made their way to **Prague and Warsaw**, where they took refuge in West German embassy buildings. By the last week of September there were 3500 people in the Prague embassy, while Czech police and *Stasi* agents tried to hold back the thousands more who hoped to gain admission. Despite strongarm tactics, increasing numbers scaled the fence and swelled the crowd of refugees inside the embassy, where living conditions were daily growing more intolerable. Relief finally came on September 30, when **Hans-Dietrich Genscher**, West Germany's foreign minister, who had himself fled East Germany during the 1950s, appeared on the embassy balcony and announced that the refugees were to be allowed to leave. Special **trains** laid on by the GDR government were to ferry seventeen thousand refugees to West Germany via East German territory. As the trains passed through towns like Dresden, Karl-Marx-Stadt and Plauen, stations were stormed by people hoping to jump on board, and there were dozens of injuries as the police sealed off the tracks.

The October revolution

Within the GDR, morale plummeted. While people who had applied to leave and were still waiting for exit permits now despaired, thousands of others who had previously been content to make the best of things suddenly began thinking of emigration. Meanwhile, fledgling **opposition groups** like **Neues Forum** emerged, as East Germans took courage from the regime's evident disarray. People risked printing and circulating *samizdat* manifestos calling for reform and dialogue. SED leader Erich Honecker, whom West Germany's *Bild Zeitung* had already assigned to the obituary column, reappeared on the scene in time to join official celebrations marking the GDR's fortieth anniversary. Among the honoured guests were Mikhail Gorbachev, whom most East Germans had eagerly awaited; a delegation from Beijing bearing thanks for the SED's public approval of the Tiananmen Square massacre; and Romanian dictator Nicolae Ceaușescu.

There was tension on all sides at the **anniversary celebrations** on October 7. Gorbachev stressed the need for dialogue, receptivity to new ideas and the West German viewpoint. Honecker took a contrary stance, praising the status quo in stock clichés, seemingly oblivious to growing public discontent. The vainglorious parade of weaponry and floats passed off calmly (only party loyalists were admitted to the televised zone), but side-street protests and scuffles took place along the cavalcade route. As the day wore on, these escalated into a huge demonstration, which the police and *Stasi* brutally suppressed. Thousands of arrests were made, and prisoners were subjected to degrading treatment and beatings. Simultaneous **demonstrations** in Dresden and Leipzig were dealt with even more harshly. But the people were growing bolder, as the regime's self-confidence diminished.

A week later, most of those arrested on October 7 were released, and sections of the press voiced oblique criticism of the party leadership's handling of the crisis. The Politburo offered to talk with the opposition, but refused to legalize it. Monday, October 9, saw **nationwide demonstrations**, which came close to bloodshed in **Leipzig**, where 70,000 people marched through the city. Honecker ordered the local security forces to suppress the protest by any means necessary, including force of arms. City hospitals were alerted, and extra plasma was rushed in to cope with the expected casualties. But the march went ahead and Honecker's orders were never executed. Whether someone in the Politburo countermanded them, or the local party secretary or security boss simply ignored them, remains unclear. The main point was that elements of the regime drew the line at wholesale slaughter.

Indeed, the whole Politburo of the SED had become disenchanted with Honecker's rigidity. He was an obvious target for public hatred, and protests were gathering momentum daily. In Leipzig, now the focal point of opposition, the latest protest brought 150,000 people onto the streets. For the leadership, the strain proved too great: after eighteen years as party secretary, **Erich Honecker was suddenly replaced by Egon Krenz** on October 18. It seems that Honecker threatened to resign unless the Politburo supported his hard line; instead, they accepted his resignation in silence, and he left the room "an old and broken man". Krenz, whom SED-watchers dubbed the "crown prince", was a 52-year-old Politburo member with a hardline reputation of his own: it was he who had congratulated the Beijing government after it had crushed the Chinese democracy movement. Confounding expectations, however, Krenz immediately announced that the regime was ready for dialogue, although his reputation was to remain a stumbling block when it came to gaining popular trust.

The continuing exodus

Over the next week, as newspaper reports criticizing the government increased in frequency, the opposition gained ground and the exodus of GDR citizens continued. On October 27, the government declared an **amnesty** for those convicted of *Republiksflucht* (fleeing the country) or jailed for demonstrating, but the pressure on the streets kept rising. On November 4, East Berlin witnessed the largest **street protest** since the workers' uprising of 1953, as over one million citizens demonstrated. The vast crowd walked from

the headquarters of the ADN state news agency to Alexanderplatz, where they were addressed by reformists, writers and priests. Banners calling for the demolition of the Wall were unfurled. The author Stefan Heym, a long-time critic of the regime, told the crowd: "It's as if someone's thrown open a window after years of dullness and fug, platitudes, bureaucratic arbitrariness and blindness." Author Heiner Müller added: "If the government should resign during the next week, it will be permitted to dance at demonstrations."

The authorities made hasty **concessions**. The same day, Krenz agreed to allow five thousand East Germans who were packed into the West German embassy in Prague to leave for the West. It was also announced that GDR citizens no longer required visas to visit Czechoslovakia – in effect, permitting emigration via Czechoslovakia. People swarmed across the border to exploit this loophole, and fifteen thousand of them had reached Bavaria by November 6. The same day, 500,000 citizens demonstrated in Leipzig, winning fresh concessions – the promise of thirty days' foreign travel a year – that satisfied no one.

Next, the SED tried placating people with **resignations**. The government of Prime Minister Willi Stoph quit on November 7, with the Politburo following suit the next day. On the new executive that replaced it, Krenz and Berlin party boss Günter Schabowski were the only relics from the old order; the new prime minister, **Hans Modrow**, had acquired something of a liberal reputation during his previous job as Dresden party chief. Simultaneously, the Ministry of the Interior accepted an application from *Neues Forum* to be considered a legal group. Across the GDR, hardline officials were resigning in the face of ever-increasing demands from the street, and the exodus of citizens was continuing. By now, 200,000 East Germans had left the country since the beginning of 1989.

The Wall opens

The **opening of the Berlin Wall** was announced almost casually. On the evening of Thursday, November 9, Schabowski told a press conference that East German citizens were free to leave the GDR with valid exit visas, which were henceforth to be issued without delay. Journalists were puzzled: did this really mean that the Wall was effectively open? As news filtered through to the East German population, they sought confirmation by calling the TV stations, which broadcast Schabowski's announcement several times in the course of the evening. Hardly daring to believe it, citizens started heading for the nearest border crossings, with or without visas. A couple who passed through the Bornholmer Strasse crossing at 9.15pm may well have been the first to leave under the new law.

In both East and West Berlin, people flocked to the Wall. Huge crowds converged on the **Brandenburg Gate**, where an impromptu **street party** broke out. As West Berliners popped champagne corks and Germans from both sides of the Wall embraced, the *Volkspolizei* gave up checking documents and simply let thousands of East Germans walk through into West Berlin, from which they had been barred for 28 years. The scenes of joy and disbelief were flashed around a world taken by surprise. West German Chancellor **Helmut Kohl** had to interrupt a state visit to Warsaw and rush to West Berlin, where the international press was arriving in droves. Inside the GDR, disbelief turned to joy as people realized that the unimaginable had happened.

The opening of the Wall was a hard act to follow, but events acquired even greater momentum. On November 10, the Jannowitzbrücke U-Bahn station reopened after 28 years, making it possible for East Berliners to go to West Berlin by U-Bahn. On Saturday, November 11, **500,000 East Berliners visited West Berlin**. There were reports of mile-long queues at checkpoints, where 2.7 million exit visas were issued during the first weekend after the opening of the Wall. West Germans – and TV-viewers around the world – gaped at the streams of Trabant cars pouring into West Berlin, where shops enjoyed a bonanza as East Germans spent their DM100 "welcome money", given to all GDR visitors by the Federal Republic. On November 12, the mayors of the two Berlins, Walter Momper and Erhard Krack, met and shook hands at the newly opened Potsdamer Platz border crossing. Just over two years earlier, Krack had spurned an invitation to the West Berlin celebrations marking the city's 750th anniversary, saying that West Berlin "does not exist for us".

Protest and further reform

Inside the GDR the pace of protest didn't slacken, although the opposition was as surprised as anyone by the rapid changes. Demonstrations continued across the country; in places like Leipzig (now known as the "hero city of the revolution") they had practically become institutionalized. Feelings were still running high against Krenz and other government figures seen as tainted by their association with the old system. Not least of the problems facing Prime Minister Modrow was the **declining value of the Ostmark**. The black market rate fell from ten to twenty Ostmarks per Deutschmark, and enforcing the official rate of 1:1 became virtually impossible. A fiscal crisis loomed on the horizon.

On the second weekend after the opening of the Wall, the GDR authorities announced that **ten million visas** had been issued since November 9 – an incredible statistic considering the whole population of the GDR was sixteen million. By now all eyes were on the Brandenburg Gate, where the western media was massing in expectation of a grand reopening. Their hopes were dashed on November 19, when Krenz announced that the opening of the Gate was a symbolic affair in which he had no interest at the moment. Attention shifted back to events in the GDR, whose parliament, the *Volkskammer*, was asserting itself – particulary the hitherto "tame" parties allied to the SED.

The *Volkskammer* motion **ending the leading role of the SED** was passed (December 1) just as pent-up feeling against the *Stasi* erupted in a series of demos and sporadic attacks on its premises and members. These calmed down with a promise from the government that the dismantling of the formidable *Stasi* security service would begin straight away. In the first week of December, **round-table talks** between government and opposition began in an attempt to thrash out the future. After some haggling, the government agreed to one of the opposition's prime demands, pledging **free elections on May 6, 1990** – these were later brought forward to March 18.

At a special **SED conference** (December 15–17), the party decided to emulate the Hungarian Communists and repackage itself as the new, supposedly voter-friendly **PDS** – *Partei des Demokratischen Sozialismus* or "Democratic Socialist Party". As one of the last representatives of the old guard, Egon Krenz was consigned to political oblivion. His successor, **Gregor Gysi**, was a previously unknown lawyer who had defended a number of dissidents under the old regime. Almost immediately, Gysi and Modrow had to respond to a new initiative from **Chancellor Kohl**, who visited Dresden on December 19. Addressing a huge, enthusiastic crowd as "dear countrymen", Kohl promised that he wouldn't leave them in the lurch, and declared his ultimate goal of a **united Germany**.

Hans Modrow took Kohl's visit as an opportunity to announce the **reopening of the Brandenburg Gate**. Initially it was opened to pedestrians only, with one channel in each direction. Almost simultaneously it was announced that the **removal of visa controls and compulsory currency exchange** for West German visitors to the GDR would be implemented ahead of schedule. By the year's end there were further signs of the two Berlins drawing closer together. Numerous joint economic, industrial and cultural projects were under consideration, and East Berlin city maps began to feature S- and U-Bahn stations in West Berlin (which had previously been represented by blank spaces).

Into the 1990s

On the face of it, Berlin's future had never looked so rosy, but for many Germans in the East, the new decade began under a palpable shadow of disappointment and fear. There was a general anxiety that the change from a planned to a market economy would push up rents, close factories and wipe out the value of pensions and savings, and already the first legal claims by former owners of apartment buildings in East Berlin were being lodged. Politically, reform seemed too slow in coming, and people suspected that the apparatus of SED control had merely gone underground, biding its time. Hence the outrage in January 1990, when the government proposed establishing a new security service based on the old *Stasi*.

Revelations of **corruption** among the former Communist leadership, and the discovery that West Germany's standard of living eclipsed anything offered by the GDR, produced massive disillusionment with the East German state. The notion of **German unification** became increasingly popular, dismaying some of the original opposition activists, who cherished hopes of a separate state, pursuing a "third way" between socialism and capitalism. Groups like *Neues Forum* began losing ground to parties modelled on Kohl's CDU, the social democratic SPD, and the far-right Republicans, all of which supported unification in one form or another.

When the GDR's first free elections were finally held on March 18, 1990, the result was a victory for a right-wing alliance dominated by the CDU under Lothar de Maizière. In reality this was a victory for Chancellor Helmut Kohl, the self-proclaimed champion of German unification. It was his promises of financial help and investment that had led people back to the CDU in the GDR, and it was to him that people were looking to ease the worsening economic plight.

During the two months following the election it began to seem possible that these hopes would be realized as, after a shaky start, the new government hammered out an agreement with the Federal Republic in mid-April about the introduction of the Deutschmark into the GDR, scheduled for July 1. The agreement on **economic union** was clearly a prelude to one on political union, for which a provisional date of autumn 1991 had been set. This was to be effected according to **article 23** of the Federal Republic's constitution, which made provision for any part of the GDR to request accession to West Germany. On June 17 a *Volkskammer* delegate called for immediate union by means of article 23: his motion was overturned but the issue of **reunification** was now firmly in the spotlight, and Kohl upped the ante by declaring 1990 the year of German unity.

However, at this stage it was the chancellor himself who was proving the biggest stumbling block en route to a united Germany. His ambiguous public stance (prompted by fear of alienating Republican support) on the inviolability of the Oder–Neisse line and other post-World War II borders was causing alarm in Poland and eliciting testy reactions from the EC countries. The advice of Foreign Minister **Hans Dietrich Genscher** finally forced Kohl to realize that he risked sacrificing German unity to party political expediency, and to affirm German commitment to existing borders.

As planned, **currency union** was rapidly effected on **July 1**, the most enduring image being that of East Berliners thronging into city centre banks to claim their allotment of Deutschmarks. With monetary union the GDR began to fade away rapidly: overnight, eastern produce vanished from the nation's shops, replaced by western consumer goods, and, superficially at least, it seemed as though a second "economic miracle" was about to begin. Yet for many people in the GDR, the expectation that economic reform and West German know-how would substantially improve their standards of living within a few years was tempered by fear of rent increases and factory closures during the transformation to a market economy.

The political background

For the time being, however, fears like these were overshadowed by **political developments**. It was time to address head-on the issue of reunification, and the "two plus four" talks between the two Germanys and the wartime Allies had established that the west would not stand in the way of the Germans – though the final approval of the Soviet Union had yet to be secured.

On July 15 Kohl met with **Mikhail Gorbachev** in the Caucasus, where they worked out a mutually acceptable series of conditions for the union of the two Germanys. It was agreed that Soviet troops would withdraw from Germany over a period of three to four years and that a united Germany would be free to decide for itself which military alliance it would belong. An important proviso was that no foreign troops or nuclear weapons would be stationed on the territory of the former GDR.

The last obstacle in the way of unification had been removed and it was now possible to set a firm date for the event. On August 23 an all-night *Volkskammer* session announced that the GDR would become part of the Federal Republic on October 3, 1990, and just over a week later East and West Germany signed an 1100-page **treaty of union**. On September 12, the Allied military commanders of Berlin and the German foreign minister signed an agreement restoring full sovereignty to Germany, and a day later the Federal Republic and the Soviet Union signed a treaty of co-operation, including a non-aggression clause.

Street level changes

The two Berlins, meanwhile, were already drawing together as the border withered away during the course of the year. Passport and customs controls for German citizens had ceased early in 1990 and, by the time of currency union, nationals of other countries, although nominally still subject to control, could cross the border unhindered. During the course of the year most of the central sections of **the Wall** had been demolished and numerous cross-border streets linked up once again.

As border controls in Berlin and elsewhere throughout the former Soviet bloc eased, Berlin became a magnet for the restless peoples of eastern Europe. First arrivals had been the **Poles**, who set up a gigantic impromptu street market on a patch of wasteland near the Wall, much to the chagrin of Berliners, who felt the order of their city threatened by the influx of thousands of weekend street traders selling junk out of suitcases. They were followed by **Romanians**, mainly gypsies, fleeing alleged persecution at home and hoping, by taking advantage of visa-free access to what was still the GDR, to secure a place for themselves in the new Germany. Post-unification visa regulations were to put a stop to the commuting activities of the Poles, but as asylum seekers the Romanians had the right to remain, and the sight of gypsy families begging on the streets of Berlin became commonplace.

The Stasi legacy

In East Berlin it was becoming apparent that a united German government was going to be plagued by questions arising from the immediate past of the GDR. In the run-up to reunification, activists from the GDR citizens' opposition groups occupied the former *Stasi* HQ in Magdalenenstrasse, demanding an end to the removal of *Stasi* **files** to West Germany. The protesters demanded that the files remain in the former GDR after reunification, mainly so that victims of the *Stasi* would have evidence of what had happened to them, enabling them to claim compensation and possibly bring their persecutors to justice. The *BND* (*Bundesnachrichtendienst* – West Germany's secret service) had other ideas, however, and was keen to get its hands on the files, presumably to dispose of potentially embarrassing revelations about the extent to which the *Stasi* had penetrated West German political life.

After a promise from the West German government that the files would remain in the GDR for the time being, the protest action fizzled out, and following reunification the German government discreetly removed the remaining files to Bonn.

Unification and beyond

On **October 3, 1990**, the day of **reunification**, Chancellor Kohl spoke to assembled dignitaries and massive crowds in front of the Reichstag. A conscious effort was made to rekindle the spontaneous joy and fervour that had gripped the city on the night the Wall was opened and during Berlin's first post-*Wende* new year, but for many ordinary people already experiencing the economic side-effects of the collapse of the GDR the celebrations left a bitter taste. On the sidelines anti-unification demonstrators marched through the streets, precipitating minor **clashes with the police**.

Just over a month later, on the night of November 13, the reunited Berlin experienced its first **major upheaval** when SPD mayor Walter Momper ordered the police to evict **West Berlin squatters** who had occupied a number of tenement blocks in the eastern Berlin district of Friedrichshain. The violent tactics of the police, coupled with the uncompromising stance of the radical *Autonome* squatters, who responded with petrol bombs and a hail of missiles from the rooftops, resulted in the fiercest **rioting** seen in the city since 1981, with dozens of police injured and over three hundred squatters arrested. Politically, the unrest resulted in the **collapse** of the fragile Red-Green SPD/Alternative Liste coalition that had governed West Berlin for the previous twenty months.

Elections and New Year problems

These events did much to ensure a **CDU victory** in the **city elections** held on **December 2** to coincide with Germany's first nationwide elections since 1933. Nationally the CDU, in coalition with the FDP (Free Democrats), triumphed easily, though in Berlin the victory was by a narrower margin. One surprise in the Berlin elections (which were marked by irritatingly facile poster campaigns from all parties) was the fact that the PDS secured 25 percent of the vote in eastern Berlin on an anti-unemployment and anti-social inequality ticket.

The immediate result of the city elections in Berlin was the replacement of SPD Mayor Momper by the **CDU's Eberhard Diepgen**, who faced the unenviable task of dealing with the united city's **mounting difficulties**: to the obvious problem of unemployment could be added a worsening housing crisis, increasing right-wing extremism, and rising crime in the eastern part of the city with its demoralized and under-equipped police force. At the start of 1991, with celebrations of the first united Christmas and New Year over, it was time for the accounting to begin in earnest. The new year brought vastly unpopular **tax increases** in the western part of Germany to

pay for the spiralling **cost of unification**, which an embarrassed government was now forced to admit it had underestimated. As the year wore on and **unemployment** continued to rise, Kohl's honeymoon with the east soon came to an end. The man who had been mobbed in the former GDR only a year previously was now conspicuously reluctant to show himself there, and when he finally did, in April, he was greeted by catcalls and egg-hurlers.

Meanwhile, **ill-feeling** between easterners and westerners, which had first become apparent the previous year, continued. Western Berliners resented the tax increases and rising rents and mourned the passing of their subsidized island existence, while easterners, grappling with economic hardship, resented the fact that their poverty had reduced them to the status of second-class citizens. However, occasional strikes and dark mutterings about a long hot summer to come aside, the early part of the year passed relatively peacefully. The only major unrest in Berlin came with the outbreak of the **Gulf War** in January, which provoked large and sporadically violent **anti-war demonstrations**, recalling the early 1980s when the German peace movement had been a force to be reckoned with.

Post-unification problems

By mid-1991 the reserves of optimism topped up by currency union and unification had evaporated, particularly in the eastern part of the city, where the full force of social dislocation was felt. The loss of subsidies and tax breaks quickly had a **severe economic effect** on the previously immune west. On July 1, over 300,000 workers in subsidized, part-time work were made unemployed; at the same time, the huge **federal subsidies** that had propped up West Berlin's economy throughout the postwar years started to be scaled down to zero, removing DM8.5 million a year – around half the city's budget – from the municipal coffers. Unemployment, spiralling rents, and the wholesale flight of businesses hit the city.

Meanwhile, events at a national level were hardly encouraging. The Red Army Faction's assassination, on April 1, of **Detlev Rohwedder**, head of the *Treuhandgesellschaft* responsible for privatizing the ex-GDR's industry, did little to bolster hopes of imminent economic improvement. Neither was general confidence in the government's ability to deal with the situation boosted by the CDU's defeat in local elections in Kohl's local powerbase of Rheinland-Pfalz, a result seen by many as a symptom of growing disenchantment with Kohl's handling of the first months of unification.

On June 20 an unexpected *Bundestag* decision to **relocate the seat of government to Berlin** (all key functions are to be transferred by 2003 at the latest) provided brief distraction, but by September attention was once more focused on the darker side of reunification. **Attacks on foreigners**, commonplace in the GDR even before the *Wende*, had been increasing steadily since the fall of the Wall. In September they mounted in intensity with one of the worst outbreaks taking place in the small Saxon town of **Hoyerswerda**, where a mob stormed a hostel housing asylum seekers, necessitating the removal of the residents under police escort.

Hoyerswerda became a symbol for a wave of anti-foreigner violence that extended into western Germany, and which the government seemed unable to deal with. Rather than condemning the attacks in a forthright manner, the political establishment concentrated on calling for the reform of Germany's liberal asylum laws. Electorally this made sense – the far right was gaining ground, as shown by the Republicans gaining 10.5 percent of the vote in Baden-Württemberg's local elections in April 1992 – but many observers felt that such moral haziness only served to offer encouragement to the extremists.

But the main social pressure, one felt particularly strongly in Berlin, was the **growing distance** between west and east Germans. After forty years of separation no one expected the social gulf between them to be bridged overnight, but western anger at higher taxes to subsidize the east, and eastern resentment of what were seen as patronizing and neo-colonialist western attitudes to the people of the former GDR, brought about an antipathy bordering on open hatred between the two peoples. Furthermore, it became apparent that the ever-increasing cost of reunification had pushed the German economy into recession.

By the end of 1992 the **civil war in Yugoslavia** had had its effect on the city, as Germany absorbed more Yugoslavs fleeing persecution and violence than any other European nation – again, much to the distaste of the far right, whose fol-

lowers were in action elsewhere: in August a Jewish memorial was attacked in the city, and in September, neo-Nazis were convicted of beating an Angolan student to death in the town of Eberswalde-Finow, 35km northeast of Berlin. The November murders of a Berlin left-winger, three Turks (two of whom had been born in Germany), and a man mistakenly thought to be a Jew were all claimed by neo-Nazi groups.

In October 1992 the ex-mayor of the city, founder of *Ostpolitik* and international statesman **Willy Brandt** died at the age of 78: fittingly, he was given the first state funeral reunified Berlin had seen, and was buried in a small forest cemetery at the edge of the city. Meanwhile the hunt for Erich Honecker on charges of having been responsible for the deaths of would-be escapees from East Germany had been abandoned on the grounds of his ill-health. Honecker was allowed to join his daughter in Chile at the start of 1993 and died there the following year.

Berlin in the mid-1990s

Berlin has now come to terms with the fact that the problems thrown up by reunification – unemployment, rising crime, tension between east and west – aren't going to go away. The city has had its share of violence against foreigners too, though not on the scale seen in places like Rostock and Hoyerswerda.

The summer of 1994 brought the **departure of the troops** of the World War II Allies, which had maintained a presence in the city since 1945. Their exit was a symbolic end to nearly fifty years of occupation and a signal that Berlin was once again in control of its own destiny. However, the fifth anniversary of the fall of the Wall in November 1994 was marked by muted retrospectives. No one was much in the mood for celebration: the continuing psychological division of the city had been made plain the previous summer, when the reformed Communist party, the PDS, secured forty percent of the vote in the eastern part of the city in the European Parliament elections.

Berlin in the late-1990s is undergoing a period of change as dramatic as any it has ever seen. Gearing up for the eventual full transfer of government from Bonn, the city centre district of Mitte is akin to a vast building site as major redevelopment schemes continue – notably along Friedrichstrasse and in the environs of Potsdamer

Platz. Elsewhere, plans are afoot to transform Alexanderplatz and Schlossplatz, and, despite its problems, Berlin has a boomtown feel with tens of thousands of workers flocking here from around Europe.

The building and bustle hide a great deal of **anxiety** however. The arrival of the national government and its legions of bureaucrats doesn't excite many Berliners. Many mourn the loss of the city's idiosyncratic flair; others are annoyed with the worsening traffic jams and crunch on housing.

Economic troubles add to the apprehensions. The huge costs of integrating the "new states" of the former GDR and belt-tightening necessitated by the Euro currency guidelines have caused deep cuts in social services and subsidies. 1997 saw huge **demonstrations** by construction unions and students protesting cutbacks, but to little avail. The cushy social net enjoyed by Germans – and particularly by Berliners – for so long is beginning to fray.

Still, Berlin is poised for success. As Germany's seat of government, as a bridge to emerging eastern Europe, and as a dynamic cultural centre, the city should take its place once again as a leading metropolis of Europe. Long a stage for others, it is now finally a city that forges its own history.

Books

Publishers are detailed below in the form British publisher/American publisher, where both exist. Where books are published in one country only, UK, US or G (for Germany) precedes the publisher's name; where the publisher is the same in the UK and US, only the publisher's name is given. Abbreviations: o.p. out of print; UP University Press.

History

Early and pre-World War II

Michael Farr, *Berlin! Berlin!* (US: Kyle Cathie). This compressed (200 page) history of the city from its earliest origins has all the main facts and plenty of colour and character. An ideal introductory text, though by no means the deepest or fullest account.

Otto Friedrich, *Before the Deluge: A Portrait of Berlin in the 1920s* (US: HarperPerrenial). An engaging social history, full of tales and anecdotes, of the city when Dada and decadence reigned. An excellent history of Berlin's most engaging period.

Mary Fulbrook, *A Concise History of Germany* (Cambridge UP). "Concise" is the key word for this post-unification history, whose brevity is simultaneously its strength and its weakness. Nevertheless, a useful basic history, and a clear introduction to a difficult subject.

Walter Hubatsch, *Frederick the Great: Absolutism and Administration* (Thames & Hudson o.p.); **Christopher Duffy**, *Frederick the Great: A Military Life* (UK: Routledge o.p.). Two contrasting biographies on different aspects of the man who brought Berlin and Prussia to the forefront of German affairs and to a place among the great powers of Europe.

Alex de Jong, *The Weimar Chronicle* (Paddington Press o.p./New American Library). While not the most comprehensive of accounts of the Weimar Republic, this is far and away the most lively. A couple of chapters focus on Berlin, and the book is spiced with eyewitness memoirs and a mass of engaging detail, particularly on the arts in Berlin. Worth hunting the libraries for.

Ebehard Kolb, *The Weimar Republic* (UK: Unwin & Hyman). The most recent study of the endlessly fascinating but fundamentally flawed state – the only previous attempt at a united and democratic German nation – that survived for just fourteen years. A bad omen?

Giles MacDonogh, *Berlin* (UK; Sinclair-Stevenson). A solid history of the city, emphasizing its early years. It's organized geographically rather than chronologically, which makes it at times confusing and repetitive. A good history, but perhaps not the best introduction to the city.

Questions on German History (G: Bundestag Press). English translation of the guide to the Reichstag exhibition of the same name. Handy if you're visiting, and, for the price, a good bargain read on the history of Germany and Berlin from 1800 to the present.

Alexander Reissner, *Berlin 1675–1945* (UK: Oswald Wolff o.p.). Subjective and often highly opinionated history of the city. A stimulating read, nevertheless.

John Willett, *Weimar Years* (Thames & Hudson/Abbeville Press o.p.). The man who has brilliantly translated Brecht's works into English here turns his attentions to the wider culture of the Weimar Republic.

Nazism and the war years

Allied Intelligence Map of Key Buildings (UK: After The Battle). This large detailed map is an excellent utility for anyone searching for Nazi and prewar remains in the city.

M. Baigent and R. Leigh, *Secret Germany* (UK: Penguin). By the authors of the superb investigative work on the Dead Sea Scrolls, this book on Claus von Stauffenberg, pivotal figure of the July 1944 bomb plot against Hitler, is a great disappointment. While the authors have dug up some facts about Stauffenberg's early life, there's little new information on the events of July 1944, and the weird quasi-mystical subplot concerning the teachings of nutty poet Stefan George would be laughable were it not linked to so tragic a conclusion.

Christabel Bielenberg, *The Past is Myself* (UK: Corg). Bielenberg, the niece of Lord Northcliffe, married German lawyer Peter Bielenberg in 1934 and was living with her family in Berlin at the outbreak of the war. Her autobiography (serialized for TV as *Christabel*) details her struggle to survive the Nazi period and Allied raids on the city, and to save her husband, imprisoned in Ravensbrück as a result of his friendship with members of the Kreisau resistance group.

Alan Bullock, *Hitler: A Study in Tyranny* (Penguin/HarperCollins). Ever since it was published, this scholarly yet highly readable tome has ranked as the classic biography of the failed Austrian artist and discharged army corporal whose evil genius fooled a nation and caused the deaths of millions.

George Clare, *Berlin Days 1946–1947* (Macmillan). "The most harrowing and yet most fascinating place on earth" is how Clare begins this account of his time spent as a British army translator. This is Berlin seen at what the Germans called the *Nullpunkt* – the zero point – when the city, its economy, buildings and society, began to rebuild almost from scratch. Packed with characters and observation, it's a captivating – if at times depressing – read.

Susan Everett, *Lost Berlin* (Hamlyn o.p./ Smithmark o.p.). A coffee-table account of inter-war Berlin. A wealth of photographs of the vanished city and some informative accounts of aspects of life in the city, with emphasis on the arts.

Joachim C. Fest, *The Face of the Third Reich* (Penguin/Pantheon). Mainly of interest for its biographies of the men surrounding the Führer – Göring, Goebbels, Hess, Himmler, et al.

D. Fisher and A. Read, *The Fall of Berlin* (Pimlico/Da Carpo). Superb account of the city's Götterdämmerung, carefully researched with a mass of anecdotal material you won't find elsewhere. An essential book for those interested in the period.

Bella Fromm, *Blood and Banquets* (US: Carol Publishing). Fromm, a Jewish aristocrat living in Berlin, kept a diary from 1930 until 1938. Her job as society reporter for the *Vossische Zeitung* gave her inside knowledge on the top figures of Berlin society, and the diaries are a chilling account of the rise of the Nazis and their persecution of Berlin's Jews.

Anton Gill, *A Dance Between Flames* (Abacus/Carroll & Graf o.p.). Gill's dense but readable account of 1920s-to-30s Berlin has lots of colour, quotation and detail but leans so heavily on a single source – *The Diary of Henry Kessler* – that you feel he should be sharing the royalties. Even so, one of the best books on the period.

Charles W. Haxthausen and Heidrun Suhr, *Berlin: Culture and Metropolis* (University of Minnesota). This collection of learned essays on twentieth-century Berlin is heavy-going in parts, but has fascinating essays on the city's cinema and the art of the Lustmord.

Adolf Hitler, *Table Talk* (UK: OUP o.p.). Hitler in his own words: Martin Bormann, one of his inner circle, recorded the dictator's pronouncements at meetings between 1941 and 1944.

Claudia Koonz, *Mothers in the Fatherland* (Methuen o.p./St Martin's Press). Recent and brilliantly perceptive study of the role of women in Nazi Germany. Includes a rare and revealing interview with the chief of Hitler's Women's Bureau, Gertrud Scholtz-Klink.

Brian Ladd, *The Ghosts of Berlin: Confronting German History in the Urban Landscape* (University of Chicago Press). Much dense talk of policy issues and urban planning, but within that discussion is an excellent history of the city.

Tony Le Tissier, *The Battle of Berlin* (UK: Jonathan Cape o.p.). Soldierly (the author is a retired lieutenant-colonel) shot-by-shot account of Berlin's final days. Authoritative, if a little dry. His *Berlin Then and Now* (UK: After the Battle) is a collection of photographs of sites in the city during the war years, contrasted with the same places today. This extraordinary book is the best way to find what's left of Nazi Berlin's buildings – a startling number are barely changed – and to correct myths (such as the position of the Führerbunker) that have long gone unchallenged. Beg, steal or borrow a copy if you have any interest in the city's past.

Martin Middlebrook, *The Berlin Raids* (Penguin/Penguin o.p.). Superbly researched account of the RAF's campaign to destroy the capital of the Third Reich by mass bombing. Based on interviews with bomber crews, Luftwaffe fighter pilots and civilians who survived the raids, it's a moving, compassionate and highly exciting read.

Cornelius Ryan, *The Last Battle* (New English Library o.p./Simon & Schuster). The Battle of Berlin turned into a sort of historic filmscript, with factual descriptions alongside speculated conversation. While reasonably accurate in its account of what happened, the style can be cloying.

William Shirer, *The Rise and Fall of the Third Reich* (Mandarin/Fawcett). The perfect complement to Bullock's book: Shirer was an American journalist stationed in Berlin during the Nazi period, and his history of the German state before and during the war has long been recognized as a classic. Notwithstanding its length and occasionally outdated perceptions, this book is full of insights and is ideal for dipping into, with the help of its exhaustive index.

James Taylor and Warren Shaw, *A Dictionary of the Third Reich* (UK: Penguin). The handiest reference book of the period, and difficult to put down, despite some glaring factual errors.

Hugh Trevor-Roper, *The Last Days of Hitler* (Papermac/University of Chicago Press). A brilliant reconstruction of the closing chapter of the Third Reich, set in the Bunker of the Reichs Chancellery on Potsdamer Platz. Trevor-Roper subsequently marred his reputation as the doyen of British historians by authenticating the forged Hitler Diaries, which have themselves been the subject of several books.

Marie Vassiltchikov, *The Berlin Diaries* (Mandarin o.p.). Daughter of a Russian emigré family and friend of the Bielenbergs (see above), Vassiltchikov's diaries provide a vivid portrait of wartime Berlin and the July 1944 bomb plot conspirators – whose members also numbered among her friends.

Peter Wyden, *Stella* (US: Doubleday). Stella Goldschlag was a young, very "Aryan"-looking Jewish woman who avoided deportation and death by working for the SS as a "catcher", hunting down Jews in hiding in wartime Berlin – including her former friends and even relatives. The author, who knew the young Stella, traces her life story and tries to untangle the morality and find some explanation for the motives behind what seem incalculably evil actions. A gripping, terrifying story made all the more chilling by the fact that its protagonist is still alive – and unrepentant.

Recent history and social studies

John Ardagh, *Germany and the Germans* (Penguin). The latest and most up-to-date characterization of the country and its people, taking into account its history, politics and psyche, and covering almost every aspect of national life. The section on Berlin, while brief, is packed with astute observations and illuminating facts.

Argonaut, *The Fourth Reich* (US: Argonaut Press). This excellent Californian review dedicated most of an issue to the rise of neo-Fascism and other problems confronting the new Germany. The title is a good indication of its slight tendency to alarmism, but there's so much unignorable factual material that the book is essential reading for those interested in contemporary Germany.

Timothy Garton-Ash, *We the People* (UK: Granta Books). An in-depth account of the revolutions in eastern Europe. There's a brief chapter on the GDR but, as ever, Garton-Ash is best when dealing with the political and intellectual background to the events in Poland and Czechoslovakia.

Norman Gelb, *The Berlin Wall* (UK: Michael Joseph o.p.). The definitive account of the building of the Wall and its social and political aftermath – as far as 1986. Includes a wealth of information and anecdotes not to be found elsewhere.

Mark Girouard, *Cities and People* (Yale UP). A well-illustrated social and architectural history of European urban development that contains knowledgeable entries on Berlin, particularly the eighteenth- and nineteenth-century periods.

Granta 30, *New Europe!* (UK: Granta). Granta's round-up of writing on and from central Europe published in spring 1990 contains pieces by Jurek Becker on German unification, and Werner Krätschell on the opening of the Wall.

Werner Hülsberg, *The German Greens* (Verso o.p./Routledge o.p.). A detailed analysis of Germany's most exciting political phenomenon, this book traces the movement's intellectual and political origins, chronicles its internal disputes, introduces the main characters, and analyzes its shortcomings.

Anne McElvoy, *The Saddled Cow* (Faber o.p.). Essays on different aspects of GDR life (interviews with border guards, pieces on the *Stasi*, etc) by the most insightful western commentator on the East. A useful document on the twilight years of the GDR.

Peter Millar, *Tomorrow Belongs to Us* (UK: Bloomsbury). A study of three generations of a family that runs, and lives above, a corner *Kneipe* in Prenzlauer Berg. Worth looking at for its interesting first-hand accounts.

David E. Murphy, Serfei A. Kondrashev and George Bailey, *Battleground Berlin: CIA vs KGB in the Cold War* (Yale University Press). A detailed account by participants of the tense, crafty skirmishing in Berlin between the spys of the two superpowers.

Amity Schlaes, *Germany: The Empire Within* (Cape o.p./Farrar Strauss & Giroux). A collection of essays on Germany, exploring its contemporary nature in interviews with people who recall the recent past. The two chapters on Berlin are much the best parts of the book.

Michael Simmons, *The Unloved Country* (UK: Abacus). Pre-*Wende* account of the GDR by the Guardian's man in eastern Europe. A bit dry and dull at times, but then so was the GDR.

John Simpson, *Despatches from the Barricades* (UK: Hutchinson o.p.). Cut-and-paste rush job about the 1989 revolutions. The GDR/Berlin chapter is serviceable enough, but short on any kind of real feel for the events.

Ken Smith, *Berlin* (Penguin o.p.). Considered, unsensational accounts of life before, during and after the fall of the Wall, including some fascinating first-hand accounts from the 1920s onwards.

Tearing Down the Curtain (UK: Hodder & Stoughton). The events of 1989 as seen by the London *Observer* team, including a strong, newsy chapter on East Germany and Berlin.

Hermann Waldenburg, *The Berlin Wall Book* (Thames & Hudson/Abbeville). A collection of photographs of the art and graffiti the Wall inspired, with a rather self-important introduction by the photographer.

Art and architecture

Peter Adam, *The Art of the Third Reich* (Thames & Hudson/Abrams). Engrossing and well-written account of the officially approved state art of Nazi Germany – a subject that for many years has been ignored or deliberately made inaccessible. Includes over three hundred illustrations, many reproduced for the first time since the war.

Alan Belfour, *Berlin, the Politics of Order: 1737–1989* (Rizzoli). A highly cerebral historical/architectural deconstruction of the area around Leipziger Platz. Through quotations, structuralist commentary, allusions and reference, a huge picture of a relatively tiny strip of the city is drawn, creating a paradigm of the richness and complexity of Berlin history. One staggering error – Columbus House recorded as headquarters of the SS, instead of Columbiadamm in a different part of the city – has resulted in the book often being sold off very cheaply.

Berlin: An Architectural History (Academy Editions o.p./St Martin's Press). Excellent – if academic – essays on the city's development from the thirteenth century to the present day. Somewhat heavy- going, but worth the effort.

Wolf-Dieter Dube, *The Expressionists* (Thames & Hudson). A good general introduction to Germany's most distinctive contribution to twentieth-century art.

Thomas Friedrich, *Berlin: A Photographic Portrait of the Weimar Years* (UK: Tauris Parke). Collection of fascinating old photos of the buildings and people that made pre-war Berlin one of the world's great cities. Has an introductory essay by Stephen Spender.

Peter Güttler (et al), *Berlin-Brandenburg: An Architectural Guide* (G: Ernst & Sohn). Brick-by-brick guide to the buildings of the city, in German and English. The definitive guide if you're interested in studying the city's architecture.

Post-War Berlin (Architecture Design Profile). A collection of scholarly essays on how the wartime legacy of destruction has been handled by the architects of the former East and West Berlin.

John Willet, *The Weimar Years* (Thames & Hudson/Abbeville). Heavily visual account of art, design and culture in pre-Nazi Germany. The seemingly Dada-influenced layout is a bit of a distraction.

Frank Witford, *Bauhaus* (Thames & Hudson). Comprehensive and well-illustrated guide to the architectural movement that flourished in Dessau and included the Berlin architect Walter Gropius (see p.130).

Guides and travel writing

Stephen Barber, *Fragments of the European City* (Reaktion Books). Written as a series of interlocking poetic fragments, this book explores the visual transformation of the contemporary European city, focusing on Berlin. An exhilarating evocation of the intricacies and ever-changing identity of the city.

Karl Baedeker, *Berlin and its Environs* (Baedeker o.p., but widely available at secondhand bookshops). First published in 1903, the learned old Baedeker is an utterly absorbing read, describing a grand imperial city now long vanished. There's advice on medicinal brine-baths, where to buy "mourning clothes", the location of the Esthonian embassy, and beautiful fold-out maps that enable you to trace the former course of long-gone streets (see also our map on pp.306–307). An armchair treat.

Andrew Gumbel, *Berlin* (Cadogan/Globe Pequot). Handy little book of walking tours. Scant practical information, but good for literary background.

Hans Peter Heinicke, *The Secret Sights of Berlin* (G: Wort & Bild Specials). Not quite as intriguing as the title suggests, but with the occasional titbit of offbeat information.

Gordon McLachlan, *Germany: the Rough Guide* (Rough Guides). Companion volume to the book you're holding, a highly readable, erudite and comprehensive guide that's packed with practical information. Essential if your travels take you further than Berlin.

John Miller and Tim Smith, *Chronicles Abroad: Berlin* (Chronicle Books). A suitcase-sized anthology of fiction, reportage and impressions of the city, including pieces by Brecht, Kafka, Isherwood, E.T.A. Hoffmann and Josephine Baker.

Karin and Arno Reinfrank, *Berlin: Two Cities under Seven Flags, A Kaleidoscopic A–Z* (Berg/Berg o.p.). Quirky observations on Berlin make this an enjoyable study of the city's background.

Uwe Seidel, *Berlin & Potsdam* (G: Peter Rump). Illustrated guide to the city that has much detail on what you can't see any more. Useful if you need more knowledge of the what-stood-where kind.

Claire Sharp, *Berlin* (UK: Lascelles). An enjoyable guide to the city with some quirky insights and an insider's knowlege of its bars and restaurants.

Fiction

Len Deighton, *Winter: A Berlin Family 1899–1945* (Grafton/Ballantine). This fictional saga traces the fortunes of a Berlin family through World War I,

the rise of Nazism and the collapse of the Third Reich: a convincing account of the way in which a typical upper-middle-class family weathered the wars. Better known is Deighton's *Funeral in Berlin* (Grafton/Ballantine), a spy-thriller set in the middle of Cold War Berlin and based around the defection of an Eastern chemist, aided by hard-bitten agent Harry Palmer (as the character came to be known in the film starring Michael Caine). *Berlin Game* (Grafton/Ballantine) pits British SIS agent Bernard Samson (whose father appears in *Winter*) against an arch manipulator of the East Berlin secret service, and leaves you hanging for the sequels *Mexico Set* and *London Match*.

Alfred Döblin, *Berlin-Alexanderplatz* (Continuum). A prominent socialist intellectual during the Weimar period, Döblin went into exile shortly after the banning (and burning) of his books in 1933. This is his weightiest and most durable achievement, an unrelenting epic of the city's proletariat.

Hugo Hamilton, *Surrogate City* and *The Love Tent* (UK: Faber o.p.). Hamilton has set two of his recent novels in Berlin. *Surrogate City* is a love story between an Irish woman and a Berliner and is strongly evocative of pre-*Wende* Berlin. *The Love Tent* is the tale of a journalist researching the history of a woman's involvement with the *Stasi* and gives a realistic account of contemporary Berlin.

Robert Harris, *Fatherland* (Arrow/HarperCollins). A Cold War novel with a difference: Germany has conquered Europe and the Soviet Union, and the Cold War is being fought between the Third Reich and the USA. Against this background, Berlin detective Xavier March is drawn into an intrigue involving murder and Nazi officials. All this owes much to Philip Kerr (see overleaf) but Harris's picture of Nazi Berlin in 1964 is chillingly believable.

Lillian Hellman, *Pentimento* (Quartet/New American Library-Dutton). The first volume of Hellman's memoirs contains "Julia", supposedly (it was later charged to be heavily fictionalized) the story of one of her friends caught up in the Berlin resistance. This was later made into a finely acted, if rather thinly emotional, film of the same name.

Christopher Isherwood, *Goodbye to Berlin* (Mandarin/Penguin). Set in the decadent atmosphere of the Weimar Republic as the Nazis steadily gain power, this collection of stories brilliantly evokes the period and brings to life some classic Berlin characters. It subsequently formed the basis of the films *I Am a Camera* and the later remake *Cabaret*. See also Isherwood's *Mr Norris Changes Trains* (Minerva/New Directions), the adventures of the overweight eponymous hero in pre-Hitler Berlin and Germany.

Philip Kerr, *March Violets* (Penguin/Viking Penguin o.p.). Well-received detective thriller set in the early years of Nazi Berlin. Keen on period detail – nightclubs, the Olympic Stadium, building sites for the new autobahn – and with a terrific sense of atmosphere, the book rips along to a gripping denouement. Bernie Gunther, its detective hero, also features in Kerr's other wartime Berlin crime novel, *The Pale Criminal* (Penguin/Viking Penguin o.p.). But his best work so far, *A German Requiem* (Penguin/Viking Penguin o.p.), has Gunther travelling from ravaged postwar Berlin to run into ex-Nazis in Vienna. All three books are available in an omnibus edition entitled *Berlin Noir* (Penguin).

Ian McEwan, *The Innocent* (Vintage/Bantam). McEwan's novel brilliantly evokes 1950s Berlin as seen through the eyes of a post office worker caught up in early Cold War espionage – and his first sexual encounters. Flounders in its obligatory McEwan nasty final twist, but laden with a superbly researched atmosphere.

J.S. Marcus, *The Captain's Fire* (US: Knopf). The complaints and reflections of a young American Jew living in the former east of Berlin. Written in an artful and self-conscious style, and spotted with references to Kafka and Walter Benjamin,

the book, though full of atmosphere, leaves the reader unfulfilled.

William Palmer, *The Pardon of St Anne* (Vintage). The story of a morally shallow Berlin photographer whose professional involvement with the Nazis forces him – and the reader – to reassess his values.

Ulrich Plenzdorf, *Die neuen Leiden des jungen W.* ("The New Sorrows of Young W."; G: Suhrkamp Taschenbuch, German-language only/Continuum). A satirical reworking of Goethe's *Die Leiden des jungen Werthers* set in 1970s East Berlin. It tells the story of Edgar Wibeau, a young rebel without a cause adrift in the antiseptic GDR, and when first published it pushed against the borders of literary acceptability under the old regime with its portrayal of alienated, disaffected youth.

Holly-Jane Rahlens, *Becky Bernstein Goes Berlin* (US: Arcade Books). A young Jewish girl from Queens falls in love with a German, emigrates to Berlin and discovers a new love for the city. A bouncy and funny novel full of New York wit.

Peter Schneider, *The Wall Jumper* (Allison & Busby o.p./Pantheon o.p.). A series of fascinating cameos that describe life under the Wall, and the intrigue, characters and tragedy it caused.

Ian Walker, *Zoo Station* (Abacus/Grove Atlantic o.p.). Not strictly fiction but a personal recollection of time spent in Berlin in the mid-1980s. Perceptive, engaging and well informed, it is the most enjoyable account of pre-*Wende* life in the city available.

Language

German is a very complex language and you can't hope to master it in a short time. As English was a compulsory subject in West Berlin's school curriculum, most people who have grown up in the west since the war have some familiarity with it, which eases communication a great deal. In the east, Russian was the language most often taught, and you won't find so many English speakers among former inhabitants of the GDR.

But wherever you are, a smattering of German will help. Also, given that the city still has leftovers of the American and British forces, who make little effort to integrate into local communities or learn German, people are particularly sensitive to presumptuous English speakers. On the other hand, most will be delighted to practise their English on you once you've stumbled through your German introduction. Of the many teach-yourself courses available, best is the BBC course, *Deutsch Direkt*. The most useful **dictionary** is the pocket-sized *Mini Dictionary* (Harrap). For a **phrasebook**, look no further than the *Rough Guide to German* (Rough Guides; £3.50/$5.00). Practical and easy-to-use, it allows you to speak the way you would in your own language.

Pronunciation

English speakers find the complexities of German grammar hard to handle, but pronunciation isn't as daunting as it might first appear. Individual syl-lables are generally pronounced as they're print-ed – the trick is learning how to place the stress-es in the notoriously lengthy German words.

Vowels and umlauts

a as in father, but can also be used as in hut
e as in day
i as in leek
o as in bottom
u as in boot
ä is a combination of a and e, sometimes pro-nounced like **e** in bet (eg Länder) and sometimes like **ai** in paid (eg spät)
ö is a combination of o and e, like the French eu
ü is a combination of u and e, like true

Vowel combinations

ai as in lie
au as in house
ie as in free
ei as in trial
eu as in oil

Consonants

Consonants are pronounced as they are written, with no silent letters. The differences from English are:
j is pronounced similar to an English y
r is given a dry throaty sound, similar to French
s is pronounced similar to, but slightly softer than an English z
v is somewhere between f and v
w is pronounced same way as English v
z is pronounced ts
The German letter ß, the *Scharfes S*, occasionally replaces ss in a word: pronunciation is identical.

Gender

German words can be one of three genders: masculine, feminine or neuter. Each has its own ending and corresponding ending for attached adjectives. If you don't know any German gram-mar, it's safest to use either neuter or male forms.

GERMAN WORDS AND PHRASES

Basics

Ja, Nein	Yes, No
Bitte	Please/ You're welcome
Bitte Schön	A more polite form of *Bitte*
Danke, Danke Schön	Thank you, Thank you very much
Wo, Wann, Warum?	Where, When, Why?
Wieviel?	How much?
Hier, Da	Here, There
Jetzt, Später	Now, Later
Geöffnet, offen, auf	All mean "open"
Geschlossen, zu	Both mean "closed"
Früher	Earlier
Da drüben	Over there
Dieses	This one
Jenes	That one
Gross, Klein	Large, Small
Mehr, Weniger	More, Less
Wenig	A little
Viel	A lot
Billig, Teuer	Cheap, Expensive
Gut, Schlecht	Good, Bad
Heiss, Kalt	Hot, Cold
Mit, Ohne	With, Without
Wo ist . . . ?	Where is . . . ?
Wie komme ich nach . . . ?	How do I get to (a town)?
Wie komme ich zur/zum . . . ?	How do I get to (a building, place)?

Greetings and times

Auf Wiedersehen	Goodbye
Auf Wiederhören	Goodbye (telephone only)
Tschüs	Goodbye (informal)
Guten Morgen	Good morning
Guten Abend	Good evening
Guten Tag	Good day
Wie geht es Ihnen?	How are you? (polite)
Wie geht es Dir?	How are you? (informal)
Lass mich in Ruhe	Leave me alone
Hau ab	Get lost
Geh weg	Go away
Heute	Today
Gestern	Yesterday
Morgen	Tomorrow
Vorgestern	The day before yesterday
Übermorgen	The day after tomorrow
Tag	Day
Nacht	Night
Woche	Week
Monat	Month
Jahr	Year
Wochenende	Weekend
Am Vormittag/ vormittags	In the morning
Am Nachmittag/nachmittags	In the afternoon
Am Abend	In the evening

Days, months and dates

Montag	Monday
Dienstag	Tuesday
Mittwoch	Wednesday
Donnerstag	Thursday
Freitag	Friday
Samstag	Saturday
Sonnabend	Saturday
Sonntag	Sunday
Januar	January
Februar	February
März	March
April	April
Mai	May
Juni	June
Juli	July
August	August
September	September
Oktober	October
November	November
Dezember	December
Frühling	Spring
Sommer	Summer
Herbst	Autumn
Winter	Winter
Ferien	Holidays
Feiertag	Bank holiday
Montag, der erste Mai	Monday, the first of May
Der zweite April	the second of April
Der dritte April	the third of April

Some signs

Damen/Frauen	Women's toilets
Herren/Männer	Men's toilets
Eingang	Entrance
Ausgang	Exit
Notausgang	Emergency exit
Ankunft	Arrival
Abfahrt	Departure
Ausstellung	Exhibition
Autobahn	Motorway
Auffahrt	Motorway entrance
Ausfahrt	Motorway exit
Umleitung	Diversion
Vorsicht!	Attention!
Geschwindig- keitsbegrenzung	Speed limit
Krankenhaus	Hospital
Polizei	Police
Nicht rauchen	No smoking
Kein Eingang	No entrance
Verboten	Prohibited
Baustelle	Building works
Ampel	Traffic light

Numbers

1	eins	11	elf	22	zwei-und-zwanzig
2	zwei	12	zwölf	30	dreissig
3	drei	13	dreizehn	40	vierzig
4	vier	14	vierzehn	50	fünfzig
5	fünf	15	fünfzehn	60	sechzig
6	sechs	16	sechszehn	70	siebzig
7	sieben	17	siebzehn	80	achtzig
8	acht	18	achtzehn	90	neunzig
9	neun	19	neunzehn	100	hundert
10	zehn	20	zwanzig	1996	neunzehn-hundert-sechs-und-neunzig
		21	ein-und-zwanzig		

Questions and requests

All enquiries should be prefaced with the phrase *Entschuldigen Sie bitte* (excuse me, please). Note that *Sie* is the polite form of address to be used with everyone except close friends, though young people and students often don't bother with it. The older generation will certainly be offended if you address them with the familiar *Du*, as will all officials.

Sprechen Sie Englisch?	Do you speak English?
Ich spreche kein Deutsch	I don't speak German
Könnten Sie bitte langsamer sprechen	Please speak more slowly
Ich verstehe nicht	I don't understand
Ich verstehe	I understand
Wie sagt mann das auf Deutsch?	How do you say that in German?
Können Sie mir bitte sagen wo . . . ist?	Can you tell me where . . . is?
Wieviel kostet das?	How much does that cost?
Wann fährt der nächste Zug?	When does the next train leave?
Um wieviel Uhr?	At what time?
Wieviel Uhr ist es?	What time is it?
Sind die Plätze noch frei?	Are these seats taken?
Die Rechnung, bitte	The bill, please
Getrennt oder Zusammen?	Separately or together?
Die Speisekarte, bitte	The menu, please
Hallo!	Hello! (to get attention of waiter/waitress)
Haben Sie etwas billigeres?	Have you got something cheaper?
Haben Sie noch ein Zimmer frei?	Is there a room available?
Wo sind die Toiletten, bitte?	Where are the toilets?
Ich hätte gern dieses	I'd like that one
Ich hätte gern ein Zimmer für zwei	I'd like a room for two
Ich hätte gern ein Einzelzimmer	I'd like a single room
Hat das Zimmer eine Dusche, ein Bad, eine Toilette . . . ?	Does it have a shower, bath, toilet . . . ?

For a detailed glossary of food terms see pp.224–226.

Glossaries

Art and architecture

ART DECO geometrical style of art and architecture prevalent in the 1930s.

ART NOUVEAU sinuous, highly stylized form of architecture and interior design; in Germany, mostly dates from the period 1900–15, and is known as Jugendstil.

BAROQUE expansive, exuberant architectural style of the seventeenth and early eighteenth centuries, characterized by ornate decoration, complex spatial arrangements and grand vistas. The term is also applied to the sumptuous style of painting from the same period.

BAUHAUS plain, functional style of architecture and design, originating in early twentieth-century Germany.

EXPRESSIONISM emotional style of painting, concentrating on line and colour, extensively practised in early twentieth-century Germany; the term is also used for related architecture of the same period.

GOTHIC architectural style with an emphasis on verticality, characterized by the pointed arch, ribbed vault and flying buttress; introduced to Germany around 1235, surviving in an increasingly decorative form until well into the sixteenth century. The term is also used for paintings of this period.

NEOCLASSICAL late eighteenth- and early nineteenth-century style of art and architecture, returning to classical models as a reaction against Baroque and Rococo excesses.

RENAISSANCE Italian-originated movement in art and architecture, inspired by the rediscovery of classical ideals.

ROCOCO highly florid, light and graceful eighteenth-century style of architecture, painting and interior design, forming the last phase of Baroque.

ROMANESQUE solid architectural style of the late tenth to mid-thirteenth centuries, characterized by round-headed arches and a penchant for horizontality and geometrical precision. The term is also used for paintings of this period.

ROMANTICISM late eighteenth- and nineteenth-century movement, particularly strong in Germany, rooted in adulation of the natural world and rediscovery of the achievements of the Middle Ages.

German terms

ALTSTADT old part of a city.

AUSKUNFT information.

ÄUSLANDER literally "foreigner", the word has come to be a pejorative term for any non-White non-German.

AUSSTELLUNG exhibition.

BÄCKEREI bakery.

BAHNHOF station.

BAU building.

BERG mountain or hill.

BERLINER SCHNAUZE sharp and coarse Berlin wit.

BEZIRK city district.

BRÜCKE bridge.

BURG mountain or hill.

BUSHALTESTELLE bus stop.

DENKMAL memorial.

DOM cathedral.

DORF village.

EINBAHNSTRASSE one-way street.

ELECTOR (KURFÜRST) sacred or secular prince with a vote in the elections to choose the Holy Roman Emperor. There were seven for most of the medieval period, with three more added later.

FEIERTAG holiday.

FLUGHAFEN airport.

FLUSS river.

FREMDENZIMMER room for short-term let.

GASSE alley.

GASTARBEITER "guest worker": anyone who comes to Germany to do menial work.

GASTHAUS, GASTHOF guesthouse, inn.

GASTSTÄTTE traditional bar that also serves food.

GEMÄLDE painting.

GRÜNEN, DIE "The Greens": political party formed from environmental and anti-nuclear groups.

HABSBURG the most powerful family in medieval Germany, operating from a power base in Austria. They held the office of Holy Roman Emperor 1452–1806, and by marriage, war and diplomacy acquired territories all over Europe.

HAUPTBAHNHOF main train station.

HAUPTEINGANG main entrance.

HOF court, courtyard, mansion.

INSEL island.

JAGDSCHLOSS hunting lodge.

JUGENDHERBERGE youth hostel.

JUGENDSTIL German version of Art Nouveau.

JUNKER Prussian land-owning class.

KAISER Emperor.

KAMMER room, chamber.

KAPELLE chapel.

KAUFHAUS department store.

KINO cinema.

KIRCHE church.

KNEIPE bar.

KONDITOREI cake shop.

KRANKENHAUS hospital.

KUNST art.

MARKT market, market square.

MOTORRAD motorbike.

NEUES FORUM umbrella group for political opposition organizations within the former GDR.

NOT emergency.

OSTPOLITIK West German policy of détente towards the GDR.

PLATZ square.

PRUSSIA originally an Eastern Baltic territory (now divided between Poland and the Soviet Union). It was acquired in 1525 by the Hohenzollerns, who merged it with their own possessions to form Brandenburg-Prussia (later shortened to Prussia); this took the lead in forging the unity of Germany, and was thereafter its overwhelmingly dominant province. The name was abolished after World War II because of its monarchic and military connotations.

QUITTUNG official receipt.

RASTPLATZ picnic area.

RATHAUS town hall.

RATSKELLER cellars below the Rathaus, invariably used as a restaurant serving *burgerlich* cuisine.

REICH empire.

REISEBÜRO travel agency.

RUNDGANG way round.

SAMMLUNG collection.

S-BAHN commuter train network operating in and around conurbations.

SCHICKIE abbreviation of "Schicki-Micki": yuppie.

SCHLOSS castle, palace (equivalent of French *château*).

SEE lake.

STAATSSICHERHEITSDIENST (STASI) the former "State Security Service" or secret police of the GDR.

STADT town, city.

STAMMTISCH table in a pub or restaurant reserved for regular customers.

STIFTUNG foundation.

STRAND beach.

STRASSENBAHN tram.

TANKSTELLE filling station.

TOR gate, gateway.

TRABI conversational shorthand for the now famous *Trabant*, East Germany's two-cylinder, two-stroke people's car.

TURM tower.

U-BAHN network of underground trains.

VERKEHRSAMT, VERKEHRSVEREIN tourist office.

VIERTEL quarter, district.

VOLK people, folk; given mystical associations by Hitler.

WALD forest.

WECHSEL currency exchange office.

WEIMAR REPUBLIC parliamentary democracy established in 1918 that collapsed with Hitler's assumption of power in 1933.

WENDE literally, "turning point" – the term used to describe the events of November 1989 and after.

ZEITSCHRIFT magazine.

ZEITUNG newspaper.

ZEUGHAUS arsenal.

ZIMMER room.

Acronyms

BRD (*Bundesrepublik Deutschlands*) official name of former West Germany.

CDU (*Christlich Demokratische Union*) ruling Christian Democratic (Conservative) Party.

DB (*Deutsche Bahn*) national train company.

DDR (*Deutsche Demokratische Republik*) official name of former East Germany.

FDJ (*Freie Deutsche Jugend*) East German party youth organization.

GDR ("German Democratic Republic") English equivalent of DDR.

NSDAP (*National Sozialistiche Deutsche Abrbeiterparte*) "National Socialist German Workers' Party", the official name for the Nazis.

SED (*Sozialistische Einheitspartei Deutschlands*) "Socialist Unity Party of Germany", the official name of the East German Communist party before December 1989.

SPD (*Sozialdemokratische Parteii Deutschlands*) Social Democratic (Labour) Party.

STASI slang term for the *Staatssicherheitsdienst,* the former East German secret police.

VOPO slang for *Volkspolizei,* a member of the East German police force.

Index

direct orders from

		UK£8.99	US$14.95	CAN$19.99
Amsterdam	1-85828-218-7			
Andalucia	1-85828-219-5	9.99	16.95	22.99
Antigua Mini Guide	1-85828-346-9	5.99	9.95	12.99
Australia	1-85828-220-9	13.99	21.95	29.99
Austria	1-85828-325-6	10.99	17.95	23.99
Bali & Lombok	1-85828-134-2	8.99	14.95	19.99
Bangkok Mini Guide	1-85828-345-0	5.99	9.95	12.99
Barcelona	1-85828-221-7	8.99	14.95	19.99
Belgium & Luxembourg	1-85828-222-5	10.99	17.95	23.99
Belize	1-85828-351-5	9.99	16.95	22.99
Berlin	1-85828-327-2	9.99	16.95	22.99
Boston Mini Guide	1-85828-321-3	5.99	9.95	12.99
Brazil	1-85828-223-3	13.99	21.95	29.99
Britain	1-85828-312-4	14.99	23.95	31.99
Brittany & Normandy	1-85828-224-1	9.99	16.95	22.99
Bulgaria	1-85828-183-0	9.99	16.95	22.99
California	1-85828-330-2	11.99	18.95	24.99
Canada	1-85828-311-6	12.99	19.95	25.99
Central America	1-85828-335-3	14.99	23.95	31.99
China	1-85828-225-X	15.99	24.95	32.99
Corfu & the Ionian Islands	1-85828-226-8	8.99	14.95	19.99
Corsica	1-85828-227-6	9.99	16.95	22.99
Costa Rica	1-85828-136-9	9.99	15.95	21.99
Crete	1-85828-316-7	9.99	16.95	22.99
Cyprus	1-85828-182-2	9.99	16.95	22.99
Czech & Slovak Republics	1-85828-317-5	11.99	18.95	24.99
Dublin Mini Guide	1-85828-294-2	5.99	9.95	12.99
Edinburgh Mini Guide	1-85828-295-0	5.99	9.95	12.99
Egypt	1-85828-188-1	10.99	17.95	23.99
Europe 1998	1-85828-289-6	14.99	19.95	25.99
England	1-85828-301-9	12.99	19.95	25.99
First Time Asia	1-85828-332-9	7.99	9.95	12.99
First Time Europe	1-85828-270-5	7.99	9.95	12.99
Florida	1-85828-184-4	10.99	16.95	22.99
France	1-85828-228-4	12.99	19.95	25.99
Germany	1-85828-309-4	14.99	23.95	31.99
Goa	1-85828-275-6	8.99	14.95	19.99
Greece	1-85828-300-0	12.99	19.95	25.99
Greek Islands	1-85828-310-8	10.99	17.95	23.99
Guatemala	1-85828-323-X	9.99	16.95	22.99
Hawaii: Big Island	1-85828-158-X	8.99	12.95	16.99
Hawaii	1-85828-206-3	10.99	16.95	22.99
Holland	1-85828-229-2	10.99	17.95	23.99
Hong Kong & Macau	1-85828-187-3	8.99	14.95	19.99
Hotels & Restos de France 1998	1-85828-306-X	12.99	19.95	25.99
Hungary	1-85828-123-7	8.99	14.95	19.99
India	1-85828-200-4	14.99	23.95	31.99
Ireland	1-85828-179-2	10.99	17.95	23.99
Israel & the Palestinian Territories	1-85828-248-9	12.99	19.95	25.99
Italy	1-85828-167-9	12.99	19.95	25.99
Jamaica	1-85828-230-6	9.99	16.95	22.99
Japan	1-85828-340-X	14.99	23.95	31.99
Jordan	1-85828-350-7	10.99	17.95	23.99
Kenya	1-85828-192-X	11.99	18.95	24.99
Lisbon Mini Guide	1-85828-297-7	5.99	9.95	12.99
London	1-85828-231-4	9.99	15.95	21.99
Madrid Mini Guide	1-85828-353-1	5.99	9.95	12.99
Mallorca & Menorca	1-85828-165-2	8.99	14.95	19.99
Malaysia, Singapore & Brunei	1-85828-232-2	11.99	18.95	24.99
Mexico	1-85828-044-3	10.99	16.95	22.99
Morocco	1-85828-169-5	11.99	18.95	24.99
Moscow	1-85828-322-1	9.99	16.95	22.99
Nepal	1-85828-190-3	10.99	17.95	23.99
New York	1-85828-296-9	9.99	15.95	21.99
New Zealand	1-85828-233-0	12.99	19.95	25.99
Norway	1-85828-234-9	10.99	17.95	23.99

UK orders: 0181 899 4036

around the world

		UK£12.99	US$19.95	CAN$25.99
Pacific Northwest	1-85828-326-4			
Paris	1-85828-235-7	8.99	14.95	19.99
Peru	1-85828-142-3	10.99	17.95	23.99
Poland	1-85828-168-7	10.99	17.95	23.99
Portugal	1-85828-313-2	10.99	17.95	23.99
Prague	1-85828-318-3	8.99	14.95	19.99
Provence & the Cote d'Azur	1-85828-127-X	9.99	16.95	22.99
The Pyrenees	1-85828-308-6	10.99	17.95	23.99
Rhodes & the Dodecanese	1-85828-120-2	8.99	14.95	19.99
Romania	1-85828-305-1	10.99	17.95	23.99
San Francisco	1-85828-299-3	8.99	14.95	19.99
Scandinavia	1-85828-236-5	12.99	20.95	27.99
Scotland	1-85828-302-7	9.99	16.95	22.99
Seattle Mini Guide	1-85828-324-8	5.99	9.95	12.99
Sicily	1-85828-178-4	9.99	16.95	22.99
Singapore	1-85828-237-3	8.99	14.95	19.99
South Africa	1-85828-238-1	12.99	19.95	25.99
Southwest USA	1-85828-239-X	10.99	16.95	22.99
Spain	1-85828-240-3	11.99	18.95	24.99
St Petersburg	1-85828-298-5	9.99	16.95	22.99
Sweden	1-85828-241-1	10.99	17.95	23.99
Syria	1-85828-331-0	11.99	18.95	24.99
Thailand	1-85828-140-7	10.99	17.95	24.99
Tunisia	1-85828-139-3	10.99	17.95	24.99
Turkey	1-85828-242-X	12.99	19.95	25.99
Tuscany & Umbria	1-85828-243-8	10.99	17.95	23.99
USA	1-85828-307-8	14.99	19.95	25.99
Venice	1-85828-170-9	8.99	14.95	19.99
Vienna	1-85828-244-6	8.99	14.95	19.99
Vietnam	1-85828-191-1	9.99	15.95	21.99
Wales	1-85828-245-4	10.99	17.95	23.99
Washington DC	1-85828-246-2	8.99	14.95	19.99
West Africa	1-85828-101-6	15.99	24.95	34.99
Zimbabwe & Botswana	1-85828-186-5	11.99	18.95	24.99
Phrasebooks				
Czech	1-85828-148-2	3.50	5.00	7.00
Egyptian Arabic	1-85828-319-1	4.00	6.00	8.00
French	1-85828-144-X	3.50	5.00	7.00
German	1-85828-146-6	3.50	5.00	7.00
Greek	1-85828-145-8	3.50	5.00	7.00
Hindi & Urdu	1-85828-252-7	4.00	6.00	8.00
Hungarian	1-85828-304-3	4.00	6.00	8.00
Indonesian	1-85828-250-0	4.00	6.00	8.00
Italian	1-85828-143-1	3.50	5.00	7.00
Japanese	1-85828-303-5	4.00	6.00	8.00
Mandarin Chinese	1-85828-249-7	4.00	6.00	8.00
Mexican Spanish	1-85828-176-8	3.50	5.00	7.00
Portuguese	1-85828-175-X	3.50	5.00	7.00
Polish	1-85828-174-1	3.50	5.00	7.00
Russian	1-85828-251-9	4.00	6.00	8.00
Spanish	1-85828-147-4	3.50	5.00	7.00
Swahili	1-85828-320-5	4.00	6.00	8.00
Thai	1-85828-177-6	3.50	5.00	7.00
Turkish	1-85828-173-3	3.50	5.00	7.00
Vietnamese	1-85828-172-5	3.50	5.00	7.00
Reference				
Classical Music	1-85828-113-X	12.99	19.95	25.99
European Football	1-85828-256-X	14.99	23.95	31.99
Internet	1-85828-288-8	5.00	8.00	10.00
Jazz	1-85828-137-7	16.99	24.95	34.99
Millennium	1-85828-314-0	5.00	8.95	11.99
More Women Travel	1-85828-098-2	10.99	16.95	22.99
Opera	1-85828-138-5	16.99	24.95	34.99
Reggae	1-85828-247-0	12.99	19.95	25.99
Rock	1-85828-201-2	17.99	26.95	35.00
World Music	1-85828-017-6	16.99	22.95	29.99

US/International orders: 1-800-253-6476

Small

but perfectly informed

Every bit as stylish and irreverent as their full-sized counterparts, Mini Guides are everything you'd expect from a Rough Guide, but smaller – perfect for a pocket, briefcase or overnight bag.

Available 1998
Antigua, Barbados, Boston, Dublin, Edinburgh, Lisbon, Madrid, Seattle

Coming soon
Bangkok, Brussels, Florence, Honolulu, Las Vegas, Maui, Melbourne, New Orleans, Oahu, St Lucia, Sydney, Tokyo, Toronto

 Everything you need to know about everything you want to do

Stay in touch with us!

The view from Johannesburg
ARE WE IN AFRICA YET?

The Final Countdown: The Last Days of
COLONIAL HONG KONG

RAINFOREST TOURISM

ROUGH*NEWS* is Rough Guides' free newsletter.
In four issues a year we give you news, travel
issues, music reviews, readers' letters and the
latest dispatches from authors on the road.

I would like to receive ROUGH*NEWS*: please put me on your free mailing list.

NAME . . . .

ADDRESS . . . .

Please clip or photocopy and send to: Rough Guides, 62–70 Shorts Gardens, London WC2H 9AB,
England or Rough Guides, 375 Hudson Street, New York, NY 10014, USA.

A heavyweight insurance for those who travel light.

Our 'hassle-free' insurance includes instant cover, medical, personal liability, legal expenses, cancellation, passport and much more.

For details call

0171-375 0011

Lines open: 8am-8pm Mon-Fri, 9am-4pm Sat.

COLUMBUS DIRECT
TRAVEL INSURANCE

2 MINS FROM LIVERPOOL STREET STATION
Visit us at 17 DEVONSHIRE SQUARE, LONDON EC2M 4SQ

VISA MasterCard SWITCH

Est.1852

World Travel starts at Stanfords

Maps, Travel Guides, Atlases, Charts
Mountaineering Maps and Books, Travel Writing
Travel Accessories, Globes & Instruments

Stanfords
12-14 Long Acre
Covent Garden
London
WC2E 9LP

Stanfords
at Campus Travel
52 Grosvenor Gardens
London
SW1W 0AG

Stanfords
at British Airways
156 Regent Street
London
W1R 5TA

Stanfords in Bristol
29 Corn Street
Bristol
BS1 1HT

International Mail Order Service
Tel: 0171 836 1321 **Fax**: 0171 836 0189

The World's Finest Map and Travel Bookshops

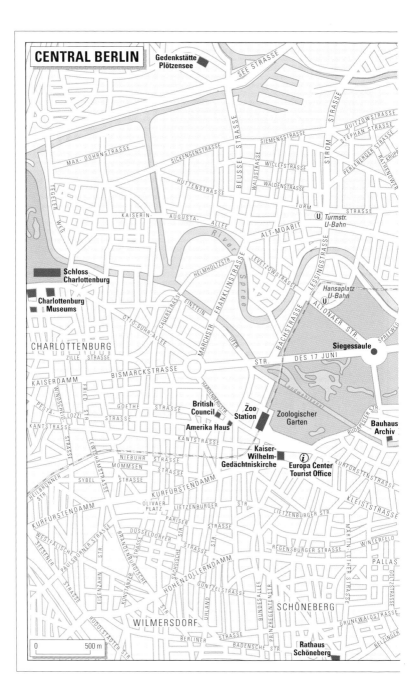

CENTRAL BERLIN

Gedenkstätte Plötzensee

SEE STRASSE

QUITZOWSTRASSE

STEPHAN STRASSE

PERLEBERGER STRASSE

KRUPP

RATHENOWER STRASSE

STROM STRASSE

SIEMENSSTRASSE

WICLEFSTRASSE

WALDSTRASSE

WALDENSTRASSE

TURM STRASSE

U *Turmstr. U-Bahn*

ALT-MOABIT

MAX. DÖHRN STRASSE

SICKENGENSTRASSE

HÜTTENSTRASSE

BEUSSE STRASSE

TEGELER WEG

KAISERIN- AUGUSTA- ALLEE

River Spree

HELMHOLTZSTR

FRANKLINSTRASSE

LEVETZOWSTRASSE

BACHSTRASSE

ALTONAER STR

Hansaplatz U-Bahn

LESSINGSTRASSE

Schloss Charlottenburg

Charlottenburg Museums

OTTO-SUHR-ALLEE

CAUERSTRASSE

EINSTEIN

MÄRCHSTR

UFER

STR DES 17 JUNI

Siegessäule

SPREEWEG

CHARLOTTENBURG

ZILLE STRASSE

BISMARCKSTRASSE

HARDENBERGSTR

LUDWIGSKIRCHSTR

KAISERDAMM

WINDSCHEID STR

FRIED

GOETHE STRASSE

STRASSE

British Council

Zoo Station

Zoologischer Garten

BUDAPESTER STR

Bauhaus Archiv

KANTSTRASSE

FESTA-LOZZI STR

Amerika Haus

KANTSTRASSE

NIEBUHR STRASSE

MOMMSEN STRASSE

Kaiser-Wilhelm-Gedächtniskirche

ⓘ Europa Center Tourist Office

KURFÜRSTENSTRASSE

HEILBRONNER STR

SYBEL STRASSE

KURFÜRSTENDAMM

OLIVAER PLATZ

LIETZENBURGER STR

LIETZENBURGER STR

KLEISTSTRASSE

LEWISHAMSTRASSE

WESTFÄLISCHE STR

STESENER STR

PAULSBORNER STRASSE

BRANDENBURGISCHE

SÄCHSISCHE STR

PARISER STRASSE

DÜSSELDORFER STRASSE

STRASSE

REGENSBURGER STRASSE

MARTIN-LUTHER-STRASSE

WINTERFELD

PALLAS

EISENZAHN

KONSTANZER STRASSE

HOHENZOLLERNDAMM

UHLAND STR

GÜNTZELSTRASSE

BUNDESALLEE

PRINZREGENTENSTR

GOLTZSTRASSE

SCHÖNEBERG

GRUNEWALDSTRASSE

RUDOLSTÄDTER STR

WILMERSDORF

BERLINER STRASSE

BADENSCHE STR

Rathaus Schöneberg

BELZINGER

0   500 m

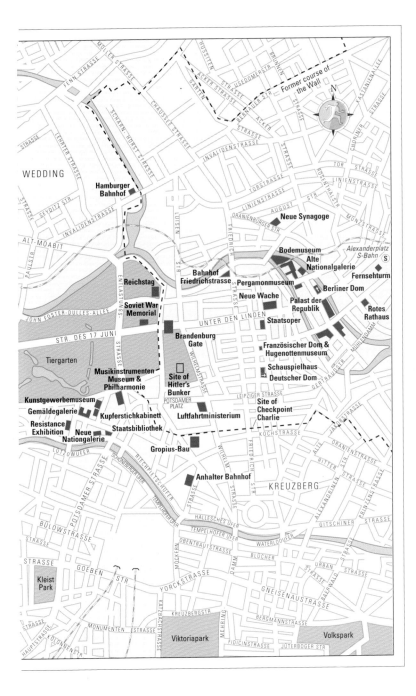

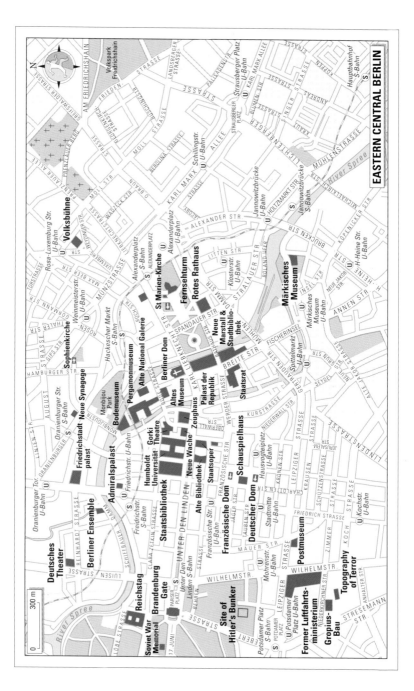

EASTERN CENTRAL BERLIN

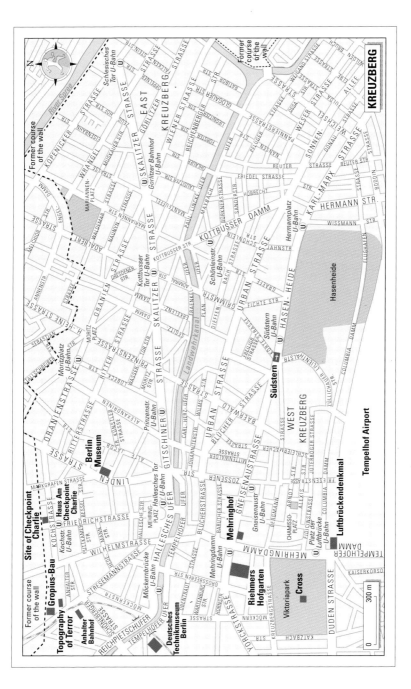

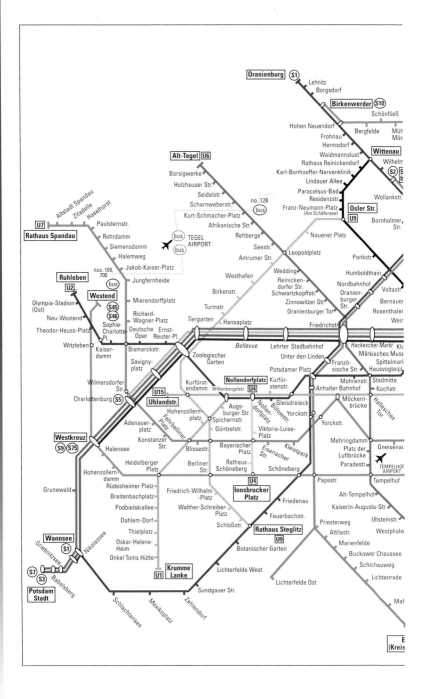

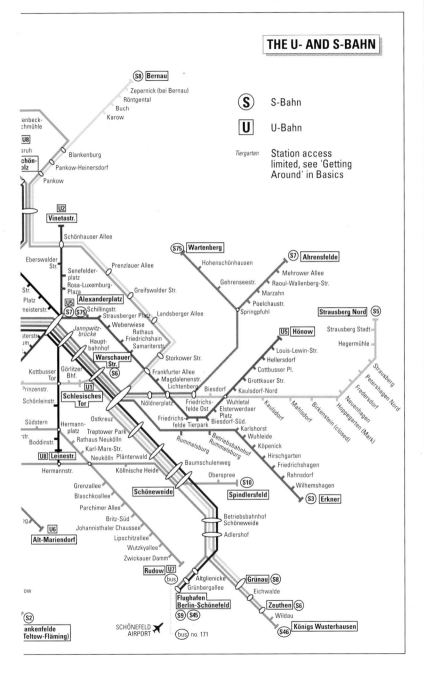

THE U- AND S-BAHN

(S) S-Bahn

U U-Bahn

Tiergarten Station access limited, see 'Getting Around' in Basics

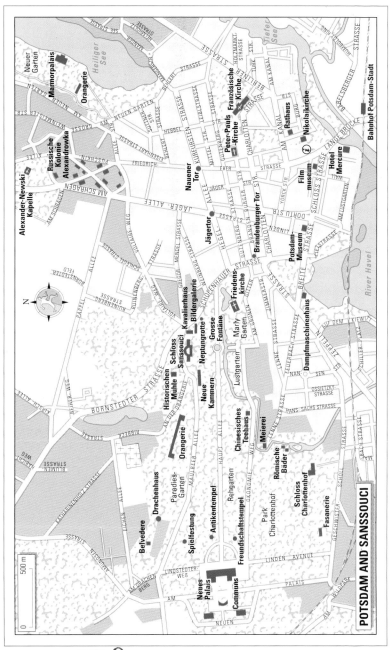

POTSDAM AND SANSSOUCI

Neuer Garten

Marmorpalais

Orangerie

Heiliger See

Alexander-Newski Kapelle

Russische Kolonie Alexandrowka

Neuer Garten

Peter-Pauls Kirche

Französische Kirche

Rathaus

Nikolaikirche

Bahnhof Potsdam-Stadt

Nauener Tor

Jägertor

Film museum

Hotel Mercure

Brandenburger Tor

Potsdam-Museum

River Havel

Bildergalerie

Kavalierhaus

Friedens kirche

Neptungrotte

Grosse Fontäne

Marly Garten

Dampfmaschinenhaus

Schloss Sanssouci

Historischen Mühle

Neue Kammern

Lustgarten

Orangerie

Chinesisches Teehaus

Meierei

Römische Bäder

Schloss Charlottenhof

Park Charlottenhof

Fasanerie

Drachenhaus

Paradies-Garten

Belvedere

Spielfestung

Antikentempel

Freundschaftstempel

Neues Palais

Communs

BORNSTEDTER STRASSE

JÄGER-ALLEE

500 m

0

4879